Encyclopedia of World's Fairs and Expositions

Edited by
JOHN E. FINDLING and
KIMBERLY D. PELLE

Foreword by
Vicente González Loscertales

McFarland & Company, Inc., Publishers
Jefferson, North Carolina, and London

Library of Congress Cataloguing-in-Publication Data

Encyclopedia of world's fairs and expositions / edited by John E. Findling and
Kimberly D. Pelle ; foreword by Vicente González Loscertales.
p.   cm.
Includes bibliographical references and index.

ISBN 978-0-7864-3416-9
softcover : 50# alkaline paper ∞

1. Exhibitions—History.   I. Findling, John E.   II. Pelle, Kimberly D.
T395.F56   2008   907.4—dc22   2008011205

British Library cataloguing data are available

Cover photograph ©2008 Shutterstock

Manufactured in the United States of America

*McFarland & Company, Inc., Publishers
Box 611, Jefferson, North Carolina 28640
www.mcfarlandpub.com*

For Lorelei Knobloch Hull
and Charles Ellis Findling

Table of Contents

Table of Contents

Table of Contents

Foreword

by Vicente González Loscertales

In the 21st century, while world expos continue to display an impressive power of attraction for both visitors and participating countries, the global context requires a continuous effort to maintain their relevance in a rapidly changing world. This is why the publication of the *Encyclopedia of World's Fairs and Expositions* is particularly timely and important.

The Encyclopedia of World's Fairs and Expositions is an impressive endeavor that matches the scale of these great events. The dictionary is both a tool for understanding the historical roots of expos while giving readers a map that helps them see how they have been able to capture the mood, the innovations, and the specific visions of their time.

Through the gathering of the international community, world's fairs attract millions of visitors around a theme. No other human event has the same force of involvement. Today, when we refer to the international community, we do not mean just countries or governments, but also civil society, corporations, and ordinary citizens.

Expos are platforms for innovation and for showing citizens the problems that the global society faces in different cultures and different latitudes. Expos also show the effort made by corporations, governments, and nongovernmental organizations in order to to meet the challenges for the day-to-day life of the citizens. This is what expos are about and their great value lies in their power to gather around a relevant theme all of humankind.

The first decade of the 21st century has brought two contradictory phenomena into the forefront. On the one hand, there are discussions as to the value and adaptability of expos to the needs of the 21st century, and on the other hand, there is a steady increase in the number of visitors at expos and a growing number of candidate countries bidding to host future exhibitions.

This situation obliges the Bureau of International Expositions and both present and future exhibition organizers to carry out a thorough reflection, in order to give expos of the 21st century the value and usefulness that public opinion demands. The globalization of political, economic, and social exchanges as well as the increasing value given to the respect of cultural diversity proves that civil society, corporations, cities, and regions all find themselves in a key position for national presentations at world's fairs.

The economic and political opening of new regions such as Asia, Latin America, and the Pacific in the last twenty years has transformed the international scene and brought new actors into the world of expos. The 140 nations that comprise the BIE reflect this new reality, which requires that these great events be taken into new geographic areas to ensure a greater equality in the distribution of future expos. Article 7 of the BIE Convention, therefore, acquires, in the 21st century, a role which had not been available throughout the 20th century.

From the very beginning, world expos have had a tremendous impact on their host cities. Although most large events tend to impact one particular sector of a city, expos manage to touch almost every imaginable aspect of the host city. No other public event needs infrastructure investment on the scale of an expo. Sporting events such as the Olympic Games are of much shorter duration, and most spectators watch them on television. Expos, on the other hand, with their six-month duration, have throughout their long history had a profound impact on the culture, economy, and urbanization of their respective hosts.

In socio-economic terms, expos have first and foremost provided a massive impulse to the local economy: the construction and exploitation of a large-scale "exhibition city" for millions of visitors requires "man-centuries" of work. That means plenty of opportunities for business and employment for citizens. But it also means substantial tax revenues for the state.

World's fairs also contribute to the development of a commercial apparatus for tourists, day-trippers, and shoppers: from department stores and restaurants to hotels and places of entertainment. Perhaps more importantly, each expo has led to a larger organization of companies involved in the realms of transport, tourism, and trade.

Article 1 of the BIE Convention regulating world expos states that their purpose is "the education of the public." The knowledge at the disposal of humankind on a given theme is to be displayed to a mass public in a way that is comprehensible to visitors from all walks of life. One could say that an expo is an "inventory" of what we know and do to meet the challenges of our time. Indeed, I would go even further. At its most successful, an expo projects a vision for the future of humankind. Key to this is the choice of the theme.

There are some fundamental criteria the theme should fulfil:

It must be of global interest.

It must be a major issue for the future of civilization.

It should be a top priority for national governments and on the policy agendas of key international organizations.

It should be important to the top echelons of the corporate sector as well as among representatives of civil society and non-governmental organizations.

It must be future-oriented and project a powerful fascination for exchange, dialogue and cooperation.

Last but not least, it should relate to citizens in their daily lives and their most vital concerns.

A world expo is an exercise in global public diplomacy. It offers national governments a unique opportunity to showcase their achievements to the world. Contributing to the theme allows them to describe major policy challenges to the general public and explain why they have chosen the solutions they are putting into practice.

For corporate participants, expos provide an opportunity to develop a culture of educated and discerning consumers. An educational approach will help people appreciate the investments involved in the research, production, distribution, and marketing of products. They will also better understand that companies are involved in making practical contributions to solving global problems and challenges.

For non-governmental organizations (NGOs) and civil society, the theme allows them to express legitimate concerns. In an interdependent society, the voice of these groups and their contributions are vital to giving the theme its full significance and global value. Finally, the theme must appeal not only to the intelligence of its visitors but also to their emotions and their imaginations. I shall come back to this essential aspect of a successful expo.

Today, a new type of expo has seen the light. Expos nowadays do not only aim at presenting progress through showcasing technological innovations in various areas of human action. Instead, they are developed and carried out with the clear objective of serving humanity. Contemporary expos personalize, exemplify, and embody the idea and ideal of sustainable development. They raise public awareness of specific sustainable development issues relating to the chosen themes and subthemes. They provide a snapshot of the current human condition and display feasible practical solutions to improve these. They display local and regional answers to specific global, environmental, economic, social, and human problems, all effecting sustainable development.

World expos provide informal public education. They contribute to the making of an active informed citizenry, which is able to distinguish between unsustainable and sustainable national policies and initiatives and which can take an active part in implementing and enacting sustainable measures.

Because of participation from countries all over the world, expos display issues relating to human development within very different physical, biological, and cultural contexts. Thereby, world expos offer not only knowledge, skills, perspectives, and values that encourage people to work toward a sustainable livelihood, but also a respect for different cultures.

Current expos display more than practical solutions to local problems and challenges. Expos symbolize and promote a new holistic and complex way of approaching sustainable development. In this perspective it is important to show that the realization of sustainable development is related and connected with many cross-cutting issues. This means that the concept of sustainable development encompasses solidarity, equity, social justice, respect for different cultures, the fight against poverty, and coherence among economic, development,

and environmental policies, all features that are more or less explicitly addressed in expos.

At the same time, expos also provide a platform for the establishing of global partnerships, which is another vital element of the concept of education for sustainable development. In conclusion, contemporary expos are carried out with a clear purpose of serving, securing, and supporting a sound course of progress for humanity. This is why world expos are a very powerful tool for education for sustainable development.

I am grateful to John E. Findling and Kimberly D. Pelle for their vision to orchestrate such a great collection of perspectives. I am equally grateful to all who have contributed to this book, because in so doing, they have helped the Bureau of International Exhibitions in its efforts to continue to promote the values and the benefits of world expos to the global society of today and tomorrow. In our past lies the key to the better understanding of our future.

The author is Secretary General of the Bureau of International Expositions.

Preface

An earlier version of this book, published in 1990, had its origin in a senior seminar on world's fairs and expositions for history majors taught at Indiana University Southeast in the spring of 1982. At that time, we encountered major problems in obtaining resource material for John's students. That book was an attempt to remedy the problem by bringing together what information existed on fairs, along with the most comprehensive bibliographical information we could find to assist scholars in their research endeavors. This revision and updating of that book is a testament to the increased scholarly interest in fairs and expositions since 1990. The number of excellent articles and monographs published since then is much greater than what had previously come to light, and the Popular Culture Association created a section on fairs and expositions that provided many scholars with a venue to present papers and research in progress on various fairs. In addition, the centennial observances of many fairs during this time, especially the World's Columbian Exposition in 1893 and the Louisiana Purchase International Exposition in 1904, triggered an outpouring of both academic and nostalgic work. With the earlier version of this book long out of print, there seemed good reason to put together a new work, and this is the result.

Although world's fairs and expositions can claim only a rather short direct ancestry prior to their beginnings in 1851, rudiments of these fairs can be traced to ancient times. There are biblical references to great feasts held at important population centers, which also included markets, athletic games, and visiting dignitaries. The Romans held numerous festivals, usually associated with religious holidays; indeed the English word *fair* derives from the Latin word for holidays, *feriae.* During medieval times, great fairs were held at major crossroads of trade and were a mixture of commerce, entertainment, and theater. They continued to grow as trade and communications improved.

These medieval European fairs were basically international, at least to the extent to which there were nations. In England, however, the fairs were national and were a blend of a trade show and a public entertainment, similar to a modern carnival. Although the fairs continued in England until at least the late nineteenth century, the more direct genealogical line to the Crystal Palace exhibition of 1851 may be said to have originated with the formation of the Royal Society of Arts in London in 1754.

In 1761, the Royal Society produced a show of its annual prize winners in the "arts, manufactures, and commerce," which ran successfully for seven weeks. The show included exhibits of a sort that we might understand as industrial arts. Thus, the exhibits were technological innovations— machines, mostly — such as miniature windmills, spinning wheels, agricultural implements, including a threshing machine and a cider press, various models of ships, and assorted machines of concern to the textile industry.

Little publicity was given to this exhibition, and people were not encouraged to come and see it after the first year. The Royal Society decided to put its prize winners on permanent display, much like a museum, where they continued to attract attention, but the idea of a special annual exhibition was lost.

Thus it was left to the French, later in the eighteenth century, to hold the first industrial exhibition that had an impact on the development of subsequent exhibitions and ultimately, world's fairs. Such an exhibition in France was the idea of the marquis d'Avèze, the commissioner of three manufacturing outlets that until 1789 had been under the authority of the king. After the onset of the French Revolution, the marquis found that business was bad and so arranged in 1797 an exhibition in Paris to display his tapestry, carpet, and porcelain products, as well as the products of other trades he had invited to the fair. This exhibition resembled a bazaar or a medieval fair in the sense that the items on display were meant to be sold.

The success of the d'Avèze exhibition was so obvious that the French government took up the idea and decided to hold an annual national exhibition of French products in three specially constructed buildings. This fair was more strictly a national exhibition, state sponsored, with nothing for sale during the time the fair was open. A good part of the motivation behind this scheme was to demonstrate the ability of the French to compete on favorable terms with their main rival, the British. Since the two nations were then at war, the British did not participate, so no direct comparisons could be made.

These French national exhibitions continued to be held intermittently, wars and government instability often interfering, until 1849. In that year, the eleventh and largest exhibition attracted more than 4,500 exhibitors and remained open for six months, four months longer than any previous fair.

In England, no such exhibitions were organized. There was no interest, and the prevailing feeling appears to have been that the French shows were nothing more than futile efforts to promote the absurd notion that French products were superior to English ones.

What did develop in England, however, were exhibitions sponsored by mechanics institutes. These institutes, designed to teach scientific principles to working-class people, began to function in English towns in the 1820s. One manner of providing instruction

was through periodic exhibitions. These exhibitions emphasized scientific inventions and mechanical devices, often miniaturized for display purposes. Often model working machines produced actual products, which were then sold to visitors. Other exhibits followed the different stages in the production of a particular item and were especially instructive.

There were other attractions in those exhibitions as well, many of which traveled around England appearing at various sites. Mr. Austin's "Happy Family," for example, featured nearly 200 different animals cohabiting peacefully in a single cage. Other attractions bordered on the miraculous—the key to the Tower of London, a bed that King Richard III slept in, and a bodice worn by Mary, Queen of Scots—and were very popular. Attractions similar to these would eventually find their way onto the midways of modern world's fairs.

In addition to scientific, mechanical, and exotic exhibits, all of the mechanics institute exhibitions included a fine arts section. Little discrimination was made among artworks, and local artists vied for space with nationally known painters and sculptors.

From their beginning in Manchester in 1837, the mechanics institute exhibitions spread to nearly every town of any size in England and collectively attracted several million visitors before 1851 and the Crystal Palace. These exhibitions were popular and successful in diffusing knowledge; moreover, they contained several attributes later found in the great international exhibitions.

Art exhibitions also form a part of modern world's fairs, although with few exceptions, they take a back seat to the industrial and technological show. Still the development of art exhibitions in England constitutes part of the heritage of the Crystal Palace and subsequent world's fairs. In eighteenth-century England, there were no art museums or other public places to view art. Paintings and sculpture were held in private collections, to which public access was understandably difficult. Only when art was to be sold at public auction was it on public view, and many people attended auctions with no intent (or any means) to purchase items offered for sale. In both Italy and France, on the other hand, art was publicly displayed at this time.

In 1760, the first public art exhibition was held in England. It was the idea of a group of artists, who were encouraged by the popularity of a few portraits given by contemporary painters to a London hospital. In addition, there was a good deal of interest expressed in the annual prize winners of the Royal Society of Arts, which made awards for a variety of artistic and applied scientific achievements. The artists' show ran for two weeks in April 1760, admission was charged, and the proceeds were used to create a fund for impoverished artists. Several thousand visitors attended this event, which stands as an important milestone in the prehistory of world's fairs. In 1768, the Royal Academy (different from the Royal Society of Art) was founded and began putting on annual art exhibitions that helped elevate the status of British artists.

From this amalgam of industrial arts displays, art exhibitions, mechanics institute exhibitions, and French national shows emerged the Crystal Palace exhibition of 1851, the first modern world's fair, and the approximately 100 subsequent exhibitions that form the body of this volume. At their core, these fairs have never strayed too far from the object stated with respect to the Crystal Palace: "to forward the progress of industrial civilization." With the inclusion of an international component, exposition organizers could allow visitors to make easy comparisons of technology and craftsmanship among the industrial and other products that many nations displayed.

As the essays that follow demonstrate, fairs have moved beyond being mere showcases of industrial progress. The evolution of fairs has come to involve such things as the inclusion of special themes; the 1876 exhibition in Philadelphia commemorated the centennial of the American Declaration of Independence; the 1915 fair in San Francisco celebrated the opening of the Panama Canal and the recovery of the host city from its devastating earthquake and fire of 1906. There has been a movement away from fairs contained in one big building, such as the Crystal Palace, and toward individual country or thematic buildings. Finally, one might note the inclusion of more and more non-industrial features, such as fine art (although that was present from the beginning on a minor scale) and amusements (beginning in a formal way with the Midway Plaisance at the 1893 World's Columbian Exposition in

Chicago). With these more diverse elements, fairs have come to exhibit comparative national life-styles rather than simply industrial (or post-industrial) progress.

In the United States, there was no tradition of national industrial exhibitions or even broadly based art shows for potential fair managers to build upon. Mechanics institute exhibitions, as well as county and state fairs, certainly existed by the mid-nineteenth century and displayed some of the same attributes as world's fairs, such as exhibits of products, competition for awards, and amusement, but these seem to have had negligible impact on the individuals who were involved in the planning of the earliest international fairs held in the United States. Rather, American fairs came about because of the experience Americans had as participants in or visitors at the early European fairs.

In these earlier fairs, U.S. participation was undertaken by private means; there was much resistance to government support among Americans used to a sense of political isolation and nonentanglement with the Old World. Not surprisingly, then, early American fairs tended to be managed privately, with little government involvement outside of official government buildings and exhibits. In addition, as Reid Badger points out in *The Great American Fair* (1979), American fairs had a greater significance for their host cities than did European fairs. Hosting a fair was (and still is) a great and obvious symbol of urban achievement and a matter of civic pride to the host city, and many of the earlier American fairs witnessed intense competition among cities vying to host them.

American fairs have also put a greater premium on the entertainment aspect. In part, this derived from a desire to make more money, almost always a major challenge for fair managers. In addition, managers noticed quite early that visitors needed diversion from the fatigue that accompanied a day of looking at nothing but machine tools and farm implements. European fairs took up the idea quickly, and by the first decade of the twentieth century, amusement zones with rides, exotic shows, and foreign "villages" had become a staple at all international exhibitions. This trend, which continued throughout the century, has caused concern to some observers who see modern fairs devoting too much of their resources to amusements and making themselves indistinguishable from theme parks like Euro Disney or Six Flags over Texas.

One final note. The international events described in this book are commonly called "world's fairs" in the United States, "exhibitions" in Great Britain and the Commonwealth, and "expositions" in France and other countries. The term "expo," a shortening of exposition, has become popular as a descriptive term since the 1960s and is now part of the formal name for some fairs. For purposes of practicality, we have chosen to use these terms interchangeably, as if they were precise synonyms. Language purists, however, will want to know that they are not. As Kenneth Luckhurst explains in *The Story of Exhibitions* (1951), exhibitions are similar to fairs but are quite different in one respect: exhibitions are solely for displaying or exhibiting goods, while fairs connote commerce, as in the sale of goods being displayed. Thus it is no accident that we usually refer to art *exhibitions* (where works of art are rarely sold) and trade *fairs* (where products are contracted for and sold). As for *exposition*, it is a word that etymologically bridges the gap between fair and exhibition. It was first used in 1649, with the meaning of displaying something or putting on a show, but in contemporary usage, its meaning has become indistinguishable from that of fair, except in a connotative sense that an exposition is larger, more extensive, and perhaps more formally organized than a fair.

Like the earlier version, this book strives to serve two purposes. First, the essays on individual fairs and the various appendixes provide a collective body of basic information on more than 95 fairs held in more than 20 countries between 1851 and 2005, along with fairs being held in Zaragoza, Spain, in 2008 and Shanghai in 2010. Our appendixes provide information on the Bureau of International Expositions (BIE), as well as fair statistics and officials, fairs that were not included in the main body of the work and fairs that were planned but never held. Authors, who in many cases, had published works on their fairs, were encouraged to emphasize features of the fairs they considered most significant. In addition, each author was asked to prepare an annotated bibliography on the fair, indicating, where possible, the location of relevant primary sources and the quality of secondary sources. These bibliographies, along with a general bibliography at the end of the book, contain commentary on archival collections, published bibliographies and checklists, collective and thematic works, and active (as of 2007) websites, should prove valuable for researchers who wish to go beyond the factual information provided in the essays and appendixes.

Many people have rendered valuable assistance to us in the preparation of this book. Indiana University Southeast, and especially Dean of Social Sciences Cliff Staten, generously provided an emeritus professor office space on campus that greatly facilitated the preparation of this book. Our editorial board, Robert Rydell, Eric Breitbart, David Dunstan, and Paul Greenhalgh, helped us navigate through some difficult rapids at points in the process of putting this book together. Tammy Lau, Jean Coffey, and Alexander Geppert were very generous in letting us mine their extensive bibliography on fairs and expositions, and Tammy and Jean offered help from their vantage point in the special collections department in the Henry Madden Library at California State University, Fresno. Martin Manning, curator of the Public Diplomacy Archives at the U.S. Department of State archives, loaned us pictures of recent fairs that would have been difficult to obtain otherwise and also made valuable suggestions for authors of various essays. Dr. Vicente Loscertales, Sandrine Toiron, Dimitri Kerkentzes, and Anca Anghel all did much to make a research trip to the Bureau of International Expositions in Paris both pleasant and profitable, and Veronique Marteau has helped us in many ways from her home in Paris. Si Yan of the Expo 2010 organizing committee gave us useful information on that upcoming exposition. Kristen Brackett prepared the list of websites found in the general bibliography, and we thank her for her computer skills and willingness to take on this task on short notice. Carol Findling provided some much-appreciated last-minute typing help, and many of our friends and family members provided much-needed moral support along the way. Most importantly, we thank our authors for the time and effort they put into the work of preparing the essays on the fairs, and for providing many of the images that enhance the text. Without them, there would have been no book. In the end, though, the final product is ours, and we accept responsibility for the good, the bad, and the ugly.

London 1851

John R. Davis

The Great Exhibition of the Works of Industry of All Nations

The Great Exhibition of the Works of Industry of All Nations opened on May 1 and closed on October 15, 1851. Housed in what had become, even prior to its opening, popularly known as the Crystal Palace in Hyde Park, the exhibition became an immediate and spectacular success. It captured the minds of Britons and foreigners. It appeared to symbolize the optimism and success of the new industrial period. The Great Exhibition was an event of significance for contemporaries. It has remained so for those looking back, becoming a milestone in historical literature, a starting point for exhibition studies, and a talisman of the Victorian age and the establishment of modernity.

The success of the exhibition was by no means a foregone conclusion. Indeed, there were many who feared and even hoped that it would be a catastrophic failure. The idea of a "great" national exhibition had been promoted most prominently by the Society of Arts. This organization had sustained a tradition of supporting good technical and artistic design through premiums and small-scale exhibitions going back to its foundation in 1754. The Royal Academy also had a long-standing tradition of art exhibitions. During the first half of the nineteenth century, however, interest had grown generally in British exhibitions. French and German organizers were showing a worrying capacity to compete with Britain, particularly in manufactured goods. Mass production was also believed to be undermining tasteful craftsmanship, meanwhile, with perceived negative consequences for artists and artisans as well as for social stability.

The concerns of economic reformers had led to a Parliamentary investigation in 1835–1836, and the subsequent foundation of a School of Design at Somerset House. Other British organizations were also beginning to take action. Mechanics' Institutes had begun holding small-scale events in different parts of Britain. This encouraged, in 1828, the foundation by the Society for the Diffusion of Useful Knowledge of a National Repository for the Exhibition of New and Improved Productions on Trafalgar Square. The Society of Arts' finances were not healthy, and it was felt that something needed to be undertaken to revive it and remind the public of its relevance. On the continent, a tradition of exhibitions had developed as a means of promoting craftsmanship, often with state support. Members of the Society looked to the continental model of exhibitions, particularly those of Paris and Berlin in 1844, and proposed transferring it to Britain. Several tentative exhibitions were held at the Society's premises in the Adelphi between 1845 and 1849, proving the financial viability of such undertakings, and encouraging plans for a "great" national event.

Two factors in particular shaped the Society of Arts' plans further. One was the assumption of the presidency of the Society by Prince Albert in 1840, whose advanced and enlightened notions about education and experience of continental practices made him the strongest and firmest advocate of an international, rather than merely national, exhibition. The other was the successful outcome of the political battle for Free Trade, marked in 1846 by the abolition of the Corn Laws by the government of Sir Robert Peel. This step testified to the general confidence of British manufacturers in their ability to compete, but also expressed a desire to internationalize the British economy. The new British government of Lord John Russell, brought in on the tide of support for Free Trade, seized on the idea of using the exhibition to showcase British goods abroad, educate domestic manufacturers about foreign suppliers, and thus put pressure on foreign governments to reduce their own tariffs.

The mixture of intentions behind the exhibition could therefore largely be described as a modernizing agenda, with a strong emphasis on industrial development and commercial liberalization. Despite the introduction of Free Trade and the support of reformers and significant sections of the country for industrialization, such an agenda was still heavily contested at the time, and it was this that meant the exhibition was opposed and its success was doubted until the day it opened. Opposition came from a range of quarters, including protectionist industry, landed interests, conservatives and socialists, for example, while many intellectuals and social commentators occupied positions of critical distance from the exhibition's aims.

Such opposition was vociferous. It was louder than it was substantial, however, and the exhibition had much to support it. One factor was the method of organization that lay behind it. Victorian concern with the maintenance of probity in government and by the monarchy led to the Society's original business contract for an exhibition being annulled, and the proposal that the exhibition be funded by donations, subscriptions and entry takings. This necessitated, in turn, a keen interest in raising public support, not least through the organization of some significant events during the run-up to the exhibition. A Mansion House Banquet, a Mayors' Banquet at York, as well as numerous other social events contributed to fundraising, publicity, and the development of a pro-exhibition movement. The voluntary funding structure also meant the exhibits were defined in part with a view to engaging the country as a whole. Local committees were set up for the whole country, which were not only crucial to fundraising but also instrumental in choosing exhibits. Visits to the exhibition were

often motivated by a desire to see how the locality had fared on the national and international stage.

Probity also led to the foundation of a Royal Commission to organize the exhibition. This displaced the Society, which was seen as too narrow a body, and which, had it been left in control, might have created an impression that the Prince Consort was involved in a money-making exercise. Still chaired by Prince Albert, the Royal Commission was carefully constructed to include as many sectors of the British economy, society, and political spectrum as possible while maintaining the broad consensus of the modernizing agenda. It included among its number politicians (Sir Robert Peel, W.E. Gladstone, Lord Stanley, Lord John Russell, Richard Cobden), commercial leaders (Henry Labouchere and Lord Granville of the Board of Trade and Thomas Bazley, the president of the powerful Manchester Chamber of Commerce), artists (Charles Barry, Charles Eastlake and Richard Westmacott), scientists (Lord Rosse, Charles Lyell and William Hopkins) and others from London's financial interests from agriculture, and from the aristocracy. Its day-to-day activities were placed in the hands of an executive committee, formed of members of the Society who had led the exhibition project, Henry Cole, Francis Fuller, George Drew and Charles Wentworth Dilke, as well as from the Board of Trade, Stafford Northcote and, crucially in terms of organization, Colonel William Reid, a man combining military organization and intellectual credibility. Coordinating the activities of the local committees was Lyon Playfair, who had helped devise the classification scheme, and who became an increasingly influential force in the Commission.

Another major factor assuring the exhibition's success, indeed, was the range of interests supporting it. The government's support was essential. A careful course had to be steered to prevent the exhibition being seen as a Free Trade or liberal project and to lend the event the status of a national undertaking. Hence substantial efforts were made to retain the backing of all political parties, and the occasion was used to build bridges with disgruntled and alienated protectionist conservatives. Nevertheless, the strongest supporters of the exhibition came from liberal and Peelite conserv-

Visitors gather near Joseph Paxton's great Crystal Palace, the innovative building that helped guarantee the success of the first modern world's fair (from C.B. Norton, *World's Fairs from London 1851 to Chicago 1893,* 1892).

ative parties, and the exhibition reflected to a great extent the ambitions of the Russell government as well as the new political consensus of the mid-century based on Free Trade. The government could not give financial backing. However, official channels such as the diplomatic service were used to make arrangements with foreign countries. Special arrangements were made by the customs authorities to allow for the free entry of goods destined for Hyde Park.

The support of the monarchy was crucial. While Prince Albert did not, as has been popularly asserted, initiate the exhibition, the event would not have taken place without him. His connections, intellectual strength, and energetic commitment made preparations possible, and his personal network of correspondents was vital. Albert's, but especially also Queen Victoria's, demonstrative support set the official seal of approval on the exhibition but also, significantly, encouraged loyal support for it particularly within aristocratic and conservative circles. If one event can be said to have shaped reception of the exhibition as a whole, it was the opening ceremony on May 1, which resembled a new coronation of Victoria in the industrial setting of the Crystal Palace. Ancient ceremonial and pageantry was extended to industry and validated it as an acceptable feature of national life. The European, colonial, and international dimensions of the exhibition

insured the message at the heart of this spectacle was absorbed widely abroad.

A final reason for the exhibition's success was Joseph Paxton's building, which captured the popular imagination, and was seen by many as a primary reason for visiting. Again in line with current views about probity, a competition had been held to find the best building design, but the winning plan, an enormous brick building with a dome similar to that at the British Museum, attracted a great deal of criticism. Somewhat inappropriately, Paxton's plan was accepted at the last minute and in desperate haste as a replacement by the Royal Commission, which recognized its practical benefits. The building could be set up and taken down, allowing the uproarious opposition of Kensington residents to its erection, exploited by protectionists, to be defused by pointing to its temporary nature. It was flexible in design, a necessity at a time when the exact proportions of the exhibition were unknown. More than anything, however, it was based on a quite modern principle of architecture, capturing in built form the spirit of the age. It utilized immense amounts of glass, giving it an aesthetic quality of light and weightlessness quite revolutionary at the time. It also exploited new techniques of production, erection, and construction, all of which were subjected to a great deal of public scrutiny, encouraged in turn by everyone involved. Constructed by the Birmingham-based contractors Fox and Henderson, the Crystal Palace was designed along modular lines, with cast iron columns placed at 24-foot intervals and creating an open-plan space enclosed by walls and ceilings of rolled glass. It was 1851 feet in length running west-east, two stories high, with an arched transept at its center, allowing for main entrances from the north and south. The transept, indeed, formed an iconic architectural feature, and founded a tradition of architectural adventure connected to exhibitions. It had not been in Paxton's original concept, but was the happy result of practical discussions about how to build around Hyde Park's trees.

Physically, the transept divided the exhibition into two general parts: British and colonial produce in the western half of the building and foreign goods in the eastern half. As visitors entered, they encountered the high, arched ceiling of glass, beneath which were two of Hyde Park's elms, ornate wroughtiron gates by the Coalbrookdale company, palm trees, statues of political and Classical heroes and, at the center, the so-called Crystal Fountain by F & C Osler, a gigantic glass Gothic spire, lit from within, and cascading with perfumed water. To either side, the display extended into the distance. Exhibits were divided into four general sections representing a hierarchy of production: raw materials; machinery; manufactured products; and fine arts. These, in turn, were subdivided into a total of 30 classes. The classification, however, was less obvious in the arrangement of the exhibits than in the exhibition catalogue, and geographic subdivision was a more obvious criterion of placement.

Reflecting the relatively advanced state of manufacture in the country, the ease of transport, and support for the exhibition's aims, the British display was by far the largest, occupying almost all the western half of the building. The priorities of the exhibition could be discerned in the proximity of fine arts to the transept, and the ornate goods of India were also placed here. In the east, visitors walked through so-called courts, passed the refined goods of Turkey and China, and then through the displays of France, Belgium, Austria, the German Customs Union (*Zollverein*), Russia, and the United States. Here, countries' ranking reflected generally perceived strengths in manufacturing. Nevertheless, logistical neces-

sities led to some unsystematic solutions, and refreshment courts, stairwells, executive offices, and the like broke up the sense of order. The coherence was even less obvious upstairs, where goods were located for their lightness more than according to any systematic rationale.

The variety of reasons for holding the exhibition was reflected in the multifaceted quality of its display. The comparative, educational aims of economic reform meant the best in technological and artistic design as applied to industry was on show. The categorization of the display, based on a sense of hierarchy of manufacture, was broken up by the insistence of foreign countries that their goods be exhibited together, and national rivalry hence cut across pedagogical abstraction. The original aim of educating industrialists had also been overlaid with the necessity to entertain the masses, and artifacts were added for their curiosity, beauty, or impressiveness rather than their didactic value.

While the exhibition had lost some of its overarching coherence, however, it gained in its impact. The photogenic building, an explosion of novelty at the time, exerted a strong pull on visitors of its own. Then there was the presence of so-called "lions" of the exhibition, artifacts which individually attracted a great deal of attention. These famously included the Koh-i-Noor diamond, Osler's fountain, the stuffed animals from Württemberg, the French Gobelin tapestries, the gigantic vases from Russia, and the sumptuous wares of India. Still, statues of famous politicians, of Victoria and Albert, sculptures, technical marvels such as telegraphs and calculating machines, vast steam hammers and whole cotton-weaving machines, also worked their influence on the public and the press. The great combination of such a vast range of products, the variety of priorities which appeared to have determined the display, and the novelty of many of the objects shown, meanwhile, insured a lasting discussion about the exhibition's meaning, value, and purpose.

Public interpretation extended beyond the already ambitious rationale of the Royal Commission, with many speaking of the exhibition as a complete view of human progress, as a harbinger of international peace and fraternity, and as evidence of the providence of God. Such themes were reflected outside the Crystal Palace in society at large. Poems, songs, plays and orchestral pieces celebrated the grand aims of the exhibition, and occasionally lampooned them. Such themes, as well as raw commercial self-interest, spawned a range of associated attractions and events across London, including Wyld's "Monster Globe" as Leicester Square, Alexis Soyer's "Gastronomic Symposium of All Nations" at Gore House opposite the exhibition, and the display of a Chinese junk on the Thames. The exhibition mania also encouraged more highbrow events, such as the reception of foreign commissioners in Birmingham, the official invitation of the Royal Commission to Paris and St. Cloud, and a dinner given by George Peabody for American exhibitors.

The contents of the Great Exhibition were recorded in detail in a four-volume *Official and Descriptive Catalogue*, published by Spicer Brothers, a work valued by many at the time as a reference of producers and suppliers worldwide, but certainly not intended to be an actual guide to exhibits on display. Again, testifying to the popularity of the exhibition, this official catalogue was accompanied by many unofficial guides of greater and lesser authority, mostly aiming to provide information in a more digestible and inexpensive format. Manufacturers, meanwhile, were prevented from displaying prices on exhibits by the Royal Commission, but produced their own brochures and catalogues for those wishing to make purchases. The *Official and Descriptive Catalogue*'s authority as a reference work could not last as economic development soon made it obsolete. However, it stands as a monumental source of information on industry in the mid-nineteenth century. The additional commemorative volume containing *Reports of the Juries*, meanwhile, is also of great significance for its photographic content, carried out early in the history of photography.

The pricing structure for entry to the exhibition was also cleverly planned. It insured, on the one hand, the entry of the wealthy classes early in the season, thus attaching social prestige to a visit. On the other it also provided for ease of access for the less well-off later on. The careful records of the Royal Commission revealed over 6 million visitors to the exhibition, though repeat visits probably made up part of this figure. More importantly, perhaps,

the exhibition made a solid profit of £186,000, a substantial amount at the time. The exhibition had proved itself against its critics financially, and had also created an avenue for future projects.

Historical literature on the Great Exhibition is extensive. Early accounts tended to be eulogistic, and works written against the backdrop of later exhibitions have tended to follow this example. A consistent interest in the exhibition and its contents down to the present has been generated by naïve and voyeuristic historical curiosity and the antiquarian obsession with Victoriana. One consequence of the popular success of the event is the continued presence of countless types of memorabilia in museums and antique stores. A more critical tone was assumed, however, when later generations began to reject the priorities, lifestyle and assumptions of the Victorians. The exhibition's artifacts were seen as aesthetically deficient. Opponents of industrial development, capitalism and modernization, often echoing and drawing on contemporary critiques, highlighted the exhibition's failure to represent the disadvantages and social costs of modernity and its inherent imperialist messages. On the other hand, economic historians since the 1960s have begun to appreciate the significance of exhibitions as important routes for technology transfer. More recently, with greater historical perspective on modernization, the Great Exhibition has been identified as an important event in that process, allowing both reflection on, and furtherance of, industrialization.

The Great Exhibition was groundbreaking in many ways. Nothing quite like it had been seen before. A good deal of the event's legacy is due to the fact that many wished to perpetuate, recapture, or replicate its success. The popular appeal of the Crystal Palace building and the exhibition generated the financial scheme to remove it to Sydenham, a suburb in south London. The Crystal Palace, rebuilt at Sydenham and housing events strongly reminiscent of the exhibition's more populist aspects, enjoyed an important cultural position in late Victorian and early twentieth-century Britain until it was consumed by fire in 1936. The more cerebral and pedagogic aims of the exhibition were taken up by the Royal Commission. Using the financial profit of the event, it purchased a large estate in South Kensington, close to the original site of the Crystal Palace, and founded there a complex of museums, colleges, and cultural institutions. Many exhibits from the exhibition would be transferred there into the Natural History and Victoria and Albert Museums. Staff closely connected with the Crystal Palace would continue their activities there, such as Henry Cole and Lyon Playfair, who took over at the Department of Science and Art. The model of the Great Exhibition was taken up by other countries, meanwhile, and a tradition of international exhibitions, expos as they would later be known, was born. The genesis, execution and results of such events, while all distinctive, follow in many respects the experiences of 1851. The success and profit, meanwhile, have been aspired to again and again, but sadly not always achieved.

The most important legacy of the Great Exhibition, perhaps, was in its contribution to the process of modernization. At a time when industrialization was causing social problems across Europe, when British politics and society were polarised, and when commitment to Free Trade and economic development was fragile, the Great Exhibition not only served an important cathartic function but also acted as a superbly effective propaganda weapon in favor of modernity. Subsequent claims that the economic boom of the 1850s was caused by the exhibition are hard to verify, and probably groundless, and it is also important to recognize that the upswing in financial fortunes might have done as much as the exhibition to stabilize the situation. However, the Great Exhibition certainly sent out a powerful message, felt not just in Britain but also abroad, where reformers and supporters of progress utilized it to bring change in their homelands. It launched many industrial careers, and created economic ties of importance, across Europe as well as at the colonial level. It brought together a significant network of personal connections. The Gladstonian liberal grouping in particular appeared to have strong roots in the Royal Commission. Reformers in Britain and elsewhere managed to use their connections via the exhibition to enhance their political positions and their objectives. Finally, the traditional aristocratic rulers of the country were brought together with the striving and capitalistic masses, and a new consensus based upon modernization was forged.

Bibliography

The primary and substantial archival collections essential to research on the Great Exhibition are held at the Royal Society of Arts, the Royal Commission of 1851, the Royal Archives Windsor, the National Art Library within the Victoria and Albert Museum, and the National Archives at Kew. Further important collections are located at the Bishopsgate Institute, the London Museum, and the British Library, while most relevant newspaper coverage is found at the British Library's Newspaper Library at Colindale. Countless collections outside Britain also exist.

The Great Exhibition's organization and extent is well recorded. The *Official Descriptive and Illustrated Catalogue* (1851), edited by Robert Ellis, with an historical introduction by Henry Cole, lists all categories and exhibits in four volumes. Further copious statistical information can be found in the first and second *Report of the Commissioners for the Exhibition of 1851* (1851 and 1852). Also useful, for its photographic record, is the presentation copy of the *Reports of the Juries* (1852), as well as R. Hunt, *Handbooks to the Official Catalogue* (1851); the Royal Society of Arts' *Lectures on the Results of the Great Exhibition* (1853); and John Tallis, *History and Description of the Crystal Palace* (1852). The reprint of the *Art Journal*'s catalogue, titled *The Great Exhibition. London's Crystal Palace Exposition of 1851* (1995), is an attractive, informative and accessible overview of artifact design.

An older, though still useful, secondary work is Yvonne French, *The Great Exhibition, 1851* (1950), while Charles Gibbs-Smith's *The Great Exhibition of 1851* (1950), provides an illustrated if orthodox accompaniment. More critical coverage is to be found in Christopher Hobhouse, *1851 and the Crystal Palace, Being an Account of the Great Exhibition and its Contents* (1937) and, more influentially, Nikolaus Pevsner, *High Victorian Design: A Study of the Exhibits of 1851* (1951). Paul Greenhalgh, *Ephemeral Vistas: The Expositions Universelles, Great Exhibitions and World's Fairs, 1851–1939* (1988), offers some revision of the significance of the Great Exhibition and points to its place in the exposition tradition. The economic significance of the Great Exhibition is evaluated most recently by Anthony David Edwards *International Exhibitions, British Economic Decline and the Technical Education Issue 1851–1910* (2000). To learn more about the destruction of the Crystal Palace, see Allison Edwards and Keith Wyncoll, eds., *"The Crystal Palace Is on Fire!" Memories of the 30th November 1936* (1998).

A substantial step in the foundation of a new historiography of the Great Exhibition and exhibitions generally is Utz Haltern, *Die Londoner Weltausstellung von 1851: Ein Beitrag zur Geschichte der bürgerlich-industriellen Gesellschaft im 19. Jahrhundert* (1971), which provides not only the most detailed history of the event, but also a powerful thesis regarding its significance to modernization. Among the valuable and essential recent studies are Jeffrey Auerbach, *The Great Exhibition of 1851: A Nation on Display* (1999), investigating the event as a reflection of, and discussion about, national identity in a new, modern setting; *The Great Exhibition and Its Legacy* (2002), edited by Franz Bosbach and John Davis, et al., which centers on the domestic ramifications and international influence of the event; James Buzard, Joseph W. Childers and Eileen Gillooly, *Victorian Prism: Refractions of the Crystal Palace* (2007), which is an edited collection bringing together recent research evaluating the event's significance; and Jeffrey Auerbach and Peter Hoffenberg's edited collection, *Britain, the Empire and the World at the Great Exhibition of 1851* (2008), which seeks to outline and explain the international dimensions of the event.

Dublin 1853

Tammy Lau

The Great Industrial Exhibition

Ireland's first international exhibition was planned with great optimism in the aftermath of the first potato famine. It was believed that the exhibition would stimulate economic growth and industrialization across the country following the example of the Great Exhibition of 1851. The organizers were convinced that the exhibition would "contribute very largely to render Ireland that which she is so eminently qualified to become ... a manufacturing country ... and that hitherto undeveloped sources of prosperity and power in Ireland will date a new era from the Exhibition of 1853." This idea was partially based on the success of the Royal Dublin Society's industrial and scientific exhibitions, which had been held every three years since 1834. The other impetus came from the first national exhibition held in Cork in 1852.

The wealthy railroad owner William Dargan, about to become mayor of Dublin, offered a loan of between £15,000 and £20,000 to expand a previously planned industrial exhibition into an international exhibition similar to the 1851 Crystal Palace exhibition in London. Dargan's associate, Cusack P. Rooney, was appointed secretary of the exhibition, and John C. Deane became his assistant. John Benson, the county surveyor of East Riding of Cork and the engineer for the Cork Harbour Commissioners, won a public competition to design the exhibition building. Built on the grounds of the Royal Dublin Society and nicknamed the Irish Crystal Palace, Benson's exhibition building in fact differed greatly from Joseph Paxton's Crystal Palace in both size (only a third as large) and style.

The American version of England's Crystal Palace exhibition caused many problems for Rooney and Deane as their efforts to secure industrial exhibits from Britain and the Continent were thwarted by Charles Buscheck, the American agent in charge of acquiring exhibits for the New York Crystal Palace exhibition, which offered a wider and much more lucrative market for European manufacturers than the Dublin exhibition, which meant that Rooney and Deane went home largely disappointed.

Because of his inability to gather industrial exhibits, Rooney turned his attention to indiscriminately accumulating art exhibits, which quickly overwhelmed all other kinds of exhibits and necessitated enlarging the exhibition building. There were four main categories (Raw Materials, Machinery, Manufactures, and Fine Arts and Antiquities) as well as thirty subdivisions, taken from the classification scheme of the Great Exhibition of 1851. However, because of the preponderance of fine arts

An interior view of the Fine Arts gallery at the Dublin 1853 exhibition (*Illustrated London News,* June 4, 1853).

exhibits, it became impossible to distribute the exhibits evenly throughout the building, resulting in a rather haphazard arrangement that displeased critics.

The manufactured items on display were, for the most part, luxury items such as ornate furniture meant for the wealthy rather than the masses. Although linen was the one native industrialized product that made an impression in the industrial sector, handcrafted lace and embroidery received more attention at the exhibition. The United States and most major European countries sent exhibits, but the vast majority were specialized luxury items or national curiosities, an indication that the Irish commercial market was not worthy of serious consideration. Only Minoy Freres of Paris sent items suitable for purchase, in this case an impressive assortment of affordable clocks. Decorative items symbolizing life in India, Japan, and China, arranged through the Lon-

don Society of Arts, were also very popular, although largely ceremonial in nature.

The admission price for the exhibition was beyond the means of most citizens, which resulted in disappointing attendance in its early months. Although the building could accommodate 15,000 people at a time, fewer than 2,000 visitors a day attended the exhibition even on days when the price was reduced. Many of the attendees were repeat visitors or season ticket holders from Dublin's upper class. Exhibition officials and exhibitors accounted for one-sixth of the daily visitors.

In an effort to stimulate interest and boost attendance, the organizers arranged for Queen Victoria, Prince Albert and two of their children to visit in late August. This did indeed give a temporary boost to attendance. Exhibition officials finally lowered the admission price for the last two months and attendance rose significantly. At the same time, the Midland Great

Western Railway was persuaded to provide special third class roundtrip exhibition fares, with admission included, from different parts of Ireland, and this enabled more people from outside metropolitan Dublin to come to the exhibition.

Not surprisingly, the exhibition failed to make a profit, but it did provide much-needed short term employment for those in the construction and tourist trades. It also resulted in a fund for a public art museum in honor of William Dargan. Built on the exhibition grounds, this became the National Gallery of Ireland.

In the final analysis, despite widespread criticism that the 1853 Exhibition did not live up to its promise of fostering industrial progress in Ireland, what the exhibition did do was demonstrate to the Irish people and the world that Ireland was capable of putting on an international exhibition of the same sort as the Great Exhibition of 1851 ... and countless others in the years to come.

Bibliography

The *Official Catalogue of the Great Industrial Exhibition in connexion with the Royal Dublin Society, 1853* is probably the best source on this exhibition. However, the official catalogue was supplemented by the *Synopsis of the Contents of the Great Industrial Exhibition of 1853 in connection with the Royal Dublin Society, and Guide to its Internal Arrangements* in which C.C. Adley, the superintendent of machinery, describes the agricultural and industrial exhibits. There is also the *Illustrated Dublin Exhibition Catalogue: the Exhibition of Art-Industry in Dublin* put out by the *Art-Journal* with descriptions and illustrations of the *objets d'art* that were on display. The weekly newspaper, *The Exposition Expositor and Advertiser* put out by John Sproule in twenty-five issues, is also an excellent primary source. A special supplement to the *Illustrated London News* (June 4, 1853), gives a very detailed description of the Dublin exhibition and its many and varied exhibits, along with a number of line-engraved illustrations. Other contemporary publications include William J. Battersby, *The Glories of the Great International Exhibition of All Nations in 1853* (1853), particularly useful on the opening ceremonies and the queen's visit; Thomas D. Jones, *Record of the Great Industrial Exhibition 1853* (1854), containing information in attendance and specific exhibits; and Henry Parkinson and Peter Lund Simmonds, *The Illustrated Record and Descriptive Catalogue of the Dublin International Exhibition 1865* (1866), drawing comparisons between the 1853 and 1865 Dublin fairs.

The one secondary source on this exhibition is Alun C. Davies, "Ireland's Crystal Palace, 1853" in J.M. Goldstrom and L.A. Clarkson, eds., *Irish Population, Economy, and Society: Essays in Honour of the Late K.H. Connell* (1981), 249–70. Davies also wrote "The First Irish Industrial Exhibition: Cork 1852," *Irish Economic and Social History* 11 (1975) which could be useful as background reading giving researchers a better sense of the social and economic context.

There is even a work of fiction, *Erin's Fairy Spell, or, the Palace of Industry and Pleasure: a Vision* by William Scribble. Scribble, whose real name was William Smith, was a comic poet; his book takes a lighter look at the exhibition.

New York 1853

Ivan D. Steen

Exhibition of the Industry of All Nations

In 1853–1854, New York City hosted the first world's fair ever held in America. The inspiration for that fair was the 1851 Great Exhibition at the Crystal Palace in London. Businessmen from the United States who attended the Great Exhibition were very favorably impressed by the fair and by the successes of American exhibitors, who won a large number of prizes. Many left London convinced that a similar exhibition should be held in the United States.

There was little doubt that if the United States were to have a world's fair it would be held in New York City. The project was promoted primarily by New Yorkers, among them Horace Greeley, who, in a May 1851 New York *Tribune* article about the London Crystal Palace, proposed erecting a similar structure in New York. The most active early promoter of such an exhibition was Edward Riddle, a Massachusetts auctioneer, who also advocated a New York site. Mid-nineteenth-century New York fancied itself, and was widely regarded as, the London of America; if London hosted a great international exhibition, New York surely would have to follow suit.

The site originally chosen for the fair was Madison Square, but opposition from local residents and others resulted in its location at Reservoir Square. This square was bounded by Fortieth and Forty-second streets, Sixth Avenue and the Croton distributing reservoir, and is now the site of Bryant Park. Clearly, this was not the best place for the fair; it was far from the center of the city, and the huge reservoir provided a poor backdrop for the building that was to be erected.

Several plans for the structure were submitted, the most interesting coming from Leopold Eidlitz, a prominent New York architect, Joseph Paxton, the designer of the London Crystal Palace, and James Bogardus, the New York architect credited with originating the use of cast-iron exteriors for business buildings. However, the plans chosen were those of Georg J.B. Carstensen and Charles Gildemeister. Carstensen was the designer of Copenhagen's famous Tivoli amusement park, and Gildemeister was a New York architect and lithographer.

Emulating the building housing the London exhibition, the New York structure also was constructed of iron and glass, though its configuration was quite different. The New York Crystal Palace was in the form of a Greek cross, with a 100-foot diameter dome at the intersection of the arms. The total exterior height of the building was 149 feet, and the arms of the cross were 365 feet long. The angles formed by the intersection of the cross were filled with 24-foot-high triangular lean-tos. At each of the eight corners of the building was an octagonal tower, 8 feet in diameter and 75 feet in height. The exhibition area of the New York

Crystal Palace was approximately 4 acres. As applications from prospective exhibitors poured in, its promoters realized that this space would be insufficient. Therefore, an additional two-story building was erected in the space between the main building and the reservoir. This building was used to house a machine arcade and a picture gallery. To lessen the heat and glare from the sun, the Crystal Palace's glass walls were enameled. The London structure had not been so treated, and so the interior of that building had to be covered with canvas. The building was supplied with both gas and water. The gas was to be used to supply adequate lighting should it be decided to open the building at night, while the water was both for drinking and for extinguishing fires. The building was heated by stoves, but this marred the interior effect, since the pipes ran through the whole height of the building.

The speed of erection of the London Crystal Palace was a marvel of the age-the entire building being erected in seventeen weeks. The New York Crystal Palace, however, was noted for the amazingly long period of time required for its construction. Although the first pillar was erected on October 30, 1852, it was not until July 14, 1853-nearly nine months later-that the New York building was in a sufficient state of completion for the exhibition to commence.

The Exhibition of the Industry of All Nations opened with great ceremony, attended by President Franklin Pierce, on July 14, 1853. Although the total number of exhibitors varied from month to month, no fewer than 4,000 were represented at the fair. More were from the United States than from any other country, and the largest single category of American exhibits was that of machinery. Generally, the classification of articles was patterned after the system used at the London exhibition. There were four divisions, each representing a nation or a group of nations. Each division occupied one quarter of the space on the first floor of the Crystal Palace. These divisions were further divided into "courts" — twenty-nine for each division — each representing a category of products. The exhibits representing American industry were particularly notable for displaying the latest applications of technology, and to a greater extent than ever had been presented previously. In addition to the displays of prod-

Colored engraving of the Crystal Palace, New York, by Capewell and Kimmell, 1853 (courtesy New York State Museum, Albany).

ucts relating to industry, the Crystal Palace housed a significant collection of sculpture — the largest such display in the United States until then. The most extensive contribution to this department came from Italy, and it consisted primarily of copies from classical works. Also on display were statues by such notable artists as Baron Carlo Marochetti, August Kiss, and Bertel Thorvaldsen. Among the works exhibited by American sculptors, most noteworthy were those of Hiram Powers, especially his most admired sculpture, *The Greek Slave*. The fair also incorporated a picture gallery. While the quality of the paintings exhibited in the picture gallery was questioned by many contemporaries, the inclusion of that gallery was significant: the New York Crystal Palace exhibition was the first world's fair to include an exhibit of this type. Visitors seeking entertainment beyond that offered by the industrial and artistic exhibits at the Crystal Palace would have to leave the fair's grounds, for unlike later world's fairs, this one contained no midways or sideshows. However, various forms of popular entertainment were to be found in the surrounding area. One of the principal attractions was the Latting Observatory, a 315-foot wooden

tower, located across the street from the Crystal Palace, which offered a panoramic view of New York City.

The opening festivities for the Crystal Palace attracted considerable attention, but the attendance figures were disappointing until the fall months. Still, between July 15 and November 30, nearly 700,000 people were admitted to the Crystal Palace, and more than $300,000 was collected; but in December and January attendance fell off precipitously. In January, the organization's president, Theodore Sedgwick, handed in his resignation but agreed to stay on until a successor could be found. P.T. Barnum was persuaded to take over that office. Although he announced that the exhibition was to become a permanent institution, even that celebrated showman could not rejuvenate it. On July 10, he resigned the presidency. The Crystal Palace Exhibition officially closed on November 1, 1854, leaving a debt of $300,000.

Several factors contributed to the disappointing attendance and insufficient receipts. While railroad construction in the United States was proceeding rapidly, a nation-wide integrated rail system was some years in the future, and travel to New York City would be

The New York Crystal Palace Polka was an example of special music that was composed for many world's fairs but seldom achieved lasting popularity (Larson Collection, Special Collections Library, California State University, Fresno).

days, the only day most wage-earning New Yorkers would be free to attend.

Although a financial failure, the Exhibition of the Industry of All Nations was of considerable significance. It was, after all, the first world's fair held in the United States and the first anywhere to include an exhibit of paintings. It was a source of some pride to New York, and it surely added to that city's economy. Not only did the exhibition draw many tourists into the city, thus providing increased business for hotels and shops, but it also proved lucrative for the construction trades and printers and publishers. Further, like many world's fairs, it served as a proving ground for new concepts. For example, it provided Elisha Graves Otis with an opportunity to have a public demonstration of a practical passenger elevator in 1854. Most significantly, at a time when the police of New York wore no distinctive attire, the special police at the Crystal Palace were outfitted with uniforms and before the end of 1853, the city police were required to be similarly clothed. It is perhaps ironic that the most celebrated day in the history of the Crystal Palace was October 5, 1858, several years after the close of the world's fair. On that day, while the building was being used for the annual exhibit of the American Institute, a fire broke out. In less than half an hour the building was consumed in a spectacular blaze.

difficult from many parts of the country. For visitors to New York, as well as for the city's residents, getting to the Crystal Palace, located three and a quarter miles from City Hall, involved time and expense. Both omnibuses and street railways provided transportation to the fair for 5 or 6 cents. Perhaps this was a small expenditure for those wealthy enough to make the journey to New York from elsewhere, but for working-class New Yorkers the round-trip fare represented a significant portion of a day's wages, especially for a family outing. Adding to that, the admission to the fair cost 50 cents, which would make it a very expensive entertainment. Further, the fair was closed on Sun-

Bibliography

The principal manuscript collection relating to the Exhibition of the Industry of All Nations is the Crystal Palace Papers at the New-York Historical Society. The papers of Samuel Francis du Pont and his wife in The Henry Francis du Pont Winterthur Collection at Longwood Library also contain a significant number of items related to the Crystal Palace.

The most extensive description of the Crystal Palace may be found in Georg J.B. Carstensen, *New York Crystal Palace* (1854). Several catalogs of the exhibits were published by the Association for the Exhibition of the Industry of All Nations, including: *Official Catalogue of the New York Exhibition of the Industry of All Nations, 1853* (1853); *Official Catalogue of the Pictures Contributed to the Exhibition of the Industry of All Nations, in the Picture Gallery of the Crystal Palace* (1853); *Official Awards of Juries, 1853* (1853). These do not contain illustrations depicting any of the items exhibited. Other catalogs and guides do contain illustrations and are generally more interesting. Of these, the most important are: Charles R. Goodrich, ed., *Science and Mechanism: Illustrated by Examples in the New York Exhibition, 1853-4* (1854); Horace Greeley, *Art and Industry as Represented in the Exhibition at the Crystal Palace, New York, 1853–54* (1853); William C. Richards, *A Day in the New York Crystal Palace, and How to Make the Most of It* (1853); and Benjamin Silliman, ed., *The World of Science, Art, and Industry, Illustrated from Examples in the New York Exhibition, 1853–54* (1854).

No books have been written about the New York Crystal Palace exhibition, but a few articles have been published. Earle E. Coleman provides a brief history of the fair and an extended discussion of manuscript and published materials dealing with it in "The Exhibition in the Palace: a Bibliographical Essay," *Bulletin of the New York Public Library* 65 (September 1960): 459–75. A lengthy description of the exhibition, its exhibits, and contemporary reaction to it may be found in Charles Hirschfeld, "America on Exhibition: The New York Crystal Palace," *American Quarterly* 9 (Summer 1957): 101–16. Brooks McNamara, *Day of Jubilee: The Great Age of Public Celebrations in New York, 1788–1909* (1997), makes brief mention of the Crystal Palace and the 1853 exhibition in the context of other public festivities in the city. Grace M. Mayer, "The New York Crystal Palace," *Museum of the City of New York Bulletin* 2 (March 1939): 50–55, is too brief to be of much value. More recent articles are Richard Reinhardt, "The Dubious Glory of New York's 'Great Exhibition,'" *World's Fair* 6, 1 (Winter 1986), and Robert C. Post, "Reflections of American Science and Technology at the New York Crystal Palace Exhibition of 1853," *Journal of American Studies* 17 (1983): 337–56. Two articles by Ivan D. Steen discuss the New York Crystal Palace Exhibition, including its significance to New York City, at some length: "America's First World's Fair: The Exhibition of the Industry of All Nations at New York's Crystal Palace, 1853–1854," *New-York Historical Society Quarterly* 47 (July 1963): 257–87, and "New York's Crystal Palace: Symbol of a World City," *NAHO* 13 (Spring-Summer 1981): 68–71. The fullest discussion of the fair is to be found in Steen's unpublished master's thesis, "The New York Crystal Palace Exhibition" (New York University, 1959). A more recent master's thesis by Thomas Gordon Jayne (University of Delaware, 1990) adds little.

Paris 1855

Barrie M. Ratcliffe

Exposition Universelle

The 1855 Paris Exposition Universelle had multiple, ambiguous, and even conflicting, objectives. To some extent, the aims of other world's fairs shared these characteristics, but the ambiguities of those behind the first Paris international exhibition are especially noteworthy. Organizers intended that the exposition would commemorate the forty years of peace since the battle of Waterloo and trumpet the benefits of international collaboration and yet, if early planning had begun in peacetime, by the time organizing began in earnest Britain, France, and their allies were at war with Russia, which, of course, did not attend (though individual Russian businessmen did). It was meant to further cement the newly crafted

Franco-British alliance, and Queen Victoria made a dazzling visit to the exposition in August 1855, the first state visit by a reigning English monarch since Henry V in 1422. However, each country used its exhibits to showcase its own achievements and build up its national identity, and each government recognized that acquiring the latest technology and to develop successful industrialization constituted the puberty of nations, and that these were the bases of national power and well-being. As a consequence, there was usually discreet rivalry and jockeying for position between the two. The French government not only attempted to ensure that their exhibition would be more successful than its British predecessor — its pavilions covered a much greater area, it had more exhibitors and more participating countries (34 as opposed to 28) — but also attributed greater space to its own exhibitors. Whereas in 1851 British exhibitors had been four times as numerous as the French and had occupied over half the space in the Crystal Palace, in 1855 the proportions were exactly reversed. It was further hoped that the technology and the bounty of consumer goods on display would signal the reality and the promise that capitalist development and progress offered to all: echoing Marx, Walter Benjamin would famously call international expositions "places of pilgrimage to the fetish commodity." Organizers wanted the working classes to attend and kept admission prices low, particularly so on Sundays, so that large numbers of them, especially those in Paris, actually did so. Unfortunately they could only gaze on what wealth could buy and high culture offer but their own condition — over two-thirds of the population of Paris, France's wealthiest city, still lived in poverty — meant they would not share in the feast on display. Their likely reaction is captured in the French proverb, "après la fête on gratte sa tête." As were other world's fairs, too, the spectacle was window-dressing for the city in which it was held. However, set up as it was in the wealthy bourgeois west of the city (in what is now the VIIIth arrondissement) and taking place before Haussmann's urban planning had shown major results, the opulent west had a hidden darker pendant: the overcrowded, and relatively poor working-class living in the city center and east end.

Organizers also hoped that the exposition would serve as an advertisement for the newly installed Second Empire, and that its spectacle would make many forget the Revolution of 1848 as well as the bloody repression of the Second Republic that marked the advent of the current regime. Others, though, had neither forgotten nor forgiven: throughout the Second Empire, but above all during the 1850s, the emperor was the object of numerous plots, some real, others doubtless invented by the forces of order. On the very day the exposition opened, one would-be assassin, who just two weeks earlier had tried to shoot Louis-Napoléon in the Bois de Boulogne, was guillotined, and there would be another attempt four months later when the exposition was still in full swing. Organizers also inaugurated in France the practice of proudly exhibiting the colonial empire, but as did the British with their vast possessions, they did so only by exoticizing and even inventing "Orientalism" and the colonial "other." Whatever their intentions, those behind the exposition could not know that 1855 and 1856 were benchmark years for the regime: the half million who attended, along with the signing of the Treaty of Paris that ended the Crimean War and the birth of the prince imperial, heir to the throne, both of which occurred in March 1856, marked what was to prove the high point of the regime's popularity.

Coming on the heels of the Crystal Palace exhibition, and two other smaller fairs, the exposition has often been seen as merely derivative. This is not the case. It was innovative in a number of ways, all of which would later be emulated. Before 1851, France rather than Britain had had the well-entrenched tradition of holding national industrial exhibitions. Beginning in the 1790s under the Directory, these had continued the public festivals of both the Old Regime and the Revolution and were usually held on the sites where these rites had been celebrated. Successive French governments, along with officially sponsored organizations, such as the Société d'Encouragement pour l'Industrie Nationale (established in 1802), recognized that bringing industrialists together and awarding medals to the most meritorious would stimulate innovation and emulation, while entrepreneurs themselves saw the advertising value of participating. As a consequence, though the first industrial exhibition, held in

1798 had attracted only 110 exhibitors, chiefly from the capital, exactly twice this number of industrialists, representing more departments, exhibited at the second in 1802, and while just 23 prizes had been given out at the first, 80 were awarded at the second. By the time of the tenth such exhibition took place in 1844, 3,960 participated and 3,253 medals were awarded. It had frequently been suggested that industrial exhibitions take place annually in the French capital, and it had even been proposed that the one held in 1849, the last before 1855, be made international. Political circumstances prevented this. The Great Exhibition of 1851 was itself closely modeled on the French example in general and on that held in Paris in 1849 in particular. The 1855 exposition, then, was less derivative than it has been made to appear. Besides, one of the aims of its promoters was to wrest back leadership in organizing such events for France. They succeeded because 1855 was the first of six that would take place in Paris down to 1937. It was innovative in a second way: to encourage attendance by the less wealthy, its admission charges were considerably lower than at London and on Sundays the charge was a mere 20 *centimes* (at 3 francs, the average daily wage for male workers in the capital was fifteen times as much). Although total attendance was a million fewer than at the Crystal Palace, the exposition attracted a larger proportion of the working classes, especially those living in the capital. A third change was introduced: for the first time inexpensive articles of everyday consumption were put on display, as were models of low-cost workers' housing. There is very little evidence, though, that these had any impact in the real world.

More significant was the fourth innovation. While the London exhibition had included only sculpture among the objects it put on show, its Parisian successor built a separate pavilion on the avenue Montaigne devoted entirely to the fine arts. Here were displayed 5,000 works by 2,054 artists representing 29 countries. France's numerical advantage was even more pronounced than it was at the Palace of Industry: 3,634 of the paintings and sculptures were by French artists. Organizers determined early that it be retrospective, that only artists still alive in June 1853 would be eligible to show, and that national juries would select the works they wanted to represent their

country. The French expected to be able to demonstrate the prowess of their artists and France's domination of high culture. They were not disappointed. French sculptors led their section: François Rude, Francisque Duret, and Augustin Dumont were awarded the highest medals. French painters were even more dominant, and entire sections of the pavilion were devoted to the works of Ingres, Delacroix, Decamps, and Vernet. At the same time, however, the exposition also served to reveal strains in the world of French art. The French jury continued to favor the morally uplifting art that had been shown at previous Salons, art that successive governments had patronized. As a consequence, though it accepted some works by the young realist painter Gustave Courbet, while it rejected two that posterity would rightly consider two of his finest: *Burial at Ornans* and *The Studio of the Painter*. In retaliation, Courbet organized his own rival exhibition in a tent set up opposite the fine arts pavilion, producing a catalog and charging admission. When viewed in a longer perspective, his gesture, mocked by critics at the time, can be seen as one of a number of crucial symbolic challenges to the power of officially sanctioned art in later nineteenth-century France. Complacency about the supremacy of French art was also shaken by the popular success that foreign and especially British art enjoyed. With both John Constable and J.M.W.Turner dead and their works therefore not on display, Britain did not possess artists of the stature of Ingres or Delacroix, and French commentators were often scathing about British genre painting and the absence in their works of what they deemed to be proper historical subjects. However, both they and the French public were brought into contact with some of the finest early Victorian artists—William Frith, Edwin Landseer, William Holman Hunt, and John Everett Millais—who until then had been very little known across the English Channel. At the same time, critics could not hide their envy that British artists were more widely supported by private patrons than were their French counterparts, still overwhelmingly dependent on government support. It was, then, the pavilion on the avenue Montaigne that attracted the most critical attention as well as one in five visitors to the exposition: it was perhaps the most important of the innovations introduced. It should be noted, too, that music also served to signal the cultural vibrancy of French, and especially Parisian, life. At the end of April 1855 Hector Berlioz conducted his *Te Deum* in the capital and, at the exposition's closing ceremony, he conducted a performance with twelve hundred participants of his *l'Impériale* cantata. In June of the same year, Giuseppe Verdi presented *The Sicilian Vespers* that he had recently composed in Paris. The year 1855 was an unequivocal triumph for French high culture.

Preparations for the Paris exposition began even before the Crystal Palace had closed its doors. On March 27, 1852, the French government approved the formation of a private company whose purpose was to build and operate a permanent structure to house future industrial exhibitions (previous exhibitions had been held either in temporary buildings or in space allocated in the Louvre museum). The state donated the land and guaranteed a minimum 4 percent annual return on the original capital; in return, it would gain possession on the building in 1898. Though the exposition itself lost money, the company that built and operated the Palace of Industry actually earned a profit. A year later, in imperial decrees of March 8 and June 22, 1853, the holding of an international exposition was announced and the following December a commission of thirty-seven was given the responsibility of organizing the event. This body, which was divided into two sections, one for the agricultural and industrial exhibits and one for the fine arts, included leading political figures, such as Jules Baroche and the duc de Morny, as well as artists such as Ingres and Delacroix. Responsibility for detailed planning, though, rested with a smaller group that included the Emperor's cousin, Prince Napoléon, who proved an effective chair, Frédéric Le Play, the engineer and leading social thinker, Michel Chevalier, a leading economist close to official circles, and Emile Pereire, the financier who was already playing a major role in the economy and the redevelopment of the capital.

It had originally been intended that the entire exhibition would be housed in the Palace of Industry that the private company was already building on the Grand Carré Marigny, an elegant promenade and recreation area along the still developing Champs Elysées, a site now occupied by the Grand and Petit Palais, them-

selves built for the 1900 exposition. The structure that was erected had two remarkable features. One was the speed with which it was completed. The other, more important, was the innovative use that its engineer, Alexandre Barrault, and, to a lesser extent, its architect, Jean-Marie Viel, made of iron frames and glass to give height and light to the building. They designed an iron frame, 250 meters long, 108 meters wide, and 35 meters high, and incorporated reinforced glass in the roof. In this respect, the Palace of Industry thus resembled Joseph Paxton's Crystal Palace. However, Barrault also drew on the examples of the metal and glass canopies of the first Parisian railroad stations, and his design would precede those of the department stores that were to develop rapidly in the Paris of the Second Empire. The Palace of Industry, though, suffered two signal disadvantages. One of these was that the daring engineering was hidden behind a façade that was a pastiche of past architectural styles: the metal frame was prudishly encased in heavy stone facing. The other was that the hall proved too small (it was not as large as the Crystal Palace) and also proved ill-suited to meet the needs of the exposition. Not only did inadequate ventilation mean the building was too hot, a problem that the installation of muslin screens only marginally alleviated in the warm summer of 1855, but, more importantly, insufficient space obliged the organizers to set up two additional temporary structures: a long gallery on the quai de Billy, parallel to the Palace of Industry, and, at one end of the avenue Montaigne, a building in the French Renaissance style, designed by the architect Hector Le Fuel, which was to house the fine arts exhibition.

The layout of the exhibits in both the Palace of Industry and in the glass gallery along the quai de Billy, which put the technology and industrial exhibits on show, was arranged according to a classification devised by Frédéric Le Play. This proved too elaborate to be fully effective, however, and visitors complained that they were unable to follow it. As it had been at London in 1851 and would be at later world's fairs, the greatest emphasis at both pavilions was laid on humanity's increasing capacity to harness nature, on the technology that was such a vital constituent of the spreading nineteenth-century faith in progress. Technology domi-

A view of the entrance of the main building at the Exposition Universelle in Paris 1855 (from Norton, *World's Fairs*, 1892).

nated the glass gallery, where different machines were all driven by a common transmission belt, thereby symbolically demonstrating the interdependence of the different processes and branches of advancing capitalism. The exposition came too soon after the Crystal Palace Exhibition for there to be major new technical advances on display. New machines and process there were, though, and among the most striking were the Singer sewing machines from the United States that successfully synthesized previous developments, the Ruolz silver-electroplating process—Louis-Napoléon purchased a 1,200-place dinner service of silver plate that wags said that since it was not solid silver, it was symptomatic of a not truly legitimate regime — and the production, albeit in small quantities, of a newly discovered metal, aluminum.

The exhibits, as well as the distribution of medals of excellence, served to reveal two significant characteristics of the British and French industries that dominated the exposition. First, the technology gap between the two, which had been considerable after the ending of the Napoleonic wars in 1815, had narrowed,

though it had not disappeared, by 1855. Tariff reformers in France would use the success of so many French industrialists in the medal awards as an argument to persuade their government to follow Britain's lead and lower and even abolish customs barriers. Five years later, the French government would sign a major commercial treaty with the British that would lower tariffs. Second, the exposition showed that if there was rivalry between British and French manufacturers, there was also complementarity: British technology was more successful in heavy engineering, metallurgy, and the preparatory, spinning, and weaving processes in textiles, but the French excelled in textile finishing processes and in producing high-quality goods that required a significant input of design and flair. As the official report on the exposition would put it: "France has its own domain, the taste that no one else has yet been able to equal."

Despite the inevitable delays that mark all such enterprises, and the fact that two additional pavilions had to be hastily erected, the exposition opened only two weeks late on May

15. It closed six months later on November 15, by which time 5,162,230 visitors had attended. When it did so, this combination of theme park, paean to Western prowess, consumerism and high culture, was deemed a success.

Bibliography

With the greater attention scholars have paid in recent years to cultural history in general and in particular to postmodernist discourse analysis, and how the West represented — and invented — both itself and the world beyond Europe, many new studies have been published on the word's fairs. These have usefully treated international exhibitions as windows not only on technical change but also, and above all, on the meaning of spectacle and how cultures and values are constructed. While these approaches are suggestive of ways of approaching international expositions in general, very little work has yet been carried out on the 1855 exhibition and its significance and this despite the attention that continues to be lavished on its better-known London predecessor. If this is so, it is not because contemporary sources, printed or primary, are not available. Achille de Colmont's *Histoire des expositions des produits de l'industrie française* (1855) and Emile Tresca, ed., *Visite à l'exposition universelle de Paris, en 1855* (1855) are still valuable descriptive accounts and may be consulted on the Gallica website of the French National Library (*Gallica.bnf.fr*). The government-sponsored atlases, guides, and reports of the commission established to organize the exposition, all of which were published between 1855 and 1856, are also most accessible published sources. These are: *Exposition universelle de 1855. Atlas descripitif. Dressé par ordre de S.A.I. le prince Napoléon; Catalogue officiel publié par ordre de de la Commission impériale; Rapports du jury mixte international publiés sous la direction de S.A.I. le prince Napoléon* (2 vols.). These have now been made available on line at the Conservatoire numérique des Arts et Métiers (*cnum.cnam.fr*). Anyone wishing to go beyond these official published sources should be aware, though, that the city and departmental police archives offer little on the exposition because in May 1871 the Communards burned both the Hotel de Ville and the Prefecture of Police and most of their manuscript holdings were lost. The archives of the Paris Chamber of Commerce and, more importantly, the Archives Nationales do have important dossiers on planning the event, bringing exhibits to Paris, and the awards made to exhibitors (especially in the F12 series from the

Ministère du Commerce and de l'Industrie and the LH series from the Grande Chancellerie de la Légion d'Honneur).

While they do not fill the void, three kinds of secondary works also offer insights into facets of the 1855 exposition. The first of these consists of recent studies of world's fairs in general and those held in Paris in the second half of the nineteenth century in particular. The most useful of these are: Julie K. Brown, *Making Culture Visible: Photography and Display at Industrial Fairs, International Expositions and Institutional Exhibitions in the U.S. 1847–1900* (2001); Zeynep Celik, *Displaying the Orient: Architecture of Islam at Nineteenth-Century World's Fairs* (1992); Paul Greenhalgh, *Ephemeral Vistas: The Expositions Universelles, Great Exhibitions and World's Fairs 1851–1939* (1988); Philippe Hamon, *Expositions: Literature and Architecture in Nineteenth-Century France* (1992, original French edition 1989); Winfried Kretschmer, *Geschichte der Weltausstellungen* (1999); Pascal Ory, *Les Expositions Universelles: Panorama raisonné, avec des aperçus nouveaux et des illustrations par les meilleurs auteurs* (1982); Werner Plum, *Les exposition universelles au XIXe siècle, spectacles du changement socio-culturel* (1977); Florence Pinot de Villechenon and Jean-Louis Cohen, *Fêtes géantes: les expositions universelles. Pourquoi faire?* (2000); Robert W. Rydell and Nancy Gwinn (eds.), *Fair Representations: World's Fairs and the Modern World* (1994); Brigitte Schroeder-Gudehus and Anne Rasmussen, *Les Fastes du progrès: le guide des expositions universelles, 1851–1992* (1992); Michael J. West, *Spectacular Ideology. The Expositions Universelles de Paris and the Formation of French Cultural Identity, 1855–1937* (on-line text at cmu.edu/courses/mjwest); Martin Wörner, *Vergnügen und Belehrung: Vokskultur auf den Weltsanstellungen, 1851–1900* (1999). A useful, though not exhaustive, bibliography of French industrial and international exhibitions down to 1867 is Régine de Plinval de Guillebon, *Bibliographie analytique des expositions industrielles et commerciales en France depuis l'origine jusqu'à 1867* (2006).

The second kind of study addresses ancillary aspects of the 1855 exposition. For an analysis of its impact on French commercial policies, see Wolfram Kaiser, "Cultural Transfer of Free Trade at the World Exhibitions, 1851–1862," *Journal of Modern History* 77 (2005): 563–590. Dewey Markham has examined the introduction of the classification of Bordeaux wines that was prompted by the government's desire to display France's best vintages at the 1855 exposition: *1855: A History of the Bordeaux Classification* (1997). Barrie M. Ratcliffe has offered an explanation for the success of Parisian industrialists at the exposition — they made up half of French and fully a quarter of all exhibitors—in "Manufacturing in the Metropolis: The Dynamism and Dynamics of Parisian Industry in the Mid-Nineteenth-Century." *Journal of European Economic History* 23 (1994): 263–328.

The fine arts exhibits are the final facet of the 1855 fair that has recently been examined by scholars. The most detailed study is that by Patricia Mainardi, *Art and Politics of the Second Empire: The Universal Expositions of 1855 and 1867* (1987).

Still useful, however, are: Marcia Poynton, "From the Midst of Warfare and its Incidents to the Peaceful Scenes of Home," *Journal of European Studies* 11 (1981): 233–261 and Elizabeth G. Holt, *The Art of All Nations, 1850–1873: The Emerging Role of Exhibitions and Critics* (1981). Pierre Sanchez and Xavier Seydoux, *Les Catalogues des Salons: VI 1852–1857* (2002) includes a chapter on the 1855 fine arts exhibition by Dominique Lobstein and offers a guide to works of art on display.

London 1862

Thomas Prasch

International Exhibition of 1862

Can a palace of glass cast a shadow? The Royal Commissioners responsible for the London International Exhibition of 1862 learned that it could. Working in the massive shadow of the spectacular success of the Great Exhibition of 1851 and the Crystal Palace that housed it, they strove in all ways to make theirs a bigger and better exhibition, one that would leave memories of the Crystal Palace "rivalled, and, I trust, surpassed" by its "beauty and success," as none other than Prince Albert himself, patron saint of 1851, promised in the June 1861 *Illustrated London News*.

And there was good reason to anticipate such success: the hugely profitable Great Exhibition had been followed by great successes at other exhibitions: the international exhibition in Paris in 1855, the Manchester Art Treasures exhibition of 1857, and of course the rebuilt Crystal Park itself, opened as a permanent exhibition site in Sydenham in 1854. Profits from the Great Exhibition had meanwhile been employed to fund a burgeoning complex of museums, gardens, and schools at South Kensington, with the South Kensington Museum (now the Victoria and Albert) at its heart; the new exhibition would be situated on grounds owned by the commissioners of the earlier success (roughly where today's Natural History

Museum stands), and visitors would thus have easy recourse to those permanent installations as well as the new exhibition. The personnel assembled for the project had a rich range of experience: Earl Granville and Wentworth Dilke were both veterans of 1851; William Fairbairn had been involved with the Manchester Art Treasures exhibition; the Duke of Buckingham and Chandos came to the committee with established business success in the railroad industry; and Thomas Baring, M.P., gave the group political clout. The team had the support of the 1851 commission, whose land they leased, the Royal Horticultural Society, whose gardens adjacent to the exhibition would be open to visitors, and the Royal Society of Arts, which as in 1851 acted as patron, and they had raised subscription guarantees of over 450,000 pounds (nearly twice what the Great Exhibition had cost) with which to put together their show.

Although he had no official role on the commission (and would only late in the process be officially named a consultant for the exhibition), the emperor behind the curtains for the 1862 exhibition was Henry Cole, the key figure involved in the 1851 exhibition, made head of the national Schools of Design in that exhibition's wake (and later folding those schools into his Department of Science and Art), and grand master of South Kensington's rapidly growing museum complex. For Cole, even before the Great Exhibition, when he was writing about how to reshape the future of British design in his *Journal of Design and Manufactures* (1848–52), periodic exhibitions provided a key mechanism for targeting multiple audiences—artisans, consumers, and producers—and reinstilling in them the sound design principles lost in the process of industrialization. As he argued (unsuccessfully) for retaining the Crystal Palace in Hyde Park after the Great Exhibition closed, one of the purposes he envisioned for it was regular future exhibitions following and expanding upon the 1851 model. In the wake of the Paris exhibition of 1855, Cole began promoting the idea of decennial exhibitions in London. In the event, Cole played a significant role, as Elizabeth Bonython and Anthony Burton have shown, in the selection of Francis Fowke as architect, in the color scheme of the building, in the classification scheme for exhibits, and in the allocation and arrangement of space.

They promised bigger and better than 1851, and bigger it was. The exhibition building was bigger, at over 23½ acres, with a front façade that ran 1,250 feet and with two temporary annexes adjoining the meant-to-be-permanent main building. Architect Francis Fowke's answer to the Crystal Palace's innovative use of iron and glass in its construction was an ironwork central nave and two massive glass domes, each greater in diameter than St. Paul's. There were more exhibitors (26,336), more of them from foreign nations (17,851), and more colonies mounting shows (35). The range was wider, most notably (in response to the exhibitions in Paris and Manchester, as well as reflecting the growing reach of the collections of South Kensington itself) incorporating a significant show of fine art to complement the ornamental arts and machinery that had provided the core of exhibited materials in 1851. The wall space of the fine arts wing doubled that of the Manchester show, allowing the display of 6,529 works of painting, sculpture, and engraving by 2,305 English and European artists.

But was bigger better? Practically no one thought so. Critics routinely compared the 1862 exhibition with the Crystal Palace, and almost universally preferred the latter. In matters both big (like the building) and little, critics found far more to carp about than to praise.

Most vociferously, Fowke's exhibition building came under sustained critical attack. Given Fowke's record to that point—he was not, strictly speaking, an architect, but a naval engineer (but then, Cole had argued, Paxton had not been an architect either), and his previous work in the district, the initial iron buildings that first housed the South Kensington Museum (and that still stands, relocated to Bethnel Green initially as a South Kensington annex and now as the Museum of Childhood) had been dubbed by summer-suffering critics the "Brompton Boilers"—the failure is perhaps not entirely surprising, and even less so given accounts of the chaotic if rapid building procedure carried out by Kelk and Lucas, the low-bidding contractors, but the harshness of the criticism remains striking. The *Art Journal* called it a "wretched shed" and a "national disgrace"; *Fraser's* countered with "monstrous piles" and "architectural fungus," its domes "colossal dish covers"; Charles Babbage recalled that it had "the threefold inconvenience of being ugly, useless, and expensive"; an ostensibly French correspondent to the *Times* wrote "even the little boy the guide he say 'dam ugly'"; the *Quarterly Review* called the building an "ignorant, presumptuous, tasteless, extravagant failure."

The building had been designed to provide a permanent structure at the site, and, in advance of the opening, Cole had written, in a pamphlet defending the work, that it "was designed to serve not merely for that Exhibition [of 1862], but for all future exhibitions—International, Colonial, and otherwise." Otherwise would win out. In response to the relentless critical response, the government refused to pay for the purchase of the building, and it was torn down after the exhibition closed (although some of its material was recycled: the glass and iron going into Alexandra Palace, and the wood to assorted London Baptist churches).

Indeed, press coverage of the exhibition's development and displays provide a litany of complaints. Exhibitors griped in advance of the opening about poor access to the site and unfair space assignments to both nations and individual exhibitors. The French demanded the right to wall off their own section, and the newspapers complained when they were allowed to do so. Just as the Crystal Palace had featured a living tree beneath its glass, so the 1862 exhibition

The main building for the London 1862 exhibition was considered a national disgrace by the *Art Journal* published that same year (from Norton, *World's Fairs*, 1892).

sought to do the same, but when the area was assigned to the metalworks of Sheffield, the tree had to be cut down lest watering it would rust the iron on display around it. The Giuseppe Verdi composition commissioned for the opening ceremony was rejected when he sent in a chorale instead of a march, and the refusal of music director Michael Costa to conduct Sterndale Bennett's choral setting of Alfred Lord Tennyson's ode for the opening became public knowledge. On opening day, there were unfinished installations of exhibits and significant signs of unpacking and chaos, as well as confusion about press privileges, the rights of season pass holders at the opening, reserved seating, and proper dress for the opening ceremonies. The ceremony itself (featuring music by Daniel-François-Esprit Abuer, Giacomo Meyerbeer, and Bennett) was dismissed by the *Art Journal* as a "meagre pageant," and others complained that the music could scarcely be heard.

Things got no better for the exhibition after opening day. To many critics, the exhibition seemed less about "progress" (the main theme of the 1851 exhibition) than mere commerce, and thus far less noble in basic aims than its predecessor. Thus Frederick Green-

wood lamented "the portentous Bedlam of peddler sovereignty" in *Cornhill's*, while the *Art-Journal* grumbled that "The Exhibition had been a bazaar ... degrading into a market what should be held as a great congress for the *true* appreciation of industrial progress." William Gibson similarly complained of exhibits "brought together more for business purposed than for the illustration of progress" in *Bentley's*, and the *Quarterly Review* griped about "puffery and shoppishness." The "trophies," large carefully arranged pyramids of products that were a major feature of many exhibits came in for particular criticism; the *Times* of London called them "very large and very ugly things," but when organizers acted to remove many of them, exhibitors complained. The *Official Illustrated Catalogue*, which was financed by paid advertisements, was dismissed by the *Times* as "dull and most unsatisfactory ... two volumes of tradesmen's advertisements," and the volumes sold far less well than anticipated. That still was better than what happened to Francis Turner Palgrave's *Handbook to the Fine Arts Collections*, which was withdrawn after complaints.

Other critics harped on bad service and high prices at the refreshments counter, poor ticket arrangements, too few of the popular shilling days, and mismanaged crowd control. Even the majolica fountain that was one of the exhibition's principal centerpieces provided grounds for criticism, because of the perfuming of its waters: the *Illustrated London News* demanded a scent with "a less cloying and sickly effect." More people, despite all this, came to the 1862 exhibition than had attended the Crystal Palace, but only barely, and fewer than anticipated: 6,211,103, compared to 6,039,195 eleven years before. As a result, when the exhibition closed on November 1, the ledgers showed a minimal profit (Adrian Duncan estimated it at 790 pounds), and that only after Kelk and Lucas sacrificed some of their outstanding claims to clear the deficit.

So what (aside from the poor choice of a building, assorted bits of bad management, and a cloying fountain scent) went so wrong in 1862? The very date — not, after all, ten years after 1851 — provides a partial clue, for timing was a problem from the outset. The Great Exhibition had been able to project an almost utopian promise of a new, peaceful forum for international competition in part because it was staged at a rare moment of relative peace, in the calm that followed the widespread revolutions of 1848. A decade later — a decade of almost continuous continental warfare later — the exhibition organizers would have no such luck. When the Society of Arts began to discuss the idea of a successor to the Crystal Palace in 1858, the outbreak of war between France and Austria and related conflict in Italy led them to decide to postpone the event for a year. But 1862 would prove no more peaceful.

Indeed, the Civil War in the United States would have wide-ranging effects on the exhibition. Most obviously, the war largely took the United States out of the exhibition, in part because of the war itself, as Representative Conklin argued in congressional debate over funding for an American display ("We have a World's Fair now in session on this continent," he proclaimed, and the London *Times* reported), and in part because of Northern hostility to the suspicion of pro-Southern sympathies in Britain (Representative Lovejoy insisted, again as reported by the *Times,* that it was "enough ... to have been humbugged, and dishonoured, and disgraced by the British nation, without now appropriating $35,000 for the purposes of

an American Exhibition there"). In the end, the Americans did participate, but on a far smaller scale than originally anticipated, on such short notice that they were given very limited exhibition space, and largely through privately organized funds. But the war also had a major impact on Britain itself, whose cotton-consuming textile mills were hit hard by the cutoff of Southern cotton supplies. Commentators noted both a dearth of textile displays in 1862 and a relative lack of workers, less able to attend the exhibition because of the depressed textile economy despite the shilling days (a tradition carried over from 1851) that were designed to encourage working-class attendance. They "have not even shillings to pay this year," a writer in *Chambers' Journal* noted.

The timing of the exhibition also suffered because of the death in December 1861 of Prince Albert, consort to Queen Victoria and one of the prime movers for the original Great Exhibition. His death plunged the queen into the deep widowhood that largely removed her from public sight for the next two decades, and presented the exhibition organizers with an eerily ominous opening ceremony: the temporary throne erected for the occasion stood empty, with busts of Albert and Victoria on either side. Every speech opened with a reference to the dead prince, and Tennyson's ode for the occasion focused on him as well, addressing the "silent father of our Kings to be," and recalling that "the world-compelling plan was thine." But it was the Crystal Palace Tennyson hearkened to, in an ode far more backward-looking than progressively forward in its tenor.

Still, for all its difficulties, the London International Exhibition of 1862 was not without its significant accomplishments. For one, it achieved Cole's most basic aim: to establish the principle of regular international exhibitions as part of the broad educative program carried out in South Kensington. It would be succeeded by a series of international exhibitions on the site in 1871–1874, and another sequence (after Cole's departure from the scene) in 1885–1886. It would also continue to promote progress in invention and technology. The 1862 exhibition would be credited, for example, with the spread of the Bessemer steel process to Germany, and would showcase Charles Babbage's Differential Engine, that precursor to the computer (although not in a way that left Babbage himself at all pleased with the results).

Further, the exhibition continued and extended Cole's central program of revivifying English design, in part through competition among European producers (the basic mechanism Cole had developed as early as his comparative reviewing of current designs in the pre-exhibition era *Journal of Design and Manufacture*, reinforced on the exhibition site through competitive display), and in part through holding up models of preindustrial craftsmanship as a curative to the flawed design ideas of industrial production. As in 1851, and as in the collecting of art that the South Kensington Museum accomplished over the intervening decade, India took pride of place in this latter project, with its extensive display of traditional handicraft again garnering enthusiastic reviews. Again as in 1851, a medieval court featured both reproductions of actual medieval ornament and Victorian neo-Gothic work, this time including the first public exhibition of the new work of Morris and Co., the medieval-style designs wrought by William Morris with his collaborators Edward Burne-Jones, Dante Gabriel Rossetti, and Ford Madox Brown. But in 1862 the design project went further, with the inclusion of an extensive display of Japanese art, much of it seen for the first time in Europe at the exhibition. And, again following the South Kensington Museum's lead, the 1862 exhibition also strongly featured the new art of photography, although exactly how to categorize photographic images in the broader classificatory scheme of the exhibition remained a problematic issue.

The 1862 exhibition went further, too, in bringing the fine arts—traditional painting, drawing, and sculpture—into the exhibitionary orbit. Here, organizers were following the precedents of Paris and Manchester, but also reflecting the growth of the fine arts collections across the street at the South Kensington Museum, with its acquisition over the previous few years of the major Sheepshanks and Soulages collections and its temporary control over the Turner bequest and Vernon collection. At the exhibition, the fine arts followed the pattern of other exhibits in allowing each nation to determine the character of its display, thus strongly encouraging the notion of national schools of art (while explicitly exclud-

ing non–European artistic production). The extensive British display (covering a full half of the space allotted to fine arts) traced a strongly naturalistic trajectory for English art, taking William Hogarth as a founding father, tracking through eighteenth-century masters of portraiture and landscape, and culminating with the work of the Pre-Raphaelite Brotherhood.

That sense of nationalistic competition evident in the arts wing in the shaping of national styles defines as well the most evident dynamic of the 1862 exhibition as a whole: the honing of the international exhibition as an arena of competitive international display. That competition can be seen even before the opening: the *Times*'s careful coverage of installations in progress tracked nation against nation, complaining early on "that the building will be open with the foreign courts complete and beautifully arranged, while the English will have their counters and cases but half-finished, and their displays, of course, proportionately ill-arranged and ill-shown." Closer to opening day, the *Times* reporter could breathe a sigh of relief: the British stood "very far in advance of the foreign competitors," and the arch-rivals, the French, were relatively behind. Similar competitive spirit drove evaluations of everything from art manufacture (Alphonse Equiros insisted, in *Revue des deux mondes*, that the French were favored there, as "an artistic race, which masters above all charm, sobriety, and taste in ornament") to everyday tools ("no people has invented so much that is useful and necessary to men as the British race," the *British Quarterly* insisted) to industrial technologies ("It will be seen that England has fallen behind Germany," German journalist Lothar Bucher wrote). Clearly, who was winning the competition among nations depended very much upon what one looked at and who one asked.

One interesting sidelight in this national competition comes in 1862 with the emergence of new nations. The progress toward national unification in two key parts of Europe, Germany, and Italy can be tracked in commentary on the productions they showed at the exhibition. The Zollverein, the trade alliance that was a precursor to a united Germany, participated together, although they then subdivided their display area to reflect the still-separate units. Edmund Yates, writing about the German displays in *Temple Bar*, saw in the display signs of national consolidation, and even in the fine art the *Illustrated London News* saw signs of "quickened political life." And Italy was presenting materials at the start of the *Risorgimento* that followed the Franco-Austrian war and would lead toward full unification less than a decade later. Again, commentators found political meanings in the material displayed, as when Dante Gabriel Rossetti found in the art shown from Italy "the impulse of a people who now feels itself free" (*Fraser's*). National identity could thus precede nation itself.

That tendency was, however, limited to European nations. With the greater representation of colonial works also came one last feature in which the London Exhibition of 1862 paved the way for future exhibitions: the application to non–Western peoples of an essentially ethnographic, and strongly racially hierarchical, framework. This can be seen in Robert Hunt's *Synopsis* of the contents of the exhibition, where Australian aborigines, Indians, and settler colonists are treated as successive levels of evolutionary development, and as all inferior to Europeans. Journalists echoed this ethnographizing in their own comments on displays by non–Western nations and colonial subjects. It would be a motif that would only become more pronounced in future exhibitions.

Bibliography

The "bigger is better" principle of the exhibition itself is reflected in official publications for the London International Exhibition of 1862: the listings in the British Library catalogue run to over 200 entries, with separate catalogs and handbooks for many of the national collections and for many of the categories of displayed objects. Besides the *Official Illustrated Catalogue*, of particular interest among official publications are Robert Hunt, *Synopsis of the Contents of the International Exhibition of 1862,* John Hollingshead, *A Concise History of the International Exhibition of 1862,* Francis Turner Palgrave's (withdrawn) *Handbook to the Fine Arts at the International Exhibition,,* John Forbes Watson, *A Classified and Descriptive Catalogue of the Indian Department,* Christopher Dresser, *Development of Ornamental Art in the International Exhibition,* and the *Catalogue of Photographs Exhibited in Class XIV.* Inde-

pendent handbooks also proliferated, notably including the *Art-Journal Catalogue to the International Exhibition of 1862,* issued both as a bound volume and as a special supplement to subscribers, Edward Macdermott, *Popular Guide to the International Exhibition*, *Routledge's Guide to the International Exhibition*, *A Plain Guide to the Exhibition*, and *Penny Guide to the International Exhibition.* Henry Cole's defense of Fowke's building appeared as the anonymous pamphlet, "Some account of the buildings designed by F. Fowke for the International Exhibition of 1862" (1861); see also Cole's posthumously published autobiography, *Fifty Years of Public Work* (2 vols., 1884). Charles Babbage's grumpy account of his exhibition experience appears in his autobiography, *Passages from the Life of a Philosopher* (1864; vol. 11 of *Works*, 1989). Lord Alfred Tennyson's "Ode for the Opening of the International Exhibition," separately published in 1862, appears in his *Poetical Works.*

The exhibition was extensively covered in the newspaper and periodical press. The most thorough coverage was offered by the *Times* of London and the *Illustrated London News*. Among the rest of the coverage, most notable are Cole's advance promotion of the exhibition in *Cornhill Magazine* (June 1861), the extensive reviews in *Art Journal*, Alphonse Esquiro's extended treatment from a French perspective in *Revue des deux mondes*, [A. J. Beresford] Hope's article in *Quarterly Review*, John Horner's two pieces in *Once a Week*, and coverage in *Fraser's, Bentley's Miscellany,* and *Temple Bar.* The quirkiest treatments are "How a Blind Man Saw the Exhibition" in *Temple Bar*, and the serialized fictional feature, "Mossoo's Visit to the International Exhibition," in *Bentley's.* See also Percy Cruikshank's illustrated treatment, *The Comic Adventures of the Young Man from the Country ... on his way to visit the International Exhibition* (1862), which is, oddly, an updated revision, in comic rather than prose form, of the premise Henry Mayhew's failed novel *1851,* for which Percy's uncle George Cruikshank has done illustrations.

Among modern commentators, see Peter H. Hoffenberg, *An Empire on Display: English, Indian, and Australian Exhibitions from the Crystal Palace to the Great War* (2001); Elizabeth Bonython and Anthony Burton, *The Great Exhibitor: The Life and Work of Henry Cole* (2003); *Survey of London* vol. 38, *South Kensington Museums Area* (1975; now also available online at *www.british-history.ac.uk*); Adrian Duncan's on-line essay on the exhibition at *www.mcgee-flutes.com/1862%20London%20Exhibition.htm*; Paul Greenhalgh, *Ephemeral Vistas: The Expositions Universelles, Great Exhibitions, and World's Fairs, 1851–1939*

(1988); Evelyn Kroker, *Die Weltausstellungen im 19. Jahrhundert* (perhaps the only treatment that prefers 1862 to 1851, albeit only because of the focus on German national and economic development); and my own earlier discussion in John E. Findling, ed., *Historical Dictionary of World's Fairs and Expositions, 1851–1988* (1990). On photography at the exhibition, see Steve Edwards, "Photography, Allegory, and Labor," *Art Journal* 55, 2 (1996); for a defense, or at least a fuller contextualization, of Fowke's architecture, and Rafael Cardoso Denis, "The Brompton Barracks: War, Peace, and the Rise of Victorian art and Design Education," *Journal of Design History* 8, 1 (1995). On ornamental art, see Charlotte Gere, "European Decorative Arts at the World's Fairs: 1850–1900," *Metropolitan Museum of Art Bulletin* 56, 3

(1998). For the impact of the exhibition on copyright, consult Lara Kriegel, "Culture and the Copy: Calico, Capitalism, and Design Copyright in Early Victorian Britain," *Journal of British Studies* 43 (2004); on Babbage's Differential Engine at the exhibition, see Louise Purbrick, "The Dream Machine: Charles Babbage and His Imaginary Computers," *Journal of Design History* 6, 1 (1993); and on the impact of Japanese art displayed at the exhibition, see Toshio Watanabe, "The Western Image of Japanese Art in the Late Edo Period," *Modern Asian Studies* 18, 4 (1984), and Anna Jackson, "Imagining Japan: The Victorian Perception and Acquisition of Japanese Culture," *Journal of Design History* 5, 4 (1992). Because of William Morris's role there, most biographies of make a (usually brief) mention of the exhibition as well.

Dublin 1865

Miglena Ivanova

International Exhibition of Arts and Manufactures

Eager to prove to Ireland and the world that Dublin was the British Empire's "second city" not just in size but also in cultural and economic magnitude, the Duke of Leinster, Lord Talbot de Malahide, and Benjamin Lee Guinness established in 1862 the Dublin Exhibition Palace and Winter Garden Company Limited with the intention of organizing an international exhibition in 1865. The company's initial capital totaled £50,000 (10,000 shares at £5 each). Benjamin Guinness had already acquired a suitable 15-acre plot of land within the city limits which he placed at the disposal of the company. Known to locals as the Cobourg Gardens, the site was in close proximity to the thriving suburbs of Rathmines, Rathgar, and Rathfarnham, the Westland Row station, and the Bray railway. With the adjoining part of the Hutchinson estate, which the company managed to lease, and the Kildare Street facilities of the Royal Dublin Society, the company had access to a total of 17 acres of exhibition grounds. Harcourt Street and Earlsfort

Terrace served as the site's western and eastern boundaries, respectively, while St. Stephen's Green and Hatch Street marked its limits to the north and south.

The call for designs, issued in June 1862, did not produce a winner as none of the projects met the required ceiling cost of £35,000. The selection committee eventually adopted the plans of Dublin architect Alfred G. Jones on the condition that they be revised under the supervision of the Company's advising architect, F. Darley. In its final design the Exhibition Palace covered an area of five acres and consisted of three structures: a brick-and-stone Main Building, a Winter Garden and Exhibition Building, whose iron and glass edifice was influenced by London's Crystal Palace, and a permanent stone annex with an iron roof and glazed skylight. A public ceremony on June 12, 1863, marked the laying of the foundations of the Exhibition Palace. Its construction was carried out by London engineers Ordish and Lefevre and Dublin contractor Beardwood and Sons; the iron work was commissioned to Liverpool's Rankin and Co. On March 31, 1865, much to the amusement of

Dubliners, 600 closely packed soldiers of the 78th Highlanders marched the entire length of the galleries giving the still unfurnished Exhibition Palace its final strength test. The Prince of Wales opened the international exhibition on May 9, 1865; it was formally closed on November 8.

On the ground floor of the three-story Main Building, a piazza led to a central entrance hall which, lined with Caen stone columns, connected to a gallery via a grand staircase. The large concert hall to the left of the entrance (seating 3,000) was paired with a smaller one (seating 1,500) to the right. The upper floor consisted of two dining rooms, a lecture hall, board rooms, offices, and an extensive picture gallery. The basement provided ample storage and service facilities. Visitors could access the exhibits in the Winter Garden and Exhibition Building on both the ground and upper levels. The permanent annex, displaying machinery in motion and at rest, bordered both the Carriage Court and the exhibition space occupied by Great Britain and its colonies. The Pleasure Grounds featured multiple fountains, extensive gardens, and a conservatory, as well as a cascade and archery field (both at the western border of the exhibition grounds).

The 1865 committee adopted a classification of exhibitors which mirrored the 1851 and 1862 London exhibitions and utilized the Royal Dublin Society's extensive experience with art exhibits since the first Irish Industrial Exhibition in 1853. The displays were divided into the following categories: raw materials, machinery, textile fabrics, manufactures (metallic, vitreous, ceramic, and miscellaneous), and fine arts. As of June 1, 1865, the combined participation of the 25 foreign countries and cities and the 23 British colonies amounted to 2,368 cases of articles.

Great Britain's contribution, including those from Ireland, totaled 2,413 cases and 775 exhibitors (compared to 1,467 British exhibitors in 1853). The fine arts department received 659 packages from abroad and 313 from the British Isles. Although the exhibition committee managed to attract foreign interest that greatly surpassed that in 1853, the number of visitors decreased by a fifth to 956,295, despite a reduction in admission prices and inexpensive excursion railway tickets. The receipts totaled £45,000, almost a quarter of which came from season tickets (£11,586). The Dublin Exhibition Palace and Winter Garden Company continued to use the site for national exhibitions of varying success until the 1880s, when the Royal University acquired the buildings. Earlsfort Terrace is the current location of Ireland's National Concert Hall.

Bibliography

Henry Parkinson and Peter Lund Simmons, *The Illustrated Record and Descriptive Catalogue of the Dublin International Exhibition of 1865* (1866) is the most useful among the 28 publications documenting the exhibition. In addition to the nearly 170 engravings of the exhibition grounds, galleries, and displays, this catalogue offers a comparative account of the events since 1851 that contributed to the 1865 exhibition. Its publisher, John Falconer, printed also the *Official Catalogue* which contains the "Report of the Executive Committee" and *Reports of the Juries and Lists of Their Awards.* It is also worth consulting *The Visitor's Guide to the International Exhibition of 1865* (1865); John Sturgeon, *Descriptive Illustrated Catalogue of the Machinery in the Exhibition* (1865); and *Notes and References Explanatory of Selected Paintings in the Dublin International Exhibition* (1865).

Dunedin 1865

Conal McCarthy

New Zealand Exhibition

The New Zealand Exhibition was the country's first world's fair. It was an astonishing achievement, as the organizers were quick to point out, only 25 years after the founding of this British colony in 1840 and barely 17 years after the European settlement of the Otago province by Scottish pioneers in 1848. Only four years before, Dunedin was a small town in New Zealand's South Island, but the discovery of gold in 1861 made it the largest and wealthiest city virtually overnight. The spirit of enterprise and boundless optimism transformed the proposal of an industrial exhibition, originally suggested by Anglican church leaders, into a major international exhibition funded partly by the general government in Wellington, and partly by the Otago provincial government. The rationale for the exhibition was scientific to a degree but mainly a practical example of extractive economics, the kind of colonial boosterism that historian James Belich has called the "progress industry." The organizers declared confidently that "It is a matter of necessity that the country in which they seek to erect another England, should contain within itself those natural elements which are necessary for the support of commercial and manufacturing prosperity."

The fair was situated on a central site and consisted of a large stone building with a series of annexes at the back which housed the fine arts, machinery, and other exhibits. Designed by distinguished local architects Mason and Clayton, the grand Italianate building with its impressive central clock tower towered over the townscape. It was by far the most impressive structure yet built in Dunedin and was later used as part of the public hospital. As well as a wide range of commercial and industrial exhibits from the provinces of New Zealand, there were exhibits from Fiji, the colonies of Australia, as well as Canada, America, France, Belgium, Holland, Germany, and Austria. The extensive exhibits from the "Mother Country" of Great Britain included a large Indian court.

The exhibition was made up of 38 classes, displaying the range of commercial and mercantile produce typical of industrial expositions of this period. The first display in a prominent position inside the main building was gold — not surprising considering the recent gold rush — in the form of a large gilded obelisk which represented the £6.7 million worth of gold exported from the region. Also prominent were exhibits on "natural history

and physical science." The first class was "Mining, quarrying, metallurgy and mineral products," a popular exhibit arranged by the provincial geologist, James Hector. In contrast to the confusing displays by "mere gatherers of pleasing natural objects," officials praised the "instructive" exhibits classified and labelled by scientists such as Hector and Julius von Haast, because they taught the viewer "valuable lessons." Surprisingly, Maori material culture was not seen at this time in purely ethnographic terms. Exhibited in the section titled "Maori and other aboriginal manufactures and implements," objects such as weaving and carving were described as useful and skillfully made, evidence of Maori intelligence, resourcefulness, and adaptability despite the prevailing acceptance of social Darwinism. The catalogue included numerous items exhibited by Maori — weapons, ceremonial objects, carving and weaving — reflecting the fact that organizers wanted Maori people to be included as exhibitors and visitors.

Despite the hyperbolic Victorian rhetoric of the day, questions remain about the fair's success. It opened unfinished due to construction delays, and there were doubts over its financial status. Governor Sir George Grey did not attend, due partly to the wars between the crown and Maori tribes on the North Island. The chief legacy of the exhibition is that it provided a precedent for events of this type and a platform for a number of individuals and institutions that were significant in New Zealand's cultural history. The leading commissioner and juror, Scotsman James Hector, was appointed director of the Colonial Museum and Geological Survey in Wellington later the same year. He became the foremost scientist in the colony, associated with many later world's fairs and closely involved in the New Zealand Institute and its journal. The busy superintendent, Thomas Forrester, who drew the geological survey map that was a feature of Hector's display, went on to become a successful architect in Oamaru. The collector and naturalist Walter Lawry Buller, who exhibited bird specimens and wrote an essay on the ornithology of New Zealand, later published the definitive book on the subject. A portion of the exhibits from Dunedin went to the Colonial Museum, while others became part of the collections of the Otago Museum, located at Otago University.

The New Zealand Exhibition building must have dominated the skyline of the small town of Dunedin in 1865 (Alexander Turnbull Library, Wellington, New Zealand PA2-0012).

The works in the fine arts gallery, particularly the popular landscapes by local artists such as William Mathew Hodgkins, John Gully, J.C. Richmond, Charles Heaphy, William Fox, and C.D. Barraud, stimulated the establishment of New Zealand's first art school in Dunedin in 1870.

Bibliography

Records and correspondence relating to the exhibition can be found in the New Zealand Room of the Dunedin Public Library, the Otago Settlers' Museum, and the Hocken Library Collections, Dunedin. Thomas Forrester's copy of the catalogue with handwritten notes is held in the Otago Settlers Museum. James Hector's papers with references to the exhibition can be found in the Hocken Collections and the archive of the Museum of New Zealand Te Papa Tongarewa, Wellington.

The official published reports are: *New Zealand Exhibition, 1865: Reports and Awards of the Jurors and Appendix* (1866) and *Official Catalogue of the New Zealand Exhibition, 1865* (1865).

For Walter Buller's essay on New Zealand birds, see *Essay on the Ornithology of New Zealand* (1865). The official reports edited by Hector and Eccles were published in vol. 1 of the *Transaction of the New Zealand Institute* in 1868, now available online at the National Library, Wellington *http://www.natlib.govt.nz.*

A very useful retrospective survey was written by the secretary Alfred Eccles and reprinted as *The First New Zealand Exhibition and Dunedin in 1865* (1925). For a concise summary of the exhibition see N. Palethorpe, *Official History of the New Zealand Centennial Exhibition, Wellington, 1939–40* (1940). For a recent study of the display of Maori culture in colonial New Zealand, see Conal McCarthy, *Exhibiting Maori: A History of Colonial Cultures of Display* (2007). The best general history of New Zealand for this period is James Belich, *Making Peoples: A History of the New Zealanders from Polynesian Settlement to the End of the Nineteenth Century* (1996). Two histories of Dunedin refer to the exhibition: K.C. McDonald, *City of Dunedin: A Century of Civic Enterprise* (1965); and Erik Olssen, *A History of Otago,* (1984). For useful biographies of the people involved in the exhibition, consult the *Dictionary of New Zealand Biography http://www.dnzb.govt. nz/.*

Paris 1867

Volker Barth

Exposition Universelle

The idea to organize the exhibition originated in the year 1863. It was after the 1862 London Universal Exhibition that French exhibitors expressed the desire to hold another exhibition in Paris, which had already hosted an event in 1855, but also offered their financial support for this project. With the initiative of the 1867 exhibition thus being established, the Emperor released an Imperial Decree dated June 22, 1863, stating that a Universal Exhibition was to be held in Paris in 1867 and that all the necessary measures for staging this exhibition were to commence immediately.

Eugene Rouher, the Minister of Agriculture and Commerce, outlined the overall concept of the exhibition as a guideline for the organizers to follow, highlighting the "general advantages" for the larger population. These included improvements of the working techniques in all sectors, the intensification of commercial exchange around the globe, and in general, the advancement of universal progress. Special measures for the working class, a decisive feature of the 1867 exhibition, were another central argument of the concept. Furthermore, the exhibition was to contribute to the development of art and science around the world and to demonstrate France's preeminent position in international politics.

That Paris was the only imaginable location for the Exposition Universelle de 1867 was never doubted nor contested. However, the exact site had to be selected. Twenty-two proposals were made ranging from the Parc des Princes in the Bois de Boulogne in the west of Paris to the Bois de Vincennes in the east. Some of them were too far from the center of the city while others were too costly to build upon. One location emerged from all the suggested sites as

the most viable and would remain to serve as the principal site for all future universal expositions in Paris: the Champ de Mars. It was an open, rectangular space with sufficient means of communication and transportation to and from the city center. The French military academy, located in the immediate South of the site, had traditionally used this open field as its drill ground. The presence of the academy not only represented the military might of the *Grande Nation*, but it also proved convenient, as security and general emergency mechanisms were already well established. But most of all the first French industrial exhibition had been held on the Champ de Mars in 1798 and it was therefore the historically most suitable place for any form of national gathering or festivity. On June 29, 1865, the French parliament officially declared it to be the exhibition site.

The budget of the exhibition was estimated at 20 million francs. On March 19, 1865, the national government and the city of Paris signed a contract committing both to provide 6 millions francs each. A stock corporation, the Association de Garantie, was established on April 7, 1865, to raise the remaining 8 million francs. It launched a public offering and encouraged subscribers to buy share certificates for 1,000 francs each with an immediate dividend of 20 francs and a share of the exhibition proceeds. The French parliament approved this financing model on July 8, 1865.

The final report of the exhibition states that the number of people involved in the exhibition was 5,250. However, this gives a rather misleading sense of the total number of individuals who had some role in the four years of exposition preparation and the seven months of its duration (April 1 to November 3, 1867), as this figure does not include all the members of the foreign commissions. Also groups like the national or regional chambers of commerce, scientific associations, or the numerous employees of the participating countries appear only as a single mention in the statistics. Therefore it seems appropriate to assume that the number of people involved in the administration and organization of the exhibition most probably exceeded 10,000. In any case, fewer than 200 of them were remunerated for their services.

The most important committee of the exhibition was the Commission Impériale. It consisted of 60 members, appointed by Napoleon III. This committee was responsible for the communication with the participating countries as well as appointments to and oversight of the numerous sub-commissions. Its president was the Prince Jerome-Napoléon, the cousin of the emperor; an appointment meant to highlight and celebrate the Bonaparte dynasty. However, on June 10, 1865, Jerome-Napoleon was removed from his post after a controversial speech on foreign policy critical of the government. In a rather symbolic gesture, he was replaced by the nine-year-old son of the emperor, Louis-Napoléon.

The imperial commissions consisted of the leading politicians and economists of the Second Empire. Beside the prefect of the Seine Department, Baron Eugène Haussmann, and the prefect of the Paris police force, Pierre-Marie Piétri, the leading ministers, such as Achille Fould, Pierre Jules Baroche, the marquis Charles de La Valette, the comte Alfred de Nieuwekerke, the comte Alexandre Walewski and the duc Charles de Morny were among its members. They were supported by important industrialists such as the owner of the Le Creusot factories and the president of the parliament, Eugène Schneider, as well as the owners of the largest railroad companies, Alfred le Roux, Émile Pereire, baron James de Rothschild and Paulin Talabot. Three English citizens were its only foreign members: the Ambassador of his Majesty in Paris, Henry Cowley; the former minister of state, Lord George Granville; and Richard Cobden, one of the leading figures of the international free-trade movement. Cobden had negotiated the Anglo-French Free Trade Treaty of 1860 with Michel Chevalier, another leading figure of the 1867 exhibition. Unfortunately, Cobden died on April 2, 1865, two years before the opening of the exhibition.

The most important member of the Commission Impériale was its commissioner general, Frédéric Le Play. Not only did he manage the day-to-day organization and administrative activities of the exposition, he also left a lasting impact on its concept and ideology. Le Play, a mining engineer and social reformer, had already played a leading role in the exhibition of 1855 and had been the president of the French delegation to the London exhibition of 1862. He was a state consultant and worked closely with the emperor on issues of social welfare. With his book *The European Workers* (*Les Ouvriers européen*, 1855), he became the leading advocate in the state-supervised reform movement for the working class, a cause so dear to the emperor that it became one of the most prominent features of the 1867 exhibition. The distinctive classification system of this exhibition and its outstanding tenth group, which addressed a wide range of social concerns, were directly due to Le Play's influence and design.

Beside the imperial commission, there were no fewer than 106 sub-commissions for the French exhibition section alone: one commission for each of the ten exhibition groups, one for the park, and one for each of the 95 classes into which the exhibits were divided. In addition to that, every participating country was urged to copy the French commission's system for the organization of its national section. However, no other nation conformed exactly to the French system, as it was, especially for smaller participants such as the kingdom of Hawaii or the Vatican, far too costly and too sophisticated.

Apart from this impressive network of organizations, there were a total of 95 admission juries (juries d'admission) responsible for the acceptance or rejection of the proposed exhibits to each class. Three additional juries were charged with the tenth group, the works of art, and a special exhibition called the History of Labor (Histoire du travail). Of equal importance was the international jury, which was responsible for the distribution of medals and honorable mentions for the best exhibit on show. Its president was Michel Chevalier.

The regional distribution of the 49 participating nations was as follows:

Africa: Egypt, Morocco, Tunisia.

America: Argentina, Bolivia, Brazil, Chile,

Costa Rica, Ecuador, Haiti, New-Grenada (Colombia), Nicaragua, Paraguay, Peru, El Salvador, Uruguay, Venezuela, United States.

Asia: Annam (part of what is now Vietnam), Cambodia, China, Japan, Liou-Kiou (the Ryukyu Islands), Persia, Siam (Thailand), Ottoman Empire.

Europe: Andorra, Austria, Baden, Bavaria, Belgium, Denmark, France, Great Britain, Greece, Hesse, Italy, Luxemburg, Netherlands, Portugal, Prussia, Romania, Russia, Spain, Sweden and Norway, Switzerland, Vatican City, Württemberg.

Oceania: Hawaii.

The sections of Mexico and China deserve special attention because exhibits from both nations were located inside the exhibition grounds although neither nation was an official participant. At the time of the exhibition, French troops were fighting in Mexico in an attempt to install Maximilian of Habsburg as Emperor. The resistance of the Mexicans, led by Benito Juárez, made an official participation of Mexico impossible. Thus, the Mexican section had been privately organized by the traveler and collector Léon Méhédin. It consisted of a reduced model of the temple of Xochicalco and contained a very limited number of objects from Mexico.

China was the only nation that had declined the invitation to the exhibition. However, the French foreign ministry managed to obtain permission for a display of Chinese objects. This section was organized by the Marquis Hervey de Saint-Denys who in 1874 was appointed to the chair of sinology at the Collège de France.

The invited nations were urged to put products on display that underlined their contribution to progress in every aspect of human activity. Thus, the key principle of nineteenth-century universal exhibitions, national participation, was respected in 1867. But the exhibition also provided early examples for the participation of civic as well as religious organizations: the Société des Secours aux Blessés Militaires (the future Red Cross), the Société Protectrice des Enfants, the Société Protectrice des Animaux, and the Société Biblique.

As host nation, France occupied almost 50 percent of the total exhibition space. Thus between the system of organization, the disproportionate number of French exhibitors,

and the corresponding large amount of square footage used, the host country exerted tremendous control over the entire exhibition.

This French ideological control of the exhibition was based on the *Règlement general*, specifying the rules of participation. Each nation received these regulations, along with the official invitation. The exhibition organizers left no possibility for discussion or modification, even though participating countries were free to arrange their national sections with objects of their choice. However, the imperial commission reserved the right to reject any exhibit without explanation. The costs of the section were to be borne by the participants. Every participating country had to name a general commissioner living in Paris. This commissioner maintained contact with his national committee and was the exclusive liaison with the Commission Impériale. Article 10 of the regulation offered a possibility, especially attractive for smaller participants, to have French architects, engineers, and scientists provided to help with the set-up of their national section. This partly explains the important influence of French commissioners in putting up many non–European sections.

Every participating country was allocated a portion of the central exhibition building, the Palais d'Exposition. It was an iron and glass structure designed by the engineer Jean-Baptiste-Sébastian Krantz. The structure was related to other buildings, such as train stations, that used a wide span to cover a vast area with minimal support. The geometric shape of the building was a hemisphere cut in half, with a rectangular section inserted in between. The total area covered 40.97 acres out of Champs de Mars' total of 113.51 acres. The palace was torn down at the end of the exhibition.

In order to meet the program of the exhibition, the structure of the supporting pillars of the Palais followed the spatial layout of seven concentric ellipse-like rings, each to house one of the first seven groups of the classification system. The corresponding logic between the classification system and the architecture was supplemented by an innovative system of movable walls that provided flexibility for the exhibitors' needs. Thus the palace was a versatile container that sheltered a very sophisticated classification system of ten groups of exhibits, subdivided into 95 classes:

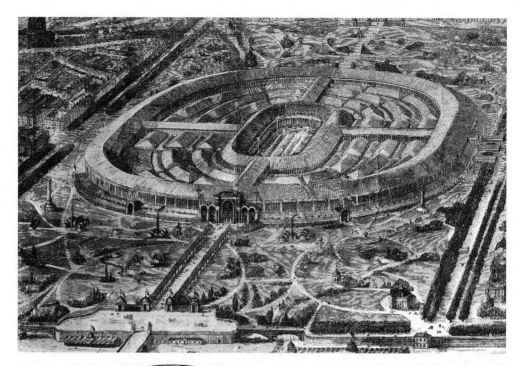

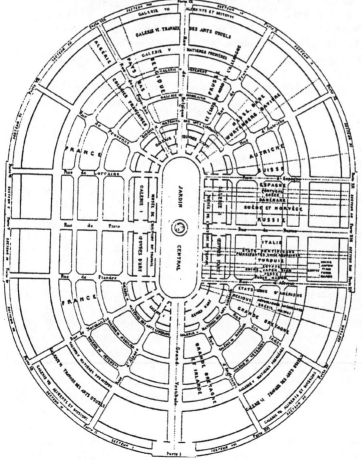

Top and bottom: The floor plan of the Trocadéro reflected the first attempt to incorporate a rational organization of exhibits (courtesy of Volker Barth).

I. Works of art (5 classes)

II. Material and applications of the free arts (8 classes)

III. Furniture and other objects for the dwelling (13 classes)

IV. Clothing (including textiles) and other objects carried by a person (13 classes)

V. Products (raw and processed) of extractive industries (7 classes)

VI. Instruments and proceedings of the industries (20 classes)

VII. Alimentation (fresh or in conservation) in diverse degrees of preparation (7 classes)

VIII. Living products and specimens of agricultural establishments (9 classes)

IX. Living products and specimens of horticultural establishments (6 classes)

X. Objects specially exhibited to improve the physical and moral condition of the population (7 classes)

The agricultural section (group VIII) was located at the Ile de Billancourt on the Seine River in the southwestern part of Paris. The horticultural section (group IX) occupied one-quarter of the exhibition park. The objects of the tenth group were scattered throughout various parts of the palace and the park. The works of art (group I) were in the inner and smallest circle, followed by the other groups in sequential order.

Visitors could explore the exhibition hall in two different ways. They could either walk around one of the circles and see the exhibits of all nations in one group, or they could make their way from the outside to the inside along any radius and see all the objects of one nation in all seven groups. This double system of classification, by object and by nation, enabled visitors to compare systematically the progress of the participating nations in every sector of human activity. In fact, the classification of objects from all fields and all countries was meant to display the totality of human endeavors; every product of human labor could be found in its particular place in one of the ten groups.

Thus, this comprehensive system aimed at nothing less than the creation of an ideal order of the universe. This is precisely what makes the Exposition Universelle de 1867 unique in the history of universal exhibitions. It lies in the tradition of the French Enlightenment based on the positivistic principle of a complete inventory of the world understood as an intelligible entity. The exposition of 1867 was conceived as a three-dimensional world encyclopedia of representative objects. The criterion for display insisted upon each nation's contribution to progress, understood as a steady and linear development geared towards perfection. By means of science and observation, organizers claimed that progress was measurable in an objective and universal manner.

In line with this reasoning, the organizers thought of the exhibition of 1867 as a contribution to universal progress. The displays only informed the public but also stimulated new inventions. The global exchange of knowledge was seen as a powerful tool to reduce what was assumed to be the backwardness of underdeveloped nations. Even though the international free-trade movement was one specifically identified aim of the exhibition, the French commissioners of 1867 by no means wanted to stage an international trade event, as is clearly indicated by the official prohibition to sell the objects on display.

The ideology of the exhibition is best seen in the tenth group (Objects specially exhibited to improve the physical and moral condition of the population) that was almost exclusively dedicated to the working classes. Here, the government of the Second Empire constructed its vision of an ideal industrial society, including libraries and models for popular education. Its most impressive features were housing prototypes for workers, displayed in the park. With special attention given to hygienic concerns, they suggested a modern, bourgeois lifestyle as a model for workers to aspire to. The key to ownership of these dwellings was a blend of credits and savings that would enable a worker to finance them over a period of time. Together with the display of cheap household objects, affordable by the same financing method, the improvement of the material condition of the working class would not only bridge the social gap between the poor and the bourgeoisie, but also serve as a cure for social ills. Thus, the tenth group provided a social model of state integration ranging from the child to the pensioner. A kindergarten, where working mothers could board their children during the exhibition day, and model schools, in which children were taught before the eyes of the public, were designed to demonstrate social progress in action. Thus, rather than accurately reconstructing society, the tenth group actually ended up staging a social utopia.

The exposition aimed at nothing less than a complete, objective and measurable control over the world in the form of a representative model. This meant first of all, control over time — or better, over evolution — through the concept of progress. The clearest example of this was the History of Labor, one of the first chronologically arranged thematic displays in an exposition. Exhibits reaching from pre-history to the end of the eighteenth century illustrated the improvement of working techniques over time that indicated steady development towards a better life. Logically this exhibit concluded with a solemn distribution of prizes on July 1, 1867, where the best objects were presented with medals. With the New Order of Recompenses (*Nouvel ordre des récompenses*), a category of special prizes was awarded to employers who contributed to social harmony by special treatment of their workers. Most of all, the exhibition claimed control over space by means of the arrangement of the exhibits in the classification system.

However, this microcosmic model of the world did not work. This was due not only to the exhibition being far from completed on its opening day, nor the fact that the prizes led more to bickering than to a universal acclamation of progress. It was unfortunate that the huge exhibition hall proved to be too small to host the totality of human products. The agriculture and the horticulture sections were displayed outside the hall, and because of the extreme diversity of its exhibits, the tenth group was scattered all over the Champ de Mars. Symbolic of this loss of control was the park, the first one in the history of international exhibitions. Designed by Adolph Alphand as an English garden, its purpose was to counterbalance the museum-like exhibition hall. The park not only held all the exhibits that were too large to be displayed inside the exhibition hall, but it also hosted all the entertainment venues.

Due to its diversity and spectacle, the park was the center of attraction and the most memorable aspect of the exhibition. Here the visitor found entertainment and excitement rather than the complicated comparative displays inside the exhibition hall. True, the principle of learning through amusement was at the very heart of the exhibition didactics: the spectacle of future industrial happiness was to be staged in a way that would the desire for its realization. The exhibitors were asked to make interesting and attractive arrangements, the machines on display were put into action, and a large variety of decorative ornaments were found everywhere. There was no general division between spectacle and entertainment as illustrated by the many restaurants at the exhibition. They were part of the seventh group (alimentation) and offered the opportunity for visitors to taste the food in a diverting setting. Servers were dressed in their national costumes and orchestras performed traditional music.

The very same features were found in the major invention of the exposition, the national pavilions. Their appearance was a logistical coincidence. The imperial commission had allotted proportionate space to the participating nations in the park as well as inside the hall. Only after the majority of the European nations had declined the offer of park space for financial reasons did the French organizers present this space to non–European nations and invited them to display their culture in a building constructed in their indigenous architectural styles. Thus, roughly 30 national pavilions were constructed in various styles. Some of them were theatres, tea-rooms, or restaurants; others were scaled-down replicas of existing buildings or a mixture of different influences. Many of them utilized native workers, and at some, artistic performances were staged for the public. These pavilions followed no clear-cut theoretical concept. Their form was due largely to financial and logistical constraints. To reduce expenses and to avoid overseas transport, many nations accepted the imperial commission's offer of assistance and hired French architects to help with the design. Most of these architects had no first-hand experience with the nation they represented.

These pavilions contributed to the transformation of the exhibition into a huge spectacle. With national pavilions displayed alongside amusement facilities such as café-concerts, theaters, or Nadar's gas balloon, a visitor could not distinguish between entertainment and education, between amusement and information. This is also illustrated by the two aquariums installed in the park. Constructed as glass cages, the aquariums surrounded visitors with water from all sides, including overhead. It was as though one was literally submerged into the world of the ocean.

Encouraged by popular success, commissioners as well as exhibitors transformed the ideal reconstruction of the universe into a giant fun fair. Many sections were rented out and transformed into additional bars, restaurants, and other attractions. Throughout the year, prostitution increased dramatically, and many legal proceedings were initiated to settle compensation disputes. In the summer of 1867, the most exotic and spectacular exhibits began to sell out. The intellectual aims of the exhibition were gradually pushed to the background, leaving the businesses and entertainment to prosper. The record-high attendance marked the success of this exhibition with more than 11 million visitors over the 217 exhibition days. The exhibition closed with a profit of 3,130,000 francs.

The legacy of the Paris Universal Exhibition of 1867 is complex and contradictory. Several of the national pavilions were sold and transported to various places in France and abroad, but no fair building remained on the site. The exposition's only remaining features are the boats on the Seine, initially intended to transport visitors between the Champ de Mars and the agricultural section. These *bateaux mouches* are today one of the most well-known tourist attractions of Paris. The fall of the Second Empire, of which the Exposition Universelle de 1867 was perhaps the most prominent symbol, only three years after the exhibition cut short to any direct political or economic legacy.

Nevertheless, the 1867 exposition remains an exceptional and important moment in the history of universal exhibitions. It was the first and the last attempt to stage a universal exhibition *à la lettre*. The aim of the event was not only to be "more universal than its predecessors"–a premise to be found throughout the history of exhibitions—but also to display "as far as possible, the work of arts, the industrial products of all nations and, in general, the manifestations of all branches of human activity," Thus, the organizers refused any preliminary thematic restriction whatsoever and conceptualized the universe as such.

At the same time, Paris 1867 marked a turning-point in the history of exhibitions. It was the first to be staged in part as an outside event with the incorporation of a large park. Moreover, the exposition was the first in history to utilize national pavilions, an innovation that became standard in universal exhibitions. Therefore, the uniqueness of Paris 1867 lies in a paradox. A microcosmic reconstruction of the universe according to a highly theorized framework based on utopian ideologies of a finite world turned into a spectacular fun fair and a rather kaleidoscopic collection of curiosities.

Bibliography

The majority of primary sources of the 1867 universal exposition are in the Archives Nationales in Paris (F^{12} 2918 — 3161). The printed sources are available in the Bibliothèque Nationale de France. A large quantity of graphic material including maps, drawings, and photographs can be found in the departments Estampes et Photographies and Cartes et Plans of the same library. Much general information is found in the final report of the exhibition, La Commission Impériale, ed., *Rapport sur l'Exposition universelle de 1867 à Paris. Précis des opérations et listes des collaborateurs. Avec un appendice sur l'avenir des expositions, la statistique des opérations, les documents officiels et le plan de l'Exposition* (1869), as well as in the extensive report of the international jury, Michel Chevalier, ed., *Exposition universelle de 1867 à Paris. Rapports du jury international publié sous la direction de M. Michel Chevalier*, 13 vol. (1868). The most comprehensive document in English is the *Report of the United States Commissioners to the Paris Exposition 1867*, 4 vols. (1870).

Some of the official documents are published in La Commission Impériale, ed., *Exposition universelle de 1867 à Paris. Documents officiels publiés successivement du 1er Février 1865 au 1er Avril* (1867). Aside from the two volumes of the exhibition catalogue (La Commission Impériale, ed. *Exposition universelle de 1867. Catalogue général, Première partie, Contenant les oeuvres d'art (Groupes I à V)* (1867) and La Commission Impériale, ed., *Exposition universelle du 1867. Catalogue général, Deuxième partie (Groupes VI à X)* (1867), some of the exhibition journals are very helpful. See especially François Ducuing, ed., *L'Exposition Universelle de 1867 Illustrée*, 2 vols. (1867); and Gabriel Richard, ed., *L'Album de l'Exposition Illustrée. Histoire pittoresque de l'Exposition universelle de 1867* (1867). Two contemporary works in English are George Augustus Henry Sala, *Notes and Sketches of the Paris Exhibition* (1868), the witty account of a London *Daily Telegraph* correspondent, and Eugene Rimmell, *Recollections of the Paris Exhibition of 1867* (1868), the recollection of a businessman who liked the park setting and the History of Labor exhibit but felt the fair as a whole was too commercialized.

Among modern works on the exposition of 1867, consult the following: Patricia Mainardi, *Art and Politics of the Second Empire: The Universal Expositions of 1855 and 1867* (1987), which discusses the social and aesthetic implications of fine arts at the exhibitions with respect to the development of modernism; Arthur Chandler, "The Paris Exposition Universelle, 1867: Empire of Autumn," *World's Fair* 6, 2 (Summer 1986): 2–8; Volker Barth, *Mensch vs. Welt. Die Pariser Weltausstellung von 1867* (2007); Fritz Walch, *Das Gebäude der Pariser Weltausstellung*, (1967), which is available in the Bibliothèque Historique de la ville de Paris; Alice von Plato, *Präsentierte Geschichte. Ausstellungskultur und Massenpublikum im Frankreich des 19. Jahrhunderts* (2001); Mehrangiz N. Nikou, "National Architecture and International Politics: Pavilions of the Near Eastern Nations in the Paris International Exposition of 1867" (unpub. Ph.D. diss., Columbia University, 1997); Volker Barth, "Kontrollierte Träume —

Der Orient auf der Pariser Weltausstellung von 1867," in: Klaus Müller-Richter and Kristin Kopp, eds., *Die Großstadt und das Primitive — Text, Politik, Repräsentation* (2004): 31–52; and Antoine Savoye, "1867, réformateurs sociaux et représentants ouvriers face à face," in *La Revue de l'économie sociale* 19 (1990): 71–96.

London 1871–1874

Catherine Dibello and the Editors

London International Exhibitions

The London International Exhibitions of 1871–1874 began with a proposal made on July 18, 1868, by the Provisional Committee of the Royal Albert Hall to Her Majesty's Commissioners for the Exhibition of 1851. To commemorate Prince Albert's involvement with the Great Exhibition of 1851 and his commitment to industrial education, the committee proposed that the commissioners organize a series of annual international exhibitions on the commissioners' estate in South Kensington, adjacent to the Royal Albert Hall and the Royal Horticultural Gardens. Pursuing the recommendations of the commissioners of the Paris exhibition of 1867, the committee suggested that the size of the exhibitions be limited, that no prizes be awarded, and that goods be organized by class, not nationality. Each exhibition would focus on a class or small number of classes of manufactured goods and on significant scientific discoveries and works of art.

After consulting with chambers of commerce, the Royal Society of Arts, the Institute of Mechanical Engineers, and other relevant groups, the commissioners declared sufficient public interest to support the exhibitions. On July 8, 1869, they approved a plan for sponsoring the exhibitions, established committees to carry out various tasks, and elected additional commissioners. The General Purposes Committee, which served as the executive committee until it was replaced by the Committee of

Management in 1872, was chaired by the marquis of Ripon and included the marquis of Lansdowne, earl of Devon, duke of Edinburgh, and Earl Granville. Henry Cole (later Sir Henry) was also a key organizer, as he had been for the exhibitions of 1851 and 1862.

Influenced by the Great Exhibition's Crystal Palace, the commissioners briefly considered building a large glass structure in the ante garden of the Royal Horticultural Society, but the cost proved prohibitive. Instead two brick halls were built on the commissioners' strips of land south of the Royal Albert Hall and east and west of the Horticultural Gardens. Annexes and temporary wooden exhibition halls were added in the remaining space. The total cost for buildings and fittings was £126, 383. Although the commissioners intended the exhibition halls, the Royal Albert Hall, and the Royal Horticultural Gardens to function as a unified exhibition site, the pu8blic did not like having exhibits separated into two halls on opposite sides of the gardens. When the Royal Horticultural Society withdrew its support after the first year and limited access to the gardens, the separation of the two halls became even more of a problem.

The halls were built under the supervision of General Henry Young Darracot Scott and James Wild, based on the design proposed by Richard Redgrave and executed by Francis Fowke at the South Kensington Museum and the exhibition of 1862. Thirty feet wide, each hall was built of red brick and decorated with terra cotta. The ground floors were 20 feet high, and the top galleries were 30 feet high with 15 feet of skylight.

In each exhibition the top-lighted galleries featured fine arts, the south and east sides of the ground floors displayed manufactured goods, and the west side exhibited machinery in motion. Except for the exhibition of 1871, which included Horticulture as a fourth category, each exhibition had three categories: Fine Arts, Manufactures, and Recent Scientific Inventions and New Discoveries of All Types. Dividing the category of Manufactures into specific classes of goods, the commissioners published a plan for ten annual exhibitions. The exhibitions closed in 1874 because of financial loses after the first year. The following classes of manufactures goods were exhibited between 1871 and 1874:

1871: pottery, woolen and worsted fabrics, educational works and appliances.

1872: cotton and cotton fabrics, musical instruments, acoustic apparatus and experiments, paper, stationery and printing.

1873: silk and velvet, steel, surgical instruments, carriages not connected with rail or tram roads, food and cooking.

1874: lace, civil engineering, architectural and building contrivances, heating leather, bookbinding, and foreign wines.

Music was an integral part of the exhibitions. In 1871 the commissioners invited notes organists from eight of the participating European countries to perform on the Royal Albert Hall's organ. In 1872, when musical instruments comprised a class of manufactured goods, instruments on display were played in the hall. That same year a series of concerts featuring oratorios, popular music, choral arrangements, and operatic and miscellaneous works was held in the hall. In 1873 a fifty-piece orchestra performed daily, and organ recitals were given frequently — daily in 1874. A military band played twice a week toward the end of the 1874 exhibition.

Because the exhibitions were intended to encourage industrial education, lectures were given on many of the displays, but the only well-attended lectures were those on cooking. In 1873 three £50 scholarships were offered, and two were awarded to people who passed the Royal Society of Arts's examinations on the Exhibition's technological subjects.

Although the exhibition of 1871 was generally considered a success, those of the following three years registered increasingly steep declines in gross receipts and attendance and showed financial loses. Gross receipts dropped from £76,433 in 1871 to just £16,399 in 1874; attendance shrunk from 1,142,154 to 466,745 over the same period. A £17, 671 profit in 1871 turned into a £17, 821 loss in 1874.

The financial decline is also reflected in the decreasing amount of ceremony associated with the exhibitions from year to year. In 1871 the prince of Wales and Princess Helena opened the exhibition in a formal state ceremony. In 1874, the exhibition opened with no ceremony at all. An article in an 1874 number of the *Practical Magazine* described the closing of that year's exhibition as the "most inglorious ending of any Industrial, especially any International, Exhibition... Not an atom of ceremony, not a word of leave-taking or explanation."

After receiving the financial results of the 1873 exhibition, the commissioners met in March 1874 and decided, on the advice of the earl of Caernarvon, chair of the Board of Management, to discontinue the series of exhibitions unless the first two months of the 1874 exhibition proved extremely popular. They were not, and the commissioners agreed to end the series after the exhibition's close.

The commissioners provided several explanations for the exhibitions' financial losses. Lord Caernarvon pointed to the competition with the Vienna exhibition of 1873 and to the Royal Horticultural Society's lack of cooperation. Henry Cole blamed the severe decline in receipts in 1873 and 1874 on the Horticultural Society's excluding visitors from the gardens and demanding payments from the commissioners for the use of a pathway between the two exhibition halls. Other deficiencies he cited included the lack of a railway link with the exhibition, the lack of a connection with the South Kensington Museum, and insufficiently convenient refreshment rooms.

Cole speculated that the arrangement of goods by class instead of by national origin may have discouraged visitors since such an arrangement is less strikingly interesting. In a twentieth-century critique of the exhibitions, Kenneth Luckhurst added that this nongeographic arrangement obscured the international nature of the displays, deprived foreign countries of the chance to arrange their goods, and confused the general public with its scientific nature. Other theories explaining the exhibitions' failure include the lack of juried awards, the interference of the Franco-Prussian War in 1871, and controversy over the right to sell exhibited goods.

While some of the exhibitions' problems were unavoidable, others stemmed directly from the commissioners' adoption of the recommendations made after the Paris exhibition of 1867. The policies of limiting the size and expense of the exhibitions, arranging goods by class, and not awarding prizes were intended to make the exhibitions more affordable and educational; unfortunately, they also made them less dramatic. Beginning only twenty years after 1851, this series was inevitably compared with the Great Exhibition. While no British exhibition, no matter how exciting, could have eclipsed that of 1851, the London exhibitions of 1871–1874 never even came close.

Bibliography

The most complete source of information on the exhibitions is Henry Cole, Her Majesty's Commissioners for the Exhibition of 1851, *A Special Report on the Annual International Exhibitions of the Years 1871, 1872, 1873 and 1874*. Appendixes, C. 2379 (1878–1879). This command paper includes copies of documents, lists of commissioners, and other pertinent materials. Another helpful parliamentary report is Her Majesty's Commissioners for the Exhibition of 1851, *Sixth Report*, Appendixes (1879). For detailed information on the 1871 exhibits, see *Official Reports on the Various Sections of the Exhibition of 1871*, ed. Lord Houghton [Richard Monckton Milnes], 2 vols. (1871). Copies of Lord Houghton's report are available in the British Museum (London), the Newberry Library (Chicago), Yale University (New Haven), and University of British Columbia (Vancouver).

In addition to these official reports, contemporary journalistic accounts of the exhibitions provide useful information. The *Journal of the Royal Society of Arts* 19–23 (1871–1874) contains many detailed articles on the exhibitions. For an overview and evaluation of the 1871 exhibition, see "The International Exhibition," *Times* (London) October 2, 1871. For a good analysis of why the exhibitions failed, see "International Exhibitions from 1851 to 1874: A Retrospect," *Practical Magazine* 4 (1874): 454. A more recent explanation of the exhibitions' failure is contained in Kenneth W. Luckhurst, *The Story of Exhibitions* (1951).

Vienna 1873

Nadine Rottau

Weltausstellung 1873 Wien

The Vienna world's fair of 1873 marks a turning point in the history of the world's expositions. The Austro-Hungarian Empire organized an event that moved the focus away from an industrial and technical orientated presentation to a more entertaining and diverting experience for a broad audience. It was the first international fair in a German-speaking region and was to remain the only one for nearly 130 years.

Since the Great Exhibition in London in 1851, the idea to host a world's fair in Austria circulated among industrial organizations within the country. A war with Italy cancelled plans for an exhibition in 1859. Another imperial resolution fixed the year 1865 for the event, but again shifting political alliances and the announcement of a world's fair in Paris in 1867 delayed the Austrian project. In 1866 Prussia won a decisive victory in the Battle of König-grätz against the Danube Monarchy and gained hegemony in Central Europe. This defeat brought about an adjustment between Austria and Hungary, strengthening Hungarian influence within the multi-ethnic state. Due to these political circumstances an international fair seemed to promise a revival of economic and social prestige for Austria in the eyes of leading industrialists as well as the foreign ministry. In 1870, the president of the Lower Austrian Trade Association, Franz von Wertheim, proposed an exhibition to the board of trade, and Emperor Franz Joseph I concurred in May. The date was set for 1873, the twenty-fifth anniversary of the coronation of the Austrian Emperor.

Vienna's most popular recreation area, the Prater, was chosen as the site for the fair. It was part of the imperial forest in the south of the city and proved to be ideal after the regulation and relocation of the river Danube. In the past the city had regularly been flooded due to the low meadows lying along the many tributaries of the river. After one of the worst floods in 1862, the city council decided to relocate the riverbed. Because of these civil works a perfect exhibition site was created that could easily be reached by rail, boat, and road. Furthermore, the chosen area was five times larger than the site of the Paris Exhibition of 1867 and even larger than all previous world's fair sites combined. A contemporary calculated that a visitor would need 40 days to see everything that was exhibited on the roughly 576 acres of the site.

During the second half of the nineteenth century what the audience expected of a world's fair changed: people wanted to travel the world in one day, become acquainted with exotic cultures and see foreign handicrafts and resources in authentic surroundings. Taking this development into account, the concept of fairs was transformed, starting in Vienna. The construction of one single exhibition hall was abandoned. Instead, under the supervision of the general director of the Austrian fair, Wilhelm von Schwarz-Senborn, the arrangement of the show was allocated among four main buildings and many smaller structures of various sizes and styles. This practice was extended to the world's fairs in America. Today's common system of pavilion-architecture at international exhibitions has its roots here.

Schwarz-Senborn had been appointed general director in 1871 because of his experience and the reputation he had gained when working for Austria at the expositions in Paris in 1855 and 1867 and London in 1862. He suggested a major building with a huge rotunda as signature structure; this was designed by the well known architect Karl von Hasenauer, who was also in part responsible for the modification of the imperial Hofburg in Vienna's city center. The Palace of Industry, as it was called, was situated in the middle of the exhibition site. Its single long nave ran from the northwest to the southeast with a gigantic rotunda in the centre that was realized by the English shipbuilding-engineer John Scott Russell. Measuring 354 feet in diameter and 284 feet in height, it was the largest rotunda ever constructed and an outstanding achievement of iron manufacture. The dome had a cone-shaped roof consisting of tapering iron plates that rested on a circular iron girder and was supported by 80-foot-high double columns. On top of the roof a lantern was installed which provided another attraction for the visitors. The lantern, 100 feet in diameter, had an outside walkway, allowing people to enjoy a magnificent view of the fairgrounds and the city, the countryside, and even the Alps. A smaller lantern, 25 feet in diameter, was topped by a cap in the shape of the Austrian crown — made of wrought iron, gilded and decorated with glass imitations of the crown jewels — that formed the peak of the palace. According to the so-called herringbone system, invented by the Austrian architects Eduard van der Nüll and August Sicard von Siccardsburg in 1844, the main nave of the palace was crossed by transepts, thus creating several galleries connected by arcades or courtyards. Because of its striking architecture, the building soon became the definitive symbol of the Weltausstellung.

Compared to conventional exhibition halls the advantages of the new building were a consistent illumination, and the ability to divide the space into smaller areas and a more efficient organization of the exhibition space. The rotunda was primarily open, but due to a shortage of exhibition space, it was utilized for exhibits as well. Since it was the most exclusive place of the Weltausstellung, the exhibitors tried to outbid one another for the space. The match company A.M. Pollak, for example, showed the Laxenburger castle made totally out of matches, while a fabricant from Hamburg showed a huge statue of Victory made of hard

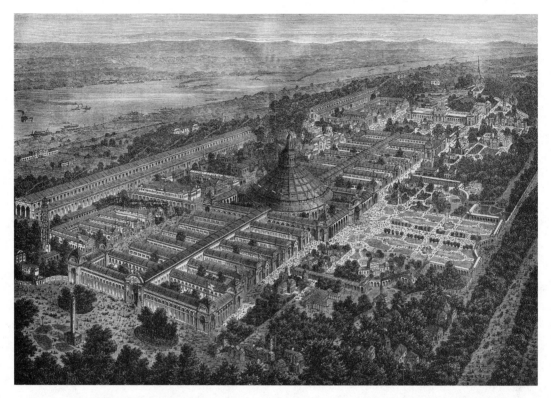

This overview of the exhibition shows its location along the Danube River (from Julius Engelmann et al., *Der Weltverkehr und seine Mittel...*, 1879).

rubber and a candlemaker erected a memorial for the inventor of stearin-candles completely made of glycerine. A monumental fountain, designed by Jean Jules Klagmann and constructed by the French foundry Durenne, was mounted in the middle of the gigantic hall. In the rest of the Palace of Industry, exhibits from the sections for nourishment and stimulants, textile-, wood- and metalworking industries, stone- and glass wares, notions industry, paper industry, and graphic arts were exhibited. It was the aim of Schwarz-Senborn to mix all branches of industry thus demonstrating their interdependence. The rotunda was not demolished at the end of the fair, but was used for diverse events and exhibitions until 1937, when a fire destroyed it.

The second largest building was the Machinery Hall, situated parallel to the Palace of Industry on the north-east side of the site. The 2,060-foot long building accommodated railroad tracks for the easy shipping of heavy exhibits. A contemporary report describes the objects inside: "We found there conventional railway- and tramway-cars, comfortably equipped delicate wagons, magnificent locomotives, steam fire engines, sew-, stitch- and weaving-machines, street-locomotives, annunciators, iron giants and dwarfs side by side, as the unfatigued human mind had devised to let fire and iron work for it."

Works of art were exhibited in one large and two smaller buildings, situated east of the Palace of Industry. Again, Karl von Hasenauer was responsible for the design. He tested a novel illumination system that was so successful that it was installed in the two imperial museums in Vienna's city center, the Museum of Fine Arts and the Museum of Natural History. Coordinated roof lights, side windows and glass vents in the roof ensured a consistent lighting for the exhibits. Despite the innovative gallery, the exhibits were mainly works presented in Paris in 1867. Two so-called *Agriculturhallen* were located between the Palace of Industry and the Machinery Hall. Austria, for example, presented its achievements in agriculture with great success. Local brewers and winegrowers offered the jury a great variety of beer and wine, and the Austrian sugar industry set up a collective exhibit with more than 90 participants.

The architecture of the main buildings of Vienna's world's fair was characterized by a variety of historical styles. The iron framework of each building was hidden behind the façade, following a trend in exposition architecture away from the functional glass and iron buildings of the previous decades towards a more ornamental and decorative style. This was influenced by another urban management project in Vienna that started in 1857: the rebuilding of the medieval defensive fortification into a grand boulevard of remarkable proportions. The aim was to connect the inner city with the growing suburbs and to transform the medieval infrastructure into a modern and progressive townscape. The new *Ringstrasse* was lined with sufficient buildings like the opera, the theatre, the parliament, the city hall, the stock exchange and museums, all carried out in eclectic styles. Although this project was not directly attached to the plans for the world's fair, it encouraged the municipality to improve the general infrastructure of the city for the event. By the time of the exposition, an upgrading of streets and bridges had been completed. A tramway pulled by horses was expanded and new routes to the Prater were built. The *Praterstern* was the junction from where the visitors entered the exhibition site. The *Ausstellungs-Strasse* (Exhibition Road) and the *Haupt-Allee* (Main Avenue) formed two sides of a triangle between which the exposition area spread. From the Exhibition Road visitors could enter the fair by passing the pavilions. From the Main Avenue, they would get to the main entrance From here the *Kaiser-Allee* (Emperor Avenue) led to the main portal of the Palace of Industry, which bore the maxim of the show: *Viribus Unitis* ("with forces joined").

The Weltausstellung in Vienna was the first to utilize the environment of the Palace of Industry extensively. The ample grounds enabled the organizers to create a kind of modern theme park with many different architectural structures alternating with avenues, small plazas, water basins and flower meadows. The officials wanted to emphasis the scenic beauty of the grounds, which would serve as an additional attraction. More than 200 different structures spread from the west side of the site over the south side of the Palace of Industry and in the southeast next to a small river called Heustadlwasser. These buildings were used in various ways: in some, companies presented products and innovations, but there were also authentic residential buildings and farmhouses, ethnic restaurants, food stalls, coffeehouses, arcades, and dance pavilions, where the Austrian composer Johann Strauss played his famous waltzes. The main attraction was the ethnic village, which illustrated the traditional ways of life found in southeast European regions like Hungary, Croatia, Romania and Transylvania. Another crowd pleaser was the oriental quarter with its typical palaces, workshops for jewelery and pipes, a mosque with dome and minaret and a bazaar. Japan participated with an extraordinarily comprehensive exhibit, consisting of some 6,000 objects, including a reproduction of the temple of Kyoto and a Japanese garden. They were allowed to sell their wares to visitors, although exposition officials prohibited sales on the exposition site. The focus on exotic countries inspired an oriental boom in central Europe.

Fair officials' decision to prioritize the Orient, the Far East and the Balkans signified a desire on Austria's part to portray itself as a kind of bridge between Europe and the Orient. This strategy turned out to be successful due in part to the diplomatic contacts of the protector, president, and general director of the exhibition, Archduke Karl Ludwig, Archduke Rainer and Schwarz-Senborn. They visited many countries and made numerous contacts abroad to promote the Weltausstellung. Many prominent guests visited the exhibition, including the Prince of Wales, the German Emperor Wilhelm I, and Tsar Alexander I of Russia. The Persian Shah Nāsir-ad-Dīn stayed several days with an entourage of 57 people and fascinated the Viennese people with his luxurious and unorthodox appearance.

The innovative allocation of space in the Palace of Industry and across the entire exhibition site also drew attention to Austria's position between the east and west. The 35 participating countries were arranged from east to west in their natural geographical proximity to one another. As the gateway between east and west, Austria was positioned in the middle.

With 9,000 of a total of 53,000 exhibitors, Austria's section was the largest, closely followed by the German Empire with 8.000. Thus the German-speaking states dominated the event, while the other major nations of the world, France, Britain and the United States were less prominent. Only Russia tried to increase its economic influence in Western Europe by sending more and qualitatively better products to Austria in comparison to previous expositions. Although France sent 5,000 exhibits and won 240 awards, critics did not regard their participation as outstanding. Great Britain's exhibits were designed to show the political and economic importance of British colonies, especially India. The United States was more interested in the organization of the event than in presenting American products. They sent a group of government commissioners that prepared a comprehensive report used in the preparation of the Centennial International Exhibition in Philadelphia in 1876.

As with previous expositions, the principal focus was on the exhibition of the products and production processes of the industrial age. But since Austria was not a leading industrial nation it emphasized its role as a leader of cultural and intellectual achievement, especially with regard to education. The official program was divided into 26 groups and then subdivided into 174 sections of which one-third concerned cultural and educational issues. Exhibits revealed a positive concern with labor, a belief in continuous progress, an appreciation of education, arts, and science and an emphasis of the social value of the family. The program reflected a bourgeois moral concept and self-image.

The somewhat all-emcompassing aim of the event "das Culturleben der Gegenwart und das Gesamtgebiet der Volkswirtschaft darzustellen und deren weiteren Fortschritt zu fördern" (to represent and advance contemporary cultural life and the complete realm of political economy)—as the official program stated—caused many contemporaries to characterize the Viennese event as the first real world's fair. Therefore it was known by the more universal term "Welt-ausstellung" instead of "Welt-Industrieausstellung," as it was initially to

Courtyard of the Egyptian viceroy's palace (from Julius Engelmann, et al., *Der Weltverkehr und seine Mittel...*, 1879).

be called. To deepen the diverse issues of the program, the general management and private associations organized 16 international congresses, of which the most important was one on international patents and one on art history, led by the Austrian curator Rudolf von Eitelberger.

On May 1, 1873, Emperor Franz Joseph opened the fair on schedule. The exposition ran for 184 days and closed on October 31. For early visitors it must have seemed quite chaotic as the buildings and grounds of the fair were not all completed. The rotunda of the Palace of Industry was bare brickwork, and some pavilions did not open until the end of June. Also, the civil works in the inner city were still under construction; only few of the great buildings along the Ringstrasse had been finished. Vienna must have appeared like a gigantic construction site rather than the cosmopolitan metropolis that the organizers wished. Nonetheless, the capital and the whole of Austria were looking forward to improving their public image. Because of the optimistic and positive mood due to the earlier period of boosterism, people had very high expectations for the outcome of the exposition. Commercial circles as well as the general public speculated in the hope of huge financial profits. But the grand opening dampened the lofty optimism. The weather was cold, rainy, and windy and a traffic snarl caused a strained atmosphere. Because of the exorbitant prices for hotel rooms many of the newly built hotels remained empty. To make things even worse, the Viennese stock market crashed on May 9. It was an international crisis and was not unexpected, but it had its beginning in Austria where too many individuals had speculated recklessly. It burdened the city and caused a severe financial depression and widespread unemployment in the country. Another setback followed shortly, when at the end of June an outbreak of cholera resulted in 2,983 deaths in the city's poorer areas. Due to these circumstances, the attendance figures were much lower than estimated. A total of 7,255,000 visitors came to see the latest advances in science and industry, education and the arts, but this was only half the number Paris had counted in 1867. However, when the weather improved during the summer and the market had stabilized, attendance increased. Entrance fees were 1 gulden on weekdays and

half a gulden on weekends. The show was open daily from 9 A.M. to 7 P.M. But the exposition incurred a large financial loss that could not be overcome by the growing number of visitors in the last month of the fair. In the end a total expenditure of 19 million gulden outstripped an income of roughly 4.3 million gulden. Unlike the Great Exhibition in London in 1851 which was completely funded by private bearers, the fair's shortfall had to be paid by the Austrian state.

Although the Weltausstellung in Vienna had to cope with a lack of visitors, bad weather, a stock market crash, a cholera epidemic, and a huge deficit, it managed to transform the Austrian capital from a rather underdeveloped medieval city into a cosmopolitan national capital. The preparations for the world's fair initiated important modernizations in the infrastructure such as bridges and public transportation. The intention of the organizers to create an exposition with spacious recreation areas for visitors and the novel pavilion system reflects the change of the fair's purpose from a trade show to an edifying cultural event for the populace. This can also be seen in the new focus on education and culture. In addition, the ethnographic concept and the oriental sections proved to be a success for the multi-ethnic state. On the whole the changes that Austria bought about in the conception of world's fairs were adopted and expanded in later expositions. The significance of the expositions as a cultural event rather than an industrial and technological event increased. The challenging and diverse program with its overwhelming number of exhibits on the huge site in Vienna served to illustrate an aspect of modern times that became more and more apparent. At the exposition, just as in real life, it seemed impossible for the individual to deal with society's industrial processes and cultural diversity in its totality. As the publicist Ferdinand Kürnberger summed it up in November 1873: "With thundering voice the Exposition universelle preaches: there are no generalists anymore. The most exclusive way of education has stopped being possible."

Bibliography

Very detailed information on the Weltausstellung in Vienna is found in the official reports on the fair by the participating countries. In these reports facts like the different exhibitors, their profession and exhibits can be consulted. The *Officieller Ausstellungs-Bericht*, hrsg. durch die General-Direction der Weltausstellung 1873 (1873–1877) accumulates in 95 issues basic data on the event. The *Amtlicher Bericht über die Wiener Weltausstellung im Jahre 1873*, erstattet von der Centralcommission des Deutschen Reiches für die Wiener Weltausstellung, in drei Bänden (1874–77) does the same with focus on the German part of the exhibition. Another example are the *Reports of the Commissioners of the United States to the International Exhibition held at Vienna 1873*, ed. by Robert H. Thurston, 4 vol. (1876), in which the U.S. role on the exhibition is covered. Most of these reports are located in the ÖNB, the national library of Austria in Vienna and usually in the national library of the respective country.

A very detailed and vivid picture of the world's fair can be gathered from the various newspapers specially issued for the event. The *Allgemeine illustrierte Weltausstellungs-Zeitung* (1872–1873) and the *Internationale Ausstellungszeitung*, a supplement to *Neue Freie Presse* between May 2 and November 1, 1873, contain articles about the presented objects, the calendar of events, information about special activities, feuilletons and introductions of important persons as well as news and stories about life in the Viennese capital at the time.

Other contemporary sources are valuable for their information on special exhibits, such as August Oncken, *Die Wiener Weltausstellung 1873*, Berlin 1873 or Carl von Lützow, *Kunst und Kunstgewerbe auf der Wiener Weltausstellung 1873* (1873), and Jacob von Falke, *Die Kunstindustrie auf der Wiener Weltausstellung 1873* (1873.) Oncken gives a very wide-ranging overview of the exhibition program and its advantages and disadvantages while Lützow and von Falke focus on the arts and applied arts with detailed descriptions and images.

The most important and comprehensive secondary publication is Jutta Pemsel's book *Die Wiener Weltausstellung von 1873* (1989.) It deals with nearly every aspect on the fair, the appendix contains a detailed bibliography and 52 pictures provide a broad survey. With a focus on urban planning the exposition and its special exhibition site are analysed in *Der planbare Nutzen: Stadtentwicklung durch Weltausstellungen und Olympische Spiele* (2001) by Monika Meyer-Künzel. The book *Smart Exports: Österreich auf den Weltausstellungen 1851-2000* (2000), by Ulrike Felber, Elke Krasny and Christian Rapp, examines the exposition of 1873 along with all participations of the Danube Monarchy at world's fairs to reveal the development of the country's self-conception over the years.

Philadelphia 1876

Alfred Heller

Centennial International Exhibition

On the initiative of Congressman D. J. Morrell of Pennsylvania, the U.S. Congress acted in 1871 "to provide for celebrating the One Hundredth Anniversary of American Independence, by holding an International Exhibition of Arts, Manufactures and Products of the Soil and Mine" in Philadelphia in 1876. The originator of the idea was Professor J. L. Campbell of Wabash College, Indiana, who in

1866 conveyed his thoughts in a letter to the mayor of Philadelphia. The Congress was pressed into action after the idea won the support of the Franklin Institute, the Academy of Fine Arts, the select and common councils of the city and the state legislature.

To oversee the first major U.S. world's fair, Congress created the Centennial Commission, to be appointed by the president from nominees of the governors of each of the existing states and territories. But Congress offered no money for the commissioners and specifically disclaimed federal liability for the expenses of the exhibition. (Nor has the United States accepted financial responsibility for any other world's fair held in the country since the Centennial.)

The city of Philadelphia put up $50,000 for the commission's operating expenses, but aside from deciding that the exhibition would be held in Fairmount Park, the commission could accomplish little without funds. Once again Morrell prevailed on the Congress, and this time they chartered the Centennial Board of Finance, which had the power "under the Centennial Commission" to sell up to $10 million in stock. This sum was never realized, however. Ultimately the board sold $2.5 million in stock, almost all of it to local supporters; the city produced another $1.5 million (not for stocks); and in 1875 Congress loosened up sufficiently to lend $1.5 million to finance the completion of the buildings. The federal government also spent more than $500,000 on its building and its exhibits. An additional $2 million was expected from admissions and payments from concessionaires.

With 2,740 acres (today more than 9,000), Fairmount Park in Philadelphia was the world's largest urban reserve and surely one of the most beautiful. On July 4, 1873, the park's commissioners handed over 450 acres to the Centennial Commission, of which 285 became the fairgrounds. North and west of Independence Square, some 115 feet above the Schuylkill River, the grounds filled a plateau that rose toward George's Hill on their western edge. Pleasing views of the river and the city, modest ravines, running water and a small lake contributed to the attractions of the site.

The commission entrusted the layout of the fair to an ambitious 27-year-old German immigrant with an engineering and architectural background, Hermann J. Schwarzmann. He had been instrumental in laying out the park and had designed its splendid zoo. For the fair he envisioned several main buildings and many separate pavilions placed within an efficient and handsome landscape. It was the grandest scheme of any world's fair to this time and fixed the pattern that has persisted to this day. An architectural competition to choose the design of the main building produced plans by some of the most famous architects of the time. The winners, the Philadelphia firm of Collins

& Autenrieth, did not receive the commission, however, because although their plans followed the official specifications, they would have proved too costly to execute. The Centennial Commission eventually abandoned all the competitors and in 1874 assigned the Main Building and the adjacent Machinery Hall to Henry Pettit and Joseph M. Wilson, engineers connected with the Pennsylvania Railroad. They entrusted the design of the exhibition's two permanent buildings, Memorial Hall (the art gallery) and Horticultural Hall, to the ever-ready Schwarzmann.

By early summer 1875, construction was underway on the large buildings and some 250 pavilions and auxiliary structures. Although all the major buildings were completed more or less on schedule, the inside work lagged, as did the fitting out of some exhibits. Four days before the scheduled opening of May 10, the *New York Times* noted that in Memorial Hall, "the larger half of the great plaster pilasters have yet to be placed in position, and much of the marble work, such as the cornices and plinths, is still undone." And even two days after the opening, Agricultural Hall was "in a deplorably backwards stage," with "empty showcases." Three days later, workers were trying to complete exhibits in the Main Building, and in the Memorial Hall, paintings and statuary were still being installed. Six days after the opening, huge shipments of exhibits from Russia and China arrived.

On May 9, the fairgrounds were soggy from two days of steady rain. The entire Congress and high officials from the other branches of the government had come up from Washington on three special trains. Visitors jammed the downtown hotels. Workmen struggled through the night to clear debris from the fairgrounds. It was raining at 7:00 A.M. on opening day, but the weather soon lifted. The sun came out at times. The *Times* was confident the Centennial would "present the grandest monument ever offered to the world of the industrial progress of the English-speaking race." The *Philadelphia Inquirer*, by contrast, brooded that the government had "refused to vote a dollar or to render help in any way, until our own citizens had completed the work and assumed obligations so vast as to shame the national authority into doing something."

The Philadelphia Centennial Exhibition was so large that several major pavilions were built to accommodate all the exhibits. Shown is the elaborate Horticultural Hall (courtesy Peter M. Warner).

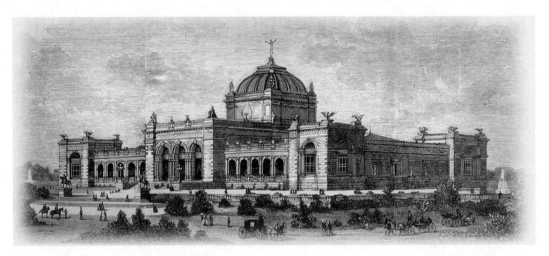

Memorial Hall at the Centennial Exhibition housed the very popular fine arts exhibit (from *Visitor's Guide to the Centennial Exhibition*, 1876).

The opening ceremonies were in front of the neoclassic Memorial Hall, where a platform had been constructed for the dignitaries, with a program affixed to each seat. The plans had been carefully laid, but some attendees were not happy. Congressmen disliked the seating arrangements, soldiers were disgruntled that their uniforms had been splattered with mud, and diplomats found themselves lost and struggling in the crowd of 200,000 (altogether, 37 nations had accepted the U.S. invitation to participate in the fair). The program began with a march composed for the occasion by Richard Wagner. The critic for the New York *Tribune* called it "one of the most original things Wagner has written since *Tristan*," but it was inaudible to the reviewer from the *Inquirer* even though, he wrote, "Wagner bears the reputation of being the noisiest of composers."

A lengthy invocation, a hymn with words by John Greenleaf Whittier, and speeches by John Welsh, president of the Board of Finance, and Joseph R. Hawley, president of the Centennial Commission, preceded the address of

President Ulysses S. Grant, who modestly downplayed the American exhibits ("Our necessities have compelled us to chiefly expend our means and time in felling forests, subduing prairies, building dwellings, factories, ... machinery") and commended displays that demonstrated "the skill and taste of our friends from other nations." Then he declared the exhibition open, and in the ensuing tumult, Dom Pedro, the emperor of Brazil, the only foreign head of state who was in attendance, stood up and waved his hat. The ceremony ended with a rendition of the Hallelujah chorus and a 100-gun salute.

After a noontime reception, the officials proceeded to the center of Machinery Hall for the most memorable moment of the entire exhibition. Beneath the towering twin cylinders of the largest of all steam engines, devised for the fair by American inventor and manufacturer George Corliss, the president and the Brazilian emperor each turned handles setting the engine in motion. Other machines in the hall, connected to the giant by 23 miles of shafting and 40 miles of belting, began heaving, clanking and whirring. The power and potential of American industry were at once made plain to all the world.

The Giant Corliss engine was the most spectacular sight at the Centennial Exhibition (editors' collection).

Visitors to the Centennial felt overwhelmed. The developed portion of the grounds was inside what might be described as a large triangle, with a narrow-gauge railroad around its periphery. Across its southern base stretched the Main Building and Machinery Hall, end-to-end some four thousand linear feet of warehousing. The Main Building, framed in cast iron, had brick walls 6 feet high, with two bands of windows above. It enclosed 20 acres of land. Square towers at the central entrances and at each corner diverted attention from the low-slung effect, as did colorful flags and streamers that flew above the length and breadth of the hall. Archways above the entrances echoed the three grand arches of Memorial Hall just across the Avenue of the Republic.

The Main Building was devoted mainly to manufactures of the United States and other countries; those of the United States occupied about a third of the space. Products arrayed in eye-catching patterns filled row on row of tall, glassed-in display cases: glassware, silverware, scientific instruments, clocks, dental instruments and ceramics. Furniture—carved, tasseled, cushioned in needlepoint—was mixed with ornate examples of industrial art: caskets, carriages, textiles, musical instruments, revolving pistols, vases, chandeliers, beer mugs, chimney pieces and a steel gun weighing 100 tons, turned out by Friederich Krupp of Essen, the largest gun ever made. Most items were grouped according to their countries of origin—the United States, Austria, Britain, France, Japan, and so forth. But everything at the Centennial was also classified in one of

France's gift to the Centennial Exhibition was the torch of the still unfinished Statue of Liberty (editors' collection).

Edison's quadruplex telegraph, machines for agricultural use and heavy industry — the cumulative impression of industrial power must have been the most stunning of all. And the United States, whose exhibits filled 80 percent of Machinery Hall, was at the center of progress.

The 700-ton Corliss engine proved to be the most popular attraction of the fair and its most celebrated artifact. At midday it would be shut down for an hour, and after the repast the crowds would gather to see the behemoth wheeze back to life. During the summer when, as contemporary historian James McCabe expressed it, "the exhibition buildings were like ovens, and the concrete paths through the grounds burned the feet like lava," Fairgoers gravitated to an annex of the hall, in which the latest in hydraulic pumps sent plumes of cooling water into a tank.

The exhibit of fine art in Schwarzmann's granitic, square-domed Memorial Hall also turned out to be exceedingly popular. An extra building had to be built hastily to accommodate some of the thousands of paintings, statues and photographs from some twenty countries. It was the first full-fledged international art exhibit in the republic and has been credited with bringing about a strong American interest in the arts, even though, as Walter Smith in *Masterpieces of the Centennial* (1876) grumbled, it included nothing from the Louvre or the Vatican. The British sent a fine collection from the Royal Academy; French and Italian works depicting large-breasted women in various stages of dishabille as allegorical figures had a large following. America had brought some of its best, including works by Frederick E. Church, Edward Moran, Winslow Homer and Albert Bierstadt. The building itself, topped by a colossal zinc statue of a gloomy Columbia bestride a globe, dominated the Centennial. Envisioned as a permanent museum for the city, it spawned numbers of beaux-arts style galleries and libraries throughout the United

seven departments (Mining and Metallurgy, Manufactures, Education and Science, Art, Machinery, Agriculture, and Horticulture), subclassified and subclassified again, in a logical scheme that later became the model for the Dewey Decimal System used in libraries. In contrast with earlier exhibitions, the Centennial made no hierarchical awards; the judges handed out more than 13,000 identical bronze medals to exhibitors in the various categories.

Machinery Hall, framed in wood, was similar in configuration to the Main Building. Most of the mechanical marvels gathered here, produced by the United States and 13 other nations, were in actual operation: mining equipment, typesetters and printing presses, locomotives, drills, lathes, fire trucks, electric engines, looms and magic lanterns, to cite a few examples. (The steam plant that powered the Corliss engine was in a separate annex.) Although many articles were first introduced to the public at the Centennial — typewriters, a mechanical calculator, Bell's telephone,

States. The hall housed Philadelphia's art museum until 1928. Today it contains, in the basement, a popular scale model of the Centennial. The model remained after an interactive children's museum opened in Memorial Hall in spring 2008. The elaborately detailed, Moorish-style Horticultural Hall was a conservatory for the display of native and exotic plants, some of great rarity. Around it and along walkways leading from it were beds of flowering plants. The building was finally torn down in 1955, a victim of neglect and damage from the elements. The fifth major building, at the top of the triangle, was Agricultural Hall, with roofs and windows pointed heavenward in Gothic peaks. The tillers of the soil, their animals, and producers of farm equipment were much exalted at the Centennial, as befitted a largely agricultural nation.

On the west side of the grounds were twenty-four state buildings, each in a regional style. The states generally showed their manufactures in the main exhibit halls, reserving these small houses as resting places and greeting centers for dignitaries and visitors from "home." The Ohio Pavilion, built of stone, and Memorial Hall, are all that

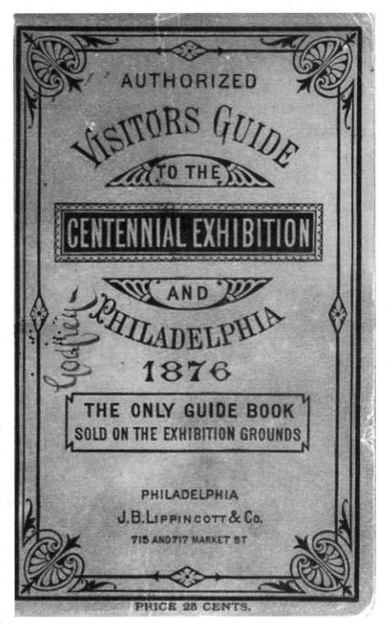

By 1876 guidebooks had become necessary for visitors to find their way around fairs (editors' collection).

remain today of the Centennial buildings. Some states of the Confederacy, notably Virginia, Georgia, Louisiana, and Texas, had no buildings and were unable to contribute much in the way of exhibits. Nor did they participate in the festivities, causing the Centennial Commission's president, General Joseph R. Hawley,

to lament, "Had the Governor of Virginia appointed a day for his people to meet here he would have received the warmest greeting he ever saw in his life."

The Declaration of Independence was on view in the large U.S. Government Building, along with exhibits from the Smithsonian Institution (Indian artifacts, mineral samples), the

War and the Navy departments (artillery, model boats), the Interior Department, the U.S. Post Office and others. The Women's Building, presided over by Elizabeth Duane Gillespie, displayed items of art, crafts and inventions by women. It represented an early achievement in the feminist struggle for suffrage and equal rights.

The Pennsylvania Railroad had built a depot on Elm Avenue, across from the main entrance to the grounds. Before entering or after leaving the fair, visitors might tarry along the avenue and its side streets for amusements provided in beer halls, cheap hotels and sideshows. One establishment claimed to recreate the 1870 siege of Paris by the German army (with its Krupp cannon); another, calling itself a "museum," featured the fierce and unregenerate "Wild Men of Borneo." (Soon after, P.T. Barnum brought this act into his circus. His wild men, if not the ones at the Centennial, were gentlemen who had grown up on Long Island.) Thus the precincts of Elm Avenue were an unofficial midway at a time before amusement zones were incorporated into the fairs.

Beside the lake near Machinery Hall was a piece of Bartholdi's Statue of Liberty — its arm, hand and torch. Visitors helped fund the statue's completion by paying to climb to the observation platform below the flame. The exhibit attracted much interest, but art critic Edward Strahan was not enthusiastic about the "titanic Hand of Liberty whose tremendous fingernails were reflected in the shuddering waters of the Lake." Another unusual structure was a public comfort station that provided reading rooms, access to the telegraph, umbrellas, messengers, barbers, hairdressers and baths, in addition to toilets. Restaurants and soda fountains were available throughout the grounds. Fairgoers could enjoy exhibits in many small pavilions erected by brewers, dairymen, shoe manufacturers, carriage makers and others. Fireworks, concerts and parades were regular activities, and sporting events, such as an international rowing regatta on the Schuylkill, accompanied the fair. Both presidential candidates that year, Rutherford B. Hayes and Samuel J. Tilden, spoke before large crowds on the fairgrounds.

In the summer when the weather was unusually hot, attendance was low. The daily average in July was just 15,207, and on the Fourth only 50,000 arrived for the country's hundredth birthday. The throngs and the enthusiasm grew in the fall. Pennsylvania Day in September brought in 257,165. By nightfall on closing day, November 10, the fair had drawn 9,789,392 visitors, of whom 8,004,325 paid to get in. If it had not been for the heat, the Sunday closings, a turn in the economy and, perhaps, the reluctance of the railroads to lower their rates, who knows how high the attendance would have gone? The Centennial suffered a loss of $1.9 million. The federal government demanded repayment of its $1.5 million, so the stockholders had to accommodate the entire amount.

"We had a nation to show," said General Hawley, and the Centennial gave ample evidence of American progress in education, industry and the arts. According to Congressman Morrell, foreign visitors saw "a polite, orderly, self-respecting and self-governing people... What [they] may be lacking in form is made up in substance." In the United States, the effect of the Centennial was deep and lasting. Sales were made through the fair; foreign trade received a definite boost. Americans could observe firsthand how their best work compared with that of others. They came to know people from other lands and to admire their accomplishments (even though, as Frank Leslie reported, the Americans' "vulgar curiosity" discouraged foreigners at the fair from wearing their native costumes). At a time when the scandals of the Grant administration had undermined the people's confidence in their leaders, the administration of the fair, led by director-general Alfred T. Goshorn, showed itself to be efficient, honest, and deserving of the public trust. The entire fair, in fact, boosted the pride and self-confidence of the sponsoring nation.

Bibliography

A great deal of primary source material for the Centennial Exhibition of 1876, including the records of the U.S. Centennial Commission and the Board of Finance, is in the Philadelphia City Archives. Other original material is located in the Historical Society of Pennsylvania in Philadelphia, and in the National Archives and Smithsonian Institution, both in Washington, D.C. The U.S. Centennial Commission published *Interna-*

tional Exhibition 1876. Official Catalogue (1876), as well as several volumes in 1879: International Exhibition 1876: Report of the Director General, 2 vols.; Appendix to the Reports of the Director General; Reports of the Officers; and Reports and Awards, 2 vols.

Contemporary publications of value include The Masterpieces of the Centennial International Exhibition, 3 vols. (1876); Frank Leslie's Historical Register of the United States Centennial Exposition, 1876 (1877), filled with vivid wood engravings and much information; James D. McCabe, The Illustrated History of the Centennial Exhibition (1876); and Thomson Westcott, Centennial Portfolio (1876), with engravings and thumbnail descriptions of the buildings. Two more whimsical works are David S. Cohen, Our Show: A Humourous Account of the International Exposition ... (1876), and A.G. Sedgwick, "The Restaurants at the Centennial," Nation 23 (1876).

Among modern works, one should begin with John Maass, The Glorious Enterprise: The Centennial Exhibition of 1876 and H.J. Schwarzmann, Architect-in-Chief (1973), which contains an excellent bibliography. A book published in conjunction with an ambitious exhibit mounted at the Smithsonian in Washington, D.C. in 1976 to mark the centennial of the Centennial contains many informative essays about the original exhibit halls: Robert C. Post, ed., 1876, A Centennial Exhibition (1976). See also Bruno Giberti, Designing the Centennial (2002), which, among other things, relates the exhibition to bazaars, museums, and department stores." In a chapter on the Centennial in All the World's a Fair: Visions of Empire at American International Expositions, 1876–1916 (1984), Robert W. Rydell documents his assertion that "from beginning to end, the exposition illustrated the consolidation and unequal distribution of power in the United States." At the site of the fair in Fairmount Park in Philadelphia, many of the fair's roads and walkways remain, as does Memorial Hall.

Paris 1878

Andrea C. Roeber

Exposition Universelle

Fewer than two years had passed since the last international exhibition had closed its gates in Philadelphia when the Exposition Universelle of 1878 was declared open on May 1 in Paris. It was to be the exhibition that, in the eyes of many critics, marked the beginning of what is commonly described as an exhibition fatigue. Exhibitors slowly began to tire of the shows and the effort they demanded, especially as the time gap between them constantly shrank. The encyclopedic presentations of the world's products were an ideal opportunity for the participating nations and manufacturers to demonstrate their technical and cultural achievements and interact with competitors. But as the exhibitions became increasingly complex, larger in scale, and more spectacular, the accomplishment of a single exhibitor was likely to be lost amid the overall vision of the exhibition itself.

Nonetheless visitors were attracted in ever greater numbers. So long as the public's fascination increased, the exhibition was legitimate in the eyes of the organizers. An additional important aspect of the 1878 exhibition was that the event had acquired political significance: a demonstration of the exhibiting nations' achievements with the host country clearly having a home field advantage. With a total of more than 16 million at Paris, exhibition attendance was at an all-time high, having increased dramatically from 9,789,382 at the Philadelphia exhibition. Still, there was eventually a financial loss of at least 28 million francs. With so many visitors coming to the fairs, why was no profit made, and why did nations continue to invest in them, despite many producers being less and less enthusiastic to exhibit?

The general significance of the 1878 Exposition Universelle can be traced in its preparations. In March 1876, the government decreed that an exhibition was to take place in 1878, leaving only a little more than two years for all preparations. Like all previous exhibitions, this one was to surpass its predecessors, even if the general background was anything but promising as France was still in a massive general crisis. After losing the 1870–1871 war to Prussia and being burdened with about five billion francs of indemnities as well as experiencing the Paris Commune Revolt in 1871, the country and Paris in particular were still suffering from their loss of significance, splendor, and self-confidence. A world's fair could strengthen the nation's status, bringing it back onto the international stage. Furthermore, the country was still in the state of political instability that characterized the early years of the Third Republic, proclaimed in 1871. From the start, the organization of this exhibition had not only been about a nation's prestige but also about a young government's need for recognition. The Second Empire had arranged two triumphant Expositions Universelles in 1855 and 1867, but after the 1870s' series of relatively unsuccessful international exhibitions, Paris and the new government now had the opportunity to outshine all earlier efforts.

The Third Republic clearly followed two main ambitions with this endeavor. On the one hand, as it remained in a state of relative instability the new administration wanted to demonstrate continuity, legitimizing its power. The last French exhibition of 1867 was naturally used as a point of orientation. This is shown in many facets of the event, notably the choice of the exhibition grounds and the decision to opt once more for a central exhibition building, but also in organizational aspects. Jean-Baptiste Krantz, who had designed the Palais d'Industrie in 1867, was appointed commissioner general. In other areas too, people who had gained experience at earlier exhibitions were trusted with important offices. Georges Berger, for instance, who had organized the foreign section in 1867, was given that responsibility again. Although one objective was to tie in with many aspects of the previous exhibition, the second objective was to outshine the Second Empire government wherever possible: in sheer size as well as in significance. The event was to demonstrate continuity and progress as well as a newly won political and economic confi-

dence. It was an ideal opportunity for the nation to show itself and the rest of the world that France was on its way up again, confirming that the state had recovered from the disastrous defeat in the Franco-Prussian War. As a consequence of this politicalization, Germany, which by then had become the German Empire under Prussian leadership, refused to take part officially. It blamed the rapid succession of exhibitions and the high expenses, which were common arguments, and sent exhibits only for the fine art section at the last minute. However, critical voices could be found inside France as well. Within the context of France's weak economy, the organizing of the 1878 Exposition Universelle was difficult to achieve. There was also some criticism as to whether the country could really afford such a financial extravaganza.

With respect to the site and architecture there was some continuity but the Republic wanted to distinguish itself from its predecessor. The Champ de Mars was chosen once more, but this time the site was extended to the Trocadéro hill on the other side of the River Seine, increasisng the exhibition space from 170 to 185 acres. At this point, the river banks were linked by the Pont d'Iéna which was widened for the occasion. The exhibition buildings, too, surpassed those of 1867 in size. The organizers opted for one central exhibition building with an arrangement similar to that of 1867, which was to be complemented by an additional building for special events. A competition was launched for the two main structures: the temporary Palais d'Industrie and the permanent Palais de Trocadéro across the river, which was to accommodate concerts, parties, and congresses during the fair and serve the city of Paris as a venue for similar events in the future. The main exhibition hall, the Palais d'Industrie, was designed by Léopold Amédée Hardy, supported by various engineers, including Gustave Eiffel, whose best-known contribution was the overhanging roof of the main entrance. The Palais d'Industrie was an enormous structure, the largest building of its time with a length of 2,316 feet and a width of 1,135 feet providing 2,690,977 square feet of exhibition space. As the oval construction of the 1867 fair had proven hard to sell after that exposition, the organizers decided on a rectangular layout which had the additional advantage of utilizing the space more efficiently. It included the Galerie des Machines, once more the largest hall with a height of 82 feet, as well as separate spaces for raw materials, general products, art industry, and the fine arts exhibition. The exhibition area was split into two halves: one occupied by France and its colonies; the other by the foreign nations. Similar to the exhibition of 1867, all goods were placed into classes (parallel to the River Seine) and countries of origin (along the main axis of the exhibition grounds), subdivided into nine groups containing a total of 90 classes. After the closing of the exhibition, the Palais d'Industrie was dismantled and recycled.

The Palais de Trocadéro and the cascade in front of it were built according to plans by Gabriel Davidou and Jules Bourdais. The palais, whose main elements were a central concert hall for up to 6,000 people, two towers of 230 feet each, and two 240 feet long colonnades embracing the Parc de Trocadéro, was an eclectic pastiche based on Romanesque and Spanish-Moorish styles. Contemporary critics were disturbed by its lack of unity but nevertheless startled by its magnificence. It would stand for 56 years until it was replaced by the Chaillot Palace for the 1937 Exposition Universelle. Although it had not been finished on the opening day, it became a center for cultural events soon after its completion. Concerts and congresses took place in the concert hall, while the rooms behind the arched colonnades served as an exhibition space for a retrospective art exhibition that was assembled from French government and private collections and opened at the end of June. Like the rest of the exhibition the show was meant to be divided into two halves—one for France and one for the rest of the world. As most of the latter did not send exhibits however, the exhibition remained almost exclusively French and the space was filled with ethnographic exhibits and Asian art. The presentation was extremely popular and stayed open even after the closing of the exposition.

Within the Palais d'Industrie and the Palais de Trocadéro, a railway system, covered over with planking to allow the visitors to walk on during the exposition, was installed to facilitate the construction and the dismantling of the fair. Nevertheless neither of the structures was completed when the exhibition was opened by the president, maréchal de MacMahon, on May 1, 1878—another tradition of the Empire that the Republic repeated. The German art critic Friedrich Pecht remarked, "Everybody realizes that an exposition such as this is never completed by the officially announced opening. The current one however, surpasses all its predecessors, being still in its swaddling clothes."

But even though many parts remained unfinished until the end of June and the 'real' opening date is sometimes given as May 20, visitors started to come from the beginning of May. The grounds surrounding the two buildings served as an amusement park. On the Trocadéro side, visitors could stroll across the monumental stairs down to the river; go for a walk through the forested Parc de Trocadéro; or visit the aquarium, one of the numerous restaurants, or one of the national pavilions scattered across the area. At the foot of the cascade, Arabian, Egyptian, Japanese, and Chinese booths had been installed where food and souvenirs were on sale.

As in 1867, the classification grid left little room for a representation of the nation as a whole. Since then, however, the interest in a demonstration of national pride within the central exhibition area had grown, not only on the part of the organizing nation, but also on that of the guests. This had led to the introduction of national pavilions at earlier shows. As a consequence, Berger proposed that every nation was given the opportunity to create an entrance to its section in the court of the Palais d'Industrie, representing their culture through architecture. The result was a pastiche of various architectural styles, which in some cases was extremely inconsistent, in particular when the façades were small, such as those of Siam or China. The so-called "Rue des Nations," though controversial among contemporaries, was an important innovation of the 1878 Exposition Universelle as it made the conceptual development of world's fairs from industry towards culture explicit. There were more autonomous national pavilions on the exhibition grounds for those who had not been able to fit into the Rue or just needed more space. A representative fair building as such, with suitable architecture, was acknowledged to be very important. The American pavilion, for instance, was widely criticized for being too nondescript. Simply presenting goods fit for

View down Rue des Nations with the Portuguese pavilion in the foreground (from Julius Engelmann et al., *Der Weltverkehr und seine Mittel...*, 1879).

competition did not suffice any longer; a cultural manifestation was needed alongside the industrial and commercial exhibits.

Not only had architecture become an important aspect of the exhibition but also the fine arts, and painting in particular. Paris had initiated this tradition in 1855, deliberately adding painting to the original plan of the Great Exhibition of 1851, which had included sculpture but left out painting. Contemporary fine arts were shown in the Palais d'Industrie where visitors could see the annual French salon, a special international exhibition salon, and contemporary decorative arts in their respective classes. The retrospective exhibition at the Palais de Trocadéro gave French culture additional prominence. It was part of a staging of national pride which drew the concept of the international exhibition further away from industry and engineering and closer to a cultural manifestation.

Even though the representation of cultural values and traditions became increasingly significant, industrial products and engineering were still a major aspect of the exhibition. An exhibit which attracted many visitors while simultaneously embodying France's growing national self-confidence was the steam hammer presented by Le Creusot. With the actual European leader in the heavy industry (the German company Krupp) not taking part in 1878, the leading French manufacturer had an opportunity to shine. The hammer with a weight of 1,200 tons and a power of impact of 100 tons was described as the "second colossus of Rhodos." It was so high that it would not fit into the Palais d'Industrie but had to be exhibited outside. Hydraulic engineering was also a major exhibit on the part of France, fitting neatly into the concept of representing national pride. It was presented at the Quay d'Orsay as well as perfectly integrated into the spectacle of the exhibition grounds. Water from the River Seine was used, for instance, to power elevators and to feed the fountains on the Trocadéro Hill and the aquarium in the Parc. The aquarium had been planned as a major attraction with sea animals from all over the world but eventually resembled a live version of a French fish market. Water was transported by four hydraulic pumps through 23 miles of cast iron and lead pipes, reaching every corner of the exhibition grounds. It was also used to cool down the Palais d'Industrie. Other exhibits illustrated the many uses of hydraulic engineering, ranging from colonial to domestic, from the building of canals to the watering of decorative ponds. A spectacular attraction on the boundary between art and engineering was the second piece of the Statue of Liberty. After the torch had been presented in Philadelphia, visitors were now able to admire the bust and climb the 43 steps inside to enjoy the view across the exhibition grounds from the head. With Eiffel realizing the engineering aspects of Auguste Bartholdi's design, this object embodied both types of exhibits represented at the exposition.

Alongside these large exhibits, the traditional steam engines, and other massive machines, smaller machines marked an important development in comparison to earlier expositions. What was new in 1878, for instance, were the ice machine, electrical lighting, the lawn mower, and the electro-magnetic motor. Moreover, the marvelous developments in French hydraulic engineering were overshadowed by the inventions of the American Wizard of Menlo Park. Thomas Alva Edison's megaphone and phonograph were featured at the exhibition. Lighting was also exhibited, but Edison's commercially successful light bulb was invented the following year. In June the streets between the Place de Théâtre and the Place de l'Opéra were illuminated by electric candles, which had been developed by the Russian Pawel N. Jablotschkow two years earlier, based on the principle of the carbon arc lamp. About 300 of these powerful street lamps were installed, replacing the faint gas light and making the streets at night brighter than ever before.

The tradition of international exhibitions as an occasion for congresses was continued in 1878. Considered an intellectual extension of the principles of international exhibitions, they were used to exchange ideas instead of goods. The organizers maintained the tradition of congresses to prevent the charges of frivolousness that had stained the image of the 1867 exposition. The 32 congresses of this exposition are considered very significant. There were, for instance, congresses on homoeopathy, on alcoholism, on blindness, and on legal medicine. The most far-reaching congresses dealt with protection of industrial property, the right to the reproduction of works of art, and

on the protection of literary property. This congress, led by Victor Hugo, eventually bought about the introduction of international copyright law.

If the Exposition Universelle with all its patriotic importance and relevance was so glorious, and if there was a growing cultural component thanks to exhibits and congresses attracting more and more visitors, why were exhibitors increasingly unhappy with the concept? Since 1867 the significance of expositions for the promotion of technical and cultural innovation had declined as they were unable to cover the growing complexity of the world. Although they remained by far the most attractive medium as far as publicity was concerned, new forms of publicity, such as journals, specialized trade fairs, and congresses had begun to threaten the supremacy of expositions, since they were much more effective and flexible with respect to the increasing pace of progress. International discourse on technical, scientific, and industrial progress found outlets other than large expositions, which required larger amounts of time and capital to bring about.

Commercial interests found that the extra work participation in the exposition created, often accompanied by a lack of immediate profit, was increasingly annoying. Expositions exhibitions had become spectacles, which forced manufacturers to develop specially created products. For the decorative arts and commodities, it had become customary to exhibit spectacular objects, but due to their nature and value, they often proved hard to sell after the show, leaving the companies with a considerate financial loss. Moreover, the barriers a company had to overcome before it could present its exhibit on the site were considerable. The national sections were usually organized by national commissions that were allocated exhibition space by the coordinators that they in turn had to distribute to their exhibitors. Due to exhibition logistics, a firm had to apply in advance for space, but learned how much space it was allocated shortly before opening, after all its preparations had been finished. The firm would not know if its exhibits would fit into the space allotted. For example, when the ceramics manufacturers Josiah Wedgwood & Sons learned about its allocated exhibition space in 1878, the firm found that it was too small for all the show pieces it had prepared and that a column restricted the effective use of the area. Indeed, most foreign exhibitors complained about inadequate space.

On the whole, the exhibition as an institution was moving away from industry and commerce towards culture. The increasing importance of cultural events such as congresses, concerts, art exhibitions, and amusement parks were testimonies to this trend, as well as the national pavilions that showcased national cultural events. Visitors were attracted in ever greater numbers by the spectacle, but those coming to the exhibitions on business were complaining about the long distances, the high expenses, and the comparatively small results. As the nature of the international exhibitions shifted further from industrial to cultural, many companies in the decorative arts realized that no commercial benefit could be expected. Even though firms had studied the market and their competitors' products, they found that the material and intellectual profits fell increasingly short of expectations. Furthermore, due to the increased general awareness of technological and artistic progress, which had been intensified by the exhibitions, the events had lost their central importance. Finally, for the purpose of doing business involving meeting new retailers, dealers, and contractors, specialized trade fairs were much more effective and much less costly. Only a few years later commercial producers would come to realize that no positive effects for business were to be expected from the world's fairs. But the fear of missing out on something by not going to the fair was stronger than the growing dissatisfaction. Participants were still drawn by the medals given as awards for outstanding products. Winning a medal could be important for an aspiring young firm, as the award could be used for marketing purposes, despite the fact that the number of medals awarded had increased exponentially since 1851. The 1878 exposition set a new record with 29,810 awards for 52,835 exhibitors. More than half of the exhibitors received a Grand Prix, or gold, silver, or bronze medal, or honorable mention. Still, manufacturers were satisfied. Only when every exhibitor received a medal at the World's Columbian Exposition in 1893, would they rebel.

From the point of view of the host nation, the exhibition was a successful despite the loss of more than 28 million francs. In the preface of *Les Merveilles de l'Exposition de 1878* the following can be read concerning the outcome of the exhibition: "Seen exclusively from the French point of view, its significance is particularly precious for us. It marks indeed the hour of resurrection of a nation so cruelly put to the test. It confirms the untameable vitality of France: it bears testimony to French artistic and industrial fecundity" (p. 3).

France had regained its political and cultural self-confidence after the crisis of the early and mid–1870s, which it demonstrated to the world at the Exposition Universelle, thus confirming the new role of world's fair as cultural and to a certain degree political exhibitions. Finally, in comparison to the "glorious" 1867 exhibition of the Second Empire, Friedrich Pecht concluded in *Kunst und Kunstindustrieauf der Pariser Weltaustellung 1878*: "The main purpose of the 1867 exhibition was to highlight the glamour of the dynasty, documenting the supremacy and the potency of France in the most palpable way. The current one demonstrates that France is no less a glamorous host today, using its advantage cleverly, but certainly much more amiably than the Empire" (p. 274).

Bibliography

As for all exhibitions, the standard sources of information are the official reports. Apart from the *Rapport administratif sur l'exposition universelle de 1878 à Paris* (1881) there are the French *Catalogue officiel: Exposition Universelle Internationale de 1878 à Paris,* published in Paris from 1878 onwards in several volumes as well as in various foreign language editions. The national reports, catalogues, and directories, such as the Austrian *Bericht über die Weltausstellung in Paris 1878* (1879) or the American *Reports of the United States Commissioners to the Paris Universal Exhibition, 1878* (1880) provide important information on exhibited goods. *Les Beaux-arts et les arts décoratives: Exposition universelle de1878,* published under the direction of Louis Gonse (1879), or *Kunst und Kunstindustrie auf der Pariser Weltausstellung 1878,* by Friedrich Pecht (1878) focus on the fine arts as well as the decorative, while *Les Beaux-arts à l'Exposition Universelle: (1867 – 1878),* by Gabriel Monod (1878) deals explicitly with the fine arts.

There are several sources published for visitors to the exposition. The *Guide de visiteur à l'Exposition Universelle de 1878: itinéraire en huit et en quatre jours objets remarquables a visiter* (1878) and the exhibition journal, *L'Exposition Universelle de 1878. Journal Hebdomadaire* and its English and German counterparts *Illustrated Paris Universal Exposition* (1878) and *Die Pariser Welt-Ausstellung 1878. Illustrierte* (1878) provide excellent details surrounding the fair, including illustrations, anecdotes, and facts on exhibits and statistics.

Helpful twentieth-century publications on the 1878 Exposition Universelle include Raymond Isay, *Panorama des Exposition Universelle* (1937), and Philippe Bouin and Christian-Philippe Chanut, *Histoire française des foires et des expositions universelles* (1979). Arthur Chandler's article, "Heroism in Defeat — The Paris Exposition Universelle of 1878," in *World's Fair* 4, 4 (1986): 9–16, which has been expanded and revised, and published on line at *http://charon.sfsu.edu/publications/PARIS EXPOSITIONS/1878EXPO.html* is a good retrospective in English. In his *Geschichte der Weltausstellungen* (1999), Winfried Kretschmer dedicates one chapter to "Machinen für jeden Zweck: Paris 1878." The most recent article on the exposition is Colette Wilson, "Memory and the politics of forgetting — Paris, the Commune and the 1878 Exposition Universelle," *Journal of European Studies* 35, 1 (2005): 47–63.

Sydney 1879–1880

Kirsten Orr

Sydney International Exhibition

In 1879 the British colony of New South Wales hosted the first international exhibition in the Southern Hemisphere. Never before had an international exhibition been held so far from the cultural and commercial centers of Europe. Exhibits and visitors from all the great nations of the world made the daunting sea journey to the remote and little-known colony that, less than forty years earlier, had been the destination mainly of convicts and their keepers.

The proposal for an international exhibition in Sydney was first advanced by the Royal Agricultural Society but the governor, Sir Hercules Robinson, argued that the reputation of the colony was at stake and convinced the colonial government to take over control. The objectives were to create new opportunities for trade and finance, to increase the international profile and status of the colony, to educate the public in the arts and sciences, and to advance nation building.

The monumental Garden Palace was designed in the Italianate style by colonial Architect James Barnet. Also built were agricultural and machinery halls, an art gallery, and several small pavilions. Sited in the Domain on land rising up from Sydney Harbor, the Garden Palace was viewed by visiting ships as the gateway to the city and symbolized the colony's progress and emergence on the world stage. The builder, John Young, devised an ingenious construction system of timber components detailed and fabricated according to what was available in the colony. The *pièce de résistance* was the marvelous dome — constructed entirely of timber and lit by clerestory windows at its base — that was not only the largest in the Southern Hemisphere, but ranked sixth in the world for size. Inside, lavish decorations incorporated all the usual devices of allegorical and emblematic art, as well as uniquely Australian imagery. The destruction of the Garden Palace by a great fire on September 22, 1882, less than two years after the exhibition had closed, devastated the community and created a profound sense of loss of identity that had been attached to its architecture and its harbor-side position.

The exhibition's opening day on September 17, 1879, was declared a public holiday and crowds lined the streets to cheer a giant parade.

The festivities continued throughout the exhibition with brass bands, daily organ and piano recitals, twice-weekly orchestral concerts of popular classical music and regular choral performances. The harbor was spectacularly covered with men-of-war from all nations flying the flags of their respective countries. For most visitors, the greatest experience was walking through the impressive exhibition and admiring the Aladdin's cave of assembled treasures—rich Turkish carpets, striking displays of ceramics and glassware, trophies of minerals and agricultural products, handsome and useful furniture, the vast range of building products, appliances to revolutionize daily life, fine art from around the world, new agricultural inventions and industrial machinery—the ordinary and the exotic side by side.

The layout of the national courts reflected the world order and the power relations among the exhibiting countries. New South Wales was located under the dome flanked by Victoria and the other Australian colonies. Diagonally opposite was Great Britain, occupying an entire quadrant of the building. The longitudinal ceremonial axis divided the Old World from the New. America was located directly opposite Great Britain as the equivalent power in the New World.

The classification system for the 14,000 exhibits was based on that used at Philadelphia in 1876. No items were exhibited by Australian aborigines, although there were occasional displays of native weaponry and pseudo-historical tableaux depicting spear-carrying natives in fern valleys populated by wallabies and kangaroos. An impressive European collection of painting and sculpture was the first public display of European art in the Australian colonies. Women from all walks of life enthusiastically exhibited. Their participation at the Sydney International Exhibition across all categories was almost three times the participation of women at the 1878 Paris Exposition Universelle.

Extraordinary numbers visited the exhibition. The attendance figure of 1,117,536 was the largest in proportion to population that had ever been recorded at any international exhibition held in any part of the world. On Foundation Day, January 26, 1880, 27,500 visitors celebrated the birth of the colony with a Temperance Holiday at the exhibition. A choir of 1,000 children clad in white sang temperance

and patriotic songs, with encores of *Rule, Britannia* and *Advance Australia Fair*.

The Sydney International Exhibition closed on April 20, 1880. It would be hard to overestimate the exhibition's cultural impact. While it may seem small in comparison to the preceding exhibitions in Paris and Philadelphia, it was hugely significant in the Australian context and came at an important turning point in the nation's history. Legacies included new museum collections, city infrastructure such as tram lines and port development, new technologies, increased immigration and trade. The exhibition was a force for developing a system of technical education in New South Wales and for establishing institutions to support it, such as the Technological Museum (now the Powerhouse Museum) and Sydney Technical College. Increased awareness of the fine arts and the acquisition of new European works assisted the development of the Art Gallery of NSW. The influx of professional artists from abroad brought significant changes to the local art scene and led to the campaign for the recognition of Australian art and to the development of a distinctive national style. The urban focus of the exhibition caused Sydney to be viewed in a new light, no longer as the outcome of a penal settlement, but as a potential metropolis of a civilized society. New building materials and technologies derived from the exhibition, combined with a strong economy and a growing population, stimulated urban improvement and led to the construction of public and commercial buildings, the development of transport infrastructure and suburban expansion.

The Sydney International Exhibition, and the two international exhibitions that followed in Melbourne in 1880 and 1888, encouraged Australians to contemplate their own identity, their cultural and economic achievements, their place in the world and the British Empire, and the prospect of nationhood.

Bibliography

The comprehensive report of the Sydney International Exhibition is the *Official Record of the Sydney International Exhibition, 1879* (1881.) It includes the history of the event, a complete list of exhibits, reports of the judges and awards, with plans of the exhibition halls and grounds. Countless small catalogues, guides to specific national courts and handbooks were also published. Most of these can be found in the Mitchell Collection in the State Library of New South Wales, Sydney. There was extensive coverage in local newspapers, The Sydney *Morning Herald* and *The Illustrated Sydney News and New South Wales Agriculturalist and Grazier*. The Sydney Powerhouse Museum contains a diversity of objects exhibited at, or associated with, the Sydney International Exhibition. Its collection represents all of the exhibition divisions—mining, metallurgy, manufactures, education, science, ethnology, art, women's work, machinery, agriculture and horticulture.

Secondary sources include Peter Proudfoot,

Roslyn Maguire, and Robert Freestone, eds., *Colonial City, Global City: Sydney's International Exhibition 1879* (2000); Peter Proudfoot and John Young, "James Barnett and the 1879 Garden Palace International Exhibition in Sydney," *Journal of the Royal Australian Historical Society* 86, 1 (2000): 1–22; Kirsten Orr, "A Force for Federation: International Exhibitions and the Formation of Australian Ethos 1851–1901" (unpub. Ph.D. thesis, University of New South Wales, 2006); and Linda Young, "Let Them See How Like England We Can Be: An Account of the Sydney International Exhibition 1879" (unpub. M.A. thesis, University of Sydney, 1983).

Melbourne 1880–1881

David Dunstan

Melbourne International Exhibition

News of Australia's gold deposits sparked one of the largest ever mass migrations of people, with 622,000 migrants venturing to geographically remote British colonies from 1851 to 1861. Victoria was the main beneficiary and Melbourne prospered, becoming "a Victorian community overseas" with its citizens attuned to the world's fair movement. Local and intercolonial exhibitions were staged in 1854, 1861, 1866, 1872, and 1875, preliminary to participation overseas in Europe and the United States. London in 1851 was a fond memory. With Paris 1878 approaching, and the French planning colonial possessions a major theme, the British urged participation. Political contests were hard fought in the 1870s. After the London-born liberal demagogue and protectionist, Graham Berry, won the 1877 election, his manufacturer supporters sought a permanent exhibition hall to display their wares. With time short Berry's commissioner to Paris, Joseph Casey, suggested an international exhibition afterwards with a grand exhibition hall built in the interim. Berry agreed but was stopped in

the Parliament. Only after a successful showing at Paris was approving legislation passed. Victoria was beaten by its neighbor and rival, New South Wales, with Sydney's exhibition in 1879.

William Clarke, Victoria's richest man, headed a five-man executive committee stacked with Berry supporters and forty commissioners with industrial or professional associations. The secretary was George Collins Levey, cosmopolitan journalist and exhibition specialist and organizer. The vice-president, James Munro, the ambitious leader of the temperance movement, secured the prized 21-acre Carlton Gardens site overlooking the city. Melbourne's leading architect, the Cornish-born but London-trained Joseph Reed won the design competition and on February 19, 1879, the foundation stone of a grand central building in brick, stone, timber, steel, glass, and slate was laid—quite the largest in the colonies. David Mitchell, a Scottish-born stonemason, directed construction. The building's cruciform structure, with naves and transepts, fanlight and clerestory windows, round arches, great barn-like interiors and elevated mezzanine galleries had echoes from early Norman church design,

Exhibition Building. — Melbourne.

The Royal Exhibition Hall may be the oldest world's fair building still in use. Recently, it was designated a World Heritage Building (editors' collection).

the Italian renaissance, Paxton's Crystal Palace (fanlight windows), and Fowkes "great barn" built for London in 1862. Surmounting all, the building boasted a 217-foot high replica of the double-shelled dome of Brunelleschi's Florence Cathedral. Local artist John Mather followed South Kensington principles in the simplicity and aestheticism of his interior designs. Only under the dome was any richness of treatment to be seen: a starry sky with a circle of clouds. The transepts were a "subdued olive green" to provide "a neutral background for setting off brilliant objects" with "deep maroon purple" backgrounds in the picture galleries. Single female figures, representing the arts and the sciences, and friezes over the four arches symbolically represented the main theme of Peace. Over the southern arch the nations were grouped with the motto: "Victoria Welcomes All Nations." Horticulturist William Sangster elaborated Reed's garden design with a central promenade and lawns giving way to flower beds and ornamental lakes all enclosed by an iron fence, an aid to ticketing and security. A fountain of painted concrete with giant mermen, Australian plants and animals—including ferns and crocodiles—and emblazoned with commercial and industrial details, including steam

engines, was an antipodean echo of the cascade of the Trocadero at Paris.

The opening on Friday, October 1, 1880, a public holiday, was a typically variable Melbourne spring day with dull, windy, and chilly weather. Crowds lined the city streets and the exhibition dome—the city's highest object—drew the procession towards it. In the western nave, a concert hall with a locally-built grand organ, a choir of 900 and an orchestra of 100 performed the exhibition cantata. French-trained musician Leon Caron had set to music local artisan and temperance lecturer J.W. Meaden's poem that proclaimed Victoria "Queen of the Southern Seas.." President Clarke spoke of the how the world fair movement that had reached these parts and "the contrast presented by the scene here displayed and that which existed less than 45 years ago where Melbourne now stands."

Massina's Popular Guide suggested approaching the exhibition from the main, southern entrance. To the north of the dome were manufactures from Britain. The Avenue of Nations was a great spine-like passageway that led from the northern transept into the central annex of temporary buildings and the leading national courts. Here "the empires, kingdoms and republics of the northern hemisphere, on the one side" were confronted "on the other, by all the British colonies that have grown up under the Southern Cross." Notwithstanding the loss of the ship *Eric the Red*, the United States attracted much interest with new gadgets, including the typewriter. Germany had five spaces—not including fine art exhibits—and pianos, furniture, toys, porcelain, lager beer, wines, armaments, cigars and perfumes, a reflection perhaps of imperial interest in the region. French exhibitors numbered 1,250 (as opposed to 300 at Sydney). The paintings hung in the first level galleries were often four or five deep with 800 works in the British collection alone, including major works from the Royal Collection. Viewing them properly took weeks. *Le Figaro's* unnamed correspondent (musician Henri Kowalski), poked fun at the British Puritanism that banished certain (nude) paintings to almost invisible altitudes. One of them, *Chloe*, by the Chevalier J.J. Lefebvre would remain in Melbourne and become a national symbol. Purchases of Italian statuary were made by the Victorian government, including G.B. Dupre's gold medal-winning *Cain*.

THE NEW TOWER OF BABEL.

This cartoon from the Melbourne *Punch* suggests that some people thought world's fairs were a costly extravagance, even in 1880 (from *Melbourne Punch*, April 22, 1880).

Nearly every exhibit at the Victorian court had "a temple, or trophy and specimens of local handiwork" constructed on a colossal scale to "demonstrate the rapid development of the colony." The South Australians had a bush scene before the arrival of the Europeans, complete with Aboriginal "gunyah" and native marsupials. "Hindoos attired after the fashion of their country" served exotic teas and told stories at the Indian court. In all, there were more than 13,000 exhibits. The awards, divided into five Orders of Merit plus honorable mentions, ran into thousands, with 2,465 in the First Order. Great Britain obtained 559 followed by Victoria with 373, France, 338; Germany, 259; Italy, 138; and the United States, 115. The Emperor of Germany's special prize chosen by his emissary Dr. Francis Reuleaux for the "most meritorious Australasian exhibit" went to the wine industry. Over seven months 1,458,896 people attended before the exhibition closed on April 30, 1881, with the final event a grand ball held on June 1. Most of the extensive temporary structures were dismantled and sold. At £277,292 the cost was less than half what had been feared. While impacts in terms of increased trade and manufacturing were slight, the exhibition was significant, especially for Victorians. It ushered in the boom of the 1880s and was a grand vehicle of colonial display, self-congratulation, and exchange that, ultimately, led to federation and nationhood in 1901. A magnificent (and now World Heritage-listed) exhibition building and gardens, new found prosperity, political peace and self-confidence were the immediate result of this successful and timely exhibition.

Bibliography

The *Official Record of the Melbourne International Exhibition, 1880–81* (1882) is an invaluable and comprehensive contemporary guide. Leon Caron, *Victoria Cantata* (1880) is the musical setting of J.W. Meaden's poem. The *Report of the Executive Commissioner on the Melbourne International Exhibition, 1880–81* (1881) is an official account from another Australian colonial perspective. See also R.P. Whitworth, *Massina's Popular Guide to the Melbourne International Exhibition of 1880–81* (1880). The exhibition received coverage in international and Australian newspapers, but notably the Melbourne press, including the *Argus*, Age, and *Herald* with the "Exhibition Supplement" to the *Argus* of October 2 and 6, 1880, particularly useful. Also, see the illustrated periodicals of the day, such as the *Illustrated Australian News* and the *Australasian Sketcher*. Manuscript records of the exhibition organization appear not to have survived.

The collections of the State Library of Victoria (SLV) *http://www.slv.vic.gov.au/* and Museum Victoria *http://www.mov.vic.gov.au/* offer scope for research. The Royal Exhibition Building *http://whc.unesco.org/en/list/1131* (the 'royal' was added on its centenary in 1980) is the museum's largest collection object. It has a special collection of memorabilia, ephemera, images and other research materials. Copies of Reed's architectural drawings are in the Bates, Smart and McCutcheon collection of the University of Melbourne Archives *http://www.lib.unimelb.edu.au/collections/archives/index.html* In addition to its printed, manuscript and newspaper collections the SLV has artifacts and images and the massive (44.5 cm wide and 17 cm deep) "Visitors Register" with the names and thoughts of 16,000 visitors to the exhibition. Exhibition-inspired vernacular verse and observations are recorded in diaries and scrapbooks held by the SLV. Its image collections and those of the National Library of Australia *http://www.nla.gov.au/* document the building and the exhibition, some available in digitized form over the internet. See also "Victoria at the Great Exhibitions" *La Trobe Library Journal* 14, 56 (1995).

The exhibition has been extensively (though by no means exhaustively) discussed in scholarly works starting with J.R. Parris' unpublished 1955 thesis (University of Melbourne) that is summarized and revised in John Parris and A.G.L. Shaw, "The Melbourne International Exhibition 1880–81," *Victorian Historical Journal* 51, 4 (1980). Graeme Davison, "Exhibitions," *Australian Cultural History*, 2 (1982), reprinted as "Festivals of Nationhood: the International Exhibitions" in S.L. Goldberg and F.B. Smith, eds., *Australian Cultural History* (1988), and his outstanding study, *The Rise and Fall of Marvellous Melbourne*, (1978, 2004), opens with it. Many exhibition participants are included in the *Australian Dictionary of Biography http://www.adb.online.anu.edu.au/adbonline.htm*. The wider imperial context is explored in Peter H. Hoffenberg, *An Empire on Display* (2001), and the life and elements of the building is the focus of David Dunstan, *Victorian Icon*, (1996). On the shaping of urban form and culture see Paul Fox, "Exhibition City: Melbourne and the 1880 International Exhibition," *Transition* Melbourne (Summer 1990) and Kirsten Orr, "A force for Federation: international exhibitions and the formation of Australian ethos (1851–1901)" unpub. Ph.D. thesis, University of New South Wales, 2006.

Atlanta 1881

James M. Russell

International Cotton Exposition

The idea of holding the International Cotton Exposition of 1881 in Atlanta originated with Edward Atkinson, a Boston textile mill magnate. Atkinson saw the exposition as a means of educating southern cotton farmers about ginning techniques so that cleaner bales would be sent to northern mills. But promoters of Atlanta, especially Henry W. Grady and others associated with the Atlanta *Constitution*, channeled Atkinson's idea into a different direction. They saw the exposition as an opportunity to demonstrate to the nation that the New South, and particularly Atlanta, had abandoned the plantation ideal and was now ready to worship the Yankees' industrial gospel.

Planning for the fair began in earnest when the International Cotton Exposition Association was incorporated in April 1880. The incorporators turned to the city's most flamboyant booster, Hannibal Ingalls Kimball, to organize the crusade for the exposition. Kimball, a native of Maine and a controversial figure in Georgia Reconstruction politics, had led a successful drive to build the state's largest cotton factory in Atlanta in 1879. Appointed chairman of the association's executive committee, Kimball immediately began looking for funds. He and others argued that outside capital could not be found for the venture unless local citizens first indicated their support. He suggested that at least one-third of the association's capital stock issue (initially set at $100,000) and later raised to $200,000 would have to have come from Atlanta. Within a 6-hour period on March 15, 1881, Kimball and his friends raised $36,600 in the city. Kimball shrewdly relayed news of this dazzling success to newspaper offices across the country. When he and other organizers of the exposition went on a whirlwind tour of northern cities later in the spring, they had no trouble finding additional capital.

In 1880, Atlanta's population was only 37,000, and Kimball was concerned that there would not be sufficient hotel space for the expected influx of visitors from out of town. He asked the fair's "Department of Public Comfort," whose job it was to look out for the comfort of visitors, to conduct a survey of available rooms in the city. The survey revealed that Atlanta could accommodate about 5,000 guests in 3,000 rooms, and Kimball decided that this was not enough. He arranged for the construction of the Exposition Hotel on the fair site. This was a 300-room hotel that could take in up to 1,000 guests, and its $2.50 per night rate was designed to limit price gouging by other hotels in the city. If there were still a room shortage, Kimball also organized a tent city adjacent to the fairgrounds, where military organizations and other large groups could stay, and to solicit local citizens to offer rooms in their homes to fairgoers. After the exposition opened on October 5, however, attendance lagged behind expectations, and the tent city idea was quickly dropped and there is no record of how many visitors were housed in private homes. In early November, railroad companies serving Atlanta were persuaded to offer special fares to visitors coming to the fair, and attendance did pick up subsequently, although it never reached the level organizers hoped for. The Exposition Hotel was never able to make a profit. In all, more than 290,000 people eventually went to the fair before it closed on December 31, 1881.

Those who visited the fair saw 1,113 exhibits from thirty-three states and seven foreign countries. The exhibits were displayed in four buildings; most were items associated with cotton cultivation or textile manufacturing, though just about everything usually seen at world's lairs of the era was available for viewing. On October 27, visitors saw an unusual demonstration. Shortly before sunrise on ibis day, enough cotton was picked and ginned on the grounds to make two suits of clothes. By the end of the day, the cotton had been woven into cloth, and the suits were worn by the governors of Georgia and Connecticut at an evening reception.

After the exposition ended, its main hall (designed in the shape of a Greek cross for the purpose) was turned into a cotton factory, the Exposition Cotton Mills, which opened for business in 1882. The mill employed 500 people, some of whom lived for a while in the Exposition Hotel. There were other intangible and indirect results from the exposition. Atlanta's hotels, restaurants, saloons, and livery stables all benefited from the presence of out-of-town visitors. Potential investors who came to the fair were lavishly courted, with the result that some $2 million was invested in Atlanta during the six months following the fair's closing. Promoters showed off what they called the "Atlanta Spirit," and a conscious attempt at sectional reconciliation was made by inviting General William T. Sherman to speak at the fair. According to Harvey Newman, the exposition launched the New South movement and placed Atlanta at its head. Much of the credit for this goes to the tireless H. I. Kimball, whose work on the exposition won him praise across the country. In addition, the International Cotton Exposition of 1881, often referred to as the South's first world's fair, spawned a number of successors in the late nineteenth- and early twentieth-century South: two in Atlanta (the Piedmont Exposition of 1887 and the Cotton States and International Exposition of 1895), one in Louisville (the Southern Exposition of 1883–1887), one in New Orleans (the Cotton Centennial Exposition of 1884–1885), one in Nashville (the Tennessee Centennial Exposition of 1897); and one near Norfolk (the Jamestown Exposition of 1907). All were expressions of the New South's urban-industrial ethos. While the region failed to industrialize as much or as profitably as the organizers of these expositions desired, it did succeed in demonstrating that its economic leadership had accepted the need for industrial development.

Bibliography

The best contemporary source is H.I. Kim-ball, *International Cotton Exposition, Atlanta. Georgia. 1881: Report of the Director-General. H.I. Kimball* (1882), although the fair was also covered in the Atlanta *Constitution*. A good comparison of this fair with the later Cotton States and International Exposition may be found in Mary Roberts Davis, "The Atlanta Industrial Expositions of 1881 and 1895: Expressions of the Philosophy of the New South" (M.A. thesis, Emory University, 1952). A short summary of the event is provided by Jack Blicksilver, "The International Cotton Exposition of 1881 and Its Impact upon the Economic Development of Georgia," *Atlanta Economic Review* 7, no. 5 (May 1957), 1–5, 11–12, and 7, no. 6 (June 1957,: 1–5, 11–12. Blicksilver overemphasizes, however, the economic spinoff from the exposition for Atlanta and Georgia. There is an adequate summary of Kimball's role in the undertaking in Alice E. Reagan, *H. I. Kimball: Entrepreneur* (1983). Many of the details and events of the fair are described most accurately in Franklin M. Garrett, *Atlanta and Environs: A Chronicle of Its People and Events*, 3 vols. (1954), 2: 29–34. The fair is described and played in historical context in a short section of Harvey K. Newman, *Southern Hospitality: Tourism and the Growth of Atlanta* (1999), and is mentioned more briefly but in a wider context in Dan H. Doyle, *New Men, New Cities, New South: Atlanta, Nashville, Charleston, Mobile, 1860–1910* (1990).

Amsterdam 1883

John E. Findling

Internationale Koloniale en Untvoerhandel Tentoonstellung

In the first half of the nineteenth century, the Netherlands experienced bleak times, characterized by little economic growth. By the 1860s and 1870s, this began to change, especially after 1876, when the Noord Canal was completed, bringing oceangoing vessels to Amsterdam. At the same time, the national rail system was rapidly improving, and in 1879, the city's new central station was completed. By this time, international expositions were commonly believed to promote economic growth and tourism, and in 1880, a French entrepreneur, Edouard Agostini, saw potential in a fair in the Netherlands.

Agostini mailed brochures and information to a group of influential Amsterdam business leaders, describing the possibilities of an exhibition to be held in their city. A local organizing committee was formed and brought Agostini to Amsterdam as a technical adviser. Because the Netherlands was not well known except for the wealth of its colonial empire, the committee decided to organize the fair as a colonial exhibition, giving it the formal name of *Internationale Koloniale en Untvoerhandel Tentoonstellung te Amsterdam.*

A preliminary report was given to King William II, who endorsed the plan, but this was about all the help the organizers received from the government. Although the committee was unable to obtain national government funding, the city of Amsterdam donated the use of 62 acres of land in the western section of the city for use as an exposition site. After some difficulty, the committee contracted a Belgian firm to develop the site and build the large exhibition hall.

Behind the newly completed Rijksmuseum rose the main building of the fair. Measuring about 1,000 by 420 feet, the building covered some 13 acres. A temporary structure, it was built of wood, with a glass roof, but it was covered with plaster and painted canvas to give the impression of marble. The façade was decorated in a grotesque Indian motif, featuring large elephant heads, lions, and other animals, all cast in plaster. Other major exhibit halls were the Colonial Building, measuring 417 by 250 feet, and the Machinery Hall and the Art Palace, both 667 by 100 feet. There were many other buildings on the site, including a pavilion for the city of Amsterdam, a Japanese bazaar, and many small shops and restaurants. A canal, traversed by a bamboo bridge, ran through the grounds, providing a home for a Chinese junk. The ethnography and fine arts exhibits were installed in the nearby Rijksmuseum, probably because it was far more fireproof than the main exhibition building.

The newly crowned King William III formally opened the exhibition on May 1, 1883. Although only the Netherlands and Belgium had comprehensive exhibits, some 40 other countries or colonies participated, including most of the other countries of Europe, as well as China, Japan, India, Siam, the Dutch East Indies, New South Wales, and Victoria. Persia, Turkey, Egypt, Tunisia, and Mauritius represented the Middle East and Africa, and the United States, Canada, Jamaica, Haiti, Brazil, Uruguay, and Venezuela came from the Western Hemisphere. Major attractions at the fair were model villages with natives brought to Amsterdam from Dutch colonies in the Caribbean and Southeast Asia. The natives displayed their way of life, foreshadowing the larger anthropological exhibits using Filipinos that were a staple of U.S. fairs in the early twentieth century. Another attraction that raised some controversy was the Indian tea house, where tea was given without charge to visitors as a way to try to popularize the colonial beverage among Europeans. The tea was subsidized by the Indian Tea Syndicate, and the effort was successful, although some of the "better class" of fairgoers were uneasy about drinking free tea in the company of working-class visitors.

By the time the exhibition closed on October 31, just over a million visitors had attended. This was the last major international exhibition held in the Netherlands, but it was an important influence on the 1885 exposition in Antwerp, Belgium, and its successors in that country.

Bibliography

There is no record of archival materials for the Amsterdam exhibition. The official report of the French commissioner, Oliver Claude Augustin Poullain Saint-Foix, *Rapport sur l'Exposition internationale industrielle d'Amsterdam en 1883* (1885), contains much general information about the fair, its theme, exhibits, and other participating nations. Another report in French is Victor Delahaye, *Rapport aux l'Exposition Coloniale et Internationale d'Amsterdam, 1883* (1886). This report is in the library of the BIE, as is the *Catalogue Official* (1883). A much narrower account is Louis Roux, *Conference faite per L. Roux...le 17 août 1883* (1883), which describes a conference held at the fair on the process of manufacturing dynamite. The Hagley Museum and Library, near Wilmington, Delaware, has a number of other catalogues or official reports from this fair. A contemporary account in English is "The Amsterdam Exposition," *Nation* 37 (1883), 350–51. A centennial work in Dutch is Ileen Montijn and Kermis van Koophandel, *De Amsterdam Wereldtentoonstellung voan 1883* (1983) Montijn also wrote *Fair of Commerce* (1983), a short pamphlet published for the centennial of the fair.

Boston 1883–1884

Noah W. Sobe

The American Exhibition of the Products, Arts and Manufactures of Foreign Nations

Running from September 3, 1883, to January 12, 1884, the American Exhibition of the Products, Arts and Manufactures of Foreign Nations was brought together by Boston's business leaders and widely referred to as the Foreign Exhibition. Because the exhibition opened on the hundredth anniversary of the end of the Revolutionary War, subdued claims were put forth that the Boston exhibition was the "true centennial exhibition." Economic growth and the hope that the fair would boost international trade brought it into being, but its most significant legacy may be in the cultural dimensions of some of its art exhibitions.

The 1883–1884 exhibition in Boston came about as plans for an 1885 Boston world's fair had to be scaled back for financial reasons. Fair boosters settled for an exhibition limited to foreign products, arts, and manufactures, organized by the Foreign Exhibition Association under the leadership of its secretary, Charles Benjamin Norton, a former civil war brigadier general. The exhibition presented almost 700 foreign exhibits, with display space offered free of charge to any manufacturers or tradesmen who shipped their goods to Boston. An unusual aspect of the exhibition was that it featured no exhibits from the United States, the host country. Though the exhibition did not receive financial support from the federal government, a June 22, 1882, act of Congress permitted all goods destined for Boston's exhibition to enter the country duty-free. Evidencing Boston's global commercial networks, a considerable number of the exhibits were arranged by specially appointed overseas commissioners, typically men of Boston families who were pursuing interests overseas.

The Foreign Exhibition Association was chartered under the auspices of the Massachusetts Charitable Mechanics Association, and it was in the 92,000-square foot Mechanics Hall of this organization that the exhibition took place. This permanent structure, at the intersection of Huntington Avenue and West Newton Street, was designed by William Gibbons Preston in 1880 and completed in 1882. One notable feature of this turreted red-brick building was that it was equipped with electric lighting that allowed the fair to remain open in the evenings. The Mechanics Hall was not built for the exhibition but for the triennial exhibitions of the Mechanics Association, and it remained standing until 1959 when it was demolished to make way for Boston's Prudential Center.

Exhibits from thirty countries as well as various parts of the British Empire were featured at the exhibition. Decorative objects such as fabric, pottery, furniture, and jewelry featured prominently in the exhibits; alongside were significant fine arts exhibits. Germany, Italy and France provided the greatest numbers of works of art and manufactured goods, though the Chinese and Japanese exhibits attracted considerable attention. The latter featured a tea room and a living ethnological display consisting of fourteen Japanese women doing traditional craftwork. The Japanese exhibits at Boston followed those at earlier world's fairs that introduced Japanese aesthetics to receptive western audiences and helped to cement the late nineteenth-century American admiration for Japan — both for its chic exoticism and the perceived cultural refinement that could be positioned as a utopian contrast to America's burgeoning consumer culture. Noteworthy works of French impressionist art were displayed by the prominent dealer Paul Durand-Ruel, thus helping to create in the United States a taste for French and later American Impressionism. A final artistic movement that the exhibition helped to popularize was the British arts and crafts movement, represented at the exhibition by a large display of the work of the influential designer and later prominent socialist, William Morris (1834–1896).

Admission to the fair cost fifty cents. In addition to touring the exhibits, visitors could listen to international music being performed in the central hall and eat at one of the several restaurants established for the exhibition. During the four and a half months that the exhibition ran, only 300,000 visitors came, a number which was considered a disappointment. Charles Benjamin Norton estimated that four-fifths of the visitors came from outside Boston and that only 5 percent of Boston's population visited. In financial terms the fair was considered a failure with contemporary newspapers setting the losses at between $25,000 and $50,000. Notwithstanding these losses, the exhibition organizers considered the event a success in educating the public and increasing overseas commerce.

Bibliography

An extremely limited number of primary sources on the exhibition are available in the Robert A. Feer Collection of World's Fairs of North America in the Rare Books and Manuscripts collections of the Boston Public Library (BPL), the Massachusetts Historical Society (MHS) and the Boston Athenaeum. BPL holdings include daily programs and newsletters associated with the fair. A brief journal of C. B. Norton's minutes from the exhibition's planning committee meetings is available at the MHS. Guides to the exhibition include C. B. Norton, ed., *Official Catalogue Foreign Exhibition Boston 1883* (1883), *Illustrated Catalogue of the Japanese Art Exhibits, Foreign Exhibition* (1883), and Morris and Company, *The Morris Exhibit at the Foreign Fair Boston* (1883) [available on-line at *http://www.burrows.com/mor.html*]. Accounts of the planning for the aborted 1885 world's fair can be found in the New York *Times*, June 2–3 and October 14, 1881, and January 17, 1882. Notable accounts of the 1883 exhibition appear in the New York *Times*, September 2, 4, 1883 and January 13, 1884; the Boston *Globe*, September 2 and 18, 1883, and the Boston *Evening Transcript*, September 3–4 and October 2, 1883. Contemporary accounts of the design and construction of the Mechanics Hall also appear in *American Architect and Building News* (May 21, June 4, 1881, January 27, 1883).

Calcutta 1883–1884

Thomas Prasch

Calcutta International Exhibition

India's first international exhibition — indeed, the first in any non-settler colony — opened inauspiciously, with unseasonable rain wetting the outdoor festivities; an overlong opening address by Lord Ripon, Viceroy of India, further dampening spirits; the exhibits themselves less than completely installed; a boycott by much of the Anglo-Indian community (incensed by the recently passed Ilbert Bill, which gave Indian courts and juries jurisdiction over white settlers) visibly emptying seats for the opening ceremonies; and a technical failure for a climax. As the London *Times* noted: "A fanfare of trumpets followed and an attempt was made to light the building by the electric light, which, however, unfortunately failed through some defect in the machinery, and left the spectators to disperse in darkness" (December 5, 1883). Despite the clouds, both literal and political, over the opening ceremonies, the exhibition eventually proved successful: it drew over a million visitors before closing on March 10, 1884. The exhibition organizers secured participation by countries in Europe and North America as well as Japan and the colonies of Australia and New Zealand (with the Australian colony of Victoria alone contributing 2,300 items to exhibit); and in all over 2,500 exhibitors displayed products (and paid for their display space at the rate of two shillings per foot, with a five shilling surcharge for frontage space facing the main avenues in the exhibit hall).

The controversy over the Ilbert Bill shadowed the exhibition in multiple ways, not only interfering with the spectacle of its opening ceremonies but also dominating press coverage of India during much of the year at the exhibition's expense. Nor was it the only political controversy that disrupted the proceedings. General Manager Jules Joubert's determination to bring women to the exhibition, by providing women-only "*zenana* days" that would in theory allow women to attend while protecting the veiling traditions of *purdah*, provided, as Peter Hoffenberg has noted, a considerable source of debate in the Indian press. But, in the end, the disputes and disruptions failed to undermine the exhibition's overall success.

That success owed much to a constellation of forces interested in promoting the essentially economic enterprise at the heart of the exhibition (for, as the *Calcutta Review* noted, its goal was "the hope of giving a new and powerful impulse to the trade and industries of the Indian empire"). Joubert, the naturalized citizen of New South Wales who was the initiator and general manager of the exhibition, came to Calcutta in the wake of successful exhibition promotion in Australia, Aggressive development of trade between the Australian colonies and India was one of his central aims, along with personal profit. His goals dovetailed conveniently with those of the British governors of India, looking for ways both to enhance Indian commerce generally and to revivify Indian craftsmanship. Earlier in 1883, the Department of Revenue and Agriculture had resolved on a program to promote Indian commerce and "art manufacture," using museums and exhibitions (and a new state-sponsored *Journal of Indian Art*) among their tools to that end. This initiative coincided, in turn, with the interests in promoting art manufacture of the developing Indian Schools of Design in Lahore, Bombay, Madras, and Calcutta, all headed, as Arindam Dutta has noted, by personnel trained at South Kensington, in the museum complex that had developed in the wake of the Great Exhibition of 1851 (and that, from the time of the Crystal Palace forward, had Indian craftsmanship at its heart, held up as a model for good design). Indian native princes employed the opportunity to enhance their own position by supporting the exhibition (and many of them, unlike Anglo-Indians, made a point of attending the opening, as did the Bengal government, who provided a direct subsidy of 50,000 rupees. Further, the Calcutta exhibition fit perfectly into the developing tradition of international exhibitions, where imperial themes, and showcases of imperial subjects, were becoming increasingly central.

In the actual structures of the Calcutta International Exhibition, a group of buildings occupying a third of the 22 acres of exhibition grounds, the divisions of empire were reflected by the stark divide between two main areas. On one side of Chowringhee Road, in a permanent brick building connected to the city's nearly new India Museum, were housed the displays of foreign nations and colonies participating in the exhibition, a cornucopia of consumer goods, with contributions "specially suited to the wants and requirements of India," as the *Times* noted. But that was not what visitors mostly came to see. Constance Fletcher, after cataloguing the civilized offerings for the *Art-Journal,* asserted that the "man of culture" soon "turns his weary eyes from beholding pyramidal biscuit towers" and "crosses a slender bridge" that spanned Chowringhee Road "to an enchanted land." That land was the temporary iron structure that housed the India courts, with the spectacular carved-stone Gwalior gateway at the entrance and "huge capisoned elephants, ablaze with golden trappings ... like Titanic sentinels on either side of the doorway." The India courts were thus the real center of the exhibition, offering, the *Westminster Review* asserted, "the most complete collection of Indian products and industries ever presented to the public," arranged in a series of regional courts and incorporating human displays of the different races of India as well as craftsmen at work. A machinery annex, a shed for military displays, a refreshments room, and a diorama completed the complex.

If Indian products and handicraft provided the center of the exhibition, the India presented at that center was a distinctive and distinctively exhibitionary one: at once deeply traditional and utterly hybrid, as Peter Hoffenberg has noted. The thrust for the revivification of Indian handicrafts came, after all, from British colonial authorities, through their Department of Revenue and Agriculture, and from those South Kensington-trained heads of the Indian Schools of Design. Their complex motives, mixing preservation of traditional design (and traditional sources of authority) with the promotion of new commerce (and the training of new artisans), contributed to the hybrid product the exhibition presented. The Gwalior Gateway that marked the India Courts' entrance typifies the process. A production arranged by Major J. B. Keith, using a thousand Indian stone carvers and completed in just four months, the gateway employed a style that incorporated multiple stone-carving traditions from the full range of Indian art history. It was thus in no sense a product of any actual Indian art tradition, but it was assembled to say "India" to the world. The same might be said for the Calcutta International Exhibition as a whole.

Bibliography

Official publications of the Calcutta International Exhibition include a two-volume *Official Report* (1885), a catalog of *Economic Products of India* (1883) assembled by George Watt and others, and a photographic collection, overseen by G. C. Du Prée, of *Indian Art-Work in the Calcutta International Exhibition* (1885). Separate catalogs exist for the contributions of New South Wales, by Alexander Mackenzie Cameron, and of the Madras Presidency and Travancore, complied by George Bidie. The resolution of the Department of Revenue and Agriculture to support collections of Indian goods for exhibitions is reprinted in the first volume of the *Journal of Indian Art* (1883). See also Jules Joubert's autobiography, *Shavings and Scrapes from Many Parts* (1890). Contemporary coverage in the English press was somewhat limited, but includes the *Times* of London, *Westminster Review, Art-Journal,* and *Illustrated London News;* Indian press coverage includes articles in *Calcutta Review, Statesman and Friend of India, Englishman, Hindoo Patriot,* and *Bengalee.*

Among modern commentators, the most extensive treatment of the Calcutta exhibition is in the work of Peter H. Hoffenberg. A number of comments about the exhibition appear in his *An Empire on Display: English, Indian, and Australian Exhibitions from the Crystal Palace to the Great War* (2001); see also his article "Photography and Architecture at the Calcutta International Exhibition" in Maria Antonella Pelizzari, ed., *Traces of India: Photography, Architecture, and the Politics of Representation* (2003). In addition, see Arindam Dutta, *The Bureaucracy of Beauty: Design in the Age of its Global Reproducibility* (2007); John Powell's essay in John E. Findling, ed., *Historical Dictionary of World Fairs and Exhibitions, 1851–1988* (1990); Deborah Swallow's fascinating history of the Gwalior Gateway (which tracks its travels from Calcutta to London, where it ended up hidden away in the Victoria and Albert Museum after again playing gateway to Indian courts at the Colonial and Indian Exhibition of 1886), "Colonial Architecture, International Exhibitions and Official Patronage of the Indian Artisan: The Case of a Gateway from Gwalior in the Victoria and Albert Museum," in Tim Barringer and Tom Flynn, eds., *Colonialism and the Object: Empire, Material Culture and the Museum* (1998); and the brief mentions of the Calcutta exhibition in Paul Greenhalgh, *Ephemeral Vistas: The Exposition Universelles, Great Exhibitions and World's Fairs, 1851–1939* (1988).

Louisville 1883–1887

Carl E. Kramer

Southern Exposition

Organized ostensibly "to advance the material welfare of the producing classes of the South and West" and "to exhibit the products and resources of the southern states to northern and eastern manufacturers," the Southern Exposition was a central component of Louis-ville's strategy to capture control of the southern market during the post–Reconstruction period. The concept of a Louisville exposition was first suggested in 1880 by Boston financier Edward Atkinson. The proposal won the immediate endorsement of *Courier-Journal* editor Henry Watterson, but Atlanta preempted the idea by holding its Cotton States Exposition in 1881.

After the Atlanta exposition closed, Watterson resurrected the concept and in August 1882 gained the support of the Louisville Board of Trade. Two months later, the board appointed a committee headed by merchant J. H. Lindenberger to incorporate the Southern Exposition at Louisville. Paper manufacturer Bidermann du Pont was elected exposition president, and J. M. Wright, superintendent of the Board of Trade, was appointed general manager. To raise the projected $300,000 budget, the exposition directors initiated a stock subscription campaign, offering 12,000 shares at $25 per share. Sales progressed well, but there is no record that the entire offering was subscribed.

Selected for the exposition site was a vacant tract located between Fourth and Sixth

streets, about 1 mile south of the central business district. Situated immediately to the north was Central Park, then owned by exposition president Bidermann du Pont and his elder brother, Alfred V. du Pont. When the brothers lent the park for exposition use, the grounds approximated 45 acres.

Louisville architects Cornelius Curtin and Kenneth McDonald designed the exposition buildings. The main exhibition hall, constructed of wood and glass over a steel frame, measured 300 by 600 feet, enclosed 13 acres of floor space, and cost $200,000. Central Park served as a promenade and picnic ground and provided sites for a 3,000-seat Music Hall and an art gallery. The Music Hall housed an enormous organ and hosted concerts directed by renowned conductors such as Walter Damrosch of the Metropolitan Opera. The art gallery eventually housed works from the collections of New York financiers J. Pierpont Morgan and August Belmont and former Louisville & Nashville Railroad president Victor Newcomb.

President Chester A. Arthur opened the Southern Exposition on August 1, 1883. The *Courier-Journal* predicted that the fair's influence would be "felt for years in cutting new channels

The main building for the Southern Exposition enclosed 13 acres of floor space and cost $200,000 (editors' collection).

for commerce, in opening new avenues of industries, and furnishing new sources of wealth and power." More than fifteen hundred exhibitors paid the $25 exhibit fee. Oriented largely toward southern industry and agriculture, exhibits gave particular emphasis to sawmilling, mining, sugar refining, and textile machinery. Much space was devoted as well to grape, hemp, tobacco, grain, silk, and rice cultivation. Fairgoers witnessed an electric lighting system that consisted of 4,600 16-candlepower incandescent lamps powered by 15 dynamos furnished by the Edison Company of New York. Complementing this innovation was an electric railway that carried passengers on a narrow track that circled Central Park and passed through an artificial tunnel lighted by incandescent bulbs.

Although primarily a regional event, the exposition also had an international dimension. The Museum of Natural History included specimens such as a mammoth from the Royal Museum in Stuttgart, Germany, an orangutan from Borneo, and the fossilized remains of a megatherium discovered in Argentina. Ethnological exhibits included a Japanese village installed in 1886, and the art gallery displayed many paintings, sculptures, tapestries, and objects of art by international artists, mainly from American collections.

By the time the exposition closed its first season on November 10, 1883, it had attracted 770,129 paid guests and an additional 200,933 admitted on passes. The exposition operated through 1887, usually from August through October.

In addition to bringing Louisville's economic advantages to national attention, the exposition was a catalyst for urban development. In 1885 alone, 260 large Victorian houses were constructed in the vicinity of the exposition. In 1890 William H. Slaughter transformed the vacant fair site into St. James Court, an exclusive residential neighborhood, which soon housed some of Louisville's most illustrious citizens.

Bibliography

The most comprehensive contemporary source on the Southern Exposition is the *Southern Exposition Guide* (1883). The official program of the event, it includes an extensive narrative detailing the range of exhibits, activity schedules, descriptions of buildings and grounds, and aims of the exposition. It also contains extensive information about Louisville itself, such as an analysis of local economic conditions and lists of visitor accommodations and entertainment opportunities. A similar publication, which appeared three years later, is *The Great Southern Exposition of Art, Industry & Agriculture*. In addition to recapitulating much of the information contained in the *Southern Exposition Guide*, it contains data on the costs of buildings and grounds, local economic advantages, ethnological and historical exhibits, and exhibitor rules and regulations. The publication claims that the exposition was a financial success, but it provides no evidence to support the statement.

Useful secondary accounts are Carl E. Kramer, *Old Louisville: A Changing View* (1982), and George H. Yater, *Two Hundred Years at the Falls of the Ohio: A History of Louisville and Jefferson County* (1979). Kramer's pamphlet focuses on the neighborhood in which the Southern Exposition was located, exploring the event's impact on the area's growth and development, as well as describing the fair's exhibits and facilities. Yater's history of Louisville provides a concise analysis of the city's desire to strengthen its control of the southern market, the primary motive behind the Southern Exposition.

New Orleans 1884–1885

Miki Pfeffer

The World's Industrial and Cotton Centennial Exposition

From December 1884 until the end of May 1885, New Orleans mounted a huge international showpiece to boost its economy and to demonstrate that the South was fully reconciled in the Union. Some observers, including journalist Edward Smalley in articles for *Century Magazine*, considered the World's Industrial and Cotton Centennial Exposition in this "ancient, easy-going, semi-tropical city near the mouth of the Mississippi" a success. Others disagreed. Although the event exceeded the Philadelphia Centennial in "magnitude" and as the "world's university," it fell short of the hoped-for investment in the region, and its finances were strained throughout its days. Nevertheless, it was a heady time for the city and its people.

The Cotton Centennial commemorated a hundred years of exporting cotton and was the third exposition to grow from Boston economist/textile mogul Edward Atkinson's idea that direct communication between cotton farmers and manufacturers during an international exposition would benefit both. Henry W. Grady's concept of a New South, proclaimed in his *Atlanta Constitution*, also influenced promoters of the Cotton Centennial. If the region could convince northerners that past animosities were set aside, investors might send money, men, and expertise southward, thus reinvigorating the distressed economy. Also, promoters eyed a new Latin American trade to regain for the New Orleans port the prominence that it lost during the Civil War and Reconstruction.

Colonel F. C. Morehead of the National Cotton Planters' Association proposed the centennial in 1882 with New Orleans as its natural site, and he became the exposition's commissioner-general and roving ambassador. Cotton magnate Edmund Richardson headed its Board of Management, but Director-General Major E. A. Burke was the event's ideological architect and was responsible for its massive expansion and excessive claims and, possibly, for its financial woes. Burke, a true believer in the New South creed, was owner/editor of the New Orleans *Times-Democrat* and also was Louisiana's state treasurer. He spearheaded solicitation of the $500,000 needed to secure a congressional loan for the exposition, but fundraising met with lukewarm response from New Orleans businessmen. Burke claimed that $225,000 had been amassed in private and commercial pledges to be paid in installments over the course of the exposition, but the director-general had a tendency to inflate statistics. Even members of the Cotton Exchange

wondered aloud if a monetary outlay for such an undertaking would add even "one bale of cotton" to their coffers.

Nevertheless, on February 10, 1883, Congress sanctioned the Cotton Centennial's international scope and gave it legal status under "joint auspices" of the United States, the National Cotton Planters Association, and the city with a thirteen-member board of management selected from the association (six members) and stockholders (seven members). By the time Congress agreed to lend the enterprise $1,000,000 and to appropriate another $300,000 for federal exhibits, it was already mid–1884. However, this congressional windfall and an alleged "demand for exhibit space" prompted Director-General Burke and management to expand the exposition to extravagant proportions beyond their capacity to administer.

The Board of Management selected a plot of 247 acres for exposition grounds four miles upriver from the central business district, between St. Charles Avenue and the Mississippi River. The former plantations were "as level as a billiard table and just as green," according to Smalley. Only rows of magnificent oaks graced the otherwise undeveloped Upper City Park (now Audubon Park). Buildings were to be set among the trees, and Gustave M. Torgerson, a Swedish architect living in Mississippi and known for his sprawling Queen Anne houses, won the architectural competition, but Director-General Burke assumed building oversight. Chronic underfunding, poor time-and-money management, continuous rain that turned the grounds to mud, and a logjam of waiting exhibits exacerbated normal construction problems. The work started late, and proceeded leisurely and without benefit of power tools so that later, at great cost, hundreds of additional men working double shifts and overtime were hired to complete the task.

No organizing architectural style seems to have been created for the Cotton Centennial. Torgerson's two largest buildings were built of southern pine in an eclectic style without much adornment but "well floored, well roofed, and admirably well lighted." Their great size lent them dignity. The Main Building imitated the style of the Louvre and housed 1,656,000 square feet of exhibition space for foreign, private, and commercial exhibits. It covered over 33 acres with no obstructing inte-

View of the 33-acre Main Building at the World's Industrial and Cotton Exposition with landscaping yet incomplete (courtesy Historic New Orleans Collection, Williams Research Center).

rior partitions other than a huge central Music Hall that seated 11,000 in the audience and 600 on the stage. Across a lagoon stood the Government and States Building (648,825 square feet) where almost every state and territory exhibited and where federal displays came from Departments of State, Navy, War, Treasury, Interior, and the Patent Office, the Post Office, and the Smithsonian Institution. Wide galleries provided a "fascinating spectacle" of exhibits below, and both buildings featured elevator systems that, in the Main Building, took visitors to the roof for a panoramic view of the grounds. The electric railway traveling between buildings was a marvel to most visitors. The city of New Orleans paid $100,000 for a permanent, predominately glass Horticultural Hall — where Mexican cacti proved most captivating — and was also to gain a developed park at the end of the exposition. Other buildings of various sizes and styles included an art gallery,

saw-mill building, and boiler house (all of iron), six livestock barns, and eight ornamental entrances. The Mexican Mining Pavilion was most admired for its octagonal structure of iron and glass and its graceful glass dome surmounting a fine portico. Mexico had the greatest presence of the twenty-one foreign exhibitors, and the Eighth Cavalry Mexican Band starred at the opening ceremonies and performed at numerous concerts, fund-raisers, and parades.

The Cotton Centennial opened with great fanfare on December 16, 1884, two weeks later than its originally scheduled opening date. The day was sunny, and colorful streamers and flags of all nations graced the street and river parades. President Chester A. Arthur waited in Washington while prayers, poems, and speeches exceeded their allotted time in the exposition Music Hall. Finally, he touched the button that was the signal to start the huge Corliss engine, than clustering similar items in his categories of agriculture, horticulture, pisciculture, ores and minerals, raw and manufactured products, furniture and accessories, textile fabrics, clothing and accessories, the industrial arts, natural history, alimentary products, education and instruction, and works of art. Mullen's unorthodox system caused *The Manufacturer and Builder* reporter to grouse that there was a "total absence of any attempt to classify or arrange its heterogeneous contents," and also that "vendors and peddlers of all sorts of trumpery" were hawking wares everywhere in the Main Building. However, the fifteen-percent commission on vendors' sales was needed to supplement poor gate receipts. Only on Louisiana Day did the number of visitors (approximately 50,000) exceed the daily figure needed to break even. By February, the director-general reported liabilities of $369,422.95 to President Arthur, and Burke spent two months in Washington securing a final grant of $350,000 ($335,000 for back payments

Patriotic bunting graces the Government and States Building at the World's Industrial and Cotton Centennial Exposition (courtesy Historic New Orleans Collection, Williams Research Center).

the largest machine powering the event. A crowd of approximately 14,000 visitors cheered the opening ceremonies, but beyond the Music Hall, they found empty or chaotic exhibit spaces, incomplete buildings, and sparse landscaping.

Negative press began immediately and continued into spring, and visitors who came early to the exposition broadcast their disappointment back home. Exhibitors complained that assignment of exhibit spaces was disorganized and favoritism shown, and they charged Burke and Chief of Installation Samuel Mullen with mismanagement. Newspapers competing with Burke's *Times-Democrat* noted the director-general's cavalier record keeping. Mullen used an arrangement of variation rather

to contractors; $15,000 for Woman's Department's expenses) with this stipulation: only the U. S. Secretary of the Treasury was authorized to pay bills and only to non-residents. Louisiana creditors were left with partial payments at best.

Visitors who paid the 50-cent admission price and arrived later in spring, when all exhibits were in place, were impressed with the Cotton Centennial's immensity and breadth of exhibits, and two special departments were notable: the first-ever Colored Department demonstrated the New South's "racial accommodation," and the Woman's Department strengthened promoters' claims of "sectional reconciliation." The two departments shared the wide balcony of the Government and States

Building with the Educational Department and a zoological exhibit. African Americans, shut out of participation in the 1876 Centennial, here proudly displayed aesthetic and industrial achievements of twenty years of freedom, although some leaders had been free persons of color and not slaves. Nonetheless, the inclusion of a Colored Department was cause for celebration, and its visitors and participants had access to all exhibit halls. The neighboring Woman's Department was presided over by Bostonian Julia Ward Howe, famous for her iconic northern patriotic song, "Battle Hymn of the Republic." Local women were hospitable but resentful that a northerner was chosen to lead, but although Howe was controversial, she devoted her vast organizational experience and energy to the department and the exposition. A frequent speaker on the grounds and around the city, she also devised "Twelve O'Clock Talks" in various departments where lecturers' topics ranged from science and travel to woman suffrage. These speeches were considered forms of entertainment in the days before the creation of midways at world's fairs.

The Cotton Centennial amused its visitors with machines-in-motion, tethered balloon ascensions, frequent fireworks displays, drills by the U. S. Life Saving Service in Exposition Lake, and torpedo explosions there. Unique displays vied for attention: "Lot's wife" of a large block of salt, a Greek temple carved from soap, a cathedral of cracker boxes, an owl of Esterbrook pens, a 35-foot-high replica of the new Statue of Liberty covered with crops from Nebraska, and the real Liberty Bell brought all the way from Philadelphia. The King of Carnival provided excitement with his "royal" visit on Mardi Gras. Daily chimes, band concerts, and music from the mammoth Pilcher pipe organ were popular, and lectures from Susan B. Anthony of woman suffrage fame and Frances E. Willard of the temperance movement drew large audiences. But the sight of stunning new electric lights—especially as they illuminated the glass of Horticultural Hall—was the true marvel of the exposition and also allowed it to remain open evenings until ten. Offsite attractions were a panoramic Battle of Sedan, Buffalo Bill's Wild West Show, and the country's new craze, a roller-skating rink. Especially important to the city's future as a destination, visitors discovered the exoti-

cism of New Orleans, often with a book of George Washington Cable's *Old Creole Days* as their guide.

The World's Industrial and Cotton Centennial Exposition closed on June 1, 1885, having hosted only 1,158,840 visitors—little more than a fourth of predictions—and with a deficit nearing $470,000. It reopened under new management from November 1885 to May 1886 as the North, Central, and South American Exposition but met with similar failure. However, some indirect successes can be traced to the sustained media attention on the Cotton Centennial and the city and its people, leading to later tourism and some emigration to the South that helped the economy. Some northern investment was made to cut vast forests of Louisiana timber, but because little reforestation was undertaken, the stripped land was resold for agricultural rather than industrial uses. The city's port did eventually regain prominence partly because of Latin American trade. The Cotton Centennial grounds remained intact and were later developed as Audubon Park, today enjoyed for its fine zoo, golf course, running paths, flora, and stately oaks (Horticultural Hall was destroyed in the hurricane of 1915). Wealthy Americans built grand houses in the surrounding area that is today still the fashionable university section. Some scholars trace the founding of Sophie B. Newcomb College to Julia Ward Howe and conversations in the Woman's Department about the urgency of higher education for women. Newcomb assumed that mission for over a century before hurricane Katrina (2005) caused it to be merged into the Tulane University system with which it long shared a campus across the avenue from the former grounds of the World's Industrial and Cotton Centennial Exposition.

Bibliography

Contemporary New Orleans newspapers are excellent resources on the World's Industrial and Cotton Centennial Exposition. The New Orleans *Daily Picayune* and the New Orleans *Times-Democrat* clearly supported the event and meticulously detailed every parade, speech, concert, and exhibit. These and other city and state newspapers are available at the New Orleans Public Library. The boosterism in the *Times-Democrat* is conspicuous, but the satirical weekly New Orleans *Mascot* balanced Burke's paper by disputing every questionable claim and often tracing problems directly to the director-general's secretive transactions. The *Mascot* is available in Tulane University Special Collections. Although the *Times-Democrat* considered Eugene V. Smalley's articles patronizing, "The New Orleans Exposition" and "In and Out of the New Orleans Exposition" in *Century Magazine* (1885) are lyrical if essentialist views of the event, and E. W. Kemble's accompanying sketches are illuminating. *The Manufacturer and Builder* magazine from January to May 1885, critiques engines and machines and provides two contrasting views of the exposition. These two magazines are available online.

Numerous illustrated guides and pamphlets were written that include diagrams of exhibit spaces, lists of hotels and transportation, and useful facts about the city. Guides, photographs, ephemera, and other files are housed at Tulane, the University of New Orleans Louisiana Collection, the New Orleans Public Library, the Louisiana State Museum, and the Historic New Orleans Collection. The role of Congress can be found in the *Congressional Record* of the 48th Congress. A dependable eyewitness account is Iowa Commissioner Herbert S. Fairall's *The World's Industrial*

and Cotton Centennial Exposition, New Orleans, 1884–1885, and for a thorough description of women's activity, see Julia Ward Howe's *Report and Catalogue of the Woman's Department of the World's Exposition, held at New Orleans, 1884–1885*. Both are available in Tulane University Special Collections.

Three modern views are important: D. Clive Hardy, in his 1964 Tulane University thesis "The World's Industrial and Cotton Centennial Exposition," was the first to rediscover the event, and his narrative is crisp and comprehensive; Thomas D. Watson, in "Staging the 'Crowning Achievement of the Age' — Major Edward A. Burke, New Orleans and the Cotton Centennial Exposition" (*Louisiana History* 25.3, 1984: 229–257 and 25.4, 1984: 341–366) traces Burke's leadership strengths and weaknesses that affected exposition finances and repute; Samuel C. Shepherd, Jr., in "A Glimmer of Hope: The World's Industrial and Cotton Centennial Exposition, New Orleans, 1884–1885" (*Louisiana History* 26.3, 1985: 271–290) assesses pitfalls and outcomes for the city as a result of hosting the event. The latter two articles were written as the 1984 New Orleans World's Fair was being examined for some of the same troubles that had plagued the Cotton Centennial a century earlier.

Antwerp 1885

Matthew G. Stanard

Exposition Universelle d'Anvers / Wereldtentoonstelling van Antwerpen

The idea to host an *exposition universelle* in Antwerp took shape among prominent members of the city's bourgeoisie after visits to the 1883 Amsterdam colonial-themed world's fair, to which Belgium had contributed an important display. In January 1884, a number of leading merchants and other "men of means" from Antwerp founded the temporary limited company Naamloze Maatschappij der Wereldtentoonstelling van Antwerpen to direct the

effort. Both Catholics and Liberals were well represented within the organizing company, indicating that commercial goals and municipal and national pride transcended politics. This was despite the tense political situation in Belgium: Catholics and Liberals had engaged in a *guerre scolaire* in the late 1870s and early 1880s over control of education, and the "social question" surrounding universal (male) suffrage only added to civic stress. Moreover, worker discontent was rising, signaled most clearly in the formation of the socialist Parti Ouvrier Belge in 1885.

The 1885 exposition had several goals. First and foremost, it was an effort at munici-

EXPOSITION INTERNATIONALE.

A formal view of the impressive main building for Antwerp's first international exposition (the Wolfson-Florida International University, Miami Beach, Florida).

pal self-promotion. Second, organizers wanted to promote Belgium as a highly industrialized country, which it was. Belgium was the first nation on the continent to industrialize, beginning in the 1830s. By the end of the century it had become a major source of products of the first and second industrial revolutions such as rolling stock and rails, and in particular intermediate or semi-finished goods such as steel, coal, and iron. Third, organizers wanted to present Antwerp as a historical shipping center in order to solidify its position as a key sea port. It is important to remember that in the latter half of the nineteenth century, Antwerp's position as a major European and world port was not preordained. In fact, the Netherlands in essence had closed the Scheldt after the 1830 Belgian revolution and had not reopened it until nine years later. This emphasis on shipping, in addition to the event's focus on industry and commerce, lent a strong atmosphere of free trade to the fair.

The 1885 Antwerp exposition opened on May 2 and closed November 2, during which time it drew 3.5 million visitors. Thirty-two foreign nations partook in the fair—although only 25 were official participants—including Great Britain, France, Germany, Austria, the United States, Canada, Spain, Portugal, the Ottoman Empire, Romania, Serbia, and a number of South American states. In total, there were 14,472 exhibitors, of which 3,411 were Belgian. The exposition's budget was around 4 million Belgian francs, and in the end, the fair broke even. The city's contributions to the budget and the fair itself were substantial, whereas the provincial government made more of a token financial offering.

Working in concert with the city administration, organizers had located the fairgrounds in a new and undeveloped urban quarter known as 't Zuid (the South or Southside), located south of the city center and near Antwerp's southern railway station. They chose, and the city agreed to, this location in order to help develop the area. Moreover, Antwerp had just renovated the quays along the Scheldt from which the fairgrounds were removed by only a few blocks, and the fair could serve to introduce the modernized wharfs to the world. The fairgrounds themselves covered 22 hectares (54 acres) in total (220,000 square meters), of which 90,000 square meters had construction on them, and of which 25,000 square meters were for Belgian constructions and pavilions.

A number of industrial displays entertained visitors. The large (for the time) Hall of Machinery and the Hall of Industry were the main attractions. Both halls focused upon the innumerable new products of the industrial age, and many visitors were awed in particular by the displays of powerful steam engines. Telephone communications between major Belgian cities were inaugurated in 1885, and exposition organizers set up lines to the fairgrounds so that visitors could listen to live concerts in Brussels, some 50 kilometers (32 miles) away. Another product of the industrial age was previewed at the French stand where visitors could see architectural plans for a 300 meter tall tower that would make history when unveiled in full scale fewer than four later.

Another attraction at the fair was the display of King Leopold II's new colony, the État Indépendent du Congo (EIC). The decision to display the Congo and Africans in 1885 was in part influenced by displays at the Amsterdam fair of 1883. Furthermore, the recently concluded Berlin Conference had recognized Leopold II's authority in central Africa, and in fact in July 1885 he had himself declared sovereign of the EIC at its capital, Boma. Nonetheless, because of the lack of colonial revenues it was not Leopold II, bur rather the Société Royale Belge de Géographie that took the lead in creating what was only a modest pavilion, in particular organizing its ethnographic section. The EIC, along with the Musée Commercial of Brussels, also contributed to the Congo displays. In addition to the pavilion, Chief Massola of Vivi and twelve other Africans were displayed as a "*village congolais*" and were asked to pose for photographs, including for those that were to appear in the exposition's Livre d'Or. Leopold II visited the Congolese at the fair and invited Massola and his "court" to the royal palace at Laeken.

The display of the Congo in 1885 was the first instance of a practice that would continue to the very end of Belgian imperialism in Africa. The Antwerp exposition coincided with the start of formal Belgian involvement in central Africa, and the ninth and last of Belgium's *Expositions universelles et internationales* took place in 1958, on the very eve of Congolese independence. Thus there was an almost exact correspondence between the timeframe of Belgian World's Fairs (1885–1958) and the era of Belgian formal rule in central Africa (1885–1960), indicating the important role expositions played in the promotion of empire as well as Europeans' attempts to rule Africa literally and figuratively.

Bibliography

For an overview of Belgian expositions to 1958, A. Cockx and J. Lemmens, *Les Expositions Universelles et Internationales en Belgique de 1885 à 1958* (1958) remains an important place to start. Another source for early Belgian fairs is Charles Mourlon, *Quelques Souvenirs des Expositions Nationales, Internationales et Universelles en Belgique 1820–1925* (n.d.).

The well-illustrated *De Panoramische Droom — The Panoramic Dream: Antwerpen en de Wereldtentoonstellingen — Antwerp and the World Exhibitions 1885, 1894, 1930* (1993) offers a number of fine interpretive essays on Antwerp's three universal expositions. On the 1885 fair specifically, see also Maria Dreesen, *Antwerpen 1885. De eerste Belgische Wereldtentoonstelling: een manifestatie van herboren stedelijk bewustzijn* (unpub. M.A. thesis (Katholieke Universiteit Leuven, 1984). The fair's Livre d'Or or Gulden Book is an important source: René Corneli and P. Mussely, *Anvers et l'Exposition universelle de 1885* (1885), was published in German, *Antwerpen und die Weltausstellung 1885*, (1887).

The Archives Générales du Royaume-Algemeen Rijksarchief (AGR-ARA) in Brussels has important resources on all Belgian *expositions universelles* up to and including the world's fair of 1935. The primary reference work for research at the AGR-ARA is R. Depoortere and L. Vandeweyer, eds., *Inventaire des archives des expositions universelles organisées en Belgique entre 1880 et 1913: Fonds provenant du Ministère des affaires économiques*, Pub. 2037 (1994). The research instrument code (*code de l'instrument de recherche*) for the *inventaire* is T182. The Stadsarchief Antwerpen also has documents on Antwerp's three fairs. Information on the Stadsarchief Antwerpen collections is available at *http://stadsarchief.antwerpen.be/*.

Edinburgh 1886

Laurie Dalton

International Exhibition of Industry, Science and Art

The 1886 International Exhibition of Industry, Science and Art was the first international exhibition to be held in Scotland, and ran from May 4 to October 30. The exhibition was under the patronage Queen Victoria and the Prince of Wales. The president of the exhibition was the Marquis of Lothian, with James Gowans, esq, Lord Dean of Guild as the chairman. Prince Albert Victor officially opened the exhibition and, during the course of the summer, the queen as well as the Prince and Princess of Wales visited the exhibition.

The location of the exposition, made accessible by the town council of Edinburgh, was in the Meadows, an expansive park just south of the city center. Design of the building, which was constructed over 7 acres of the park, was conceptualized by the architects John Burnet and Son and Charles Lindsay. The entrance to the main building was capped by a large central dome and flanking towers. The building had architectural features faced with stone but was constructed predominantly of steel and glass, new building materials that would be fitting to an exhibition of science, industry, and art. Outside, in front of the main entrance, was a large fountain; just past the entrance was an art gallery, while the main central court was composed of various temporary buildings and exhibits. The grounds around the main building had various features, including walkways, a stage, and areas for refreshments.

There were many committees for the exhibition, ranging from finance and building construction to those dealing with aspects of admissions, transportation and entertainment. Classification for objects was varied in scope, from natural materials such as minerals and agriculture to manufactured objects to art. Although other countries did participate, the prospectus for the exhibition noted that an important goal was to showcase the resources, manufactured objects, and art of Scotland. In addition, there were special sections dedicated solely to women's art, including embroidery and art needlework. There was also an artisan section, made free to exhibitors, which was aimed to provide an opportunity for the working classes to display their various crafts. An interesting feature of the exhibition was a large re-creation of "Old Edinburgh," composed of historical buildings from the fourteenth, fifteenth, and sixteenth centuries, including facsimiles of Luckenbooths, West Port, Lawn Market, and West Bow. This section was under the direction of architect Sydney Mitchell, a prominent Scottish architect, who had previously worked on projects for the Commercial Bank of Scotland and the Crichton Royal Institution. In this area the organizers hoped to present "living history" to the visitor in not only the re-created buildings but also in requesting that all exhibitors dress in period costume. Marshall Wane was one of the primary photographers for this section and documented it in the form of postcards, cabinet prints, cartes de visite, and a book.

One key factor affecting the exhibition was the fact that the Colonial and Indian Exposition in South Kensington also occurred in 1886. As a result, the organizers of the exhibition in Edinburgh were not only hoping to attract large numbers from Scotland, but also additional visitors who made trips to see the other exhibition. However, the venue in South Kensington also affected the number of foreign countries who participated, as many could not provide two exhibits simultaneously. For example, Canada did not participate in the Edinburgh exposition, having already committed to the Colonial and Indian Exhibition.

The 1886 exposition in Edinburgh was meant to show the depth and breadth of the industry, science, and art of Scotland. However, aspects of the exhibition design also spoke to larger political and social implications, such as the section of Old Edinburgh. While very successful at re-creating old historical Edinburgh, this area also pointed to the fact that many towns were permanently affected by the Industrial Revolution. Initially, it was hoped that the main building of the exposition would be kept in the Meadows after the end of the exhibition. Yet, due to a Parliamentary decree from 1827, which did not allow for any building on the Meadows, the structure was taken down. Nevertheless, several elements from the exhibition can still be found in the host city. A group of whale jawbones, which had previously been part of the Zetland and Fair Isle Knitting stand at the exposition, now form an arch over one of the walkways in the park, now know as Jawbone Walk. There are also tall Mason's Pillars in the park, which were built originally for the exhibition. Many trades and guilds, including the masons, spent large amounts of money in order to erect sculptures at the exhibition that would highlight and identify their trade. Overall the organizing of the exposition was successful, boasting a profit of £5,555 and treating visitors to the first large display of electric lights in Scotland. Remnants of the exhibition are still found throughout Edinburgh, and its success led to the organizing of subsequent fairs in Scotland.

Bibliography

There is a substantial amount of primary source material on the exhibition ranging from the prospectus of the exhibition to other planning and marketing materials. Many of these documents can be found in the Edinburgh Room of the Edinburgh City Library or at National Archives of Scotland, *http://www.nas.gov.uk//* (accessed 10–01–06). The Exhibition Committee published a considerable quantity of guides and programs to the exhibition. See, for example, *Cameron's Guide Through the International Exhibition of Industry, Science, and Art and Old Edinburgh)* (1886); *Daily Programme of Exhibition Arrangements, Amusements and Music* (1886); *International Exhibition of Industry, Science, and Art, Edinburgh 1886: The Official Catalogue* (1886); and *The Official Guide to the Exhibition with Notes of What to See in Edinburgh* (1886). Other contemporary articles of interest appeared in the periodicals *Builder* and *Building News*. Issues of the *Builder* for May 8, May 15, June 5, July 31, August 21, and October 30, 1886, have useful articles, as do issues of *Building News* for May 7, May 14, June 4, and June 25, 1886.

The National Library and Archives of Canada also hold specific records of Canada's correspondence with the organizers as well as a copy of the prospectus. For a discussion of the section of Old Edinburgh, see John Charles Dunlop and Edward Topham, *Edinburgh Life 100 years Ago*, (1886). J.K. Gillon, "The Edinburgh International Exhibition," an online publication found at *http://members.fortunecity.com/gillonj/edinburghinternationalexhibition/* (accessed 10–01–06) provides an overview and description of the exhibition. In addition, Juliet Kinchin, "International Exhibitions: 1851–1938," *http://www.arthist.arts.gla.ac.uk/int_ex/index.html* (accessed 10–01–06), provides general descriptions of each fair, along with thematic discussion and images. For research into the remaining public monuments and sculptures consult the Public Monument and Sculpture Association National Recording Project, *http://pmsa.cch.kcl.ac.uk/index.htm* (accessed 10–01–06) as well as the The Royal Commission on the Ancient and Historical Monuments of Scotland *http://www.rcahms.gov.uk/highlightsappp.html* (accessed 10–01–06), which provides extensive information on Scottish-built heritage.

London 1886

Thomas Prasch

Colonial and Indian Exhibition

At the opening of the Colonial and Indian Exhibition on May 4, 1886, Queen Victoria and the Prince of Wales (the exhibition's official patrons) led a grand procession through the Indian Courts, with Indian artisans and Beefeaters lining their path, to Albert Hall, where the queen took her place on a golden throne looted by the British, as Peter Hoffenberg has noticed, after the capture of Lahore. After the usual speeches and pomp, a wildly varied musical entertainment was offered up: an occasional ode by Lord Alfred Tennyson, set to music by Arthur Sullivan (of Gilbert and Sullivan fame), which invoked a vision of unified imperial subjects undercut by curious question marks ("Brothers, must we part at last?/ Shall we not thro' good and ill/ Cleave to one another still? ... one imperial whole/ One with Britain, heart and soul!/ One life, one flag, one fleet, one throne!"); the singing of "God Save the Queen," with two verses translated into Sanskrit by Oxford professor Max Müller to honor the Indian contribution (apparently, no Indian scholars were deemed adequate for the translation); those standard hymns of British patriotic zeal, Hayden's Hallelujah chorus and "Rule Britannia"; and, sandwiched between these last two, the already-old-chestnut of a popular tune, "Home Sweet Home," with its sentimental avowal, "Be it ever so humble, there's no place like home." The odd musical mishmash signaled the essential incoherency of message in an exhibition designed to celebrate the unity of empire at its height.

The Colonial and Indian Exhibition, the last great exhibition on the Crystal-Palace-hallowed grounds of South Kensington, followed three successive years of annual thematic international exhibitions, devoted to fisheries (1883), health (1884), and inventions (with a secondary emphasis on music, 1885). Indeed, the exhibition not only used the same spaces as the previous years' shows, a series of temporary arcades built over 24 acres surrounding what was left of the Royal Horticultural Society's gardens, with the South Kensington Museum across the road, it also re-used some of the earlier exhibits' more popular features: an aquarium left over from the year of the fish and an Old London Street, featuring recreated buildings from the Tudor-Stuart era through the eighteenth-century, which had been the most popular feature of the Health Exhibition (although what it had to do with health is an open question). In contrast to the relatively tepid public and press reception for the preceding years' events—indeed, the previous year's inventions exhibition had closed in the red—the Colonial and Indian Exhibition was

a clear success, drawing exhibitors from across the empire, garnering enthusiastic and extensive press coverage, bringing in 5.5 million visitors by its closing on November 10 (including 400,000 working-class visitors whose reduced-fare passes were underwritten by the London Trades Council), and earning a profit of around 35,000 pounds, enough to repay the debt of the past year's exhibition and to underwrite the establishment of the Imperial Institute in South Kensington.

This success came in spite of the fact that, officially, the Colonial and India Exhibition was not an international exhibition at all. As the *Official Guide* pointed out, "The Exhibition is in no sense international. It is confined exclusively to our Colonial and Indian fellow-subjects, both British and Foreign Exhibitors being excluded." The aim was, the guide continued, "to bring prominently under notice the development and progress which has been made in the various parts of Empire" in order to underscore "the vast fields of enterprise and commerce which exist throughout the British Dominions." The timing for such an event was especially propitious, with increased international competition in the colonial sphere, the scramble for Africa in full swing in the wake of the Berlin Conference of 1883–1884, struggles for Home Rule intensifying in India (the Indian National Congress having been founded just one year before) even as the British state sought to consolidate its hold there (with the declaration that made Queen Victoria the Empress of India a decade before), and the settler colonies of Australasia more strongly asserting their own autonomy. The exhibition would not only feed into the consolidation of British imperial spirit (manifest in both the founding of the Imperial Institute and the more colonial emphasis of subsequent exhibitions, as well as in the imperial trappings of the Queen's Jubilee the following year), but would, as John MacKenzie has pointed out, place colonial possessions and colonial subjects at the center of subsequent international exhibitions (even when, as in the major American exhibitions of the later nineteenth century, there were few actual colonies).

But that powerful imperial theme did not mean the empire would speak with a single voice. Indeed, a range of constructions of empire would find space in the exhibition, in part because the organizers chose to abandon any overall scheme of organization and classification in the exhibition, instead allowing each exhibiting government to arrange its own contributions. The result was that the exhibition provided a forum for competing visions of empire. The official view of imperial unity and common British imperial identity was expressed most clearly in the opening ceremonies, in the language of the guidebooks, in wall decorations that linked paintings of towns throughout empire with a vista of London, and with the conjunction of emblematic imperial panels with the adjacent Old London display. But that vision of empire competed with, and was to an extent undercut by, everything else in the show.

India provided, predictably, the real heart of the show, reflecting both its place in the imperial imagination and its centrality to South Kensington's collections from the Great Exhibition onward (most notably with the addition of the India Museum to the complex in 1880). Occupying almost a third of the overall exhibit space, and with displays five times as large as at any previous exhibition, the jewel of the empire was represented with materials in five separate sections: a panoramic array of Indian arts; an economic and commercial section; a military/geographic display; a court of private exhibitors vending tea, cocoa, coffee, and tobacco; and an Indian Palace that included a Durbar Hall, used as a reception hall for the Prince of Wales throughout the exhibition, with adjacent shops manned by native artisans. The "India" offered at South Kensington, however, was an increasingly hybrid beast, the product of British imperial management over the production of "traditional" Indian arts and crafts.

This hybridity is clearest in the exhibition's most dramatic architectural monuments: the Gwalior Gate, which provided an entrance to the Indian Palace (initially made, as Deborah Swallow has shown, for the Calcutta Exhibition of 1883–84 by native stone carvers under the guidance of Major J. B. Keith, who chose to echo in its structure a range of Indian stone-carving traditions; the *Art-Journal*'s reviewer found in the mixed result "a strange incongruity"); the Durbar Hall itself (carried out by Indian artificers, but to designs by South Kensington's Caspar Purdon Clarke to reflect "typical" Indian architecture); and the Jaipur Gate

that provided an entrance to the Indian courts (again, the work of Indian craftsmen, but the design of Englishmen, Col. Samuel Swinton and Surgeon-Major Thomas Holbein Hendley, who sought to revive a past "Indo-Saracenic" architectural style in the work). But even in subtler details the constructed character of the exhibition's India were evident. Saloni Mathur has shown, for example, that the artisans who worked the exhibition halls were brought to the site through a subcontracting arrangement with Dr. John William Tyler, superintendent of the central prison in Agra, where most of the workers were obtained. Their skills as artisans were clearly secondary to their recruitment.

A different image of empire was projected by the installations of the major settler colonies, those of Australasia and of Canada (each region getting about a quarter of the exhibition space): one of increasingly autonomous, commercially competitive, white settlement. Thus, no indigenous artists were featured in the Colonial Arts Gallery, which instead featured white artists working in traditional European genres; Rowland Ward's safari-inspired taxidermic installations ("animal trophies," to use the guidebook parlance) were featured throughout the site; and areas designated specifically for the settler dominions featured strong showings of economic prosperity in displays of goods and machinery. Even in the language of the *Official Guide*, the message seems clear: "Australia will ere long cease to require supplies of manufactured goods from Britain"; in the New Zealand section, "one might fancy one's self in … some Yorkshire manufacturing town"; and Canada "is already … a manufacturing power." Such messages, reinforced by a strong commercial presence (with sales of everything from Australian wines to Canadian pianos to Montserrat lime juice), argues on the one hand for the success of the colonies, but on the other for the increasing irrelevance of supervision from the mother country.

Meanwhile, in ethnographic displays (perhaps especially those of Australian aborigines, who appeared in the exhibition in clay models featured in natural dioramas) and in the West African courts (where, the *Times* of London noted, "Mumbo Jumbo with his gods and his gauds has taken complete possession"), yet another version of empire was told: one in which Social Darwinian constructions of racial difference and competition predominated. A congress on "Native Races of the British Possessions" sponsored by the Royal Anthropological Society on the site, and employing examples from the exhibition to anchor their arguments, reinforced the point, often bluntly. As J. Bonwick decreed in his contribution to that congress, "All the Tasmanians have gone, and Maories will soon be following. Pacific Islanders are departing childless. Australian aborigines as surely are descending to the grave. Old races everywhere give place to the new." A more distant vision of empire from Tennyson's brotherly embrace is difficult to imagine.

The disunity of the imperial message perhaps perfectly fits the times, as the struggles over imperialism intensified in the last decades of the nineteenth century. Perhaps such disunity fits the place as well at this, the final great exhibition on the South Kensington grounds. None of it seemed significantly to trouble contemporaries, who flocked to the exhibition to see the spectacle of empire, and seemed scarcely to notice the shadows that spectacle cast.

Bibliography

Some of the primary sources for the Colonial and Indian Exhibition were lost when the British Library was damaged during World War II, but many relevant records can still be found there, as well as at the Victoria and Albert Museum Library, the Royal Commonwealth Society Library, the Bodleian Library at Oxford University, and the Greater London Record Office.

Official publications of the Colonial and Indian Exhibition are extensive, including, in addition to an *Official Guide* and an *Official Catalog*, in the listings of the British Library, over 100 more focused publications: catalogs or handbooks for the exhibits of many of the separate colonies (India, Victoria, Queensland, South Australia, West Australia, Canada, New South Wales, Natal, Cape of Good Hope, West Africa, Jamaica, Malta, etc.), a *Statistical Handbook of India* prepared for the occasion, a number of lectures presented at the site, a guide to the opening ceremonies, Tennyson's ode (which also appears in his *Collected Poetry*), pamphlets on a range of particular products (teas, sugar, fibers), judge's reports, a railway guide, and much more. See also the independently published *Penny Popular Guide to the Colo-*

nial and Indian Exhibition (1886) and Frank Cundall, *Reminiscences of the Colonial and Indian Exhibition* (1886). The full proceedings of the conference on "native races" were published in that year's *Journal of the Royal Anthropological Institute*. Among the extensive contemporary press reports of the exhibition, see especially the Indian state-sponsored *Journal of Indian Art* (which devoted six issues entirely to the exhibition; 2: 11–16), the *Art-Journal* (which published a special supplement for the exhibition), London *Times*, *Illustrated London News*, and *Westminster Review*.

For modern treatments of the exhibition, see Peter H. Hoffenberg, *An Empire on Display: English, Indian, and Australian Exhibitions from the Crystal Palace to the Great War* (2001); Tim Barringer, "The South Kensington Museum and the Colonial Project," in Tim Barringer and Tom Flynn, eds., *Colonialism and the Object: Empire, Material Culture and the Museum* (1998); John MacKenzie, *Propaganda and Empire: The Manipulation of British Public Opinion, 1880–1960* (1984); Vladimir Steffel's essay on the exhibition in John E. Findling, ed., *Historical Dictionary of World's Fairs and Expositions, 1851–1988* (1990); Arindam Dutta, *The Bureaucracy of Beauty: Design in the Age of its Global Reproducibility* (2007); and Paul Greenhalgh, *Ephemeral Vistas: The Expositions Universelles, Great Exhibitions and World's Fairs, 1851–1939* (1988). Ethnographic and living displays at the exhibition are treated by Saloni Mathur in "Living Ethnological Exhibits: The Case of 1886," *Cultural Anthropology* 15:4 (2000) and by Raymond Corbey, "Ethnographic Showcases, 1870–1930," *Cultural Anthropology* 8:3 (1993); the architecture of the exhibition is analyzed by Swati Chatoopadhyay in "A Critical History of Architecture in a Post-Colonial World" in the on-line journal *Architronic* at *http://architronic.saed.kent.edu* 6:1 (1997); the positioning of Fiji at the exhibition is evaluated by Ewan Johnston in "Reinventing Fiji at 19th-century and early 20th-century Exhibitions," *Journal of Pacific History* 40:1 (2005); the role of the exhibition in further developing Indian collections at South Kensington is covered by Robert Skelton in "The Indian Collections: 1798 to 1978," *Burlington Magazine* 120:902 (1978) and, more obliquely, by Carol A. Breckenridge, "The Aesthetics and Politics of Colonial Collecting: India at World Fairs," *Comparative Studies in Society and History* 31:2 (1989); the construction of domesticity in the opening ceremonies is read by Alison Blunt in "Imperial Geographies at Home: British Domesticity in India, 1886–1925," *Transactions of the Institute of British Geographers* n.s. 24:4 (1999); and the exhibition is handled as a prelude to the creation of the Imperial Institute in G. Alex Bremner, "'Some Imperial Institute':

Architecture, Symbolism and the Ideal of Empire in Late Victorian Britain, 1887–93," *Journal of the Society of Architectural Historians* 62:1 (2003). Individual objects displayed at the 1886 Colonial and Indian Exhibition have also received recent scholarly attention, including the Gwalior Gateway (Deborah Swallow, "Colonial Architecture, International Exhibitions, and Official Patronage of the Indian Artisan: The Case of a Gateway from Gwalior in the Victoria and Albert Museum," in Barringer and Flynn, *Colonialism and the Object*), the Durbar Hall and the Jaipur Gate (David Beevers, "'From the East Comes Light': Two Relics of the Raj in Surrey," *Apollo* [November 2000]), and relics of Agra's red fort displayed there (Ebba Koch, "The Lost Colonnade of Shah Jahan's Bath in the Red Fort of Agra," *Burlington Magazine* 124:951 [1982]).

Adelaide 1887–1888

Lara Anderson

Jubilee International Exhibition

Sir E.T. Smith, mayor of Adelaide, chose 1887 as the date for an international exhibition because it was the double anniversary of the Queen's Jubilee Year and 50 years since the foundation of the colony. According to Smith, the goal of the exhibition was to illustrate "not only what we in this colony have done during the last fifty years but by inviting comparison with the skilled products of other countries to show to our artisans what may be accomplished in the future." This statement is reminiscent of commonly held beliefs on the function of nineteenth-century exhibitions. While Smith's discussion in the *Handbook for the Adelaide Jubilee International Exhibition* of the function of the Adelaide exhibition adheres to standard thinking about exhibitions, it occurs alongside comments about South Australian colonization and the new theories of colonization which informed this process. Articulated in the act (cited in the handbook) authorizing the colonization of South Australia, these new theories demanded that "the colony was not to be a charge on the Mother Country ... [and] settlers should be capitalists able to profitably work the land." Suffice it to mention that colonial self-sufficiency was a source of pride for South Australians, its mention in the handbook providing the backdrop against which the industrial and artistic achievements of this colony were to be measured at the Exhibition.

Coinciding with the rail network linking Sydney, Melbourne, Brisbane, and Adelaide for the first time, a further goal of the exhibition was to bring the colonies of Australia together. It is estimated that more than 12,000 people traveled overland to the exhibition. A number of exhibitors from other parts of Australia were also present at the exhibition: 500 from Victoria and 469 from New South Wales, both numbers very close to South Australian representation, which figured at 536 exhibitors. In addition to this, Great Britain sent more than 600 exhibits and approximately 300 exhibitors came from Austria, Belgium and Germany.

Although several buildings were erected on the site, only the main building, designed by the local architectural firm of Withall & Wells, was meant to be permanent. The governor of South Australia, Sir William Robinson, opened the exhibition on June 21, 1887, and it received a total of 753,592 visitors throughout its 172-day duration. It operated daily from 11 A.M. to 5 P.M. (except Sundays), and in the high season it also opened three evenings a week. The biggest day was September 26, with a total of 16,229 visitors and the smallest, December 9, with 1109 visitors. All in all, the attendance figures far exceeded the initial expectations of the organizers. Ticket prices were less than the recent exhibitions in Sydney and Melbourne. Season passes cost one guinea, while daily admissions were one shilling for adults and sixpence for children. Children on school trips paid only threepence. Entertainment included concerts, military and fireworks displays, and a "tableaux of savage life," with aborigines from two mission stations. The exhibition buildings were situated upon the slope of a hill and of the main building, it was claimed that "[f]rom its summit a bird's eye view can be had of the country for twelve miles surrounding Adelaide."

The members of the organization committee agreed that the profit from the exhibition — assured from the outset since the promoters did not have to draw upon the guaranteed fund and expected substantial gain from the sale of the buildings — would be spent in the erection of works of public utility. Indeed, section D of the exhibition, "Physical, Social, and Moral Condition of Man," hosted a number of exhibits of this nature, including, among many others, Lying-in Asylums, Treatment of Paupers, and Treatment of Aborigines. This last topic, in particular, state protection of the Aborigines, also received substantial mention in the exhibition handbook. According to the handbook, depots were established in order "to ameliorate the condition of the natives by industrial pursuit, as well as moral and religious training and thus render their labor more useful and profitable to themselves." This discussion in the handbook of the aims of the civilizing nature of the depots and the presence of exhibits dedicated to illustrating this same belief were reminiscent of the self-justificatory colonial discourse of the time. The exhibition, therefore, in addition to showcasing the industrial and artistic achievements of the South Australians, also demonstrated both the benefits of British colonization and the particularly positive path that it had taken in South Australia.

The *Report of the Royal Commission for the Exhibition* was generous in its praise of the event. In addition to its high attendance and financial success, the exhibition was also praised for its social and cultural achievements and for the greater love of the fine arts it had engendered in the minds of a large number of South Australians to the number of "men and women of high distinction in the old land" that it had brought to South Australia. There was also mention made in the *Report* of the history of South Australian colonization and in particular how the exhibition had "served to prove

that the same spirit of courage, self-reliance, and energy which marked the founders of [the] colony [had] descended to those upon whom the burden of a strong and healthy national life now rests" (p. 366).

The legacy of this exhibition was a boost to South Australia's beleaguered economy by means of the 2,700 jobs the event created, as well as the boost that visitors' spending gave to the city's businesses and the optimistic outlook that the exhibition created. Remnants of the exhibition remained in Adelaide until 1962 when finally the main exhibition building was pulled down.

Bibliography

Records of the Jubilee International Exhibition are available in the Netley repository of the State Records Office of South Australia in Adelaide. They are in General Record Group (GRG) 47, and consist of committee meeting minutes, letter books, financial records, lists of exhibitors, visitor books and attendance statistics, exhibition building plans, and much more. Other publications, including most noted below, may be found in the Mortlock Library of South Australiana, a division of the State Library of South Australia. Additional information may be found in the *South Australian Parliamentary Debates* and the *Notice Papers of the Adelaide City Council* for the years 1885–1888. Contemporary publications include the official documents, *The Adelaide Jubilee International Exhibition 1887: Reports of Juries and Official Lists of Awards* (1889), which contains lists of jurors, exhibitors, promoters, officials, as well as the Exhibition Ode and the balance sheet for the fair, and Henry Matthews and Commissioners, *Report of the Royal Commission for the Adelaide International Exhibition of 1887 to the Queen's Most Excellent Majesty* (1888), the report of the British commissioners. H.J. Scott (ed.), *A Handbook for the Adelaide Jubilee International Exhibition with an Introduction by Sir Samuel Davenport, K.C.M.G., L.L.D.* (1887) includes information on the purpose of the exhibition J.C. Neild, *Report of the Executive Commissioner for New South Wales to the Adelaide Jubilee International Exhibition, 1887–88* (1890), details that colony's participation in the exhibition and also contains information about the site and exhibition building. The book can be found in the Larson Collection at the California State University at Fresno library. John Fairfax Conigrave, "Adelaide Jubilee International Exhibition 1887,"

(1886), a brochure prepared before the event, contains advance information for exhibitors and visitors. H.J. Scott, *South Australia in 1887* (1887), provides historical context and some information

on the exhibition. Two South Australian newspapers, the *Advertiser* and the *Register*, also covered the exhibition in some detail.

Barcelona 1888

Gary McDonogh

Exposició Universal de Barcelona

Spain's first international exposition dramatized Barcelona's resurgence as an industrial, commercial, and cultural center for the Catalonia region and Spain as a whole, amid attendant and conflictive questions of national strength and state identity. The exposition celebrated the region's power and international connections while orienting the city and its growing environs towards a seemingly bountiful future.

Barcelona had declined from its medieval splendor as capital of an independent Aragonese-Catalan empire as a unified Spanish nation shifted interests toward the New World. After military repression following the eighteenth-century War of Spanish Succession, Catalan agriculture, textiles, and colonial trade underpinned strong redevelopment in the nineteenth century. The population of Barcelona mushroomed from 34,000 in 1717 to 273,000 in 1887, and the city broke through its ancient walls into a fashionable new expansion district of palaces and boulevards, called the Eixample. Economic growth also fueled the arts and architecture, language and literary revival, and nationalist political aspirations.

Eugenio Serrano de Casanova initiated the exposition as a private venture in 1886. When he failed, Barcelona Mayor Francesc Rius i Taulet adopted the idea, enlisting the growing urban bourgeois elite in the venture. Although originally scheduled for 1887, Serrano's troubles and strikes postponed the opening for a year.

The fair's 115-acre site, the Ciutadela Park, held deep historical associations. A fortress had been built there to dominate the city in 1716 on

the razed ruins of a rebellious neighborhood. Barcelona regained the site in 1869 and sought to erase this symbol of state repression. Josep Fontseré's 1873 development plan created the city's largest park space and opened the area for new urban development beyond Barcelona's congested medieval core. The exposition incorporated Fontseré's *Umbracle* (1883), an arched cast-iron greenhouse that still stands.

Josep Vilaseca's Arch of Triumph crowned the exposition's entrance from an elegant new boulevard, the Passeig Sant Joan. Inside, the twenty-four naves of the 17-acre Palace of Industry housed local and international exhibits. Nearby were the Palace of Fine Arts (designed by Font Carreras) and the Hall of the Colonies. Architect and politician Lluís Domènech Muntaner created his first major work, the neo-Gothic Castell dels Tres Dragons café-restaurant, ornamented with ceramic shields, that today houses the Museum of Zoology. Antoni Gaudí's pavilion for his patrons, the López shipping family, was later torn down, but his monumental fountain for Fontseré remains a landmark of the park. Other companies, clubs, and cities erected smaller pavilions. Across cast-iron bridges, a harborside section showcased naval, trade, and electrical exhibits. Beyond the park, Domènech's International Hotel drew comments both for its style and its rapid construction (in sixty-nine days).

The infant King Alfonso XIII of Spain and his regent-mother María Cristina opened the exposition on May 8 and witnessed the Jochs Florals (Floral Games), a revived historical competition that promoted interest in the literary heritage of Catalan. Some Catalanists boycotted the opening; fearing that it would fail and bring ridicule on the region and its nationalists. Others, however, used the renascent Jochs and the exposition to promote cultural and national revitalization.

One peseta bought admission to the marvels of 12,203 exhibitors from 27 countries, including the United States, China, and Japan, whose displays proved especially popular. Exhibits from Europe and Latin American vied with showcases for Spain's remaining possessions in the Caribbean, Africa and the Far East. International naval squadrons filled the harbor. Triptychs by Hieronymous Bosch, on loan from Madrid, joined local art treasures. Concerts were frequent: the Catalan Isaac Albéniz, already a virtuoso, performed in the French exhibition area. National congresses of archaeology, economics, and medicine met during the exposition, while lighter entertainment included "magic" fountains, photographers, and a "captive" (tethered) balloon.

The Universal Exposition closed on December 9 after hosting more than two million visitors. It became a watershed in the growth and visibility of Barcelona as a modern European city and for the assertions of the new *haute bourgeoisie* who would shape its economic and political life for decades. Meanwhile, on August 8, Barcelona also hosted the first meeting of the Unión General de Trabajadores, a leftist trade union that would champion the working classes through decades of class conflict within a divided state. While few physical legacies of the fair remain beyond the park (where the Catalan Parliament now meets), its position in the history, growth, and divisions of the city and the road to the 1992 Olympics and Universal Forum of Cultures 2004 remains significant.

Bibliography

The centennial of the 1888 Exposition produced major new studies of the fair, its meanings and impact, brought together in the lavishly illustrated, 600-page *Exposició Universal de Barcelona: Libre del Centenari 1888–1988* (1988). This includes important texts by historians, geographers, and urbanists under the editorial direction of Ramon Grau. Pere Hereu Payet, *et al.,* focus on history and urbanism in *Arquitectura i ciutat a l'exposició universal de Barcelona* (1988). These have replaced Josep Maria Garrut's short *L'Exposició Universal de Barcelona de 1888* (1976) which drew on primary documents held at the Institut Municipal d'Història de Barcelona. The institute remains the major repository for primary sources, newspapers, photographs, and published guides, including *Catálogo de la sección oficial del Gobierno, Exposició Universal de Barcelona de 1888* (1888), *Catálogo oficial general* (1888) and *Estudios sobre la Exposición Universal de Barcelona* (1888).

The historical context of the exposition has been the subject of increasing research available in Castilian, Catalan, and English. Relevant works include Gary McDonogh, *Good Families of Barcelona* (1986), Alejandro Sánchez, ed., *Barcelona 1888–1929* (1994), and Pere Anguera, ed. *La consolidació del món burgès, 1860–1900* (2004). Robert Hughes, *Barcelona* (1992), Manuel Vázquez Montalbán, *Barcelonas* (1992), and Jaume Fabre and J.M. Huertas, *Noticiari de Barcelona* (1992) all provide longer popular overviews of the city. The catalogue of the 2006 exhibit on Barcelona and Modernity shared by the Cleveland Museum of Art and the Metropolitan Museum of Art provides important essays and wonderful illustrations of the sociocultural and artistic evolution of this period (W. Robinson, J. Falgàs and C. Belen Lord, eds., *Barcelona and Modernity*, 2006). Finally, Eduardo Mendoza's *La ciudad de los prodigios* (1986); and published in English as *City of Marvels* (1988), offers a provocative, picaresque fictional vision of the exposition and its context.

Glasgow 1888

Susan Bennett

Glasgow International Exhibition

The city of Glasgow decided to show off its great achievements, emphasise its position as the Empire's "Second City," and raise funds for a purpose-built art gallery and museum, by holding its first international exhibition in 1888.

Kelvingrove Park, which had been designed in 1853 by the Crystal Palace architect Sir Joseph Paxton, was chosen as the site. The Glasgow architect James Sellars chose an Oriental design that combined Moorish, Byzantine and Indian influences for his prize-winning design. The buildings occupied 11.5 acres of the nearly 60 acre site. The floor area of the main building (474,500 sq ft) was calculated to exceed that of Manchester's exhibition building, and included a great nave crossed by a transverse avenue with a grand central dome (170 feet high, including the vane). A square annex for machinery was added to the west end providing the largest display space in Great Britain since the 1862 London exhibition.

Exhibits were divided into twenty-one classes covering agriculture, natural resources, engineering, transportation, machinery, weaponry, chemistry, food science, fishing, education and the fine and decorative arts. Two-thirds of the exhibitors were from Scotland, with the most international aspect of the exhibition represented in the women's section.

Important external features included a Doulton fountain, 85 feet high, presented to the city by the manufacturers, and which, with a basin 60 feet in diameter, was claimed to the largest terracotta structure ever built. A fairy fountain, illuminated at night by electric light that shone through colored glass, proved to be one of the best-loved features of the exhibition. An exact reproduction of the ancient Episcopal palace, "The Bishop's Castle," was constructed out of realistically painted canvas on a wooden frame and used as a museum of Scottish antiquities for the duration of the exhibition. Dairymaids from Switzerland, Holland, Ireland and Scotland demonstrated their skills in a working dairy constructed in the park. The Queen's Jubilee presents were put on display in the nearby Kelvingrove Mansion Museum. Entertainments included a switchback railway, a shooting gallery, a curling rink, an Indian jungle, and various boating events on the Kelvin River, including rides on a gondola imported from Venice and operated by gondoliers. There were many dining rooms and tea rooms serving refreshments, with the Glasgow School of Cookery's tearoom producing enough profit to cover the school's running costs for a number of years.

The exhibition opened on May 8 following an inaugural visit by the Prince and Princess of Wales, and ran for six months, closing on November 10. Special railway and steamship fares encouraged many to make the visit to Glasgow leading to an attendance of 5,748,379, which made it the largest British exhibition held outside London to this date.

The exhibition was further boosted by a state visit by Queen Victoria on August 22, during only her second visit to the city. The well-known artist, Sir John Lavery, was commissioned to record this visit, and his painting is in the collections of the Glasgow Museum and Art Galleries.

The exhibition made a profit of £41,700, which was put towards the costs of building the Kelvingrove Art Gallery and Museum. This museum was completed and formally opened at the 1901 Glasgow international exhibition.

Bibliography

The Glasgow Room of the Mitchell Library holds some of the exhibition archives, together with catalogues, programs, and guides, including commercial versions published in 1888. These include: *Elliot's Popular Guide to Glasgow and the Exhibition with Excursion Notes*; *How to View the Exhibition: Hints to the Casual Visitor*; *MacDonald's Guide to the City*; *Sneddon's Guide to Glasgow International Exhibition*; *Wilson's Penny Guide to Glasgow and the Exhibition of 1888, Comprising Notices of Every Object of Interest to Strangers and All About Town*. Also in the Glasgow Room are special editions of contemporary publications dedicated to the exhibition, especially various supplements to the *North British Daily Mail*. The Special Collections section of the University of Glasgow Library provides an online listing of its resources for the 1888 Glasgow Exhibition at *http://special.lib.gla.ac.uk/teach/century/glasgow.html*. The learning resource SCRAN holds 582 images relating to the 1888 Glasgow exhibition which can be viewed online at *http://www.scran.ac.uk*.

Full descriptions and reports on the exhibition can be found in contemporary publications, in particular *The Builder*, an excellent resource in the areas of architecture and design. The *Illustrated London News*, *The Pictorial World* and *The Graphic* provide a useful resource for images of the exhibition. T. Raffles Davison, *Pen and Ink Notes at the Glasgow Exhibition*, (1888) has some interesting pictures of the exhibition. Alastair L. Goldsmith, "The Glasgow International Exhibitions, 1888–1938" (unpub. Master's thesis, University of Strathclyde, 1985) and Perilla Kinchin and Juliet Kinchin, *Glasgow's Great Exhibitions: 1888, 1901, 1911, 1938, 1988* (1988), are useful modern works.

The Glasgow Museum and Art Galleries holds Sir John Lavery's large oil painting depicting the visit of Queen Victoria to the exhibition in August 1888, together with many of the portrait studies for the audience at this event.

Melbourne 1888–1889

David Dunstan

Centennial International Exhibition

Governor Arthur Philip's proclamation of New South Wales in 1788 began the British colonial conquest of Australia and a century later spawned a world's fair. Just as the United States had in Philadelphia in 1876 and the French would do in 1889, the Australian colonists held an exhibition to celebrate their nationhood, as achieved and impending. But the foundation metropolis of Sydney was not to be the fair's host. New South Wales' leader, Sir Patrick Jennings, sought instead to curb public debt. Sydney's exhibition building, the Garden Palace, had been lost to a fire in 1882. With due deference to the older colony, Victoria offered to host the event. It had a booming economy and a building leftover from the Melbourne International Exhibition of 1880 1881.

The Chief Justice of Victoria, George Higinbotham, was appointed president of a commission rich in commercial and establishment influence. A nineteen-person English committee headed by the former leader, the now knighted former radical, Sir Graham Berry, was composed of many wealthy former colonists returned "home." In January 1887, the commissioners determined the opening and closing dates, resolved to open the exhibition in the evenings and provide motive power to the exhibits free of charge. The fastidious and controlling Higinbotham lost support and resigned. He was succeeded by a pliant Tory, Sir James McBain, with Frederick Sargood as executive vice-president. McBain was an energetic plutocrat with enthusiasms, notably militaria and music. There were no more fears of excessive expense. Tenders were called for new permanent annexes facing Rathdowne and Nicholson streets to provide additional space for exhibitors and machinery in motion. Local architect George Raymond Johnson was successful, perhaps because Joseph Reed, the architect for the 1880–1881 exhibition, was not a contender for the appointment. Electricity was new technology, and a brave and costly decision was taken to light the buildings; this required generating machinery and more than a thousand arc and two thousand incandescent lights. Exhibitors of moving machinery had power from pulleys driven by the commissioners' engines or steam pipes, or with gas or fuel as required. The anticipated area was thirty one acres— with the main building and permanent machinery annex occupying nine acres. This was more than double the area of Sydney in 1879, and even more than London in 1851 (20 acres) and only one-third smaller than Philadelphia in 1876. Eventually, with thirty-eight acres it was the biggest public event ever attempted by Australians and remained so for many decades afterwards.

The public entrance was now from the east at Nicholson Street. A new "Aesthetic style" interior by the American-trained decorative artist, John Clay Beeler, saw the 1880–

1881 colors painted over and a more lavish use of gilding. "Radiating gold rays" under the dome typified "the riches and glory of the British Empire." The motto "Victoria Welcomes all Nations" was retained, with the Biblical text, "The Earth is the Lord's and the Fulness Thereof" taken from the ill-fated Garden Palace and placed above the arch of the western transept. As with London in 1862, British national colors of red, white, and blue predominated. Nearby were fine exhibits, including gold, silver and plated ware, jewellery, "artistic glass," porcelain, and other delicate decorative objects, as well as watches, perfumery, cutlery, books, stationery and the like. Looking directly north from the dais of the opening ceremony into the distance was the Grand Avenue of the Nations.

The theme of the six-part exhibition cantata at the opening ceremony on August 1, 1888, was again the coming of European civilization. The *Argus* newspaper's eight-page supplement guide foreshadowed a display showing the "immense progress and development and the splendid natural resources of this Greater Britain in the Southern Seas." With more than ninety countries exhibiting, the show was truly an international one. But many exhibits were not complete. The British "industrial court" had shields of coats of arms and weapons on alternate pillars draped with flags with emblematic and geographic connections. Suspended above were improving mottoes of the industrial age: "Ability is a Poor Man's Wealth." Marble statues of royalty introduced the visitor to exhibits of men's mercery, whisky, hats, Irish linen, cotton, brass and silver ware, lenses and glassware, musical instruments, and pottery. The British Loan Collection — one of "the finest ... to leave the shores of the old country"—featured paintings by J.M.W. Turner, Lord Leighton, Landseer, and others.

The German court, the exhibition's second largest, featured a display of pianos from eighty-five exhibitors. The French were disappointed with their contribution overall and preoccupied with their forthcoming exhibition, but their large-scale model of Mr Eiffel's tower adorned with champagne bottles grabbed fairgoer's attention. The United States' frontage was given over to sewing machines, with the Singer Company occupying two large stands with ladies busily demonstrating. American novelties included the petrol engine, chewing gum, and Edison's latest invention, the phonograph. There was a separate court for weapons of war with Aboriginal and "native" weapons, including examples from Borneo, and arms from China. With twice the space of any other nation, Victoria presented displays of manufacturing prowess and the satisfaction of material wants befitting the newly rich community. A "Renaissance Chateau" housed Wallach Brothers' furniture displays that so well expressed "the luxury of modern life" according to the *Argus*. Displays of brewing and winemaking were opposed unsuccessfully by the powerful temperance-minded commissioner, James Munro. The Germans had a "lagerbier kiosk," a "Manila tobacco-house" had cigars and the cool and extensive cellars were given over to wines and dairy products. Bakers and confectioners manufactured and sold their goods with free samples of tea and cocoa.

The English conductor and composer Frederic Cowen was paid the astronomical sum of £5000 over the six months. A full orchestra was formed and major works of Beethoven, Brahms, and Wagner were performed for the first time in Australia. Cowen brought a group of professional musicians and added to their number, creating a real enthusiasm for orchestral music. The city and citizens of Melbourne were on display with the viewing platform around the great dome accessible by elevators. An Anglican vicar's wife, Mrs G.F. Cross, visited many times with her children. "You could live there all day long, with every comfort, including free education worth years of school," she recalled. A popular novelist, Ada Cambridge, revealed those places monopolized by lovers. The commissioners added more sideshows when attendance declined in November. An electric railway and shooting gallery, then Swiss singers and yodellers, organ recitals, bicycle rides, athletic and acrobatic feats, conjuring, and balancing went on until the exhibition closed in February 1889.

The total attendance was more than two million, nearly double the population of Victoria. The overall cost was nearly £238,000, bringing about more than twice the loss anticipated. The original estimate had been £25,000. Organizers justified the loss by pointing out that the money had gone to Victorian artisans and laborers, had increased revenue to the railways and customs, had attracted well-heeled visitors, and had created new channels of trade and commerce. But Melbourne's real estate values peaked with the exhibition's closure early in 1889 and soon fell. In its wake came unemployment, retrenchments, recrimination, the flight of British capital, and, finally, the collapse of banks and the financial system in 1893. Although the exhibition was an important expression of intercolonial cooperation and expression of national sentiment, it has not been seen as seminal in leading to the eventual federation of the Australian colonies in 1901. Rather, it was the last great fling in an era of extravagance. Its memory banished thoughts of an international event conducted on a comparable scale for a very long time.

Bibliography

The Centennial International Exhibition, Melbourne 1888–89. The Official Catalogue of Exhibits (1888) and *Official Record of the Centennial International Exhibition, Melbourne, 1888–1889* (1892) are replete with detail pertinent to the exhibition, especially the organisation, participants and exhibits. The exhibition received extensive coverage in the Melbourne press, including the *Argus, Australasian, Age,* and *Herald* with the Exhibition Supplement to the *Argus* of August 2, 1888, particularly useful for background information and for illustrations and site plans. Also, researchers should consult the illustrated periodicals of the day, such as the *Illustrated Australian News* and the *Australasian Sketcher.* Manuscript records of the exhibition organization appear not to have survived. The United States' role is covered in the *Reports of the United States Commissioners to the Centennial International Exhibition at Melbourne 1888* (1889) and in official documents contained in the National Archives, Record Group 43. Also, see R. Burdett Smith, *Report of the Executive Commissioner for New South Wales, Centennial International Exhibition, Melbourne 1888–89,* (n.d.) and *Report of the Royal Commission for the Melbourne Centennial International Exhibition of 1888 to the Queen's Most Excellent Majesty* (1889).

The collections of the State Library of Victoria (SLV) *http://www.slv.vic.gov.au/,* the Victoria Museum *http://www.mov.vic.gov.au/,* the State Library of New South Wales *http://www.sl.nsw.gov.au/,* and the National Library of Australia *http://www.nla.gov.au/* offer scope for further research. Exhibition inspired guides and souvenirs, verse and observations in diaries offer further insights. Consult *The Popular Guide to the Centennial Exhibition* (1888) and *Souvenir of the Melbourne Exhibition 1888* (1888). The picture collections of the public libraries document the exhibition, some available in digitized form over the internet. Memoirs and fiction include Oscar Comettant, *Au Pays des Kangourous et des Mines d'Or* (1890), translated by Judith Anderson, *In the Land of Kangaroos and Gold Mines,* (1980). See especially chapter 21. Also useful are Ada Cambridge, *Thirty Years in Australia* (1903) and Elizabeth Morrison, ed., *Ada Cambridge, A Woman's Friendship* (1988). See also "Victoria at the Great Exhibitions," *La Trobe Library Journal* 14, 56 (1995).

The exhibition is the subject of J.R. Thomson "The Melbourne Centennial International Exhibition 1888–89: public ostentation in an era of extravagance" unpub. BA (honors) thesis, Monash University, 1968. It is discussed in a general context in Graeme Davison, J.W.McCarty and Ailsa McLeary. *Australians 1888* (1987); Graeme Davison, "Exhibitions," *Australian Cultural History,* 2, (1982), reprinted as "Festivals of Nationhood: the International Exhibitions," in S.L. Goldberg and F.B. Smith, eds., *Australian Cultural History* (1988), Davison's outstanding study, *The Rise and Fall of Marvellous Melbourne* (1978, 2004); and general histories covering the period, most notably chapter 9 of Geoffrey Serle, *The Rush to Be Rich: A History of the Colony of Victoria 1883–89* (1971). Many participants are included in the *Australian Dictionary of Biography. http://www.adb.online.anu.edu.au/adbonline.htm* The wider imperial context is explored in Peter H. Hoffenberg, *An Empire on Display* (2001). The building, exhibition complex, and activities are the focus of David Dunstan, *Victorian Icon* (1996). On the wider influence of the exhibition, see Kirsten Orr, "A force for Federation: international exhibitions and the formation of Australian ethos 1851–1901" (unpub. Ph.D. thesis, University of New South Wales, 2006).

Paris 1889

Anthony Swift

Exposition Universelle

The Paris Exposition universelle internationale of 1889 was not the first world's fair to remain open at night, as is sometimes claimed. Nor was it the first to have a separate exhibition category for electricity — the Antwerp world's fair gained that distinction four years earlier. What was unique about the 1889 exposition was its spectacular demonstration of the power of technology to transform the natural environment on an unprecedented scale by creating a manmade wonderland of light, color, sound, engineering, and amusement that raised the bar for subsequent world's fairs. The harbinger of Coney Island and Disney's Magic Kingdom, it was a tremendous success. The exposition drew more than 30 million visitors over six months, boosted the prestige of France's Third Republic both at home and abroad, and made a profit. It left behind one of the modern world's most iconic structures, Gustave Eiffel's 300-meter tower of iron, which has since become the symbol of Paris and continues to attract millions of visitors each year. It also drew a line over the Boulanger Affair and the threat the ambitious general and his supporters had posed to the young republic.

Prime Minister Jules Ferry first proposed the exposition in 1880 and planning began in 1884, when the ministry of commerce commissioned a preliminary study. Despite objections that the exposition would be a financial extravagance in an economic depression, it would cause inflation, Europe's monarchies would refuse to participate in an exposition commemorating the French Revolution, or the money would be better spent on social programs, the government decided in November 1884 to go ahead with the exposition, arguing that it was continuing the custom of holding expositions at eleven-year intervals as well as marking the centennial of the revolution. A commission headed by Antonin Proust, a former minister of arts, submitted its recommendations in March 1885. Although the Proust commission considered a number of sites in or near Paris, in the end it went along with the recommendation of the Paris municipal council and selected the traditional Champ de Mars site for the main exposition buildings, with other pavilions located across the Seine on the Trocadéro Hill or along the Esplanade des Invalides. It also suggested that the exposition be financed by the state, the city of Paris, and private investors.

Preparations for the exposition began did not begin in earnest, however, until Edouard Lockroy become Minister of Commerce in December 1885 following a cabinet reshuffle and threw his support behind the event. In early 1886 French ambassadors sounded out foreign attitudes towards the proposed exposition, emphasizing that the date chosen was merely a coincidence and that any commemorations of the centennial of the revolution would be entirely separate. Although monarchical governments made it clear that they would not be inclined to participate, the French government nonetheless issued a decree in February 1886 affirming its support for the exposition. In April the government submitted its financial plans to the National Assembly for approval, proposing that the state contribute seventeen million francs, with an additional eight million francs from the city of Paris and 18 million francs to be provided by an Association de Garantie composed of private shareholders. Notwithstanding some opposition to the exposition on economic grounds, the National Assembly approved the government's plans in July 1886.

Lockroy generally followed the recommendations of the Proust commission, but wanted a special attraction that would entice exhibitors and attract visitors. In 1885 the engineer Gustave Eiffel had proposed a 300-meter iron tower, and Lockroy appears to have already decided that he preferred Eiffel's project when he announced an architectural competition for the major exposition buildings on May 1, 1886, for the instructions specified an iron tower whose dimensions matched Eiffel's design. On June 12, Eiffel's proposal was adopted, with the government eventually agreeing to contribute one-fifth of the construction costs and to give Eiffel all the revenue from visits to the tower for twenty years. Despite the ensuing polemic over whether its iron skeleton would permanently disfigure Paris, in the course of which 47 French artists and writers published a signed protest against the "useless and monstrous" tower, Lockroy remained steadfast in his support for the project. Along with Eiffel's tower, the government also selected Ferdinand Dutert's plan for the Gallery of Machines and Jean-Camille Formigé's designs for the Palace of Industry, the Palace of Fine Arts, and the Palace of Liberal Arts. A proposal by Charles-Louis Chassin for a museum of the revolution was vetoed, and in November 1886, Lockroy announced that the exposition would be entirely separate from the centennial celebrations. This diplomatic attempt to disassociate the exposition from the controversial centennial and instead focus on the economic achievements of the past century failed, however, and when invitations to the exposition went out in March 1887 Europe's monarchies declined to participate officially, although in the end nearly all of them were represented by privately organized exhibits. By the time the exposition opened on May 6, 1889, some 35 nations had accepted the French invitation, including the United States, Hawaii, Mexico, Argentina, Chile, Uruguay, Venezuela, Paraguay, Norway, Serbia, Switzerland, Greece, Japan, and Morocco.

The French, with some justification, blamed the European monarchies' refusal to take part in the exposition on the machinations of German chancellor Otto von Bismarck, and in some quarters the idea of a centennial exposition was revived, although the government remained determined to keep the commemoration of the revolution separate. Consequently the opening of the exposition was scheduled for May 6, the day following the celebrations held at Versailles to mark the 100th anniversary of the meeting of the Estate-General. International congresses held in conjunction with the exposition were not allowed to focus on political or religious topics. Even more disturbing than the monarchical boycott of the exposition was the growing instability of the Third Republic, threatened by the rising popularity of the right-wing militarist General Georges Boulanger. The charismatic general's election to the Chamber of Deputies in 1888 raised the possibility of a coup d'état or a landslide victory by his supporters in the 1889 general elections. In response to the crisis the government politicized the coming exposition to mobilize support for the republic and its institutions, organizing a banquet for mayors on the Champ de Mars on July 14, 1888, to demonstrate republican solidarity against the backdrop of the rising Eiffel Tower. As a conservative commentator remarked, "Everyone knows that the Exposition and the centennial have as their single purpose to aid the Republic in overcoming the obstacle of the general elections and to trick France into renewing republican contracts for another four years" (*Le Gaulois*, 5 July 1888).

By the time the exposition opened on May 6, 1889, the Boulanger threat had subsided and the general had fled abroad to avoid arrest, although the outcome of the forthcoming elections remained uncertain. The opening ceremony was a celebration of French political and economic achievements, in which President Marie François Sadi-Carnot dedicated the Statue of the Republic that stood atop the central dome of the Palace of Industry and presided over a military review before more than 100,000 people. That evening — and every evening until the exposition closed in early November — there were fireworks, concerts, and balls, with gas spotlights atop the Eiffel Tower casting their beams over the exposition and the city and illuminating the sky with blue, white, and red lights. The tower itself was lit up by thousands of colored electric light bulbs, as were the exposition grounds, creating an atmosphere of fantasy and carnival that Parisians quickly dubbed the *cité féerique*. Only low-ranking diplomats from Britain, Germany, and Italy participated in the ceremony, and Austria and Russia sent no representatives at all, but international reaction was largely very favorable.

The British *Pall Mall Gazette* acknowledged that once again the French had outdone all rivals in mounting an exposition that demonstrated their artistry and taste, predicting that "If the gloomy clouds gathering on the political horizon do not break out into a storm, half the civilized world will be lured to Paris, and most certainly with good reason, for this is the most beautiful exhibition the world has ever seen."

The central axis of the exposition on the Champ de Mars ran under the Eiffel Tower to the entrance of Palace of Industry, which was flanked by the Palace of Fine Arts and the Palace of Liberal Arts. Behind the Palace of Industry stood the Gallery of Machines, which had been designed by Dutert but largely realized by the railway engineer Victor Contamin. More than 80 buildings on the Champ de Mars contained various exhibits and attractions, while on the opposite side of the Seine the Palais du Trocadéro, built for the previous Paris exposition of 1878, housed an ethnographic exhibition that included examples of African, Oceanic, and pre–Columbian art. Exhibits devoted to agriculture, food products, colonies, the French military, and social economy were located to the northeast of the Champ de Mars along the Quai d'Orsay and Esplanade des Invalides. The exposition covered some 237 acres and had 61,722 exhibitors, of whom about 40 percent (25,364) were foreign. The official classification system divided exhibits into ten groups: the arts, education, furniture and accessories, textiles, extractive industries, mechanical industries, food products, agriculture, horticulture, and social economy.

Not since the Crystal Palace had a world's fair produced such striking examples of innovative engineering. Although the French writer and poet Joris-Karl Huysmans found it "strikingly ugly," likening it to a "hideous birdcage," the Eiffel Tower's popularity with visitors

Perhaps the most famous world's fair structure ever is the Eiffel Tower, shown here in a 1900 photograph. It was built for the universal exposition of 1889 (editors' collection).

exceeded all expectations. By the time the exposition closed nearly two million people had ascended the elevators or stairs of the towering iron monument, including the Prince of Wales, W.F. "Buffalo Bill" Cody, Sarah Bernhardt, and Thomas Edison. A popular pastime among visitors was to drop a small balloon containing a request that the person who found it return it to the sender's address. Unlike the grand structures at earlier world's fairs, the tower had no other purpose than to impress and amuse with its observation platforms, bars, and restaurants. The other wonder of engineering at the exposition, the Gallery of Machines, had a more utilitarian function. It enclosed 15 acres of exhibition space without support from internal columns, the enormous glass roof balanced on hinged supports set into concrete foundations. Electrically powered moving platforms, suspended 20 feet above the gallery, carried visitors over the humming machinery below for a panoramic view of the vast interior.

Although many new and innovative products were on display in 1889, among them stock-quotation printers and Daimler and Benz gasoline-powered motor cars, the accent was on the perfection and publicizing of existing technologies. The telephone and phonograph were sensations, for example, but they had already been crowd-pullers at several world's fairs since each made its debut at Philadelphia's Centennial Exhibition in 1876. Thomas Edison exhibited all 493 of his inventions and charmed visitors with his electric phonograph, which alternately played recordings of the American and French national anthems. The "King of Light," as he was called, demonstrated his talent for showmanship in a display of 20,000 incandescent electric bulbs arranged in the form of a pear, which emitted enough light for a small town. Electric lighting was hardly new, of course, having already been employed at a number of world's fairs and specialist trade exhibitions such as the Paris International Exposition of Electricity in 1881, but the 1889 exposition used it on an unprecedentedly lavish scale to amaze and amuse. It also provided competing electrical firms with the opportunity to demonstrate to the public the achievements and advantages of their various generating systems and lighting technologies. The Edison, Gramme, and other companies

operated six oil-fueled dynamos that provided the vast quantities of electrical power consumed by the exposition.

In effect, the exposition was a milestone not so much for what it displayed but in how it presented industry and technology, which it presented not only as exhibits and lessons but also transformed into magic. The cartoonist Ferdinand Bac wrote that he seemed to have been reborn in a new world created by "ingenious sorcerers." Electricity produced not merely power and light but also spectacle, the extravagant light shows and magically changing colors of the illuminated fountains lending the exposition a phantasmagorical air at night. A French visitor tried to convey the effect:

> The view in the evening is indescribable. It's astonishing to view that magical illumination. It's an orgy of light like we've never seen. Everything shines, glitters, blazes in a perpetual feast for the eyes. It's as if a skilful artist had used a sparkling palette to cover the exposition in light, to sprinkle gold dust on the grand domes, to mark the lawns and pavilions with lines of fire. From far away it looks like a mosaic of glistening colors, then gleaming spots on dark masses, flashes of lightening through stained-glass windows, flames in the mountains. We are in the middle of an enchanted garden.

The 1889 exposition exemplified the growing emphasis on spectacle in world's fairs towards the end of the nineteenth century. As Antonin Proust had noted in his preliminary report during the planning stages, it was essential to "offer visitors an ensemble of suitable diversions to attract them and keep them there," and the exposition provided a multitude of sensory stimulations. Visitors could ascend Eiffel's tower to see all Paris laid out before their eyes, take in the exposition from one of the two trains that ran through and around the grounds, watch the lithe Javanese dancers in the Dutch colonial section, wander among the exotic plants and flowers of the horticultural exhibits in the Trocadéro Gardens, or ride to the top of the great Terrestrial Globe in the Palace of Liberal Arts. Balls, theater performances, and concerts of contemporary and historical music were regularly held at the exposition, where composers such as Claude Debussy and Maurice Ravel made their acquaintance with Annamite, Javanese, Romanian, and Russian music. There was even a Children's Palace with games and a puppet theater. Under pressure from the radical republicans and the

Traditional works of arts dominated the fine arts exhibition in the $1,350,000 Palais des Beaux-Arts at the Paris exposition (from Norton, *World's Fairs*, 1892).

city of Paris, the government expanded the program of festivities to include more commemorations of the centennial of the revolution, such as the enormous concert with 2,000 musicians that marked Bastille Day and the gigantic banquet for 13,456 mayors and other guests held in the Palace of Industry in August. Many other events were held throughout the city during the exposition, among them Buffalo Bill's Wild West Show, which brought cowboys, "savage" Indians, and Annie Oakley to perform before Paris audiences. Franco-American friendship was celebrated on July 4, when President Carnot dedicated a miniature replica of the Statue of Liberty on the Isle aux Cygnes in the River Seine, just a stone's throw from the Eiffel Tower, where it still stands today.

Although the exposition had no rue des Nations as in 1878, it was nonetheless replete with an eclectic assortment of picturesque replicas of historic buildings from all over the world. Beside the brash modernity of the Eiffel Tower stood dozens of detailed examples of housing from prehistory to the present designed by Charles Garnier, the renowned architect of the grandiose Paris Opéra. The

Suez company constructed an Egyptian temple to house its exhibits, Mexico's pavilion was an "Aztec Palace," while for its pavilion, Ecuador drew on its Inca past for inspiration. There was also a reconstruction of the Bastille and the neighboring Faubourg Saint-Antoine, although it was relegated to a site outside the exposition grounds due to its association with revolutionary violence. As at other world's fairs of the period, the colonial section contained recreations of villages from Europe's far-flung imperial possessions, inhabited by indigenous peoples who made handicrafts and performed for visitors, as well as an assortment of palaces and temples designed by French architects that included a facsimile of a pagoda from Angkor Wat. Paul Gauguin made his first acquaintance with Tahiti's "noble savages" at the exposition's Tahitian village, which inspired his subsequent voyage to the island. The rue du Caire, a reproduction of a Cairo street that had made its first appearance at the 1878 Paris exposition, this time featured not only North African artisans, bazaars, and cafés but also a novel and somewhat scandalous form of entertainment — belly dancing. Another kind of adventure was a ride in one of the rickshaws pulled by Indochinese men. Outside the gates of the exposition, several commercial amusement parks vied for the public's cash with roller coasters, halls of mirrors, performing animals, cabarets, and ascents in balloons.

More didactic were the History of Work and the exhibits devoted to education, social economy, and hygiene. The History of Work, inspired by a similar display at the 1867 Paris exposition and organized by Jules Simon, was an anthropological examination of the process of manual and mechanical labor of each historical epoch to the present. The education exhibits demonstrated the Third Republic's much vaunted commitment to mass education, while the section devoted to social economy was the largest presentation of means for improving the moral and material condition of the working class at any world's fair thus far, with 1,171 exhibitors from France and abroad. Organized by liberal industrialists determined to demonstrate that there was no need for the state to intervene in social issues, the social economy exhibition took the form of a picturesque workers' village with model housing, a health center, a temperance café, an inexpensive restaurant, and a gallery with colorful murals, charts, graphs, photographs, and plans informing the public about savings societies and employer-sponsored institutions such as schools, hospitals, and libraries. In keeping with the organizers' paternalistic ethos, charities, socialist groups, and workers' associations were not invited to exhibit. Although the employers sought to show that private initiative was the best means to alleviate social problems, exhibits in other locations called attention to the need for public intervention in matters of social welfare, such as the city of Paris's demonstration of the fundamentals of good sanitation and hygiene, which consisted of two physically identical apartment blocks, the "healthy building" and the "unhealthy building." In any case, the anti-state views of the organizers of the social economy section failed to convince, and Alfred Picard's official report on the exposition predicted that the state would increasingly intervene in social and economic issues in the twentieth century.

There were fewer national pavilions than at the 1878 exposition, due to the absence of official exhibits from most of Europe's monar-

chies, but the empire of Brazil and the Latin American republics were a very visible presence. No previous world's fair had attracted so much interest from the nations of Central and South America, and they used the exposition as an opportunity to demonstrate their distinct identities as well as to assert their membership in the modern community of nations. Their pavilions, clustered together on the Champs de Mars at the foot of the Eiffel Tower, were in a variety of national styles, some referring to their pre–Columbian or colonial heritage, others drawing on European influences. Argentina, with 1,473 exhibitors, had a large display of its wheat, leather, cattle, and sheep. The United States, often regarded by the French as their sister republic, was a major exhibitor but had no pavilion of its own, for by the time Congress approved the necessary funds all the best sites had already been taken. In addition to Edison's exhibits, which took up about one-fifth of the exhibition space allotted to the Americans, the Tiffany lamps attracted much attention, as did the educational exhibits, agricultural machinery, and locomotives. Britain's privately funded exhibition was strong in metallurgy, chemicals, and textiles. The ornately decorated Russian *izba*, which was actually a French architect's interpretation of a traditional dwelling, contained peasants in national costumes making handicrafts and drew much favorable comment, as did Russia's exhibits of cereals, furs, minerals, and petrol. While there was somewhat less foreign participation than was usual for a major world's fair, some 69 international congresses devoted to scientific and social topics brought specialists from all over the world to Paris. Two unofficial socialist congresses also took place during the exposition, one of which founded the Marxist Second International and adopted May First as the international holiday of labor.

Like the previous French world's fairs, the 1889 exposition gave a prominent place to the fine arts and two major exhibitions were mounted at the Palais des Beaux-Arts. The Centennale was a retrospective celebration of 1,600 examples of French artistic achievement from 1789 to 1889, featuring canvasses by Géricault, Delacroix, Ingres, Corot, Courbet, and Millet, while the Décennale was devoted to more recent work. Following what was now a tradition at French world's fairs, Paul Gauguin

The Grand Fountain from the 1889 exposition in Paris shows the trend for greater ornateness in world's fair architecture (from Norton, *World's Fairs*, 1892).

organized an unofficial alternative exhibition of paintings by the "excluded" impressionists in the Caté Volpini, located under the arcades of the Palais des Beaux-Arts. There were also works from foreign nations, most importantly Belgium, Britain, Italy, Germany, the Scandinavian countries, and the United States. More sensational were the painted panoramas on display at the exposition and around the city. Théophile Poilpot's *Petrol Panorama*, in the rotunda of the Transatlantic Company's pavilion on the Champ de Mars, gave spectators the illusion of boarding a ship and crossing the ocean to view the oil fields of Pennsylvania and the Caucasus. Another panorama, Charles Castellani's *All of Paris* on the Esplanade des Invalides, depicted some 1,500 famous contemporary French personalities in the arts, literature, politics, and science.

The 1889 exposition attempted to make instruction fun, to entice visitors to apprehend the progress achieved in the past decades by stimulating their senses and curiosity. As the organizing commission put it, "It is not so much to instruct the learned as to arouse a sense of wonder in the unlearned; the visitor

doesn't come for science: he seeks above all to amuse himself but is not averse to learning while having fun." Some critics charged that it was all too much fun, claiming that the public sought only amusement and neglected to learn from the exhibits. Nonetheless, the exposition demonstrated that the success of a world's fair in part depended on its ability to achieve the right balance between edification and pleasure. The retrospective exhibits, such as the History of Work and the History of Human Habitation, together with the colonial villages and historical recreations of buildings and streets populated by people in period dress, were an important step in the evolution of world's fairs away from the mere display of technical innovation and towards the use of technology to create simulated environments to amuse, instruct, and advertise.

The exposition was so popular that it remained open a week later than planned. When it finally closed on November 6, its success had surpassed all expectations. Over 32 million visitors had passed through its gates, and the exposition had made a profit of 8 million francs. It had boosted the economy, created jobs (if only temporarily), and demonstrated to the world that republican France was a vital, dynamic nation. Many contemporaries even attributed the defeat of Boulanger's supporters in the September elections to the exposition, although it is dubious that there was a direct connection between the two events. Perhaps, as the economist Alfred Neymarck said in a speech to a group of industrialists in mid–November, the most important consequence of the 1889 Exposition universelle was that it restored French self-confidence — at least until the next crisis engulfed the Third Republic.

Bibliography

The best published primary sources on the Paris Exposition of 1889 are Alfred Picard, *Rapport général. Exposition universelle internationale de 1889 à Paris*, 10 vols. (1891–92); *Rapports du jury international sur l'Exposition universelle de 1889*, 19 vols. (1890–91); Émile Monod, *L'Exposition universelle de 1889*, 4 vols. (1890); *Revue de l'Exposition universelle de 1889*, ed. Louis de Fourcaud, 2 vols. (1889); and *Reports of the United States Commissioners to the Universal Exposition of 1889 at Paris*, 5 vols. (1893). Other rich and detailed contemporary accounts are *L'Exposition de 1889. Guide bleu du Figaro et du Petit Journal avec 5 plans et 31 dessins* (1889); *Guide Illustré de l'Exposition universelle de 1889* (1889); and *Les merveilles de l'exposition de 1889* (1889).

Major newspapers and journals throughout the world gave lavish coverage to the exposition, and are an invaluable guide to perceptions of and reactions to the exposition. The most useful French periodicals include *Le Figaro, Le Temps, L'Illustration, Le Monde Illustré, Le Petit Journal,* and *L'Exposition de Paris de 1889. Journal hebdomadaire.* The novelist and historian Eugène-Melchior de Vogüé published an insightful series entitled "À Travers l'exposition," in *La Revue des deux mondes,* vols. 94–96 (1889), and several important articles by various authors are found in *Les Annales politiques et littéraires,* vol. 2 (1889). Important British sources include The *Times* of London, *The Illustrated London News,* and *The Builder,* while extensive American coverage can be found in the New York *Times,* the New York *Tribune, The Nation,* and *Harper's Weekly,* among others.

The French Archives Nationales contain extensive holdings on the exposition in Série C (Procès-verbaux des assemblées) and Série F (Administration générale de la France). Materials on the participation of the United States are located in the National Archives, Record Group 43 ("Miscellaneous Records of the United States Commission, 1889–1891" and "Photographs of American Exhibits, 1889"). The Library of Congress has a collection of photographs of American exhibits (Manuscript Division, Brackett Collection).

There is still no scholarly monograph devoted to the Paris exposition of 1889, although Pascal Ory's impressionistic *1889: L'Exposition universelle* (1989) is a useful introduction. *1889: La Tour Eiffel et l'exposition universelle* (Paris 1989), a catalog published in conjunction with an exposition held at the Musée d'Orsay in the summer of 1989, contains articles devoted to the architecture and other aspects of the fair. Another useful catalog is Miriam R. Levin, ed., *When the Eiffel Tower Was New: French Visions of Progress at the Centennial of the Revolution* (1989). Barbara Nelms, *The Third Republic and the Centennial of 1789* (1987), examines the exposition's place in the context of the celebrations of the centennial of the French Revolution, and contains a helpful if dated bibliography of published and unpublished sources. Annegret Fauser, *Musical Encounters at the 1889 Paris World's Fair* (2005) explores the exposition from a musicological perspective and is particularly insightful in its treatment of Parisians' reception of "exotic" music. Annette Blaugrund, *Paris 1889 American Artists at the Universal Exposition* (1989), is an illustrated catalogue of a traveling exhibition of 90 of the 336 paintings that Americans exhibited at the exposition, with insightful commentary about the artists and their work. Deborah L. Silverman, *Art Nouveau in Fin-de-Siècle France* (1989) and Mauricio Tenorio-Trillo, *Mexico at the World's Fairs: Crafting a Modern Nation* (1996) each have large sections devoted to the 1889 exposition.

Among the more important and informative articles on various aspects of the exposition are Deborah L. Silverman, "The 1889 Exhibition: The Crisis of Bourgeois Individualism," *Oppositions* 8, 1 (1977); Wolf Schön, "Der Triumph des Industriezeitalters: Paris 1889 und die Weltausstellungen des 19. Jahrhunderts," in *Das Fest: Eine Kulturgeschichte von Antike bis zur Gegenwart* (1988); John W. Stamper, "The Gallerie des Machines of the 1889 Paris World's Fair," *Technology and Culture* 30, 2 (1989): 330–53; Hélène Trocmé, "Les États-Unis et l'Exposition universelle de 1889," *Revue d'histoire moderne et contemporaine* 37 (April-June 1990): 283–96; Lois Marie Fink, "American Art at the 1889 Paris Exposition: The Paintings They Love to Hate," *American Art* 5, 4 (1991): 34–53; Laurence Aubain,

"La Russie à l'Exposition universelle de 1889," *Cahiers du monde russe* 37, 3 (1996), 349–67; Pauline Racquillet, "Les Pays d'Amérique du sud à l'Exposition universelle de 1889," *Bulletin de l'Institut Pierre Renouvin* 3 (Spring 1997): 9–24; Ingrid E. Fey, "Peddling the Pampas: Argentina at the Paris Universal Exposition of 1889," in *Latin American Popular Culture: An Introduction* (2000): 61–85; Lynn E. Palermo, "Identity Under Construction: Representing the Colonies at the Paris Exposition Universelle of 1889," in Sue Peabody and Tyler Stovall, eds., *The Color of Liberty: Histories of Race in France*, (2003): 285–301. For a somewhat different perspective on the exposition, see Carter Vaughn Findley's account of a Turkish writer's visit, "An Ottoman Occidentalist in Europe: Ahmed Midhat Meets Madame Gulnar, 1889," *American Historical Review* 103, 1 (1998): 15–49. A special issue of the journal *Le Mouvement social* 149 (October-December 1989) is devoted to the 1889 exposition and contains articles on electricity, diplomatic relations, social economy, the American pavilion, and colonial displays. Finally, no one interested in the exposition's most enduring legacy should neglect Roland Barthe's seminal 1964 essay "The Eiffel Tower," in *The Eiffel Tower and Other Mythologies* (1979), 3–17.

Dunedin 1889–1890

Conal McCarthy

New Zealand and South Seas Exhibition

The New Zealand and South Seas Exhibition was the third world's fair in New Zealand, and like the first one of 1865 was held in the city of Dunedin in the South Island. Held to commemorate the jubilee of the proclamation of British sovereignty over the colony of New Zealand in 1840, the fair was also intended to promote closer economic and political relations with the Australian colonies and the Pacific Islands. The fair was organized by a private company that received a subsidy from the government. The leading officials, R.E.N. Twopeny and Jules Joubert, who had had experience with fairs in Australia, were involved in an exhibition in Christchurch in 1882 that had suffered a substantial loss. This undertaking was more successful, however, with a modest profit and an attendance of more than 600,000 (equivalent to the population of New Zealand at that time).

After some controversy a large site was chosen on Harbour Board property, bounded by Crawford Street, Anderson's Bay Road, Cumberland Street, and Jervois Street. The ancillary buildings had a simple exterior construction of corrugated iron, while the art galleries were brick, and the main entrance was a more pretentious but undistinguished domed classical structure designed by local architect James Hislop. In addition to the New Zealand exhibits, there were entries from a handful of European countries, Great Britain, the Australian colonies, Japan, and several Pacific Islands, including Fiji, Samoa, the Solomons, and Hawaii. Aside from the typical commercial and industrial produce, much of which had been exhibited at the Melbourne Centennial Exhibition in 1888, there were courts devoted to natural history, government exhibits on minerals, education, and tourism, as well as a concert hall, an amusement zone with a switchback railway, and a garden and fernery providing a "truly New Zealand sylvan scene."

One novel feature of the science court was the "anthropometrical laboratory," operated by H.O. Forbes of the Canterbury Museum, modelled on the Health Exhibition in London of 1884, which tested and measured the "human faculties" of 10,000 visitors. Another court worthy of mention is the "Early history, Maori and South Seas court" that reflected the growing interest not only in ethnology, but also in *Pakeha* (European) explorers and pioneers.

A view of Dunedin with the buildings of the New Zealand and South Seas Exhibition, visible on the right (courtesy Alexander Turnbull Library Wellington, New Zealand V2-18833F).

This court was organized by a committee headed by Dr. T.M. Hocken, a noted bibliophile who wrote the introduction in the catalogue. The Maori court brought together comprehensive displays by leading collectors such as F.R. Chapman, John White, Gilbert Mair, Walter Buller, and Augustus Hamilton. These were the *Pakeha* men whose enthusiasm for things Maori led them to support various ethnological projects in later years, such as the founding of the Polynesian Society and its journal in 1892. There were an unprecedented range and quality of objects—weapons, implements, items of personal adornment, carving, weaving, and even large house structures. Buller included a *pataka* (food storehouse), and Hamilton, who later wrote an influential book on Maori art, exhibited the partially reconstructed interior of a Maori *wharenui* (meeting house). Increasingly, these objects were coming to be seen by *Pakeha* not just as curios or specimens, but as a form of art in their own right. Regardless of the fashion for Maori culture among Europeans, there is little evidence of a Maori presence at the exhibition either as exhibitors or as visitors, compared to the first Dunedin exhibition.

The Exhibition Art Gallery was a highlight of the fair, and was declared "the most important art display ever held in the colony of New Zealand." A total of 1,500 works were displayed in six galleries, comprising prints, watercolors, and oils by colonial, Australian, and British artists. Particularly popular were the etchings and engravings by European masters such as Mantegna, Durer, and Rembrandt from the collection of Bishop Monrad, a Danish settler and politician, left to the government in the 1860s. Another magnet was the loaned collection of selected British art arranged by Sir Francis Dillon Bell, the New Zealand Agent General in London, which included examples of the work of leading academic painters such as Sir Frederic Leighton. Four major works from this exhibition, including a large canvas of a market scene in Brittany by Stanhope

Forbes, were purchased by public subscription for the city of Dunedin. The report of the fine arts committee, which included notable painters such as W.M. Hodgkins, endorsed moves to establish a public art gallery in Dunedin, and one was eventually set up in part of the former exhibition buildings to house the works that had been purchased. Once again, as in 1865, a world's fair proved to be a considerable stimulus to building the infrastructure of the colonial art world.

Bibliography

Primary sources are not extensive but some documentary material from the exhibition can be found in local archives: the New Zealand Room at the Dunedin Public Library, the Otago Settlers' Museum, and the Hocken Library Collections, Dunedin. An exhibition scrapbook and Dr. T.M. Hocken's papers, journals, notebooks, and letters are held in the Hocken Collections. Contemporary accounts of the exhibition appear in the local newspaper, the *Otago Daily Times*. The official published reports are relatively complete, including: *New Zealand and South Seas Exhibition, Dunedin, 1889–90: Official Catalogue* (1889); D. Harris Hastings, ed., *Official Record of the New Zealand and South Seas Exhibition held at Dunedin, 1889–90* (1891). In the latter volume, see the interesting reports by exhibition committees, especially those written by W.M. Hodgkins about fine arts and T.M. Hocken on the "Early history, Maori and South Seas court."

For a concise summary of the exhibition, see N. Palethorpe, *Official History of the New Zealand Centennial Exhibition, Wellington, 1939–40* (1940). A useful history of the city with reference to the exhibition is K.C. McDonald, *City of Dunedin: A Century of Civic Enterprise* (1965). The best general history of New Zealand is the two volumes by James Belich: *Making Peoples: A History of the New Zealanders from Polynesian Settlement to the End of the Nineteenth Century* (1996); *Paradise Reforged: A History of the New Zealanders from the 1880s to the Year 2000* (2001), but a shorter, one-volume work is Tom Brooking, *The History of New Zealand* (2004). For a survey of the origins of the Otago Museum and the Dunedin Public Art Gallery in relation to the exhibition, see: Keith W. Thomson, *Art Galleries and Museums of New Zealand* (1981). For a comprehensive survey of New Zealand at world's fairs, see: Ewan Johnston, "Representing the Pacific at International Exhibitions 1851–1940" (unpub. Ph.D. diss., Auckland University, 1999). On the subject of art in New Zealand courts at world's fairs see Rebecca Rice, "Picturing Progress in Paradise: New Zealand on Display at International Exhibitions, 1873–1886" (unpub. M.A. thesis, Victoria University, 2003). For a recent interpretation of Maori displays at international exhibitions, see: Conal McCarthy, "Objects of Empire? Displaying Maori at International Exhibitions, 1873–1924," *Journal of New Zealand Literature: Special Issue* 23, 1 (2005): 52–70. For useful biographies of the people involved in the exhibition, consult the *Dictionary of New Zealand Biography* http://www.dnzb.govt.nz/.

Kingston 1891

Ronald J. Mahoney

Jamaica International Exhibition

The success of the Jamaica Court at the Colonial and Indian Exhibition held in London in 1886 encouraged A. C. Sinclair, superintendent of the government's Jamaican Printing Office, to campaign for an exhibition in Jamaica. In 1889, he persuaded the chairman of the Institute of Jamaica, William Fawcett, to approach Sir Henry Blake, the new governor of the island. The exhibition would demonstrate Jamaica's natural resources and products, encourage trade, and exhibit foreign machinery useful in developing the island's natural resources. The event could also attract winter tourists from the United States. Sir Henry enthusiastically supported the idea, and, to anticipate the World's Columbian Exposition scheduled to begin in 1892, he planned for the Jamaica fair to open in 1891. Prince George (later King George V), the son of the prince of Wales, was on duty with the West Indian squadron and agreed to open the exhibition. The £30, 000 needed to pay for the exhibition was fully funded from money raised on the island, and a professional exhibition manager, S. Lee Bapty, was brought from Edinburgh to supervise the event. A local architect, George Messiter, was hired to design the exhibition buildings.

The main building was built of wood and glass in the popular cruciform floor plan with a Moorish-styled exterior of minarets and a central dome. The building was painted and illuminated at night with electric lights and a searchlight. Originally the main building was to have been prefabricated in the United States and erected by Americans. But enough local craftsmen were eventually located on the island so that only the raw materials of lumber and iron were obtained in the United States. Native trees and plants were gathered from throughout the island and used extensively inside and outside the building, and exotic gardens were laid out. An illuminated cascade was planned but never built; however, a large fountain was constructed in the front of the building and illuminated with a searchlight mounted on one of the minarets. Behind the main building were located smaller annex buildings erected to accommodate any unplanned expansion, a machinery building to power the exhibition and exhibit machinery, a separate Canadian overflow building, a poorly lighted exhibition hall for theatrical and musical performances, a tiny fine arts gallery consisting of regionally collected artworks, a vivarium (small zoo), and an industrial village containing a model school, an apiary, a working dairy, and several self-supporting native families occupied in local cottage industries. Several small amusements were available for diversion.

The primary purpose of the exhibition was to encourage and develop trade between Jamaica and the United States, Canada, and Great Britain. Although 66 percent of Jamaican exports went to the United States and the island received 34 percent of its imports from Amer-

Although photographs of the Kingston 1891 exhibition are hard to find, the Jamaica post office depicted the main exposition building on a postage stamp issued in 1919 (editors' collection).

ica, the United States was not officially represented because of a diplomatic misunderstanding regarding the invitation. However, hastily gathered displays were sent by a group of New England businessmen attempting to take some advantage of the exhibition. Canada eagerly filled the void created by the lack of official U.S. participation. Although the Canadian products were considered inferior by U.S. standards, the Canadians did show that they were interested in Jamaican trade. Canada was by far the largest and most enthusiastic foreign supporter of the fair, although it was not able to develop the hoped-for trade with the island. Sixteen foreign nations, as well as the British Caribbean colonies, exhibited, but only Canada, Great Britain, Barbados, and St. Vincent offered other than minor displays. A special exhibition postal cancel was available from January 27 to May 16 at the branch post office located in the main building. (In 1919, a commemorative ½ pence postage stamp was issued depicting the exhibition building in 1891.)

The 23-acre exhibition was held on the grounds of "Quebec Lodge" in northern Kingston from January 27 to May 2. Typical of the times, the fair was closed on Sundays. Opening day was full of parades and pomp to impress and honor the prince royal. Nearly 8,000 people visited the fair on that day. By the close of the exhibition, 302,831 visitors had been admitted (the island population was only

650,000). The final receipts showed a £4,500 loss and a bleak trade forecast. The recently enacted McKinley tariff, an island depression the following year, and the disastrously run Jamaican hotels ruined any hope for a favorable economic reward from the exhibition.

One purpose of the fair was to bring together all the people of the island in their support of the endeavor. However, the response expected from the governor's call throughout the island for a vigorous promotion of the island's local crafts was dampened by fear created among the rural population. This fear was based on rumors circulated by obeahmen (local sorcerers) and village merchants that slavery was to be reintroduced into the island or that the natives would be taxed heavily for bringing their products to Kingston. The governor was never able to dispel these rumors fully, and the expected benefits to Jamaica and its people from exposure to this exhibition were never realized.

Bibliography

There are almost no publications or other records relating to the international exhibition available in the United States. The National Library of Jamaica has significant runs of Jamaican newspapers of the period on microfilm. Of these newspapers, *Gall's Newsletter* and the *Daily Gleaner* seem to be the most entertaining and informative. The *Official Catalogue* (1891), compiled by S. Lee Bapty, apparently was to have been revised, but only the first printing is recorded. The *Jamaica Exhibition Bulletin* was published at least until a few months before the exhibition opened. There are photocopies of three issues (December 1889 to June 1890) in the Larson Collection, which also holds *Report of the Honorary Commissioner (Mr. Adam Brown) representing Canada at the Jamaica Exhibition, Held at Kingston, Jamaica, 1891* (1891), consisting of sixty-eight pages and two reproduced photographs. There are no references to any other official government reports.

The Larson Collection also has photocopies of the *Official List of Awards* (1891), *Regulations* (1891) [with classification system], and the *Handbook of Jamaica, 1890–1891* (1891), which contains preexhibition information. The London newspapers carried little on the fair, but the New York *Times* found it newsworthy. The only two modern studies of the exhibition are Karen Booth, "When Jamaica Welcomed the World: The Great Exhibition of 1891," *Jamaica Journal* 18, 3 (1985): 39–51, which is well written, illustrated, and contains a twenty-three-item bibliography, and Frank Fonda Taylor, "The Resurrection of Jamaica: The International Exhibition of 1891," *Review/Revista Interamericana* 14, 1–4 (1984): 167–96.

Madrid 1892

David R. Watters

Exposición Histórico–Americana

Efforts by Spain in 1892 to commemorate the fourth centenary of the discovery of America were overshadowed by the magnitude of the World's Columbian Exposition held the following year in Chicago. Spain's two chief events— the *Exposición Histórico-Americana* and *Exposición Histórico-Europea*— were adversely affected by problems of planning and implementation that delayed their opening, among other consequences. These special-themed expositions commemorated Columbus's discovery within its historical contexts, particularly emphasizing the Hispanic nations in Latin America that came into being as a consequence of the voyages and the Iberian peninsula whence those voyages departed. While these expositions were international in the sense that nations from Europe and the Americas participated, their emphasis on history set them apart from many other late nineteenth-century international expositions, where progress in industry and technology was the focus. Spain had hosted its first international exposition devoted to commerce and industry, the *Exposición Universal de Barcelona* in 1888, only four years earlier.

The Spanish government, in pursuance of a Royal Decree of January 9, 1891 proposed a series of international celebrations, the management of which was entrusted to the Prime Minister, His Excellency Don Antonio Cánovas del Castillo, serving as President of the *Junta Directiva del Centenario*. Lead-time was short, only slightly more than eighteen months before the commemoration was to begin, and Cánovas del Castillo's report to the Queen Regent, María Cristina, discloses the reason. The initial decrees regarding the fourth centenary commemoration had been proclaimed on February 28, 1888, but almost three years had passed with little having been accomplished by the Commission established under the previous Ministry. Cánovas del Castillo's leadership brought about dramatic changes, including a commitment to develop two complementary historical expositions centered respectively on the Americas and Europe, among other events. Both expositions were held in a newly constructed facility *El Palacio de la Biblioteca y Museos Nacionales*, a building that still houses the *Museo Arqueológico Nacional*.

Native cultures in the Americas, the focus of the Historic-American Exposition, were to be presented from a decidedly European perspective, using a three-fold system of classification covering pre–Columbian, Columbian, and post–Columbian periods. Spain invited nations throughout the Americas to join in its *Exposición Histórico-Americana*, and the response was most favorable from former Spanish colonies in the Caribbean, Mexico, and Central and South America. The Dominican Republic, Cuba (then still a colony), Mexico, Guatemala, Nicaragua, Costa Rica, Colombia, Ecuador, Peru, Bolivia, Uruguay, and Argentina accepted Spain's invitation. The United States of America was the only English-speaking Western Hemisphere country to participate, and its decision to do so clearly was associated with the upcoming exposition in Chicago. Besides Spain and Portugal, a number of European nations, most of which had possessed colonies in the Western Hemisphere,

contributed materials to the *Exposición*, including Sweden and Norway (then united), Denmark (still in possession of its Virgin Islands), and Germany. Conspicuously absent were Britain, France, and the Netherlands, the principal remaining European colonial powers in the Americas, and the independent nations of Canada and Brazil.

The exhibits of the Historic-American Exposition occupied the perimeter of the ground floor of the *Palacio*, with the main entrance being from the *Paseo de Recoletos*. Visitors first encountered the exhibits of the European nations on the left, followed by those of Colombia, Mexico, the United States, and then the rest of the Latin American nations, ending with Costa Rica. Total exhibit area was approximately 5,000 square meters (c. 53,000 square feet). The United States and Mexico had the largest exhibit spaces, occupying six and four rooms respectively, followed by Spain, Portugal, and Costa Rica with two rooms each, and with the remaining nations each having a single room or sharing one. Quality of exhibits varied due in part to the brief lead-time, but also dependent on the time and effort expended by each nation, the kinds of objects selected to represent the three time periods, and the differing sources drawn upon to obtain items, with contributors ranging from private individuals to public institutions to government agencies. No truly systematic or uniform exhibit scheme came into being because the responsibility for arranging materials displayed within in its own space rested ultimately with each nation, notwithstanding Spain's guidelines for classification that organized 12 groupings within the three time periods. Estimates of the number of objects on display ranged from 200,000 to 250,000.

Information about layout and content of exhibits in the *Exposición Histórico-Americana* comes mostly from government reports and articles in scholarly publications of the time, with the exhibits mounted by Costa Rica, Mexico, the United States, and Colombia being highly acclaimed. Documentation about collections and the individuals and institutions contributing them is surprisingly plentiful, in view of the overall poor state of knowledge about this exposition. Spain prepared a fourteen-volume *Catálogo especial* in which were listed the objects and exhibitors for each nation.

In view of this exposition's intent to commemorate the discovery of the New World, it is interesting to see that Norway displayed a one-quarter sized scale model of a Viking ship, depicting the kind of vessel that had crossed the North Atlantic Ocean to the Americas centuries before Columbus's voyage. The identities of antiquarians loaning objects from their private collections, scholarly associations and public institutions contributing artifacts, persons responsible for mounting exhibitions in Madrid, and official representatives and delegates to the *Exposición* can be gleaned from separate catalogs prepared by some countries and even individuals. Scholarly writings in some documents augmented the exhibits with commentaries on historical matters, including exploration and colonization, indigenous populations, and antiquarianism, archaeology, and anthropology.

Participating nations expressed a common concern about the brief time available to prepare exhibits after having accepted Spain's tardy invitation. Nations such as Costa Rica, Mexico, and the United States, since they had mounted historical exhibits at earlier international expositions and already were planning displays for the World's Columbian Exposition in Chicago, were more readily able to respond. Some other exhibits revealed their hasty preparation. The Historic-American Exposition opened to the public on October 30, delayed some six weeks from the scheduled date of September 12, and it remained open a month longer than originally proposed, closing January 31, 1893. Their Majesties the Queen Regent of Spain and the King and Queen of Portugal presided at the formal inauguration on November 11, thus reinforcing the exposition's scope as being the whole Iberian peninsula.

Yet, European countries for the most part ignored the exposition, regarding it as little more than a nationalistic celebration by an aged Spanish empire. Other problems existed. Issues arose between the national government and city of Madrid. Many of the provinces of Spain were not enthusiastic. France and Spain were experiencing a period of economic confrontation. Some countries opted to reinstall exhibits from Madrid in Chicago the next year, but others chose to forsake the *Exposición Histórico-Americana* in favor of the far larger World's Columbian Exposition.

Spain acquired archaeological and ethnographic collections from the Western Hemisphere, contributed by some countries participating in the Historic-American Exposition. These collections remained in the *Museo Nacional* at the *Palacio* until they were transferred to a separate museum, the *Museo de América*, in the twentieth century. The *Museo Arqueológico Nacional* still resides in the original facility, but its collections now are Old World in scope.

Spain hosted other commemorative events for the fourth centenary. The second special-themed exposition, the *Exposición Histórico-Europea*, located on the upper floor of the *Palacio*, dealt largely with Spanish civilization during the period of Columbus's voyages and Spain's exploration and colonization in the next two centuries, drawing upon objects from museums, religious establishments, royal collections, and private holdings. Relics attributed to Columbus were displayed alongside many thousands of ecclesiastical and secular items including tapestries and other textiles, arms and armor, manuscripts and printed books, ecclesiastical art, plate and chalices, and pottery and glass objects. Spanish sources refer to the *Exposición Histórico-Americana* and *Exposición Histórico-Europea*, when considered together, as the *Conmemoración del Cuarto Centenario*, whereas they are labeled in English the Columbian Historical Exposition (e.g., the Smithsonian Institution records). Spain also hosted the *Congreso Internacional de Americanistas* in Huelva, at which the sessions dealt mainly with Columbus, the origin of the name America, and Spanish voyages of exploration, and *Congreso Internacional Geográfico Hispano-Portugués-Americano* in Madrid, among other celebratory events.

The *Exposición Histórico-Americana* is poorly known and has been of very little interest to present-day scholars. It was not well attended, was ignored by many European nations, appears to have been fairly quickly disregarded if not actually forgotten, and was soon eclipsed by the World's Columbian Exposition. Yet, Spain's ability to attract an array of archaeological and ethnographic exhibits, especially from its Latin American "off-spring" nations, is noteworthy. The geographic coverage of the participating nations facilitated the comparison of artifacts from throughout the

Western Hemisphere. It is a very early example of a single venue at which scholars were able to conduct systematic, comparative archaeological studies. It also offered the casual visitor the opportunity to observe objects, ranging from the beautiful and highly crafted to the common and mundane, which represented many different Native American cultures from the New World. The *Exposición* contained aspects of antiquarianism as well as elements of the emerging discipline of anthropology, and thus well illustrates the scholarly transition occurring in the late nineteenth-century. The *Exposición Histórico-Americana*'s explicit historical orientation and its Iberian focus distinguished it from most other international expositions of that period at which industry, technology, and progress were the overriding themes. Almost forty years later, in 1929–1930, Spain would reiterate the Iberian and Hispanic American themes at its *Exposición Ibero-Americana* in Seville, but would segregate the industry and commerce themes at its concurrent *Exposición Internacional de Barcelona*.

Bibliography

Spanish archives of the *Exposición Histórico-Americana* are held in the *Archivo General de la Administración* in Madrid (IDD (09) 002 008 and IDD (10) 003 004). The Smithsonian Institution, lead organizer of participating American institutions, archives its Columbian Historical Exposition records in Record Unit 70, Series 9. The Smithsonian Institution did a great service when it compiled a listing of its publications regarding the Madrid exposition in *The Books of the Fairs: Materials about World's Fairs, 1834–1916, in the Smithsonian Institution Libraries* (see publications #807 through #822 on pages 144–145) and made these rare materials available on microfilm to researchers. The especially valuable documents of a general nature are publications #810 (*Catálogo de los objetos que presenta la nación Española a la Exposición Histórico-Americana de Madrid*), #811 (*Catálogo especial* containing lists of artifacts exhibited by the participating nations), and #821 (*Report of the United States Commission to the Columbian Historical Exposition at Madrid*, 1895), containing informative chapters by Commissioner Admiral Stephen B. Luce and noted anthropologists Daniel G. Brinton, Thomas Wilson, J. Walter Fewkes, Zelia Nuttall, Walter Hough, and Stewart Culin, among other scholars). The plan of the *Palacio* and adjacent landscape is detailed in document #820, *Cuarto Centenario del Descubrimiento de América, Plano de la Exposición Histórico-Americana de Madrid, 1892*. Discussions of layout and content of exhibits appear in Walter Hough's 1893 article "The Columbian Historical Exposition in Madrid," *American Anthropologist* (old series), volume 6:271–277 (#813), and Charles Hercules Read's *Report on the Historical Exhibition at Madrid on the occasion of the fourth centenary of Columbus in 1892*, prepared for the British Museum in 1893, which also contains a discussion of the *Exposición Histórico-Europea* (#822). Costa Rica's materials are especially well documented in two publications, *Catálogo de las Antigüedades de Costa Rica ...* (#809) and *Etnología Centro-Americana ...* by Manuel M. de Peralta and Anastasio Alfaro (#817), and a chapter in the *Catálogo especial*.

Recent publications about the *Exposición Histórico-Americana* are very scarce. Worth checking are David R. Watters and Oscar Fonseca Zamora's 2005 article "World's Fairs and Latin American Archaeology: Costa Rica at the 1892 Madrid Exposition" in the *Bulletin of the History of Archaeology* 15(1):4–11; Erika Gólcher's 1991 article "Costa Rica en un mundo de imperios: las exposiciones internacionales" in *Revista del Colegio de Licenciados y Profesores en Letras, Filosofía, Ciencias y Artes* 1, 3 : 23–30; Juan Rafael Quesada Camacho's 1993 book *América latina: memoria e identidad, 1492–1992*, Editorial Respuesta, San José, Costa Rica (see especially pages 43–52 and 67–72 for a discussion of other commemorative events); and Staffan Brunius's 1992 article "Did Swedish Americanists do anything special for the Columbus Year of 1892?," in *SAMS Årsskrift för 1991*: 67–72 . Salvador Bernabeu Albert's excellent book, *1892: el IV centenario del descubrimiento de América en España: coyuntura y conmemoraciones* (1987), places this exposition within the context of other celebratory events in Spain revolving around the fourth centennial, and it has a good bibliography of primarily Spanish sources. Spain's Ministry of Culture has produced volumes on the *Museo Arqueológico Nacional* (situated in the *Palacio* that originally housed the 1892 exposition) and *Museo de América* in which are discussed the collections acquired from various expositions that subsequently were transferred among Madrid museums. Cruz Martínez de la Torre and Paz Cabello Carro discuss similar topics in their volume *Museo de América, Madrid* (1997), produced by Ibercaja in its *Colección monumentos y museos* series.

Chicago 1893

R. Reid Badger

World's Columbian Exposition

The World's Columbian Exposition, also known as the Chicago World's Fair of 1893 and — in culturally more revealing terms — the "White City," was the most elaborate and extensive public exhibition produced by the United States in the nineteenth century. It was also, unquestionably, one of the greatest world's fairs of all time.

It is probably impossible to determine the individual responsible for first publicly proposing that the United States sponsor a world's fair to celebrate the four hundredth anniversary of Columbus's first voyage to the New World, but the success of the Philadelphia Centennial Exhibition in 1876 naturally encouraged suggestions that a similar event be considered as part of any festivities that might honor Columbus's achievement. In 1882, the Baltimore *Sun* endorsed such a plan, and that same year the Chicago *Times* carried a letter arguing not only that an international exposition would be an appropriate way to commemorate the European "discovery" of the Western world but also that the city of Chicago — because of its central location, physical capacity, and remarkable growth — was the most appropriate site. The idea gained national interest over the next three years as local business and civic groups in various cities — New York, Philadelphia, St. Louis, Cincinnati, and Washington, D.C., as well as Chicago — began promoting their respective cities.

Following glowing descriptions of the third universal exposition being planned for Paris in 1889, however, it became clear that in the United States, only New York, and perhaps Chicago, possessed the private financial and physical resources required even to approach, much less surpass, the extensiveness and artis-

tic elegance of the French standard. The subsequent battle that was fought out in the newspaper editorials of the established eastern urban giant and its younger western challenger was one of the most vitriolic in American history, but it did serve to stimulate national interest in a prospective fair and to spur organizational efforts in both cities. In the fall of 1889 in Chicago, a corporation entitled the World's Columbian Exposition of 1892 was established with members appointed by the mayor from its professional and business leaders and chartered with an initial capital of $5 million. New York had established a similar group somewhat earlier.

In December, as the U.S. Congress assembled to begin its regular session, the scene of the debate among the competing cities shifted to Washington, D. C. Numerous world's fair bills were immediately introduced, and special committees of each legislative branch were appointed to begin consideration in early 1890. Although there was now general agreement as to the desirability of holding a world's fair in the United States in 1892, the question of the site was very much unsettled, and hearings continued until February 24, when the House committee announced that it had endured all the arguments it could stand and that, due to the intensity of the debate, a roll call of the entire body would settle the issue. Finally, after eight ballots, Chicago, the most vocal representative of the newer western states, received a majority. The Senate soon followed suit. Even so, the bill that officially authorized the exposition and designated Chicago as the city was delayed while the Chicago corporation convinced the Congress that its stock subscriptions were valid (New York, in a last-ditch effort, offered to underwrite the fair by $10 million — twice what the Chicago corporation had originally guaranteed — and the Chicagoans were forced to match that amount). Eventually, on April 28, 1890, President Benjamin Harrison signed the bill authorizing an international exposition to take place in Chicago during the spring and summer of 1893, rather than 1892, in order to provide an additional year for preparation.

The provisions of the world's fair bill of 1890 made it clear that doubts existed about the ability and appropriateness of Chicago to produce a major international world's fair that would be both representative and a credit to the entire United States. In particular, the bill established a national commission to oversee and approve all significant decisions relating to the choice of physical site in Chicago, design of the grounds, construction of the exhibit buildings, and conduct of the exposition. Thus two different organizations — the local Chicago Corporation and the National Commission — were charged with the responsibility for deciding what kind of fair it was to be and for putting those decisions into effect. This duplication of authority considerably complicated the process of producing the fair. The additional problem of raising another $5 million by the Chicago Corporation was eventually solved by enlisting the aid of both the state of Illinois and the city of Chicago. The most immediate and practical problem facing the world's fair officials in the summer of 1890, however, was to determine the specific physical site for the fair.

During the spring and summer, while the Chicago Corporation and the National Commission were being organized and the financial backing was being confirmed, the initial steps were being taken toward deciding upon an appropriate location. At least some of the space needed could be obtained from the system of city parks, which had been established following the great Chicago fire of 1871, several of which remained undeveloped. The lakefront area was also attractive because of its scenic setting beside Lake Michigan. The Chicago Corporation brought in Frederick Law Olmsted, who had been involved in planning the original park system, to advise it and, although Olmsted favored the use of the lakefront, difficulties in obtaining rights to that property coupled with the unwillingness of the city's park board to allow the fair to be built on previously improved parkland eventually led to the decision to make Jackson Park, an unimproved 600-acre site alongside the lake but 8 miles south of the city's center, the principal location of the fair.

On November 25, 1890, the National Commission certified that the Chicago Corporation had met the requirements of the congressional act, and a general plan for the exposition was adopted. The basic features of the November plan for Jackson Park were primarily the work of four individuals: Daniel H. Burnham and John W. Root (of the Chicago architectural firm of Burnham and Root), and Frederick Law Olmsted and Henry S. Codman (of Olmsted's Boston company). The initial plan envisioned taking advantage of the natural characteristics of the site by utilizing water as a major element in each of the two principal aspects of the physical design. The first of these, probably a result of Olmsted's influence, was a large lagoon surrounding a wooded island. The second, undoubtedly inspired by the recent French exposition, called for a grand architectural Court of Honor surrounding a formal basin, with a system of interconnecting canals and lagoons. All of the major exhibition buildings constructed around the large lagoon and the basin were to be provided with water as well as land frontage. Also in November, the National Commission approved a classification system for the major departments (agriculture, horticulture, livestock, mines and metallurgy, fisheries, manufactures, machinery, transportation, electricity, fine arts, liberal arts, ethnology, and miscellaneous exhibits) under which the exhibits would be organized and arranged. This system, which dictated to a large degree the major buildings to be constructed on the fairgrounds, was the work primarily of George Browne Goode, an assistant secretary of the Smithsonian Institution in Washington, D.C., who was brought in as an adviser to the National Commission.

The responsibility for recommending the architects and the architectural style for the major buildings logically fell to the consulting architects, Burnham and Root. Given the time pressures, and in the interest of national harmony, Burnham recommended five leading national firms (Richard Morris Hunt, McKim, Mead and White, and George Post of New York, Van Brunt and Howe of Kansas City, and Peabody and Stearns of Boston) to design the

This photograph of the interior of the Manufactures Building gives some idea of the clutter and density of the various exhibits (editors' collection).

buildings in the Court of Honor and five Chicago firms (Adler and Sullivan, S.S. Beman, Burling and Whitehouse, Jenney and Mundie, and Henry Ives Cobb) to design the others. Burnham and Root chose not to design any of the buildings themselves, but in their capacity as consulting architects, elected to supervise and coordinate the overall plan. The recommendation was approved in January 1891. John Root, the creative designer of the firm, was expected to play an important role in determining the overall architectural style, but during the first gathering of the architects in Chicago in January, he was suddenly struck down with pneumonia, and his influence on the fair was lost. Whether Root's presence could have changed the eventual outcome remains a matter of conjecture, but it true that following his death, formal, symmetrical, and monumental stylistic values—those expressing authority and order—gained prominence, especially in the central Court of Honor where a uniform neoclassical style and color (white, thus the "White City") were agreed upon. It is also true that with the loss of his partner, a greater amount of direct responsibility and authority for constructing the fair was concentrated in the hands of Daniel Burnham, who was appointed Chief of Construction. Burnham selected Charles B. Atwood, an academically-trained New Yorker, to replace Root as designer in charge, and it was in this capacity that Atwood came to have a major influence on the overall architecture of the exposition, designing the formal peristyle group that closed off the lake end of the Court of Honor, the Art Building (320'×500'—now the Museum of Science and Industry and the sole surviving structure from the fair), plus dozens of lesser buildings. Final assignments for designing the

other major buildings were as follows: Hunt—
Administration (262'×262'—intended as the
formal entrance point to the fair); Peabody and
Stearns—Machinery Hall (492'×846'); Post—
Manufactures and Liberal Arts (787'×1687'—
the largest enclosed building ever constructed);
Van Brunt and Howe—Electricity (345'×690');
Beman—Mines and Mining (350'×700'); Adler
and Sullivan—Transportation (256'×960');
Cobb—Fisheries (165'×335'); Jenney and
Mundie—Horticulture (250'×998'); McKim,
Mead and White—Agriculture (500'×800').
Due largely to the influence of Augustus Saint-
Gaudens, America's leading sculptor who had
been brought in as an advisor, and Frank Millet, Burnham's director of color, many of the
best-known artists and sculptors in the United
States (Phillip Martiny, Lorado Taft, Mary Cas-
satt, Gari Melchers, Kenyon Cox, Elihu Vedder,
and Karl Bitter among them) were enlisted to
produce the finishing decorative details. Extensive use of a novel plasterlike substance, called
"staff" and first introduced at the French exposition in 1889 (thus "plaster of paris"), permitted the artists an "architectural spree." Daniel
Chester French (perhaps best known for his
statue of the seated Lincoln in the Memorial at
Washington, D.C.) was commissioned to create the statue of the Republic for one end of the
Grand Basin, and Frederick MacMonnies was
chosen to provide the Columbian Fountain to
balance it at the other. A greater number of
American artists and architects were drawn
into the creation of the World's Columbian
Exposition than had ever been brought together
to work on a single project before, and perhaps
since. Aided by the most extensive use of electric lighting ever attempted, the imposing and
elaborate visual impression of the formal exposition buildings, grounds, and waterways in the
Court of Honor and the Lagoon was undoubtedly the greatest exhibit of the Chicago world's
fair.

Financial problems and construction
difficulties plagued fair officials throughout the
period prior to opening in May 1893, and it was
only through great perseverance and an additional $2.5 million appropriation from the fed-
eral government (in the form of souvenir
coins) that the exposition was ready to receive
the public at all. One of the major problems,
recognized early on, was that Chicago, unlike
New York or Philadelphia or Paris, was only

vaguely known by most Americans living in the
east and hardly at all by citizens of other countries. If the fair was to attract the numbers of
visitors and exhibitors required to rival the
recent exposition in Paris or to have an expectation of financial success, serious effort would
need to be expended to circulate information
and awaken interest. In December 1890, the
Department of Publicity and Promotion was
established under the leadership of Moses P.
Handy, a successful eastern newspaperman
who had a modern appreciation of the importance of the press in molding public opinion.
Handy immediately organized a staff of writers and translators to produce a weekly newsletter and to provide pictures and articles about
the fair for a mailing list that grew to some
50,000 foreign and domestic organizations,
newspapers, and magazines. There had been
publicity bureaus at earlier world's fairs, but
the extensiveness and efficiency of the Promotion Department of the Columbian Exposition
was something quite new. R.E.A. Dorr, Handy's
chief assistant, estimated that one-third of all
that was printed about the fair by the newspapers, at home and abroad, was written by the
department itself.

There was one group, however, that
needed little convincing to become excited
about the prospect of a world's fair in Chicago.
Long before the exposition was formally
announced in December 1890, the Chicago
Corporation had begun receiving scores of
requests from amusement vendors, restaurateurs, circus acts, musical troupes, and specu-
lators of all sorts for space on the grounds. Fair
officials had expected from the beginning to
allow for an amusement and concessionary side
to the exposition; recent experience had shown
their value in drawing crowds and providing
revenue. But as the plan for the exposition
developed—with its formal emphasis—what
to do with the show business element became
a real question. The solution was to locate the
amusement features along the narrow strip of
land called the Midway Plaisance that connected Jackson and Washington parks. Under
the supervision of a young entrepreneur, Sol
Bloom, who replaced the less commercial-
minded Harvard ethnologist F. W. Putnam, the
midway at Chicago became one of the most
successful and famous amusement areas of any
of the world's fairs, and it established a pattern

The ferris wheel, first introduced at the Columbian Exposition, became the most prominent attraction at many later world's fairs as well as state and county fairs (from *Official Views of the World's Columbian Exposition*, 1893).

for mass entertainment that soon found application in such independent parks as Coney Island.

Within the midway were to be found such exotic and popular attractions as German beer halls, Turkish bazaars, Algerian jugglers, Dahomean drummers, Egyptian belly dancers, the World's Congress of Beauty ("40 Ladies from 40 Nations"), balloon rides, wild animal shows, and ostrich omelets. The great composer Antonin Dvorak, who conducted a gala concert on "Bohemian Day," and who spent nearly two weeks at the fair, could be found in the evenings at the Old Vienna Tavern on the Midway where he enjoyed real imported Pilsner beer. Here, also, was to be found George Ferris's giant mechanical marvel, the ferris wheel, which took as many as 2,000 people at a time 264 feet in the air. The Barnumesque

eclecticism and "exuberant chaos" of the midway provided visitors with an alternative to the beaux-arts neoclassicism of the Court of Honor, but it also offered a relief from the almost overwhelming complexity of the 65,000 exhibits of human progress displayed in the major exhibition halls. There were displays of book publishers, architectural firms, schools and colleges, chemical and pharmaceutical products, paints, dyes, typewriters, paper, agricultural implements, furniture, ceramics, metal art work, glass, railroad cars, jewelry, clothing, toys, leather goods, hardware, printing presses, refrigerators, the 46-foot long Krupp cannon, the "largest gold nugget in existence," a 22,000 pound block of Canadian cheese, and a 1,500 pound chocolate Venus de Milo. In the Fine Arts Building the seventy-four galleries of sculpture and paintings (some 9,000) from

Jackson Park, Chicago.   Field Columbian Museum.
Largest South Side Park, area 540 acres.

The Fine Arts Building at the Columbian exposition was built as a permanent structure and later became the Field Columbian Museum, and still later the Museum of Science and Industry, a popular attraction in Chicago today (editors' collection).

Europe and the United States made it nearly impossible to locate any particular work, in spite of the division into nationalities and the extensive cataloging. Given this situation, the small collection of French impressionists was obscured by the much larger number of traditional romantic allegories. The diversity and extensiveness of the exhibits in Machinery Hall and in the Electricity Building, however, did announce in their aggregate that the United States had entered a new technological age. Add to this the exhibits provided by eighty-six foreign nations, colonies, and principalities (including those housed in the separate buildings that nineteen foreign governments erected), and it is not difficult to understand why many visitors felt overwhelmed.

In addition to the main exhibition halls and those of foreign countries, some thirty buildings were erected by federal, state, and territory governments (the United States and the state of Illinois were given the better sites around the lagoon), and nineteen foreign nations erected their own structures. One building that drew special attention during the course of the fair was the Women's Building (199'×388'),

designed by Sophia G. Hayden of Boston. Indeed, due especially to the efforts of Susan B. Anthony, women played a more visible and active role in the Columbian Exposition than in any previous world's fair. Not only was there the Women's Building, housing exhibits demonstrating women's accomplishments in education, the arts, science, and industry, and a separate Women's Department, but also a 115-member national commission (labeled the "Board of Lady Managers") was established. "More important than the discovery of Columbus," Bertha Honoré Palmer, president of the board, told her audience of over 100,000 at the dedication ceremonies in October 1892, "is the fact that the General Government has just discovered woman."

Participation of women in the Columbian Exposition was especially prominent in the World's Congress Auxiliary; an organization presided over by Charles C. Bonney, which sought to provide a comprehensive series of intellectual conferences to be held concurrently with the fair's demonstration of material progress. The auxiliary, whose motto was "Not Matter, But Mind: Not Things, But Men," was

By 1893 individual countries frequently constructed their own buildings at fairs. Shown here is the German Building at the World's Columbian Exposition (editors' collection).

eventually organized into some twenty departments, which sponsored an unprecedented series of 1,283 sessions on such subjects as the public press, medicine and surgery, temperance, moral and social reform, commerce and finance, music, literature, education, and labor, and which drew an extraordinary number of prominent national and international leaders to Chicago during the course of the exposition. John Dewey, Woodrow Wilson, William Jennings Bryan, Henry George, Hamlin Garland, George W. Cable, Charles Dudley Warner, Samuel Gompers, Josiah Royce, Charles Francis Adams, James McCosh, Seth Low, John Fiske, and Lester Ward were among the American luminaries who delivered addresses during the summer of 1893. One of the most significant presentations occurred in the Congress of Historians (presided over by Henry Adams) where Frederick Jackson Turner pre-

sented his paper "The Significance of the Frontier in American History," which changed the course of American historiography.

Overall, the most extensive, and most internationally representative, of the World's Congresses were the World's Congress of Representative Women, which began May 15, and the World's Parliament of Religions, which convened during the last month of the exposition. May Wright Sewell, president of the National Council of Women of the United States, was chosen as chair of the women's congress, and an advisory council of more than 500 women representing twenty-seven countries was selected to organize the eighty-one meetings held at the Art Institute downtown and at the Women's Building on the grounds. Some 330 women (including Jane Addams, Frances Willard, Elizabeth Cady Stanton, Lucy Stone, and Susan B. Anthony) addressed the congress, whose total attendance exceeded 150,000. The World's Parliament of Religions, headed by John Henry Barrows of Chicago's First Presbyterian Church, began its even more notable conference on September 10. From then until the last session on September 17, almost every conceivable theme of a religious nature was discussed, and almost every conceivable sect or persuasion was given an opportunity to be heard. As historian David Burg has written, it was "the longest, most ambitious, most visited, most admired of the many congresses; and it evoked the most extensive comments in books, newspapers, and magazines." The published speeches and reviews from the congress alone required four separate volumes and thousands of pages.

Special admission prices for children promoted the educational aspects of world's fairs and encouraged family visits as well (editors' collection).

When the World's Columbian Exposition of 1893 closed on October 30, over 21.5 million paid admissions had been registered. Even more remarkable was the fact that the Chicago Corporation was able to realize a small surplus with which to repay its private investors—and this was accomplished during a year that witnessed one of the most crippling depressions of the century. But the tangible results, financial or otherwise, were insignificant compared to the value of the fair as a great cultural event. To many Americans at that time, the fair was considered a convincing demonstration of the coming of age of the United States as a world power, the cultural as well as material equal of any of the great imperial powers of the Old World. Writers in search of answers to the confusing multiplicity and cutthroat competition of the modern age, like Henry Adams and William Dean Howells, believed they sensed in the White City the first expression of unity and utopian cooperation. For Chicagoans, the fair became a landmark in the history of their city, changing former opinions of Chicago as "Porkopolis," and opening up a new era of civic commitment and cultural flowering in America's Midwest.

Chicago's White City also exerted a strong influence on American architecture—

classicism dominated American public building into the 1930s—and upon urban planning in what became known as the City Beautiful movement. Daniel Burnham played a leading role in the movement; designing unified city plans for Chicago, Washington, San Francisco, and Cleveland. The debate over the architectural style of the White City began with the opening of the exposition, but the most sweeping condemnation came much later, in 1922, from one of the fair's architects, Louis Sullivan. Sullivan, whose non-classical Transportation Building with its gilded "Golden Door" was not widely admired at the time, pronounced the White City an authoritarian, academic "virus," which "penetrated deep into the constitution of the American mind, effecting there lesions significant of dementia."

Several recent historians have agreed with Sullivan's basic assessment but have found the authoritarian disease manifest in the fair's centralized organization and operation, as well as in the architectural design. Others have emphasized the significance of the exposition as both providing a new model of democratic urban recreation (the midway) and as perpetuating, in its demeaning presentation (or exclusion) of various ethnic groups, including African Americans and Indians, Western imperialism, and "scientific" racism. Yet, it was at Chicago that Americans first heard the sound of a new music, ragtime, that was both African American and American and which would transform the emerging field of American popular music forever. Because the fair was as extensive as it was and attracted as much attention as it did, the World's Columbian Exposition of 1893 will likely continue to be seen as one of the most revealing events of that period which Henry Steele Commager once called the "watershed of American history."

Bibliography

Published material about the 1893 fair is voluminous. Newspapers and magazines in the United States especially covered the fair from the early planning stages to closing day, and literally hundreds of guidebooks, photograph albums, memorial and souvenir volumes were issued. Among the most informative are Rand McNally's *A Week at the Fair* (1893) and William E. Cameron, ed., *The World's Fair, Being a Pictorial History of the Columbian Exposition* (1893). The publicity department printed its own eight-page paper, the *Daily Columbian*, during the fair's operation, and a large number of exhibit catalogs, collections of speeches and papers from the World's Congresses, and official state documents were published at the time or shortly thereafter. The fair spawned hundreds of works of fiction (including children's literature), poetry, music (primarily marches), paintings, and an overwhelming number of professional and amateur photographs. Julie Brown, *Contesting Images: Photography and the World's Columbian Exposition* (1994), provides the most thorough analysis of the use of the camera at the fair. U.S. government participation is documented in National Archives holdings, which contain the final report of the president of the National Commission and the list of exhibit awards (Record Group 43), and the Smithsonian Institution Archives (Record Groups 70, 95, and 192). In Chicago, archival material may be found at the Art Institute, the Chicago Public Library, the Chicago Historical Society, and the University of Chicago Library. Several of the major participants in the fair also recorded their experiences. See, for example, Daniel H. Burnham and Francis D. Millet, *The World's Columbian Exposition: The Book of the Builders* (1894).

Contemporary histories of the fair include Huber Howe Bancroft, *The Book of the Fair* (1894); Rossiter Johnson, ed., *A History of the World's Columbian Exposition* (1898); and Ben C. Truman, ed., *History of the World's Fair* (1893). Julian Hawthorne, *Humors of the Fair* (1893), and Denton J. Snider, *World's Fair Studies* (1895) take a broader, somewhat more interpretative view. G.L. Dybwad and Joy Bliss, *Annotated Bibliography: World's Columbian Exposition, Chicago 1893*

(1993) and *Supplement* (1999) and David J. Bertuca, Donald K. Hartman, and Susan M. Neumeister, eds., *The World's Columbian Exposition: A Centennial Bibliographic Guide* (1996), heroically attempt to organize the published material.

David F. Burg, *Chicago's White City of 1893* (1976), and Reid Badger, *The Great American Fair: The World's Columbian Exposition and American Culture* (1979) place the exposition in a larger, primarily American, cultural context, as do Robert W. Rydell, John E. Findling, and Kimberly D. Pelle in *Fair America: World's Fairs in the United States* (2000). The fair also figures prominently in Alan Trachtenberg, *The Incorporation of America: Culture and Society in the Gilded Age* (1982), Robert W. Rydell, *All the World's a Fair: Visions of Empire at American International Expositions, 1876–1916* (1984), John E. Kasson, *Amusing the Million: Coney Island at the Turn of the Century* (1978), Neil Harris, *Cultural Excursions: Marketing Appetites and Cultural Tastes in Modern America* (1990), and James Gilbert, *Perfect Cities: Chicago's Utopias of 1893* (1991). Norman Bolotin and Christine Laing, *The World's Columbian Exposition: The Chicago World's Fair of 1893* (1992), John E. Findling, *Chicago's Great World's Fairs* (1994), and Neil Harris, De Wit Wim, James Gilbert and Robert W. Rydell, *Grand Illusions: Chicago's World's Fair of 1893* (1993) provide lively tours of the fair at its one hundred-year anniversary.

A somewhat more recent examination of the fair and its impact on Chicago and Chicagoans is Arnold Lewis, *An Early Encounter with Tomorrow: Europeans, Chicago's Loop, and the World's Columbian Exposition* (1997). Christopher Robert Reed, *"All the World Is Here": The Black Presence at White City* (2000), takes a look at the African American experience at the fair, as does Robert W. Rydell, "The World's Columbian Exposition: Racist Underpinnings of a Utopian Artifact," *Journal of American Culture* 1, 2 (Summer 1978): 253–75.

A number of books and articles published in recent years explore specific aspects of the World's Columbian Exposition. Julie K. Brown, *Contesting Images: Photography and the World's Columbian Exposition* (1994) explores the significance of official photographs taken at the fair, as does Peter Bacon Hales, *Constructing the Fair: Platinum Photographs by C.D. Arnold of the World's Columbian Exposition* (1993), which deals with a series of photographs taken as the fair buildings were under construction. Judith A. Adams, "The Form Emerges: The World's Columbian Exposition," in Judith A. Adams, ed., *The American Amusement Park Industry: A His-*

tory of Technology and Thrills (1991): 18–40, analyzes the influence of the Midway Plaisance on the development of the amusement park in the United States. Adams also published "The Promotion of New Technology through Fun and Spectacle: Electricity at the World's Columbian Exposition," *Journal of American Culture* 18, 2 (1995): 45–55. The architectural legacy of the fair is the subject of Andrea Oppenheimer Dean, "Revisiting the White City: The Lasting Influences of the 1893 Chicago World's Columbian Exposition," *Historic Preservation* 45, 2 (March/April 1993): 42–49, 97–98. The important international religious conference at the exposition is the subject of Richard Hughes Seager, *The World's Parliament of Religions" The East/West Encounter, Chicago, 1893* (1995) and in Eric Ziolkowski, "Heavenly Visions and Worldly Intentions: Chicago's Columbian Exposition and World's Parliament of Religions

(1893)," *Journal of American Culture* 13, 4 (Winter 1990): 9–15. Finally, the colorful postcards sold as souvenirs at the fair are examined in Gordon Bleuler and Jim Doolin, "World's Columbian Exposition, 1893: Official and Unofficial Postal Cards," *American Philatelist* 94, 8 (August 1980): 713–26.

Expo: Magic of the White City, a documentary film (2003) produced and directed by Mark Bussler, and especially Erik Larson's national best seller, *The Devil in the White City: Murder, Magic, and Madness at the Fair that Changed America* (2003), have rekindled interest in the fair. Stanley Appelbaum, *The Chicago World's Fair of 1893: A Photographic Record* (1980) offers a wonderful selection of photographs from the collections of Columbia University and the Chicago Historical Society.

Antwerp 1894

Matthew G. Stanard

Exposition Universelle d'Anvers / Wereldtentoonstelling

The 1894 fair was directed by a group largely similar to the one that organized the 1885 exposition, that is to say, prominent industrialists, merchants, and other "men of means" from Antwerp. Between 1885 and 1894, this group had kept momentum for the promotion of the city by means of the Maatschappij van het Paleis voor Nijverheid, Kunst en Handel. As in 1885, a short-term limited company—in which both Catholics and Liberals again were well represented—planned the 1894 event. The Antwerp expositions set a precedent in the sense that all Belgian world's fairs henceforth would be organized and financed by temporary limited companies.

The 1894 exposition was designed to promote the city of Antwerp, to tout Belgium's advanced industrialization, and to bolster Antwerp's position as a major shipping center. It is important to point out that while Antwerp already was a key European port, it had not yet

secured a role as a major importer-exporter of rubber, ivory, and other colonial products, as it would by the end of the century. It was not until 1895 that the first major shipments of Congo ivory and rubber began to reach Belgium, and not until 1896 that Leopold II's colonial budget was balanced for the first time. Again, it was not until 1897 or 1898 that E. D. Morel first noticed the objectionable guns-for-rubber exchange in and out of Antwerp that led him to start a campaign against Leopold II's rule in Africa. Thus, Antwerp's middle classes in 1894 still had good reason to feel the need to continue to promote their city as an important shipping center.

This second exposition in Antwerp was located on the same site as the 1885 event, just off the Scheldt River in 't Zuid (the South), and some pavilions from the earlier exposition were even reused. The site was expanded to cover around 290,000 square meters, of which around 110,000 were occupied by buildings for the 32 participating nations and the 12,095 exhibitors. Large areas of the fairgrounds were

Congo, Vue du Village.

Belgium had become a colonial power by 1894. Its largest colony was the Congo, in central Africa, and a native village was constructed for this exposition to show off the exotic people whom Belgium now ruled (Wolfson-Florida International University, Miami, Florida).

landscaped as open gardens that included numerous trees, plants, and shrubs. The 1894 exposition contributed to the eventual development of the southern part of the city as growth in 't Zuid accelerated after the turn of the century.

Whereas in 1885 the Hall of Machinery and the Hall of Industry had been two of the biggest draws, the preindustrial past gained more attention in 1894: One of the fair's foremost attractions was "Old Antwerp," a section of the grounds built to look like a neighborhood from sixteenth-century Antwerp. Because of the great popularity of Old Antwerp, future Belgian expositions would build similar historical neighborhoods as attractions. An important legacy of the 1894 event was the Royal Museum of Fine Arts, a museum actually built from 1884 to 1890, but which served as a main attraction during the exposition. Following up on the tremendous world's fair in Chicago, the American presence in 1894 was one of the more significant contributions, housed in a large Renaissance-style pavilion.

Aside from Old Antwerp, one of the other most remarkable displays was the Congo exhibit. The pavilion included ivory sculptures, displays of products such as rubber, copal, cotton, coffee, and cocoa, and a diorama by artists Robert Mols and Henri Meunier showing railroads and caravan routes in the Congo. The *Mouvement antiesclavagiste* contributed exhibits about the antislavery campaign that included portraits of Belgian heroes, instruments used by slave traders such as "*la cangue*, pitchforks, chains, iron collars, wrist and ankle shackles," even captured Arab booty. Organizers gave the pavilion a touch of authenticity by having it guarded by soldiers of the Force Publique, the Congo's armed force. In addition to the soldiers, organizers brought in an ethnically heterogeneous group of 144 Congolese. Along with mules, cows, pigs, and other animals from the Congo, these Congolese were put on display in a "village" where visitors could see them going about everyday activities or swimming in the nearby Bassin de Batelage. Organizers made the Congolese available to scientists to be measured, photographed, and studied.

The Congolese village was not the only display of empire in 1894. The British erected an "Indian City" that housed South Asian weavers and metalworkers who fashioned goods before the public's eyes. One could note at the exposition the competition among colonial powers that was a hallmark of universal expositions of the age, and indeed, of the age itself. One Belgian publication, for example, accused "several European powers" of being "jealous of the success of the Belgians in the Congo" that the Congo pavilion demonstrated, and went on to claim that it was this jealousy that had incited those powers to occupy the rest of Africa.

The exposition, which had a budget of between 4 and 4.5 million francs, attracted approximately 5 million visitors between May 5 and November 5. Investors in the fair's temporary limited company reaped a profit of 15 to 25 percent; an increase in the city's contribution (from that of 1885) to around 500,000 francs certainly helped, whereas the provincial government's contribution again was comparatively small.

Bibliography

For an overview of Belgian expositions to 1958, see A. Cockx and J. Lemmens's *Les Expositions Universelles et Internationales en Belgique de 1885 à 1958* (1958). Another source for early universal expositions in Belgium is Charles Mourlon's *Quelques Souvenirs des Expositions Nationales, Internationales et Universelles en Belgique 1820–1925* (n.d.).

For the 1894 exposition see *De Panoramische Droom — The Panoramic Dream: Antwerpen en de wereldtentoonstellingen — Antwerp and the World Exhibitions 1885, 1894, 1930* (1993). A contemporary source is Alph. Hertogs, *Exposition Universelle d'Anvers, 1894: Revue rétrospective* (1896). The periodical of the Maatschappij van het Paleis voor Nijverheid, Kunst en Handel was *Palais de l'Industrie*, published from 1888 to 1892.

The Archives Générales du Royaume-Algemeen Rijksarchief (AGR-ARA) in Brussels has important resources on all Belgian fairs up to and including the Brussels world's fair of 1935. The main reference work for archival research on world's fairs at the AGR-ARA is R. Depoortere and L. Vandeweyer, eds., *Inventaire des archives des expositions universelles organisées en Belgique entre 1880 et 1913: Fonds provenant du Ministère des affaires économiques*, Pub. 2037 (1994). The research instrument code (*code de l'instrument de recherche*) for the *inventaire* is T182. The Stadsarchief Antwerpen also has documents on Antwerp's three world's fairs. Information on the Stadsarchief collections are available at *http://stadsarchief.antwerpen.be/*.

There are a few works on the 1894 Congo displays: *Le Congo à l'Exposition universelle d'Anvers 1894: Catalogue de la Section de l'État Indépendant du Congo* (1894); V. Jacques, *Les Congolais de l'exposition universelle d'Anvers: communication faite à la société d'anthropologie de Bruxelles, dans la séance du 24 septembre 1894* (1894); Ch. Lemaire, *Congo & Belgique: A propos de l'Exposition d'Anvers* (1894). For the Congo in general at Belgian fairs see A. de Burbure, "Expositions et Sections Congolaises," Belgique d'Outremer, 286 (January 1959): 27–29, and Matthew G. Stanard, *Selling the Tenth Province: Belgian Colonial Propaganda 1908–1960* (unpub. Ph.D. diss., Indiana University, Bloomington, 2006).

San Francisco 1894

Arthur Chandler and Marvin Nathan

California Midwinter International Exposition

The story of San Francisco's first world's fair — the first exposition held west of the Mississippi — begins in Chicago, in May 1893. As Michael H. de Young, the energetic publisher of the San Francisco *Chronicle*, stood at the entranceway to the California building at the World's Columbian Exposition in Chicago, he marveled at the huge numbers of fairgoers who streamed through the gates—crowds that enriched the exposition vendors, the merchants of the city, and virtually everyone in Chicago, whether directly connected to the Columbian Exposition or not.

The Columbian Exposition clearly brought prosperity to Chicago. Seated at his desk in Arthur Page Brown's mission revival-style California pavilion at the Chicago fair, de Young's thoughts turned to home. Times were troubled there. San Francisco, along with the rest of the nation, was suffering through a severe recession in 1893. Though the city boasted a growing population of over 300,000, its economy was in deep trouble. Many banks had failed. Labor and management had clashed repeatedly, and an atmosphere of confrontation and bitterness loomed over the city's business enterprises.

As the official Commissioner of the California Exhibits and vice president of the National Commission at the Columbian Exposition, de Young could view both the difficulties and the opportunities of San Francisco in perspective. But was there some way to ameliorate the social and economic divisions that pitted so many factions against one other? How could some measure of prosperity be restored to the troubled community? The Columbian Exposition had unquestionably benefited Chicago in a number of ways. San Francisco could surely profit from launching its own world's fair.

De Young, realizing that he could capitalize on the impetus the Chicago fair had created, decided that San Francisco would host its own exposition, and that it should open on January 1, 1894. San Franciscans would stage this great cooperative venture, which would both announce and demonstrate the city's greatness and, at the same time, make money for local entrepreneurs. The world would come and behold the advantages of the city and the promise of the Golden State.

The more de Young thought it over, the more determined he became. But it had taken Chicagoans seven years to conceive, plan, and build the Columbian Exposition. How could a San Francisco newspaperman hope to bring about such a complex and expensive venture

in seven months? A decade earlier, New Orleans businessmen had found to their great disappointment that hosting a world's fair was no guarantee of financial success. Poor planning, bad weather, adverse political or economic conditions—there were many perilous roads to failure, but no guaranteed path to success.

However, de Young was determined to bring into being his dream of "the Sunset City," as he would call the Midwinter Fair. He summoned the San Francisco businessmen at the Columbian Exposition and set forth his dream. Though there were some skeptics among them, the majority liked what they heard and at once pledged over $40,000 for the enterprise. Thus reassured, De Young sent telegrams to the governor of California, the mayor of San Francisco, and numerous business organizations in order to gather support for his grand scheme.

Not all local leaders were convinced. Golden Gate Park Superintendent John McLaren was vehemently opposed to the plan, which he warned would desecrate his park's newly planted flora and, even worse, set a precedent for holding large-scale commercial ventures in an area originally created as a woodland retreat from urban life. McLaren's main ally was W. W. Stow, a millionaire supporter of the park and a dedicated conservationist. At one emotional meeting with the Golden Gate Park Commission, Stow denounced de Young's plan in the strongest terms: "You come in here and destroy a tree that has been growing for twenty years. The fair will be here for six months. Trees will be here for a thousand years." De Young, nevertheless, was not to be denied. He replied to Stow, "What is a tree? What are a thousand trees compared to the benefits of the exposition?" De Young won the day; and on January 27, 1894, the California Midwinter International Exposition — popularly known as the "Midwinter Fair" — opened its grounds to the world.

What the visitors saw at the California Midwinter International Exposition in 1894 was a Californian image of the world: the international spread of "Progress"—the application of technology for the improvement of human life—in which San Francisco was determined to win its rightful place. Though proud of his exposition, de Young feared that the San Francisco fair would suffer by comparison if it tried to imitate the carefully coordinated Greco-

Roman architecture of the Columbian Exposition. Consequently, he forbade any references to the classical tradition in the major Midwinter fair buildings. San Francisco architects proved more than equal to the challenge. They were adept at turning out non-traditional Victorian fantasies for their wealthy local clients, and therefore felt quite at home devising the eclectic extravaganzas that adorned the Grand Court of Honor at the Midwinter fair. The major buildings at the Chicago exposition all drew on the established architectural traditions of Europe and the ancient world. But at the Midwinter Fair, highly personalized syntheses of world architecture flanked the Court of Honor. In Chicago, the main buildings were all painted white, in deference to Daniel Burnham's notion of classical purity. In San Francisco, the "Sunset City" drew its color scheme from the spectrum that suffuses the skies over the Pacific horizon at evening time.

Though much smaller in scope than the Columbian Exposition, the Midwinter fair saw the participation of 38 nations, five American states, the Arizona territory, and 36 California counties. The marketing of an event of this magnitude, and on such short notice, fell to the eight members of the Department of Publicity and Promotion. Using mailing lists from the Chicago exposition, this small group exerted Herculean efforts to publicize the San Francisco exposition, churning out an average of 10,000 words a day on the progress of the fair, its attractions, special celebrations, and important visitors. These reports were wired and mailed to thousands of newspapers throughout California, the United States, and, in several different languages, the world. A total of 2,462 publications worldwide carried articles about the Midwinter fair, none of which were paid advertisements. In addition, the department sponsored the publication of a newspaper devoted exclusively to the exposition, commissioned artist Charles Graham to produce colorful lithographs of the major buildings, and liberally granted free passes to members of the press who came to report on the event. The official marketers of the fair also benefited from the fact that the director-general of the exposition owned one of San Francisco's major newspapers in which article after article on every aspect of the fair appeared on a daily basis.

All of the major buildings of the Court of

Honor were designed by local architects. But the central "spike"—a soaring tower of steel modeled on the Eiffel Tower—of the court was designed by a Frenchman, Leopold Bonet. Though the Bonet Tower, at 272 feet, was less than one third the size of the Eiffel Tower, it surpassed its Parisian counterpart in two significant respects. The Eiffel Tower was constructed out of iron, a building material destined to give way to the greater structural advantages of steel. Bonet fashioned his tower of steel, making it the first structure of its kind in the United States. In addition, Bonet's version had more spectacular lighting effects. The Eiffel Tower had also been adorned with Thomas Edison's recent invention, the electric light bulb, and even boasted a searchlight powerful enough to allow one to read a newspaper by its light at a distance of one mile from the tower. But the Bonet Tower delighted fairgoers with its own special magic. During the day, the Electrical Tower stood as the central symbol for the promise of Progress—power in the service of the human race. At night the lights of the tower seemed to come alive. The girders were covered with interconnected lines of 3,200 incandescent light bulbs which were programmed to change by means of a coded metal cylinder. And at the tower's crown, "the most powerful searchlight in the world" shone across the newly planted trees of Golden Gate Park, and far beyond. One commentator stated that he could read a newspaper at midnight ten miles away by the light of the tower's beams— a substantial improvement over the Eiffel Tower searchlight.

Ever since the French *Exposition Universelle* of 1867, world's fairs had offered visitors a chance to combine education with amusement. Fair organizers realized that it was the "Midway," or amusement section, that very often spelled the difference between financial success or failure for an entire exposition. Borrowing heavily from the Parisian and Chicago fairs, the Midwinter Exposition offered a substantial and diverse array of amusements in a zone called, in emulation of the Columbian Exposition, the Midway Plaisance.

One of the most astonishing amusements at the Midwinter fair was the "Haunted Swing." Twelve to fifteen visitors at a time would pay their admission fee, and then take their seats on a large swing situated in the mid-

The 272-foot Bonet Tower dominated the California Midwinter Exposition grounds, and its electric lights dazzled visitors at night (courtesy of Arthur Chandler).

dle of a comfortably furnished parlor. The swing was suspended from a bar which crossed the room below the ceiling. Once settled in their places, visitors looked around at their surroundings and saw familiar objects: chairs, dressers, pictures on the wall, and a lighted kerosene lamp upon a table. Then, little by little, the swing appeared to move back and forth. It described greater and greater arcs until at last the astonished (and sometimes frightened) participants appeared to be hanging upside down in the room — yet their hats remained on their heads! Around and around they seemed to go, and many passengers became dizzy — some even fainted at this point. Finally the swinging ceased, and the giddy visitors reeled from the room. In fact, the "swing" had remained stationary. The walls and ceiling of the room itself were mounted on a revolving drum with all the furnishings and fixtures cleverly and securely bolted down. The room itself revolved around the stationary swing; but so complete was the conviction that a room could not revolve, and that a kerosene lamp would spill its contents (it contained no oil; a hidden incandescent light bulb provided the light), no one suspected that

the room itself rotated. Even those who came away dizzy from the experience had to admit that the "Haunted Swing" was one of the most clever illusions they had ever encountered.

There was at least one major advantage in holding a world's fair in San Francisco soon after the Chicago exposition: Many national and foreign exhibitors were easily persuaded to ship their treasures to the West Coast for another six months of exhibition before returning them home. Because the Midwinter fair organizers could make arrangements with prospective exhibitors in Chicago without having to travel to, or correspond with, foreign governments, the task of lining up participants was vastly easier. Exhibits, commissioners, concessions — all could be sent to California with a minimum of inconvenience. The net result was that the commissioners of the Midwinter fair could bring to the public a sizable representation of world culture. Art and artifacts, industrial exhibits and exotic amusement concessions, a treasure that had taken Chicago some years to assemble, were present in Golden Gate Park for San Franciscans to contemplate and admire from January to July of 1894.

Another real advantage that the Midwinter Fair organizers emphasized strongly in its publicity statements was the mild climate of the city during the winter months. And indeed, the mild temperature and verdant winter landscape mightily impressed visitors from the Midwest and East Coast. It is possible that the heavy migration to San Francisco during the last several years of the nineteenth century might be attributable to the reputation that California had acquired as a veritable Eden in all seasons. Between 1890 and 1900, San Francisco's population jumped from 300,000 to nearly 400,000 inhabitants.

The planners of the Midwinter Exposition believed that San Francisco's first world's fair should do more than house exhibits and provide amusement. A serious exposition, they felt, should also sponsor serious discussions of ideas by bringing together respected authorities in the fields of economics, politics, religion, literature, education, and science. Such events, following the precedent of previous world's fairs, were called "congresses." Millionaire patron of the arts and future San Francisco mayor James Phelan was chosen president of the Midwinter Exposition Congresses Committee, whose task was to organize and promote discussions that would "advance the cause of Progress in human endeavor."

The liveliest of the exposition meetings was the Woman's Congress. The fair organizers had already encountered some strong criticism from women about their lack of presence on the planning committees. Discussions were centered on those activities which, in the world of the 1890s, constituted acceptable activities for women: education, charities and missionary work, and the decorative and pictorial arts. However, as the discussions progressed, topics such as educational reform, the immigration question, the disadvantages of female costume in the workplace, and women's suffrage, were hotly debated. A budding militancy pervaded many of the meetings, especially in the panel devoted to the topic of exclusion of women from the business world.

Despite the pride and enthusiasm which the exposition engendered among the business owners and the general population, the Midwinter fair was not without its problems. There was, of course, the ongoing resentment of those who felt that the exposition desecrated Golden Gate Park. There was also a good deal of skepticism among local labor groups about the potential advantages of the exposition for local working people. The dissenters asserted that the business leaders supporting the exposition were not creating new jobs which would permanently improve economic conditions, but were merely moving laborers from other projects around the city to temporary work on the fairgrounds.

In addition, there were other difficulties that arose at the fair itself. During one of the animal shows a lion turned on his trainer and mauled him to death. An Eskimo child died from hereditary syphilis in the "Esquimaux" village. To the consternation of citizens who learned of the fact later, the child was buried in Golden Gate Park by the Eskimos, without the knowledge of park or exposition officials. The exposition suffered one major scandal during its closing days. The Society for the Suppression of Vice, ever vigilant to keep the exposition wholesome, was scandalized to learn that there was to be a nude dancer at a special event held at the exposition aquarium. The subsequent scandal and arrests were an embarrassment to all concerned, especially the exposition commissioners.

Other difficulties resonated with the international tensions alive in the decade before the turn of the century. At one point, the delegation from Japan strongly objected to a proposal that local Japanese would pull visitors around the grounds in jinrikishas. This delegation vowed openly that they would kill any Japanese found degrading the honorable reputation of their nation by performing such menial tasks. The crisis was averted at the last minute by hiring Germans, who painted their faces and dressed up in Oriental costume!

A more urgent and costly dilemma, from the standpoint of the exposition directors, arose in the business dealings of the fair. All vendors were supposed to turn over a percentage of their daily receipts to the Midwinter Exposition General Fund. It was widely believed, though, that the vendors were not reporting their earnings honestly. In response, the directors devised a system of "rotating cash register clerks" to deal with the problem before it arose. Every day, a management-appointed clerk would take in all receipts from each exhibit. On the next day, the clerk would be shifted to another exhibit, in order to prevent familiarity and collusion arising between clerks and exhibitors. The vendors growled at this system, but the directors were determined that the fair should show a profit; and the surest way of securing that profit, in their minds, was to be rigorous in the collection of its contractual receipts.

The policy paid off. When the California Midwinter International Exposition officially closed its doors on July 4, 1894, Director-General de Young could boast that the fair had accomplished all of its goals. The exposition had earned $1,260,112.19 in revenues, as against $1,193,260.70 in expenditures, netting a profit of $66,851.49 — this without asking for or receiving a single penny of support from federal, state, or local government sources. And after the fair closed, the Fine Arts Building would remain in Golden Gate Park as the city's first municipal museum. The Japanese Tea Garden, several works of statuary, and an improved water and electrical system all contributed to Golden Gate Park's future development.

Best of all was the recovery of San Francisco's businesses in the months before the fair was opened, As de Young put it, "Stagnation and business depression were everywhere. There was a threatened run on our banks, and a want of confidence was universally apparent. Look today at the situation. There is a complete restoration of confidence; business is progressing as of yore, our streets are crowded, and the general community is in a better frame of mind." De Young's optimism seems to be confirmed by the fact that there were no major labor strikes in San Francisco for the remainder of the century, and by the emergence of a building boom in the years immediately after the fair, resulting in such structures as the Emporium Department Store, the new Cliff House, the Sutro Baths, and the Ferry Building. By all measures, San Francisco's first world's fair had proved a resounding success.

Bibliography

The Bancroft Library at the University of California, Berkeley has a number of contemporary published sources for the Midwinter Fair. Among these are the *Official Guide to the California Midwinter Exposition* (1894), the *Official History of the California Midwinter Exposition* (1894), and the *Official Catalogue, Fine Arts, California Midwinter Exposition* (1894). See also Adolph Witteman, *Souvenir of the California Midwinter Exposition* (1894), for a pictorial tour of the fair. San Francisco's several newspapers also covered the exposition in considerable detail.

Among modern works, Arthur Chandler and Marvin Nathan, *The Fantastic Fair* (1993) is a short, scholarly history of the event. Raymond Clary, *The Making of Golden Gate Park: The Early Years: 1865–1906* (1980), traces the early history of the site of the Midwinter fair and devotes a chapter to the event. A recent pictorial history of the Midwinter fair is William Lipsky, *San Francisco's Midwinter Exposition* (2002), part of Arcadia Press's Images of America series.

Hobart 1894–1895

Lara Anderson

Tasmanian International Exhibition

The organizers of the Tasmanian International Exhibition held the exhibition in the summer of 1894–1895 in the hope that exhibits would flow on from the World's Columbian Exposition in Chicago. This did not eventuate; indeed as one well-known Tasmanian, James Backhouse Walker, noted in his diary: "Our International Exhibition can hardly be said to be a success—neither England nor America, nor indeed any other country has contributed." The failure of the exhibition to attract international or even national exhibitors and visitors meant that "[o]nly five years after its closure it had all but ceased to be considered an event of importance worth noting in the history of Tasmania." This is certainly confirmed by the 2005 *Companion to Tasmanian History*, which contains only one reference to the Tasmanian International Exhibition under the heading of "Choral Music," an entry that notes that the opening of the exhibition featured a choir of 276, with an orchestra, performing F.A. Packer's specially composed cantata *The Land of Beauty*.

The successes of the New Zealand and South Seas Exhibition at Dunedin, New Zealand (1889–1890) and of the Inter-colonial Exhibition in Launceston (1891–1892) motivated the decision to hold the Tasmanian International Exhibition from November 15, 1894, to May 15, 1895. Also contributing to this decision was the belief that it would be more beneficial for Tasmania to mount a local exhibition rather than send a delegation to the fair in Chicago because it was thought that a Tasmanian display would be lost in such a huge complex. From the outset, very high hopes were held for the exhibition, in particular the belief that it would improve the economic conditions in Tasmania as had happened with Western Australia and the Perth Exhibition of 1882; Adelaide and its exhibition in 1887, and Dunedin in 1889. While the exhibition was certainly not an economic success, although it registered an attendance of 290,000, it was a modest cultural one as many pieces of art remained in Tasmania at the new art gallery. Indeed the bringing of fine art to Hobart for the exhibition was seen as a way of refining the national character. In addition to artworks exhibited at the exhibition, there was also particular excitement expressed about the "sodawater machine" brought from Sydney.

An internationally acclaimed expert on exhibitions, Jules Joubert, was engaged as chairman of all the committees for the Hobart Exhibition. Of French origin, he had been involved in the management of a number of exhibitions: Philadelphia (1876), Paris (1878), Sydney (1879) and Launceston (1891–1892), among others. Many different views circulated about why, in contrast to other exhibitions, the Hobart Exhibition was such a failure. Some cited the high charges for space or the lack of participation by rich pastoralists, while others blamed the lack of showman's skill among the promoters and high customs duties that kept foreign exhibitors away.

The government provided the site, Queen's Domain (634 acres), free of charge. The site was described as "large enough to be the lungs of a center of population much bigger than Hobart is ever likely to become, and sufficiently beautiful to excite the envy of most other cities" It was also pointed out that whatever use the aborigines might have made of the Domain before Lieutenant Bowen anchored in 1803, the history of the reserve had been peaceful since. The question of permanent buildings of the site was hotly debated, raising suspicions among the poor about the use of *their* public recreation land for a bourgeois enterprise.

The contract for the design of the exhibition buildings was won by Thomas Searell in a competition held in 1892. The main building was of the Italian Renaissance style and was described as "bold and striking" in design. The main vestibule was decorated with four enriched Corinthian pillars supporting bold frieze cornice and pediment, the recess being filled by a strikingly worked Royal coat-of-arms carved in Huon pine. Following the closing of the exhibition, there was much debate about whether the buildings should be left standing. On the one hand were those opposed to such a relic of "Joubertian exaggeration," with all the potential costs its retention would entail, and on the other were those who saw the value in keeping such a good space. The realists won and by 1896 the site had been returned to its original condition.

The removal of the exhibition buildings from Queen's Domain in 1896 was just the first step in the obliteration of the exhibition from Tasmania's collective memory. Indeed, as already mentioned, there is no entry dedicated to this event in the *Companion to Tasmanian History* (2005). Attracting very little national and foreign interest, the Tasmanian International Exhibition was an economic failure and perhaps an all too harsh a reminder of Tasmania's insignificance both nationally and internationally.

Bibliography

Records of the Tasmanian International Exhibition may be found at the Archives Office of

Tasmania, the Tasmanian Museum and Art Gallery, and in the Tasmaniana Collection at the State Library of Tasmania. The archives hold a number of documentary records, including some correspondence files, photographs of season ticket holders, and some committee records. An index may be accessed at *www.archives.tas.gov.au*. The records at the museum and state library are mostly published records, including the official record, the catalogue of exhibits, records relating to the exposition association, photographs, various guidebooks and programs, and other printed ephemera. For the museum, consult *www.tmag. tas.gov.au* and for the library, *www.statelibrary. tas.gov.au/home*. The exposition was covered extensively in the Hobart *Mercury*, the colony's main newspaper. See especially the issues of May 14, November 7, and November 15, 1894.

The only secondary source of significance is Peter Mercer, "Tasmanian International Exhibition 1894–5." *Tasmanian Historical Research Association Papers and Proceedings* 28, 1 (1981): 17–41, which is based primarily on newspaper sources, but is very thorough regarding the details of the exposition. Mercer's article was reprinted in a catalogue published for an exhibition at the Tasmanian Museum and Art Gallery that celebrated the exposition's centennial: David Hansen, ed., *The Exhibition Exhibition* (1994). Another secondary source of note is Alison Alexander, ed., *The Companion to Tasmanian History* (2005), which has practically nothing to say about the exhibition but does provide some historical context.

Atlanta 1895

Charlene G. Garfinkle

The Cotton States and International Exhibition

The third, largest, and most ambitious of Atlanta's "cotton expositions," the Cotton States and International Exposition of 1895 was intended to spark the city's recovery and economic development while taking on an international scope. The point of the exposition was to show off the resources of the cotton states and encourage the development of trade with Latin America. Atlanta advertised itself as a transportation and commercial center, merging new industrial methods with its traditional agricultural roots and the resources of its existing railroads. The Cotton States and International Exposition promoted regional products such as steel and cotton that were ready for a European market and was a vital event in the emergence of Atlanta as a major city of the "New South."

The 1895 Cotton States and International Exposition was planned during the financial panic of 1893 in an effort to expand on the lim-

ited representation by the South at Chicago's World's Columbian Exposition. When business capital was unavailable, a guarantee fund of $209,000 was raised from private subscription and city council appropriation, with additional funds coming from the U.S. Congress, concessions fees, and exhibition space rent. Under the leadership of exposition President W. A. Hemphill and Director-General H. E. W. Palmer (both later replaced by C. A. Collier as president and director-general), the exposition company ultimately spent $2,000,000 to create the fair.

The Cotton States and International Exposition hosted fewer than 800,000 visitors who paid to view its 6,000 exhibits from 37 states and 13 foreign nations between September 18 and December 31, 1895. Located two miles north of Atlanta, the exposition grounds spanned 189 acres of land leased from the Piedmont Exposition Company. The overall architectural style of the Atlanta fair was neither classical nor Renaissance-revival but instead was inspired by the early Romanesque design.

Grant Wilkins of Atlanta laid out the site, which included an oblong space, called The Plaza, that included limestone walkways, plantings and a central fountain, and thirteen-acre body of water named Clara Meer. In contrast to Chicago's "White City," the Atlanta fair employed a color scheme that would harmonize with the landscape of Piedmont Park. In response to this pastoral setting, the buildings were stained a natural wood gray with moss green roofs. Southern materials, such as Georgia pine for the framing and yellow pine shingles for the exterior were used to construct the major buildings. Bradford L. Gilbert of New York was supervising architect and designer of ten of the thirteen principal structures. Gilbert's buildings included Administration, Manufactures and Liberal Arts, Agriculture, Machinery, Minerals and Forestry, Electricity, Transportation, Fire, the Negro Building, and the Auditorium. In addition Walter T. Downing of Atlanta designed the Fine Arts Building, Elsie Mercur of Pittsburgh designed the Woman's Building, and government architect Charles S. Kemper did the U. S. Government Building.

The Machinery, Mineral and Forestry, Transportation, and Electricity buildings encircled Clara Meer, on which gondolas and electric launches transported visitors from building to building. West of Clara Meer was the main entrance to the exposition grounds, the Administration Building, and the buildings surrounding The Plaza — Agriculture, the Auditorium, Fine Arts, Fire, the U. S. Government Building, and many of the state buildings. The Women's Building was situated between Clara Meer and the Plaza while the Negro Building sat at the outskirts of the grounds, between the grandstand of Buffalo Bill's Wild West Show and the Midway attractions. South of the main exposition grounds was Midway Heights, a German Village, a Moorish Palace, the Dahomey Village, a Japanese Village with a tea garden, an Old Time Plantation, and the Streets of Cairo, as well as rides, such as the Phoenix Wheel, and recent inventions, including a motion picture projector called the Phantascope, by Charles Francis Jenkins.

Exhibits in all the exposition buildings represented regional, national, and international displays of products, manufactures, art, and educational and social achievements. Once again, a Woman's Building was planned, designed, and decorated by women and displayed the work of women in such fields as fine arts, agriculture, literature, nursing, and education, as well as housing a colonial display. The most notable exhibit was, no doubt, the Negro Building. Correcting the lacuna of the World's Columbian Exposition, which did not invite full participation by African Americans, the Atlanta organizers established a prominent exhibit in the form of the Negro Building. "This is the first instance in the history of expositions where a building has been especially devoted to the Negro race. Here are shown the results of the efforts of the race in the art of civilization and educational advances" (*Official Guide*, pp. 38–39). Success of the fair was in part due to the early solicitation by exposition planners of African American support.

Healing and recovery was the hallmark of many aspects of the fair. The most noteworthy event took place at the opening day festivities with the address by African American Booker T. Washington, the first time in the post–Civil War south that a Negro spoke publicly to an integrated audience. In honor of his aid in securing Congressional funding for the exposition, Washington was invited to take part in the opening ceremonies. In his address, Washington presented his controversial "five finger" analogy for the acceptance of segregation, later called the "Atlanta Compromise" speech, in which he suggested that "in all things that are purely social we can be as separate as fingers, yet one as the hand in all things essential to mutual progress." Racial reconciliation was not the only progress that was evident. Just three days after Washington's so called "Atlanta Compromise" speech, Blue and Gray Day featured the thirty year reunion of Union and Confederate veterans, indicative of social reconciliation as well.

Unfinished buildings and exhibits caused low attendance and near financial ruin during the opening month and a half of the exposition, but almost daily spectaculars, special programs, and days of honor eventually lured more visitors to the fair. John Philip Sousa's "King Cotton March," written for the exposition and adopted as its official march, was performed many times at the fair over a three-week period, which also helped increase attendance. Although plagued by financial problems, the

Cotton States and International Exposition ultimately survived midway foreclosure and fell short of financial success by only $25,000. However, organizers claimed that the fair had stimulated capital investment and construction in the city at a level high enough to deem the fair a successful venture.

After the close of the exposition, the main buildings were cleared and, over the next decades, the fairgrounds were transformed into a city park. At Piedmont Park today, the stonework from the original parapet remains, as does Clara Meer, but new to the site is Atlanta's Botanical Garden, tennis courts, and other park facilities for public use.

Bibliography

The Atlanta History Center Archives, part of the Kenan Research Center in Atlanta, houses the most complete collection of materials from the Cotton States and International Exposition. Primary published sources include: Walter G. Cooper, *The Cotton States and International Exposition and South Illustrated* (1896); *The Official Catalogue of the Cotton States and International Exposition* 1895); *Official Guide to the Cotton States and International Exposition*, compiled by P. S. Dodge (1895); and *Report of the Board of Commissioners Representing the State of New York at the Cotton States and International Exposition held at Atlanta, Georgia 1895* (1896). For photographs, see: *Official Views: Cotton States and International Exposition, Atlanta, 1895* (1895); *Souvenir Album of the Cotton States and International Exposition, Atlanta, Ga, 1895* (1895); and *Photo-Gravures of the Cotton States Exposition, Atlanta, 1895* (1895).

The Smithsonian Institution handled most U.S. Government exhibits and correspondence and other documents relating to federal participation can be found in the National Archives Record Group 43, Records Relating to the Cotton States and International Exposition at Atlanta, 1895 and in the Smithsonian Institution Archives, Record Group 70, Series II, The Cotton States and International Exposition.

A contemporary account of the fair is found in W. Y. Atkinson, "The Atlantic Exposition," *North American Review* 161 (October 1895): 385–93. Articles were published throughout the planning and operation of the fair in the Atlanta *Journal*, Atlanta *Constitution*, *Leslie's Weekly*, and *Harper's Weekly*. Booker T. Washington's speech can be found in his autobiography, *Up from Slavery*, (1901).

Modern studies include coverage in "The New Orleans, Atlanta, and Nashville Expositions: New Markets, 'New Negroes,' and a New South" chapter of Robert Rydell's *All the World's a Fair* (1984), a master's thesis by F. H. Boyd Coons, "The Cotton States and International Exposition in the New South: Architecture and Implications" (University of Virginia, 1988), and three journal articles: W.Y. Atkinson, "The Atlanta Exposition," *North American Review* 161, 467 (October 1985): 385–93, Bruce Harvey and Lynn Watson-Powers, "'The Eyes of the World Are Upon Us': A Look at the Cotton States and International Exposition of 1895," *Atlanta History* 39, 3–4 (Fall-Winter 1995): 11; and Sharon M. Mullis, "Extravaganza of the New South: The Cotton States and International Exposition, 1895," *Atlanta Historical Bulletin* 20, 5 (Fall 1976): 17–36. Also, Harvey K. Newman, *Southern Hospitality: Tourism and the Growth of Atlanta* (1999), devotes several pages to the fair.

For fairground history and information on Piedmont Park, see *Piedmont Park: Celebrating Atlanta's Common Ground*, edited by Darlene Roth and Jeff Kemph (2004).

Brussels 1897

Matthew G. Stanard

Exposition Internationale de Bruxelles

The capital of Belgium had to wait until after the port of Antwerp had twice hosted a universal exposition before it was to have its turn. Brussels was from the outset in a great position to host a universal exposition: It benefited from a central location, a well-developed tram system, and an extensive national railway infrastructure whose main lines had been completed as early as the 1840s. Brussels would take advantage of its location and infrastructure to secure hosting privileges for three world's fairs in the following century: in 1910, 1935, and 1958.

While the 1897 universal exposition was Brussels' first, the event had little impact on the layout of the city. Like Vienna and Paris, Brussels had undergone a period of deliberate urban renewal in the latter half of the nineteenth century, during which time extensive construction turned the city "into a permanent work-site." Among other projects, in the twenty years before 1897, the Senne river was bridged over, a colossal new Palais du Justice was built, and covering 3,400 more square meters than St. Peter's in Rome, the Jardin du Roi was landscaped, and the Palais Royal was restored. Furthermore, just as Vienna's *Ringstraße* had been converted from a military training area to broad avenues, so had military training grounds outside Brussels been transformed into the spacious Parc de Cinquantenaire, beginning in 1875. The Parc du Cinquantenaire accommodated the 1888 *Grand Concours International des Sciences et de l'Industrie* — a major exposition, if not officially international and universal — and was ready to function as the location for the exposition less than a decade later. Thus the urban landscape did not undergo any significant changes for the 1897 *Exposition Internationale de Bruxelles*, in contrast to future expositions in the capital.

Heavy rains slowed down construction at the Parc de Cinquantenaire and forced a delay of the inauguration from April 24 to early May. The opening was further postponed to May 10 out of respect for the Duchess d'Alençon, who died in a fire in Paris on May 4. Pavilions for 26 nations and buildings for 10,668 exhibitors covered 100,000 square meters and acted to frame the spacious rectangular green lawn of the Parc du Cinquantenaire. Looming largest, to the southeast, was the Arcade du Cinquantenaire with its two wings of exhibit halls, and behind it, a large exposition hall. (The Arcade itself was a triumphal single arch with a wooden façade. The triple arch of today would not be completed until 1905, and then by Leopold II with funds from the Congo.) One of the most interesting displays in 1897 was the Bruxelles-Kermesse (Brussels-Fair), for which fair organizers clearly took as a model the "Old Antwerp" section of the last *Exposition Uni-*

verselle d'Anvers. Bruxelles-Kermesse was a reproduction of a fourteenth century Brussels city quarter where visitors could see shop girls, patrolling soldiers, and other people at work dressed in period costumes.

While the Parc du Cinquantenaire drew 6 million visitors before the fair closed on November 8, the most striking exhibits were located not in Brussels but rather a few kilometers away in Tervuren. There the fair's colonial section, *Exposition coloniale 1897*, had opened as planned on April 24. The centerpiece of the inanimate colonial exhibits at Tervuren was the *Palais des Colonies*. Visitors entered the *Palais* through a *Salon d'Honneur* filled with works of art, especially chryselephantine sculpture, before passing through several rooms dedicated to ethnography, imports, transportation, and exports. An underground gallery joined the two ends of the U-shaped *Palais*; passing from one side to the other, guests would see the "aquarium" (preserved tropical fish suspended in tanks of formaldehyde) before they entered into the other side of the building through a working greenhouse. The tour would end at the *Salon des Grandes Cultures* that played up three colonial products: coffee, cocoa, and tobacco.

But the main draw was outside of the *Palais* on the surrounding grounds: several so-called *village nègres* in which, according to one observer, Africans were to be seen penned-in "like animals in a competition, flesh to white onlookers." Counting the *Force publique* soldiers present, the exposition included over 260 Congolese from Leopold II's domain. After arriving June 27, the Congolese in the *villages nègres* continuously drew large numbers of onlookers, the large crowds facilitated by the tramway line Leopold II had had built from the Parc du Cinquantenaire area to Tervuren expressly for the exposition. Because some visitors were inclined to give the Africans food to eat, organizers erected a sign that read, "Do not feed the blacks. They are already being fed." By the time the colonial section closed, it had attracted between 1.2 and 1.8 million people. Many of the Africans were housed above local stables during part of the exposition, and seven of them died as a result of poor housing and living conditions. Tombs of those who died are still located in Tervuren. Despite what may have been primitive living quarters, one Bel-

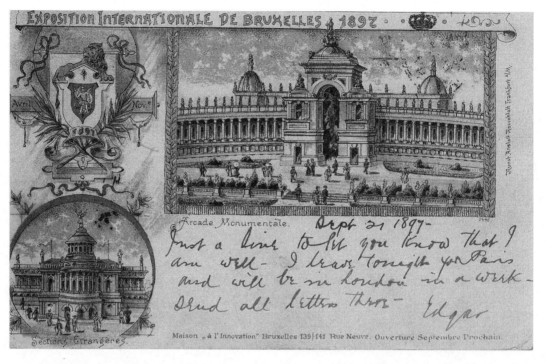

EXPOSITION INTERNATIONALE DE BRUXELLES 1897

Arcade Monumentale.

Sections Étrangères.

Maison „à l'Innovation" Bruxelles 139|141 Rue Neuve. Ouverture Septembre Prochain.

By 1897 picture postcards were becoming popular mementos from expositions. Shown is an elaborate postcard from the Brussels 1897 fair (editors' collection).

gian reported from the colony that one returning Congolese's account of the stay in Belgium and the fair was nothing but positive.

The Tervuren exposition also marked the first effort to use film as a means of Belgian colonial propaganda. Visitors to the colonial section could visit the *Zoographe* pavilion that showed colonial films. Moreover, photographer/director Alexandre (Albert Edouard Drains) created a number of colonial film shorts at the fair including *Les Congolais à Tervueren*.

While the exposition's architecture was unremarkable and while it did not contribute significantly to the urban landscape of Brussels, the *Exposition coloniale* did provide the catalyst for the eventual creation of the *Musée du Congo Belge*. The *Palais des Colonies* was reopened to the public in 1898 as the *Musée du Congo*, and as collections grew Leopold II decided to build a larger museum. A new building, begun in 1904 and finished by 1909, became both the colonial section of the 1910 *Exposition Universelle et Internationale de Bruxelles* and the *Musée du Congo Belge*, the main repository for Africana in Belgium. In symbiotic fashion, the museum and its collections

contributed to, and benefited from, the more ephemeral Belgian *expositions universelles* throughout the colonial period.

Bibliography

Comparatively little has been written on the main international section of the 1897 exposition. For a brief overview see A. Cockx and J. Lemmens, *Les Expositions Universelles et Internationales en Belgique de 1885 à 1958* (1958). Another source for early universal expositions in Belgium is Charles Mourlon, *Quelques Souvenirs des Expositions Nationales, Internationales et Universelles en Belgique 1820–1925* (n.d.). As with most world's fairs, a number of specialized catalogues were created for the 1897 event, such as those for certain national participations.

For the 1897 Tervuren colonial section, see above all Maurits Wynants' beautifully illustrated and well-documented *Des ducs de Brabant aux villages Congolais; Tervuren et l'Exposition coloniale 1897*, translated by Chantal Kesteloot (1997). Th. Masui's *Guide de la Section de l'État Indépendant du Congo à l'Exposition de Bruxelles-Tervueren en 1897* (1897) is a basic primary source on the Tervuren section. For the Congo at Belgian fairs in general see A. de Burbure, "Expositions et Sections Congolaises," *Belgique d'Outremer*, 286 (January 1959): 27–29, and Matthew G. Stanard, *Selling the Tenth Province: Belgian Colonial Propaganda 1908–1960* (unpub. Ph.D. diss., Indiana University–Bloomington, 2006).

The Archives Générales du Royaume-Algemeen Rijksarchief (AGR-ARA) in Brussels has important resources on all Belgian expositions up to and including the 1935 *exposition universelle*. The main reference work for archival research on world's fairs at the AGR-ARA is R. Depoortere and L. Vandeweyer, eds., *Inventaire des archives des expositions universelles organisées en Belgique entre 1880 et 1913: Fonds provenant du Ministère des affaires économiques*, Pub. 2037 (1994). The research instrument code (*code de l'instrument de recherche*) for the *inventaire* is T182.

Guatemala City 1897

Laurie Dalton

Exposición Centroamericana

Having participated in the Paris 1889 and Chicago 1893 world's fairs, Guatemala organized its own Central American Exposition in 1897. The exhibition ran from March 15 to 30 June and occupied 800 acres near Guatemala City. Although the fair did include participants from United States, Chile, Italy, Spain, Great Britain, Germany, France, Switzerland, and Belgium, it was staged against a tumultuous political backdrop; based on a perceived need to form a Central American union that would be better able to resist foreign aggression. This was not a new idea in Central America; a loose confederation, the United Provinces of Central America had existed between 1823 and 1838. But British occupation of the Nicaraguan port of Corinto reawakened the need for unity, and later in 1895, Honduras, Nicaragua, and El Salvador had formed the Greater Republic of Central America, with the hope that Costa Rica and Guatemala would also join. Another goal of the exposition was to highlight the various flora, fauna and agriculture of Central America.

In 1873 Justo Rufino Barrios had taken office as president of Guatemala. He made political and social changes to the country, widely encouraging agricultural development in the form of export products such as coffee, with detrimental effects to the local native population. The Central American Exposition was initiated under the government of his successor, José María Reyna Barrios, a supporter of Central American union. In conjunction with the exposition, the government began an ambitious phase of urban renewal based on the model of European cities. In 1897 the Boulevard 30 de Junio (now known as the Avenida La Reforma) was unveiled. It was a large expansive street modelled after the Champs-Elysées, and was to serve as a symbol of the progress and modernization of Guatemala City. Excessive amounts of funds were spent on the building projects as well as the exposition, which alone had an estimated cost of $2 million. Since the Barrios government had allocated only $600.000 for the exposition, a financial crisis ensued, and the government was unable to pay its debts or its employees' salaries. In May 1897, Barrios decreed new fiscal policies that relieved banks of their obligation to redeem paper money in specie, or coin, and made bank notes legal tender for the rest of the year.

Virtually all the exhibits were housed in three buildings that covered a space of 10 acres, and in order to encourage foreign participation, goods from overseas were admitted duty-free. Exhibits at the exposition were placed in one of twelve different categories, including fine arts, mechanics' and construction, fauna and flora, mining, and immigration. Approximately $200,000 was budgeted for prize money, to be split between foreign and local exhibitors.

An interior view showing the Chilean exhibit at the Central American Exposition in Guatemala City.

Products from California made up a large portion the United States exhibit at the Central American Exposition in Guatemala City (Both photographs are from *Catálogo Illustrado de la Exposición Centro América y internacional*, 1897).

Although the Central American Exposition of 1897 carried with it economic implications it also was the site of many cultural initiatives. As part of the festivities of the exhibition, the national anthem for Guatemala was officially presented on March 14, 1897, in the Columbus theatre. As a result of its participation in the Central American Exposition, Nicaragua created *Museo Nacional de Nicaragua "Dioclesiano Chaves,"* which was its first museum. While a treaty forming a provisional treaty of union between Guatemala, Costa Rica, and the Greater Republic was signed in January 1898 in the wake of the exposition, the legislatures of Costa Rica and Guatemala failed to ratify the pact, and the dream of Central American unity never became reality.

Bibliography

For an overview of the social and political climate of Guatemala see: Mario Rosenthal *Guatemala* (1962), and Jim Handy, *Gift of the Devil: A History of Guatemala* (1984). Information on the political climate of late nineteenth-century Central America, including efforts at union, can be found in Alberto Herrera, *La Unión de Centro América* (1964), Thomas Karnes, *The Failure of Union* (1985), and John E. Findling, *Close Neighbors, Distant Friends: United States-Central American Relations* (1987). The Guatemalan newspaper *El Progreso Nacional* published a collection of articles, *Guatemala en 1897,* that includes photographs and the official *Guía de la Exposición.* Other primary documents of the period can be sourced from the library at the University of San Carlos, in Guatemala, *http://www.usac.edu.gt.* The BIE in Paris has P.J. Pierson, *Catalogo Ilustrado, Lista Oficial de Recompensas de la Exposición Centro-América e Internacional, 1897* (1899), that includes an informative introduction and many photographs, in addition to lists of exhibits and prize winners. Finally, the New Orleans *Times-Picayune* (March 16, 1897) contains some information about the exposition.

Nashville 1897

Charlene G. Garfinkle

Tennessee Centennial and International Exposition

With the boom of a gun, the machinery was started, the band began to play, and the crowd went wild. In a momentary lull, Exposition President J. W. Thomas proclaimed the Tennessee Centennial Exposition "open to the world." The Tennessee Centennial and International Exposition was held to celebrate the 100th anniversary of its statehood in 1796. It was one of the largest and grandest of the U. S. expositions of the 1890s as well as a hallmark of the New South era. With exhibits of industry, agriculture, commerce, and transportation of the state, technological progress of the machine age, and examples of educational and cultural achievements, the Tennessee Centen-nial lauded the shift from rural antebellum culture to a progressive industrial economy. Financial improvements through technological progress and social improvement through science, technology, and education were the ever present themes at the exposition. As with Atlanta's exposition of 1895, the Centennial Exposition functioned to display the spirit of the New South in post-war reconciliation with the north.

The exposition was planned by Nashville businessmen and funded largely by the railroad company (in an effort to counteract negative public opinion regarding railroad monopolies). John W. Thomas, board chairman of the Nashville, Chattanooga and St. Louis Railway, was a major contributor and was made president of the exposition. The exposition's director-general, Eugene Castner "E.C." Lewis, also worked for the railroad. Due to the influence of the railway and particularly J. W. Thomas in the realization of the exposition, a unique structure to the Tennessee Centennial was the railroad exhibit building which housed products of Tennessee, Alabama, and Georgia found along the line of the Nashville, Chattanooga and St. Louis Railroad.

Nearly 1.8 million people visited the Tennessee Centennial and International Exposition between May 1 and October 30, 1897. Already a centennial site, having held its own city centennial in 1880, Nashville was selected to host the Tennessee Centennial. Funding and organizational problems, along with construction delays, prevented the planned Centennial Exposition date of 1896, but, once opened, it was a success. The exposition grounds spanned 200 acres of elevated land located about two miles west of Nashville on the site of West Side Park (a former racetrack). In honor of the exposition, the site was renamed Centennial City in 1897. According to the *Tennessee Encyclopedia*, Centennial City was granted full powers as a separate city and became a model of progressive era "good government" with its strict regulations of liquor and vice.

Like Chicago's World's Columbian Exposition of 1893, the overall architectural design of the Tennessee Centennial was classical revival; but, this was not the only source for its classical style choice. Nashville had acquired its nickname of "Athens of the South" as early as the 1840s. It referred to Nashville's dedication to education and its schools' focus on a classical education. The nickname influenced the theme of the centennial in its classically inspired buildings, especially the full-scale replica of the Athenian Parthenon.

Typical of world's fair designs of the 1890s, the exposition site featured a large body of water faced by the main exposition buildings, with the addition of state and city buildings and specialty exhibits (over 35 major buildings) as well as a midway in the surrounding area. The main exposition buildings included: Commerce, Mineral and Forestry, Agriculture, Transportation, Machinery, Horticulture, Live Stock, the Auditorium, and Administration, the latter serving as the "clubhouse for gentlemen and ladies." A Woman's Building and Children's Building had been part of both the Chicago Columbian Exposition and the Atlanta Cotton States Exposition, and were also part of the Tennessee Centennial. Following Atlanta's example, a Negro Building was included in the exposition plan, too. The U. S. Government Building featured exhibits from the departments of War, Treasury, Justice, Post Office, and the Smithsonian Institution. Nonstructural displays, such as a military encampment, provided regular dress parades on the site. Gondolas and steamboats allowed water transportation to the principal exposition buildings along Lake Watauga, a man-made lake. By land, rolling chairs and guides to push them were available (for a fee) outside the main gates and at key points throughout the grounds for those unable to walk the expansive exposition site.

After entering the grounds through the main entrance, visitors crossed Lake Wautauga via a reproduction of Venice's Rialto Bridge and headed to the architectural center of the grounds, the Fine Arts Building, known as the Parthenon. It was Director-General E.C. Lewis who envisioned a full-scale replica of the exterior of the Parthenon of the Athenian Acropolis as the focal point of the Tennessee Centennial. Lewis, who was in charge of commissioning the architects for the fair, hired William C. Smith to design the replica. The Parthenon, the first exposition structure under construction, set the tone for the rest. The final product was the most admired building on the grounds (and the only one to remain extant, although greatly restored). To further emphasize Nashville's claim as the Athens of the South, a monumental Pallas Athena statue, by Enid Yandell (who had previously worked at the Chicago Columbian Exposition), was located in front of the Parthenon and was the largest statue ever executed by a woman to that time. Created of staff around an armature, it is no longer extant. Flanking the Parthenon was an equally impressive structure, the Memphis (Shelby County) Building, known as the Pyramid of Memphis. In recognition of its Egyptian namesake, the exhibit by Memphis was housed in a large replica of the Pyramid of Cheops. The third structure clearly inspired by the ancient world was the History building, with its Erechtheum-like exterior. It housed an exhibit of historical artifacts and manuscripts related to Tennessee history.

As with other U.S. fairs of the time,

A replica of the Parthenon was the main building at the 1897 Tennessee Centennial Exposition in Nashville (courtesy Peter M. Warner).

Nashville's goal was to showcase technological, social, economic, and cultural progress in the south in general and in Tennessee in particular. Progress was often presented in a "before" and "after" manner. Visual examples of technological advances were presented via juxtapositions of outmoded cottage industry methods and tools with those of the modern machine age which replaced them; e.g., a handloom might be placed beside an electric powered textile machine. This technological progress represented the future of the New South. Other exhibits might take advantage of the temporal aspect of the fair by presenting an ever-changing display-in-progress; for example, cotton and tobacco were planted in front of the Agriculture Building where they could be observed during their entire growing season.

Social progress was represented by the special buildings devoted to the advances of women, blacks, and children. Not part of the principal buildings, their architectural styles were not classically inspired. The Woman's Building, designed by Sara Ward Conley, was based on the Hermitage, home of Andrew Jackson, and featured exhibits of women's contributions to society in education and the arts

from the early settlers to the 1890s. The Spanish-Revival style Negro Building, designed by Frederic Thompson, displayed exhibits showing the progress of African Americans via social, educational and profession organizations. The Rococo-style Children's Building held a series of entertainments and displays of interest to children and housed a kindergarten. In addition to the displays of art, education, and organizations in these buildings, lectures by visiting experts were part of each building's offerings, providing further emphasis on the advances made by each social group.

There were many exhibits beyond those in the exposition buildings. The 285-foot tall flagpole was built with a base of 15 columns, each of a different Tennessee wood and each representing a state that preceded Tennessee into the Union. The flagpole itself represented Tennessee as the sixteenth state. The structure was held together by northern steel, thereby creating in the flagpole a physical symbol of the re-unification of north and south as well as their associated industries.

Of course, there were also special events such as the two-day visit by President William McKinley, itself a symbol of reconciliation between north and south. McKinley, a Union veteran, was escorted by Confederate veterans, and the large crowd at the public event was enthusiastic and supportive. Kate Kirkman Day (September 30), which paid tribute to the president of the Woman's Board and wife of Exposition First Vice President Van Leer Kirkman, was celebrated with a floral parade of carriages.

What would a world's fair be without a midway? Located at the western corner of the grounds, the so-called "Vanity Fair" had some old favorites, such as the exotic scenes and performances of the Streets of Cairo, the Chinese Village, and Moorish Palace, and modern technological wonders, like the Cyclorama. The Giant Seesaw lifted riders over 200 feet in the air for just 10 cents, while "Shooting the Chutes" hurled a cab full of visitors down a ramp into a pool of water. Typical of southern expositions, the Old Plantation was an exact reproduction from the antebellum south.

The Tennessee Centennial and International Exposition was a great promotional success with 1.2 million paid admissions and 1.8 million visitors. A final profit of $39.44 meant it was a minor financial success as well. Within two years of the close of the fair, the exposition grounds were cleared, and Centennial City was converted into Centennial Park, which became the center of Nashville's city park system. Centennial Park today is an open space containing Lake Watauga, sunken gardens, and a band shell. All the exposition buildings were temporary structures, made of wood and staff, and not meant to last beyond the close of the fair. Most were destroyed but some were relocated, such as the Knights of Pythias Building which became a private residence in Franklin, Tennessee. Only the Parthenon replica remains as a symbol of the exposition's theme and grandeur. Escaping destruction, due to public sentiment, the plaster Parthenon was restored and made permanent in the 1920s using synthetic granite. Unlike the Centennial version, its interior was remodeled as a replica of its Greek predecessor as well. Today, it is the centerpiece of Centennial Park and serves as Nashville's art museum.

Bibliography

The papers of the Tennessee Centennial and International Exposition are housed at the Tennessee State Library and Archives in Nashville. The materials include financial records, correspondence, minutes, scrapbooks, photographs, and memorabilia from the exposition and the exposition company covering the years 1895–1900 (a finding aid is available at *http://www.state. tn.us/tsla/history/manuscripts/findingaids/ 1785.pdf*). Primary published sources include Herman Justi, ed., *The Official History of the Tennessee Centennial Exposition, May 1-October 30, 1897* (1898), *The Official Catalogue of the Tennessee Centennial and International Exposition* (1897), and *Official Guide to the Tennessee Centennial and International Exposition and City of Nashville* (1897). Another valuable source for fair research is the *Report of the United States Government Exhibit at the Tennessee Centennial Exposition, Nashville, 1897* (1901), which can be found at the special collections department of the library at the University of Tennessee, Knoxville. The *Report* features reports, event data, illustrations, and grounds layout. *Catalogue (Illustrated) Fine Arts Department Tennessee Centennial* (1897) contains an article by William. C. Smith, architect of the Parthenon, describing his various design sources.

For photographs, see *Art Album of the Tennessee Centennial and International Exposition, photographs by W. G. and A. J. Thuss* (1898); *Centennial Album of the Nashville Tennessee International Exposition* (1896) which contains watercolor renderings of the exposition buildings and photographs of the architects and prominent exposition figures; and *Souvenir of the Tennessee Centennial and International Exposition, Nashville, Tenn.* (1897), one of many souvenir publications, with lithographs and descriptive captions of the buildings.

Modern studies include coverage in "The New Orleans, Atlanta, and Nashville Expositions: New Markets, 'New Negroes,' and a New South" chapter of Robert Rydell, *All the World's a Fair* (1984), and Bobby E. Lawrence, *Nashville's Tennessee Centennial 1897* (1998), a pictorial history. The most informative websites are: *http://www. nashville.gov* and "The Tennessee Encyclopedia of History and Culture" at *http://tennesseeencyclo pedia.net* (University of Tennessee Press and Tennessee Historical Society).

Two good secondary sources contain limited but interesting information about the exposition and help place the event into the context of Nashville history: Jesse C. Burt, *Nashville: Its Life and Times* (1959), and Henry McRaven, *Nashville: Athens of the South* (1949). For information on Centennial Park, see Leland R. Johnson, *The Parks of Nashville: A History of the Board of Parks and Recreation* (1986).

Stockholm 1897

Lars F. Johansson

Allmänna Konst- och Industriutställningen

The Stockholm Great Art and Industrial Exhibition of 1897 took place at a time that has been described both as *la belle époque* and *fin-de-siècle*. Stockholm's exhibition had been in the making since 1893. Initially proposed in 1885, the exhibition did not truly materialize until some intense lobbying by Sweden's business community convinced the powers that be that it was the Swedish capital's turn to show what this country, tucked away in the far north, had to offer the world. Fortuitously for Swedish business interests, King Oscar II's 25th anniversary as a regent was coming up in 1897, thus paving the way for the city's exhibition. The fact that Sweden was experiencing an expansionary phase in the business cycle surely helped bring about the actualization of the exhibition as well. The exhibition was to be primarily a Scandinavian affair. But as a goodwill gesture for neighborly as well as political reasons, it also grew to include Russian and Finnish exhibits.

Construction on the site for the exhibition began in July 1895. The exhibition was situated on *Djurgården* encompassing an area of 200,000 square meters. To the north the area faced the city of Stockholm, to the west Stockholm Harbor (*Saltsjön*), to the east *Djurgårdsbrunnsviken*, and to the south Skansen.

King Oscar II opened the exhibition on May 15, 1897. It was divided into two categories: the art department and the industrial exhibit. The industrial exhibit showcased what Sweden and Scandinavia had to offer in the realm of engineering and industrial entrepreneurship. One of the focal points of the exhibition was the Industrial Hall (*Industri Hallen*) designed by Ferdinand Broberg and Fredrik Lilljekvist. The hall was the largest wood building in the world at the time, totaling 17,000 square meters. Its cupola (inspired by Istanbul's Hagia Sofia mosque) measured close to 100 meters. Approximately 34,000 trees were required for the construction of the hall, so that it came to be seen as a true testament to Sweden's wood and forest industry.

The art department was housed in the Art Hall (*Konst Hallen*). Also designed by Broberg and painted entirely in white, this building was described by many spectators as an artwork in itself. A number of the most well-known artists from Europe and the United States displayed their works, including luminaries such as Edvard Munch, Anders Zorn, Peter S. Krøyer, August Rodin, John Singer Sargent, and James Whistler. There were a number of other artists (such as Paul Gauguin, Edgar Degas and William Morris) scheduled to exhibit, but they backed out at the last minute.

Also located on the eastern portion of *Djurgården* was the Nordic Museum (*Nordiska Museet*). The museum was a beautiful, palatial structure of 5,000 square meters housing exhibits of science, child rearing, education, and health care. The western portion of the exhibition housed the Machinery Hall (*Maskin Hallen*) a colossal building of 10,000 square meters of iron and glass.

The most popular venue at the exhibition, with 12,000 visitors per day, was Old Stockholm (*Gamla Stockholm*), which showcased Swedish history. It was made to resemble Stockholm during the sixteenth century reign of King Gustav Vasa, the unifier of Sweden, and his descendants. The centerpiece of this piece of the urban past was the castle Three Crowns (*Tre Kronor*) and the Great Church (*Stor Kyrkan*) where Olaus Petri first proclaimed the reformation to the Swedes. More modern exhibits included the Tourist and Sport Exhibit (*Turist och Sportutställningen*) which displayed scenes from the country's outdoor and sporting life.

The theater and music exhibit featured a large Jenny Lind collection. And in spite of Sweden's frequently harsh climate, a Garden Exhibit (*Trädgårdsutsällningen*) was also developed. It consisted of three seasonal displays: Spring Exhibit (May 15–18), Summer Exhibit (July 30 — August 2), and the Fall Exhibit (September 23 — October 1).

The opening day of the exhibition was not for everyone. The high entrance cost of 10 crowns (2.5 days wages for a dock worker) meant it was primarily an affair for the wealthy. Later, the admission price was lowered to two crowns and eventually was reduced to 50 öre to attract working-class people. To attract citizens from outside Stockholm, there were "People's Trains" which provided discounted fares to people from smaller towns and villages to come and sample what Stockholm and the exhibition had to offer. Some employers were even footed the bill for their employees, and the more generous subsidized not only travel and admission costs, but also lodging for one night and spending money. Despite this egalitarianism, the exhibition management had monitors — occasionally members of the police — to watch over working class fairgoers. The bourgeoisie no doubt felt it necessary to keep the "under class" under control.

When the exhibition came to a close on October 3, 1897, a total of 1.5 million visitors had attended. These numbers were dwarfed by the 32.4 million attending the Paris exposition of 1889 and the 27.5 million who went to Chicago in 1893. Yet, the 1.5 million added up to 30 percent of Sweden's population at the time. In the end, the ticket receipts were bigger than had been expected. There was a deficit, but it was smaller than expected.

All in all, the Stockholm exhibition was a success, a glittering showcase of all that Sweden and Scandinavia had to offer the world. However, it ended on a sour note in the form of mass looting at the close of the exhibition, when rich and poor alike ransacked many of the exhibits in search of a souvenir. Nonetheless, Sweden had come a long way since exhibiting some of its products to less than stellar reviews at the London Exhibition of 1851.

Bibliography

Major sources in Swedish include the following: *Allmänna Konst- och Industriutställningen I Stockholm, 1897,* (1897); *Allmänna konst- och industriutställningen: Officiel katalog* (1897); and a more recent and descriptive analysis of the exhibition by Anders Ekström in *Den Utställda Världen: Stockholmsutställningen 1897 och 1800-talets Världsutställningar* (1994).

Contemporary sources in English include a translation of the official guidebook, *Official Guide to Stockholm and the Great Art and Industrial Exhibition* (n.d.); W.S. Harwood, "The World's Fair in Stockholm," *Outlook* (July 24, 1897) is a tourist's description, and J. Douglas, "The Scandinavian Exhibition at Stockholm," *Nation* (November 4, 1897) discusses the exhibits. For those interested in the exhibition buildings, the February 20, May 15, and May 29, 1897, issues of the *Builder* may be useful. Helpful scholarly works in English include Allan Richard, *Recognizing European Modernities: A Montage of the Present* (1995); "Spectacular Articulations of Modernity: The Stockholm Exhibition of 1897," in: *Geografiska Annaler.* Series B, Human Geography 73.1 (1991): 45–84; and Anders Ekstrom, "International Exhibitions and the Struggle for Cultural Hegemony," *Uppsala Newsletter* 12 (Fall 1989): 6–7.

Omaha 1898

Christine G. Garfinkle

Trans-Mississippi and International Exposition

"On June 1st, President McKinley touches the button which starts the great machinery of the Trans-Mississippi Exposition, at Omaha, and a well planned and executed enterprise is opened to the public," wrote Elsie Reasoner in her account of the exposition for *Godey's Magazine* (p. 609). After four years of planning, the Trans-Mississippi and International Exposition hosted more than 2,500,000 visitors viewing its 4,062 exhibits between June 1, 1898, and November 1, 1898. Located on a plateau overlooking the Missouri River, the exposition grounds spanned 184 acres of northern Omaha between 16th and 24th Streets and Pinkney and Pratt Streets on land provided by real estate developer and exposition corporation treasurer Herman Kountze.

The impetus for the Trans-Mississippi and International Exposition was to advertise the advancements of the states and territories of the west and to laud their material and cultural achievements. By 1898, the region was rebounding from the results of westward expansion — land acquisition by the transcontinental railroad, excessive homesteading, the failed attempt to turn a grazing region into a farming region, and declining support of local outfitting businesses. Fair organizers wanted to focus the exposition on the positive outcomes of this history, such as the establishment of cultural institutions, the broadening of agricultural and live stock products, and domination over the land by the pioneers. In true exposition fashion, progress was seen as moving westward from the earliest fairs of the east in New York and Philadelphia, then heading west to Chicago and on to Omaha. Just one year after Chicago's World's Columbian Exposition of 1893, the first Trans-Mississippi commercial congress of representatives from the western states and territories met to plan their exposition. Omaha was selected as the exposition site and on January 25, 1896, the Trans-Mississippi and International Exposition Corporation, headed by President Gordon Wattles, was formed. With help from various commercial sources, including business leaders and corporations, and national and local government, the corporation began work on the exposition in November 1897. In less than one year, the Omaha fair opened on time and with its main buildings completed, an unusual world's fair achievement.

The Columbian Exposition set the architectural theme for U. S. fairs with the use of classical- and Renaissance-revival style structures surrounding a central body of water and adorned by iconographic exterior sculptural ornamentation. Two local Omaha architects, Thomas Rogers Kimball and C. Howard Walker, were appointed supervising architects and, along with landscape architect Rudolph Ulrich of New York, were responsible for the overall plan of the fairgrounds. Kimball and Walker designed several smaller exposition buildings and also supervised the various architects, brought in from cities throughout the West, who were assigned the task of creating the main exposition buildings. These principal structures formed the Grand Court, a quadrangle of buildings around the 2,000-foot-long central lagoon. Visitors could promenade along the entire Grand Court, shaded from the sun and protected from the rain by a series of connected colonnades. They could glide along the lagoon in giant swan boats and Venetian gondolas and witness thousands of incandescent lights (serviced by the exposition's own power plant) illuminating the fair at dusk. The Trans-Mississippi Exposition broke with the predominantly ivory coloring of the buildings at the Columbian Exposition by applying color to their buildings' trim and decorations (although like the Chicago fair the Omaha fair was called the "White City").

The buildings of the Grand Court included the Government Building (Supervising Architect, Washington, D.C.), Fine Arts (Eames and Young, St. Louis), Liberal Arts and the Auditorium (Fisher & Lawrie, Omaha), Mines and Mining (J. J. Humphreys, Denver), Agriculture (Cass Gilbert, St. Paul), Manufacturers (S. S. Beman, Chicago), Machinery and Electricity (Dwight Perkins, Chicago), and the Administration Arch and Girls and Boys (Walker and Kimball Omaha and Boston), the latter funded through cash donations by grade school students. Exhibits within the exposition buildings emphasized western culture, production, and materials.

The exposition grounds continued to the east and north of the Grand Court. The Bluff's Track was the site of the state buildings and the Horticulture building (Charles Reindorff, Omaha). At the East Midway could be found a variety of attractions — the German Village, Moorish Palace, Mirror Maze, as well as the Streets of Cairo, with its camel rides, a Cairo Café, and dancing girls. The North Midway, accessed from the Grand Court via the Administration Arch, included sideshows and amusements, including the Wild West Show, Chinese Village, and Chiquita, the twenty-six-inch tall woman, as well as the "Giant See Saw" and "Shooting the Chutes" rides. There were also educational exhibits and ethnological displays. Here was found "A Street of All Nations," the Cyclorama (recreating the battle between the *Monitor* and the *Merrimac*), and recent inventions like those found in the Baby Incubators display. Beyond the North Midway were the Transportation (Walker and Kimball), Apiary (John McDonald, Omaha), and Dairy (F. A. Henninger, Omaha) buildings. West of the Transportation section were the Indian Exhibits and continuing north were the Stock Exhibition and Live Stock Shows for cattle, horses, swine, sheep, and poultry. Exhibits in all the exposition buildings represented the history, strengths, and future of the region by displaying products, manufactures, art, and the educational and social achievements from the states and territories west of the Mississippi River.

Various Congresses—musical, educational, religious—were held, but most notable was the Indian Congress that boasted representation by every known tribe still extant. Funded by the Bureau of American Ethnology and under the guidance of James Mooney, the Indian Congress opened in August 1898 with more than thirty-five tribes represented and five hundred Native Americans, including Apache Chief Geronimo, in attendance, displaying their native dwellings, costumes, industries, and utilitarian items, ceremonies, and customs. Unlike their representation in Wild West shows, the Indian Congress was intended to provide an educational and cultural forum for the exposition visitor regarding the current status of Native Americans. Reservations were seen as a temporary institution—it was planned that through the education and training of Native American children in government schools, assimilation was just a generation away. The Indian Congress, therefore, was touted as the last chance to view Native Americans in their "natural" environment. Unfortunately, the public taste leaned more to viewing the staged dances and sham battles than in the Native American mode of life.

"While the Exposition is an essentially Western enterprise, and has for its main object the demonstration of the material advantages of the Trans-Mississippi States," wrote Reasoner, "yet all America will join in making the Exposition a success" (p. 617). And so it was. The net revenue of the Trans-Mississippi and International Exposition was $215,812.62. At the close of the fair, the buildings were cleared of their displays and the grounds, with its remaining holdings, were sold to the Greater American Exposition for $17,500. Organizers of the Greater American had hoped to carry on the financial success of the Trans-Mississippi but failed after just three months. The grounds were cleared of the remaining structures, the lagoon was filled in, and Kountze Park was established as a public park. In 1998, Kountze Park was the site of the centennial celebration of the Trans-Mississippi and International Exposition.

Bibliography

The records of the Trans-Mississippi and International Exposition are housed at the Nebraska State Historical Society in Lincoln. The Omaha Public Library contains artifacts from the Trans-Mississippi and International Exposition, including a set of photographs by F. A. Rinehart, the official photographer for the exposition, memorabilia such as, programs, stock certificates, and medals awarded at the exposition, and the original "A History of the Trans-Mississippi and International Exposition," also known as the "Secretary's Report," completed by Exposition Secretary John Wakefield in 1903, which documents the exposition events.

Primary published sources include: James B. Hayes, *History of the Trans-Mississippi and International Exposition of 1898* (1910), the official history of the exposition commissioned by the board of directors; *Official Guide Book to the Trans-Mississippi and International Exposition, Omaha, U.S.A., June 1 to November 1, 1898* (1898); and *Official Catalogue of the Trans-Mississippi and International Exposition* (1898), an illustrated catalogue with exhibition descriptions. For photographs, see *Views of the Trans-Mississippi and International Exposition held at Omaha, Nebraska, June 1st to November 1st, 1898, Omaha, 1898* (containing views of the exposition buildings, interiors, streets and fair activities). Thumbnail-sized images that link to the full-size images are available via the internet at: *http://www.omaha.lib. ne.us/transmiss/research/thumbhtml/tmitable. html.*

Among contemporary publications, the

most informative accounts are found in Elsie Reasoner, "A National Wonder; the Trans-Mississippi and International Exposition," *Godey's Magazine* (June, 1898): 609–17, and Charles Howard Walker, "Great Exposition at Omaha," *Century Magazine* 55 (February 1898): 518–21. Articles were published throughout the planning and operation of the fair in the Omaha *Bee*, Omaha *World-Herald*, and *Harper's Weekly Magazine*. A history of the economic conditions in the Trans-Mississippi states prior to the exposition is found in Albert Shaw's "The Trans-Mississippians and Their Fair at Omaha," *Century Magazine* 56 (October 1898): 836–52.

A chapter on the Trans-Mississippi and International Exposition, "Concomitant to Empire," is included in Robert Rydell's *All the World's a Fair* (1984). Other modern studies are articles by Patrice K. Beam, "The Last Victorian Fair: The Trans-Mississippi International Exposi-

tion," *Journal of the West* 33 (1994): 10–23, which is an overview of the fair put into historical context, by Sarah J. Moore, "Mapping Empire in Omaha and Buffalo: World's Fairs and the Spanish-American War," *Bilingual Review* 25, 1 (2000): 111–126, and by Patrice Kay Beam, "The Last Victorian Fair: The Trans-Mississippi International Exposition," *Journal of the West* 33, 1 (January 1994): 10–23, and two monographs— Liz Cajka, *Westward the Empire: Omaha's World's Fair of 1898* (1998) and Jess R. Peterson, *Omaha's Trans-Mississippi and International Exposition* (2003).

The Omaha Public Library at *http://www.omaha.lib.ne.us/transmiss/* is the site for "Westward the Empire: Omaha's World Fair of 1898," (1998) a documentary video on the exposition produced by the University of Nebraska at Omaha Television.

Paris 1900

Robert W. Brown

Exposition Universelle

On July 13, 1892, not quite three years after the close of the successful 1889 exposition, the French Third Republic announced an Exposition Universelle for 1900. Jules Roche, the minister of commerce, noted the symbolic importance of this year, the end as well as the beginning of centuries of astonishing achievement, adding: "The Exposition of 1900 will synthesize the nineteenth century and ascertain its philosophy." No doubt—but rumors circulating in June that Kaiser Wilhelm II planned a world's fair for Berlin in 1900 supplied a more immediate stimulus. Mixed motives aside, the French mounted in 1900 the largest of the world exhibitions to date, and it celebrated more by recapitulating the expiring century than by anticipating the nascent one, the ideals, values, and accumulated industrial triumphs of European civilization at its height, all within a comparative historical framework. It also allowed exhibiting nations to boast peace-

fully about their wealth and power, while providing both an architectural fantasia and an entertaining miscellany of attractions and diversions, not to mention a surfeit of consumer products. The exposition accordingly mirrored fin-de-siècle Europe while revealing harbingers of the coming century.

Formal planning began on September 9, 1893, when a decree named Alfred Picard head of the Governing Commission. An official at the 1889 exposition as well as author of its report, an engineer by training and a civil servant by profession, Picard received almost complete autonomy in preparing the 1900 exposition. Within a month, he announced as its site the Esplanade des Invalides, the Champ de Mars, the Trocadéro, and the neighboring quays. And by November 1895, he had sketched its themes, projected attendance figures of 60 million, and suggested financing schemes. Of the fifty-three foreign powers invited, over forty had accepted, including all the great powers; for the first time, the German empire was to attend a Paris exposition. Noisy opposition in the legislature and the press notwithstanding, the authorization bill passed easily, becoming law on June 13, 1896. Approved was an expenditure of 105 million francs, to be raised from subventions of 20 million francs each from the French state and the city of Paris and the sale of 65 million francs of coupons redeemable for admission tickets.

While Picard and his commission supervised the preparation of the site, the construction of exhibition buildings, and the organization of the exhibits, matters beyond their control affected attitudes toward the fair, the content and reception of certain exhibits, and attendance figures. Deep-seated uncertainties, economic and social as well as political and international, prevailed in France during the exposition's planning, and advocates hoped it would not only stimulate the economy but renew domestic accord. Naturalism, positivism, and scientism, the reigning ideas of those who, like the planners of the exposition, retained faith in reason, progress, and human potential, were contested by metaphysical idealists and by a mood of intellectual and social decadence. And both long-term political and social divisions and their more immediate manifestations during the 1890s were aggravated by the Dreyfus affair, which split Paris until the presidential pardon of September 19, 1899, issued, some argue, because foreign supporters of Dreyfus threatened to boycott the exposition.

French international anxieties, the legacy of the German victory of 1870–1871, the Paris Commune, and the subsequent diplomatic isolation engineered by Otto von Bismarck, were lessened by the Russian alliance of 1894. Meanwhile, imperialistic ambitions led to clashes like that between the Marchand expedition and British troops at Fashoda (1898), the humiliating withdrawal poisoning relations with England, as did French support for the Afrikaners in the Boer War. Such events, together with eruptions of momentary concern like the Boxer Rebellion in China, made their presence felt at an exposition that was far from ready when the inaugural ceremonies took place on April 14, 1900.

Visitors to this *bilan du siècle* found its classification and layout bewildering, its size dismaying, and its transportation inadequate.

Within the main grounds, most walked, the moving sidewalk and the electric train having left large areas bereft of transportation. Worse, the arrangement of the exhibits begot confusion rather than the intended comprehension of industrial processes. According to official figures, exhibits totaled 83,047 — 38,253 by France and 44,794 by some forty foreign nations, over half European. Largest of the foreign exhibitors, the United States dispatched 7,610 exhibits, filling some 337,000 square feet of space. Picard organized these displays by methods traditional at the time, classifying them not by nation of origin but by 18 subject groups, subdivided further into a total of 121 classes, and ranked hierarchically from education and the fine arts to colonization and the military. More complexity resulted from the inclusion within each group of a historical exhibit illustrating advances since 1800. Outside this formal taxonomy were the official foreign pavilions, diverse exhibits, attractions, and entertainments.

The 1900 exposition occupied a site larger than any previous Paris exposition, with its main grounds in Paris (279 acres) and an annex at the Bois de Vincennes (274 acres). The former consisted of five sections arranged along three axes, the whole forming an immense letter A laid across the topography of central Paris. Arrayed along one axis were the fine arts exhibits (Group II) in the Grand and Petit Palais and displays of decorations and furnishings (Group XII) and miscellaneous Industries (Group XV) in two rectangular buildings facing each other on the Esplanade des Invalides.

The principal exhibition area extended from the Ecole Militaire to the Trocadéro. Parallel to the Ecole Militaire, the Galérie des Machines housed displays of agriculture (Group VII) and food and drink (Group X), separated by the Salle des Fêtes, site of both the opening and the awards ceremonies. Following exhibits of mechanics (Group IV) and electricity (Group V), the exhibition palaces bifurcated, reaching in parallel rectangles along the Champ de Mars toward the Seine and enclosing a garden with the Chateau d'Eau at one end and the Eiffel Tower at the other. To the left were chemical industries (Group XIV), civil engineering and transportation (Group VI), education and teaching (Group I) and letters, sciences, and arts (Group III), while opposite

The Algerian Palace was a popular attraction at the 1900 Exposition Universelle in Paris. In the background, through the Eiffel Tower opening, one can see the Palais d'Electricité (from *Peerless Paris and Its Marvelous Universal Exposition of 1900*, 1900).

were mechanics again, threads, cloth, and clothing (Group XIII) and mines and metallurgy (Group XI). At the base of the Eiffel Tower clustered restaurants and a potpourri of unclassified attractions, including the Panorama du Tour du Monde and displays by motoring and climbing clubs. Across the Pont d'Iéna and beneath the Palais de Trocadéro, built for the *Exposition universelle* of 1878 and demolished for that of 1937, sprawled the colonial exhibits (Group XVII), the exotic harvest of European imperialism.

Linking these axes were the displays that lined the quays of the Seine from the Pont d'Iéna to the Pont Alexandre III. Here were forestry, hunting, fishing, and gathering (Group IX), military displays (Group XVIII), social economy, sanitation, and public assistance (Group XVI), and horticulture (Group VIII). Also flanking the Seine were the foreign pavilions of the rue des Nations, halls for schol-

arly conferences, and assorted unclassified exhibits, attractions, and entertainments. Overall the exposition grounds in Paris created an unforgettable visual impression, one oriented around celebrated monuments and replete with splendid vistas, an image quite similar to that found in the Paris rebuilt by Baron Haussmann in the 1850s and 1860s.

Relegated to the Vincennes annex around Lake Daumesnil and little visited even after the Métro opened were exhibits, attractions, and competitions unsuitable for central Paris. Yet more agricultural exhibits, automobiles, and a Hall of Railways joined displays of heavy farm equipment, such as that sent by the McCormick Harvester Company. In addition to the second modern Olympic Games, competitive events ranged from the equestrian to ballooning, from tennis and croquet to motorcycle and automobile racing.

Exposition exhibits created a mosaic of

European civilization at its summit of power and influence. Most displays, especially those in the national pavilions, celebrated national pride as well. Appreciation of these achievements, however, eluded many, since the exposition lacked a self-evident theme, and the classification system not only separated exhibits that belonged together but also placed them in unexpected locations. Perfumes appeared with the chemical displays, while visitors interested in planned worker housing had to visit the Palais des Congrès, the German pavilion, and the Vincennes annex. And because the retrospective exhibits were segregated by classification group, it was all but impossible to gain a historical overview. Perhaps the exposition offered the promised synthesis of the nineteenth century, but if so, even the learned Henry Adams failed to ascertain it.

Exposition architecture incorporated existing buildings, permanent new structures, and temporary exhibition palaces. The Palais du Trocadéro remained from the 1878 exposition, while the Galérie des Machines and the Eiffel Tower survived from 1889, the latter two making evident that the architecture of 1900 would be less innovative than these austere structures of iron and glass.

The single enduring transformation of urban space occasioned by the exposition affected a site enclosed by the Seine and the Champs Elysées, the former Avenue d'Antin, and the Place de la Concorde and then occupied by the Palais de l'industrie erected for the 1855 exposition. Picard won approval for its replacement with an aesthetically unified complex, the Grand Palais, the Petit Palais, and the Pont Alexandre III, which would restore the vista from the Champs Elysées to the façade of the Invalides. Construction began when Félix Faure, then president of the Third Republic, and Czar Nicholas II of Russia laid the cornerstone of the Pont Alexandre III on October 7, 1896. Modern in design yet traditional in ornamentation, it realized a long-contemplated project for a Seine bridge and celebrated in both name and decoration the Franco-Russian Alliance of 1894.

Built to face each other across the new avenue Nicolas II, the Grand Palais, designed by Henri Deglane, Louis-Albert Louvet, and Albert Thomas, and the Petit Palais, the work of the Prix de Rome winner Charles-Louis

Girault, remain as representatives of late beaux-arts splendor. Since affiliates of the Ecole des Beaux-Arts dominated the selection of exposition architects, the design of these permanent buildings, as well as of the temporary exhibition palaces, derived from this school's concept of public architecture. Behind neo-baroque or neo-rococo stone façades, historically eclectic in style as well as allegorical and ennobling in decoration, these architects concealed innovative and modern uses of iron and glass.

The temporary exhibition palaces inspired the American publisher of a photographic album and most visitors to proclaim the exposition a dream city. Yet critics disparaged these buildings as chaotic and bizarre, likening them to the extravagant productions of a demented pastry chef or an opium smoker. With a few exceptions, the exhibition pavilions adhered to the same beaux-arts principles as the Grand and the Petit Palais, although they were more mannered in design and embellishment. With iron or steel frameworks covered by light colored plaster façades, they featured massive ornate porticoes, long colonnaded galleries, sweeping staircases, and semicircular arcades of rounded arches. Seeking novelty in decoration rather than originality of design, architects covered exterior surfaces with free standing statues and didactic sculpted groups, colored frescoes and friezes, while roof lines were broken by yet more sculpture and a jumble of domes, towers, pinnacles, and urns.

The panorama created by the twenty-two foreign pavilions along the Seine invited praise, and critics no less than visitors admired the "rue de Venise" of exposition. However arresting, this picturesque ensemble of juxtaposed façades, towers, and cupolas offered neither original nor significant architecture but rather, as recommended by exposition officials, examples of each contributing nation's historical or indigenous style. Most preferred complete historical re-creations, as did the British and the Germans, or pastiches of celebrated details as did Hungary, Italy, and Spain. With its wooden pavilion by Eliel Saarinen, Finland honored native traditions. Incongruous in contrast was Charles A. Coolidge's neo-classical American pavilion.

A miscellany of structures completed the exposition's architecture. The polychromed

This interior view of the Grand Palais, built for the 1900 Exposition Universelle in Paris, shows crowds admiring many fine works of sculpture (from *Peerless Paris and Its Marvelous Universal Exposition*, 1900).

Porte Binet, Réné Binet's monumental entrance on the place de Concorde could pass 60,000 visitors an hour beneath a dome flanked by two minarets, the ensemble topped by a controversial figure representing the city of Paris and illuminated by thousands of multicolored lights. Besides the art nouveau buildings, only Charles Gautier's horticultural pavilions of iron and glass appeared modem. To accommodate railway traffic for the exposition, Victor Laloux designed the Gare d'Orsay, reopened in 1986 as the Musée d'Orsay.

Within the exhibition buildings, cluttered and often pedantic displays awaited visitors. Some scrutinized model classrooms, while others marveled at the linotype composing machine, the new motion picture machines, or the operation of X-rays. The few still drawn by the machinery of the nineteenth century admired steam engines, a selection of railway equipment, hot-air balloons, and experimental flying

machines. Still others ambled among horticultural, agriculture, and foodstuff displays. And in each foreign pavilion exhibits celebrated national character: Bosnia's artisans working in precious metals and cloth; historical traditions, such as Hungary's Hall of the Hussars; scenic panoramas, like Sweden's dioramas; and the fine arts, such as Germany's re-creation of the library rooms from Sans-Souci. The United States sent an "Exhibit of American Negroes," organized in part by W. E. B Dubois, but it appeared in the Social Economy section, not in the American pavilion.

But by 1900 such displays no longer thrilled the imagination. What did was that "fairy electricity." Visitors crowded the Palace of Electricity to watch steam driven dynamos power the exposition's machinery and the thousands of lights that transformed the Trocadéro, the Seine panorama, and even the Porte Binet into a nocturnal fantasy. Visitors marveled at the

The Palais d'Electricité was perhaps the most ornate building in world's fair history (editors' collection).

newly invented automobile and viewed — some with pride, others with misgivings— the military might of the great powers. With extensive colonial displays, the French not only celebrated their acquisitions but also educated the public with displays of native life, like the Dahomey village, and re-creations, such as the newly discovered temples at Angkor Wat. The Boer and the Chinese pavilions received special attention owing to contemporary events.

Much applauded were the fine arts displays at the Grand Palais and the Petit Palais, the latter housing a historical survey of French arts from provincial libraries, museums, and churches. The Grand Palais sheltered both the "Centennale," a retrospective exhibit of nineteenth-century French paintings, and the "Décennale," an international exhibition of fine arts from the previous decade. In the French portion of the Décennale beaux-arts painters predominated, exhibiting their customary portraits, landscapes and seascapes, religious and genre scenes, nudes, and sentimental historical tableaux, often with Napoleonic associations. Notably absent were the impressionists and the post-impressionists. Bolder foreign exhibitors showed works by James Ensor, Gustav Klimt, and Ferdinand Hodler. The sculpture displays were likewise

conservative, and Auguste Rodin showed the Gates of Hell in a separate pavilion. For the Centennale, Roger Marx selected works by the impressionists for display along side recognized masterpieces by Jacques-Louis David and Gustave Courbet. Connoisseurs and artists in search of more modem art had to quit the exposition grounds for the Parisian galleries.

Art Nouveau enjoyed a special prominence at the exposition, notably in the decorative arts and the architecture of smaller buildings, but the frequent assertion that the 1900 exposition saw its triumph remains controversial. Examples of this fin-de-siècle style, with its emphasis on the long and sinuous line and its celebration of the fanciful, the bizarre, and the exotic, may be found in the grand staircase of the Grand Palais, the iron gates of the Petit Palais, the Métro stations of Hector Guimard, the Pavillon Bleu, and the dance pavilion designed for the American Loïe Fuller by Henri Sauvage and Pierre Roche. Art Nouveau rooms, featured in the German and Austrian exhibits, filled the pavilions of the art dealer Samuel Bing and the Union Centrale des Arts Décoratifs; a room from the latter, designed by Georges Hoentschel and containing jewelry by René Lalique and glassware by Emile Gallé, survives in the Musée des Arts Décoratifs in Paris.

Entertainments included commercial attractions, festival days with themes, special banquets, music, theatricals, dance, and sports. Of the admission-charging entertainments clustered beneath the Eiffel Tower and along the Rue de Paris on the right bank of the Seine, some were superficially educational, offering vicarious travel in space or time. At the Tour du Monde, plaster re-creations and dioramas of exotic scenes in Europe, North Africa, the Middle East, and the Far East predominated, and the Celestial Globe promised an imaginary journey into space. For the less adventurous, the Swiss Village provided, with its Alpine landscape, farms, and a village inhabited by costumed peasants, a bucolic and historical respite. The more historically minded could stroll the streets of Albert Robida's *Vieux Paris*, a full-scale picturesque evocation of medieval and Renaissance Paris, or view the historical tableaux at the Palais du Costume.

Seekers of thrills rather than edification favored the giant ferris wheel or the Manoir à l'Envers ("inverted house"). Exposition festivals, in addition to the opening and closing ceremonies and the inauguration of a statue of Lafayette by the United States on July 4, celebrated flowers, wine, automobiles, and military music. At the famous Banquet of Mayors of September 22, a crowd of 20,777 dined simultaneously. And along the Rue de Paris were grouped small theaters and cabarets like the Maison du Rire. Scattered pavilions, such as the Palais Lumineux, a sort of oriental-rococo fantasy of colored glass illuminated by thousands of electric lights, captivated evening visitors. Even within serious displays entertainments lurked. At the Russian pavilion, visitors could sit in a mock coach of the Trans-Siberian Railway and eat Slavic foods while painted scenery rolled by, creating the illusion of a journey from Moscow to Peking.

Total attendance for the Exposition universelle (April 15–November 12) was 50,860,801 (48,368,504 in Paris and 2,492,297 at Vincennes). Festivals organized by worried officials bolstered attendance, which lagged behind predictions until August. September saw the most visitors (9,555,059) and the midpoint for total paid attendance. On October 7, the greatest single day for attendance, 652,082 visited the exposition. Foreign visitors came chiefly from Germany; the English stayed home, a result of

French sympathy for the Boers and anti–British sentiments in Parisian newspapers. Also reducing attendance from the projected 60 million were the tardy completion of the exposition grounds, summer heat, international resentment engendered by the Dreyfus affair, and the absence of visiting monarchs, many of whom viewed Paris as home to anarchist assassins. Despite disappointment that attendance did not exceed official estimates, the figures established a long-standing record for a one-season fair.

Drawing up a financial balance sheet for the Exposition universelle proves difficult, though few would dispute that the French economy benefited, directly or indirectly. Operators of the admission-charging attractions, like the Tour du monde (cost: 2 million francs; receipts: 691,245 francs), however, experienced losses, as did restaurateurs and other concession holders. Reports of profits or losses for the exposition itself vary, often depending on the accounting procedure. Picard's initial estimates (January 1901) set the loss at 2 million francs, less than 2 percent of expenditures. Figures of April 30, 1903 (expenses 119,225,707 francs; receipts: 126,318,169 francs) indicate profits of 7 million francs, while others suggest profits as high as 9½ million. Even the loss figures are insignificant when juxtaposed with the additional revenues taken in by the state, the city of Paris, the railroads, and the Bank of France, not to mention the increased income enjoyed by Parisian hotels, restaurants, stores, and theaters. The exposition must be reckoned a financial success.

The Exposition universelle of 1900 was the last, as well as the greatest, of a cycle of five Parisian expositions that began in 1855. With respect to attendance figures or impressions carried home, most contemporaries regarded it a success but not the astonishing success anticipated. Among Frenchmen who believed expositions provided an opportunity for France to show its best face, some concluded that it revealed instead a second-rate power, a nation overshadowed by the Germans, the Americans, and even the Japanese. Both foreign commentators and their French counterparts wrote of the exposition with an ambiguous mixture of optimism and fin-de-siècle pessimism. Among the favorable, Patrick Geddes descried beneath a glittering surface its retrospective character as a "literal museum of the present" and an "incipient museum of the History of Civilization," though he found overwhelming the exposition's size and diversity. And while some lamented the absence of revolutionary advances in technology, Henry Adams contemplated the gigantic dynamos and saw a world of power he could not understand. Those sharing Adams's pessimism perceived, as Richard Mandell has suggested, the dim outlines of the twentieth century, where material progress would race ahead of humanity's ability to deal with it, where things and knowledge would so accumulate that people could neither adequately classify nor fully comprehend them, and where simple faith in science, reason, and progress was about to be shattered. The exposition accordingly mirrored Europe of the belle époque, a brilliant, if often arrogant and naively optimistic, civilization that all too rarely examined itself with discernment.

Bibliography

Study of the 1900 exposition begins with the annotated bibliography in Richard D. Mandell, *Paris 1900: The Great World's Fair* (1967). Listed are specialized bibliographies, official documents, guidebooks, contemporary newspapers and journals, and secondary accounts. Because this book is readily available, only the more important sources will be listed here, together with works omitted by Mandell or published since his book appeared. Of the two works by Alfred Picard, general commissioner of the exposition, the *Rapport général administratif et technique*, 8 vols. (1902–1903) is essential; also see his *Le Bilan d'un siècle* (1801–1900), 6 vols. (1906). Of much interest are the *Catalogue général officiel*, 20 vols. (1900), the commercial guidebooks (especially the Hachette guide, which is available in English), as well as the separate guides for each exhibit and for each nation's displays. For U.S. participation, see the *Report of the Commissioner-General for the United States to the International Universal Exposition. Paris. 1900*, 6 vols. (1901), published as Senate Document No. 232, 56th Cong., 2d sess., vols. 27–32. At the National Archives are the records of the U.S. Commission; see the inventory for Records Group 43. A short and relatively accessible preview of U.S. participation is Ferdinand Peck, "The United States at the Paris Exposition in 1900," *North American Review*, 168 (January 1899): 24–33.

Contemporary opinion concerning the exposition may be found in the periodical literature of the exhibiting nations, beginning in the mid–1890s. For France, see especially: *L'Illustration* (for maps and pictures), *Revue des deux mondes*, *Revue de Paris*, and *Gazette des beaux arts*. A collection of translated excerpts relating to art and architecture is in Elizabeth Gilmore Holt, ed., *The Expanding World of Art, 1874–1902, vol. 1: Universal Expositions and State-Sponsored Fine Arts Exhibitions* (1988). For visual impressions of the exposition, consult the many illustrated albums, such as José de Olivares, *The Parisian Dream City: A Portfolio of Photographic Views of the World Exposition at Paris* (1900), and James Penny Boyd, *The Paris Exposition of 1900: A Vivid Descriptive View ...* (1900). For architectural views, see A. Raguenet, *Les Principaux Palais de l' Exposition universelle de Paris* (1900), and *L'Architecture et la sculpture: Exposition de 1900* (1900?). Verbal descriptions are legion; among the available are Paul Morand, *1900 A.D.*, trans. Mrs. Romilly Fedden (1931) and vol. 9 of William Walton, *Paris from the Earliest Period to the Present Day*, 10 vols. (1899–1902). For the reflections of Henry Adams, see *The Education of Henry Adams. An Autobiography* (1918) and the *Letters of Henry Adams [1892–1918]* (1938). Delightful as an antidote to the usual ponderous accounts is Gaston Bergeret, *Journal d'un nègre a l'Exposition de 1900* (1901).

Secondary works include: Jean-Christophe Mabire, ed., *L'Exposition universelle de 1900* (2000), a centennial book, Adolphe Démy, *Essai historique sur les Expositions universelles de Paris* (1907), 438–688; Philippe Jullian, *The Triumph of Art Nouveau. Paris Exhibition 1900*, trans. Stephen Hardman (1974); Pascal Ory, *Les Expositions universelles de Paris* (1982); and Franco Borsi and Ezio Godoli, *Paris 1900: Architecture and Design* (1989). Useful for the mood of *fin-de-siècle* France are Jacques Chastenet, *La Republique triomphante, 1893–1906* (1955), vol. 3 of his *Histoire de la Troisième république*. 6 vols. (1952–1963); Charles Rearick, *Pleasures of the Belle Epoque: Entertainment and Festivity in Turn-of-the-Century France* (1985); Eugen Weber, *France Fin de Siècle* (1986); and Theodore Zeldin, *France, 1848–1945*, 2 vols. (1973–1977). Of considerable interest is Rosalind H. Williams, *Dream Worlds: Mass Consumption in Late Nineteenth-Century France* (1982); she views the exposition as a "scale model of the consumer revolution." Art Nouveau can be studied in Jean-Paul Bouillon, *Art Nouveau, 1870–1914* (1985), Franco Borsi and Ezio Godol, *Paris 1900*, trans. J. C. Palmes (1977), and Paul Greenhalgh, *Art Nouveau: 1890–1914* (2000). Beaux-arts architecture and the Petit Palais are discussed in Derrick Worsdale, "The Petit Palais des Champs-Elsyées: Architecture and Decoration," *Apollo* 107

(March 1978): 207–11; superb notes make this article a guide for further work. And also of interest are: Emmanuelle Toulet, "Le Cinéma à l'Exposition universelle de 1900," *Revue d'histoire moderne et contemporaine* 33 (April-June 1986): 179–209; William H. Schneider, "Colonies at the 1900 World Fair," *History Today* 31 (May 1981): 31–36; Arthur Chandler, "Culmination: The Paris Exposition Universelle of 1900," *World's Fair* 7, 3 (Summer 1987): 8–14; Jeannene M. Przyblyski, "Visions of Race and Nation at the Paris Exposition, 1900: A French Context for the American Negro Exhibit," in: William L. Chew, III, ed., *National Stereotypes in Perspective: American in France; Frenchmen in America* (2001): 209–244; Elizabeth Emery, "Protecting the Past: Albert Robida and the *Vieux Paris* Exhibit at the 1900 World's Fair," *Journal of European Studies* 35

(2005): 65–85; Emmanuelle Toulet, "Le Cinéma a l'Exposition universelle de 1900," *Revue d'histoire moderne et contemporaine* 33 (avril-juin 1986):179–200 (available in English as "Cinema at the Universal Exhibition, Paris, 1900," *Persistence of Vision* 9 [1991]: 10–36), and Robert W. Brown "Albert Robida's *Vieux Paris* Exhibit: Art and Historical Re-creation at the Paris World's Fair of 1900," William E. Grimm and Michael B. Harper, eds., *Year Book of Interdisciplinary Studies in the Fine Arts.* (1991): vol 2, 421–445. On-line sources include Jeffrey Howe, *A Digital Archive of Architecture* (*http://www.bc.edu/bc_org/avp/fnart/arch/1900fair.html*) and the University of Maryland, *A Treasury of World's Fair Art and Architecture* (*http://www.lib.umd.edu/digital/worldsfairs/index.jsp*).

Buffalo 1901

Lewis L. Gould and Kris L. Brackett

Pan-American Exposition

The opening of the Pan-American Exposition was announced by the Buffalo *News* on May 1, 1901 with great excitement: "The promise that the Pan-American would be the electrical marvel of the opening century has been kept." With over 2,000,000 light bulbs and the 375 ft. Electric Tower that could be seen some twenty miles away, visitors would certainly continue to enjoy their experience after dusk. But high expectations for the exposition were shadowed by the assassination of President William McKinley on September 6, 1901 and economic concerns as losses exceeded $3 million by the time the exposition ended. Despite these troubles, the Pan-American Exposition was, in McKinley's words, "a timekeeper of progress ... a record [of the] world's advancement."

The idea to hold an exposition in Buffalo, NY, originated in 1895 when businessmen attending Atlanta's Cotton States and International Exposition were inspired to host a similar event back home. The arrival of low-cost electric power from Niagara Falls in 1896 provided the technological advancement to be celebrated and the Pan-American Exposition Company was formed. In September 1897 the directors chose Cayuga Island near the falls as the site of the exposition, and planning for the event continued. The company issued bonds and filed for aid from New York State and the federal government. The organizers aimed to promote the material progress of the New World while also creating better relations and opportunities for trade with Latin America. In July 1898, the U.S. Congress adopted a resolution that said, "A Pan-American Exposition will undoubtedly be of vast benefit to the commercial interests of the countries of North, South, and Central America." Though the aims were ambitious, planners were filled with optimism and confidence.

Unfortunately these early plans for the exposition were halted by the rising tension between the United States and Spain over the fate of Cuba, resulting in the culmination of war in

Temple of Music. Buffalo. N.Y. Pan American Exposition
Building in which President Mc. Kinley was shot September 6th, 1901.

President McKinley's assassination in the Temple of Music at the Pan-American Exposition in 1901 cast a pall over the fair (editors' collection).

April 1898. The organizers, not wanting to compete with the Paris Exposition of 1900, chose the period from May to November 1901 to hold the event. Congress appropriated money for a U.S. Government building and New York State provided $300,000 for its own exhibit. The State Department invited the governments of all countries of the Western Hemisphere to take part. Popular subscriptions, primarily in the Buffalo area, brought in $1.5 million. Though the exposition leaders expected an abundance of participation by Latin American countries, the degree of local support and South American participation failed to reach the amounts projected during the planning phase.

Local leaders were then faced with the problem of deciding where the exposition should be located. The site finally chosen was the Rumsey property, together with a portion of Delaware Park, for an area that comprised 350 acres. Also important was the existence of trolley car lines along three sides of the grounds. For merely five cents, a visitor could ride to the exposition from any point in the city, and it was located only twenty minutes from downtown Buffalo.

William I. Buchanan, an American diplomat who had been involved with the 1893 Columbian Exposition, was named director general of the Pan-American Exposition in late 1899. He discovered quickly the many weaknesses in the plan for the exposition. The venture was not financially secure and the city was not yet prepared to handle the number of visitors expected. Furthermore, Buchanan was disappointed by the limited role Latin American countries would actually have in the exposition. He attempted to overcome these problems through an extensive advertising campaign to promote the exposition across the nation, a campaign that proved to be momentous in the history of American advertising. *Profitable Advertising* reported, "It is universally admitted that no similar enterprise has ever been so well advertised, and the methods used have met with the public's unqualified approval."

Despite the success of Buchanan's advertising campaign, the exposition faced more difficulties in early 1901. Bad weather consistently delayed construction efforts and forced the fair's board of directors to delay the open-

180. Pan-American Exposition, Buffalo, N. Y.: In the Streets of Cairo.

This colorful postcard shows the flags of the nations of the Western Hemisphere and the natives that were a part of the Streets of Cairo attraction (editors' collection).

ing ceremonial activities by three weeks to May 20, Dedication Day. Leaders were determined however, to keep the opening date of May 1, even though many of the exhibits were not in place and the grounds were in great disorder. "Early visitors went away with a grievance, to vent their disappointment at home," said one Cleveland newspaper, "and they did much to keep people away from Buffalo all through the season."

Dedication Day itself was a success. At noon there were exercises to dedicate the U.S. Government buildings followed by an explosive salute with 45 aerial bombs fired from the esplanade while "The Star Spangled Banner" blared from the bands. Over 100,000 people came to see Vice-President Theodore Roosevelt and other dignitaries. President McKinley was traveling on the West Coast and sent his greetings by telegram: "I earnestly hope that this great exposition may prove a blessing to every country of this hemisphere." Everything, however, was not blessed at the exposition. Visitors were few in number, hovering around 10,000 daily, as the exposition was plagued by heavy rains, labor disputes, and rumors amidst the public that the fair could not possibly be completed before June 15. The exposition lacked a

clear vision of what it hoped to achieve, opened late without being finished, and suffered from both bad luck and bad policy.

The exposition might have been largely a disappointment to visitors but it received great reviews from the press. After surveying the exposition, Mary Bronson Hartt said that it was "industrially too significant, educationally too important, and aesthetically too superb to be passed by." Another writer observed that when the lights went on each night the first-time visitor understood "something of the ecstasy of the sun-worshipper when the red disk appears the Persian Hills." The Pan-American Exposition was the first time that electricity formed the chief organizing theme of a fair. Artificial lighting and the Electric Tower attraction proved to be very popular attractions and captured the attention of visitors. Every building was outlined in incandescent lights with a staggering effect. The editor of *Atlantic Monthly*, Walter Hines Page, commented that, "At a distance the Fair presents the appearance of a whole city in illumination. The tower is a great center of brilliancy. It shines like diamonds, a transparent, soft structure of sunlight." Page was a big supporter of imperialism and the exposition, and saw the Electric Tower as an "epiphanous achievement, a masterpiece of human skill, a monument to the genius of man."

The color scheme of the exposition elicited even more praise. Hamilton Wright Mabie wrote, "The Pan-American Exposition adds to the charm of order and grace the beauty of color." The color scheme and the organization of sculpture came from the collaboration of Karl Bitter and Charles Y. Turner. They decided to make their particular areas assert the larger themes of the fair. Color schemes were worked out in advance using models with nearly every color imaginable being used but with special emphasis on all shades of gray and yellow, as well as blue, green, red, violet, orange, gold, and ivory. There were over 2,000 pieces of sculpture, many of which were made by famous American sculptors. The structures were done in Spanish Renaissance style, chosen to suggest "the historical continuity of life in the Americas" and as a compliment to Latin American neighbors.

The general plan of the exposition was arranged by John M. Carrère with main buildings surrounded by a broad court in the form of an inverted "T." There was a large plaza with sunken gardens, a bandstand, and a terrace for the music audience. A court of fountains sat between the Ethnology Building and the Temple of Music, beyond which were the Manufacturers and Liberal Arts Building and the Machinery and Transportation Building. Further along were the magnificent Electric Tower, the Electricity Building, and the Agriculture Building. Nearby these colorful buildings was the midway, which offered a Trip to the Moon, Dreamland, House-Upside-Down, Scenic Railroad, Colorado Goldmine, Darkness and Dawn, Merry-Go-Round, Ostrich Farm, Wild Animal Arena, and small villages occupied by a variety of ethnicities

The Electric Tower at the Pan-American Exposition stood at the center of the fairgrounds and dazzled fairgoers with its nighttime light shows (editors' collection).

including Indians, Mexicans, Eskimos, Africans, and others. The midway promoters spent over $250,000 preparing this area for visitors and it was promoted heavily.

The transplanted native villages were promoted as an educational experience, but they were also embraced by the U.S. government as a means of countering the rising sentiment of anti-imperialism. The government directed ethnologist Frank F. Hilder to collect artifacts from the Philippines to be featured in an

In this scene of the midway of the Pan-American Exposition, visitors could buy Mexican cigars and arrange to go see Niagara Falls (Larson Collection, Special Collections Library, CSU, Fresno).

exhibit highlighting the newly acquired possession. This display was opened in the government building, along with a Filipino village on the midway that became "one of the most thoroughly native things on the Street of Streets" and "almost as good as a trip to the islands." The Philippines Exhibit was the focal point of the colonial exhibits and was so successful that it shaped the exhibits planned for the St. Louis exposition. Though the presence of Latin American countries at the fair was less than hoped for, promoters of the fair felt that at least one of their goals had been met by demonstrating the linkage between the United States and the other nations of the Western Hemisphere. Mabie wrote, "The word American has never received a broader or deeper interpretation; and the thoughtful visitor will find in the beautiful unity of the Exposition a parable which Americans of English descent will do well to study."

By July attendance at the fair began to rise and by August there were over 40,000 visitors each day. September was expected to be a great month for visitors and improved profits due to a scheduled visit by President McKinley on September 5, when he was to deliver a major presidential speech followed by a public reception at the Temple of Music the next day. A record-breaking 116,000 people arrived at the fair for observance of President's Day at the exposition. McKinley stood before a crowd of 50,000 to praise the exposition that stimulated "the energy, enterprise, and intellect of the people and quicken human genius." The Pan-American theme was the perfect setting to advance the central purpose of the President's second term. His speech, which argued for reciprocity, sensible trade arrangements, and an expanding outlet for America's ever-increasing level of production, was met with enthusiastic cheers from the crowd. At sunset the grounds were lit with colorful fires, lighted balloons, firing rockets, shells, and streamers. For the fireworks finale, thousands of tiny fire balls exploded at once, creating a gigantic sparkling image of the President and spelled out the greeting: "Welcome to McKinley, Chief of Our Nation."

On September 6, the second day of the president's visit, McKinley went sightseeing thirty minutes away at Niagara Falls before his afternoon reception at the Temple of Music. The exposition was a promotional windfall for the falls as thousands were attracted to this nearby wonder making it an internationally famous tourist site. He walked along the gorge and toured the Niagara Falls Power Project, and viewed the American Falls from the International Bridge. McKinley returned to Buffalo for lunch and then to the exposition for his 4:00 reception at the north side of the fairgrounds. When the doors to the Temple of Music opened, hundreds of people filled the auditorium where President McKinley, John Milburn, and George Cortelyou were waiting. The president, his Secret Service men, and management for the exposition were all aware of potential security issues but a combination of factors enabled a lone assassin to appear in the receiving line for the president. It was an oppressively hot day and the temperature inside the auditorium had reached ninety degrees. Most everyone was holding handkerchiefs to wipe their brows and to wave at McKinley.

Leon Czolgosz, a self-identified anarchist who had suffered a breakdown as a young man before moving to Buffalo in 1901, stood in the receiving line holding a handkerchief that hid his gun. When the fast-moving line brought him directly in front of the president, Czolgosz shot him twice in the stomach. Attending soldiers and guards jumped on the assassin as McKinley was carried out amid the chaos and taken to the exposition hospital. The president was mortally wounded but lasted eight days. Dr. Matthew Mann, a leading Buffalo gynecologist was placed in charge of McKinley's care but he had limited experience in abdominal surgery. The newly invented x-ray machine was on exhibit but was not chosen for use on the president. He died on September 14 from gangrene caused by the doctors' failure to locate one bullet and to adequately cleanse the wounds. Leon Czolgosz was executed on October 29, 1901.

The exposition, which has been closed in McKinley's honor September 14 and 15 reopened and continued on through its originally scheduled closing date of November 2. The final month of the fair brought in an initial surge of visitors. Clever merchants profited from sales of McKinley memorabilia. But visitors began to lose interest in the exposition after the death of the president. William Buchanan declared that November 1 would be "Buffalo Day" and he pleaded to residents of the city to make closing day a success but they didn't come. He asked business leaders to grant half-day holidays to their workers but they refused. The small number of visitors who did show up left a path of destruction as they wrecked the exposition. Light bulbs were smashed, windows were broken, and doors were kicked down by the unruly visitors who created vast amounts of damage.

The official end of the exposition was much less climatic. William Buchanan had already left to represent the United States at a conference in Mexico City and was not present to commemorate in any way the end of the fair. At midnight ten buglers sounded taps from the Electric Tower. Exposition President John Milburn extinguished all of the decorative lights. The Pan-American Exposition had come to an end. By December the exposition buildings were sold to a Chicago company and the grounds were deserted.

In March 1902, Director General William Buchanan submitted his final report on the Pan-American Exposition. He lavishly praised its benefits for Buffalo, the nation, and the Western Hemisphere, for fulfilling its mission and promoting "commercial well being and good understanding" among participants. Business had never been so prosperous in the city and brought to western New York general growth in bank deposits, steady employment, rising rages, and national recognition. The exposition was a great stimulus to the industrial and cultural growth of the city. As one Philadelphia newspaper claimed, "The city has never been so advertised, a new life infused into all its channels, and several million dollars have been left there by visitors."

More than 8 million visitors came to the Pan-American Exposition, with 5.3 million of them paying the entrance fee and spending more throughout the grounds. Yet on closing day the deficit was in excess of $3 million and stockholders lost another $2.5 million from their investment. Many of the bonds issued were defaulted. Lawsuits increasingly were filed against the Pan-American Exposition Company. It was difficult for promoters of the exposition to share the enthusiasm and optimism of the Buchanan's report. The disappointment from financial failure and the inability to attract more visitors left an impact on the city of Buffalo, which lost some of its prestige and confidence and failed to become more than a respectable urban center in upstate New York. Some historians believe that it marked the decline of the city for the twentieth century.

The broader aim to encourage Pan-Americanism and future peaceful cooperation between the nations was mostly unrealized. Exhibits promoted the technological and cultural advancements of the United States with the lesser advanced countries of Latin America, influencing how Americans viewed the cultures of these countries. The *Official Catalogue and Guide* referred to exhibits as "the customs and institutions of wild and barbarian tribes." Modern scholars regard the Pan-American Exposition as an expression of cultural chauvinism and racial hegemony that marked the era of William McKinley's presidency, promoting the need for Americans to embrace imperialism.

The lasting legacy of the Pan-American Exposition is the historical importance of McKinley's assassination, which made it possible for Theodore Roosevelt to lead America in the new century. The Pan-American will always be associated with this tragic event that changed the course of modern American history.

Bibliography

Primary source materials for the Pan-American Exposition may be found in the following manuscript collections: William I. Buchanan Collection, Buffalo and Erie County Historical Society. This collection features Buchanan's correspondence as director general, along with other documents related to the exposition. The society also has a permanent exhibit entitled "Spirit of the City: Imagining the Pan-American Exposition" which contains the revolver used to assassinate McKinley, materials housed in the Pan-American Exhibition Hall, and numerous other items. *http://www.bechs.org/exhibits/exhibits.htm* See also Buchanan's published report, William I. Buchanan, *Pan-American Exposition, Report of William I. Buchanan, Director General* (1902).

Smithsonian Institution, Group 70, Series 14 covers the participation of the institution at Buffalo. The incoming and outgoing correspondence of Frederick W. True pertains to the organization, preparation, and administration of the Smithsonian exhibits. Of special interest are True's correspondence and records related to the Outlying Possessions Exhibit of the Government Board, including F. F. Hilder correspondence. *http://siarchives.si.edu/findingaids/FARU0070.htm.*

William McKinley Papers, Manuscript Division of the Library of Congress. This collection includes papers relating to the arrangements for the president's visit to the exposition. *http://www.loc.gov/rr/mss/text/mckinley.html.*

Theodore Roosevelt Inaugural National Historic Site, National Park Service. Here there is a permanent and virtual collection to commemorate the 100th anniversary of the Pan-American Exposition. *http://www.nps.gov/archive/thri/PanAmExhibit.htm.*

Films of McKinley and the Pan-American Exposition, 1901, Library of Congress. These films include footage of President William McKinley at his second inauguration; of the Pan-American Exposition in Buffalo, New York; of President McKinley at the Pan-American Exposition; and of President McKinley's funeral. The films were produced by the Edison Manufacturing Company from March to November 1901. *http://memory.loc.gov/ammem/papr/mckhome.html.*

Illuminations: Revisiting the Buffalo Pan-American Exposition of 1901, University of Buffalo. Based in part on a series of exhibits installed at the University of Buffalo in 2001, this site presents a wide range of both primary texts and original essays on the history of the Pan-American Exposition. *http://ublib.buffalo.edu/libraries/exhibits/panam/.*

The most useful contemporary periodical articles concerning the exposition include the *Official Catalogue and Guide Book to the Pan-American Exposition* (1901), published by the Pan-American Exposition Company; Mary Bronson Hartt, "How to See the Pan-American Exposition," *Everybody's Magazine* 5 (October 1901): 488–91; Charles Edward Lloyd, "The Pan-American Exposition as an Educational Force," *Chautauquan* 33 (July 1901): 333–36; Hamilton Wright Mabie, "The Spirit of the New World as Interpreted by the Pan-American Exposition," *Outlook* (July 10, 1901): 529–47. William I Buchanan, "The

Organization of an Exposition," *Cosmopolitan, 31* (September 1901): 317–21, provides the perspective of the director general during the fair. Also helpful are: "Opening of the Pan-American Exposition at Buffalo," *Literary Digest* (June 22, 1901): 753–54, and "The Pan-American Three Million Dollar Deficit," *Literary Digest* (November 9, 1901): 561–62.

Modern writing on the fair includes Kerry Grant, *The Rainbow City: Celebrating Light, Color and Architecture at the Pan American Exposition, Buffalo 1901* (2001), which revisits the exposition to reveal the ambitious color and architectural scheme that symbolically depicted and celebrated the progress of civilization. Austin Fox, *Symbol and Show: The Pan-American Exposition of 1901* (1995) is a heavily illustrated informal account of the fair. Thomas Leary and Elizabeth Sholes, *Buffalo's Pan-American Exposition* (1998), explores the exposition using pictorial items from the Buffalo and Erie County Historical Society. Barbara A. Seals Nevergold, "Doing the Pan": The African-American Experience at the Pan-American Exposition, 1901," *Afro-Americans in New York Life and History* 28, 1 (2004): 23–41, discusses the race issue at a sensitive time, and Sarah J. Moore, "Mapping Empire in Omaha and Buffalo: Wordl's fairs and the Spanish-American War," *Bilingual Review* 25, 1 (2000): 111–126, discusses the fair in relation to the war that gave America an empire. William Irwin, *The New Niagara: Tourism, Technology, and the Landscape of Niagara Falls* (1996), includes a chapter on the Pan-American Exposition and places the fair in the context of the growth of Niagara Falls as a source of electric power and as a tourist attraction. Lauren Belfer, *City of Light* (1999), is a work of historical fiction that tells the story of the Pan-American Exposition, as is Barbara Soper, *Carnival of Rainbows: A Novel of the Pan-American Exposition* (2002). The centennial of the Pan-American Exposition saw the production of two video documentaries: *The Pan-American Experience* (2001), directed by Lynne Bader-Gregory, and *Rainbow City: Reflecting Buffalo's Century of Progress* (2002), which emphasizes Buffalo's relationship with electricity.

Glasgow 1901

Cristina Carbone

Glasgow International Exhibition

Despite the half mourning requested by the new king to honor Queen Victoria's recent death in January and the prolonged debacle of the Boer War, the second Glasgow Exhibition opened under auspicious skies on May 2, 1901. The Duchess of Fife turned the golden key opening the 75-acre Kelvingrove park site, virtually the same that had been developed for the 1888 exhibition. Held to commemorate both the fiftieth anniversary of that first world's fair and the opening of the city's Art Gallery and Museum, the 1901 Glasgow International Exhibition proved to be the largest of its kind in Great Britain to date, its 11.5 million visitors doubling the attendance of the Great Exhibition of 1851.

While the museum was a red sandstone Spanish-Jacobethan bulwark from the designs of Simpson and Allen of London, the main exhibition building was in the Spanish Renaissance-Baroque style popularized at the Chicago 1893 and Buffalo 1901 exhibitions. Perhaps intending to counter the dark solemnity of the museum, architect James Miller broke up the white staff façade of the 200,000 square foot Industrial Hall into delightful massings that were by turns pseudo-Spanish, Turkish, and Venetian. Four Spanish wedding-cake towers flanked the corners of the great golden dome, atop of which stood an Angel of Light, bearing aloft her electrically illuminated torch. As at Buffalo, the buildings and fairgrounds were effectively illuminated by colored electric bulbs, creating a virtual fairyland after dark. A Shuckert searchlight, first seen at Chicago, was turned on the buildings and crowds to announce daily closing time. Directly under the dome of Industrial Hall stood an 18-

foot statue of the new king, Edward VII. Rather disrespectfully, His Majesty's subjects made rendezvous "under King Edward's nose."

Angled toward one another at the top of Kelvingrove Park, the Art Galleries and Industrial Hall formed an impressive backdrop to the foreign and commercial display pavilions scattered below. Machinery Hall, so important to the display of Glasgow's major industries, including steel, railways, and shipbuilding, was sadly hidden behind the museum but was ingeniously connected to Industrial Hall by a 75-foot-wide, 1000-foot-long glazed hall known as the Grand Avenue. Along with the more sober displays, visitors could watch Singer sewing machine demonstrations or could have a walking stick made to measure. Exhibitions were arranged in eight classes covering raw materials, industrial manufactures, machinery and power, transportation, marine engineering, lighting and heating (in a separate hall), science and music, and sport. Women's contributions were incorporated into displays through-out the exhibition grounds under the direction of the Women's Committee. Across the Kelvin, and in front of the two major buildings, stood Glaswegian ironfounder Walter MacFarlane's Saracen Fountain. One of the few remainders of the 1901 exhibition, it was relocated to Alexandra Park in 1914.

Individual national and commercial pavilions were erected by those with economic ties to Glasgow. Japan, with which Glasgow had exchanged exhibits since 1878, was installed in the half-demolished Kelvingrove Mansion. The building was painted white with a large black sun placed over the statue of Britannia, and the whole building was surrounded by a traditional Japanese garden. To one side of the Stewart Memorial Fountain stood the Canada pavilion with its informational displays for would-be emigrants and to the other side were quaint Irish cottages which must have had a folkloric appeal. The nearby Lever Brothers Sunlight worker's cottage may have pricked the ears of Glasgow's enlightened industrialists (the Tudor revival cottage still stands). Farther past the fountain, a Russian village consisting of four wooden pavilions was built under the direction of Tedor Shektel. The czar lavished some £30,000 on the display, a considerable testimony to the strong trade relations between Russia and Scotland. The primitive working method of the 180 laborers was an attraction in itself to the sophisticated Scots. Architectural delights, such as Glasgow carpet manufacturer James Templeton and Company's Thousand and One Night's mosque-like pavilion, were scattered about the exhibition grounds. Miss Cranston's Tea Room was given a prime location directly in front of the art galleries.

Glasgow's own artistic rebel Charles Rennie Mackintosh designed four pavilions for various titans of industry and for the Glasgow School of Art, in which a lady book-binder could be seen plying her craft inside a green and white cage-like booth. While Mackintosh's bold designs for the major exhibition halls had been roundly rejected, the Glasgow Style was in evidence in George Walton's starkly modern portrait studio for official photographers T&R Annan. Photography itself was recognized as an art form for the first time at a world's fair, when it was displayed in the art galleries by native son James Craig Annan and the American Alfred Stieglitz, who mounted the much acclaimed exhibition of Pictorialist Photography. Photography was also shown as a worthwhile employment for women in the Trades section. Edward Burne-Jones' *Danae* or *The Tower of Brass* (1887–88) and a plaster version of Auguste Rodin's *Burghers of Calais* (1888) were among the most modern works shown, amid the rather encyclopedic exhibition of modern English art. Both were later given to the city. William Burrell alone loaned 160 works of art that would become the basis for his generous gift to his city, including James MacNeill Whistler's *La Princesse du pays de la porcelaine* (1863–64), now in the Peacock Room in the Freer Gallery of Art, Washington, DC.

Less highbrow entertainments were available in the form of motor-car trials, football matches, a water chute, a switchback railway, and an Indian theater featuring jugglers and snake charmers. The Cinghalese waiters at Prince's Restaurant evidently surprised the locals with their ability to speak perfect English. Soap sculpture in the form of Queen Victoria, marzipan polar bears, and an Eddystone lighthouse made of sewing spools were among the requisite curiosities at the fair. Equally curious must have been the appearances made by the King of Siam and the incognito Empress Eugenie.

The 1901 Glasgow Exhibition recorded a considerable surplus of more than £35,000,

Overview of the buildings and grounds of the 1901 Glasgow exhibition (editors' collection).

surely demonstrative of that city's economic flowering at the close of the Victorian era and the dawn of the new century.

Bibliography

The largest collection of primary sources is housed at the Glasgow Room of the Mitchell Library in Glasgow. Among the holdings are personal souvenirs such as photo albums, souvenir printed ephemera, catalogs, guides, and publications of the exhibition committee and commercial publications. These include *Glasgow International Exhibition, 1901: The Official Catalogue* (1901); *The Exhibition Illustrated: A Pictorial Souvenir of the Glasgow International Exhibition* (1901): *Glasgow International Exhibition Viewbook* (1901): *Photographic Souvenir of Glasgow International Exhibition* (1901): and *White's Pictorial Souvenir and Guide to International Exhibition Glasgow 1901* (1901). The University of Strathclyde and the Smithsonian Institution's Special Collection's World's Fair Collection also have a considerable number of primary printed materials.

The *Builder* ran a series of articles on the exhibition between April 1901 and March 1902 that dealt with matters of building, design and aesthetics, and various other details. Consult issues of April 6, June 8, 22, and 29, July 20, August 17, 24, and 31, and September 14, 1901 and March 15, 1902. Contemporary texts related to the photography exhibit are included in William Buchanan, J. *Craig Annan: selected texts and bibliography* (1994).

Perilla Kinchin and Juliet Kinchin, *Glasgow's Great Exhibitions, 1888, 1901, 1911, 1938, 1988* (1988) is the best secondary source for all areas of the exhibition. See also Alastair L. Goldsmith, *The Glasgow International Exhibitions, 1888–1938* (M. Litt. thesis, University of Strathclyde, 1985). For an explanation of the politics surrounding the photography exhibit see Jane Van Nimmen, "F. Holland Day and the Display of a New Art; 'Behold It is I,'" *History of Photography*, 18, 4 (Winter 1994).

Charleston 1901–1902

James M. Beeby

The South Carolina, Interstate, and West Indian Exposition

The South Carolina, Interstate, and West Indian Exposition (also known as the Charleston Exposition) was the third major fair in the South in six years, following the Atlanta Cotton States Exposition of 1895 and the Nashville Tennessee Centennial Exposition of 1897. It also occurred a year after the tragic Pan-

American Exposition in Buffalo. The fair was planned to promote the port city of Charleston, increase trade with the West Indies and the Caribbean after the Spanish American War, attract new businesses to the area, and show off the agricultural products of the South and increase sales of cotton and other commodities.

The idea for an exposition in Charleston came from Colonel John H. Averill in 1899 and once *The News & Courier* and its editor, J.C. Hemphill, supported the idea, others came on board. Progressive-minded businessmen and civic leaders who hoped to modernize the old city and increase trade worked hard to procure the local support, funds, and the site for the fair. The fair was designed by Bradford L. Gilbert, who had designed the Atlanta exposition. Eventually a 250-acre site was located close to the Ashley River that encompassed an old racecourse and a plantation owned by the president of the fair's board, F.W. Wagener. There were fourteen exposition buildings, some built in traditional Colonial South style and others in Spanish Renaissance and Mexican missionary styles, as well as a lake, a sunken garden and plaza, and various other attractions. The impressive buildings included the Palace of Agriculture, the Palace of Commerce, the Exposition Auditorium, the Woman's Building, and many other buildings named after individual states. The most impressive building, perhaps not surprisingly, was the Cotton Palace, a 350-foot long structure with a 150-foot high dome, which celebrated the major crop of the region and the various products and machinery associated with the New South. Electric lighting dazzled the visitors and illustrated the modern thrust of the fair. The most popular section for visitors was the Midway with its "ethnic" attractions such as Akoun's Streets of Cairo, Fair Japan, the Cuban-American Theatre and a Wild West show — to name but a few.

In keeping with the racial climate of the South, the impressive Negro Building was segregated from the rest of the fair. African American leaders from Charleston used the fair as an opportunity to showcase black industrial and agricultural advancement in keeping with Booker T. Washington's philosophy of racial progress. The African American exhibits were excellent and received high praise in both the black and white press. Many African Americans visited the fair and celebrated the variety of exhibits in the Negro Building.

The two most famous visitors to the Fair were the Liberty Bell and the president of the United States, Theodore Roosevelt. Both visitors reflected the attempts of the fair's planners to rise above southern regionalism and promote patriotism and national unity. The Liberty Bell arrived by train in early January 1902 and was afforded a huge parade and an artillery salute. The bell was housed in the Philadelphia Building and was on display for the duration of the fair. In the spirit of easing sectional tensions, the visit of Theodore Roosevelt in April 1902 was celebrated by the city of Charleston; indeed, more than 24,000 people attended the fair on the day of the president's visit. Roosevelt impressed invited dignitaries with his praise for Civil War veterans, support for the endeavors of Charleston to increase trade with the West Indies, and the modernism of the fair. The fair also hosted many special events, such as Midway Day, Military Day, and South Carolina College Day, all in an attempt to boost the number of visitors.

If the South Carolina exposition attracted famous sons and daughters from across the South, it did not draw enough paying customers. The fair opened on December 1, 1901, and ended on May 31, 1902, and pulled in approximately 675,000 visitors, a number much lower than expected; indeed, estimates suggest that more than 350,000 received free passes. An unusually cold and wet winter in the Palmetto state kept many would-be visitors away, and the railroads did not provide substantially reduced rates. In addition, many "old monied" interests in Charleston, as well as the federal government, did not provide financial support for the fair, and thus financial trouble ensued — a large deficit led to bankruptcy for the exposition company and the selling off of buildings and exhibits at auction to raise money. But the fair did bring some new business to Charleston and reconnected the city and state back with the nation, some 40 years after the firing on Fort Sumter. And the local economy was boosted during the fair's duration while many in the city and state did take great pride in the South Carolina, Interstate, and West Indian Exposition.

Bibliography

Primary source information for the South Carolina, Interstate and West Indian Exposition is quite abundant. See for example, *Official Guide to the South Carolina Interstate and West Indian Exposition* (1901). The lead-up to the fair and the fair itself was covered extensively in Charleston's newspaper, *News and Courier*. Other privately produced contemporary guidebooks include Alexander D. Anderson, *Charleston and its Exposition* (1901); *Charleston, S.C. and its Vicinity Illustrated: South Carolina Inter-state and West Indian Exposition* (1901); and *Charleston and the South Carolina Inter-state and West Indian Exposition and Historic Places and Prominent Features of the City* (1902). Contemporary magazine articles also provide details and some analysis on the fair. See T. Cuyler Smith, "The Charleston Exposition," *Independent* (January 16, 1902): 142–51; Lillian W. Betts, "Sunny Days at the Exposition," *Outlook* (May 10 1902): 120–24; and "Charleston and Her 'West Indian Exposition,' *American Monthly Review of Reviews*, 25 (January 1902): 58–61, which contains some illustrations.

The following secondary works provide the best background, analysis and interpretation of the South Carolina, Interstate and West Indian Exposition: Sidney F. Bland, "Women and World's Fairs: The Charleston Story." *The South Carolina Historical Magazine* 94 (1993): 166–184; Anthony Chibbaro, *The Charleston Exposition*. (2001); Bruce G. Harvey, "An Old City in the New South: Urban Progressivism and Charleston's West Indian Exposition, 1901–1902" (unpub. M.A. thesis, University of South Carolina, 1988); Bruce G. Harvey, "World's Fairs in a Southern Accent: Atlanta, Nashville, Charleston, 1895–1902" (unpub. Ph.D. diss., Vanderbilt University, 1998); and Bruce G. Harvey, "'Struggles and Triumphs' Revisited: Charleston's West Indian Exposition and the Development of Urban Progressivism," *Proceedings of the South Carolina Historical Association* (1988): 85–93. William D. Smyth, "Blacks and the South Carolina Interstate and West Indian Exposition," *The South Carolina Historical Magazine* 88 (1987): 211–219.

Torino (Turin) 1902

Christa Carbone

Prima Esposizione Internazionale d'Arte Decorativa Moderna (First International Exposition of Modern Decorative Art)

Torino stands as the high water mark of the Art Nouveau, an artistic style that juxtaposes the planarity of the building or designed object with sinuous and flowing surface decoration. An outgrowth of the Arts and Crafts movement, it was also known as the Stile Floreale and Stile Liberty in Italy, Secession in Austria, Nieuwe Kunst in Holland, and Jugendstil in Germany, countries that were all represented at Torino The inspiration for the Torino exposition may have been the first Italian Exposition of Architecture, held in the city in 1890. Architects from all over Italy sent drawings and sketches that filled 34 rooms in the exhibition building and attracted 40,000 visitors in its ten-week run. This exposition was designed to promote the creation of a distinctive Italian national architecture, and the 1902 exposition was planned to renew Italian architecture and decorative arts in view of the current popularity of Art Nouveau. There was some thought given to holding an exhibition in 1899, focused on applied and industrial arts, but the coming universal exposition in Paris in 1900 forced planners to delay their event until 1902, when it could be coordinated with the *Esposizione Quadrienniale di Belle Arti*, scheduled for that year. In this context, the Torino exposition was not a true world's fair but it fits within the important category of late-nineteenth and early twentieth-century international design exhibitions.

In early 1901, a competition was held to select a chief architect for the 1902 exposition. Raimondo D'Aronco, who had won a similar competition for the 1890 exposition, again was the winner. Held in the English garden style Parco del Valentino alongside the River Po, the exposition stood on the site used previously for expositions in 1884 and 1898. D'Aronco closely modeled his pavilions on Joseph Maria Olbrich's Artists' Colony at Darmstadt, so much that he was accused of plagiarizing the Secession master. Annibale Rigotti, an Italian architect who had once worked for D'Aronco and who had won second prize in the competition, carried out much of the work for D'Aronco, who had to go to Constantinople. Buildings were at once Beaux Arts in plan and boldly modern in their undulating silhouettes and decoration. For the centrally located Pavilion of Honor, D'Aronco drew inspiration from the Hagia Sophia in Constantinople with its dome seeming to hover over a drum pierced by windows. The edges of D'Aronco's dome lifted upward and were held aloft by supporting sculptural maidens. A drawing by D'Aronco indicates that the interior was painted with an Arcadian theme, depicting flowering trees rising from the ground level to the frieze of Arcadia at window level, which was then surmounted by a golden dome, interwoven with tendril-like ribbons of smoke from the altars of art below. D'Aronco's designs for the photography and automobile pavilions were equally colorful and boldly modern, the latter featuring automobile outlines traced onto its surface. Several of the structures at the exposition were built around existing buildings to mask their neo-classical styles. The automobile pavilion, for example, was an industrial shed with an 80-meter-long façade in D'Aronco's modernist style and that rose high enough to block the view of classical university buildings in the distance.

A number of remarkable interiors were assembled for the Torino exposition, an innovative method of showcasing both decorative art objects and their holistically designed interior settings. Among the most influential were those by Italian designer Agostino Lauro and Scottish architect-designer Charles Rennie Mackintosh. Glasgow School of Art Director Francis "Fra" Newberry assembled two room sets by the Glasgow Four to make up the Scottish section. Frances Macdonald McNair and James Herbert McNair created a room set called "A Lady's Writing Room" that featured pale pink walls with a stenciled pale green rose petal frieze and a small settle (backed bench) with a stylized peacock feather motif on both the fabric and wood inlay. Charles Rennie Mackintosh and Margaret Macdonald Mackintosh's room set was "The Rose Boudoir," which contained Mackintosh's iconic attenuated white-painted high back chairs and pink glass wall lights suggestive of rose petals. Over the mantel hung Macdonald's two gesso panels depicting highly stylized and ethereal females, the Heart of the Rose and the White Rose and the Red Rose; a duplicate of the latter is in the now at the Mackintosh House, Glasgow.

The English section, shown to great disadvantage in glass vitrines, was assembled by Walter Crane, president of the Arts and Crafts Exhibition Society, and included works by William DeMorgan, William Morris and Company, Edward Burne-Jones, Charles Robert Ashbee, William Arthur Smith Benson, Charles Francis Annesley Voysey, James Powell and Sons, and Crane. Joseph Maria Olbrich constructed three room sets for the Austrian section, furniture from which is now in the Wolfsonian collection.

During and after the Torino exposition, art and architecture critics debated D'Aronco's Torino exposition buildings and whether they really did contribute to a national architecture for Italy. Most had their doubts, pointing out the similarities between the Torino buildings and those of Olbricht in Darmstadt, or various Secession style structures in Austria or the fact that D'Aronco's buildings were more suitable in places like Finland and Japan where wood construction was the standard, rather than in Italy, where most major buildings were constructed of marble or travertine. The discussion may have been purely academic. As Schudi Madsen points out in *Art Nouveau* (1967), Art Nouveau was soon to go into steep decline as a popular architectural and decorative style French designers had turned to more classical motifs by the Franco-British Exhibition in 1908, leading Belgian architects and designers drifted away from art nouveau by mid-decade, and in Germany, the style was taken over by inferior designers who made kitschy items and sold them until the outbreak of World War I.

Only in Austria, where Art Nouveau started later, did the style persist, although in a more geometrical variant that contributed to the modern architecture of the 1920s. All of these changes left Italian architects with no place to go with their versions of Art Nouveau, and despite the Torino exposition and the innovative work of DAronco and Rigotti, the style never became influential in Italy.

Bibliography

Research materials for the Torino exposition are scattered and piecemeal. Richard Etlin, "Turin 1902: The Search for a Modern Italian Architecure," *Journal of Decorative and Propagande Art* 13 (Stile Floriale Theme Issue [Summer 1989]): 94–109, is the best place to start. Etlin's article contains a number of photographs from the exposition, and he cites a number of contemporary works in both Italian and English, on the exposition and the state of Italian architecture. See also Terry Kirk, "Architects of the Avant-Garde, 1900–1920," in *Architecture of Modern Italy, Volume 2: Visions of Utopia, 1900-Present* (2005) and Gabriel P. Weisberg, "The Turin Exposition of International Design 1902: The Mystery of the Stile Floreale and the Palazzina of Augostino Lauro," *Arts Magazine* 62 (April 1988): 32–36. A modern source in Italian is Valeria Garuzzo, *L'esposizione del 1902 a Torino* (1999). A very recent book, Cristina Della Coletta, *World's Fairs Italian-Style: The Great Expositions in Turin and their Narratives, 1860–1915* (2006) should be useful. Finally, Walter Gamba, a resident of Torino, operates a website, *www.1902.info/* that provides information about the 1902 exposition, including a map of the site, as well as on Art Nouveau in general.

Hanoi 1902–1903

Robert W. Rydell

Exposition Français et Internationale

The idea of holding an international exhibition in Tonkin (now Hanoi) originated in the 1890s and received additional impetus at the 1900 Paris Universal Exposition when French colonial authorities and the French Committee on Foreign Expositions determined to organize a fair in French-controlled Southeast Asia to highlight the economic resources of the region and the possibilities of trade with colonies of other nations and to underscore French colonial prowess.

Under the direction of Paul Bourgeois, secretary of the French Committee on Foreign Expositions, an exposition complex operated between November 16, 1902, and February 15, 1903, on 41 acres of land near the railroad station in Hanoi. The exposition buildings were designed in the beaux-arts style, and included pavilions devoted to displays from the Philip-pines, Malaya, Siam, Japan, China, Formosa, and Korea. In addition to these national and colonial exhibition halls, the fair included galleries of machines and agriculture, as well as a pavilion devoted to the beaux-arts movement. The latter building, designed by Roger Marx, housed artistic displays assembled by nearly 200 French artists.

Exposition planners grouped exhibits from over 4,000 exhibitors into three general categories: fine arts and sciences, natural resources, and machinery. Exhibits ranged from musical instruments and theatrical art to forest products and perfumes to electrical generators and early airplanes. In addition, the fair boasted cabarets, ethnological parades of indigenous people, and a Philippine village organized by the French vice-consul in Manila with the approval of the U.S. government.

It is difficult to measure the impact of the fair. The published official history does not provide attendance figures, but reports indicate that, after opening day, despite free admission to the fair, attendance sharply declined. Most of the exhibition buildings and galleries were demolished after the close of the fair, with the notable exception of the Grand Palace, which was intended as a permanent structure to house a colonial museum. Perhaps the most important aspect of the fair was that it represented one more link in the chain of colonial fairs that Western imperial powers stretched across the Third World. It provided lessons in imperial hubris and, if reports of limited attendance are any indication, of colonial resistance.

Bibliography

Sources from the Hanoi fair are limited. Some manuscript materials are available in the Archives Nationales in Paris and Archives d'Outre Mer in Aix-en-Provence. The most complete record of the fair is found in Paul Bourgeois and G. -Roger Sandoz, *Exposition d'Hanoi, 1902–1903; Rapport général* (1904). Also consult the critical report issued [by M. le capitaine Ducarre], *Mission a l'Exposition de Hanoi et en Extreme-Orient, Rapport général* (1903). Other accounts are scattered in such journals as the *Bulletin de la société de geographie commerciale du Bordeaux* and the *British North Borneo Herald*. For a quick summary of the purposes of the fair, consult the 1901 *Consular Reports* on file in the Larson Collection, Department of Special Collections, California State University, Fresno. A good assessment of the imperial context in which the colonial fairs took place can be found in William H. Schneider, "The Image of West Africa in Popular French Culture" (unpub. Ph.D. diss., University of Pennsylvania, 1976), and Thomas G. August, "Colonial Policy and Propaganda: The Popularization of the Idee Coloniale in France, 1919–1939" (unpub. Ph.D. diss., University of Wisconsin, 1978).

St. Louis 1904

Astrid Böger

Louisiana Purchase International Exposition

Commemorating the centennial of the massive land acquisition known as the Louisiana Purchase, which had doubled the area of the United States in 1803 and was perhaps the greatest feat of Thomas Jefferson's presidency, the Louisiana Purchase Exposition was a thoroughly imperialist spectacle. Opening with a delay of one year needed to increase international participation through elaborate public relations efforts, the fair simultaneously celebrated the related ideas of Manifest Destiny and the superiority of Western civilization over the rest of the world with its expansionist "man over nature" theme. At a time when the United States was divided over the question whether it should colonize overseas territories in the Pacific region not yet claimed by the imperial European nations, it provided a welcome opportunity to put on display the perceived progress of those "less civilized" peoples recently conquered by the United States, most notably from the Philippines, which had become a U.S. protectorate as a result of the Spanish-American War in 1898. Moreover, while the fair allowed the United States to demonstrate its role as emerging rival of the European nations, on a more local level it provided the social and economic elites the opportunity to prove that St. Louis had become not only an economically powerful, but also a rather cultured and, not least due to improved municipal structures, highly desirable Midwestern city very much *unlike* the hotbed of political corruption and labor unrest it had long been notorious for and which had resulted, among other things, in a violent railroad strike at the turn of the century. From the start of the fair's planning, it was the stated goal of its organizers to outdo the great success that

Chicago had achieved with the 1893 World's Columbian Exposition. Consequently, David R. Francis, president of the St. Louis World's Fair Commission, made it his prime ambition to change the tarnished image of his city by promoting the fair both nationally and internationally. When civic leader and progressive industrialist Rolla Wells became mayor in 1901, he and fellow Democrats supported the exposition plans as they hoped it would help implement a set of reforms that would lead to a great cooperative effort which became known as the "New St. Louis." However, their ambitious plans reached far beyond the local level, as technological innovations and civic improvements popularized at the fair would potentially benefit all of mankind they believed — or at least all Americans.

Choosing an appropriate site for a world's fair is always a decisive step, and often a matter of much debate. In St. Louis as well, several possible locations were considered, but in the end fair officials decided upon a heavily wooded area nowadays known as Forest Park located toward the western end of town, miles away from the unsightly slum areas in the east. By many accounts the citizens of St. Louis first objected to having their "Wilderness," as the site was affectionately called, turned into a fairground, but site development went forward as planned once considerable technical and logistical difficulties could be solved. Among other things, the Des Peres River flowing through the area had to be redirected and moved underground to prevent recurring flooding, making it necessary to install a completely new water system representing at the same time one of the most successful long-term benefits of the fair. Also, a natural lake was drained and reshaped into a great, artificial water basin, which became the central focus of the St. Louis fair. When it turned out that the fair outgrew the area originally planned for, officials reacted promptly by negotiating a lease with Washington University, whose newly built but still unused campus bordering on the fair site made for an ideal extension — including the use of Brooking's Hall, the campus' landmark building, as the fair's Administrative Hall — so that it now covered 1,272 acres making it the largest world's fair site to this day.

Despite or rather perhaps because of the massive size of the fair site, a great effort was made to create a coherent site plan or "main picture" which would allow visitors impressive vistas from which they could take it all in. Thus, no building was to exceed 65 feet in height, and much attention was paid to their rhythmic positioning between open, carefully landscaped spaces resulting in a harmonious overall scheme. Moreover, the main buildings were arranged in a fan-like layout devised by New York architect Cass Gilbert and Frank M. Howe of Kansas City. All of them were equipped with windows that could be opened, which provided both airiness and natural light benefiting visitors and exhibits alike. The central point and most frequently photographed structure of the fair was the domed and elaborately decorated Festival Hall crowning Art Hill, also the site of the Palace of Fine Arts also designed by Gilbert and still serving as the St. Louis Art Museum today. Festival Hall contained the world's largest pipe organ, which thousands of visitors admired during daily concerts in an auditorium seating 4,500. The surrounding Colonnades of States was a monument to the thirteen states and the Indian Territory coming out of the Louisiana Purchase. From Festival Hall sprang the Cascades designed by E.L. Masqueray, which flowed down into the Grand Basin and were beautifully lit in the colors of the rainbow. This visual spectacle was the central magnet of the fair; simultaneously, it impressively demonstrated the fair's "man over nature" theme, as it was visual proof of the major accomplishment of controlling and redesigning the natural environment. Harking back to the 1893 World's Columbian Exposition, the main buildings in St. Louis were built in an unified, harmonious Beaux-Arts style, though on the whole still more ornamentation was added than in Chicago. Also, the hue chosen for the main buildings' exterior was not white but ivory, giving them a less austere look and making for the fair's unofficial name, "Ivory City" sounding even nobler than "White City," which Chicago's fair had been dubbed.

Among the exposition's main buildings organized around the Great Basin, the Palace of Agriculture designed by E.L. Masqueray was at twenty-three acres the largest structure on the fairgrounds, giving impressive testimony to Jefferson's ideal of an agrarian society and its ongoing relevance to the U.S. economy. Agricultural products from fifteen countries and

The Cascades was an impressive water feature at the Louisiana Purchase International Exposition. Such water features were standard at most fairs of this era (from *1904 Louisiana Purchase Exposition*, 1904).

forty-two states were on display, and viewers fondly remembered the impressive sculptures made from unusual materials, such as almonds, cereal, and cotton. The Palace of Electricity and Machinery by the architects Walker and Kimball demonstrated the significance of electrical power for the twentieth century. Visitors were particularly impressed with the De Forest Wireless Telegraphy tower which made it possible, not unlike today's wireless telephony, to send wireless messages, in this case to Chicago and Springfield. Next to this there was another separate, and even bigger, Palace of Machinery designed by St. Louis architects Windman, Walsh and Boisselier which housed, among other things, the power plant for the whole fair built by General Electric. The neighboring Palace of Education and Social Economy by St. Louis architects Eames & Young displayed actual classes in session, covering the whole educational spectrum from kindergarten to college, which curious visitors could just watch or actively participate in. The Department of Social Economy put on display exhibits on the most pressing municipal problems and proposed solutions, such as housing, labor, and health programs. The Palace of Mines and Metallurgy by Theodore Link of St. Louis contained exhibits of raw materials and the varied products made from them. Adventurous visitors could take a ride through a reproduction of a coal mine to get an idea of the actual work environment. The Palace of Liberal Arts, designed by Haynes & Barnett of St. Louis, housed myriad exhibits that demonstrated how science and technology were used to produce manufactured

goods from natural resources, thus providing ample evidence of human progress and its material manifestations. The neighboring Palace of Varied Industries, the first exhibit structure built on the fairground after a design by Van Brunt & Howe, put on display objects that were artistically pleasing rather than merely practical, such as decorative furniture, pottery, and silver and goldsmith wares. The largest collections came from Germany and Japan, testifying to both countries' longstanding arts and crafts traditions and also their well-established international marketing schemes. The Palace of Transportation designed by Masqueray, finally, reminiscent of a modern railroad station, displayed assembled modern and historical transportation solutions including the latest developments in urban infrastructure developments, such as motor boats, cable cars and, above all, automobiles.

After seeing the myriad official, educational or otherwise edifying displays, many visitors felt inclined to go over to the fair's less formal, popular entertainment section known as the "Pike," stretching along the northern end of the fairgrounds for about a mile. Here, they could choose among over 50 amusements for which individual entrance fees were charged while access to the Pike itself was free, inviting many to just stroll around and see the sites and thus creating a serious competition for the official part of the fair. Comparable to a giant carnival sideshow, the Pike featured many exotic displays such as the Cliff Dwellers exhibit, a reproduction of the Tyrolean Alps, and various Native American tribes per-

The Palace of Varied Industries boasted a façade 1200 feet long and contained more than 650,000 square feet of exhibition space (from *1904 Louisiana Purchase Exposition*, 1904).

forming in traditional garb, next to more typical sideshow fare including contortionists, exotic dancers and Jim Key, the famous Educated horse. Another crowd pleaser was a display of live babies in incubators then only recently introduced and of great interest to the public. One of the Pike's chief attractions, however, was the Streets of Cairo exhibit which had first appeared at the 1889 Universal Exposition in Paris and had since then become a regular feature at world's fairs. Presenting exotic Arabian Nights themes and thereby re-inscribing Middle Eastern stereotypes by showing a traditional culture by all appearances uncontaminated by modernity, the show's greatest attraction by far was the performance of the "Princess Rajah Dance" more popularly known in St. Louis as "hoochie-coochie," a rather vaudevillian variation of the belly dance adapted for Victorian tastes and more often than not performed by dancers from the area rather than by actual Middle Eastern women. Most exhibits on the Pike blended reality and

fantasy into a similarly alluring visual spectacle. Reminiscent of today's Walt Disney Company's Epcot center, its amusements presented a colorful mix of cultures from around the globe, or more precisely from about thirty countries in this case, often relying on stereotype for convenient recognition and fast consumption.

Another site that particularly fascinated visitors at the St. Louis exposition was the large Philippine Reservation located on 47 acres at the southwestern end of the fairgrounds, set apart from the rest of the fair by an artificial, triangular body of water appropriately named "Arrowhead Lake." The exhibit represented the various native cultures of the Philippine Islands, recently occupied by the U.S. as a result of the war against Spain. Its larger aims were to gain public support for U.S. foreign policy but also, more specifically, to familiarize Americans with their recent acquisition, and further to promote the Philippine's natural resources. On the other hand, the reservation was intended

Exotic natives in traditional dress, doing traditional activities. Here Negritos from the Philippines strike a threatening pose with their weapons (courtesy Library of Congress).

to introduce the over 1,000 native Filipinos who lived on the site in buildings typical of Philippine architecture to American culture and its civic virtues. To achieve this aim, there was a virtual army of Filipino scouts who were trained by American military personnel and whose role was, among other things, to insure discipline and order in the camp. Moreover, daily drills effectively demonstrated to American audiences the successful integration of these foreigners into American culture, and considering the visual appeal of such spectacles together with their implicit message it is perhaps not surprising that the Philippine Reservation became such a particular favorite in St. Louis, which never failed to attract huge crowds. Whereas the Filipino scouts were positioned relatively high up on the social Darwinist scale that native peoples were placed upon, a group of Igorot warriors, a Filipino tribe deemed far less civilized, were considered to

mark its opposite end. Countless visitors marveled at the natives' alleged savagery which was only confirmed, in their eyes, not only by the Igorots' scanty dress but also by the fact that they supposedly considered dog meat a delicacy. In fact, the part of the city from where many poor dogs they ate came from after supposedly having been captured by city authorities for the purpose is still referred to as "Dogtown" today. Igorot warriors frequently posed for photographers displaying their weapons, but this was always recognizable as a ritual performance and hence perceived as "tame" and therefore non-threatening to visitors clearly fascinated by the spectacle of "savage war."

The St. Louis world's fair was also the site of the first Olympic Games in the Western hemisphere, thus providing peaceful competition in the arena of sports as well. There were no national teams then, which only became common at later Olympic Games. Most competitions took place in late August and early September and focused especially on track and field, the traditional Olympic disciplines. While the overall theme was improved health through proper physical exertion, the games were also used by anthropologists, most notably W.J. McGee, head of the fair's Anthropology Department, to "demonstrate" the supposed superiority of the Euro-American race. This was done, for instance, by making non–Westerners compete without proper instruction beforehand. Unsurprisingly, the results confirmed racial stereotypes based on then-current pseudo–Darwinist schemes found elsewhere at the fair as well, according to which the white race constituted the pinnacle of evolution.

With so many sights spread out over such a vast territory, many visitors took pleasure in going on a ride in the giant ferris wheel, which gave them a welcome opportunity to not only to rest their feet but also to survey the whole scene from 265 feet above the fairgrounds at its highest point. The structure was "imported" from Chicago, where it had been used at the World's Columbian Exposition eleven years earlier. Whereas Chicagoans are said to have been slow to accept the attraction basically out of fear that it could collapse, people in St. Louis turned out to be more adventurous and rented whole cars for weddings and other parties and generally enjoyed the visual and technological spectacle the giant revolving structure afforded them. Following the fair the wheel was allegedly taken apart and sold for scrap medal, and more than one hundred years later there are still a number of world's fair enthusiasts who dig their way through Forest Park in their search for pieces of the beloved but sadly lost object.

Fortunately, a few structures from the 1904 world's fair remain, such as the St. Louis Art Museum still scenically located, after numerous reconstructive efforts, on Forest Park's Art Hill. The museum has been maintained over the years through funding generated by the Art Museum tax the citizens of St. Louis passed in 1907 and which can be considered a direct outcome of the fair as it indicates the recognition of art as a civic resource in the wake of the fair. Nearby the Bird Cage, a large steel structure that housed the Smithsonian's walk-through Aviary exhibit in 1904 still stands

as another permanent remnant of the fair. Shortly after its close, the people of St. Louis bought the cage for $3,500 rather than see it dismantled and shipped to Washington, D.C., laying the foundation for the St. Louis Zoo, another important municipal improvement originating at the fair.

When it closed on December 1, 1904, to fireworks and the solemn farewell speech of President Francis, the world's fair had attracted roughly 20 million visitors in seven months and was unanimously considered a great success, also in financial terms. Apart from the numerous civic improvements it prompted, profits were also used toward building the Jefferson Memorial in Forest Park, the first monument to honor the third president of the United States. Now known as the Missouri History Museum, the building also houses the records of the Exposition Company and the collections of the Missouri Historical Society, as well as exhibits on such diverse historical subjects as the Lewis and Clark expedition and the resulting Louisiana Purchase, the 1904 world's fair commemorating it, and Charles Lindbergh's life and times, among others.

Beyond such permanent institutions and official repositories of collective memory, popular culture is the arena in which the fair has been most fondly remembered. Thus, there are several popular foods which are said to have originated at the fair (whereas most likely, they were first *popularized* in St. Louis but had previously been invented and introduced elsewhere) such as hot dogs, iced tea and ice cream cones—the latter two indirectly testifying to the hot summer of 1904. There is also a popular Hollywood musical based on the St. Louis world's fair titled *Meet Me in St. Louis*, which was directed by Vincente Minelli and came out in 1944. More than a century after its close the fair is still fondly remembered largely because of this movie and, in particular, its title song memorably rendered by young Judy Garland. Perhaps it is also thanks to this movie regularly featured at public viewings that the world's fair is a matter of much civic pride in St. Louis even today, where it can happen that strangers greet each other with the cheerful phrase "see you at the fair" occurring throughout the movie. In general, St. Louisans seem to embrace the legacy of "their" fair more wholeheartedly than citizens of the other cities that have hosted world's fairs, which is also reflected by the numerous world's fair societies, civic organizations such as "Forest Park Forever and Today" concerned with the material legacy of the fair, and several groups of world's fair enthusiasts and collectors of memorabilia meeting regularly. Sadly, however, this ongoing enthusiasm for the fair may also be due to the fact that St. Louis has lost much of its economic as well as cultural significance since 1904, when it was the central hub of the Midwest and ranked among the four most important cities in the United States. Certainly in hindsight, the Louisiana Purchase Exposition marks the historical moment when the people of St. Louis first realized the great potential of their city and felt ready to invite the world to celebrate.

Bibliography

The Missouri Historical Society (MHS) holds most archival materials relating to the 1904 world's fair in its Louisiana Purchase Exposition Collection. This includes the papers of David R. Francis, president of the Louisiana Purchase Exposition Company, as well as the first official *Illustrated History of the Louisiana Purchase Exposition*, edited by Mark Bennitt (1905). Moreover, the MHS also has a vast photographic archive and a substantial amount of collectible items, world's fair memorabilia and rare ephemera. Some of these artifacts are on permanent display in the MHS's Jefferson Memorial Building. Additionally, visual materials can be found in the special collections of the St. Louis Public Library, and also in the special collections of the main library of Washington University. Finally, as with all other American world's fairs, the Smithsonian Institution Library and the National Archives in Washington, D.C., hold considerable archival sources. For the Smithsonian records, see Series 16, Louisiana Purchase Exposition (St. Louis, 1904), 1901–1906. For the National Archives records, see Record Group 43, No. 17, Records Relating to the Louisiana Purchase Exposition at St. Louis, 1904, Numbers 591–603.

Contemporary sources for the fair are abundant. The exposition company published the *Official History of the Fair* (1905), as well as an exposition bulletin, while local newspapers covered it extensively, and magazines published articles on various aspects of the event. Among the more helpful are Montgomery Schuyler, "The Architecture of the St. Louis Fair," *Scribner's Magazine* 35 (April 1904): 385–95; F. K. Winkler, "The

Architecture of the Louisiana Purchase Exposition," *Architectural Record* 15 (April 1904): 336–60; W. J. McGee, "The Anthropology Exhibit," *Harper's Weekly* 48 (September 1904): 683; and Thomas MacMeeken, "Down 'the Pike,' The Boulevard of Gayety at the St. Louis Exposition," *Pacific Monthly* 12 (July 1904): 30.

The St. Louis world's fair has attracted much scholarly interest, reflected in numerous publications. Robert W. Rydell's chapter in *All the World's a Fair* (1984) remains an important point of reference, especially in its discussion of the racially biased anthropological schemes behind many of the exhibits of foreign peoples. A dated but detailed biography of David R. Francis is Harper Barnes, *Standing on a Volcano: The Life and Times of David Rowland Francis* (1937). There is a more recent discussion of the imperialist nature of the turn-of-the-century world's fairs in *Fair America* by Robert Rydell, John E. Findling and Kimberly D. Pelle (2000). Eric Breitbart has published a thought-provoking book on foreign peoples at the fair but focusing exclusively on photography, *A World on Display: Photographs from the St. Louis World's Fair 1904* (1997). He has also produced a video by the same title (New Deal Films, Inc., 1994), which includes interviews with elderly citizens of St. Louis who had visited the fair in their youth.

For those interested in the early cinema pioneered at the fair, there is a compilation of world's fair films available through New Deal Films, Inc. which includes several short films made at St. Louis, *Early Motion Pictures of World's Fairs and Expositions, 1900–1905* (1997). Among them is a film version of the famed "Princess Rajah Dance," also discussed by Astrid Böger in "The Princess Rajah Dance and the Popular Fascination with Middle Eastern Culture at the St. Louis World's Fair" in Heike Schefer, *America and the Orient* (2006). The role of novelty foods introduced in St. Louis is the subject of a book by Pamela J. Vaccaro, *Beyond the Ice Cream Cone: The Whole Scoop on Food at the 1904 World's Fair* (2004).

There are a number of other useful secondary sources on the fair, many published in connection with the either the seventy-fifth anniversary or the centennial of the event. For example, see Martha B. Clevenger, ed., *Indescribably Grand: Diaries and Letters from the 1904 World's Fair* (1979); Dorothy Daniels Birk, *The World Came to St. Louis: A Visit to the 1904 World's Fair* (1979); Tim Fox, *From the Palaces to the Pike: Visions of the 1904 World's Fair* (1997), an elaborately illustrated coffee-table book; Bert Minkin, *Legacies of the St. Louis World's Fair* (1998); Elana V. Fox, *Inside the World's Fair of 1904* (2003); and Diane Rademacher, *Still Shining Discovering! Lost*

Treasures from the St. Louis World's Fair (2003). Jose D. Fermin, *1904 World's Fair: The Filipino Experience* (2004) deals with the Philippine Reservation and the experiences of its inhabitants; as do Clayton D. Laurie, "An Oddity of Empire: The Philippine Scouts and the 1904 World's Fair," *Gateway Heritage* 15, 3 (1994–1995): 44–55, and Sharra L. Vostral, "Imperialism on Display: The Philippine Exhibition at the 1904 World's Fair," *Gateway Heritage* 13, 4 (Spring 1993): 18–31. George R. Matthews, *America's First Olympics: The St. Louis Games of 1904* (2005), discusses the controversial Games of the Third Olympiad. Martha R. Clevenger, "Through Western Eyes: Americans Encounter Asians at the Fair," *Gateway Heritage* 17, 2 (1996): 42–51, and Matti Goksyr, "One Certainly Expected a Great Deal More from the Savages: The Anthropology Days in St. Louis, 1904, and Their Aftermath," *International Journal of the History of Sport* 7, 2 (September 1990): 297–306, both deal with touchy race-related issues at the fair. Finally, Nancy J. Parezo and Don D. Fowler, *Anthropology Goes to the Fair (2007)*, is a densely detailed monograph that describes all

of the anthropological exhibits and performances at the fair and places them into the historical context of anthropological studies.

In 1944, the St. Louis world's fair was indirectly celebrated in the Hollywood manner by the film, *Meet Me in St. Louis.* Directed by Vincente Minelli and starring Judy Garland and Margaret O'Brien, this musical comedy deals with a St. Louis family during the fair, and the final scenes of the film are set at a sound-stage representation of the fair.

Finally, there are several useful internet sites. The Missouri Historical Society offers not only an overview over the fair but also a virtual fair visit at *http://mohistory.org/content/fair/wf/html/Overview/page3.html. The 1904 World's Fair Society*, consisting of a group of world's fair enthusiasts, founded in 1986, and dedicated to preserving memories and exchanging memorabilia of the fair, can be found at *http://www.1904 worldsfairsociety.org/index.htm*. Finally, there is an online version of the official guide to the fair available at *http://washingtonmo.com/1904/index.htm*.

Liège 1905

Matthew G. Stanard

Exposition Universelle et Internationale de Liège

The idea for a world's fair in Liège was aired in the early 1890s, but the city faced tough competition from both Brussels and Antwerp. It was not until the 1897 Brussels exposition that Florent Pholien and industrialist Victor Dumoulin took the first concrete steps to produce a universal exposition *liégeoise*. By 1899, Dumoulin, Pholien and others had created the Société Anonyme de l'Exposition de Liège with a target date of 1903 for a fair, although due to a variety of delays they eventually pushed this date back to 1905.

Liège was a former prince-bishopric located in eastern francophone Wallonia, an area already heavily industrialized by the turn of the century, and the city intended for the fair to

demonstrate Liège's important past and present. The exposition also celebrated the 75th anniversary of Belgian independence and coincided with the 40th anniversary of Leopold II's accession to the throne. This was the fourth universal exposition in Belgium in only twenty years and established Belgium as a major exhibitory power. Belgium would follow up the Liège fair with two others in less than a decade: Brussels in 1910 and Ghent in 1913.

The fairgrounds were located at the confluence of the Meuse and Ourthe rivers toward the south of the city, incorporating three discontinuous parts of the city that the rivers separated: Les Vennes, La Boverie, and La Fragnée. Organizers located the main exposition halls in Les Vennes, an area that as late as 1900 was prone to flooding. Because of work on the quays and banks of the rivers along Les Vennes and the other areas of the fairgrounds—including a partial deviation of the Ourthe River—the city of Liège acquired a new city quarter after the fair. The Parc de la Boverie, already a public park before 1905, also benefited from exposition construction, in particular from the newly-built Palais des Beaux-Arts. The building was left to the city at the end of the fair and was turned into a new museum, called today the Musée d'Art Moderne et d'Art Contemporaine. Because the fair was situated in parts of the city separated by the Ourthe and Meuse rivers, planners constructed a number of bridges to link the different sections, the most significant of which were le Pont de Fragnée and le Pont de Fétinne. The city unveiled two monuments during the fair: local son Zénobe Gramme, inventor of the continuous current dynamo, was honored with a monument by sculptor Thomas Vinçotte; another memorial honored adoptive son Charles Rogier, who had participated in the 1830 Belgian revolution and who had been an important nineteenth century statesman. Because of these new monuments, the new bridges and buildings, the development of the fairground zones, and construction on river quays, the fair led to important changes for the city.

The Exposition Universelle et Internationale de Liège itself, the first of two fairs in the city, opened on April 27 and closed on November 6. The fairgrounds covered a total of 70 hectares (700,000 square meters), with an annex of 20 hectares. Of this area, 135,000 square meters were under roof, that is to say, they were occupied by national pavilions and other buildings that housed the fair's 17,004 exhibitors. Altogether there were more than 80 pavilions and other buildings on the fairgrounds. In terms of the number of exhibitors and the size of the exposition, the 1905 event was the largest fair to date outside of the United States and France. With more than 7 million visitors, the Liège universal exposition drew more people than any other such European event to date except the 1900 Paris Exposition universelle.

By successfully courting foreign governments the Société Anonyme de l'Exposition de Liège managed to obtain the participation of 39 nations, including France, Germany, England, the United States, Turkey, Persia, and China. Organizers even secured the participation of

A bird's-eye view of the 1905 Liège exposition (editors' collection).

Exposition Universelle de Liège 1905.
Entrée principale   No. 78

Visitors gather around the main entrance to 1905 Liège exposition dressed in their finest fair-going clothes (editors' collection).

Russia and Japan, two countries that were at war with each other throughout most of the exposition. One of the most popular attractions was "Le Vieux Liège," a section comprising dozens of buildings replicating the Liège of the prince-bishops that had existed before the 1789 revolutions in Liège and the Austrian Netherlands and the subsequent period of French rule. There was also a Village Sénégalais, panoramas and theaters, ballooning, and a number of congresses. Musical, singing, cycling, and other competitions entertained visitors throughout the months of the exposition. Visiting dignitaries added to the excitement: from May to November, King Leopold II of Belgium, King Vittorio Emanuele III of Italy, the Shah of Persia, and Prince and Princess Arisugawa of Japan visited the exposition.

Of all the foreign participations, that of France was by far the most extensive and significant. The French section covered 30,000 square meters and included 7,950 exhibitors. In addition to the pavilions l'Alimentation française, l'Horticulture française, and others, France erected buildings to house exhibits of its Asian and African colonies, including Algeria and Tunisia.

In comparison to the French imperial displays, as well as earlier Belgian colonial exhibits, the 1905 showing of Leopold II's État Indépendent du Congo (EIC) was minor. Architect Sneyers built a small pavilion for the Congo in La Boverie whose exterior resembled the colonial governor's residence in Boma. Displays included ivory sculptures, an enormous 80 meters square color relief map of the entire EIC territory (with miniature steamboats and locomotives), a Société d'Études Coloniales exhibit, and ethnographic objects. Even though the EIC pavilion won a number of awards, the colony does not seem to have elicited a great deal of interest among fairgoers, perhaps due to a lack of African subjects on hand.

Bibliography

A new publication put together concurrent with the centenary of the fair is Christine Renardy, ed., *Liège et l'exposition universelle de 1905: Urbanisme dans un espace de confluence et reflet d'un apogée* (2005). The essential primary source on the fair remains Gustave Drèze's massive *Le Livre d'Or de l'Exposition Universelle et Internationale de*

1905: Histoire complète de l'Exposition de Liège, 2 vols. (1905–1907). Drèze's two-volume work runs to well over fifteen hundred pages and in addition to providing the fair's history and unfolding, it reprints numerous primary sources including photographs, drawings, correspondence, and flyers. Another primary source is the periodical *Liège Exposition*, which was created especially for the event. For the important French colonial participation at the 1905 fair see J. L. Brunet et al., *Exposition Universelle et Internationale de Liège 1905: Les Colonies Françaises*, (1905).

The Archives Générales du Royaume-Algemeen Rijksarchief (AGR-ARA) in Brussels has important resources on Belgian fairs up to and including the Brussels 1935 exposition. The main reference work for archival research on expositions at the AGR-ARA is R. Depoortere and L. Vandeweyer, eds., *Inventaire des archives des expositions universelles organisées en Belgique entre 1880 et 1913: Fonds provenant du Ministère des affaires économiques*, Pub. 2037 (1994). The research instrument code (*code de l'instrument de recherche*) for the *inventaire* is T182.

For an overview of Belgian expositions to 1958, see A. Cockx and J. Lemmens's *Les Expositions Universelles et Internationales en Belgique de 1885 à 1958* (1958). Another source for early universal expositions in Belgium is Charles Mourlon's *Quelques Souvenirs des Expositions Nationales, Internationales et Universelles en Belgique 1820–1925* (n.d.).

Portland 1905

Carl Abbott

The Lewis and Clark Centennial and American Pacific Exposition and Oriental Fair

Portland entered a new era with the celebration of the Lewis and Clark Exposition.

In official rhetoric, the industrial and scientific fair was a "school of progress" to inform and entertain its visitors. For civic leaders in their clubrooms and real estate offices, it was also an international advertisement to attract investors and immigrants. The ostensible purpose was to memorialize the great explorers, but the impetus and organization came from bankers, brokers, and the Board of Trade who wanted to demonstrate that Portland could mount a major civic enterprise and pull it off. Portland had a solid record of economic growth since its founding in 1845, but it was competing for investment and immigration with dozens of other cities throughout the American west-with nearby Seattle, Spokane, Tacoma, Bellingham, and Everett and with more distant places like Denver, Billings, Oakland, and San Diego. A successful world's fair could do wonders for the city's reputation as a safe and sound place to do business.

Portlanders also had an extra incentive. Their event would come only one year after St. Louis put on the enormously successful Louisiana Purchase Exposition. St. Louis was one of the most important cities in the country, and a fair that held its own with the Missouri metropolis would do wonders for Portland's reputation.

The first serious efforts toward an exposition came from J. M. Long of the Portland Board of Trade, who organized occasional meetings during 1900 to consider a northwest industrial exposition. The date and the theme came from the Oregon Historical Society. Led by *Oregonian* editor Harvey Scott, the society, on December 15, 1900, endorsed the suggestion that a commercial exposition be held in conjunction with the centennial of Lewis and Clark's exploration of the Oregon country. Two months later, the Oregon legislature endorsed the suggestion and pledged state aid once an effort was underway. Organizers filed articles of incorporation on October 12, 1901. The corporate name summed up the dual goals of historic commemoration and regional boosterism: Lewis and Clark Centennial and American Pacific Exposition and Oriental Fair. Banks, railroads, hotels, utilities, department stores, and breweries took the lead in subscribing the initial stock offering of $300,000 within two days. The board of directors for the exposition company reconfirmed business leadership.

A successful fair required participation by the state of Oregon, other western states, and the national government. Oregon's legislature acted early in 1903 to appropriate $450,000 for an exhibition of the state's "arts, industries, manufactures, and products" to be held in Portland in cooperation with the work of the Lewis and Clark Exposition Company. The legislators established the Exposition Commission with four members from Portland, four from downstate, and Jefferson Myers of Salem as chair. The corporation was to organize, promote, and manage the exposition the state commission was to pay for many of buildings, obtain state and county exhibits, and keep an eye on the businessmen who were running the show in Portland. In addition to Oregon, sixteen states sent exhibits to the fair. Ten of these constructed special buildings, the largest by Missouri, Massachusetts, New York, California, and Washington.

Federal participation was obtained in 1904. As the authorization bill moved through Congress, an original appropriation of more than $2 million shrank to $475,000 as congressmen worried about the cost of the 1904 exposition in St. Louis and a pending request for the planned Jamestown exposition in 1907. According to the official account, Harvey Scott's influence with Theodore Roosevelt played a decisive role in securing a federal building and exhibit.

The corporation had picked the site in 1902. The 400-acre tract at Guild's Lake was located just beyond the settled section of the city to the northwest of the central business district. It included a low bluff, market gardens, pasture, and marshes that were periodically inundated by high water from the Willamette River. John Olmsted, of Olmsted and Sons Landscape Architects, received $5,000 for a site plan in 1903. Careful dredging plus water pumped from the Willamette turned the marshes into a shallow lake that formed the

center of the site. Visitors entered from the southeast corner through a gate flanked by Ionic columns and crossed the Pacific Court to a sunken garden between the Agriculture and European exhibit buildings. Beyond the balustraded garden was Lakeview Terrace, with a view of Mount St. Helens on clear days, and a grand staircase down the bluff to the bandstand, boat landing, and waterfront esplanade. The Federal Building lay on a peninsula on the far side of the lake. It was reached by a causeway lined for part of its distance with the amusements of "The Trail," built on pilings over the lake.

The buildings as well as the formal design expressed the aesthetic of the City Beautiful era. With one exception, they followed the agreed style of Spanish Renaissance with domes, cupolas, arched doorways, and roofs covered with red tile or red paint. Because the exposition company had leased its land with promises to return it in its original condition, the exhibition structures were constructed with relatively light wood frames covered with lath, plaster, stucco, and white paint. Most were designed by local Portland architects such as Edgar Lazarus or Ion Lewis, of the prominent local firm of Whidden and Lewis. The federal building, a cross between a railroad terminal and a Mexican cathedral, was designed by James Knox Taylor.

The only truly distinctive building at the Lewis and Clark fair was the Forestry Building, with pine cone decorations, samples of lumber, and dioramas of elk and panthers. The building was an immense log cabin, stretching 105 by 209 feet, fronted by a portico of tree trunks with the bark intact. The interior was modeled on the nave of a cathedral, with colonnades of tree trunks supporting a high ceiling and setting off side galleries and balconies. The largest foundation logs weighed 32 tons and measured 5 feet across.

From opening day on June 1 through closing on October 15, the fair attracted 1,588,000 paid admissions-540,000 from Portland, 640,000 from elsewhere in Oregon and Washington, 250,000 from California and the Rocky Mountain states, and 160,000 from east of the Rockies. They found a fair that was heavy on exhibits relating to western resources. In addition to the forestry exhibits and the farm produce in the Oregon and Washington Buildings,

A scene of Lake View Terrace at the 1905 Lewis and Clark Exposition. Notice the early automobiles sharing the roadway with bikers and pedestrians (editors' collection).

A comic and somewhat racist postcard depicting the difference of "being on the Trail" in 1805 and 1905 (editors' collection).

the U.S. building included working models of the Salt River and Palouse (Washington) irrigation projects, Haida and Tlinget totem poles from Alaska, and an aquarium and hatchery from the Fish Commission. Foreign exhibits were weighted toward Asia. The nine European nations represented in the Foreign Exhibits Building were balanced by the equally large Oriental Exhibits Building, where Japan had the most extensive display.

Like all of the expositions during the great century of world's fairs from the Crystal Palace Exhibition in London in 1851 to the New York and San Francisco world's fairs of 1939–40, the Lewis and Clark Exposition was a showcase for progress. In the era before television and websites, people came to world's fairs to learn about scientific and technological progress. In Portland they could take in moving picture shows, watch motorized blimps maneuver in the sky, cheer the winner of the first transcontinental auto race, and marvel of the power of electric lighting.

Technological progress seemed simple, but social progress was more complex. A deeply racist exhibit of Filipino "savages" along the fair's amusement trail contrasted with the forward-looking speeches at the National American Woman Suffrage Association convention. The official program for Portland Day showed a lonely Indian looking down from the hills at the fairgrounds, a reminder of the power of European Americans to push aside other peoples.

The exposition was a practical success, opening on time and operating without major hitches. Portland's leaders hoped that the Lewis and Clark Exposition would garner reams of attention favorable publicity. When they emblazoned "Westward the Course of Empire Takes Its Way" on the arch over the entrance gate, they hoped that visitors would decide that empire was actually taking its way westward to Oregon. Indeed, national newspapers and magazines were generally complimentary. Walter Hines Page summarized the consensus when he told readers of the *World's Work* that "the enterprise has from the beginning been managed with modesty, good sense, and good taste." It made an operating profit and returned 21 percent of the capital to the original investors (over the protest of the state commission, which argued that the operating profits should go to the state of Oregon).

The fair had a substantial impact on the economic development of Portland. It coincided with the substantial expansion of railroads, farming, and stock raising in Portland's natural hinterland of eastern Oregon and eastern Washington. The years from 1905 to 1912 were flush times in the northwest, with Portland gaining substantially in commerce and manufacturing. Local businessmen identified the summer of 1905 as the start of a sustained real estate boom and gave the fair credit for attracting new investment.

Impacts on the physical form of Portland, however, were minimal. The neo-Mediterranean buildings of the disposable kingdom were soon dismantled, with only the Forestry Building remaining until a spectacular fire in the early 1960s. John Olmsted had suggested that the site of the fair could be incorporated into a citywide park system; however, delays in the purchase of parklands and the attractions of land speculation combined to end the idea of a riverfront park in northwest Portland. Guild's Lake itself disappeared under a deluge of silt in the 1910s, when land developers used high-pressure hoses and sluices to cut building lots and streets out of the hills behind it. Dredge spoils from the Willamette were added to the fill.

The majority of the site remained unoccupied for another generation while the mud settled. The area housed shipyard workers in temporary housing in World War II and is now the Northwest Industrial District, one of the city's "industrial sanctuaries" that protect manufacturing and wholesaling businesses. The site of the Forestry Building is new upscale housing.

Bibliography

The starting point for information on the exposition is Henry E. Reed, "Official History of the Lewis and Clark Centennial Exposition" (1908), available in the Reed Collection at the Oregon Historical Society in Portland. Other sources of documents are: the official report of the State Commission; the central office correspondence of the Exposition Company and the photographic collections at the Oregon Historical Society; mayor's office correspondence at the Portland City Archives; records dealing with construction and with the St. Louis fair of 1904 at the Oregon Division of Archives, Salem; and records relating to the fair at the Multnomah County Public Library, Portland.

The contemporary public view of the fair and its city can be found in the locally edited *Pacific Monthly* and the *Lewis and Clark Journal* (the official bulletin of the fair) and in the daily Portland *Telegram* and *Oregonian*. The role of the federal government can be followed in the record of hearings before the U.S. House of Representatives Committee on Industrial Arts and Expositions and in the correspondence of the State Department representative on the Government Board of Management relating to the transportation of federal exhibits (National Archives, Record Group 43).

Comprehensive analyses of the Lewis and Clark Exposition can be found in Carl Abbott, *The Great Extravaganza: Portland's Lewis and Clark Exposition* (3rd ed., 2004), and in Holly J. Pruett, "A Sense of Place ... Pride ... Identity: Portland's 1905 Lewis and Clark Fair" (bachelor's thesis, Reed College, 1985). Another discussion of the fair by Carl Abbott is available on-line through the website of the Oregon Historical Society (*http://www.ohs.org/education/oregonhistory/index.cfm*). The architecture of the fair is treated in George McMath, "The Lewis and Clark Fair," in Thomas Vaughan and Virginia Ferriday, eds., *Space, Style, and Structure: Building in Northwest America* (1974). The exposition in relation to the development of urban planning is covered in Carl Abbott, *Portland: Planning, Politics, and Growth in a Twentieth Century City* (1983). A chapter in Robert Rydell, *All the World's a Fair* (1984), discusses the Portland fair (in conjunction with the Seattle fair of 1909) with emphasis on the anthropological aspects of many of the exhibits. Lisa Blee, "Completing Lewis and Clark's Westward March: Exhibiting a History of Empire at the 1905 Portland World's Fair," *Oregon Historical Quarterly*, 106 (Summer 2005): 232–53, explores the ways in which American Indians and Pacific peoples were represented in the iconography of the fair.

Milan 1906

John E. Findling

L'Esposizione Internazionale del Sempione

The international exposition at Milan in 1906 was planned as a celebration of the completion of the Simplon tunnel, a 12.3-mile railroad tunnel through the Italian Alps that was an engineering achievement comparable in some ways to the Panama Canal. With the support of the government and King Victor Emmanuel III, some 12 million lire was subscribed to finance the fair, and building commenced at two sites in Milan, located 2 miles apart but connected by a specially constructed electric railway.

Buildings housing fine arts exhibits and cultural events were located in the Parco Real, an existing municipal park, while in the Piazza D'Armi, formerly an open space, a more formal site plan included foreign pavilions and structures housing industrial and engineering exhibits. The planners' notion of separating art from engineering at the two sites was blunted somewhat by the fact that many of the foreign pavilions were highlighted by fine arts displays.

Although the architecture of this lair was not highly rated by contemporary critics, there were a few significant structures, including the Galleria del Sempione, which featured a tunnel-like entrance and contained a replica of the actual tunnel. The concert hall was an incredibly ornate building in a combination of baroque and rococo styles, termed "barocco" by one critic, and the Marine Transport Building, with its 200-foot lighthouse tower, afforded the best view of the fairgrounds. There were two quite distinctive pavilions from a topical standpoint: one dedicated to hygiene, containing medical exhibits ranging from Red Cross uniforms to surgical instruments, and the Motor Car building, probably the first at a world's fair.

Amid great ceremony, King Victor Emmanuel opened the fair on April 28 in the Parco Real; a second ceremony two days later provided the king's blessing to the exhibits at the Piazza d'Armi. In addition to the pavilions already noted, visitors enjoyed the aeronautic section, a large enclosure from which tethered balloon ascents were made, and the many exhibits featuring railway engineering. Next to the engineering displays, Italian and Hungarian art exhibits attracted the most attention. The fine arts pavilion was entirely given over to Italian national art, and a concerted effort was made to feature the works of younger artists, sculptors, and designers. The Hungarian exhibit in an adjacent building received much praise for its lack of commercialism and the interesting Byzantine motifs seen in many pieces. Tragically, both the Italian and the Hungarian art exhibits were destroyed in a fire on August 2.

Foreign nations participating included most of the countries of Western Europe, as well as Japan, China, Turkey, and Canada. Several South American nations had a combined pavilion, and the United States participated but only in a minor way. Special displays and events included Pope Pius IX's railway car, given to him by Louis-Napoleon in 1848, Buffalo Bill's Wild West Show, a special parade of automobiles on May 26, in conjunction with an international congress on the automobile and the conclusion of the Coup d'Or race, and a Streets of Cairo village with exotic attractions and performances. By the time the fair closed on October 31, about 5.5 million visitors had attended. Contemporary observers labeled the fair a success in its demonstration of Italian industrial and engineering progress and as a showplace for artists and designers beginning to reflect the influence of modern art.

Postcard depicting the symbol of the Milan 1906 exposition, which was held to celebrate the completion of the great Símplan tunnel (editors' collection).

Bibliography

The principal source for the Milan 1906 exposition is E. A. Marescotti and E. Ximenes. *Milano e l'Esposizione Internazionale del Sempione 1906* (1906), an illustrated chronicle of the fair in forty-two parts (652 pages), with lavish illustrations and articles on all aspects of the fair. For German readers, *Die erste italienische Weltausstellung: ihr Schauplatz und ihre Vorge-schichte* (1907), by Alfons Leon, provides a general description of the exposition and its background, with additional information on the Simplon tunnel and rail travel into northern Italy. The official report of the French section at the Milan Fair is *Exposition Internationale de Milan / 906* (1906?); by Paul Dreyfus-Bing and G. Roger Sandoz. In English, the most general description is "The Milan Exposition," by Dexter G. Whittinghill, in *World To-Day* 12 (January 1907): 69–75. The fair's architecture is described by Ruben W. Carden in "The Milan International Exposition," *Architectural Record* 20 (September 1906): 353–68. Alfredo Milani discusses Italian and Hungarian art at the fair in "Italian Art at the Milan Exhibition," and "Hungarian Art at the Milan Exhibition," *International Studio* 29 (August and October 1906): 147–56, 300–9.

Christchurch 1906–1907

Conal McCarthy

New Zealand International Exhibition

The world's fair at Christchurch in New Zealand's South Island, held 16 years after the Dunedin exhibition of 1889–1890, was the country's largest to date and the first to be wholly financed by the government. The idea came from Premier Richard Seddon, who originally planned an inter-colonial exhibition in Hagley Park. James Cowan, the editor of the *Official Catalogue*, observed that exhibitions were "landmarks of industrial progress." Another promoter was T.E. Donne, the general manager of the recently established Department of Tourist and Health Resorts, who had organized the New Zealand court at the Louisiana Purchase International Exposition of 1904. Aside from tourism, industry, and trade, the fair was a visible expression of a fledgling sense of "national" identity marked by the achievement of dominion status in 1907, though this was articulated within a loyalist vision of New Zealand firmly tied to the "old country" as the "better Britain of the South Pacific."

The 14-acre centrally located site in Hagley Park, facing the Avon River and Park Terrace, was dominated by a quarter-mile long building that was the largest the country had yet seen, "like a palace of white and gold above the oak trees." Christchurch architect J.C. Maddison designed the façade in a French Renaissance style that had been popular in the 1880s, with an impressive main entrance made up of a domed projecting bay flanked by twin towers. The triangular pediment at its apex contained a clock and was decorated with the words *"haere mai,"* meaning "welcome" in the Maori language. The entrance led to a spacious grand hall where visitors could look up to the lofty dome 90 feet from the floor. From here a series of corridors and avenues, decorated with Italianate arches and bronzed plaster sculptures and greenery, were laid out in a rectangular plan giving access to the exhibition halls. Most of the government and foreign exhibits were contained in this building, but there were a number of detached buildings: a machinery hall, a concert hall seating 1,600, a fire-proof art gallery built of brick and asbestos, a fernery and formal gardens, an aquarium, a very popular side show called "Wonderland," and in "Geyserland," a replica of the natural geothermal attractions found in the scenic resort of Rotorua including functioning mechanical geysers.

Exhibitions in New Zealand never attracted a great number of foreign countries and were barely "international" in scope. At Christchurch separate courts were devoted to the United Kingdom, Canada, Fiji, and several states of Australia with exhibits sent by the United States, South Africa, and eight European countries. In addition to the usual agricultural and mercantile displays, which conveyed the picture of New Zealand as a fertile land of plenty, and the elegant tourist court which celebrated its beautiful lakes and mountains, there were a number of new initiatives and events. Among a large group of government courts, the Department of Labour reflected the agenda of the reforming Liberal government, which had been the first in the world to grant women the vote. These exhibits presented an image of New Zealand as a "social laboratory" through displays such as the model workers cottages designed by architects Samuel Hurst Seager and Cecil Wood. New Zealand's first professional orchestra performed to large crowds. It was conducted by local musician Alfred Hill who composed a commemorative ode for the occasion. There was an unprecedented amount of space devoted to fine arts, with a comprehensive display of paintings in the British Art section, which incorporated a very fashionable display of arts and crafts organised by William Morris's disciple Walter Crane. The Colonial Art section, however, was rather cursory, with work by artists from Australia and New Zealand. Planned as a stimulus and model for local artists, the fine arts exhibition, with its overwhelming display of British art, in fact stifled the development of New Zealand art.

The Christchurch fair was an unparalleled success, with an astounding 2 million visitors (twice the national population). A daily average of 14,000 flocked in every day, but still the exhibition lost money. The lasting legacy of the exhibition was its significance for scholars, as a public event that furnished a snapshot of New Zealand society and culture at this pivotal point in its history. Historian Jock Phillips has written that New Zealand presented itself to the world as "Maoriland" by appropriating aspects of Maori culture to serve the needs of a distinctive identity for *Pakeha* (European) settler culture. The clearest example of this was the extraordinary Maori *pa*, or fortified village, set up in Hagley Park where Maori people from around the country lived and performed for paying visitors. Despite the picturesque exoticism of this spectacle, and the ethnographic intentions of organizer Augustus Hamilton, there is evidence that the *pa* had different meanings for the Maori involved, who generally liked the exhibition and enjoyed meeting with other tribes and the Fijians and Cook Islanders also present. Maori leaders and artists such as Hori Pukehika, Tuta Nihoniho, and Neke Kapua took an active role in the construction and running of the *pa*, and said that it celebrated the survival and adaptability of their culture in

A crowd of fairgoers waits outside the entrance to the main building of the Christchurch exhibition (editors' collection).

contrast to the prevalent myth that they were "dying out."

Bibliography

The documentary records of the exhibition are scattered among several archives: the Canterbury Museum, the New Zealand Room at the Christchurch Public Library, the Alexander Turnbull Library, Wellington, and the Department of Internal Affairs and other government departments, Archives New Zealand, Wellington. There is a full series of files and correspondence related to the Maori *pa* in the archives of the Museum of New Zealand Te Papa Tongarewa, Wellington. Photographs and visual images may be found at the Museum of New Zealand Te Papa Tongarewa and the Alexander Turnbull Library, the latter

Wonderland, the Christchurch exhibition's popular amusement area, provided an array of activities to entertain children, including camel rides (editors' collection).

Group outside the large meeting house at the Maori *pa* (fortified village) at the New Zealand International Exhibition of 1906–1907 (courtesy Alexander Turnbull Library, Wellington, New Zealand).

through its excellent searchable database *Time-frames http://timeframes.natlib.government.nz/*.

The official published reports are*: Official Catalogue and Souvenir of the New Zealand International Exhibition, 1906–7* (1907), and *Souvenir: New Zealand International Exhibition Christchurch 1906–7* (1907). The most comprehensive and lively coverage is provided by amateur historian and journalist James Cowan, *Official Record of the New Zealand International Exhibition of Arts and Industries Held at Christchurch, 1906–07: A Descriptive and Historical Account* (1910). The Canterbury Museum holds a rare copy of the catalogue to the art gallery, *New Zealand International Exhibition 1906–7, Fine Arts Section Official Catalogue* (1906). Shorter official reports can be found in government publications *New Zealand Official Yearbook* (1907–08); and *Appendices to the Journals of the House of Representatives* (1907–08). There is a long illustrated article about the Maori *pa* by Augustus Hamilton in *Dominion Museum Bulletin, No.3* (1911). In addition to the special exhibition newspaper *The Exhibition Sketcher*, there is extensive contemporary coverage of the exhibition in the local newspapers: *The Press, Star,* Lyttelton *Times,* and *Weekly Press.*

Secondary published studies of the exhibition, particularly the art and ethnographic aspects, are relatively common. For a concise summary of the exhibition see N. Palethorpe,

Official History of the New Zealand Centennial Exhibition, Wellington, 1939–40 (1940). For a recent detailed analysis of the Maori art and artists the best source is Roger Neich, *Carved Histories: Rotorua Ngati Tarawhai Woodcarving* (2001). An excellent overall study of the exhibition is John Mansfield Thomson, ed., *Farewell Colonialism: The New Zealand International Exhibition Christchurch, 1906–7* (1998). This book includes useful chapters on trade and business (Gavin McLean), architecture (Peter Shaw), art (Linda Tyler and Jane Vial), and the Maori *pa* (Bernie Kernot). Particularly recommended in this volume is the introductory chapter by historian Jock Phillips that sets the exhibition in its broader historical context: "Exhibiting Ourselves: The Exhibition and National Identity," 17–26. Special mention should be made of the article by Margaret Orbell that translates material in Maori newspapers: "Maori Writing about the Exhibition," 141–163. For a recent analysis of the exhibition from the perspective of museum display, see Conal McCarthy, "From Curio to Taonga: A Genealogy of Display at New Zealand's National Museum, (1865–2001)" (unpub. Ph.D. diss., Victoria University of Wellington, 2004). For useful biographies of the people involved in the exhibition, consult the *Dictionary of New Zealand Biography http://www.dnzb.govt.nz/.*

Dublin 1907

Miglena Ivanova

Irish International Exhibition

The idea to hold an international exhibition in Dublin in 1906 originated during an Irish Industrial Conference held on April 15, 1903, on the premises of the Royal University, Dublin. Presided over by Lord W.J. Pirrie, owner of Belfast's shipbuilding firm, Harland and Wolff, the meeting's main purpose was to establish an Institute of Commerce for Ireland in the hope of improving the trade in Irish goods at home and abroad. As the organizers' motivation was largely in agreement with cur-

rent socio-economic and political aspirations for Irish Home Rule, the exhibition was designed not only to promote the development of Ireland's agricultural and industrial resources along modern scientific lines, but also to improve the productivity and standard of living in rural Ireland by providing suitable farming and industrial education to the rural people. Among the anticipated long-term effects were the curbing of Irish emigration and internal migration to congested Dublin. Drawing on successful smaller exhibitions in Cork in 1901 and 1902, the executive council realized

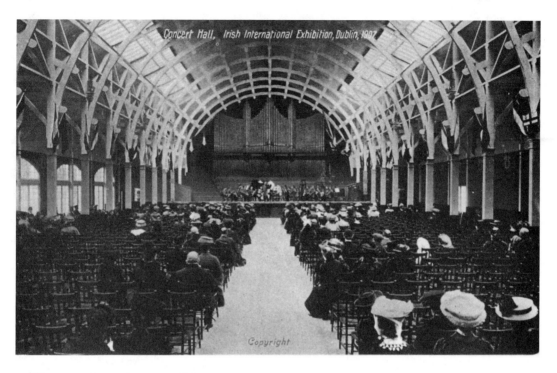

This postcard view shows a small but attentive crowd enjoying a performance in Concert Hall at the 1907 Dublin exhibition (editors' collection).

for the first time the enormous economic potential that heritage tourism held for both strengthening the Irish home industries and attracting foreign investment in Ireland.

The executive council of the Irish International Exhibition included prominent figures like the Marquess of Ormonde, Archbishop Healey, the Earl of Meath, and the Earl of Mayo. It raised a guarantee fund that exceeded £160.000, but difficulties in finding a suitable site resulted in the exhibition's postponement till 1907. The organizers' first choice, Phoenix Park, had to be abandoned due to inadequate transportation facilities. Finally, the Earl of Pembroke, one of the Council's Vice-Presidents, managed to secure a better site: Herbert Park in Ballsbridge. A mile and a half southeast of the city center, it was served by three tram lines and offered 52 acres of exhibition grounds in close proximity to the Dublin, Wicklow, and Wexford Railways. The site also bordered the grounds of the Royal Dublin Society where the prestigious annual Irish Horse Show was held in August. The exhibition was officially launched on May 4, 1907. and it remained open until November 9.

The design and construction of the exhibition buildings were entrusted to the London firm of Humphreys Ltd., renowned for their work on exhibition halls in Great Britain and the colonies. A Celtic Court at the main entrance led to the Grand Central Palace whose floor plan, façade, and interior evoked images of cultural and economic renewal: a central hall designed in the Florentine School of the Italian Renaissance enhanced the symbolism of the four radiating wings that represented Ireland's four provinces. A large statue of Erin, a reproduction of the Monasterboice Cross together with a detailed model of the Battle of Waterloo (in the Celtic Court), and an extensive Napoleonic exhibit that drew visitors' attention to famous Irishmen who served under Napoleon indicated it was no coincidence that Irish and British displays now occupied separate exhibition halls. Together with the French pavilion and the Palace of Mechanical Arts, special attention was given to the Canadian pavilion and New Zealand's section in the Palace of Industries, as both countries demonstrated a clear socio-economic autonomy from the Empire.

nal Exhibition, Dublin, 1907.

This flume ride, shown on a contemporary postcard, represents the increasing attention given to entertainment at world's fairs by this time (editors' collection).

The most popular attraction, however, proved to be the Home Industries Section, located in a building of its own, close to popular amusements like the Rivers of Ireland, the Helter Skelter Lighthouse, the Flip Flap, the Switchback Railway, and the Somali Village. In addition to the two industrial exhibition halls, the Home Industries Section contained three prize-winning model laborers' cottages, a village hall with a village green, and a village hospital that housed a Women's Section and special displays in hygiene and cottage industries. Although the exhibition generated enormous interest at home and abroad, attracting almost 2.75 million visitors, including King Edward VII and Queen Alexandra, and King Leopold of Belgium, the total earnings of £340,000 were insufficient to fill the revenue-expenditure gap of about £100,000, which was covered by the guarantors.

Bibliography

The Irish International Exhibition 1907, Inc. sponsored a large number of publications, printed in 1907 by Hely's Limited, Dublin or M'Caw, Stevenson & Orr, Ltd., Dublin and Belfast. Among the most useful are *Irish International Exhibition: The Official Catalogue, Irish Rural Life and Industry with Suggestions for the Future,* and *Record of the Dublin International Exhibition 1907,* containing maps, ground plans, financial details, economical analyses and forecasts, detailed descriptions of the exhibition grounds and buildings, photographs and illustrations, and special articles on traditional Irish arts, crafts, and manufacture.

Jamestown 1907

J.D. Bowers

Jamestown Tercentenary Exposition

The Jamestown Exposition, situated on 340 acres of land at Sewall's Point, Virginia, six miles from Norfolk (the official host city) and thirty-five miles from the original Jamestown settlement, opened to mixed reviews on April 26, 1907, three hundred years to the day of Christopher Newport's landing at Cape Henry.

The Jamestown Exposition Company was formally incorporated by an act of the Virginia Legislature in 1901, stemming from the efforts of Dr. Lyon G. Tyler, president of the College of William and Mary and the Association for the Preservation of Antiquities. This was not the first time that the settlement at Jamestown had been commemorated; beginning in 1807 the founding of the colony had been celebrated with great fanfare every fifty years. The Tercentennial was to be the third such event. Although locally conceived of as a regional fair to celebrate the tercentennial of the first permanent English settlement in the new world and revive tourism in the state's Tidewater region, the exposition was transformed into a showcase for the nation's new militarism and imperialism and as a venue to show the nation's people and the world the country's naval force, the "Great White Fleet."

Although the exposition was named for the place of settlement, Jamestown was not directly involved with hosting or planning the fair. That role went to the collective cities of Norfolk, Hampton, Newport News, and Portsmouth, as well as Norfolk County. It was an auspicious choice and many claimed that the site was unmatched by previous fairs, with the combination of its waterfront location and its exquisite wilderness, traversed by a canoe path as well as shaded walking trails. The fair's plan-

ners and builders were plagued by delays, however, stemming from issues of labor scarcity, cost overruns, bad weather, site complications, and inadequate transportation facilities. At its opening, while estimates varied wildly, the exposition was less than half finished, and two buildings were never fully completed according to plan. It was not until mid–August that the exposition director declared the show complete, just in time for the expected rush of northern fair-goers who hoped to avoid the region's summer heat and humidity.

The fair was promoted on the basis of the region's historical character, which few Americans had seen in person and which was said to have changed little in character from old Virginia. The surrounding region, rife with sites of historical significance owing to its role in both the Revolutionary and Civil War histories, was equally touted, along with an accompanying and justified militarism that stemmed from the past.

President Theodore Roosevelt arrived, via private yacht, to open the fair. His first order of business was to review the Great White Fleet and entertain the commanders, reminiscent of the 1857 anniversary celebration when former President John Tyler spoke and reviewed a naval flotilla and military parade of sixteen companies. Roosevelt's opening day address included a welcome to the peoples of the world, followed by a lengthy statement that honored the diverse origins of the nation while attributing the principal character, laws, and direction of the nation to the efforts of the first English settlements. To all of this he added a policy declaration against the abuses of trusts, in particular the railroads, as an anti–American practice.

The exposition centered on three major architectural features. The first, Raleigh Square, was the central area around which was built the state buildings and exhibit halls (Colonial Revival was the prominent architectural style, though there were several notable exceptions). There were state buildings from twenty-one states, city buildings representing Baltimore and Richmond, and territorial or national buildings from Alaska, Cuba, the Dominican Republic, Panama, and Puerto Rico. No fewer than seventeen nations sponsored exhibits of various kinds, including displays on manufacturing, arts, and economy. Georgia built a replica of Bulloch Hall, the home of President Roosevelt's mother, giving the president one more occasion to show up at the celebration, and Massachusetts constructed a replica of her old statehouse. The second major feature was Hampton Roads itself, giving the fair its aquatic and naval character, drawing in the sites of Fortress Monroe, Rip-Rap Fort, the fledgling Navy Yard, the basin encompassed by a newly constructed pier, a major means of transportation to the fair, and its only real link to Jamestown itself. The third focal point was the Lee Parade grounds for the military encampments, bordered by a forested area that completed the grounds and drew in the spectators of daily drills, maneuvers, and demonstrations.

African Americans were determined not to be left out of the exposition. After petitioning for inclusion in the fair, noting that Roosevelt's initial invitation to prospective participants did not include them, a substantial and widely praised exhibit was built under the auspice of the Negro Development and Exposition Company, specifically chartered for the occasion. Another positive aspect of the exposition for blacks was that, unlike previous world's fairs held in the United States, there was no antebellum plantation exhibit on the grounds, which had been one of the most popular exhibits in St. Louis just three years earlier, depicting black life, song, dance, and humor from the pre–Civil War era. However, as a reminder to their continued status as second-class citizens, Virginia had recently passed Jim Crow legislation segregating transportation, leaving few opportunities for blacks to visit the fair and feel welcome, and just one of the many reasons that many blacks encouraged a boycott of the exposition.

The midway amusements were along the "War Path"—the name echoed the militaristic theme — and included numerous respectable and dignified entertainments side-by-side with the "couchee couchee" shows and exploitive venues. There were actually two War Paths, one in and one outside of the formal exposition grounds, but the people paid as little heed to the boundaries as did the entertainers. Visitors who came to Jamestown could experience Comanche Dan's "Wild West" show and the competing Bostock's "Call of the Wild" animal show. There were demonstrations of the new marvel in modern medicine, baby incubators, side-by-side with the "International Congress of Beauty" show, the panoramic light and shadow show, "The Destruction of San Francisco," Ferrari's "Marvels of the Jungle," gambling, fortunetellers, shooting galleries, and countless other catchpenny entertainments. In one of the more interesting juxtapositions of history and a possible affront to Southern sensibilities, reenactments of Sheridan's equestrian conquest of Winchester alternated with Roman chariot races. Like previous fairs, the midway also included expansive "anthropological" exhibits, such as the five acre Philippine settlement with five different tribes including the "savage" Bagobos, an Alaskan village, a Swiss village, and several displays from the Far East. All of these easily fit into the same mold that had been created at previous fairs.

Jamestown itself was only a sideline to the exposition, accessible by car or by a ferry than carried passengers up the James River. There was not much to see on the island, save the ruins of the original church, a few cemeteries, and the foundations of a few period buildings. Reenactments of the history surrounding the settlement took place at the island's Ye Olde Jamestown Theater, depicting the stories of John Smith, Princess Matoaka (Pocahontas) and the Powhatan peoples. The only contributions to Jamestown as a result of the exposition were four monuments: statues of Pocahontas and John Smith, respectively, a monument commemorating the establishment of the House of Burgesses and one in commemoration of the Tercentenary celebration itself.

Back in Norfolk, there were military displays to entertain the crowds. Two were panoramic cycloramas of the Battles of Gettysburg and Manassas (balancing the victories for each side of the conflict, thus presumably pleasing all visitors) as part of the official War

Railroad exhibits were a central feature in world's fairs of this era. Here the Pennsylvania Railroad exhibit shows off a full size section of one of its tunnels (editors' collection).

The Jamestown Tercentenary Exposition of 1907 reflected a strong militaristic sense as evidenced by this postcard showing ships of many nations participating in a naval parade (editors' collection).

Path. Another, outside the grounds, "Lee and his Generals" was unabashedly southern and made no mention of his military opponents, perhaps making up for Sheridan's ride. But by far the most popular show on the midway was the depiction of the famous Civil War battle between the *Monitor* and the *Merrimack*, following which many visitors could stroll to the end of the Government Pier to witness a naval restaging of the battle using ships modified to resemble the first two ironclad vessels.

A disturbance on the War Path in July was cause for great alarm. Some 400 uniformed National Guardsmen who felt exploited by several of the entertainment proprietors marched into the midway, took it over, and shut down those venues which they believed were dishonest and fakes. Their first target was two burlesque shows, "The Far East" and "The Orient," which, though separated on the exterior by numerous other vendors and shows, was actually the same show. Many of the guardsmen and (presumably) others had paid to see both before realizing that they had been duped. They were met, after some time, by the exposition police (aptly named the Powhatan Guards) and after a general melee and a few non-fatal injuries, the National Guardsmen retreated and order was restored.

The success of the fair was further threatened by a bureaucratic controversy and a fire. Many commentators had noted that the Jamestown Exposition seemed heavily bureaucratic, having both a president and a director general, along with myriad other committees and leaders. Both executive positions had been held by several individuals over the life of the exposition, from the planning stages to the opening, and a feud erupted between them over who was responsible for hosting visiting dignitaries. When the dispute could not be resolved, James Barr, the director, resigned, leaving Harry St. George Tucker solely in charge with only an interim director to finish out the fair. In late July a catastrophic fire swept away several dozen hotels and War Path venues. Although only one life was lost, that of an African American man, the fire's major impact was economic, further devastating the exposition's attractions, monetary intake, and damaging its reputation in the press.

Militarism definitely played a central role in the exposition. Seventeen nations, including the European nations of Austria, France, Germany, Great Britain, and the Netherlands, along with Argentina and Brazil of South America, sent warships or troops to appear alongside those of the U.S. fleet and encampments. Fifty-two ships in all, forty-three of which were from the United States, led by the USS *Georgia* as the flagship, and nearly 14,000 troops were present in a show of international military power. The sailors remained on their vessels, taking launches to the fairgrounds for their assigned duties and activities, while the troops camped surrounding the Lee Parade Grounds, named in honor of both the first president of the Exposition, Maj. Gen. Fitzhugh Lee, and his uncle Robert E. Lee. There were also daily airship flights and athletic contests between the troops to keep the crowds entertained.

A mixed concrete and wood pier, constructed for $400,000, was central to the naval aspects of the exposition. It consisted of two separate walkways, each jutting out more than 2,500 feet into Hampton Roads then joined at the far end with the single-largest span of concrete in the nation, thus forming a lagoon. Here visitors could interact with sailors, see naval maneuvers, and witness the many aquatic demonstrations that took place within the enclosed basin.

While a great deal was made about the presence of the U.S. fleet and it was scheduled to set out in December for its world tour, the irony was that the fleet was already outdated and many of the vessels were due to be decommissioned soon after their return. The fair was thus the appropriate venue from which to launch such a voyage — both were fleeting and impermanent. There was a great debate about the degree to which the military and its war machines pervaded the atmosphere of the fair and protests as well as a public debate took place over these issues throughout the duration of the exposition.

There was no shortage of notable speakers or guests to the exposition. King Edward VII was on site for several days to help celebrate the British connections, and so too were other notables, in recognition of the fair's industrial and expansion exhibits, including Samuel Gompers, William Randolph Hearst and Cornelius Vanderbilt. In May, William Jennings Bryan, the famous orator, made an appear-

This postcard view shows the main concourse of the Jamestown exposition, where most of the major pavilions were situated (editors' collection).

ance on Patrick Henry Day, in honor of the nation's other leading orator. Booker T. Washington also came to visit the African American exhibit and pay tribute to its originator, Giles B. Jackson, of Richmond. Finally, in late September, Mark Twain showed up on Robert Fulton Day to honor the prominent role played by the invention of the steam vessel. Following Twain's departure a report appeared in the New York *Times* claiming that the famous essayist was missing at sea, to which Twain replied he would have been certain to notify the paper of his disappearance.

There were definitely different assessments of the fair — northerners and the northern press seemed less taken in by the exposition and less understanding of its shortcomings, while southerners lauded its charm and made allowances for its apparent failings. Despite criticisms of its incomplete nature, the exposition attracted more than 2.85 million visitors (of which 1.25 million were paid admissions) during its seven month run. Both transportation problems and the initial negative publicity contributed to its failure to garner the anticipated crowds of 3.5 million and resulted

in a debt topping $2.5 million, putting the fair into receivership when it was all complete. Many decried the expenses associated with the fair, from the national leadership who had loaned them substantial sums of money, to the visitors themselves, citing price gouging by the hotels, transportation companies, restaurants, and even the costs of admission to many of the exposition attractions and entertainments. Initial calls and efforts to reopen the fair for a second season in 1908 understandably fell upon deaf ears and the exhibit closed, as planned, in late November of 1907. Several years later the government bought the fair grounds, minus the amount of debt owed on the original loan, and incorporated the site into the Norfolk Naval Base.

Bibliography

The most detailed coverage of the fair can be found in Amy Waters Yarsinkske's two volume illustrated history, *Jamestown Exposition: American Imperialism on Parade*, (1999), part of the Images of America series. It contains the largest collection of images, context, and details about the fair, but Robert Taylor, "The Jamestown Tercentennial Exposition, 1907," *Virginia Magazine of History and Biography* 65 (1957): 167–208, has much more text and fewer pictures. The exposition company published a sixteen-page brochure, "Jamestown Exposition," that is also helpful. For information on the US Government's role see U.S. Senate, 60th Cong., 2^d sess., no. 735 (Vol. 16), *Final Report of the Jamestown Ter-Centennial Commission* (1909). Guidebooks, such as Charles Russell Kiehy, *The Official Blue Book of the Jamestown Ter-Centennial Exposition* (1909) and J. E. Davis, *Round about Jamestown* (1907), contain a great deal of information about Jamestown and the fair. The bulk of the material on the Tercentennial can be found in the newspapers and periodicals of the day, especially the Richmond *Times-Dispatch,* the Norfolk Dispatch, and the *Virginian-Pilot.* See also a series of reports by Franklin Fyles in the Chicago *Tribune,* particu-

larly his reports on the War Path from July of that year.

Among the many magazine articles on this fair, the most useful are William Inglis, "troubles at Jamestown," *Harper's* Weekly (June 8, 1907): 834–37, which is critical of the fair's opening; Plummer F. Jones, "The Jamestown Tercentenary Exposition," *American Review of Reviews* 35 (March 1907): 305–18; George Harvey, "The Singularity of the Jamestown Exposition," *North American Review* (March 15, 1907); and Helen A. Tucker, "The Negro Building and Exhibit at the Jamestown Exposition," *Charities and the Commons* (Sept. 21, 1907). For the information on Mark Twain, see "Twain and Yacht Disappear at Sea" in the New York *Times,* May 4, 1907. A great many of these articles, and more, have been collected by Robert Zwick at *http://www.boondocksnet.com/expos/jamestown.html,* making this site the single best place to start for a look at the fair as it was viewed during the early 1900s.

London 1908

Jane Kimber

Franco-British Exhibition

The Franco-British Exhibition, which took place at the new White City exhibition site in Shepherds Bush, West London, embodied the spirit of the Entente Cordiale in its spectacular presentation of the industry, commerce, and culture of the French and British empires. The French Chamber of Commerce and the British Empire League started to plan the exhibition in 1905, working with Imre Kiralfy, an established entrepreneur in the exhibition field, whose company was charged with creating the exhibition. A site in Britain was being sought for the 1908 Olympic Games, and it was decided to place the Olympic Stadium alongside the new exhibition ground. An area of agricultural land in Shepherd's Bush, owned by the Ecclesiastical Commissioners, was purchased to provide a site of about 140 acres close to good transport facilities. Groundbreaking took place

on January 3, 1907, and building work went on apace.

The exhibition was formally opened on May 14, 1908, a miserably wet day, by the Prince of Wales. On the opening day, 123,000 people visited the exhibition, the busiest day until August 31, when 130,000 visitors came. Admission was 1 shilling for the day, or one guinea for a season ticket, plus an extra sixpence for each of the special amusements. About 5,000 staff worked at the exhibition, of whom some 1,000 remained on the site every night, including those living in the reconstructed villages.

The prevailing architectural style of the exhibition featured white buildings, designed by a number of architects under the supervision of John Belcher and Marius Toudoire and constructed of steel frames and concrete covered with ornamental plasterwork. The site was divided into themed areas. Visitors entered first the Court of Honour, which contained water-

This stadium was built for the 1908 Summer Olympic Games, which were held in conjunction with the Franco–British Exhibition (editors' collection).

ways, pavilions in the Indian style, and the Palaces of Industry. Beyond lay the Court of Arts, where the principal buildings were the Palaces of Decorative Art, Fine Art and Applied Art, the Palace of Music and the Palace of Women's Work. Then came the Élite Gardens, where flowerbeds were laid out and bands played, while to the west was the Garden of Progress and the Machinery Halls. The northern part of the site contained the fairground amusements, the native villages, and a radiating series of avenues with names recalling the French and British empires, where halls and pavilions displaying the products and arts of colonial countries such as India, Canada, Australia, and Ceylon were clustered. Many of the buildings were outlined with electric lights and illuminated at night. Refreshments were provided by the caterers J. Lyons and Co., and private dining rooms could be booked.

There was a wide range of exhibits, combining trade fair with cultural exposition. The Palace of Decorative Art, for example, contained furniture, cooking ranges, billiard rooms, carpets, upholstery, ceramics, and many other goods designed to gladden the heart of an Edwardian homeowner, as well as rooms outfitted in the styles of previous centuries.

Heavy industry was represented by displays on subjects such as mining, iron and steelwork, armaments manufacture, shipbuilding, electricity generation, and printing machinery. Light industries and crafts were also included and some processes, such as glass-making, were carried out on site for the benefit of spectators. Halls were devoted to the education, science, agriculture, and nutrition of both countries, while a major display of French and British fine arts was assembled from museum and gallery collections.

The amusements section was substantial. It was dominated by the Flip Flap, a counterpoised metal structure whose arms could lift a viewing carriage to a height of 150 feet. When in motion each arm rotated 180 degrees, passing the other at the top of the rotation and affording the passengers a marvelous view of the White City and beyond. A total of 48 people could ride in each of the two cars at any one time, and the trip took three minutes. Other attractions included the mountain scenic railway, on which an electric train, reaching a speed of 50 miles an hour, carried passengers past re-creations of mountains, lakes, waterfalls, and caves. The Spiral consisted of cars which ascended and descended a corkscrew track, while the Toboggan was a type of switchback ride. A reconstruction of the Johnstown Flood, which had taken place in the United States in 1889, involved mechanical and electrical machinery weighing 54 tons. During the exhibition there were numerous concerts and fireworks displays to add to visitors' enjoyment.

The Franco-British Exhibition was intended partly to celebrate and publicize what were then perceived by the authorities as the achievements of empire. Among the attractions of the exhibition were four villages, representing Ireland, Senegal, India, and Ceylon. Native citizens of these countries lived in the villages, staying onsite for the duration, and exhibiting their crafts and other aspects of their culture in recreated buildings typical of their countries. The Irish village, named Ballymaclinton, contained cottages, an ancient Irish Cross, a village shop, a farm, and a priest's house, as well as the Round Tower of Old Kilcullen, a Galway fisherman's cottage, and the Abbey at Donaghmore. Irish industries were exhibited, including carpet manufacture, handloom weaving of damask linen, lace-making, and embroidery, and cakes were baked in peat ovens. The Ceylon village had a bazaar and pagoda, and visitors were entertained by dancers, musicians and jugglers.

The exhibition closed on October 31, 1908. Total attendance was estimated at 8.4 million, with receipts of over £420,000. Although visitor numbers had not been as high as was hoped, the exhibition was still judged to have been a success. The site continued to be used for international exhibitions until World War

Thrill seekers delighted in riding the Flip Flap, which took visitors up 150 feet and gave them great views of the exhibition grounds (editors' collection).

I, and then for wartime purposes such as tent-making. Between 1921 and 1937 the exhibition sheds that ran between the main site and the Uxbridge Road entrance hosted the British Industries Fair, an important trade show. Thereafter the White City fell into disuse and was subsequently demolished. The site was converted a residential area and the BBC Television Centre. No physical evidence remains of the Franco-British Exhibition.

This patriotic postcard hailing Franco-British friendship might be seen as an ominous prelude to World War I, just six years away (editors' collection).

Bibliography

The most important source of primary research material on this topic is the Imre Kiralfy Collection at the Museum of London, which includes manuscript and printed material, a photograph album showing the construction of the White City, and another of the Franco-British Exhibition itself. Hammersmith and Fulham Archives and Local History Centre also holds printed and photographic material concerning the exhibition, including programs, postcards, and tickets.

Contemporary printed items include the *Official Guide* (1908), which ran to several editions, and an official souvenir, *The Franco-British Exhibition: Official Souvenir* (1908). A program of events, *Daily Programme* (1908), was published each day. Other guidebooks published that year also referred to the exhibition, such as *A Pictorial and Descriptive Guide to London and the Franco-British Exhibition, 1908* (1908). There are numerous contemporary newspaper accounts, particularly in the national dailies such as the *Times* and the *Daily Mail*. The local paper, the *West London Observer*, covered the event, and there was an exhibition paper, the *White City Herald*. A few days before the exhibition closed, a banquet was given, and an account was published as a *Report of the Proceedings at the Complimentary Banquet at the Garden Club of the Franco-British Exhibition in Honour of Mr Imre Kiralfy, the Commissioner General, Wednesday 28th October 1908* (1908). Material concerning the 1908 Olympic Games includes the program, *Pro-*

Visitors who preferred not to walk could be transported around the fairgrounds by rickshaw (editors' collection).

gramme [of the] Olympic Games of London 1908, IV International Olympiad (1908), and the official report, *The Fourth Olympiad, Being the Official Report of the Olympic Games of 1908 Celebrated in London ... and Issued under the Authority of the British Olympic Council* (1908). The Games were also covered extensively in the contemporary press, especially the *New York Times,* the *Times* of London, and the *Los Angeles Times.* For more modern work on the Games, see Max Howell and Reet Howell, *The Olympic Movement Restored: The 1908 Games* (1978), and James Coates, "London 1908," in John E. Findling and Kimberly D. Pelle, eds., *Encyclopedia of the Modern Olympic Movement* (2004): 51–56.

After the exhibition closed, a detailed account was published, *The Franco-British Exhibition: Illustrated Review, 1908* (1908), edited by F.G. Dumas. In 1910 a film was made showing the exhibition ground and the buildings, called *Farmer Jenkins' Visit to the White City* (1910), which is available for viewing at the British Film Institute. A short book was published to coincide with the seventieth anniversary of the first exhibition: Donald Knight, *The Exhibitions: Great White City, Shepherds Bush, London* (1978), and a thesis has also been researched that includes consideration of the Franco-British Exhibition: Brendan Gregory, *The Spectacle Plays and Exhibitions of Imre Kiralfy, 1882 — 1914* (unpub. M.A. thesis, University of Manchester, 1988). A copy of the unpublished thesis is held by the British Library. Hammersmith and Fulham Archives and Local History Centre has a transcript of reminiscences by C. Hayward, who worked at the Franco-British Exhibition as a boy.

Seattle 1909

J. D. Bowers

Alaska-Yukon-Pacific (AYP) Exposition

Originally conceived of as a fair in and for Alaska, the planning and prospects quickly turned toward a more inclusive venue and approach, eventually evolving into the broadly-themed AYP, as a way to assure success and gain notoriety. It was a fair designed to, in the words of President William Howard Taft, "exploit the natural resources and marvelous wealth of Alaska and the development of trade and commerce on the Pacific slope." It was further intended to demonstrate that the wild frontier which so often seemed to characterize the region in the myths and legends was no more. Taft opened the exposition by touching a telegraph key in the White House studded with Klondike gold that sent a direct signal to Seattle to set in motion several of the exposition's attractions and displays, which sent the throng of 90,000 people who attended the opening day ceremonies into a frenzy. James J. Hill, chairman of the Great Northern Railroad, gave the opening address in which he spoke of this exposition as a transformative event in the way that the peoples of the Pacific would regard the rest of the nation and how the rest of the nation would now regard both the peoples and resources of the Pacific.

Unlike many earlier expositions, the AYP was almost completely finished on opening day. It took just over two years and $10 million to construct, and it was laid out in one of the most scenic and compact sites of any exposition held in the United States. Furthermore, it was the first of the international expositions held on American soil not to solicit funding from the government. Great care was taken to preserve the character of the northwestern forest lands on which it was built. The 250-acre site was four miles from the heart of the city and nestled between Lakes Washington and Union, using them as a backdrop and a major venue. The dominant architectural style was French Renaissance and the grounds were illuminated by 150,000 lights.

The fair was international in character, design, and conduct. The opening day ceremonies included Japanese fireworks, naval forces (including two Admirals from the Japanese Fleet who served as dignitaries), and cultural representations. Furthermore, both Japanese naval forces and American troops were on hand throughout the fair. Even the statue of James J. Hill that was dedicated on August 3 was covered in the flags of Japan, the United States, and Great Britain before its unveiling. September 4 was Japanese Day at the AYP and more than 7,000 citizens of Japanese ancestry were reported to have attended. The day was preceded, however, by some controversy over the use of a Japanese flag as part of a rickshaw concession on the midway that was seen as contributing to anti–Japanese and cheap labor sentiment.

Puget Plaza was the central square, marked by the intersecting streets of Olympic Place and Alaska Avenue. From there one could travel down the avenue to a large, natural amphitheatre that held more than 1,500 people and sloped downward toward Lake Washington. Within the AYP grounds there was a model farm, separate buildings sponsored by the Masons and Swedish governments, an athletic stadium, a stock exhibit, miles of natural trails weaving in and out of park lands, and both water was supplied by a direct line coming in from nearby Cedar Mountain. By far the largest exhibitor was the U. S. government, with two separate buildings and the bulk of the square footage. One of the two buildings, occupied by the U.S. Forestry Service, was built from logs taken from the Snohomish forests to the north of the city. The exhibitions for Hawaii and the Philippines shared a building, but this was not occupied at the outset of the fair, reports noting that the ship bringing both the people and their materials had been delayed in Honolulu. There was also a fully functioning, model life saving structure that was used throughout the AYP as a first-aid station and to ensure the safety of all participants in water sports. State buildings were sponsored by Washington, New York, Oregon, California, Idaho, and Utah. In keeping with the theme, the only national buildings that were constructed were those of Japan and Canada, while the rest of the world's nations spread their exhibits across the site in the more broadly-themed buildings dealing with forestry, manufacturing, the arts, and industry.

Alaska had its own building at the fair and it was among the most popular owing to the novelty and interactive nature of the displays on gold mining, fishing, trapping, forestry, transportation, and the state's flora and fauna. Alaska's prominence in the fair's inception and conduct was marked by the fact that the entire final week was named in its honor, but the territory was also given five other days, spread throughout the course of the fair, in which to honor various members of its citizenry, including former Secretary of State William H. Seward, who had purchased Alaska in 1867.

Pay Streak was the name given to the midway, honoring the traditions and heritage of the Yukon. It differed very little in character from earlier midways, and even contained many of the venues and entertainments that had been in Jamestown two years earlier. It was the usual spate of exotic shows, souvenirs, food booths, palmistry, new product demonstrations, and penny-catching entertainments. The AYP flair was heightened with unique concessions that centered on boat tours, Alaskan hunting, the Klondike, and gold-themed venues. Likewise, there were the perennial Philippine Igorot and Chinese villages. True to form (and entertainment) the Igorots were presented as the dog-eating, head-hunting, primitive and wild people of the Philippines; they were truly the noble savages. The Chinese village was a little less sensationalist, but still attempted to shock visitors with its depiction of opium dens, and the wild-eyed violence of the country-side people that recalled accounts of the recent Boxer Rebellion in China.

Despite the fact that Alaska had its own exhibit among the buildings of prominence, there was still an Eskimo Village along the Pay Streak, a village that countered the notions of progress and civilization that was given as the message elsewhere. As the largest concession on the Pay Streak, the Eskimo Village housed both Siberian and Alaskan Eskimos and their animals in recreated villages. There was a separate concession for the Inuit from Labrador, the "Land of the Midnight Sun" exhibit, which showed the peoples of Labrador in a much more civilized light than the Eskimo Village. One of the peoples on display in the Inuit village was Columbia Eneutseak, who had been

The first decade of the twentieth century marked the high point of the display of ethnic and racial minorities at fairs. This postcard shows an Eskimo child from Alaska and an Igorot child from the Philippines (editors' collection).

born in the Eskimo Village at Chicago's World's Columbian Exposition in 1893. She became "Queen" of the Pay Streak and her notoriety increased late in the fair's run when the discovery of the North Pole was announced in September. She also led her people in a protest against discrimination during President Taft's visit, asking why the role of the Inuit people was not acknowledged in the so-called "discovery" of the Pole.

Perhaps one of the most distinctive days was September 2, known as Smith Day. Anyone with the surname Smith, the nation's most common, was honored that day; and nearly 5,000 Smiths came. Many people associated with the fair, including Columbia Eneutseak and other entertainers in the Pay Streak, became honorary Smiths for the day and participated in the parades, speeches, and special events. Yet another unique event associated with the AYP was a New York-to-Seattle automobile race sponsored by Robert Guggenheim that sought to tout the grandeur of transcontinental automobile travel and its advantages over rail.

As with any coastal fair, and especially with one centered on the notion of a greater Pacific, the aquatic aspects played a central role. Naval vessels from China, France, Great Britain, Germany, Japan, and Russia, all the great exploring and colonizing nations of the Pacific, were anchored in Puget Sound for display, and their sailors routinely came ashore to represent their nations and participate in specially designated events. Water sports, in general, occupied a central place in the events of the AYP. There were yacht races held for the honor and prestige of winning one of several international cups, a long-distance sailing race to Juneau and back, collegiate regattas, and Eskimo kayak races, all designed to showcase the region's close relationship with the sea.

The future of the west was a major theme as well. John Johnson, governor of Minnesota, addressed the exposition on that state's day (August 3) and spoke of the growing identity and independence of the west and its need to assert itself in terms of its political and economic power. The northwest, he noted, was

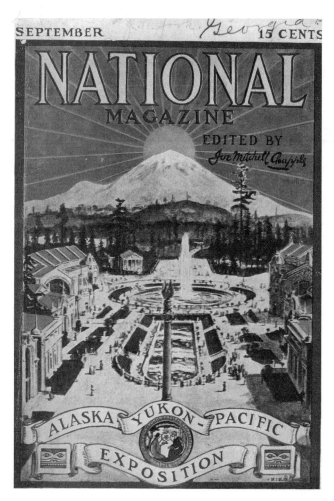

Popular magazines of the day often devoted much space to world's fairs as shown here in the September 1909 *National Magazine.*

they all planned and carried out their own efforts to host the world. But the organizers and people of Seattle overcame the apparent weariness of people toward expositions and hosted a very successful fair. The total attendance at the AYP was listed as 3,750,000 and the numbers who came west to see the exposition was a testament to the organization, the readiness, and the ability of six of the nation's transcontinental rail lines to carry them all to Seattle.

At the conclusion of the exposition many of the exhibits were packed in crates and shipped to Chicago for the U. S. Land and Irrigation Exposition held at the Coliseum between November and December. As for the buildings and the site, the intention had been all along to construct the buildings for permanent, long-term use at the conclusion of the AYP. According to plan, most of them were turned over to the University of Washington to further its mission and to provide much needed space for residential and academic facilities.

one of the nation's leading sources of raw materials and growing commerce with Asia. Thursday, September 30, was Taft Day at the AYP and the president spent the better part of two days at the exposition as part of his extended fifty-seven day tour of the nation. While at the AYP he toured the Pay Streak, delivered an address at the amphitheater reinforcing the desire to see the northwest fully assimilated into the American economic and political future, and met with dignitaries from Seattle as well as Japan to discuss the future.

The AYP was conceived of and planned during a period of "exposition fever" in the United States, crossing paths with St. Louis, Jamestown, Baltimore, and New Orleans as

Bibliography

The Manuscript Division of the Suzallo Library at the University of Washington houses the official records of the AYP. The relevant papers of the Olmsted Brothers, who were responsible for the landscaping, are also at this library. In addition, the Pacific Northwest Collection at the library includes an array of published guidebooks, other contemporary publications, and ephemera from the fair. The official guidebook is *Alaska-Yukon-Pacific Exposition: Official Guide* (n.d.). Another useful and comprehensive guide to the AYP was published by the fair's curiously-named Department of Exploitation Seattle, *Seattle and the Pacific Northwest* (1909). The exposition was covered well by the local newspapers, notably the Seattle *Post-Intelligencer, Pacific Northwest Commerce,* and a special promotional publication, the *Alaska-Yukon Magazine.* See also a pre-fair article by exposition president J.E. Chilberg, "The Alaska-

Yukon-Pacific Exposition," *The Coast* 12 (1906): 289–92.

  U.S. government records reveal much information about the planning for the exposition, as well as the federal government's role in it. Interested researchers should consult the *Hearing before the Committee on Industrial Arts and Expositions, U.S. House of Representatives, Alaska-Yukon Rxposition, January 27, 1908* (1908), U.S. Senate, 61st Cong., 3rd Sess., No. 671 (vol. 29), *Report on Alaska-Yukon-Pacific Exposition* (1911) The Smithsonian Institution was responsible for many of the federal government exhibits, and its report is *The Exhibits of the Smithsonian Institution and the United States National Museum at the Alaska-Yukon-Pacific International Exposition* (1909).

  Many contemporary newspapers and magazines ouside of Seattle ran articles that covered the fair, such as: "The Fair That Will Be Ready," *The World To-Day* 16 (April 1909); "Alaska-Yukon Fair Will Open Tuesday," New York *Times* (May 30, 1909); "An Exposition in the Golden West," Atlanta *Constitution* (June 1, 1909); R. S. Jones, Jr., "What the Visitor Sees at the Seattle Fair," *American Review of Reviews* (July 1909); "Japanese Flag Struck at Seattle Fair," Chicago *Tribune* (June 8, 1909); "Japanese

Day at Seattle Brings Host of Orientals," Los Angeles *Times* (September 5, 1909); "Smith Family Has Reunion," *Nevada State Journal* (Sept. 3, 1909). Many of these articles have been collected by Robert Zwick at *http://www.boondocksnet.com/expos/ay pexpo.html*, making this site the best place to research the fair as it was viewed by contemporaries. Among modern work on the AYP, consult George A. Fryman, "The Alaska-Yukon-Pacific Exposition, 1909," *Pacific Northwest Quarterly* 53, 3 (July 1963): 89–98; Janet A. Northam, "Sport and Urban Boosterism in the Pacific Northwest: Seattle's Alaska-Yukon-Pacific Exposition, 1909," *Journal of the West* 17, 3 (July 1978): 53–60; Georgia Ann Kumor, "'Doing Good Work for the University of Washington': The Alaska-Yukon-Pacific Exposition, 1906–1909," *Portage* (Winter/Spring 1986): 14–21; and Terrence M. Cole, "Promoting the Pacific Rim: The Alaska-Yukon-Pacific Exposition of 1909," *Alaska History* 6, 1 (Spring 1991): 18–34. For the general context of cultural politics in which the fair took place, see Robert Rydell, *All the World's a Fair* (1984), as well as his article, "Vision of Empire: International Expositions in Portland and Seattle, 1905–1909," *Pacific Historical Review* 52, 1 (February 1983): 37–65.

Brussels 1910

Paul Greenhalgh

Exposition Universelle et Internationale

  This exposition confirmed Belgium's role as a major host of international events. Staged only thirteen years after the previous Brussels exposition, and a year after an imperial international exhibition in London in which Belgium had a very large pavilion, the 1910 fair revealed the heavy commitment of the Belgian government to international display. The major part of the organization was carried out by the Ministry of Finance and Public Works, with the Ministry of War providing administrative support for the military and imperial elements. M. le Comte de Smit de Naeyer, minister of finance and public works, was the controlling figure

within the organizational structure. Above him, King Albert carried the symbolic role of *Haute protecteur de l'exposition*. The major participants were France, the Netherlands, Great Britain (including Ireland), Russia, Germany, Brazil, Spain, and Italy. A pavilion for all other nations was erected, in which several dozen countries put up stands. The number of nations committing themselves to a major investment was therefore fewer here than at any other Belgian event.

  About half way through its run, the exposition was marred by an event that might have been, but for good fortune, a tragedy. Shortly before nine on the evening of Sunday, August 14, after most of the day's crowd had left, a fire broke out near the central gallery and quickly

On the night of August 14, 1910, a fire destroyed several buildings at the Brussels exposition (editors' collection).

No people were killed in the fire that burned several buildings at the 1910 Brussels exposition, but these two crocodiles were not so lucky (editors' collection).

Buildings devoted to women's accomplishments had been a fixture at world's fairs since 1890. This view shows the Palace of Women's Work at the 1910 Brussels exposition (editors' collection).

spread to the British section, the city of Paris pavilion, and a French restaurant. After several hours, the fire was brought under control, the rest of the site was saved, and no lives were lost. What remained of the British industrial exhibit was then moved to the Salles de Fetes. The incident greatly increased the publicity surrounding the fair.

The site was southwest of the parc de Solbosch and northwest of bois de la Cambre. Its most striking feature was a series of lavish ornamental gardens, which led up to the Jardin de la Ville de Paris and the Jardin Hollandais at the core. The popular literature surrounding the event made repeated claims that this was the most beautiful site ever used for an international exposition, a dubious assertion but nevertheless one that served to highlight the unusually green site and the pleasant atmosphere. The site architecture was almost exclusively historicist—that is, verbose and superficial copies of earlier styles. A heavy neobaroque, evident in Paris in 1900 and London in 1908, dominated the skyline. Perhaps the only structure of note among the official sections was the vast Machine Hall, which had a greater total floor space than the legendary

Galeries des Machines of the Paris expositions of 1889 and 1900.

The exhibits were not divided in the traditional manner of raw materials, manufactures, machinery, and fine arts but were classifies into twenty-two groups, each with its controlling executive and judges. The most significant groups were Education, Works of Art, Appliances relating to Literature, Science and Art, Engineering, Electricity, Agriculture, Mining, Decorative Arts, Textiles, Chemical Industries, Social Economy, Woman's Labor, the Army and Navy, and Colonies. There was also a Congress Hall, in which numerous commercial and academic conferences and conventions were held.

Perhaps the two most popular areas, not for the last time at a Belgian exposition, were the colonies and the fine arts. In the former, it was the French who put on the most dramatic display, with stunning pavilions for Indochina, West Africa, Algeria, and Tunisia. The latter two attracted the most attention; they were built in indigenous North African styles, surrounded by gardens with exotic plants and with large numbers of Algerians and Tunisians in traditional costumes servicing the buildings.

The interiors of these pavilions contained serious and quite dry displays of the economic prosperity France had brought. This was unusual; the French normally preferred an exotic splash of decorative splendor or serve as imperial propaganda. There was also a general colonial pavilion for smaller French dependencies and a building for the colonial press. The pavilions dedicated to the Belgian Congo were impressive but outdone by the French display. The British expended little energy on the colonial area, unusual for them.

The fine arts were divided into old and the new art, the former of which was enhanced by a Maison de Rubens. Without any doubt, the show of Flemish art was the key attraction here, with masterpieces gathered from the best public and private collections in Belgium. The modern section was chiefly of interest for the fine collection sent by the French, a surprisingly liberal selection in relation to the normal French contribution to official expositions. The usual *grands pompiers* were all present, notably Leon Bonnat (three works), Jean Beraud (one work), and Albert Besnard (one work), but apart from these, Claude Monet (three works), Auguste Renoir (three works), and Auguste Rodin (three works) gave a different view of the older generation. More surprisingly, Edouard Vuillard (two works), Pierre Bonnard (two works), Maurice Denis (one work), Paul Signac (one work), and Henri Matisse (two works) were allowed to represent their country. This was most unusual and must be put down to the enlightenment of chief commissioner for the fine arts, Andre Saglio.

Bibliography

The general features of the Brussels exposition, including its organization and exhibits are found in these official reports and catalogs: *Brussels Exhibition 1910: Official Catalogue of the British Section* (1910); *Catalogue général, Exposition universelle et internationale, Bruxelles 1910* (1910); *Catalogue special official de la section français* (1910); *Livre d'or de l'exposition universelle et internationale de Bruxelles 1910* (1910). The fair's organizers published a journal of fair-related news, beginning in November 1907 and continuing through December 1910. Published monthly before the fair's opening and more frequently during the run of the fair, *Moniteur de l'exposition universelle et internationale Bruxelles 1910* contained both general interest articles and articles on specific features of the exposition. Both the New York *Times* and the *Times* of London carried occasional articles about the exposition, especially about the mid–August fire.

Modern works that mention this fair include A. Cockx and J. Lemmens, *Les Expositions universelles et internationales en Belgique de 1885 à 1958* (1958), which devotes a brief chapter to it, and John Allwood, *The Great Exhibitions* (1977).

Nanking 1910

Kimberly D. Pelle

Nan-Yang Ch'Uan-Yen Hui (Nanking South Seas Exhibition)

On December 15, 1908, Governor-General Tuan Fang of the Liang-kiang provinces proposed that China hold an international exhibition to promote the country's national products and to advance the modernization of its economy. Tuan believed that an international exposition would increase the growth of the Nanking area, stimulate national industry, inspire necessary educational and social reforms, and encourage the provinces to participate in "healthy competition." The last resulted in small exhibits and trade shows, with each province or region displaying its most distinctive wares months before they were to be shown at the international exhibition. This helped to promote interest and excitement among the people, and fair officials hoped that it would affect the attendance figures. It did not.

After numerous delays, the exposition finally opened on June 5, 1910, with Viceroy Chang Jen-chun and Adjudicator-General Yang Shih-chi leading the opening ceremonies. By then, numerous news articles describing the political turbulence and anti-foreign sentiment in China had been released, and this adverse publicity most likely accounted for the lower than estimated attendance figures. But despite the fear of outbursts and anti-foreign violence, the opening ceremonies were quite peaceful.

The site selected in Nanking seemed to be a perfect place to stage an exposition. Located on the Yangtze River and near the Nanking railway station, the land available for such an endeavor was also adjacent to a popular and scenic park, containing approximately fifty lakes and various bamboo patches.

Ground was broken in July 1909, and construction immediately began. Stagnant and disease-infested lakes were transformed into beautiful lagoons, and many of the natural features, such as the bamboo patches, were incorporated into the overall landscaping scheme. Flowers, shrubbery, shady walks, and beautiful water fountains were added, creating a relaxing atmosphere and enhancing the overall scenery.

The grounds covered an area of 90 to 100 acres, and the exposition was dubbed the "White City." All (except for one red-brick Georgian house) of the site's 26 buildings and pavilions, designed by the Shanghai-based architectural firm of Messrs. Atkinson & Dallas, were white. China's fair officials wanted to recreate well-known western expositions of Europe and the United States, so most of the buildings were modernistic in design, even though they contained distinctive Chinese ornamental features. Although some exposition buildings were unfinished at the beginning of the fair and some were not scheduled for completion until September, when the lair was half over, what was there was said to be a credit to the promoters.

There were two main gateways to the exhibition grounds. The main entrance, facing south, was decorated in an ornate traditional palace style and was intended for public entry. The other gate, done in a European style, was intended as an exit, and it faced west. Large buildings, such as the Industry, Education, Machinery, Public Health, and Transportation buildings were all one story and lined a broad avenue that passed through the fairgrounds. The Fine Arts building was the only two-story structure on the grounds and was considered impressive.

China's first world's fair attracted 14 other nations and 78 private companies or agencies. In addition 15 Chinese provinces participated, erecting pavilions as well. The spirit of competition had caught on, and so displays, most of which were exhibited in a Western style, were spectacular. Each province, not wanting to be outdone by a neighbor, displayed its best commodities. Exhibits included Chinese and foreign products, manufactures and machinery, model schools and factories, traditional handcrafted items, textiles, agricultural products such as tea, grains, and liquors, and modem armaments. There were foreign restaurants, a race track, a botanical garden, and a zoo located on the grounds. The site also featured a brick clock and observation tower.

Although this exposition did not make a profit or attract as many tourists as was hoped, it should not be considered a failure in all regards. Visitors who did go to the fair had a grand time, and despite the political uneasiness, participants felt a certain camaraderie toward each other. Tuan's vision of a "healthy competition" between the provinces was realized, and his reasoning "that progress in one country or area could inspire another" was correct. That is precisely what world's fairs and expositions are all about. It is nations and people putting aside their petty differences and coming together in friendship, proudly showing off their most prized possessions and inventions and bringing with them the potential for technological advancement that ultimately benefits all humanity. And that is exactly what China's first world's fair accomplished. It was a brilliant endeavor by a country facing political unrest.

Bibliography

Primary sources are limited for this fair; however, researchers will find a well-written article by Michael R. Godley, "China's World's Fair of

1910," in *Modern Asian Studies* 12 (1978): 503–22, to be a very helpful and resourceful piece. The article is informative in regard to the historical aspects of the fair and in depicting the political turbulence of the time. "China's First World's Fair," *American Review of Reviews* (June 1910): 691–93, although brief, provides some good background in information and also includes photographs of pavilions under construction. Selected articles in the London *Times* provide information on the opening ceremonies, the exhibition grounds, and the site's architecture.

See especially the issues dated June 6 and July 1, 1910. See also Susan R. Fernsebner, "China's Participation in World's fairs and Expositions, 1876–1955" (unpub. Ph.D. thesis, Department of History, University of California, San Diego, 2002).

London 1911

Susan Bennett

Festival of Empire

Because of the death of King Edward VII two weeks before its planned opening in 1910, the Festival of Empire, designed to celebrate the connections between empire, state and crown was postponed to form part of the 1911 coronation celebrations for George V.

Opening on May 12, 1911, the exhibition covered the whole area of the Crystal Palace and park at Sydenham to display imperial economic wealth and self-sufficiency. The first distinct part of the exhibition was the Palace, which had been redecorated by the unemployed for the event, and was devoted to an All-British Exhibition of Arts and Industries, with special provision for a Women's Work section.

The second distinct part was the construction of two-thirds scale, architecturally accurate models of nearly 300 buildings representing all parts of the British Empire, including parliamentary buildings. All these buildings were used to exhibit products of the relevant countries and were served by a miniature railway on the "All-Red Route," which gave visitors to the festival a tour of this scaled-down British Empire. Visitors could stop off at various locations to see a South African diamond mine, a Jamaican sugar plantation, a jungle (with a variety of animals running wild), a bazaar or an Indian tea plantation.

The third distinct part was "The Pageant of London," an outdoor theatrical spectacle involving a total of 15,000 volunteers recruited from the London boroughs. Designed by the pageant master Frank Lascelles for the proposed 1910 exhibition under the title "Heart of Empire," and enlarged and made more elaborate for the 1911 event, the pageant was designed to show the growth and development of the English nation, as seen through the history of London as an imperial city. The architect, Sir Aston Webb, designed an amphitheatre to seat 8,000 for this event, at a cost of £7,500.

An Imperial Inventions exhibition was included in the Festival which, unlike previous exhibitions held in Great Britain, included only inventions by British subjects residing either in the United Kingdom or in the dominions. In addition, many and varied kinds of entertainment were provided; for example: an inter-empire wrestling tournament, a Boy Scout rally, a baby show, military tattoos, balloon ascents, fashion shows, concerts, and firework displays, including a representation of the Great Fire of London in 1666.

The Festival ran for five months from May 12 to October 28. The entrance fee to the Festival itself was one shilling. Tickets for the pageant ranged from one shilling to 21 shillings, or £10 10s for a private box for six. A total of 144,234 attended on opening day, possibly hoping to catch a glimpse of the recently crowned King George V, and another 22 members of the

The 1911 Festival of Empire Exhibition was located in the shadow of the great Crystal Palace, which had housed the first modern world's fair in 1851 (editors' collection).

royal family at the time, who attended the opening concert of nearly 4,500 voices. Attendance continued to be good during the summer, despite competition from the smaller Coronation Exhibition at Shepherd's Bush, a well-known park, and amusement areas located elsewhere in the city.

Although organizers had estimated in 1909 that the cost for mounting a Festival of Empire in 1910 would be £49,000, the actual cost of preparations for that event was £70,000, including the construction of an amphitheatre at £7,500. In June 1910, the committee estimated that it would cost a further £50,000 for the resumption and enlargement of the Festival in 1911. It was estimated that the receipts for the 1911 Festival would be £119,000, but records detailing actual receipts are not available. Whatever the financial losses were, they brought about the bankruptcy of the Crystal Palace Company. The magnificent building passed into public ownership in 1913 and continued to host various events until its destruc-

Right: Ground plan of the site of the Festival of Empire exhibition in 1911 (courtesy Susan Bennett).

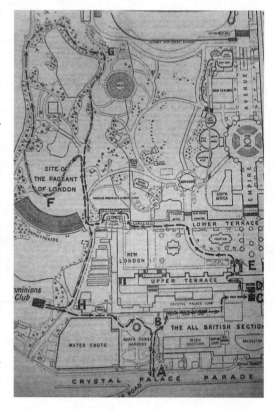

tion by fire on November 30, 1936. The Festival of Empire was the biggest event ever staged at Crystal Palace. Perhaps the greatest legacy of the Festival of Empire was the staging of the first sporting competitions, called "Inter-Empire Games," between teams representing Britain and its dominions. These events laid the foundation for today's Commonwealth Games.

Bibliography

Minutes of the Executive and Finance Committees for the Festival of London 1909–1910 are held at the archives of the London School of Economics, under Coll. Misc. 0459. The Bromley Local Studies Library holds a number of guides and catalogues, including souvenir picture postcards depicting the Great Pageant of London. Additional information may be obtained from the Crystal Palace Foundation. The guidebook to the Festival is *Official Programme, Festival of Empire*

Exhibition (1911). A contemporary published source is Sophie C. Loomis, ed., *Festival of Empire: Souvenir of the Pageant of London* (1911). M. P. Noel compiled a publication, *Scrapbook containing materials relating to the Pageant of London,* which was given as part of the Festival of Empire (1911). More accessible in terms of contemporary information about the Festival of Empire is the *Times* of London, which published a number of detailed articles on the event during 1911. See, in particular, the issues of February 6, May 5 and 13, June 5, July 5, and August 7, 1911.

Patrick Beaver, *The Crystal Palace* (1970) is a history of the building and the events, like the Festival of Empire, that occurred there. While the book says relatively about the festival, it does include a number of photographs of the event. Felix Driver and David Gilbert, eds, *Imperial Cities: Landscape, Display and Identity* (1999) discuss the Pageant of London and its representation of the British Empire. Nigel Burton, "Festival of Empire," *History Today* 52, 8 (August 2002): 2–3, examines the Festival of Empire in relation to the origins of the Commonwealth Games.

Ghent 1913

John E. Findling

Exposition Universelle et Industrielle

This star-crossed exposition was the largest and most elegant of the several fairs Belgium hosted before World War 1, and it was the last European fair before the outbreak of that war. Ghent, located halfway between Brussels and the coast, is a textile and garden center, and these two elements played a central role in the planning and execution of the fair and its exhibits. A site of 309 acres, developed around a city park, served as a backdrop for the pavilions and was laden with banks of flowers in nearly every conceivable location. Belgium, France, and Great Britain dominated the exposition; each of the four largest Belgian cities had its own pavilion, and France and Britain con-

structed large buildings flanking the Court of Honor. Other nations, including the United States, Canada, the Netherlands, Germany, Persia, and the Belgian Congo, also participated.

King Albert of Belgium opened the exposition on April 26, initiating seven and a half months of intense activity based on the theme of "Peace, Industry, and Art." The fair hosted over sixty international congresses on topics as diverse as agriculture and the sport of fencing. There was the usual panoply of fine arts attractions, including artworks in the fine art pavilion thought to be so scandalous that Cardinal François Joseph Mercier forbade priests, school principals, and parents to visit it. More generally acceptable were special performances of the Russian ballet, featuring the renowned Nijinsky.

Le Palais du Congo Belge
Het Paviljoen van Congo
Congo-Palast
The Palace of the Belgian Congo

Gand
1913

Many European fairs of this era showcased their colonial empires. This postcard portrays the Palace of the Belgian Congo at the 1913 Ghent exposition (editors' collection).

The most distinctive pavilion was that of the Belgian Congo, a circular structure 50 feet high and 500 feet in circumference, which featured an immense panorama of the Congo, created by Belgian artists Paul Matthieu and Alfred Bastien. A good deal of emphasis was placed on showing both Belgian imperialists and the Belgian empire in a favorable light; King Albert, in a speech opening the Belgian section on May 15, exhorted his parliament to adjust its relations with the Congo to give the natives mere autonomy and work to improve their standard of living in order to benefit the empire. After seeing the Congo pavilion, visitors could amuse themselves at the highest water chute in the world, a 3-mile scenic railway ride around the fairgrounds, a rapid "joywheel" of "improved design," or Mr. Bostock's Menagerie, which had also been popular at the recent Festival of Empire in London.

This, however, was an exposition plagued with more than its share of disaster. At least six fires struck the fair, destroying, among other things, the Indochina pavilion, a German restaurant, and much of Old Flanders, an area built in the style of a medieval city. On July 28, a gold ingot valued at $20,000 was stolen from the Belgian colonial pavilion; only later was it discovered that what had been stolen was merely an imitation worth just $200. In the Filipino village, an anthropological exhibit doubtless modeled after those in recent U.S. fairs, the natives were reported to be starving, and nine of the fifty-five had died from exposure by early November. The Filipinos complained they had received no wages for eight months, since the agency that had brought them to Ghent had gone bankrupt. A U.S. congressman pleaded with the Belgians to send them back home lest they all starve or be jailed as vagabonds.

By the time the fair closed in early December, some 11 million visitors had been counted. Negative publicity from the fires and the plight of the Filipinos probably contributed to keeping the attendance 2 million below that of the Brussels fair of 1910, but the extensive flower beds and the impressive textile machinery exhibits received high praise from contemporary observers. Within a year, however, Belgium would be overrun by German armies, and not until 1930 would its tradition of international fairs be resumed.

Bibliography

As with most of the earlier Belgian fairs, material on the Ghent 1913 exposition is hard to find. A. Cockx and J. Lemniens. *Les Expositions universelles et internationales en Belgique de 1885 à 1958* (1958), is a general work on Belgian fairs and contains information of value on this one. An official report was published by the Ministére de l'industrie et du travail, *Exposition universelle et internationale de Gand* (1913), and the exposition committee published a journal of fair-related news, *Organe official de l'Exposition universelle et internationale de Gand*. From March 1911 until the opening of the fair, this was published monthly, and during the run of the fair, it appeared more frequently. Although contemporary magazines in Great Britain arid the United States generally ignored the lair, the New York *Times* and the *Times* of London ran occasional articles on it, and French and Belgian papers doubtless gave even more space to it.

San Francisco 1915

Burton Benedict

Panama-Pacific International Exposition

In 1915, just nine years after a devastating earthquake and fire and one year into a world war, San Francisco put on a highly successful world's fair in which twenty-eight foreign nations and thirty-two states and territories participated. A virtual city, 2½ miles long by ½ mile wide, was constructed. There were more than 18 million paid admissions in the ten months that it was open.

As early as 1904, the San Francisco Chamber of Commerce had proposed a world's fair to advertise the city's growing commercial potential. Such advertisement became urgent after the earthquake and fire of 1906. Businessmen and politicians wanted to show the rest of the world that San Francisco had recovered from this disaster. A postcard of the period, labeled "Undaunted," shows a wounded California bear rising from the ashes with an idealized exposition at its feet.

From the beginning, an exposition had been planned to celebrate the completion of the Panama Canal, which occurred in 1914. But San Francisco was not the only city wanting such a fair. Southern California was also interested in self-promotion, and San Diego, strongly backed by the Los Angeles business community, made a bid for the exposition. Taking advantage of this rivalry, New Orleans announced its intention to hold the Panama Canal exposition. The Californians, realizing that their continued squabbling might lose them the fair altogether, worked out a compromise whereby San Francisco would receive full state support for its exposition in return for support of a more limited exposition for San Diego. The latter became the Panama-California Exposition of 1915–1916. New Orleans mounted a strident campaign in which it claimed to be the logical point for the fair because it was more centrally located. It also lined up an impressive number of congressmen on its side. San Francisco countered with a blizzard of postcards (at one point the West Coast ran out of cardboard) urging people to write their congressmen to support a San Francisco fair. In the end, California won largely because, unlike New Orleans, it was willing to accept federal recognition without federal funds.

The exposition was financed by the merchants of San Francisco. Charles Moore, owner of an engineering firm, became president of the exposition, and directors included leading bankers, publishers, department store owners, shipping magnates, and executives of the utilities and railroads. On April 28, 1910, the businessmen held a public meeting at which they raised over $4 million in two hours. Municipal and state bond issues of $5 million each guaranteed adequate financing of the exposition.

Federal recognition enabled the exposition's organizers to solicit foreign participation, but the whole enterprise was put in jeopardy by the outbreak of World War 1. Germany and Britain mutually agreed not to participate, but France stayed on and constructed a replica of the Palace of the Legion of Honor, which it shared with Belgium, overrun by the Germans before the exposition opened.

The contest now shifted to the choice of a site in San Francisco for the fair. Developers, businessmen, and politicians fought over proposed sites. For a time Golden Gate Park (site of the 1894 California Midwinter Exposition) was favored, and President William Howard Taft actually broke ground there in 1911. But eventually an undeveloped site on San Francisco Bay was chosen, and it was here and in the neighboring Presidio that the 635-acre fair was built.

Early plans for the exposition had envisaged a totally remodeled San Francisco with wide boulevards and chains of parks. Daniel Burnham, director of the World's Columbian Exposition in Chicago in 1893, drew up plans, but by 1912 they had been abandoned as too expensive and too impractical. The fair did stimulate the rebuilding of the Civic Center with an Exposition (now Civic) Auditorium and a new City Hall, but none of the buildings of the exposition itself survived except for the Palace of Fine Arts, which had to be almost entirely rebuilt in the 1960s and which now houses a popular science museum. The site itself was developed in the 1920s to become the Marina District, facing a yacht harbor and park on the waterfront.

The Panama-Pacific International Exposition (or PPIE, as it was commonly called) opened, as scheduled, on February 20, 1915. San Franciscans were awakened at 6:00 A.M. by whistles, steam sirens, horns, and fifteen marching bands. A procession 2½ miles long wound its way toward the exposition, and by 10:00 A.M., more than 100,000 people packed the grounds. In Washington, President Woodrow Wilson touched a key that started the Fountain of Energy. The fair was open.

The design and layout of the fair were innovative. Instead of great avenues of imposing beaux-arts palaces, the PPIE was laid out in

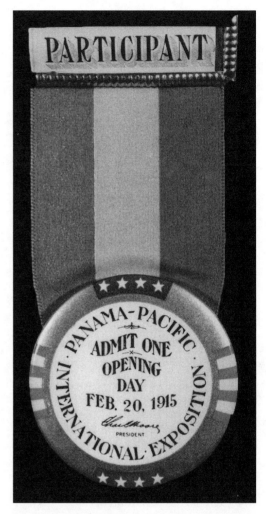

Participants at opening day ceremonies for the Panama-Pacific International Exposition wore this badge to display their status (Larson Collection, Special Collections Library, California State University, Fresno).

courtyards, each designed by a different architect. The exhibition buildings formed the walls of these courtyards and at the same time protected fairgoers from the winds of the Pacific. They also made the exposition compact and thus easier on the feet. The layout was the inspiration of Ernest Coxhead. There were three major courts: in the center: the Court of the Universe designed by the firm of McKim, Mead and White and enclosed by the Palaces of Transportation, Manufactures, Liberal Arts, and Agriculture; to the east of this, the Court of Ages (later renamed the Court of Abun-

The Palace of Fine Arts, which still stands in the Marina district in San Francisco, was designed by Bernard Maybeck, a prominent California architect, and was the most memorable structure from the fair (editors' collection).

dance), designed by Louis Christian Mullgardt and enclosed by the Palaces of Transportation, Mines and Metallurgy, Varied Industries, and Manufactures; and to the west, the Court of the Four Seasons, designed by Henry Bacon and enclosed by the Palaces of Agriculture, Food Products, Education and Social Economy, and Liberal Arts.

Each exhibition palace was surmounted by a central dome, with smaller domes and half-domes at the corners of each building. But the "City of Domes," as the fair was often called, was not limited to these. South of the courts rose the Palace of Horticulture, an immense glass dome bigger than that of St. Paul's Cathedral in London, and the Festival Hall, another vast domed building that was the exposition concert hall. To the east was the huge Palace of Machinery, in which Lincoln Beachey flew an airplane, a publicity stunt billed as the world's first indoor flight—an occupation with a limited future. To the west, separated from the courts by a lagoon, rose Bernard Maybeck's Palace of Fine Arts, a colonnade partially surrounding a domed rotunda. The most visible feature of the PPIE was the 432-foot Tower of Jewels. Its arches were larger than the Arc de Triomphe, and it dripped with

allegorical statues and murals depicting the triumph of the West. It was covered with more than 100,000 faceted glass jewels, each backed by a tiny mirror.

The tight harmonious layout of the fair unraveled at the edges with national and state pavilions in a myriad of styles fanning out west of the Palace of Fine Arts. Beyond these were livestock buildings, athletic grounds, and a race track. To the east was the visual jumble of the amusement area, dubbed the Joy Zone.

The older nations constructed their pavilions in traditional architectural style: a Renaissance palace for Italy, teahouses for Japan, a bit of the castle of Kronberg at Elsinore for Denmark, a Norwegian chieftain's medieval castle, a Siamese palace. Newer nations—Australia, New Zealand, and those of Latin America—tended to build in classical or beaux-arts style. States followed a similar pattern. Those that had notable buildings—the State House in Massachusetts, Independence Hall in Pennsylvania—reproduced them in reduced versions at the fair. Those that did not tried something else to impress visitors. Oregon constructed a reproduction of the Parthenon with forty-eight columns of Douglas fir with the bark left on. The California pavilion was in the form of a huge mission —far larger than any actual mission in the state. Within were elaborate agricultural displays from various counties and a ballroom in which dances and the principal exposition social functions were held. It also housed the administration and was the headquarters of the Women's Board, which was in charge of reception and entertainment.

The PPIE was the first world's fair to make extensive use of indirect lighting. Previous fairs had been lit almost entirely by outlining buildings in light bulbs, as was the common practice on theater marquees. The PPIE relied on more than 370 searchlights and 500 projectors on roofs and at other vantage points. These lights reflected the texture and color of the buildings and highlighted statuary and planting. The dome of the Palace of Horticulture glowed like an opal, and lights played on the Tower of Jewels each night producing dazzling and incandescent effects. A squad of U.S. Marines changed colored filters on a battery of forty-eight searchlights located on a pier in the bay. On foggy nights, the mist took on various hues as it drifted across the exposition grounds, and on clear nights, a stationary locomotive produced clouds of steam to give a similar effect.

Plaster and lath had been the standard building materials for most other world's fairs, producing glaring white structures. The PPIE used artificial travertine, a material developed by McKim, Mead and White for the Pennsylvania Station in New York. Not only did this material look like the real travertine marble of Rome, but also it could be tinted. Jules Guerin, who was known for his theatrical designs and watercolors, coordinated the color scheme of the exposition. His inspiration was the California landscape. The buildings were in pastel shades of green, blue, pink, lemon, and ochre. Even the plantings were color coordinated to complement the buildings.

John McLaren, who had been largely responsible for creating Golden Gate Park, was in charge of the landscaping. Hundreds of full-grown cypresses, palms, and orange trees were transplanted. A living green wall 1,150 feet long formed the southern boundary of the exposition. It was made by planting cuttings in boxes measuring 2 by 6 feet but only 2 inches deep. Chicken wire was nailed over the top to retain the plants, and the boxes were upended to form

the wall. It took 8,700 of them to complete the wall.

The grounds and courts abounded with sculpture. In charge was A. Stirling Calder (the father of Alexander Calder). His giant sculptural groups, *Nations of the East* featuring an elephant and *Nations of the West* featuring, rather chauvinistically, a covered wagon, surmounted the immense triumphal arches in the Court of the Universe. His massive *Fountain of Energy* epitomized the thrust of progress in the west. Mullgardt's Court of Ages was devoted to Social Darwinism, with bas-reliefs depicting creatures from invertebrates to humans creeping up the walls. In the center was Robert Aiken's *Fountain of the Earth* surrounded by friezes with such titles as "Survival of the Fittest" and culminating with "Intellectual Attraction." The most famous sculpture of the exposition was James Earle Frazier's *End of the Trail*, which depicted an exhausted Indian on an exhausted horse, sentimentally epitomizing what was thought to be the fate of Native Americans. When the fair closed, *End of the Trail* was sold to Tulare County and was erected in Mooney Grove Park, Visalia. There it remained, gently decaying, until at some point it was removed and lost track of, though reproductions of it were to be found all over the United States. Even Frazier (who was also the designer of the buffalo nickel) did not know where it was. In 1968 a group of wealthy westerners located it and wanted to buy it for the National Cowboy Hall of Fame in Oklahoma City. The citizens of Visalia would agree only if the purchasers would give them a full-sized reproduction of the statue in bronze. The original plaster version is now in the museum in Oklahoma City, and a bronze *End of the Trail* graces Mooney Grove Park.

The Palace of Fine Arts housed the first major international contemporary art exhibition to be held on the West coast. There were more than 11,400 works of art, all of which were supposed to have been produced within the previous ten years. Two-thirds of the works came from the United States and included such artists as Childe Hassam, Arthur F. Matthews, John Singer Sargent, James McNeil Whistler, Gertrude Vanderbilt Whitney, and N. C. Wyeth. There was a room devoted to Edvard Munch from Norway, and the Italian futurists were shown for the first time in the United States.

More than 2,200 concerts were given at the exposition. Fritz Kreisler, Ignace Paderewski, Victor Herbert, Mme. Schumann-Heink, and the Boston Symphony performed. The aged Camille Saint-Saëns composed "Hail California" in honor of the exposition and gave three concerts in the Festival Hall. Bands, of which the most famous was John Philip Sousa's, played every day, and there were daily recitals on the giant festival organ (now in the Civic Auditorium).

Classification of exhibits at the PPIE reflected the general theme of uplift that was so characteristic of the fair. Art headed the list, followed by Education. Third came Social Economy, which included agencies for social betterment, eugenics, hygiene, labor, cooperatives, banks, and charities. Next came Liberal Arts, which covered everything from printing to medicine, architecture, and musical instruments. It was followed by Manufactures and Varied Industries, Machinery, Transportation, Agriculture, Live Stock, Horticulture, and Mines and Metallurgy. Each had a separate exhibition building except for the livestock, which were in pens and outbuildings at the western end of the fairgrounds

A popular exhibit was the Ford assembly line in the Palace of Transportation, which turned out eighteen Model Ts a day. Henry Ford toured the fair with his friend, Thomas Edison, and on one occasion took a place on the assembly line. Another wonder was the first transcontinental telephone line, which had been completed on January 25, 1915. Visitors could hear readings of headlines from the New York papers and the pounding of the waves of the Atlantic Ocean. Aeroplanes (as the word was then spelled), a great attraction, made daily flights over the fairgrounds. At night flares were attached to the wings and tail of Art Smith's fragile plane as he looped the loop over the bay. Moving pictures were utilized by exhibitors at the PPIE probably to a greater extent than at any previous exposition. It is estimated that over a million feet of film was shown in sixty cinemas. Eastman Kodak displayed two-color Kodachrome photographs, and General Electric showed 'The Home Electrical" with built-in vacuum cleaner outlets in each room and an electric piano. The Underwood Typewriter Company attracted attention with a working typewriter 15 feet high, 21 feet long, and weigh-ing 14 tons. There was a full-sized coal mine that "blew up" at 2:00 P.M. each day, bringing a full rescue apparatus into play. A two-story color press was capable of producing 1,728,000 newspaper pages an hour.

The railroads played a crucial rote at the PPIE. They not only brought the goods but also the people to the fair, vying with each other in providing bargain fares from the east. In the end it was the railroads and not the Panama Canal that brought prosperity to the West coast. In addition to their extensive exhibits in the Palace of Transportation, several railroad companies build separate pavilions. Union Pacific produced a miniature Yellowstone Park with working geysers, and Santa Fe reproduced the Grand Canyon and a full-sized Hopi village with living inhabitants.

Nearly every day witnessed special events. There were days for nations, states, and counties, for learned and not so learned associations, for Theodore Roosevelt, Luther Burbank, and Thomas Edison. The American Association for the Advancement of Science held its first Pacific Coast meetings at the fair. There were sports events such as horse racing, motor car racing for the Vanderbilt Cup, a golf tournament, and a dog show. Perhaps the greatest publicity stunt of the fair was the progress of the Liberty Bell from Philadelphia across the nation to San Francisco. It was greeted by bands and local dignitaries at every stop. People kissed it, threw flowers, and burst into tears. Nearly 115,000 people greeted it in the exposition grounds on July 17, 1915, when they heard Champ Clark, Speaker of the House of Representatives, proclaim that he was not a jingo but that peace at any price was demoralizing and degrading. Though the United States had not yet entered the war, the military was in evidence at the fair. The army and marines paraded daily, and warships rode at anchor in front of the exposition

The garish color and strings of naked lights of the Joy Zone contrasted with the harmonious pastels and indirect lighting of the main fair. Dominating the zone was an effigy of a suffragette and two tin soldiers about 90 feet high. A 120-foot gilded Buddha marked the entrance of "Japan Beautiful" (which had been seen at other fairs) with its shops and tea stalls. There were an ostrich farm and an alligator farm and the usual rides. A novelty was the Aeroscope, a long metal arm terminating in a

1505. JAPAN BEAUTIFUL ON "THE ZONE".

Exhibits from Asia had been popular at world's fairs since the Crystal Palace. Shown is the Japanese pavilion at the Panama-Pacific International Exposition (editors' collection).

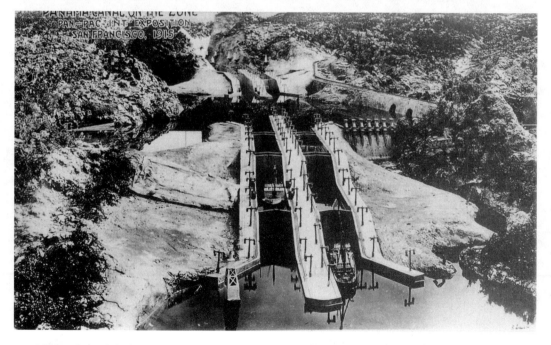

This scale model of the recently completed Panama Canal was a popular attraction on the midway of the Panama-Pacific International Exhibition (editors' collection).

two-storied house and capable of liftingg 120 people 265 feet in the air. Ethnic exhibits included villages of living Samoans, Hawaiians, Mexicans, Maoris, Egyptians, Filipinos, Japanese, and Native Americans.

The most important exhibit in the zone was a working model of the Panama Canal, which covered nearly 5 acres. A moving platform of seats transported spectators around the exhibit while they held telephone receivers to their ears to hear recorded lectures on what they were seeing. The mechanism foreshadowed the famous General Motors "Futurama" at the 1939 New York World's Fair.

When the Panama-Pacific International Exposition closed on December 4, 1915, there had been 18,876,438 admissions. This figure does not represent separate individuals; most people came more than once. In one way, the war had helped the exposition. Easterners who were in the habit of visiting Europe each year came to the West Coast instead. Unlike most other world's fairs, the PPIE made a profit. By August 30, 1915, two-thirds through the season, it bad made enough money to pay off its mortgage. Ex-president William Howard Taft burned it publicly on a toasting fork at the exposition grounds. The exposition profits amounted to $2,40l,911.

The 1915 exposition did more than just commemorate the completion of the Panama Canal. It celebrated the rebuilding of San Francisco; it asserted the importance of California and the American West; it turned American attention toward the Pacific and South America. It epitomized a whole view of American society, a view conceived in optimism and carried through despite the outbreak of World War I. It was, perhaps, the last collective outburst of this sort of naive optimism.

Bibliography

The most extensive archival collection on the Panama-Pacific International Exposition is in the Bancroft Library of the University of California at Berkeley. Other important collections may be found in the History Room of the San Francisco Public Library and in the libraries of the California Historical Society and the Society of California Pioneers, both in San Francisco. These collections also contain a wealth of ephemera from the fair. A videotape, with original footage, *1915 Panama Pacific Fair,* by Burton Benedict is available from the educational television department at the University of California at Berkeley.

The most comprehensive printed source for the PPIE is Frank Morton Todd, *The Story of the Exposition,* 5 vols. (1921), characterized by a highly readable writing style. Two short guides are Ben Macomber, *The Jewel City* (1915), and John D. Barry, *The City of Domes* (1915, reprinted 2006). Barry's book, written as a dialogue between author and reader, after an introduction on the fair's background, is particularly good for the architecture of the PPIE. A contemporary tribute to the fair is Louis John Steilman, *That Was a Dream Worth Building* (1916), with a poetic text and attractive color plates of fair scenes. A more comprehensive pictorial record is *The Blue Book of the Panama Pacific International Exposition at Sam Francisco* (1915).

Recent analyses may be found in the essays in *The Anthropology of World's Fairs* (1983) by Burton Benedict, *et al.* See especially the essay by George Starr, "Truth Unveiled: The Panama Pacific International Exposition and Its Interpreters." Robert W. Rydell, *All the World's a Fair* (1984), contains a chapter on the anthropological exhibits at the PPIE. For art at the exposition, see Eugen Neuhaus, *The Art of the Exposition* (1915). Rose V. S. Berry, *The Dream Citv: Its Art in Story and Symbolism* (1915), Juliet James, *Palaces and Courts of the Exposition* (1915), and Stella G. S. Perry, *The Sculpture and Murals of the Panama Pacific International Exposition* (1915). All of these offer critical interpretations of the works. More objective is the two-volume *Catalogue of the Department of Fine Arts* (1915), edited by John E. D. Trask and J. Nilsen Laurvik, which lists the works displayed in the Palace of Fine Arts.

The Panama-Pacific International Exposition continues to attract attention from writers, a trend that will doubtless accelerate as the fair's centennial approaches. A general pictorial history of the fair is William Lipsky, *San Francisco's Panama-Pacific International Exposition* (2005), a volume in Arcadia Press's *Images of America* series. The Golden Gate Parks Conservacy has published a short work, *The Last Great World's Fair: San Francisco's Panama-Pacific International Exposition, 1915* (2004), for the benefit of tourists. Laura Bruml, *Electric Lights Dazzling: An Account of One Family's Visit to the 1915 Panama-Pacific International Exposition, from the Diary of Laura (Foote) Bruml* (1999), is a travel account based on a family diary. And, finally, Chris Pollock, Ken Garcia, and Erica Katz make frequent mention of the exposition in their pictorial history of Golden Gate Park, *San Francisco's Golden Gate Park: A Thousand and Seventeen Acres of Stories* (2001).

San Diego 1915–1916

Matthew Bokovoy

Panama-California Exposition

The city of San Diego held the Panama-California Exposition in 1915–1916 to commemorate the opening of the Panama Canal. The fair became the most important event in the cultural history of the American Southwest. Writing in *Sunset Magazine,* David C. Collier, the first director general of the fair, introduced readers to the theme of the exposition, "The Progress and Possibility of the Human Race." He believed the "most interesting things in the world are its peoples," and the exposition would show what different cultures and peoples "are doing; what they are thinking about and what they are accomplishing." With a focus on the culture of the southwestern borderlands, Mexico, and Latin America, the Panama-California Exposition strove to educate the people of the American West and the United States about the antiquity, culture, history, and peoples of the Americas and their human connections to the rest of the globe. Southwestern writer Charles Lummis believed the fair should "Humanize Science," and not merely "popularize as fads and fakes may be spread, but to make knowledge the right, title, and interest of every common man, woman, and child instead of a privilege of the aristocracy." In the elaboration of this theme, the organizers of the exposition sought to weave the history of Spain, Mexico, and Native America into the tapestry of American memory.

In July 1909, prominent local banker Gilbert A. Davidson approached his colleagues in the Chamber of Commerce to argue San Diego required a world's fair to commemorate the opening of the Panama Canal in 1915. Members of the Chamber formed the Panama-California Exposition Corporation (PCEC) to begin planning for the exposition, thus mak-

ing the Chamber and corporation one. The city would be the first U.S. port of call. The PCEC hoped to promote San Diego and the Southern California region, particularly the city's twenty-two square mile harbor, growing local manufacturers, agricultural development of county lands, and the elusive, direct railroad route to East Coast markets that had bedeviled the city since the 1880s. With roughly forty thousand people by 1910, San Diego's leaders had to rely on national political connections and local determination to receive federal recognition for the fair. The city also overcame opposition from northern California's congressional delegation for the event. Led by real estate investor Collier, San Diego's leading citizens prepared for congressional sanction. The Los Angeles Chamber of Commerce lent its support to the San Diegans for a Southern California world's fair. In December, San Francisco announced its intent to hold a similar world's fair, named the Panama-Pacific International Exposition, led by Charles Moore and Michael De Young of the *San Francisco Chronicle.* With the chances slim, Collier and his colleagues prepared to fight against California's most powerful city.

The two California cities approached Congress to wrest the Panama Exposition from one another in spring 1910, however, the city of New Orleans entered the congressional arena for the event. New Orleans had previously staged the World's Industrial and Cotton States Exposition of 1884-1885. The Southern bid caused serious concern among California's congressional delegation, especially when Louisiana governor Jared.Y. Sanders claimed a unique Spanish heritage for New Orleans first pioneered by enterprising Californians. Unifying their ranks around the Panama-Pacific International Exposition, California's congressmen defeated the New Orleans bid when they revealed

The official seal of the 1915 Panama-California Exposition indicates clearly that the fair celebrated the completion of the Panama Canal (editors' collection).

and county improvements to accommodate the anticipated millions of tourists. The committee granted San Diegans their much desired federal recognition.

Before the Chamber of Commerce decided to hold the Panama-California Exposition, George W. Marston, a wealthy department store owner, headed the Civic Improvement Committee to hire an urban planner to lay San Diego anew. They choose John Nolen of Brookline, Massachusetts, to bring City Beautiful Movement ideals to remake downtown into a modern metropolis. With Nice, France, as his inspiration, Nolen believed "San Diego's opportunity appears to me without equal in the broad land." Planning experts agreed, like Charles Mulford Robinson, who had a plan pending with the L.A. Municipal Art Commission. "I hope that the receipt in Los Angeles of such a fine report from San Diego," he thought, "may stir up the larger city." Despite the efforts of Nolen and Marston, the plan would never be. Downtown real estate interests and the forthcoming exposition defeated the Nolen Plan. All San Diego urban planning would center on the Panama-California Exposition.

The PCEC agreed the fair would be built in the 1400-acre City Park, renamed Balboa Park in 1910. Debate about its location caused considerable local intrigue during a time of great labor unrest in San Diego. The PCEC originally hired John C. and Frederick Olmsted, Jr. to design the fairgrounds. Envisioning Mission Revival architecture to evoke Franciscan era California, the Olmsteds selected thirty-seven acres in the Howard Tract near the southwest corner of the park, closer to downtown for nighttime attractions. They decided the park's central mesa be left undisturbed so San Diegans and visitors could enjoy it, following their father's philosophy for Central Park in New York City. The Olmsteds recommended Bertram G. Goodhue to design the buildings,

murky charges of embezzlement of federal funds during the 1885 event. Congressional Republicans would not deliver a world's fair to the South, especially with William Howard Taft in the White House and midterm elections in the fall. By supporting San Francisco against New Orleans, northern California congressmen considered a second look at the Panama-California Exposition in San Diego. When David Collier spoke to the House Committee on Industrial Arts and Expositions in May 1911, he claimed San Diego had raised $2,000,000 in private subscriptions for the fair. San Diego had approved a $1,250,000 municipal bond for the event with an additional $5,000,000 for city

Visitors to the Panama-California Exposition enjoyed the singing and dancing provided by this troupe of musicians from Spain (editors' collection).

and Goodhue preferred Spanish Colonial over Mission Revival. Supported by George Marston and the city's Park Board, the plan appeared sound. The PCEC, however, sought control of park improvements to benefit some board members' real estate investments north of the central mesa. Led by John D. Spreckels, the city's most powerful businessman, Joseph Sefton, Jr. and John Burnham, they helped the PCEC gain control of the location. They defeated the Olmsted Plan and refused payment to the firm. Goodhue and Frank P. Allen, the director of works, proposed a plan for the central mesa amenable to the Spreckels interests. Goodhue designed a Mediterranean Renaissance city on the central mesa. With his apprentices Clarence Stein, Carleton Monroe Winslow, and William Templeton Johnson, Goodhue envisioned the California Quadrangle, with the California and Fine Arts Buildings, as premier architectural contributions to the fair. Allen conceived all the other fantastic buildings along the El Prado, in Mission Revival Style, with Coney Island and the Venice Beach Boardwalk in mind.

The Panama-California Exposition made a lasting imprint on American culture by cre-ating cultural connections with the Southwest Museum of Charles Lummis, the Museum of New Mexico and School of American Archeology directed by Edgar Lee Hewett, and the United States National Museum headed by William Henry Holmes. All cultural institutions involved with Native American and Spanish Southwest research formed a powerful network to highlight "ancient America" through comparison with classical Greece, Mesopotamia, and the "Orient." Where European "tradition" oriented itself towards the Mediterranean, the United States could look to the antiquity of the Americas for cultural inspiration, thus a home-grown nationalism. Edgar Hewett and Jesse Nusbaum organized the ethnology exhibitions, furnished by the Atchison, Topeka, and Santa Fe Railway and Museum of New Mexico. Tourists found the Santa Fe Railway's "Painted Desert" Indian village the most fascinating exhibition, a ten-acre Indian village with about 100 Southwestern Indians with Pueblos the most numerous, and Apache, Hopi, and Navajo Indians as well. The acclaimed San Ildefonso village potters María and Julian Martínez attended, as well as artists Crescencío Martínez and Alfonso Roybal (Awa Tsireh). The MNM

The San Diego fair included a number of exhibits featuring American Indian culture from the Southwest (editors collection).

furnished exhibits within the Indian Arts and Fine Arts Buildings, with dramatic Spanish Catholic paintings completed by Donald Beauregard and frescoes of ancient American cities executed by Carlos Vierra. In tandem with the nostalgic thrust of the New/Old Santa Fe cultural revival of 1912 to make a "city different," the MNM impressed their interpretation of the Spanish heritage in Southern California.

The United States National Museum and its division of physical anthropology designed exhibitions to showcase three areas in anthropology, namely the physical evolution of humanity, the evolution of culture, and the native races of America. Led by physical anthropologist Aleš Hrdlička and William Holmes, the displays sought to move the study of humanity and race into a comparative, global dimension, and favorably assess the artistic life of Amerindian civilizations. The exhibits spread among the California, Fine Arts, Indian Arts, and Science of Man Buildings. The displays would highlight the racial origins, ancient history, arts and crafts, and archeological artifacts of the ancient Americas, American Indian civilizations, and New Spain.

Using an array of bronze busts, clay casts, architectural models, archeological artifacts, and other material culture, the "Races of Man" displays signaled the transition of anthropology from a self-trained amateur's discipline to a modern science. Notable features of the exhibition were the dignified, male and female pairs of bronze busts of the world's people created by sculptress Malvina Hoffman, known for her artistic, racial egalitarian perspective.

Previous world's fairs in Europe and the Americas impressed Social Darwinist understandings on audiences, and civilizations had been ranked in terms of technological development from savagery, barbarity, to civilization. Public displays of anthropological science had been overtly racist for social and political purposes. Hrdlička and Holmes found the distinctions uncomfortable and arbitrary, so the USNM, with funding from the PCEC, undertook global expeditions to counter the claim. The science of Hrdlička presented a genetic model to account for cultural history by linking physical types, cultures, and languages, thus bringing physical anthropology into conversation with his colleague Franz Boas, the founder of an anti-racist, cultural anthropology. As a Czech-Bohemian immigrant, he also saw flaws in science that linked race and blood heritage to individual achievement and racial behaviors, as well as arguments that inferior races came from a different genetic pool than races deemed superior. For Hrdlička, the family of humanity was one. In an exhibit showing the progression of human forms from the lemur to man, he cautioned it "must not be taken as representing the line of man's evolution." William Holmes, the foremost illustrator of Latin American antiquity, created sculptures based on Vierra's murals of the temple cities of the Americas, Quirigua, Copán, Palenque, Tikal, Uxmal, and Chichén Itzá. He believed Aztec, Mayan, and Incan civilizations had architecture of "exceptionally high order, indicating great progress in architecture." As he stressed international historic preservation efforts of these great ruins, Holmes thought the cities of antiquity demonstrated elaborate engineering feats equal to the religious devotion given to the cathedrals and synagogues of Judeo-Christian tradition. Ancient Amerindians may have appeared far above the level of savagery, perhaps embracing the tenets of civilization when compared to the crude state of European society before 1492. Despite the re-evaluation of American beliefs in the savagery of indigenous cultures, the message was lost on the average exposition tourist.

The Panama-California Exposition provided tourists with other popular and educational entertainments, such as the Southern California Counties "Model Farm," the International Harvester Demonstration Field, the War of the Worlds concession, a Panama Canal diorama, and the underground Chinatown. These exhibits ranged from instructive to playing on the racial fears of European American tourists. Following the Native American theme of the fair, white fairgoers were treated to an Indian costume carnival in August 1915, where Anglos could "play Indian" for an evening. The composer Charles Wakefield Cadman brought Cherokee singer Princess Tsianina Redfeather to the exposition to perform modern traditional renditions of Cherokee hymns.

The Panama-California Exposition attracted 3,747,916 visitors when the 1916 season ended on December 31. The fair had brought the tiny hamlet of San Diego to national attention.

The poster stamp advertising the Panama-California Exposition was one way in which organizers publicized the fair (editors' collection).

The Spanish fantasy heritage theme of the fair created a modern regional tradition, where the built environment and promotional image of Southern California was set firmly in the Indian and Spanish past. Local historic preservation of the Spanish mission and presidio began as well. Balboa Park became the center for cultural institutions in San Diego. The fair also brought the harbor of San Diego to the attention of Naval Department, which decided to headquarter the Pacific fleet and eleventh naval district in the city. The fair made an architectural imprint on Southern California, and the entire southwest and southern plains during the 1920s. California's eminent critic Carey McWilliams believed there had been "'Spanish,' and 'Mission,' and 'Moorish' structures in Southern California before the San Diego Exposition, but the appearance of these structures had never assumed the proportion of an epidemic." The influence can be seen in numerous homes and public buildings stretching from San Diego to Tulsa, Oklahoma. In the end, through public memory and the invention of tradition, the Panama-California Exposition unveiled the difficult, but promising, past at the core of California history.

The author appreciates permission to excerpt from Matthew F. Bokovoy, *The San Diego World's Fairs and Southwestern Memory, 1880–1940* (Albuquerque: University of New Mexico Press, 2005).

Bibliography

Historians cannot begin to study the Panama-California Exposition (PCE) without consulting the vast collections of newspaper clippings, national archival materials, and published articles amassed by San Diego lay historian and critic Richard Amero. More than 150 linear feet, Amero's folders on the fair and all related major events are at the San Diego Historical Society (SDHS). Articles from newspapers and magazines such as the San Diego *Union,* San Diego *Herald,* and San Diego *Sun* as well as *Sunset Magazine, West Coast Magazine, the Overland Monthly (Out West Magazine),* and *El Palacio* are included. The collection is comprehensive and includes records from the Avery Architectural Library at Columbia University, the Smithsonian Institution, and the National Anthropology Archives in Washington, DC. The SDHS holds the most significant collections of manuscript sources, scrapbooks and diaries, and ephemera related to the exposition. Notable are the three volumes of Panama-California Exposition Corporation minutes that detail the weekly operations, such as finance, contracts, and internal discussion about the planning, maintenance, and politics of the fair from 1911 to 1917. The photographic archive contains official photographs of the PCE, as well as the excellent photographs taken by Jesse Nusbaum, an all-around tradesman for the Museum of New Mexico who became an expert in southwestern antiquities and director of John D. Rockefeller's Laboratory of Anthropology in Santa Fe during the 1930s. The George White Marston Papers detail urban planning and exposition politics very well from a progressive point of view, and indicate the machinations of city-wide politics. There are also old films of the fair at SDHS as well.

The San Diego Public Library, California Room research archives holds some architectural drawings for the fair, notably the Olmsted Plan and the drawings of Bertram Goodhue and John Nolen. There are also several boxes of fair records that are incidental and redundant about the event. Clippings files and published items on the fair can be found there as well. Since the fair was staged in Balboa Park, researchers should consult the numerous boxes of San Diego Park Commission records. To understand San Diego's connection with Los Angeles, Santa Fe, and Washington DC, the Charles Lummis Papers at the Southwest Museum (now part of the Autry National Center) are instructive. To understand the role of Santa Fe, the Edgar Lee Hewett and Jesse Nusbaum Papers at the archives of the Laboratory of Anthropology, Museum of New Mexico details the state's involvement. The Western History Collection at University of Oklahoma contains the author Alice Marriott's papers, which reveal information on Pueblo Indians at the fair, particularly María Martínez. The National Anthropology Archives, Smithsonian Institution hold the Aleš Hrdlička Papers, and the Smithsonian Institution "Office of the Secretary Records" offers insight into the museum's role and commitment to the fair. The American Philosophical Society's Franz Boas and Charles Davenport Papers detail conversations among anthropologists about the San Diego fair. The Hiram Johnson Papers at the Bancroft Library, University of California, Berkeley, indicate the governor's role with San Diego leaders like George Marston and information about the Museum of New Mexico. U.S. Government publications like the Bureau of American Ethnology annual reports, research monographs, and Smithsonian Miscellaneous Collections indicate the progress of field research related to the fair. The files of the Congressional Record include the congressional committee hearings on the Panama Exposition.

A number of secondary sources are helpful. Richard Pourade's *Gold in the Sun* (1965) and the *Glory Years* (1964) provide an overview of San Diego history from the 1870s to 1916, with a chapter and photographic essay devoted to the PCE. A critical history of San Diego by Mike Davis, Jim Miller, and Kelly Mayhew, *Under the Perfect Sun: The San Diego Tourists Never See* (2003) is a well-researched, sweeping synthesis of San Diego looking at promotion, working class radicalism, and political corruption. To start, researchers should consult Robert Rydell, *All the World's a Fair: Visions of Empire at American International Expositions, 1876–1916* (1984) for the chapter on San Diego's fair. See also Richard Amero, "The Making of the Panama-California Exposition, 1909–1915," *Journal of San Diego History* 35, 1 (Winter 1990). Matthew Bokovoy has written a history of the two San Diego expositions, *The San Diego World's Fairs and Southwestern Memory, 1880–1940* (2005) and interested researchers should consult its extensive bibliography. He has also written numerous articles on the fairs, urban planning, and the development of modern Spanish heritage in the San Diego and the Southwest, "'The Peers of Their White Conquerors': The San Diego Expositions and Modern Spanish Heritage in the Southwest, 1880–1940," *New Mexico Historical Review* 78, 4 (Fall 2003); "The Federal Housing Administration and the 'Culture of Abundance' at the San Diego California-Pacific International Exposition of 1935–1936," *The Journal of the American Planning Association* 68, 4 (Autumn 2002); "Humanist Sentiment, Modern Spanish Heritage, and California Mission Commemoration, 1769–1915," *Journal of San Diego History* 48, 3 (Summer 2002); "Inventing Agriculture in Southern California," *Journal of San Diego History* 44, no. 2 (Spring 1999); and "Ghosts of the San Diego Rialto," in Jim Miller, ed., *Sunshine/Noir: Writings from San Diego and Tijuana* 1, 1 (2005). Phoebe Kropp, *California Vieja: Culture and Memory in a Modern American Place* (2006) devotes an entire chapter to the fair and places the event within the broader context of European-American memory and cultural landscape history. She has also written a definitive essay on the fair, "'There is a little sermon in that': Constructing the Native Southwest at the San Diego Panama-California Exposition of 1915," in Barbara Babcock and Marta Weigle, eds., *The Great Southwest of the Fred Harvey Company and the Santa Fe Railway* (1996) that probes the display of imperialist nostalgia at the fair.

The *Journal of San Diego History* provides a number of good articles related to Balboa Park

and cultural development in the city. Essays by Gregg Hennessey, Abraham Shragge, and Gregory Montes should be consulted, especially Montes' three Balboa Park articles (1977, 1979, 1982). All the *JSDH* articles are available online at the SDHS website. There are also popular histories of Balboa Park by Florence Christman, *The Romance of Balboa Park* (1985) and Roger Showley, *Balboa Park: A Millennium History* (1999). There are a number of works that mention the influence of the Santa Fe cultural revival on the PCE. They are Chris Wilson, *The Myth of Santa Fe: Creating a Modern Regional Tradition* (1997); Don Fowler, *A Laboratory for Anthropology: Science and Romanticism in the American Southwest, 1846–1930* (2000); and Beatrice Chauvenet, *Hewett and Friends: A Biography of Santa Fe's Vibrant Era* (1983). To understand Spanish fantasy heritage more broadly, one should consult two works by Carey McWilliams, *Southern California Country: An Island on the Land* (1946) and *North from Mexico: The Spanish-Speaking People of the United States* (1948). Dydia DeLeyser, *Ramona Memories: Tourism and the Shaping of Southern California* (2005) examines the role that Helen Hunt Jackson's Indian justice novel played in the development of regional promotion and heritage tourism.

Rio de Janeiro 1922–1923

Bruno Bontempi, Jr., and Noah W. Sobe

Exposição Internacional do Centenário do Brasil

The Brazilian Centennial Exposition, one of the few major international world's fairs to be held in South America, was initially proposed as a national celebration marking one hundred years of independence. Early on in the planning, however, the scope was changed, and the fair was turned into an international exposition in which twenty countries participated. While not a financial success, the Brazilian Centennial Exposition was hailed at the time for bringing Brazil into closer contact with Europe and North America. It has had a last-

ing impact on the city of Rio de Janeiro and played a role in the consolidation of a Brazilian national identity.

The Brazilian Centennial Exposition had considerable significance for the urban design and development of Rio de Janeiro, the coastal city which served as Brazil's capital from the eighteenth century through 1960. Commissioner General Carlos Sampaio's plans for the exposition grounds were joined to a larger urban reform program designed to eliminate architectural remnants from the Portuguese colonial period as well as rundown and unsalubrious housing. Both the Centennial Exposition and this plan for urban renewal (as in the

Nighttime illumination of one of the main buildings at the Rio de Janeiro exposition (editors' collection).

cases of Paris and Vienna on which the urban restructuring was modeled) were also intended to help cultivate a distinct, progress-oriented national identity. Portuguese-era buildings including a Jesuit seminary (São José) and a fort (São January) on the Morro do Castelo were torn down. Failure to provide any alternative housing for the considerable numbers of impoverished residents who were displaced as a result of the exposition construction spurred the development of the favelas, or hillside slums, that are a feature of Rio de Janeiro to this day.

The 62-acre exposition site was divided into to national and international sections. The principal architects involved in designing the Brazilian buildings were Morales de los Rios, A. Memoria, and F. Couchet. Many of the buildings were in the Brazilian neo-colonial style, a hybrid architectural movement attempting to craft a national identity (in juxtaposition to the internationalist Beaux-Arts movement). The largest Brazilian exposition hall was the Palace of Industries, which survives today as a national historical museum. The national section also included a limited amusement area (Parque das Diversões) which featured a carrousel, theater, cinema, and roller-skating

rink. Other buildings in the national section included the Festival Palace, the Pavilion of Hunting and Fishing, the Palace of Minor Industries, the Pavilion of Statistics, and the Pavilion of States—a number of which are still standing today. The fair's Administration Building dated from 1906 and was itself a reproduction of the Brazilian pavilion featured at the 1904 Louisiana Purchase International Exposition. Named the Monroe Palace, for its role in the Third Pan-American Conference in 1906, it also variously housed Brazil's Chamber of Deputies and Federal Senate and was ultimately demolished in 1976 to make way for the Rio de Janeiro subway system.

The international exhibits were grouped along the Avenue of Nations and were provided by 3,913 of the Brazilian Centennial Exposition's 9,926 exhibitors. Among the 20 participating nations were Argentina, the United States, Japan, France, Great Britain, Italy, Denmark, Mexico, Czechoslovakia, Norway, Belgium, Sweden, and Portugal. The French pavilion, a replica of the Petit Trianon, was donated by the French government to the Brazilian Academy of Letters in 1923 and remains part of this institution to the present day. Japan built its pavilion at the Brazilian

Centennial Exposition in the style of an ancient pagoda, as it had at earlier expositions. Japanese silk, porcelain and handicrafts were displayed. The U. S. exhibits were stored in temporary quarters until the official pavilion was completed on December 23, 1922, more than three months late because of construction delays. Designed by Frank L. Packard, the pavilion and exhibits were funded by a $1 million appropriation from the U.S. Congress. Various government agencies sent displays, including the Agriculture and War departments. There were also notable displays on mining, forestry, hygiene, public health, and public education. The U. S. pavilion later served as the U.S. embassy to Brazil until the capital was moved to Brasilia in 1960.

Brazilian President Epitácio Pessoa opened the exposition on September 7, 1922, one hundred years to the day after the Portuguese empire was split in two and an independent Empire of Brazil established under the rule of Dom Pedro I. Admission was free on opening day. The opening also marked the first significant radio broadcasts in Brazil, as proceedings were broadcast from a tower at the top of the Corcovado hill and heard in Niteroi, Petropolis, and in São Paulo. For Pessoa the exposition was a way to reinforce centralization in the face of regional conflicts that were threatening the country. Notable visitors included the U.S. Secretary of State, Charles E. Hughes, who visited in part as a gesture intended to reciprocate the visit of a Brazilian delegation to Philadelphia in 1876. Though initially scheduled to close on March 31, 1923 the exposition was extended to run through July 2, 1923.

Bibliography

The Museu Histórico Nacional and Biblioteca Nacional in Rio de Janeiro possess good collections of materials related to the exposition, including Portuguese-language catalogues. The records of the U.S. commission to the exposition are housed in the National Archives, Record Group 43. The exposition was well covered in the *New York Times*, notably September 24, and December 25, 1922, and March 25, 1923; also in the *Times* of London, July 29, August 26, September 2, 5–9, 1922, and April 11, June 25 and November 10, 1923. Notable secondary literature on the exposition includes Marly Silva da Motta, *A Nação faz cem anos: a questão nacional do Centenário da Independência* (1992); Lucia Lippi Oliveira. "As Festas que a República manda guarder" *Estudos Históricos* 2, 4, (1989): 172–89; Maurício Tenorio "Um Cuauhtémoc carioca: comemorando o Centenário da Independência do Brasil e a raça cósmica," *Estudos Históricos*, 7, 14, (1994): 123–148; and José Antônio Nonato, "O Passado morro abaixo," *Nossa História*, 9 (2004): 68–73.

Wembley 1924–1925

Alexander C. T. Geppert

British Empire Exhibition

The British Empire Exhibition, held in 1924 and repeated in a year later, was neither the first nor the last imperial exposition in Great Britain but certainly the most important one. While there were no great exhibitions as such in London during this period, the medium had established itself with the Colonial and Indian Exhibition of 1886 as the first British exhibition exclusively devoted to imperial themes and had developed into a spectacular exposition type, as seen in Imre Kiralfy's large-scale Franco-British Exhibition held in Shepherd's Bush in West London in 1908 and its annual sequels through 1914. Wembley's continental counterpart, sometimes dubbed the "French Wembley," was staged seven years later in the Bois de Vincennes in southeastern Paris. As the first Parisian exhibition solely devoted to French overseas expansion on such a scale, the Exposition Coloniale et Internationale of 1931 corresponded to Wembley in many ways.

Like its Parisian counterpart, the Wembley exhibition was planned to take place long before the outbreak of World War I. Initial proposals by the British Empire League and other similar organizations for holding an imperial exposition dated back to 1902. They were again put forward by the Canadian high commissioner in London, Lord Strathcona, influential exhibition impresario Imre Kiralfy, and the South African Captain Sir Pieter C. Van B. Stewart-Bam in November 1910. Together, Strathcona and Kiralfy had been involved in organizing events of a comparable kind before, and Stewart-Bam had served as the chairman of the General Executive of the 1907 South African Exhibition. In 1910, the Wembley project still figured under the heading "Imperial Exhibition" and was intended to be held in 1915 to coincide with the Prince of Wales' coming of age. Yet, the realization of these plans was delayed, first, by organizational difficulties and then by World War I, but similar proposals continued to be made.

Once the war was over, a provisional committee was appointed, and the project eventually launched by the Prince of Wales — the future King Edward VIII — at a meeting held under the auspices of the Lord Mayor of London at the Mansion House on June 7, 1920. The motives for reviving these pre-war plans were twofold. The exhibition was intended to ensure the empire's stability after World War I had led to an increased awareness of its domestic significance and, at the same time, of the fragility of the empire's precariously maintained unity. At the same time, such a large-scale endeavor could help the process of postwar demobilization and was envisaged as a means to counter wide-scale unemployment and the threatening economic decline. More than a year later, a second meeting was organized, this time with the colonial secretary and future prime minister, Sir Winston Churchill, and the mayors of numerous provincial towns present. As the president of the exhibition's General Committee the Prince of Wales announced that the exhibition would include a "great national sports ground" as its center-

piece. In 1923, businessman and public servant James Lord Stevenson was appointed chairman of the Board of Management, with Lieut.-Gen. Sir Travers E. Clarke as deputy chairman and chief administrator.

In the meantime, the scheme had also been approved by the Board of Trade whose newly established Department of Overseas Trade under civil servant and diplomat Sir William Henry Clark was to become directly involved in the organization. The government arranged for a special guarantee fund by passing a special Act of Parliament on December 23, 1920, to facilitate the private financing of the endeavor. Otherwise, however, it proved reserved in its support. Except for contributing £100,000 to the guarantee fund, the government did not at this time provide for any direct subventions or subsidies. Therefore, the British Empire Exhibition was neither state-initiated nor state-sponsored, even if the government increased its financial contribution several times and eventually participated more actively than before. This came about as a consequence of a new policy formulated by the Board of Trade's Exhibitions Branch, set up permanently on the recommendation of a 1907 survey committee, and because the vast majority of colonies and dominions had unanimously agreed to take part with their own displays.

Finding and eventually choosing the venue had proved far less controversial and intricate than in previous cases. Faced with the alternative of either re-using an existing site — such as the Crystal Palace in Sydenham or Kiralfy's White City — or creating an entirely new one, the latter option was chosen, first and foremost for financial reasons. Although it would have been possible to make use of pavilions already built for the largely unsuccessful Festival of Empire held in 1911 at the Sydenham site, the palace itself had already been in decline for some years. With trees and water left over from its previous function as a park, Wembley in North London seemed a much more suitable alternative, and was, in 1921, selected as the future exposition venue. Although it had previously been earmarked for development as an upper-class garden suburb, Wembley was chosen mainly for reasons of its size and accessibility by rail. Work on the exhibition grounds including the stadium began in early 1922.

13

The Empire Stadium, with the white twin towers in the foreground, remained in use long after the exhibition, hosting a variety of international sporting events (Larson Collection, Special Collections Library, California State University, Fresno).

The new sports arena was placed on the exact site of the so-called "Watkin's Folly," London's notorious imitation of the Eiffel Tower, and in itself a direct conceptual transfer from the Parisian 1889 Exposition Universelle. Begun in June 1893, construction was never completed due to structural defects and the fragment of a tower was demolished in September 1907. Erected in less than 300 days to hold more than 125,000 spectators, the so-called Empire Stadium — as it was known well into the 1950's— opened to the public a year before the exhibition itself with the Football Association Cup Final in 1923. This game, later known as the legendary "White Horse Cup Final," attracted an estimated crowd of 150,000 spectators. Soon, the stadium was not only described as the central *clou* of the British Empire Exhibition but it also became to be seen as a national landmark and genuine *lieu de mémoire.*

While taking the form of a city within a city, the venue in Wembley, although well connected to public transportation and within a quarter of an hour's distance from Piccadilly Circus, was some way out of London. After the Colonial and Indian Exhibition of 1886 held in the Royal Horticultural Society Gardens in South Kensington, London exhibitions were increasingly driven out of the city center, and thus by and large suburbanized. It was only on the occasion of the Festival of Britain in 1951 that town planners and urban designers realized the enormous possibilities for redevelopment connected with the holding of such a mega-event and decided to bring the spectacle back into the city center. Hence, Wembley could be interpreted as a further attempt in a long line of comparable urban development projects at permanently imperializing London's character, and thus lessening its inferiority complex with regard to competing cities such as Paris.

Although the original intention was to open the Empire Exhibition in May 1921, the date had to be postponed several times, first to 1923, and, in the summer of 1922, once more to 1924 — mainly for organizational reasons and to allow the participating dominions and colonies more time for preparation. Finally, King George V opened the British Empire Exhibition on April 23, 1924, St. George's Day, and it was to remain open through November 1, 1924. The final words of George V's speech — "I declare this exhibition open" — was the first sentence by a head of state ever transmitted live on radio. Simultaneously a cablegram was sent around the entire world and arrived back in Wembley eighty seconds later.

Wembley's spatial structure was strictly symmetrical and, just like any other exhibition, this one tried to create an imaginary structure by assigning both objects and people their "right place." However, the entire world on display at the Wembley site was reduced to its British imperial variant, i.e. the British overseas dominions, colonies and possessions. There were no attempts to include other foreign countries. The exhibition's two architectural directors, Sir John William Simpson and Maxwell Ayrton, and its principal engineer, Sir Owen Williams, applied the standard pavilion system, widespread in the international exhibitionary system since the 1880s, to the explicit and officially exclusive subject matter of *this* exposition, i.e. the entire British Empire. Thus each colony was assigned its own pavilion. The largely triangle-shaped venue was 216 acres in size (4000 ft. x 3000 ft.) and divided by a double axis shaped like a St. Andrew's cross — with a huge garden and the main entrance at its northern apex, the Empire Stadium at its southern, the pavilion of New Zealand at its western and the Indian pavilion at the eastern end. Still further to the east, this rather "serious" part, including a special building for the British government, together with pavilions devoted to Fiji, Newfoundland, the West Indies and British Guiana, was supplemented by a 47-acre amusement park. The two largest buildings on the site were the Palace of Industry and the Palace of Engineering, at that time the two largest buildings in the world. A number of lakes, connected with each other, and various

parks divided the northern and southern parts of the venue. Situated around these lakes and other gardens were exhibition complexes of the four most important territories of the empire — New Zealand, Australia, Canada, and India. Of the 58 countries which comprised the empire at that time, 56 participated with displays and pavilions of their own, with only Ireland and Gibraltar missing. The majority of these colonies were located in the southern part of the venue. They included, from west to east, Malaya, Southern Rhodesia, Bermuda, Sierra Leone, Nigeria, the Gold Coast, Palestine, South Africa, West and East Africa, Burma, Ceylon and Hong Kong. They were all considered "representative of the characteristic architecture of the different countries," although their architects and designers were more often than not of British rather than indigenous origin. All the roads on the site were named by Rudyard Kipling, Britain's foremost author of tales of the empire.

During its 150 days of existence, the exhibition featured numerous spectacles and attractions, such as the first-ever complete church to be built in an exhibition in order to display ecclesiastical art, a lavish Queen's Doll's House, now on display in Windsor Castle, designed by the architect of New Delhi, Sir Edwin Luytens, a replica of the recently discovered tomb of Egyptian King Tutankhamen, a mock-up of an entire coal mine and, in the Canadian pavilion, a full-size model of the Prince of Wales completely made of butter to emphasize its production capacities in the dairy industry.

Although a minimum of 25 million visitors had been expected, some 17,403,267 visitors made the British Empire Exhibition nevertheless a resounding success, although not with regard to its revenues. The financial loss amounted to more than £600,000 before the sale of the buildings. A great deal of speculation set in as to whether the exhibition would reopen in 1925, with the intention of reducing the deficit suffered during the first year. Although always having insisted that the exhibition was run by private enterprise, the government eventually decided to assume more responsibility. In consequence — and most unusually — the exhibition reopened the following year for another full season (May 9–October 31, 1925), with slight conceptual changes, some new pavilions, and a number of

The pavilions of East and West Africa at the Wembley 1924–1925 exhibition (Larson Collection, Special Collections Library, California State University, Fresno).

extensions, especially in the amusement park. However, some colonies, such as India and Burma, did not participate in 1925, mainly for financial reasons. In the second year, attendance figures dropped to 9,699,231, making a total of 27,102,498 visitors over the two seasons. With construction and maintenance costs adding up to more than twelve million British pounds, the exhibition took a financial loss of £1,581,905 over the two years, which had to be covered by private donations and the guarantee fund.

The site's future was, at the time of closing, quite uncertain. Hopes for a further continuation in 1926 soon proved futile and unrealistic. Although four complexes—the Palaces of Art, Industry and Engineering, and the British government building, in addition to the stadium, had been intended to be permanent, grandeur and gravity, rather than durability or sustainability, were the main criteria at the time of their construction. Most of

the pavilions were completely dismantled after the exhibition's close, and some were sold at a private auction and moved to other sites. Only a very few of the original structures remained at the site. The Burmese pavilion was shipped to Australia to form part of the Melbourne centenary celebrations. In the 1970s, the site was transformed into an industrial park. The British government pavilion was demolished in 1973, the Palace of Engineering six years later. While all contracts had originally included a special clause that made interfering with the use of the land or buildings for the purpose of another exhibition at any time within a period of five years legally impossible, no further grand-scale exhibition was ever held at the Wembley site again. The first remained the last.

The only building that continued to be used for its original purpose was the stadium, at least through October 2000. In 1927, the entrepreneur and sports promoter Sir Arthur

James Elvin had assumed control and turned the whole complex into a national sports venue where, in 1948, the first Olympic Games after World War II were held. As the venue of the 1966 World Cup, numerous concerts and music festivals such as Live Aid in 1985 and the European Championship in 1996, this world-famous sports ground with its prominent white twin towers developed into a veritable icon of Englishness— until Britain's Sports Council decided in 1996 that the "most spectacular stadium in the world," in the words of Prime Minister Tony Blair should be erected in its place, a new "superstadium," designed by the renowned architect, Lord Foster, and more expensive than any other sports arena in the world. With the demolition of the original Wembley Stadium in the fall of 2002, the final remains of the British Empire Exhibition were irretrievably swept away.

Wembley's overall significance was ambiguous. On the one hand, the exhibition certainly served to renew and perpetuate the importance of empire to the British in the interwar years. Never before had the imperial theme been so central and dominant in a European exhibition on such a scale, and — as official and semi-official publications did not tire of repeating time and again — never before had an area as large as this been given to the dominions, colonies and "dependencies" to present themselves in the metropolis. Yet, neither the exhibition's prevailing language nor its specific modes of representation were as original and innovative as its promoters took pleasure in claiming. Indeed one could even diagnose a formal, both representational and discursive "hangover." On the other hand and in complete contrast to all expectations, Wembley also epitomized the symbolic beginning of the empire's end. Since the British Empire Exhibition had originally been planned to take place in a pre-war setting it was not altogether appropriate when it eventually came about, with a time-lag of almost a decade and the first global war in between. The first signs of dissolution in both the 'exhibitionary complex' and the exposition's subject could no longer be overlooked. From such a perspective, the British Empire Exhibition of 1924–1925 represented another attempt at reinventing the empire. Simultaneously, however, it foreshadowed the empire's subsequent political disintegration.

Bibliography

Although its exhibition-related holdings were severely damaged during World War II, the best of all places to start research into the British Empire Exhibition is the British Library in London. Many of the numerous publications occasioned by the Wembley exposition can be found there. Another extensive collection is kept at the Community History Archive, Cricklewood Library and Archive, London Borough of Brent. It includes musical recordings, commemorative items, and various publications produced by amateur historians and members of the Wembley History Society. Large quantities of contemporary postcards, both blank and inscribed, can be found in the Noble Collection, Guildhall Library.

The most convenient route to study any exhibition is not through its ephemera but rather through its official publications. In this case, the exhibition authorities did not produce a comprehensive official report after the event but issued an official catalogue, *British Empire Exhibition: Official Catalogue 1924* (1924), an official guide, Lawrence, George Clarke, ed., *The British Empire Exhibition 1924: Official Guide* (1924) and a handbook, *British Empire Exhibition 1924 Wembley, London April-October: Handbook of General Information* (1924) before or throughout its duration. Among the numerous catalogues and guide books specifically published for many of the sections and features, see in particular F. A. Chetwynd Jessett, *British Empire Exhibition: What You Want to Know about the Exhibition* (1924); Harras Moore, *The Marlborough Pocket Guide to the Empire Exhibition at Wembley, 1924* (1924); *The Wonders of Wembley, and Souvenir Guide to London* (1924); *Daily News Souvenir Guide to the British Empire Exhibition: With Maps and Photographs, Concise "Where Is It" Index and Complete Train, Tram and Bus Guide* (1924). Special issues of newspapers such as the *Times* (see in particular the four supplements published on April 23, May 24, July 29, September 30, 1924) or of the *Illustrated London News* (May 24, 1924) appeared on the occasion of the exhibition. A year and a half before its opening, the exhibition authorities also launched a newspaper of their own, the *Empire Exhibition News: The Organ of the British Empire Exhibition (1924), Wembley* (1922–1924), to create the necessary degree of long-term publicity. For a critique of the exposition's architecture see Hubert C. Corlette, "The British Empire Exhibition Buildings," *Journal of the Royal Institute of British Architects* 31, 20 (Oct. 18, 1924): 653–665. From the experience gained during his involvement with the exposition as director of United Kingdom exhibits, Sir Lawrence Weaver later published two influential volumes *Exhibitions and the Arts of Display* (1925) with numerous illustrations of the various British stands and posters, and *The Place of Advertising in Industry* (1928).

The correspondence and papers of the Board of Trade's Department of Overseas Trade are held at the National Archives in Kew. Further archival material can be found in the records of the Colonial Office, the Dominions department, and the India Office. Issues discussed include government participation, financial arrangements, negotiations with the colonies and dominions in regard to subsidies for their participation, the reopening of the exhibition in 1925, and its final winding-up. Additional archival sources are available at the Victoria and Albert Museum, Archive of Art and Design. The papers of Lord Stevenson are kept at the University of Sussex Library, Special Collections. A very limited number of oral history interviews also exist; and transcripts can be consulted at the Grange Museum of Community History in Neasden in northwest London and at the East Midlands Oral History Archive, Centre for Urban History, University of Leicester. Last but not least, large quantities of contemporaneous newsreels and other film footage are available at the British Film Institute National Archive in London.

Unlike most other exhibitions of the same size, scale, and significance, the British Empire Exhibition has hitherto received comparatively little scholarly attention. To date there is no large-scale historiographical analysis that could completely meet professional standards. The only book-length account, Donald R. Knight and Alan D. Sabey, *The Lion Roars at Wembley: British Empire Exhibition 60th Anniversary 1924–1925* (1984) was written by two local ephemera collec-tors and tends towards the celebratory, and makes no pretence at analysis or interpretation. The best place to start is still the broad chapter in John M. MacKenzie's pioneering *Propaganda and Empire: The Manipulation of British Public Opinion, 1880–1960* (1984): 96–120. Denis Judd mentions Wembley briefly in his survey *Empire: The British Imperial Experience, from 1765 to the Present* (1996). Among the older literature, see Kenneth Walthew, "The British Empire Exhibition of 1924," *History Today* 31 (August 1981): 34 39. So far the best researched and most convincing analyses are, however, written from an art historian's perspective. See, for example, Jonathan Woodham, "Images of Africa and Design at the British Empire Exhibitions between the Wars," *Journal of Design History* 2, 1 (1989): 15–33, and, seen from the sports historian's angle, Jeff Hill and Francesco Varrasi, "Creating Wembley: The Construction of a National Monument," *The Sports Historian* 17, 2 (November 1997): 28–43. For Wembley's treatment by a literary scholar consult Scott Cohen, "The Empire from the Street: Virginia Woolf, Wembley, and Imperial Monuments," *Modern Fiction Studies* 50, 1 (Spring 2004): 85–109. Last but not least, from the perspective of a cultural historian with an emphasis on different forms of space, see Alexander C. T. Geppert, "True Copies: Time and Space Travels at British Imperial Exhibitions, 1880–1930," in Hartmut Berghoff, *et al.*, eds., *The Making of Modern Tourism: The Cultural History of the British Experience, 1600–2000* (2002): 223–248, and "London vs. Paris: Imperial Exhibitions, Transitory Spaces, and Metropolitan Networks, 1880–1930" (unpub. Ph.D. thesis, Department of History and Civilization, European University Institute, Florence, 2004).

Paris 1925

Philip Whalen

Exposition Internationale des Arts Decoratifs et Industriels Modernes

The Paris International Exposition of Industrial Design and Decorative Arts in Modern Life affirmed the importance of modern industrial design and decorative art in the twentieth century. Situated on seventy acres on either side of the Seine River, running through the center of Paris, the exposition extended

The entrance gate to the Place de la Concorde shows clearly the influence of Art Deco architecture that this fair helped popularize (editors' collection).

along two perpendicular axes: west to east from the Champs-Elysées to the Place de la Concorde and north to south from the Grand Palais to the Place de l'Hotel des Invalides. This project was financed by the sale of 50 franc bonds each equal to 20 admission tickets; hefty subsidies from the Ministry of Fine Arts and the France's national manufactories (Sèvres, Gobelins, and others) as well as a 3 million franc grant from the city of Paris. Inspired by the futurist orientation of the Turin International Exposition in 1902 and the Decorative Arts Exposition in Munich in 1910, the Society of Artists-Decorators planned a decorative arts exhibition for Paris in 1915. The Paris exposition overcame substantial delays in its efforts to reclaim France's desired position as center of fashion and arbiter of refined taste. French organizers sought international cooperation and conceptual unity by showcasing contemporary works "original in conception and modern in design" Disrupted by World War I, it could only be scheduled after the Marseilles Colonial Exposition in 1922, the Franco-Belgian Fashion Exposition of 1922, and the Spanish Interior Decoration Exposition of 1923. Inaugurated by

France's President Gaston Doumergue on April 30, 1925, the Paris decorative arts exhibition welcomed an estimated 14 million visitors before closing on October 15, 1925.

A total of 13 different monumental gates set the tone for the exposition's fairy tale landscape. The Gate of Honor (Porte d'Honneur), designed by Henri Favier and André Ventre, ran between the Grand and Petit Palaces. Bronzed geometric grillwork hung between polished columns that supported neon lit bas-relief metal panels depicting artisans making decorative products. Another entrance, the Gate of Concord, was noteworthy for its 10-meter tall allegorical female figure surrounded by ten massive 22-meter high concrete pylons. Once through, fairgoers entered a "glittering fairyland" that they remembered with delight.

If the Paris exposition's ephemeral landscape "made no heavy intellectual or moral demands on the visitor," it amused, dazzled, and overwhelmed visitors' aesthetic sensibilities with obtrusive radiance, extravagant luxury, cheeky sumptuousness, and occasional austerity. The exhibition's director of landscaping, Louis Bonnier, transformed pre-existing green spaces into a continuous garden carpet embellished with dramatic lighting, stunning fountains, abundant statuary, trellised arcades, crushed marble alleys, and flowered terraces. Following one of the *Official Catalogue*'s six suggested itineraries, capacity crowds visited 131 different pavilions. They refreshed themselves at colorful kiosks and aboard floating restaurants moored along the Seine while galas, concerts, nightclubs, and festivals animated incandescent evenings. The Alexander III Bridge, which served as the principal entrance to the exposition from either side of the river, was cleverly embellished with 44 boutiques and surrounded by Venetian gondolas. At night, the fair was transformed by powerful floodlights and cascading water fountains highlighted by an illuminated pedestal topped by the Eiffel Tower's thirteen different lighting patterns (delivered through 200,000 bulbs configured into 60 foot letters to advertise Citroen).

The 1925 exposition sought to showcase a mutual understanding between art and industry. It favored fashionable tendencies associated with a new international aesthetic, Art Deco. This movement rejected the derivative and highly ornamental classical motifs of the past, and, if its early phases were influenced by whimsical and sinuous motifs characteristic of 1890s Art Nouveau, Art Deco increasingly borrowed from Cubist art, Bauhaus architecture, Soviet Constructivism, Machinism, Italian Futurism, Egyptology, and African Primitivism to develop a strikingly geometric and angular aesthetic. Banishing Corinthian columns, Victorian fig leaves, mythological heads, ornamental "egg and dart" motifs, crawling larvae, sinuous serpents, tortuous tentacles, and libidinous satyrs, Art Deco embraced moderate cubism's geometry of straight lines, angular forms, and smooth surfaces. These were attractively standardized into an iconography of floral bouquets, prolific nymphs, ubiquitous fawns, recurring chevrons, and sharp lightning bolts executed in cool colors and innovative materials.

Visitors and critics either loved or hated the new style; few remained indifferent to the exposition's "exhilarating mix of avant garde structures." Fairgoers saw in the Art Deco pavilions a "dependence upon effects produced by a proportion of a richness of material rather than elaborate carving or applied ornament."

A number even found that the aesthetic combination of simplicity and rationalism suggested a "tension between art and mechanism" to be cold, dismal, and preposterous. Others, by contrast, fondly remembered decors rich in beauty and emphasizing common sense. Charles Richards, director of the American Association of Museums, was rather impressed and bemoaned that American artists, engineers, and manufacturers missed an important and valuable opportunity to showcase their skills and wares at the exposition.

Projects of exposition scale required workshop collaboration and the coordination of finished works into a harmonious arrangement: mass, contour, color, and line were harmonized by an *ensemblier* into a work of art in its own right — a decorative *ensemble*. The best were commissioned to supervise the assembly of some of the most fabulously designed and decorated pavilions ever created for a world's fair. Abrupt angularity and exuberant moods could be softened with textures calculated to import warmth, comfort, and luxury. Unexpected materials such as platinum, aluminum, zinc, horn, ivory, exotic hardwoods, glass, and celluloid introduced surprise and novelty. Color retained gaiety and was considered a priority by the 1920s *ensembliers*, who employed bright lavenders, orange-reds, and hot pinks, juxtaposing them with lime-green yellows to generate a psychedelic palette that some later critics compared with the 1960s.

Universally acknowledged as unrivalled, Pierre Patout's spectacular Pavillon d'un Riche Collectionneur (a Rich Collector's Home) offered one of the century's most celebrated room settings, described as "an embarrassment of riches, and an icon both in its entirety and in its individual pieces." Decorated by the celebrated Jacques-Emile Ruhlmann and associates, this graceful pavilion housed a luxurious private apartment filled with contemporary masterpieces: paintings, sculptures, crystal fixtures, rich carpets, a piano, and elegant furniture. The structure's vaguely neo-classical lines greatly influenced Art Deco architectural evolution toward the *moderne* style of the 1930s.

A flamboyant leftover from the 1900 international exposition, the Grand Palais served as the exposition's center for official ceremonies and receptions. Its central foyer and vestibule were converted into a multi-tiered staircase capable of staging theatricals that included over 2,000 participants such as the "Oriental Nights" production of June 16. Exhibit spaces on the two main floors were allocated either to individual nations or categories of finished products including woodwork, toys, musical instruments, scientific instruments, draperies, lace, embroideries, tapestries, screens, carpentry, furs, flowers, furniture, and much more. A new feature at such exhibits was Alfred Agache and Maurice Neumont's street scene showcasing "street arts" with storefronts and urban fixtures such as benches, signs, water fountains, lightposts, and urinals.

The French Embassy pavilion was France's official entry; a prototype "to be installed at an indefinite date in some unnamed foreign capital" The Ministry of Fine Arts granted Paul Leon, director of the Ecole des Beaux-Arts and assistant commissioner-general for the exhibition, a million francs to construct a pavilion furnished by France's leading artists, decorators, craftsmen, and designers. The Society of Artist Decorators outfitted 25 spaces (including vestibules, and hallways) like department store showrooms that constituted a display of an idealized residence capable of addressing an embassy's private needs and official functions. The U-shaped pavilion surrounded a Crafts Courtyard (Cours des Metiers) designed by the exposition's chief architect, Charles Plumet, to celebrate French trades. From the vantage of this spiritual center, visitors gained an unobstructed view across the Alexander III Bridge to the Main Gate (Port d'Honneur) on the other side of the Seine a third of a mile away.

The largest Parisian department stores— Galleries Lafayette, Au Bon Marché, Au Printemps, and Les Magasins du Louvre —flaunted their dominance as premier purveyors of taste within the home furnishings industry by constructing grandiose Art Deco pavilions. Located at the Alexander III bridge's left bank entrance and of similar dimension and construction materials, each structure offered a distinctive example of the Art Deco style replete with multiple planes, numerous angles, and decorated flat surfaces. Each pavilion occupied one corner of the Place des Invalides. These icons of mass consumption underscored the exposition's commercial rather than dem-

ocratic orientation: they offered original and opulent creations for exclusive clients who could afford them.

The Galleries Lafayette's white marbled La Maitrise pavilion (designed by Joseph Hiriart, Georges Tribout, and Georges Beau) was distinguished by four massive columns topped by emblematic sculptures designed by Leon Leyritz and representing fashionable decorative materials: fur, lace, ribbon and leather. Rooms were thematically arranged, such as the softly lit rose, black and silver "Vie en Rose" display thought to represent "the quintessence of the Exhibition and indeed the period." The surface of Printemps' concrete-domed Primavera pavilion (designed by Andree Mare, Louis Süe, and Emile Ruhlmann) was encrusted with glass and metal and resembled an oversized Roman ice house. Laplade's Studium Louvre pagoda was noted for its covered upper-level, three-sided garden terrace and glass storefront windows. Au Bon Marché's Pomone Pavilion, by Louis Boileau, was monumentally rectangular with a pattern of geometric motifs decorating the exterior surfaces.

Despite a perceived tension between the extravagant exteriors and their more conventionally designed interior space, few buildings achieved significant modernist departures. Banished to the shadows of the Grand Palais by the exposition's organizing committee and surrounded by a thirty-foot fence until the minister of Fine Arts intervened to have it removed, Le Corbusier's Esprit Moderne pavilion proposed a "standard cell for habitation" in the form of two cubes: one for living space furnished with materials "industrially" available; the second empty with three walls and a large circular hole cut out of the ceiling provided garden space and accommodated a pre existing tree. Abhorring the notion of "decorative arts" and notorious for stating that a home should be "a machine for living," Le Corbusier embraced functionality as a supreme architectural law. An adjacent structure exhibited Le Corbusier's 1922 plans for a futuristic, 3-million-person city that featured twin rows of skyscrapers housing up to 3,000 people and connected by arched walkways. On the eastern side of the Grand Palais stood a startling Tourism Pavilion, designed by Robert Mallet-Stevens, that boasted a 36-meter clock tower. Inside, Louis Barillet's wrap-around leaded

One of the focal points of the 1925 Paris exposition was the Place des Invalides, where the four largest department stores in Paris built similar Art Deco pavilions on each corner as shown in this view (editors' collection).

glass window depicted a cubist landscape viewed from a car traveling 120 kilometers per hour.

The Soviet Union's austere rectangular glass pavilion by Konstantin Melnikov offered a constructivist integration of industrial, structural, and aesthetic practice in architecture. Painted in red, grey, and white, it was built with inexpensive materials on a minuscule budget. The Danish pavilion also merged form and function. Standing like an ancient monolith in the shape of the Danish cross, with one large opening serving as the entrance, the edifice was entirely built of red and white bricks layered to produce alternating horizontal and vertical surface patterns.

Four identical towers prominently occupied the four corners of the Invalides Esplanade. Promoting France's agenda of "internal tourism," each tower represented one of France's wine regions (Bordeaux, Burgundy, Champagne and the Rhone Valley) and was equipped with a restaurant to promote that region's gastronomy.

Interesting pavilions that also deserve mention range from Paul Poiret's theatrical sets exhibited on three barges moored along the Quai d'Orsay to the oversized kiosks representing a host of popular newspapers and magazines such as *L'Intransigeant, Femina, Le Quotidien, l'Illustration* and *Le Monde Illustré*. Provincial France held its place with municipal pavilions representing regional capitals, communications entrepôts, and manufacturing centers. These included Roubaix, Nancy, Saint-Etienne, Lyons, Tourcoing, Bordeaux, Nantes, Marseilles, and Mulhouse. Contributions from the private sector beyond the big Parisian department stores were also in evidence. The purveyors of Baccarat crystal and Christofle tableware shared an elegant pavilion on the Invalides Esplanade, while Lalique's pavilion, directly facing the colonnade of the French Embassy, reflected the glassmaker's art in its design, which included an obelisk-shaped fountain. The Sèvres manufactory took the prize for most eccentric décor with its garden display of 20-foot-tall concrete urns appearing like stranded extraterrestrials. Many complained that these were distracting and obstructed the Esplanade.

Few exhibits actually addressed the needs of ordinary citizens. The French Village showcased a church, an inn, a school, and homes

As a decorative arts exposition, Paris 1925 included many interiors for the display of furniture and decorative objects. Shown is a lady's bedroom in Galeries Lafayette Pavilion, complete with a bearskin rug (from *Intérieurs en couleurs,* 1926, courtesy of Hagley Museum and Library).

that might appeal to rich provincials or Parisian bourgeois on vacation. A few austere interiors intended for "ordinary" people could be found in the Colonial Pavilion, and in René Gabriel's workers kitchen in the Society for Applied Arts Pavilion.

Foreign pavilions representing Austria, Denmark, Finland, Poland, Belgium, Great Britain, Italy, Sweden, Japan, Holland, Estonia, Denmark, Turkey, Latvia, Luxembourg, the Soviet Union, Switzerland, Monaco, Czechoslovakia, Yugoslavia, Greece, and Spain were arranged in the Court of Queens on the Left Bank. None represented the Americas. Although offered an enviable site along the Seine River, the United States declined to participate, and its site was given to Japan. Overlooking skyscraper architecture and the 1913 New York Armory Show, U.S. Secretary of Commerce Herbert Hoover explained that America had no modern art and thus nothing worthwhile to display. Germany, not yet forgiven for its role

in World War I, was not invited. Additional pavilions represented French colonial possessions: North Africa, French Equatorial Africa, Indo-China, Morocco, Tunisia, and France's colonial administration.

Popular amusements could be found alongside the exposition's fine-arts exhibits. These included belly dancers, a dunking booth whose victims were colonials and women wearing pajamas, assorted shooting galleries, operator-controlled miniature cars (Le Dodgem), rolling carpets that amused those who watched the riders fall down, and a medley of beauty contests, parades, concerts, comedy acts, and fireworks displays. A "Parisian Life" merry-go-round replaced traditional animals with eighteen contemporary characters including a merchant, a cook, a delivery boy, a gangster, a flapper, and a bourgeois. Old and young children also marveled at an oversized Toy land.

From its monumental architecture to decorative surfaces, the legacy of Art Deco is debated. Early critics who observed its evolution characterized Art Deco as transitional. Subsequent art historians, however, have judged this sumptuous style as a "legitimate and highly fertile chapter in the history of the decorative arts." Beyond original creations of "uncompromising geometry" and great value; now either worn or in museum collections, only works rendered in the softer, watered-down *moderne* style have retained popular currency. The ocean-liner *Normandie* (1935) remains a recognizable example of this aesthetic. Architecturally, the style dominated the modern skyline for the next half century. The streamlined aerodynamic survives in Paris through the Palais de Chaillot (1937) and the Colonial Museum (1931). In the United States, such buildings as the Rockefeller Center complex (1931–1938), the RCA (1931), Empire State (1930) and Chrysler (1928) buildings in New York City, the Ramsey County-Saint Paul Courthouse in Saint Paul, Minnesota (1930), the Hoover Dam (1931), the Golden Gate Bridge (1933), the Seattle Art Museum (1932), the Union Terminal (1931) in Cincinnati, Ohio, and countless others are surviving Art Deco structures.

The Danish pavilion at the exposition took the new Art Deco form to an extreme in geometric simplicity (from *Encyclopédie des arts décoratifs et industriels modernes,* 1927. Courtesy of Hagley Museum and Library).

Bibliography

Significant secondary and archival collections pertaining to world's fairs and expositions are located at the Henry Madden Library at California State University at Fresno and the Hagley Museum and Library in Wilmington, Delaware.

Among useful primary sources are *Album Souvenir, Exposition Internationale des Arts Décoratifs. Paris 1925* (1925); *Encyclopédie des arts décoratifs et industiels modernes,* 12 Vols. (1928–32), a beautiful and comprehensive work covering all artistic aspects of the exposition; *Catalogue Général Officiel: Paris 1925* (1925); Gaston Que-

nioux, *Les Arts Décoratifs Modernes* (1925); United States Commission on International Exposition of Modern Decorative and Industrial Arts, 1925, *Report ... upon the International Exposition ... in Paris, 1925* (1926); and Alistair Duncan, "Introduction," *Authentic Art Deco: Interiors from the 1925 Exposition* (1925, 1989). Frank Scarlett and Marjorie Townley, *A Personal Recollection of the Paris Exhibition* (1975) and Elbert Baldwin," The Paris Decorative Arts Exposition," *Outlook,* (July 29, 1925): 454–56, are two visitor's accounts.

Secondary sources of note include Susan M. Matthias, "Paris 1925: Exposition Internationale des Arts Decoratifs et Industriels Modernes," in John E. Findling, ed., *Historical Dictionary of World's Fairs and Expositions, 1851–1988* (1990); David Gebhard, *The National Trust Guide to Art Deco in America* (1996); Arthur Chandler, "Where Art Deco Was Born," *World's Fair* 9. 1 (1989): 1–7; Simon Dell, "The Consumer and the Making of the Exposition Internationale des Arts Décoratifs et Industriels Modernes, 1907–1925," *Journal of Design History* 12, 4 (1999): 311–25; Tag Gronberg,

"Speaking Volumes: The Pavilion de l'Esprit Nouveau," *Oxford Art Journal* 15, 2 (1992): 58069; Bevis Hillier and Stephen Escritt, " Strictly Modern: The 1925 Paris Exposition and the State of European Decoration," in Bevis Hillier and Stephen Escritt, *Art Deco Style* (1997); Laetitia Bonnefoy, "L'Éclairage monumental," in *Les Expositions Universelle à Paris de 1855 à 1937*

(2005), 52–59; Victor Arwas, *Art Deco* (2000); Emmanuel Bréon, "Les Arts décoratifs en mouvement," in *Les Expositions Universelle à Paris de 1855 à 1937* (2005): 154–162; Philippe Rivoirard, "La Modernité á l'Exposition," in *Les Expositions Universelle à Paris de 1855 à 1937* (2005), 163–166; and Marc Gaillard, *Les Expositions Universelles de 1855 á 1937* (2003).

Dunedin 1925–1926

Jennifer Wagelie

New Zealand and South Seas Exhibition

In the years leading to the opening of the New Zealand and the South Seas Exhibition on November 17, 1925, the port city of Dunedin, on the east coat of the South Island, had been experiencing difficult financial and economic times. After enjoying many years of prosperity as the center of New Zealand's commercial world and site of the 1861–1863 gold rush, the city had taken a downturn. Some of the factors for this were its removal from global shipping routes after the opening of the Panama Canal and an economic depression that occurred after World War I. More New Zealanders were moving to the North Island in response, and those who stayed formed the Otago Expansion League that was instrumental in advocating the idea of having the exhibition to bring attention to both the South Island of New Zealand and the fair city of Dunedin. With the country's financial and commercial future improving, the idea for the fair was unveiled in the January 27, 1923, edition of the *Evening Star* newspaper. The exhibition was to be financed by both private funds and New Zealand government subsidies and loans. By October 1923, an exhibition board of directors, headed by prominent Dunedin businessman J. Sutherland Ross, had been formed.

After much debate regarding the suitability of several different sites, the fair board settled on 65 acres of reclaimed land from Lake Logan, an idyllic location at the foot of the Opoho Hills, and one whose close proximity to the railroad station provided ease in delivering supplies and, after the fair opened, bringing visitors to the grounds. Edmund Anscombe, a well-known New Zealand architect, designed the site that consisted of seven pavilions situated on two sides of the Grand Court. All of the buildings converged on Festival Hall that featured a dome similar to that of the U.S. Capitol building. The buildings were connected so that visitors would never have to walk outdoors to visit the pavilions, courts, and exhibits.

The pavilions and courts at the fair represented countries both inside and outside the British Empire, including Australia, Fiji, and Canada. The New Zealand Government Pavilion featured the country's many industrial, commercial, and agricultural interests, as well as social welfare advances in the health care and prison systems. The provincial courts displayed the "bountiful resources of the Dominion," with displays highlighting each region of New Zealand, including Otago, the Southland, Canterbury, Marlborough, Wellington, and Auckland.

The British Court displayed a Hall of Empire that contained a central frieze depicting scenes from the "history and pageant of the Empire," and a 400-square-foot map of the world that had New Zealand at its center. The Australian, Fijian, and Canadian courts were located within the British pavilion. The Queensland exhibit, within the Australian court, was

The commercial exhibits at the Dunedin exhibition included a wide range of enterprises including one devoted to the rabbit skin trade (from L.S. Fanning, ed., *The Pictorial History of the New Zealand and South Seas International Exhibition, Dunedin 1925–26*, 1926).

noted for having the finest display of canned fruit at "any exhibition, ever." The Fijian Court was described as, "one of the most picturesque spots in the Exhibition." Island fruits, sugar, and coconut byproducts were featured, and a small pavilion made of Fijian mahogany housed native Fijians. Weapons of war were also displayed. Large gates welcomed the visitor to the Canadian Court. Exhibits stressed Canada's grain trade and the diverse nature of its resources. Maple leaves and beavers were carved into the court's arches and illustrations of Canada's natural resources covered the walls.

Other exhibits included the Education Court, the Women's Section, and Motor Pavilion. The last was noted for its comprehensive display of motor vehicles and cycles in New Zealand. Additionally, visitors enjoyed an art gallery that included work from the National Academy of Design in New York, and the Fernery, a 100 by 65 foot area constructed of fern tree

trunks, displaying the fifty different types of New Zealand ferns. With streams and waterfalls, it was one of the most popular areas of the fair, described as a "fairyland" at night. The Fernery was also the site of a Maori meetinghouse that had been returned to New Zealand for the first time since 1879, having previously been on display at the fair at Melbourne and most recently, the Wembley Exposition. The art of the Maori was also included in the Dominion Museum's display in the New Zealand Government Pavilion.

Another popular area of the fair was the Amusement Park. Seven "devices" were installed, including the Scenic Railroad, the Water Ride, the Whip, Dodgem Juniors, the Fun Factory, the Caterpillar, and the Merry Mix-Up. Football and cricket were additional amusements, with games and matches played in a stadium built at one end of the fairgrounds.

By all accounts, the exhibition was a suc-

The Fun Factory was a place of laughter and challenge, as visitor walked and balanced their way through the various attractions and obstacles (from L.S. Fanning, ed., *The Pictorial History of the New Zealand and South Seas International Exhibition, Dunedin 1925–26,* 1926).

cess—the attendance was three times the entire population of New Zealand at the time. Financially, all of the fair's shareholders enjoyed a large dividend at the end of the fair, and all loans that the government had made were repaid in full. Considered the largest and most successful world's fair in New Zealand, the Dunedin and South Seas Exhibition realized the goals of the Otago Expansion League, albeit only briefly, since the financial doom of the Great Depression began just four years after the fair closed.

Bibliography

Primary source materials are located in the Hocken Library at the University of Otago (ARC-0049). Other useful sources include photographic records such as Leo Fanning, *The Pictorial History of the New Zealand and South Seas Interna-*tional Exhibition (1929) and Hugh Neill, *Official Photographic View Album 1925–6: New Zealand and South Seas Exhibition, Dunedin* (1926) as well as G.E. Thompson, *Official Record of the New Zealand and the South Seas Exhibition* (1927).

The most extensive newspaper coverage is found in the *Otago Daily Times* and *Evening Star.* Both the Hocken Library and the Dunedin Public Library contain files of these newspapers, and the Hocken Library additionally has three books of clippings on the fair and a file containing "exhibition special" newspapers.

Among secondary works, the most useful is Miriam Smith's thesis, "The History of the New Zealand Exhibitions with Particular Reference to the New Zealand and South Seas International Exhibition, 1925–1926" (Auckland University, 1974), available at the Hocken and Auckland University libraries. Another work of interest is Edward Anscombe, *The Inside History of the Exhibition* (1929), in which Anscombe, the fair's architect, revelas the shortcomings of the organizers.

Philadelphia 1926

David Glassberg

Sesqui-centennial International Exposition

Philadelphia's Sesqui-centennial International Exposition of 1926 was widely regarded as a flop, especially when compared with the city's dazzling Centennial Exposition a half-century earlier. Planning got off to a late start; most of its buildings remained incomplete until well after opening day; the Philadelphia city government spent millions of dollars to bail out the bankrupt Sesqui-centennial Exhibition Association after the exposition closed its gates, and it rained 107 of the 184 days the exposition was open. Critics of proposed international expositions in Chicago and New York City in the 1930's cited the Philadelphia experience as proof that the day of the giant world's fair had ended.

Yet another look at the Sesqui-centennial International Exposition reveals many innovations— the use of talking motion pictures, public address systems, colored lighting, radio advertising — that contributed to the success of subsequent world's fairs. And while the exposition did little to influence the nation's concept of its future in the manner of the international expositions in Chicago in 1933–1934 and New York City in 1939–1940, it did much to shape the nation's concept of its past.

The shadow of the 1876 Centennial fell on the Sesqui-centennial Exposition from it inception in 1916, when John Wanamaker, a member of the finance committee in 1876, proposed that the city stage an international exposition to commemorate the 150th anniversary of the signing of the Declaration of Independence. Serious planning did not get underway until 1921, with the formation of the Sesqui-centennial Exposition (later Exhibition) Association. The association's appeals to the federal government for $20 million and to the Pennsylvania state government for $2.5 million were ignored, despite President Warren G. Harding's message to Congress in 1922 endorsing the exposition idea. In the end, the state and federal government provided approximately $1 million and $2 million, respectively, barely enough to cover the cost of their own buildings at the exposition.

Most of the money for the exposition came from the city government. In 1924, Mayor W. Freeland Kendrick assumed the presidency of the Exposition Association, and the following year the Philadelphia city council voted to back the exposition with a $5 million guarantee fund. Few expected that the exposition would use it all, but by the time the Sesqui-centennial Exhibition Association closed its books in 1929, the city had made seven appropriations to the exposition totaling nearly twice that amount — $9.7 million — much of it used to reimburse the association's numerous creditors.

The city also provided an estimated $5 million worth of services to the exposition, the bulk of it from the Department of Public Works, which prepared the exposition grounds for visitors. The association considered 14 different sites for the exposition, including the site of the 1876 Centennial in Fairmount Park, before deciding on 1,000 acres adjacent to the League Avenue Navy Yard in South Philadelphia. This site had the advantage of already being largely owned by the city — but the disadvantage of being swampland. Transforming the South Philadelphia marsh into level fairgrounds required dumping several million cubic yards of fill, in places 20 feet deep. The spongy soil conditions also dictated that the foundations of the exposition buildings be placed on pilings sunk deep into the ground.

One of the most spectacular features of the 1926 Philadelphia Sesqui-centennial Exposition was the 200-foot Tower of Light with two 62-inch searchlights at its top (editors' collection).

halls from five to three, combining categories that had been displayed in buildings at other fairs. The three principal exhibit halls were the Palace of Liberal Arts and Manufactures, the Palace of Agriculture and Foreign Exhibits, and the Palace of U.S. Government, Machinery, and Transportation, the last not completed until July 20, nearly two months after the exposition opened to the public. Several smaller buildings, the Palace of Education and Social Economy and the Palace of Fine Arts, also opened well after the rest of the exposition. Only seven buildings came from foreign nations, while six came from states. Other exposition structures included an auditorium, in which the American Kennel Club organized the first dog show in its history; the administration building; the amusement concessions in the Glad Zone; and a gaudy 80-foot high, 30-ton Liberty Bell outlined in 26,000 electric lights. A 100,000-seat Municipal Stadium built for the exposition hosted extravaganzas such as the $1.7 million heavyweight championship fight in which Gene Tunney dethroned Jack Dempsey. Renamed John F. Kennedy Stadium, it remained in use for special events such as the annual Army-Navy football game and the Live Aid benefit concert for African famine relief in 1985 until it was demolished in 1992 to make way for a new sports arena for the Philadelphia Flyers hockey team and the Philadelphia 76ers basketball team.

Exposition planners declared that the multicolored stucco and rounded edges of the fair's official buildings struck a contemporary look, suggesting neither a particular historical style, such as beaux arts, nor the ultramodern. But the most influential architectural style at the exposition was a historical one, that of colo-

Because of the late start, the enormous task of site preparation, and the exposition's uncertain funding, businesses and state and foreign governments were slow to purchase exhibit space, and consequently buildings were slow to rise on the fairgrounds. The exposition's first director general, David Collier, a veteran of the 1915 Panama-California Exposition in San Diego, quit seven months before opening day when it became clear that his elaborate plans for the fair could not be realized. His successors reduced the number of exhibit

While most world's fairs tend to look to the future, the 1926 Philadelphia exposition looked back into history with its replica of colonial High Street (photograph by John D. Cardinell, in *Sesqui-Centennial International Exposition, Philadelphia 1926*, 1926).

nial revival. New York State reproduced two colonial buildings on the fairgrounds—replicas of Washington's headquarters in Newburgh and of Federal Hall in New York City where George Washington was sworn in as president. Ohio erected a replica of William Henry Harrison's home and the National Society of Colonial Dames of America a replica of Sulgrave Manor, ancestral home of the Washington family in England. The Philadelphia YWCA built a replica of Mount Vernon on the exposition grounds as headquarters for its visitor services. Even the Jell-O Company dispensed samples of its quivering product in a replica of a colonial cottage within the Palace of Agriculture and Foreign Exhibits.

Far and away the most extensive exercise in colonial revival architecture at the exposition was High Street, a collection of 20 homes along a replicated colonial Philadelphia street. Organized by the Women's Committee with a grant of $200,000 from the Exhibition Association, the exteriors were built in collaboration with the Philadelphia chapter of the American Institute of Architects and architectural historian Fiske Kimball, the new director of the Pennsylvania Museum (renamed the Philadelphia Museum of Art). Responsibility for furnishing the interior of each building went to a different women's organization, such as the National League of Women Voters and the Daughters of the American Revolution. Sponsoring organizations also staffed their houses with members in period costume. A replica of Indian Queen Inn served meals, in the tradition of the "New England Kitchen" restaurants at earlier world's fairs. *Good Housekeeping* magazine sponsored a replica of the home of colonial physician Thomas Shippen, installing the latest in modern kitchen, bathroom, and laundry fixtures behind the imitation eighteenth-century façade to "demonstrate that one can possess one's ancestral home and be moderately at home in it." The popularity of High Street set the stage for the opening of outdoor museum villages such as Greenfield Village and Colonial Williamsburg in the 1930s, as well as offering a boost to the fledgling historic preservation movement.

While High Street's version of the world of the colonial urban gentry demonstrated the Anglocentrism of American elite culture in the 1920's, other parts of the Sesqui-centennial International Exposition displayed the cultural pluralism of the modern city. A Roman Catholic Mass celebrated by Cardinal Dougherty packed even more visitors into the new Municipal Stadium than the Dempsey-Tunney fight. The exposition remained open on Sundays, flaunting Pennsylvania's blue laws. If the official exposition historical pageants, "America" and "Freedom," slighted the role of African-Americans in the nation's past, two other pageants at the fair were explicitly devoted to black history. One, "Loyalty's Gift," featured a 500-voice chorus with young soloist Marian Anderson. It appears, however, that public facilities at the exposition remained segregated. The Women's Committee constructed a separate "hostess house" for blacks, with a cafeteria and emergency health station, not far from the High Street it erected for white visitors.

The Sesqui-centennial International Exposition embodied many of the contradictions of its decade. In years known for economic boom and ballyhoo, the fair was a financial and public relations disaster. In a decade in which the automobile transformed American life, the fair's most striking exhibit was a replica of the walking city of the eighteenth century. Like the Shippen House on colonial High Street, the fair employed the latest in modern technology — to drain the swamps, advertise on radio, automate exhibits through moving pictures — but wrapped inside a façade playing homage to the world of the founding fathers. Many Americans felt more at home in this world, constructed on the exposition grounds in accordance with their idealized image of the past, than in their own.

Bibliography

The principal work on the Sesqui-centennial International Exposition is the official history written by E. L. Austin and Odell Hauser, *The Sesqui-centennial International Exposition: A Record Based on Official Data and Departmental Reports* (1929). To get behind this history, researchers should consult the extensive records of the Sesquicentennial Exhibition Association (Record Group 232) in the Philadelphia City Archives. These records include the names of subscribers to the association; minutes of the board of directors; files of the officers of the exposition and of the directors of the various divisions and departments; official publications, such as press releases, guidebooks, and daily programs; approximately 4,000 photographs; and eighteen volumes of newspaper clippings and miscellaneous memorabilia.

Other Philadelphia repositories with materials concerning the exposition include the Manuscripts Department of the Historical Society of Pennsylvania, which houses the papers of Elizabeth F. L. Walker, and of Albert M. Greenfield, chairman of the Finance Committee; the Free Library of Philadelphia, which has several volumes of photographs and site plans; and the Temple University Urban Archives, which contains records documenting the participation of many local groups, including blacks, in the fair's activities. The Atwater Kent Museum has a collection of paintings of the twenty houses on High Street by Arrah Lee Gaul, official artist of the Women's Committee.

Outside Philadelphia, materials pertaining to the exposition are in the National Archives (Record Group 43, files 607–18), which document the preparation and construction of federal government exhibits; and in the Library of Congress, in the papers of Frank Lamson Scribner who prepared exhibits for the U.S. Department of Agriculture at Philadelphia, as well as Rio de Janeiro (1922–1923) and Chicago (1933–1934).

There is little in the secondary literature that adds to an understanding of the exposition, but a sympathetic contemporary work is Sarah D. Lowrie and Mabel Stewart Ludlum, *The Sesqui-centennial High Street* (1926). A check of the standard indexes will lead to contemporary journal and newspaper articles on the fair. Modern works include Alan Axelrod, ed., *The Colonial Revival in America* (1985), Steven Conn, *Museums and American Intellectual Life, 1876–1926* (1998), which devotes a chapter to the Sesqui-centennial Exposition, and Charlene Mires, *Independence Hall in American Memory* (2002).

Long Beach 1928

Kaye Briegel

Pacific Southwest Exposition

Late in 1927 leaders of the Long Beach, California, Chamber of Commerce decided to organize an international exposition to promote trade through the city's improved harbor. By the time it opened, the Pacific Southwest Exposition had become the biggest international fair in the west since those in San Francisco and San Diego in 1915.

Long Beach was a seaside resort and commercial city of 145,000 people. Near its center was the Signal Hill oil field, where oil had been discovered in 1921, and on its western boundary was Los Angeles harbor. Adjacent to that older harbor, Long Beach was building its own harbor, financed by a $5 million bond issue approved by the voters in 1924. In May 1928, while the exposition was being planned, voters sustained the local mood of optimism and approved $2 million of additional bonds to expand the harbor.

To emphasize the significance of harbor development, the 63-acre site chosen for the exposition was at the end of a peninsula between two newly dredged channels in the inner harbor. The site had a dock, so visitors could arrive by boat, and a regatta was one of the exposition's featured events. Promoters arranged free use of the previously undeveloped land for the duration of the exposition. When the exposition closed, a Proctor and Gamble plant was built there.

Exposition promoters chose Tunisia as their architectural theme, they explained, because it was a coastal land of traders with a climate similar to Long Beach's. Local architect Hugh R. Davies designed exposition buildings with white walls and low, flat roofs topped by domes and pinnacles. Davies's buildings were made of plasterboard with an outer covering

of stucco and roofed with stretched canvas, almost like movie sets, in response to the need to keep building costs low, build quickly (Davies was commissioned just ten and a half weeks before the exposition opened), and return the site to its owners at the end of the exposition. Inside the walls, landscaping transformed the harbor sand, which promoters said looked like the Sahara Desert, into an oasis.

Exposition buildings were called Palaces; there was one for General Exhibitions and others for Education, Fine Arts, and Aeronautics and Transportation. Organizers offered trophies and medals to attract exhibitors; for example, Maynard Dixon's "Wild Horses of Nevada" won a silver medal for oil painting. There was also a Street of Nations whose sponsors from Europe, Asia and the west coast of Latin America celebrated their products and culture. In addition there was the Amusement Zone, an outdoor stadium, and a bandstand surrounded by a reflecting pool where the municipal band played twice daily. A daily pageant represented the history of the Southwest "from the time of the Indians."

The exposition was open for 40 days and official attendance was 1.1 million, stimulated by a series of special days dedicated to cities, clubs, businesses, and special interest groups of every imaginable type. On opening day, for example, the annual Nebraska Picnic adjourned from a local park to visit the site; Herbert Hoover established a campaign office there and visited to canvass for votes. Officials set the cost of the exposition, which was "self-sustaining," at $650,000.

On the last day of the exposition, the tower atop the Palace of Fine Arts collapsed, perhaps reflecting its insubstantial construction. Like the tower, which stood long enough that its collapse was of minor significance, the

Pacific Southwest Exposition celebrated the boom of the 1920s in Long Beach at a time when reports that the boom might not go on forever seemed insubstantial and of minor significance.

Bibliography

When the exposition was over, one of its organizers, John W. Ryckman, compiled and edited *Story of a Epochal Event in the History of California: The Pacific Southwest Exposition ... 1928* (1929). It includes Bruce Mason, "The Pacific Southwest Exposition at Long Beach, California," *American Architect* (October 5, 1928), 431–34 and William L. Wollett, "Architecture of the Pacific Southwest Exposition, Long Beach, California," *Architect and Engineer* 94 (August 1928), 57–59. Woollett, an architect, praises the exposition's buildings while noting their insubstantial construction and the small scale of the event. Mason, a Long Beach city attorney and the architect's brother-in-law, also praises the exposition and its buildings. *Overland Monthly* also featured an article on the exposition in its April 1928 issue.

Long Beach Public Library became the depository of the official books of clippings and ephemeral materials from the exposition. Four volumes of these materials have been microfilmed. They contain copies of most of the large number of articles about the exposition published in local and out-of-town newspapers. One notable exception is "Woman Injured by Tower Crash; Structure at Long Beach Exposition Falls," *Los Angeles Times* (September 5, 1928). There are several exposition publications such as its preliminary announcement, "Long Beach Invited the World, July 27 to August 13," "Official Souvenir Guide," and "Catalogue of Invited Works by Painters, Sculptors and Craftsmen."

Barcelona 1929–1930

John E. Findling

Exposición Internacional de Barcelona

Following the successful international exposition held in Barcelona in 1888, civic leaders planned a second fair, the Electrical Industries Exhibition, for 1913 to celebrate the recent electrification of the city. But the coming of World War I forced planners to delay the exposition, and in the early 1920s, the idea surfaced again. This time, however, the plans escalated as the new government of General Miguel Primo de Rivera, a military dictator, sought an event that would glorify Barcelona and win him favor among Europe's leaders, most of whom had come to power more democratically than he. In addition, a major exposition was seen as a way to showcase Spanish industry, which had never fully recovered from the turn-of-the-century wars in Cuba and the Philippines, and had suffered more in the hard times following World War I. Financing for the fair came from both the Barcelona city government and the Spanish national government, which saw the fair as an event that would play well in European diplomatic circles. A contemporaneous exposition in Seville, the Ibero-American Exposition, was also held, and the two together were known as the General Exposition of Spain.

The exposition covered an area of almost 300 acres in front of and atop a hill named Montjuich, formerly the site of a grim prison where executions were common. Pedro Domenech headed a team of regional architects in planning the site, and he and his team transformed the area (that became a permanent city park) with the construction of landscaped avenues, palatial museums, water gardens, and a 60,000-seat sports stadium. The most important structure was the National Palace (originally called the Central Palace), a huge neoclassical building that hosted not only the art exhibits, including the massive Arte de España exhibition, but also many musical perform-

The Palace of Textile Art of the 1929 Barcelona International Exposition was one of 11 pavilions devoted to Spanish and foreign industrial achievements (editors' collection).

The Art Deco lighting that surrounded the Palacio Nacional, around which the Barcelona International Exposition was staged, was spectacular (editors' collection).

ances featuring world-famous composers, such as the Brazilian Heitor Villa-Lobos. A broad roadway, the Avenida de la Reina María Cristina, connected the palace with the Plaza de España, a circular plaza that served as the main entrance for the exposition. Many of the foreign pavilions flanked the avenue connecting the plaza with the palace. .In addition, the exposition brought about significant improvements to streets and squares all over the city. The metro was moved underground and different lines were linked to create a more coherent subway system, and a new railroad station to handle trains to and from the north was constructed.

The king and queen presided over the opening ceremonies on May 19, 1929, and the exposition continued until January 1930. A total of 14 European nations participated officially, but other countries, such as Japan and the United States, were represented by private exhibitors. Most of the exhibits dealt with industry, Spanish art, and sport, but the Spanish hosts took advantage of the occasion to mount impressive displays of Spanish industrial accomplishments in such areas as textiles, chemicals, and electricity. Also notable were Spanish displays in city planning and agriculture. Spanish electrical successes were especially admired when a spectacular light show, with large searchlight beams rising from behind the National Palace, lit up the skies every night at closing time.

However, the Barcelona exposition is remembered most for two features situated some distance away from the main avenue. The Pueblo Español, or Spanish Village, was a honeycomb of 320 buildings in various Spanish styles that was the result of ten years of research. Most of the buildings contained shops or were "homes" to artisans who crafted swords, did leatherwork, created woven goods, or worked in any number of other traditional arts and crafts. At another site not far from the National Palace, the German pavilion, designed by modernist architect Mies van der Rohe and constructed of Roman travertine, green marble, onyx, and glass, stunned visitors with its clean, unadorned lines and simple structure. The Barcelona pavilion, as it became known, became the prototype for a generation of architects who designed residences and commercial buildings in this style. Although it was dismantled after the fair, it was reconstructed in the

1980s and used as the press office for the 1992 Summer Olympic Games in Barcelona. It remains today as an important tourist site in the city.

The Barcelona International Exposition transformed the city into a whirlwind of civic activity. During the fair, there were military parades, bullfights, theatrical and musical productions, and Zeppelin flights. Under the aegis of the exposition, there were conferences and seminars on topics as widely diverse as cancer and dry cleaning. When it was over, the city was left with a substantially improved international reputation. Because of the coming of the Great Depression in the early 1930s, however, the exposition did not bring about any lasting economic benefits of significance.

Bibliography

The records of the Barcelona International Exposition are housed in the Instituto Municipal de Historia and the Archiva Administrativa Municipal, both in Barcelona. The exposition published several guides with photos of key pavilions and maps of the grounds, including *Catálogo official* (1929); *Guía official* (1929); and *Exposición Internacional, Barcelona: Su significación y alcance* (1929). A description of the Arte de España exhibit, illustrated with thousands of plates, appears in the two-volume *Catálogo Histórico y Bibliográfico de la Exposición Internacional de Barcelona, 1929–30* (1931, 1933).

General descriptions of the architecture and attractions of the Barcelona and Seville expositions can be found in "Spain and Her Two Great Expositions," *Living Age* 336 (April 1929): 136; and Arthur Stanley Riggs, "The Spanish Expositions," *Art and Archaeology* 27 (April 1929): 147–64. In the same issue of *Art and Archaeology*, Joseph Pijoan, "The Spanish Village," provides a detailed architectural discussion of this exhibit.

Modern works on the exposition include Juan Pablo Bonta, *An Anatomy of Architectural Interpretation: A Semiotic Review of Mies van der Rohe's Barcelona Pavilion* (1975), Caroline Constant, "The Barcelona Pavilion as Landscape Garden, Modernity and the Picturesque," *AA Files* 20 (Fall 1990): 56–68; and Rubio Sola-Morales, Ignasi Christian Cirici, and Fernando Ramos, *Mies van der Rohe: Barcelona Pavilion* (1993), all on the famous modernist structure, and Oriol Bohigas, "Comentários al "Pueblo Español" de Montjuich," *Arquitectura* 35 (noviembre 1961): 15–23.

Seville 1929–1930

Cristina Carbone

Exposición Ibero-Americana (Ibero-American Exposition)

Seville's Ibero-American Exposition of 1929 is a unique example of an early twentieth century world's fair in that its grounds and so many of its buildings remain intact. The brightly colored and grandiose structures are situated in the lush Parque María Luisa, named in honor of the Bourbon princess who donated the lands of her Palace of San Telmo. A part of this park is aptly named Las Delicias.

Seville first planned to hold an international exposition in 1914 but was stymied by world events. Despite the disturbance of World War I, work went forward on the Alfonso XII Canal, which linked Seville with the Atlantic. The canal met the Guadalquivir River to the south of town and later formed the western boundary of the exposition. When it opened in 1926, the canal could accommodate 14,000-ton liners, surely a boon to Seville's tourism industry. It was here that a replica of Columbus's caravel, the *Santa María,* was moored during the exposition. In 1914, engineer J.C.N. Forester laid out some 170.5 acres of previously undeveloped land, taking advantage of the nearby water source to create a modern Mozarab paradise of avenues, vistas and waterways. A garden city-style worker's quarter was built at the same time just below the park. In 1926, José Cruz Condé became the director of the exposition, which had by then metamorphosed into an Ibero-American exposition aimed at restoring Spain's prestige on the world stage. To best effect this last point, Spanish officials deemed it advantageous to hold a concurrent international exposition in Barcelona. Together the two fairs were called the General Exposition of Spain.

While Barcelona and Seville shared in the Exposición Nacional de Bellas Artes, the Barcelona exposition concentrated on world-wide commerce, and Seville emphasized Spain's cultural ties with its former colonies. Among the attractions were the Exposición del Libro, which examined the historic role of printing and publishing as a method of exporting Spanish culture, and the Historia de Sevilla, featuring rare artifacts from the Roman, Visigoth, Moorish, Christian, and romantic eras of the city's history. Seville emphasized its role in the European discovery of the New World with the Historia de América exhibit, which displayed important maps and other documents from Seville's famed Archivo de los Indios.

To one side of the exposition entrance was the Royal Tobacco Factory where the city's most famous cigarrera, Carmen, worked, and to the other was the grand hotel Alfonso XIII which was built specially for the exposition and which conformed to its architectural idiom. Native son Anibale Gonzalez laid out the major plazas and designed most of the Ibero-American exposition's 74 buildings. An advocate of national romanticism, Gonzalez drew inspiration from a variety of Spanish architectural styles to create monumental stage sets. His Plaza de España literally became a stage when it appeared in David Lean's *Lawrence of Arabia* (1962) and George Lucas's *Star Wars Episode Two: Attack of the Clones* (2002). The Plaza de España is a 200-meter wide hemi-cycle, surrounded by a colossal curving, colonnaded neo-Renaissance exposition building, at either end of which is an 80-meter high rendition of Seville's famous Giralda tower. At the center of the plaza is a great fountain and pool with four bridges honoring the Spanish provinces of Leon, Castile, Navarre and Aragon. All of these are fantastically decorated with *azulejos,* or glazed tiles,

The spectacular Plaza de España was the centerpiece of the 1929 Seville exposition and remains an important landmark today (editors' collection).

manufactured in the Traina quarter of Seville. The 49 provinces of Spain are represented in tiled alcoves that run the length of the Plaza, each with historical scenes specific to the province shown at the back of its center bench, and an illustrated map is on the ground to its front. To either side of the bench are open shelves that housed books and pamphlets on each province during the exposition.

Further in the Parque María Luisa is the elliptical Plaza de Américas for which Gonzales designed each of the three major buildings in a historical style evocative of great moments in Seville's history: the Palace of Decorative Arts is neo–Mudéjar (Ibero-Moorish), the Palace of Fine Arts is neo–Spanish Renaissance-Plateresque, and the Royal Pavilion is neo–Spanish Gothic. Each of these buildings is now a museum.

At least 13 foreign nations participated in the Ibero-American exposition. Spanish architects designed pavilions for Colombia, Venezuela, and Guatemala, while native architects designed the pavilions of Portugal, Brazil, Peru, Uruguay, Argentina, Mexico, Chile, Santo Domingo, Cuba, and the United States. The United States devoted $700,000 to erect one permanent and two temporary buildings designed by San Diego architect William Templeton Johnson, whose Spanish colonial revival buildings would have been equally at home in Southern California as in Seville. Johnson evoked Hollywood more than Spain, with his domed cinema auditorium, but this was not a venue for Hollywood celluloid; rather it was an early endeavor by the U. S. government to use informational films as a cost-efficient means of communication and propaganda at world's fairs. Some 20 government agencies contributed films on such subjects as child welfare reform, women in industry, scenic grandeur, and road building in the United States.

Argentina initiated airmail service between Seville and Buenos Aires on the opening day of the exposition via the launching of a dirigible and built the largest national pavilion. Mexico's building was universally acclaimed as the best example of a national pavilion. Mexican architect Manuel Amabilis designed an Art Deco-Maya pavilion that was pointedly pre–Hispanic in inspiration, expressive of the political currents then running strong in post–Revolutionary Mexico. The interior featured frescos by Victor Reyes that did not shy away from inflammatory topics such as the Spanish and Indian wars. Like the other Mexican muralists, Reyes understood Mexico's current glory to be rooted in its Hispanic and Indian past. But like Spain and Seville, Mexico was looking to its future.

Much like the later 1992 exposition in Seville, the Ibero-American Exposition spurred the modernization of Seville's infrastructure through the construction of new hotels and hostels, the expansion of unran parkland, and other public works. The exposition also brought about the in migration of many skilled artisans, whose work augmented the attraction of the city as a tourist destination.

Bibliography

The archives of the Ibero-American Exposition are housed in the Hemeroteca Municipal in Seville. The *Libro de Oro Iberoamericano* (1929) is the first of a proposed two-volume official guide to the exposition, volume 2 of which was never published. The local newspaper ABC de Sevilla published a 32-part series of articles on the exposition between August 30 and October 12, 1961. The city of Seville issued a number of studies on the history of exposition in 1992, in conjunction with its second world's fair. Published that year was Sylvie Assassin, *Seville: Exposición Ibero-americano, 1929–1930* (1992), which focuses on the architecture of the fair. Three other modern works in Spanish are Francisco Narbona, *Sevilla y la Exposición de 1929* (1987), Manuel Alfonso Rincon, *Sevilla y su Exposición 1929* (1992), and Eduardo Rodriguez Bernal, *Historia de la Exposición Iberoamericana de Sevilla de 1929* (1994).

One of the few English language texts to deal with the fair is Mauricio Tenorillo-Trillo, *Mexico at the World's Fairs: Crafting a Modern Nation* (1996), which includes a chapter on the 1929 exposition. Arthur Stanley Riggs covered both fairs in "The Spanish Expositions," Art and Archaeology 27 (April 1929): 146–64. *Living Age* 336 (April 1929) offers a general description of the grounds. Frances Parkinson Keyes focuses on the American pavilions in her, "A Little Window in Seville," *Good Housekeeping* 89 (September 1929): 34. And the architecture of the fair is featured in Alberto Villar Movellán, *Arquitectura del regionalism en Sevilla, 1900–1935* (1979).

Antwerp/Liège 1930

Paul Greenhalgh

Exposition Internationale Coloniale,
   Maritime et d'Art Flamand
Expositon Internationale de la
   grande Industrie, Science et
   Application Art Wallon

It would be a mistake to assume from the title of this entry that there were two international exhibitions in Belgium in 1930. Rather there was one held on two sites. Antwerp was by far the bigger and more lavish venue, with the subtitle Coloniale, Maritime et d'Art Flamand, while Liège had the sciences, industry, social economy, agriculture, and music. The split was due to the discord and rivalry caused during the deliberations as to which city should be chosen as focus for the celebrations of Belgium's centenary of independence from Spain. Brussels had staged the most impressive earlier expositions, and Antwerp and Liège decided it was their turn. Ultimately Brussels built the Heysel Stadium to mark the anniversary, and Antwerp and Liège agreed to split the exposition between them.

Antwerp proved by far the more successful site, for two reasons. The display of Flemish art from the previous five centuries proved a tremendous attraction throughout Europe, and the colonial sections, as at all other expositions in the early twentieth century, were staggeringly impressive. It was these latter sections that dominated the official literature and set the atmosphere for the exposition.

Belgium had profited handsomely out of the scramble for Africa at the close of the nineteenth century, and the government had taken care to exhibit its empire at all expositions from 1900. Antwerp staged the most lavish display of empire ever held on Belgian soil, partly due to the city fathers' zeal and partly to the willing-

ness of other empires to display their gains. Great Britain, France, the Netherlands, Italy, and Portugal built substantial pavilions along the Avenue de la Colonie, with pride of place going, naturally enough, to the Belgian effort, the Palais du Congo. With various colonial villages, filled with peoples from various conquered lands, dotted around the area, the whole was a spectacular, exotic expression of European imperialism, surpassed in Europe only by British and French efforts, revealing the extent to which empire had come to grip the economy and imagination of Belgian government and population.

The Flemish art exhibition was the most complete and impressive since the Brussels exposition of 1897 and included examples from many European collections. This showing was complemented, in terms of atmosphere at least, by the attraction Vieille Belgique, a reconstructed medieval city, which had by 1930 become an absolute standard in Belgian fairs. The period feeling of Renaissance Flanders was enhanced by various sideshow and entertainment features around the site.

In contrast, there were impressive examples of modern architecture, notably the Finnish, Norwegian, Dutch, and Italian pavilions, and the Pavillon des Villes Hanséatiques. This last piece, sponsored mainly by Bremen and Hamburg, has in hindsight an air of tragedy about it, as its international style would soon become proscribed in the midst of the National Socialist pogroms. By the same token, the Italian pavilion was one of the last pieces of modernism to come out of Italy with government approval. By 1937, at Paris, Mussolini had firmly harnessed classicism to the cause of Italian fascism. Marcel Schmitz, an architect and writer chosen by the central committee to report on the architecture of the site, felt pos-

The French pavilion, one of the largest at the 1930 Antwerp exposition, was situated along the avenue de la Colonie (editors' collection).

itive about the prospective effects of the exposition: "Taken as a whole, one can see a marked advance on previous manifestations, and one is able to say that there has been a clear benefit for the evolution of modern architecture in our country." Apart from the buildings already mentioned, Schmitz pointed to the various edifices put up by the Belgians themselves, including the Decorative Arts Palace, the Pavilion of the City of Antwerp, and the Electricity Pavilion. Indeed, photographic evidence indicates that these were full-blooded examples of international-style modernism. These were steel-framed buildings sheathed in concrete, with an emphasis on fenestration, the manipulation of space, and abstraction. Decoration was wholly absent, roofs were flat, and walls were white. It was quite progressive for a government to allow itself to be represented by architecture much more modern than, say, that of the French in the 1925 Paris Art Deco show. Indeed, the architecture at Antwerp can be compared with that shown by Mies van der Rohe, Le Corbusier, J.J.P. Oud, and others in Stuttgart at the 1927 Weissenhof housing exhibition, which drew much attention to the most forward looking concepts in architecture, construction techniques, and even furniture design.

By comparison the Liège exposition had more of the air of a trade fair or conference about it, having been stripped of those features normally thought to be most colorful at these events. Nonetheless, in terms of international participation and the trade it created, it remains a significant event in the recent history of the city.

The size of the attendance is not contained within the official reports. Everything indicates, however, that the two sites had good attendance throughout and that the events were officially considered successful. The large amounts of money the British, French, Italians, and Portuguese spent on their contributions confirms that they considered them events of the first class with massive audience potential.

Bibliography

For the Antwerp exposition, see *Exposition internationale, coloniale, maritime, et d'art Flamand: Rapport general* (1931) for the factual aspects. The Liège fair is similarly treated in Leon Michel, *L'Exposition internationale de Liège 1930* (1929). The *Times* of London published several articles of interest dealing with this joint exposition; see, especially, the issues of March 4, 24,

April 26, 28, May 9, July 18–19, 23, and October 9, 1930.

Among modern works, Paul Greenhalgh, *Ephemeral Vistas* (1988) discusses Antwerp-Liège in the context of their imperial displays, while John Allwood, *The Great Exhibitions* (1977), briefly mentions the Antwerp fair and provides some statistical data on the fair at both sites.

Stockholm 1930

Ursula Lindqvist

Stockholm Exhibition

The Stockholm Exhibition of 1930 is considered a watershed event in Sweden's cultural history as well as in Western architectural and design history. The exhibition modeled a new unifying social aesthetic, called functionalism, which would fuel the political agenda of the Social Democrats who would come to power in Sweden in 1932 and forge ahead with the now famous Scandinavian Model of social welfare. For Swedish cultural historians, the 1930 Stockholm exhibition signaled the moment when this agrarian nation-state in northern Europe became modern. For the rest of the Western world, the 1930 Stockholm Exhibition introduced what some contemporary critics called the only viable form of modernism in architecture and design. This form, known alternatively as "functionalism" and "Swedish Modern," has become ubiquitous in modern life through its mass-market appropriation by the global home furnishings giant IKEA. The 1930 exhibition focused simultaneously on advocating for functional, affordable, and comfortable living spaces for the masses, and for transforming a class stratified society into a more egalitarian and democratic one. Tellingly, the colloquial name that Swedes use for their social welfare model is *folkhemmet*, or "the people's home." The planners and architects of the 1930 exhibition successfully crafted a prototype of Sweden's future social welfare society on the banks of Djurgårdsbrunnsviken, the main canal that runs through Sweden's capital city, from May to September of 1930.

This was the second major exhibition to be staged on the banks of the canal, following the exhibition of 1897. While this land today comprises the largest public park in Stockholm, called Djurgården ("Animal Park"), in 1930 these were the king's private hunting grounds and normally off-limits to the public. The absence of permanent structures on the site made it ideal for erecting a prototype for a futuristic Swedish city, and its main entrance was strategically placed down the street from Stockholm's Embassy District, in walking distance for the entire foreign diplomatic corps. The 1930 exhibition differed dramatically from its predecessor in that it did not focus on Sweden's industrial progress, but rather on its skill in social engineering, with new advances in building and design serving this greater good. The working class Swedish writer Ivar Lo-Johansson, who attended the 1930 exhibition, makes explicit this connection between the new modern cityscape and the new modern human being in his memoir *Författaren* (1957):

> The shining machine limbs of the exhibition halls demanded a new poetry. The exhibition area's high steel mast rose like a signal, like a shiver of happiness toward the bright blue sky. The functionalist era had blown in. The style of the new age was really the scraping away of styles. Its naked language is called facts. I directly translated the language of architecture to that of literature. I walked and looked about for the new human being [quoted in Allan Pred, *Recognizing European Modernities* (1995), 109].

Functionalism's governing principle mandated that sanitary, affordable housing of good quality should be available to the masses as well as upper classes. Furthermore, the simplicity, rationality, and functionality of the new architecture communicated a new ideal for beauty, security, and contentment in the home environment that was a radical departure from the traditional, highly decorative and baroque Oscarian style of bourgeois drawing rooms and ornamental furniture. Functionalism was therefore deemed to be highly democratic. In her book *Nation and Family* (1940), Swedish sociologist Alva Myrdal, whose work shaped many of the social welfare state's public policies, described the tenets of Swedish modern design, which grew out of the 1930 Stockholm exhibition, as follows:

1. high quality merchandise for everyday use, available for all by the utilization of modern industrial resources;

2. natural form and honest treatment of material, with pure and simple lines, rational forms, white buildings, open floor plans with lots of glass to let in natural light; and

3. aesthetically sound goods, resulting from the close cooperation of artist and manufacturer [p. 230].

In addition to highlighting close cooperation between artist and manufacturer as a hallmark of Swedish design, Myrdal noted that close cooperation between government and civic organizations was a hallmark of Swedish social democracy. This was particularly true of the 1930 exhibition, which continued a tradition of longstanding collaboration between government and industry in staging home exhibitions. Two civic organizations that played a pivotal role were the *Svenska Slöjdföreningen* (The Swedish Society for Crafts and Design), and *Centralförbundet för Socialt Arbete* (The Central Federation for Social Work). The handicrafts society was founded in 1846 in response to the state's abolition of the guild system, which opened the field of handicrafts to all. "The society's ambition," according to art historian Eva Rudberg, "was to develop craftsmen's skills and promote good public taste." The federation for social work, known as the CSA, formed in 1903 to address pressing socioeconomic problems, the foremost of which was a widespread lack of sanitary, affordable housing for the working classes. The lack of decent housing was considered a leading cause of many other urban ills, namely poverty, poor public health, prostitution, weakened family support structures, and a low birth rate. The respective ambitions of these two civic societies

merged in 1917 into a single ambition: to redesign the home environment, when the CSA urged the handicrafts society to sponsor a competition for quality housing and furniture for the working classes. The result was the Home Exhibition of 1917, displayed in the newly designed Liljevalchs art gallery in Stockholm. This exhibition, while still designed in the classic "Swedish grace" style of this earlier period, highlights three important developments in the ideological system that produced the 1930 exhibition: the coming together of different civic organizations for a common goal, the attempt to disseminate these ideas widely in a public space, and the focus on the home environment — traditionally a private, individual space — as the point of departure for massive social change.

It was at a 1927 board meeting of the Society for Crafts and Design that the idea was presented to stage a major exhibition that would sell functionalism's forms and ideas to the public. The society soon received pledges of financial support from the state, the city of Stockholm, and private individuals. In spring of 1928, the Swedish government appointed an executive committee of financiers and bankers to oversee the exhibition's planning, and on June 6 of that year, Gregor Paulsson, the society's director, was named commissary-general. Gunnar Asplund, who had designed the new Stockholm city library in the functionalist style in 1925, was named chief architect. Departing from the traditional world's fair model, which typically invites foreign nations to build pavilions, the 1930 exhibition would feature only Swedish exhibits and invite the entire world to come and see them. In addition, it would focus almost exclusively on the home, with its layout divided into three sections: household goods; the home itself, featuring various apartments and terrace homes in the functionalist design; and the extra-domestic urban framework, including public transport, streets and gardens, stores and restaurants, media, and public amusements. According to world's fair scholar Elias Cornell, "The Stockholm Exhibition had a more thoroughly thought-through and unified programme than any of its forerunners."

Asplund designed the exhibition's dominant architectural structures to be either entirely white or an off-white, "neutral" color. A variety of brightly colored and festive elements—curtains, marquees, awnings, canopies, landscaped flower beds, waving flags, advertising posters, neon signs, costumed employees, and even the (presumably) colorfully dressed fairgoers themselves—accented the scene and gave it life. Asplund, who had been deeply influenced by the ideals of the German Bauhaus architectural school, nonetheless wanted to avoid Bauhaus' ascetic rationalism and create a festive, rather than dogmatic, atmosphere. He viewed his white structures as a holistic background upon which the social life of a city could be inscribed. Asplund's vision was to design functional architectural forms that would not call attention to themselves—a deeply imbedded Nordic cultural value—and rather showcase the "color" of human life in the city as a *tableau vivant*. Although the exhibition had the long daylight hours of Nordic summer working for it, Asplund nonetheless worked with local power companies to generate the most ambitious lighting system ever attempted in Sweden to keep the exhibitions' structures lit up at night. Because the restaurants and nightclubs were built with glass facades, the effect was to highlight the human activity inside even more vibrantly after dark. The entire exhibition served, in this sense, as a living museum of the past, present and future. While Nordic architects already had established their reputations on buildings that were light, harmonious, and blended with the natural environments, Asplund's "White Town," as the newspaper *Social-Demokraten* called it, was striking in its sheer mass of white geometric forms working together to create a unified idiom.

Asplund and his assistants, the most prominent among them Sven Markelius and Uno Åhrén, drew their stylistic, technical and philosophical influences from many recent major developments in modern architecture elsewhere in Europe. The strongest influences came from the Swiss architect Le Corbusier's Purism and from the Bauhaus school. Le Corbusier and Bauhaus architect Walter Gropius gave lectures in Sweden in the 1920s and remained in close contact with Asplund, Markelius, Åhrén, and Paulsson. Purism celebrated the simple and harmonious beauty of geometric forms working together in a functional, systemic way. Le Corbusier incorporated this ideal into an interior design exhibit at the 1925 exhi-

bition in Paris, titled *Pavillon de l'Esprit Nouveau*, which bears a striking resemblance to the apartment interiors Markelius later designed for the 1930 Stockholm exhibition. In a review of the 1925 Paris exhibition published in Sweden, Åhrén used the term *funktionalistisk* (functional) to praise Le Corbusier's modern forms and spatial arrangement. A Swedish columnist, drawing on a vernacular idiom, soon shortened this term to *funkis*, which entered the Swedish vocabulary as the name for this new style of architecture. *Funkis* also became the name of a popular restaurant and nightclub built for the 1930 exhibition.

Worldwide publicity for the event began in 1928, two years prior to its opening. This was the first Swedish exhibition to have its own publicity department, which held a competition to design an advertising poster and a symbol. Sigurd Lewerentz' "wings of progress" symbol, a geometric appropriation of the wings of the ancient Egyptian bird-man, won the competition and was featured both on the poster and as a three-dimensional structure atop the 74-meter-high advertising mast that rose from the exhibition's main square. All advertising featured new "grotesque" fonts associated with modernist styles, particularly one called Futura. The exhibition's publicity department printed its exhibition poster in fourteen languages and displayed it on the European railways and in travel agencies worldwide. The advertising campaigns, both local and global, was considered a success: of the exhibition's 4 million visitors, 25,000 were estimated to have come from outside Sweden, whose population in 1930 was only 6 million people. The admission price of 2 Swedish crowns for an adult and one crown for a child was high for the average Swede, particularly at the onset of a global depression. In all, the exhibition cost 8 million crowns to put on and was an estimated 200,000 to 300,000 crowns in the red when it closed.

The exhibition's designers knew from the start that their toughest audience would be the Swedish public and the Swedish press, who were likely to resist this new, "functionalist" idea of Swedishness. The press was built a special vantage point from which to survey the exhibition: a press box midway up the advertising mast at the heart of Festival Square. The mast, modeled on the Russian Constructivist

Vladimir Tatlin's famous model communications tower of 1919, featured the names of Swedish companies in oversized geometric fonts leading up to the wings of progress symbol at the top. While substantially shorter than Tatlin's tower, the mast was extraordinarily high for Stockholm's cityscape. When lit up at night, it could be seen from passing ships in Stockholm's archipelago. The exhibition's geography also attempted to win fairgoers and critics to warm to the *funkis* social aesthetic. For example, the broad, flag-lined, open walkway from the main entrance to the Festival Square was called *Il Corso*, Italian for "the way." At the end of *Il Corso* was the main restaurant, called *Paradiset*, or "The Paradise," a structure that showcased the new *funkis* architecture most strongly. The idea, then, was that *funkis* was the way to a utopian society for modern Sweden.

To sell the functionalist way of living even more aggressively to the Swedish public, exhibition designers built a national museum just beyond Paradiset titled *Svea Rike* ("The Kingdom of Sweden"). Its closed facades and its monolingualism — all exhibit displays were in Swedish only — made its target audience clear. The goal of Svea Rike's designers was to create an educational space that exuded the authority of science but in a language, both written and displayed, that was highly accessible to, and "fun" for, the average Swede. Svea Rike represented a seminal work of interactive advertising. These fun and interactive displays ensured that millions of Swedes participated in these "fun house" activities despite the additional admission price of one Swedish crown. This fun–house styled museum also had the very serious purpose of cultural education. For example, the museum featured a display of "scientific" research conducted by Professor Herman Lundborg, head of the Uppsala Institute for Racial Biology, which had been founded in 1921. The display's location right at the entrance made it the starting point of an allegory that constituted a single, linear narrative of Sweden's progress. Svea Rike's story, then, began with the presupposition that *Moder Svea* ("Mother Sweden") was a progenitor of a superior Germanic race, and thus all of Sweden's accomplishments to date are only the logical manifestation of its biological destiny. Because Lundborg's work was not widely known in the general public at that time, and

because it bore the stamp of scholarship and science, the press, despite their critical comments on most other aspects of the exhibition, accepted [the racial biology display] without question. The exhibition's clear semantic link to the inception of Sweden's social welfare society here underscores one of that society's more unsavory aspects: a state eugenics policy, including forced sterilizations, perpetuated in Sweden from 1935 to 1975.

The global impact of the functionalist ethos, however, is undeniable. Functionalism still predominates in building throughout the Nordic countries, where building codes often require office spaces to have windows. In addition, the IKEA Concept, published on the company website, "offering a wide range of well-designed, functional home furnishing products at prices so low that as many people as possible will be able to afford them," is nearly identical both to Myrdal's description of "Swedish Modern" and of the manifesto, titled *acceptera!* ("accept!") that the exhibition's designers published in 1931. IKEA was founded in Sweden in 1943, capitalized on the Swedish government's affordable housing programs following World War II, and by 2006 had built 237 showrooms on four continents. Thus the impact of the 1930 Stockholm exhibition has transformed not only Sweden and Scandinavia, but also the private homes of many families worldwide.

Bibliography

In English, the most complete information available on the exhibition is found in art historian Eva Rudberg's monograph, *The Stockholm Exhibition 1930: Modernism's Breakthrough in Swedish Architecture* (1999). Geographer Allan Pred also devotes a substantial chapter of his book *Recognizing European Modernities: A Montage of the Present* (1995) to the 1930 exhibition. The August 1930 issue of London-based *Architectural Review* provides ample contemporary coverage and reviews. *Modern Movement Scandinavia: Vision and Reality* (1998), published by DOCOMOMO Scandinavia, contextualizes the 1930 exhibition in light of Nordic architectural and design trends during the twentieth century. Ylva Habel's recently published doctoral dissertation from Stockholm University, *Modern Media, Modern Audiences: Mass Media and Social Engineering in the 1930s Swedish Welfare State* (2002), not only devotes a chapter to the 1930 exhibition, but also places the exhibition within critical and popular discourses on social engineering and the Swedish social welfare state in that decade. A recent doctoral dissertation by Ursula Lindqvist, "The Politics of Form: Imagination and Ideology in 1930s Transnational Exhibitions and Socially Engaged Poetry" (University of Oregon, 2005) includes a chapter on the exhibition.

In Swedish, Per G. Råberg, *Funktionalistiskt genombrott* [Functionalistic Breakthrough] (1970), which traces the development of functionalism generally, includes a chapter on the exhibition. The Swedish Museum of Architecture has published a book, *Funktionalismens genombrott*

och kris: svenskt bostadsbyggande 1930–80 [Functionalism's breakthrough and crisis: Swedish residential building 1930–80] (1980), which takes the exhibition as its starting point. The museum also has published a more recent anthology on twentieth-century Swedish architecture, *Att bygga ett land* [To Build a Country] (1998) that includes two chapters by Rudberg that contextualize the exhibition in light of Sweden's architectural trends and socio-political developments. Finally, the Museum of Architecture in Stockholm has a rich archive of materials from the exhibition itself, including photographs, catalogs, design sketches, news reports, and memorabilia.

Paris 1931

Marc Lagana

Exposition Coloniale Internationale

The French empire had an important place in national and international expositions from the beginning of the Third Republic. Great expositions such as those held in Paris in 1889 and again in 1900, as well as the colonial expositions of 1906 and 1922 in Marseille, exposed millions of visitors to the economic, political, social and cultural dimensions of colonial imperialism. The promotion of empire, and with it the idea of a "greater France," reached its zenith with the International Colonial Exposition of Paris in 1931.

For the French colonialists, whose multiple political and cultural associations and powerful economic organizations made up the colonial party, national and international expositions were a privileged moment in the promotion of empire. Not surprisingly, members of the colonial party were very much involved in the conception and organization of the 1931 exposition. In every way the International Colonial Exposition of 1931 corresponded to the objectives pursued by the French colonial party: to show what France had accomplished

in its colonies and what the colonies had given France, thus providing a justification for empire and building an imperial consciousness. The French government, and the colonialists in general, wanted to convince the French public of the economic potential represented by the colonial empire, especially in an era of economic crisis. Thus the exposition became a propitious event to present the colonies as a fertile ground for economic development.

When the inauguration of the International Colonial Exposition finally took place in May 1931, after five years of intensive preparations, the entire colonial world could be proud of the achievement. Most of the colonial empires were present on the impressive Vincennes site in the east end of Paris. But the British government had pleaded financial constraints in order to justify a very limited participation in the exposition, while Spain, Germany, and Japan simply refused to participate. The other European colonial powers (the Netherlands, Portugal, Belgium, Italy, Denmark) and the United States each had its own national pavilion.

The French empire took up most of the 148 acres of the Vincennes site. At the entrance of the exposition, visitors were welcomed by an imposing international information center that housed all the data on the exposition and offered a number of activities, including permanent film projections in a 1,500-seat auditorium (80 kilometers of film had been produced just on the French colonies for the occasion). Moreover, businessmen could obtain practical information on the colonies and the various agencies dealing with colonial matters.

Visitors could view many different facets of the French empire in the exposition's museum. In order to inform and educate public opinion, a major objective of the exposition, the museum offered a full retrospective on French colonial history since the Crusades. It also showed the colonial influence on French literature, art, and music. The museum's prominent themes included the educational effort made by various establishments, such as the Ecole colonial in Paris, the provincial institutes, and the technical and professionl schools in the colonies. The general commissioner of the exposition and past colonial administrator, Marshal Hubert Lyautey, gave a substantial place to the religious missions as well as the military in the museum. Moreover, in order to underline their role in the colonization process and the triumph of empire, Lyautey had encouraged the construction of independent pavilions for the Catholic and Protestant missions as well as for the Army and the Navy. Today, the museum, which is the work of the architects Leon Jaussely and Albert Laprade, remains a permanent symbol of the 1931 exposition.

Beyond the information pavilion and the museum, the new and fabulous world of the colonies unfolded before the eyes of the visitor with the Grande Avenue des Colonies. Among the numerous themes at the exposition, the most pervasive and constant clearly was the economic dimension of empire. Thus there appeared, in a variety of forms, multiple colonial economic activities.

Aside from the colonial business groups, the metropolitan business community played a significant role in the exposition. Not only did it make a major contribution to the organization of the exposition, but a variety of enterprises also had their own impressive exhibitions, including a number of pavilions. At the Palace of Industrial Groups, the latest products of the electrical, metallurgical, mechanical, automo-

tive, and chemical industries—along with many more—found a prominent place. The luxury trades were also present, In fact, a special pavilion had been built to house beauty products, jewelry, fashion, and other consumer products. The textile industry had a large window on the Vincennes site, exhibiting numerous items dear to colonial trade, such as clothes, threads, and fabrics.

Exhibits of colonial industrial and agricultural products stressed the commercial relations between France and its colonies. Each colony naturally wanted to demonstrate its particular value to France and thus expand its trade and attract investments. The various exploitable primary products, the agricultural resources, the progress of public works (along with graphics of rail and road networks, maquettes of harbors, and the like), and data on the state of the local economy and the development of trade since the beginning of the century were displayed in every colonial pavilion.

Beyond this wealth of information offered by the colonial governments, industrial, public works, financial and commercial enterprises held their own exhibitions. The pavilion for Algeria contained about 400 exhibits by local enterprises, Morocco had 224, and Tunisia 220. Even for the French colonies south of the Sahara, where business was less active, 72 enterprises had a stand in the French West Africa pavilion and 33 in the French Equatorial Africa pavilion, while Madagascar and Indochina had their share.

In general, the colonial pavilions were colorful and demonstrated artistic imagination. Such was the case with the Indochinese temples designed by the firm of Charles and Gabriel Blanche, under the general supervision of Joseph Albert Tournaire (1862–1958), chief architect for the 1931 exposition. At the heart of the Indochinese complex, which took up a tenth of the Vincennes site, stood a replica of the Cambodian Angkor Wat temple. The massive central building with its five life size towers (as high as 53 meters), dominated the colonial exposition site, thus symbolizing not only the prestige and wealth of Indochina among the colonies but also French imperial power. At the center of the 5,000 square meters temple, visitors could admire the opulence and economic potential of Indochina through the elaborate exhibits of its products and the presence of its

The 1931 Paris exposition featured the achievements of France's colonial empire. The Morocco pavilion contained displays from more than 200 Moroccan enterprises (from a presentation album for the 1931 exposition).

enterprises, as well as its rich artistic and ethnographic heritage.

The exposition featured numerous special attractions. For the purpose of authenticity, ritual processions and religious ceremonies were organized on a regular basis. Frequent concerts brought music from all parts of the empire to the exposition, and African and Indochinese dances were regularly scheduled. At night the moving and colorful lights—to which fireworks would often be added—of the Vincennes site offered a dazzling background for these performances. Another sort of special attraction were the native villages constructed for the occasion, and the use everywhere of colonial natives as extras. The zoological garden, a living museum of exotic animals, attracted much attentions with over 5 million visitors, and remains today one of the few relics from the exposition.

Conservatively estimating at least 8 million visitors, most contemporaries considered the exposition a tremendous success. Indeed, the ordinary citizen could not help but be impressed by the exposition as well as informed on the empire. The exposition had an even wider impact throught the simultaneous proceedings of 200 congresses and symposiums, including the congress of the International Institute of African Languages and Civilizations, one on intercolonial transportation, and another on the National Congress on Cotton and Natural Fibers. These events fostered the exchange of ideas and the circulation of information among all those interested in the future of the empire and allowed debate on colonial policy as well as on the multiple problems— especially those dealing with energy, transportation and agriculture—facing the empire in those years of economic and political crisis.

The International Colonial Exposition of 1931 demonstrated the economic and political

This replica of the temple of Angkor-Wat was probably the most impressive colonial pavilion at the 1931 Exposition Coloniale Internationale in Paris (editors' collection).

A view from the rear of the Cambodian pavilion, showing the towers of Angkor Wat in the background (from a presentation album for the 1931 exposition).

success of French colonial imperialism. The empire had a world dimension second only to the British, and trade, production, and even investments and experienced continuous, even if often modest, growth. Moreover, the 3,000 reports produced by the congresses and symposiums represented the most complete contemporary knowledge on the colonies, placing the colonial economy squarely in the service of the mother country, and thus offering a veritable colonial charter for the future development of the empire. Finally, the exposition educated public opinion, stimulated the imagination of ordinary citizens, and offered the world an imperial vision of "greater France,"all of which operated as a dynamic symbol of the French republic and contributed to the national myth of France's conqering destiny.

The view of some of the detail of the Cambodian pavilion shows the care with which architects designed fair buildings, even though they were, for the most part, only temporary structures (from a presentation album for the 1931 exposition).

Bibliography

The principal archival sources for the International Colonial Exposition of Paris are located in the Section Outre-Mer of the French National Archives, which contains reports on all aspects of the exposition, as well as detailed information on the preparations for each colonial section, the pavilions, the exhibits, and other attractions. They are catalogued under Agence de la France Outre-Mer (FOM). See, notably, FOM, box numbers 527–28, 530, 538–39, 544, 824, 829. 832, 873, 892, 948. The Section Outre-Mer also holds the papers of the Service de Liaison avec les Originaires des Territoires d'Outre-Mer (SLOTFOM). In these records may be found much information on anti-colonial groups and activities, along with numerous reports concerning natives from the French colonies at the time of the exposition. See SLOT-FOM, série III, especially box 5. The U.S. National Archives contains primary sources concerning U.S. participation in the exposition. These include the records of the Commission Representing the United States at the International Colonial Exposition at Paris in 1931. In particular, consult the General Correspondence files for 1930–1932, especially the correspondance of C. Bascom Slemp (the commissioner general), and the Record of Disposition or Shipment exhibits, 1931–1932 (see Record Group 43).

A basic published primary source on the exposition is the *Rapport général*, by Governor General Marcel Olivier, titled *Exposition colonial internationale de Paris*, 5 vols. (1933). This monumental work contains a complete catalog and description of the exposition, its organization, historical background, and objectives, along with a detailed description of each section. Furthermore, *Les Enseignements généraux de l'exposition coloniale* (1932) by Du Vivier de Streel, a major figure in the French colonial party, contains a contemporary analysis of the educational and ideological dimensions of the exposition.

Among secondary sources, Catherine Hodier and Pierre Michel, *L'Exposition coloniale* (1991) is the best short synthesis on the 1931 exposition and an excellent reference work. Charles-Robert Ageron, *France coloniale ou parti colonial?* (1978), contains an insightful analysis of the colonial exposition's impact, notably on public opinion, and provides an overview of colonial France. Ageron also discusses the mythic nature of the fair in "L'Exposition coloniale de 1931: mythe républicain ou mythe impérial?" in Pierre Nora (ed.), *Les Lieux de mémoire*, vol. 1: *La République* (1982). Raoul Girardet also mentions the exposition in his analysis of French colonialism, *L'Idée coloniale en France, 1871–1962* (1972). Patricia Morton, *Hybrid Modernities: Architecture and Representation at the 1931 Colonial Exposition* (2000) offers a detailed discussion of the various architectural styles and what they were intended to signify. Panivong Norinder, "Representing

Indochina : The French Colonial Fantasmatic and the Exposition Coloniale de Paris," *French Cultural Studies* 6, 1 (1995) : 35–60, deals specifically with one French colony. On the occasion of the fiftieth anniversary of the fair, Jean-Pierre Gomane briefly surveyed the French colonial experience in "L'Héritage colonial: souvenirs d'une exposition," in *Études* (June 1981), while Thomas August dwelt on the same theme in "The Colonial Exposition in France (1931) : Education or Reinforcement?" *Proceedings of the 6th and 7th Annual Meetings of the French Colonial Historical Society* (1980–1982). A short descriptive article by Arthur Chandler, "The Exposition Coloniale internationale de Paris 1931," appeared in *World's Fair* 8, 4 (Fall 1988):15–20. *L'Impérialisme à la française, 1914–1960* (1986), by Jean Bouvier, René Girault, and Jacques Thobie, is a lucid discussion of the nature of French colonial imperialism and offers a conceptual and historical framework for understanding an event such as the colonial exposition. There is also the work *Le Parti colonial français: éléments d'histoire* (1990), by Marc Lagana. For the most recent general works on French colonial imperialism see Françoise Vergès et al., *La République coloniale* (2003), and Pascal Blanchard, Nicolas Bancel, and Sandrine Lemaire, *La Fracture coloniale: La Société française au prisme de l'héritage colonial* (2005).

Chicago 1933–1934

John E. Findling

A Century of Progress Exposition

The idea for an international exposition to celebrate the centennial of the founding of Chicago was suggested by various civic leaders in the mid–1920s, and on April 8, 1926, Mayor William L. Dever called a meeting to create a planning body. Mayor William H. Thompson, who replaced Dever in 1927, initially rejected the idea of a fair but was persuaded to change his mind, and planning resumed in December 1927. In January 1928, a board of directors was formed with Rufus G. Dawes, an oilman and brother of former vice-president Charles G.

Dawes, as chairman. In April 1929, the board chose Lenox R. Lohr, a retired army officer, as general manager of the fair. Lohr and his administrative assistant, Martha McGrew, ran the day-to-day operations of the fair with great order and efficiency, and in the process, preserved every scrap of paper for posterity.

While the official name of the fair, A Century of Progress, was not formally adopted until June 1929, the notion of using as a theme the scientific and industrial progress over the century since Chicago's founding dated from at least 1927. In the fall of that year, Dawes held the first of a series of meetings with represen-

A CENTURY OF PROGRESS! — CHICAGO 1933

Different people interpreted the idea of "Century of Progress" in different ways (editors' collection)

tatives of the National Research Council, a little-known organization created in 1916 to facilitate cooperation among science, industry, and the military. After World War I. The council had become an agency to coordinate scientific research in industry and academia and, in general, to promote (the benefits of science to humanity and the corporate state. Clearly, to focus a major world's fair on this theme would suit the council's objectives. During the planning process, the Science Advisory Committee, created by the National Research Council and funded by the fair corporation, provided a great deal of input on what should be exhibited in the areas of pure and applied science. The idea of having cooperative industrial exhibitions arranged along thematic lines was dropped in favor of letting larger industries prepare exhibits and, in some cases, entire pavilions, on their own; industrial giants such as General Motors and Sears, Roebuck and Company were willing to pay to have their own pavilions because of the highly favorable publicity that would be generated. By the time the fair opened in 1933, the trauma of the Great Depression

made the positive, upbeat theme of scientific progress even more popular among visitors.

Early on, fair planners decided to finance the exposition independent of government subsidization. Instead, an array of innovative schemes was used to raise funds. Beginning in April 1928, the public was invited to purchase for five dollars a certificate of membership in the Chicago World's Fair Legion, good for ten admissions to the fair: $634,000 was raised in this manner, as well as a great deal of free publicity, significant because the board of directors had decided to avoid paid advertising, and let the newsworthiness of their activities publicize the exposition

A much more important source of funds was a $10 million bond issue, secured by 40 percent of the gate receipts, that ironically was announced one day before the stock market crash in October 1929. Despite the unfortunate timing, about $7.74 million of bonds had been subscribed by June 1932, and about $6.11 million actually paid in, providing sufficient funds to pay for the construction of the Hall of Science, the Travel and Transport building, and the Electric Group. Exhibit space in these buildings was offered to industry, which paid nearly $2 million. In addition, some $3 million in concession contracts came from fifteen food, transportation, and entertainment providers. The federal government appropriated $1 million for the erection of a pavilion and an official government exhibit, and 18 participating states paid out another million dollars for their exhibits. Virtually every observer commented favorably on the careful financial planning done for the Century of Progress exposition.

From the beginning, the board was determined to site the fair on parkland along Lake Michigan and land reclaimed from the lake just south of Chicago's Loop. The state legislature

This night view of the Hall of Science highlights the Art Deco features of the exposition architecture (from a presentation album for the 1934 season of the Century of Progress Exposition).

gave its approval in June 1929, and the fair was built on a 427-acre strip of land, seldom wider than a quarter of a mile, that stretched 3 miles from Twelfth Street down to Thirty-Ninth Street. Included in the site were two large lagoons that occupied about 86 acres.

Rufus Dawes and the fair board appointed an Architectural Commission to design the buildings for the fair. Not since Chicago's previous fair in 1893 had a world's fair enjoyed the services of so many of the nation's most distinguished architects. Daniel H. Burnham, son of the man responsible for the architecture of the 1893 fair, was the commission secretary, and the other members included Edward H. Bennett. Arthur Brown. Jr. Hubert Burnham, Harvey Wiley Corbett, Paul Philippe Cret, John A. Holabird, Raymond Hood, and Ralph T. Walker. Joseph Urban, a well-known stage set designer, was named director of color, and Louis Skidmore, and Nathaniel Owings, later to become two-thirds of the noted architectural firm of Skidmore, Owings, and Merrill, were in charge of exhibit design and concessions, respectively.

Given that the theme of the fair was scientific progress and that the members of the commission had been identified with the beginnings of modern architecture in the United States, it is not surprising that the decision was made to avoid a derivative classical style of architecture and build instead on the precedents of the Bauhaus and the successful modernism seen in the Paris 1925, Barcelona 1929, and Paris 1931 fairs. Not only did such unornamented and generally functional architecture seem to suit the times and the theme of the exhibition well, but also it was economical to build. The fifteen-cent per cubic foot cost was less than the cost of some buildings for the World's Columbian Exposition in 1893.

Fair buildings were constructed very simply by using ½-inch wallboard over a steel framework and, for the most part, shunning the use of windows. The lack of windows freed exhibitors from worrying about the vagaries of daylight illumination, provided more interior space for exhibits, and saved money. In place of applied ornamentation, the commission decided to use color and illumination to provide the desired decorative scheme, and Urban's color palette consisted of 23 intensely bright colors, usually three or four to a building, with black, white, blue, and orange predominating. The color scheme also utilized a zoning principle, with the same color scheme used for related groups of buildings or exhibits in order to help visitors find their way around. Exterior lighting was handled cooperatively by Westinghouse and General Electric and consisted of a variety of functionally designed fixtures that provided white light at ground level and colored light coordinated with the buildings at higher levels.

Most of the fair buildings had some kind of distinctive architectural feature, often a tower or pylons. The Federal Building, for example, had three such pylons rising 150 feet into the air and representing the three branches of the federal government. The General Motors Building, designed by Albert Kahn, boasted a 177-foot tower, and the Electrical Building had two 100-foot pylons framing a water gate through which visitors could enter by boat after crossing the lagoon. The most distinctive building from a design and engineering standpoint was the Travel and Transport Building, which featured a domed roof suspended 125 feet high by cables attached to twelve steel towers around the exterior perimeter of the building. This provided an interior exhibition space of over 200 feet, uncluttered by columns or interior load-bearing walls. The dome was made with expansion joints, which allowed it to rise or fall by as much as 18 inches, depending on the weather.

The commission was pleased with its work. Harvey Wiley Corbett, the chairman of the commission, remarked, "The fair stands as a symbol of the architecture of the future — the icons of the past cast aside, the ingenuity of the designers of the present thrown on their own resources to meet the problems of the day. But many other architects scorned the Century of Progress design. Frank Lloyd Wright, whose checkered past had denied him a place on the

A view of some of the detail of the Travel and Transport Building, the most innovative structure on the site (from a presentation album for the 1934 season of the Century of Progress Exposition).

commission, said, "There is nothing in the fair except wholesale imitation, hit or miss," and Ralph Adams Cram, the dean of neo-Gothic architecture, termed the fair architecture "a casual association of the gasometer, the freight-yard, and the grain elevator." Clearly there were some design problems The irregular site, with its lagoons, made it all but impossible for the architects to plan a coherent layout comparable to that employed at most previous fairs. The fair buildings, while colorful and built according to the same construction scheme, often did not relate well with their neighbors. And the entire scale of the fair and its buildings was badly damaged by the looming presence of the Sky-Ride, with its 628-foot-high steel towers bisecting the site and destroying its sense of proportion.

Louis Skidmore and the exhibits committee emphasized their desire to show processes in action rather than static machines. It was also decided to encourage innovation by eliminating any competition for blue ribbons. Exhibits, especially those in basic science and medicine, were understandable even by the uneducated, while applied science exhibits leaned heavily toward miniaturized or replicated processes. Visitors could see an operating oil refinery, an automobile assembly line, a radio-controlled tractor, and a toothpaste tube-packing demonstration. Other exhibitors employed film, talking dioramas, and pageants using actors.

There were a number of exhibits of special significance. "The World a Million Years Ago" featured six dioramas and lifelike dinosaurs and other prehistoric animals. The Golden Temple of Jehol, the summer residence of Manchurian emperors, was reproduced in 28,000 pieces in China and sent to Chicago for assembly. Chicago's history was reflected in reconstructions of Fort Dearborn and the cabin of Jean Baptiste Point du Sable, the first person to settle in the Chicago area, whose black ancestry provided a focal point for some mild protests against racial discrimination.

Foreign participation in (the Century of Progress was originally encouraged by a delegation of fair officials who toured Europe in the fall of 1930 and established an office in London run by Sir Henry Cole. a veteran fair organizer who had played a major role in Britain's Wembley fair of 1924–1925. In January 1931, the Bureau of International Expositions gave its consent for members to participate in the Century of Progress, but problems arose with respect to America's high tariff rates and European resistance to the fair board's suggestion that foreign exhibits be designed to attract American tourists rather than display scientific progress or industrial products. Eventually Congress allowed foreign merchandise for display to enter duty free but demanded that customs duties be paid on items sold. Meanwhile, Belgium built a model village as a means of attracting tourists; it was so successful in 1933 that several other nations did the same for the 1934 season. Among foreign participants, China, Czechoslovakia, Italy, Japan, Sweden, and the Ukraine had their own pavilions, while other nations exhibited in a Hall of Nations located in the Travel and Transport Building.

A view of the detail of the Travel and Transport Building at the Century of Press Exposition reveals the severe geometry of the fair architecture (from a presentation album for the 1934 season of the Century of Progress Exposition).

In addition to the domestic and foreign exhibits, the Century of Progress offered art lovers an expan-

Exposition planners wanted to emphasize process rather than finished products, as exemplified by this picture of women bottling Canadian Club whiskey at the fair (editors' collection).

The Century of Progress Exposition marked the centennial of Chicago's founding in 1833. Fort Dearborn was the first building in Chicago and a replica was constructed for the fair (editors' collection).

sive show held at the Art Institute on Michigan Avenue, a few blocks north of the fairgrounds. An agreement was made in June 1932 by which the Art Institute would provide and conduct an art exhibit connected with the fair and have control over the selection and display of works exhibited. In return, the fair board agreed to give the Art Institute 20 percent of any surplus remaining at the end of the fair. This arrangement spared the board from having to build a fireproof, secure structure for an art show without which it could not have obtained loans of important works of art.

The art exhibit theme for 1933 was "A Century of Progress in American Collecting," which brought together an assemblage of works, all but one borrowed from private collectors in the United States. In 1934, the theme was simply "American Art," seen in the context of world art. The exhibit showed masterpieces borrowed from Europe, including many works of the French impressionists, which set off a survey of American art from the Revolutionary era to the twentieth century. Special attention was paid to James McNeill Whistler, whose centenary was being celebrated, and to Thomas Eakins and Winslow Homer, considered among the most important of all American artists. Just under 3 million visitors paid a twenty-five cent fee to see the art exhibits in 1933 and 1934.

Special attractions of an entertainment nature were a staple at the Century of Progress. The Sky-Ride, with its giant towers, transported visitors 1,850 feet across the fairgrounds in "rocket cars" 200 feet above the ground. The Enchanted Island was a 5-acre playground for children that also functioned as a day-care center for parents who wanted to see the fair free from requests to buy cotton candy or find the bathroom. The Midway included such attractions as Spoofs Spectaculars, with giant movie screens and 64-mm films: the Odditorium, with exhibits from Ripley's "Believe It or Not"; Bring 'Em Back Alive, the well-known Frank Buck wild animal show; and Midget Village, where sixty midgets lived in tiny houses and put on plays and other entertainment.

Among the entertainment at the fair, the most controversial was Sally Rand and her fan dance, a revealing act that tested the moral scruples of midwestern fair officials and visitors from all parts of the nation. Rand, who was born Helen Gould Beck in Hickory County, Missouri, was a former Kansas City model, silent movie actress, and vaudevillian before entering the world of burlesque in the early 1930s, where she found steady work and plenty of notoriety. For the fan dance, she completely covered her nude body with white "cosmetic whitewash" and powder and then danced behind two large feathery fans. At the end of her performance, she raised her fans high, revealing her entire body, which, with the whitewash and powder, made her look much like an alabaster statue. Although she began dancing at the fair and at downtown clubs in late May, she was not arrested until August 4, at which time she was fined $25 and told to wear clothes beneath her fans. Arrested again on September 23, she was fined $200 and sentenced to a year in jail, but the case was dismissed on appeal, and her popularity was enhanced by virtue of the publicity. At the beginning of the 1934 season, fair directors announced their intention of raising the cultural level of the entertainment presented, but by July, Sally Rand was back again, this time in a "bubble dance," with a 5-foot semitransparent bubble.

The Century of Progress Exposition did not shy from lending its name or association with a large number of special events and special days, both on and off the fairgrounds. The first major league baseball all-star game was played at nearby Comiskey Park, the home of the Chicago White Sox, on July 6, 1933. Five college football games were played at Soldier Field, adjacent to the fairgrounds, in the fall of 1933, and a national boys' marbles championship was held there as well. The National Roque League staged the annual tournament of this croquet-like sport in early August as a collateral event to the fair. The Chicago Symphony, under the direction of Frederick A. Stock, presented a series of concerts for fairgoers, and public school bands and choruses seemingly never ceased performing.

At the fair, most states and many ethnic groups had their own special days, and fair officials designated still other days as special for one reason or another. To commemorate the end of prohibition, the fair provided free beer and sandwiches on November 8. Fifty thousand visitors showed up, drank 1,000 barrels of beer, and ate almost 200,000 sandwiches

One of the attractions at the Century of Progress was the Goodyear blimp which took visitors on short flights (editors' collection).

on that day, dubbed Personal Responsibility Day. On November 10, all people on relief rolls were admitted free upon presentation of their identity card.

Between May 27, when Postmaster General James A. Farley officially opened the fair, and November 12, when the 1933 season closed, a total of 22,320,456 visitors attended; another 245,403 tickets were sold but not used, making the grand total of ticket sales 22,565, 859. In October 1933, the fair board decided to open the exposition for a second season. Although all agreed that the fair had been a success and that it would be a shame not to take advantage of the expertise gained during the first season, the principal reason for reopening was to enable the bondholders to be paid off in full, since receipts for 1933 had fallen short of that goal. Support came from state and city governments, and most of the industrial exhibitors renewed their contracts for 1934, while new ones, including the Ford Motor Company, were added.

In most respects, the 1934 version of the Century of Progress was similar to the 1933 one. Physically, some changes were made to the

entryways, the lagoons, and the lighting. Joseph Urban had died, and his successor, Otto Teegen, adopted a new, simpler exterior color scheme but one still based on bright, intense colors. The success of the Belgian Village led other nations to construct their own model villages, featuring typical food, drink, and entertainment. In general, exhibitors relied more on dramatized entertainment or live demonstrations then they had in 1933. Chrysler used its quarter-mile track for stock car races, and Standard Oil Company replaced its film on the oil industry with a free wild animal act, called "Cage of Fury." Hupmobile placed would-be drivers in front of a film that reacted to their driving skills, and the Safety Glass demonstration invited visitors to throw a rock at a window. Armour meatpacking used "auburn-haired beauties" in a bacon slicing and wrapping exhibit, and even Petrolagar, a laxative, enjoyed popularity with a diorama showing a doctor treating a critically ill child.

The most significant addition to the 1934 Century of Progress was the Ford Motor Company pavilion, a 900-foot-long building with a rotunda in the center displaying a 20-foot globe indicating Ford's international operations. On the walls of the rotunda was a mural by Walter Dorwin Teague, a noted industrial designer, showing an automobile assembly plant. The pavilion contained the Industrial Hall, showing Ford's latest technological innovations, and the Industrial Barn, containing farm machinery and a replica of Henry Ford's father's barn as it was in 1863, the year of Ford's birth. The Detroit Symphony played daily in a band shell located in a garden setting in front of the pavilion; the garden was inside a 2,000-foot oval with 21 sections representing different historic highways. The Ford exhibit occupied 11 acres, cost a reported $5 million to produce, and received the personal attention of Henry Ford in most of its detail. It paid off, however, as 70 percent of the daily visitors toured the pavilion, making ii the most popular of the 1934 season.

On the last day of the fair, October 31, 1934, nearly 375,000 visitors came. The mayor declared a half-holiday for city workers, and many businesses and schools were closed. That day, the fair received its sixteen-millionth visitor of the year, a Chicago grandmother making her fiftieth visit, and bestowed a truckload of gifts upon her, including 5 acres of land and a monkey. Late in the evening, a near riot ensued as visitors, sensing the finality of the fair, spontaneously began disassembling and taking with them fair fixtures and anything else portable that seemed a likely souvenir. Police were called in, and many people were forced to leave their prizes behind, but only one arrest was made — a man had wrapped a toilet seat in an American flag and was charged with desecration of the flag. Since most of what the fairgoers had tried to take was scheduled for demolition anyway, the actual damage amounted to only about $5,000. Altogether, the 1934 season saw ticket sales of 16,486,377, with actual attendance of slightly over 16 million. The city council, recognizing the continuing popularity of the fair, passed a resolution authorizing the formation of a committee to explore ways in which the Century of Progress could be maintained as a permanent attraction for tourists. The committee was also assigned the task of raising $2.5 million to reopen the fair on a sound financial footing. The fair board, however, discouraged such plans, asserting that "the orange has been squeezed dry" and nothing ever came of the council's resolution.

The Century of Progress Exposition ended its two-year run with a surplus of $688,165, out of which demolition, future claims, and corporate dissolution expenses had to be paid. Most of the buildings were torn down, although the fair's administration building served the same function for Chicago's parks for a number of years. The final profit amounted to $160,000, with the South Park Corporation and the Museum of Science and Industry each receiving 25 percent, the Art Institute 20 percent, and the Adler Planetarium 10 percent. The remaining 20 percent was divided among a number of other participating groups.

By most standards, the Century of Progress Exposition was a success. It was carefully financed and turned a profit, even during a period of national economic crisis. Although many contemporary architects had serious reservations about the style of the fair's buildings, the bold and colorful architecture sustained the modernist movement and showed its influence in the streamline style of industrial design in the 1930s and in the architecture of the New York World's Fair of 1939–1940. Finally, the fairyland architecture and futuristic exhibits based on the theme of scientific progress were, for most visitors, a vehicle that transported them for a day out of the real world of unemployment, bread lines, and human misery. It was, almost literally, a dream world on the shores of Lake Michigan.

Bibliography

The official records of the Century of Progress Exposition are housed in the Special Collections Department of the library at the University of Illinois at Chicago. These records include correspondence, reports, minutes of meetings, legal and financial records, press releases, clippings, photographs, blueprints, and other material relevant to all phases of the fair. There is an unpublished guide to these records available at the library.

The Chicago *Tribune* and other Chicago newspapers covered the fair on a daily basis and are a source for detailed information on special days and events. The official guide to the fair was called *Book of the Fair*. Nearly 200 pages in length, it provided a comprehensive overview for visitors. Contemporary magazines published an abundance of articles on all aspects al the fair, and some are quite useful. For the architecture of the fair, see E.H. Klaber, "World's Fair Architecture," *American Magazine of Art* 26 (June 1933): 292–98; Arthur F. Woltersdorf, "Carnival Architecture," *American Architect* 143 (July 1933): 10–20; and "Branding the Buildings at the Chicago Fair," *Literary Digest* (August 12. 1933): 14. A recent book on the same subject is Lisa D. Schrenk, *Building a Century of Progress: The Architecture of Chicago's 1933–34 World's Fair* (2007). "Science and the Century of Progress Exposition in 1934," *Scientific Month/v* 39 (November 1934): 475–78, is a useful summary, and J. Parker Van Zandt and L. Robe Walter, "King Customer at a Century of Progress." *Review of Reviews* (September 1934): 22–27, presents some interesting insights on the changes made for the 1934 season. Finally, Rufus C. Dawes. in his *Report of the President of a Century of Progress to the Board of Trustees* (l936), and Lenox R. Lohr, the general manager of the fair, in *Fair Management: A Guide for Future Fairs* (1952), present detailed accounts of their roles in the planning and execution of the Century of Progress Exposition.

There has been relatively little historical research done on the Century of Progress. Most recent histories of Chicago give only passing mention to the fair, and John Allwood, *The Great*

Exhibitions 1977), also surveys it. Robert W. Rydell, in "The Fan Dance of Science: American World's Fairs in the Great Depression," *Isis* 76 (December 1985): 525–42, explains the important work of the National Research Council in establishing and carrying out the theme of scientific progress. Rydell gives a more complete picture of the fair in *World of Fairs: The Century of Progress Expositions* (1993), as does John E. Findling in *Chicago's Great World's Fairs* (1994). Cheryl Ganz, *A New Deal for Progress: The 1933 Chicago World's Fair* (2008) is the first full-length book devoted completely to all aspects of the Century of Progress. The relationship of black Chicagoans to the fair is described in "Negro Protest at the Chicago's World's Fair," *Journal of the Illinois State Historical Society* 59 (Summer 1966): 161–71, by August Meier and Elliott M. Rudwick. And, finally, in "The Lost City of the Depression," *Chicago History* 4 (Winter l976–1977): 233–42, Cathy Cahan and Richard Cahan provide a retrospective view of the lair through the reminiscences of Martha McGrew, Lenox Lohr's assistant.

Two collateral works may also be of interest. The eminent historian Charles Beard was commissioned to edit a book outlining the advances of industry and applied science during the past century; the result was *A Century of Progress* (1933). David Mamet's play "The Water Engine," which is set in Chicago during the Century of Progress, was first produced in 1977.

Brussels 1935

Johan Lagae

Exposition Universelle et Internationale

Between April 27 and November 6, 1935, an estimated 20 million visitors toured the Brussels Universal and International Exposition, the third in a series of such events that the city had hosted since 1897. Initially planned in 1930 to celebrate the centennial of the Belgian nation, a honor that was finally bestowed on the cities of Antwerp and Liège, the Brussels fair coincided with the centennial of the inauguration of the first railroad in Belgium, as

well as with the fiftieth anniversary of the founding of the Congo Free State. The Brussels 1935 exposition was organized in a context of worldwide economical depression and political turmoil in Europe. More than the previous fairs in Belgium, the 1935 exposition was proclaimed by its organizers as a "leap of faith" and presented as a key instrument to counter economic hardship in Belgium by stimulating trade and creating jobs. The fair furthermore acted as a playground for the affirmation of national identities at a moment when Europe's political context was being shaped by the rise of Nazism in Germany, and the consolidation of Fascism in Italy and of Stalinism in the Soviet Union. While the Brussels fair lacked an iconic image of clashing nationalisms similar to the opposition of the German and Soviet pavilions at the 1937 Paris world's fair — in Brussels, Germany and the Soviet Union did not participate, and the United States and Japan were present only through non-official displays. National ideology was nevertheless explicitly downplayed at the 1935 exhibition. Even so, its optimism and its recurrent motto "peace among the races" would soon be silenced by the political realities of late 1930s Europe.

Brussels mayor Adolphe Max was one of the driving forces of the event, together with a series of Belgian personalities and entrepreneurs, most of whom had previous experiences with the organization of major expositions. While Brussels had already hosted two major exhibitions (1897 and 1910), all of them located on sites within the existing fabric of the city, Max saw the 1935 fair as a means to develop a new urban area, the so-called Plateau du Heysel, situated between the Royal Palace in Laken and the city. In 1926, the Belgian government had donated this site, a former property of King Leopold II who himself had envisioned it as a future residential area, to the city council. Large infrastructure works including a tram connection to the city center were executed to provide the area with all the necessary amenities required for its future function as a new neighborhood. In 1930, a new sports stadium had been completed as the first evidence of this future urban extension.

The designer of the stadium, Joseph Van Neck, also was the architect-in-chief of the 1935 exposition. His master plan for the fair drew both on Beaux-Arts planning principles and picturesque design. A central, monumental boulevard lined with the pavilions of the main participants and ending in a symmetrical vista on the imposing Grand Palais was combined with meandering routes and the inclusion of gardens and a large park, the layout of which was executed by a team of prominent landscape architects. At night, extensive use of artificial lighting of buildings and water fountains further enhanced the exhibition's fairy-like atmosphere of a "One and a Thousand Nights" landscape. To help visitors get around the immense 312-acre site, a circular tramway route was constructed, connecting various entry points to the fair ground.

Even if in the 1980s some architectural historians still termed the 1935 fair "not very original," it did offer an interesting survey of 1930s architecture with some striking achievements. Many national pavilions, such as those of France and the United Kingdom, were designed in a monumental, stripped classicism that was common in 1930s public architecture and was to dominate the appearance of the Paris 1937 fair. Fascist power Italy, present in Brussels with no fewer than 16 pavilions, opted for a more modern idiom. At the explicit demand of Mussolini, the official pavilion of the Italian section (the *Padiglione del Littorio*) was designed by Adalberto Libera and Mario de Renzi in box-like architectural style with four gigantic abstract *fasces* standing in front, reiterating their project for the Palazzo del Expositione of the 1932 Mostra della Revoluzione Fascista. The competition entry of Mies Van der Rohe for the German pavilion, which was never built, was an equally interesting example of contemporary monumental modern architecture representing national identity.

Some of the smaller nations in Europe opted for a more outspoken functionalist idiom, the purpose of which was to embody their democratic policy, as is the case in the Czechoslovakian and Scandinavian pavilions and in the elegant Swiss structure, with some interior decorations executed by Max Bill. Such formal language also characterized a large number of the commercial pavilions, such as the publicity pavilions designed by the prominent Belgian architect Louis-Herman De Koninck that were reminiscent of the fair architecture of the Stockholm Exposition of 1930. In other national pavilions, such as those of Greece, Egypt, and Palestine, national identity was represented by means of a regionalist formal language that referred to the so-called "traditional" or "authentic" vernacular styles of the country of origin. In colonial sections, such tendency towards regionalism was blended with an exoticism, turning these pavilions into architectural forms of "invented traditions." For instance, the official pavilion of the Belgian Congo, notwithstanding its Africanizing appearance and decorative schemes, by no means presented a genuine African vernacular.

The 1935 Brussels fair rehabilitated orna-

Mabel and Ted stop to pose for a picture in front of a fountain at the 1935 Brussels International Exposition (editors' collection).

mentation as a genuine means of architectural expression, and the *Livre d'Or* explicitly underlined the intense collaboration between architects, sculptors, painters, and typographers. Striking examples are the pavilions designed by Henri Lacoste, which have been described as some of the most sophisticated examples of Art Deco in Belgian architectural history, although they sometimes triggered ambivalent reactions. While Lacoste declared that the design of the Pavilion of Catholic Life was inspired by Byzantine church architecture, a prominent contemporary art critic decried it a "blasphemy" because its cupolas and minaret-like chimneys made it look like a mosque. The centerpiece of the exhibition, the *Grand Palais*, was an architectural hybrid. The ziggurat-shaped volume and the monumental classicist façade, designed by architect Joseph Van Neck, in fact completely masked the constructional *tour de force* achieved by engineer Louis Baes, who managed to create an immense column-free inner space by means of concrete *arches à trois routulles* spanning 282 feet (86 meters) with their center point at 97 feet (30 meters) above ground level.

With the tense political climate of the

mid–1930s, the exhibits at the Brussels fair were often instruments of nationalist propaganda, sometimes employing new visual strategies, as in the official Italian pavilion, where large-scale photomontages of the achievements of the Fascist regime were on display. At that time, however, world's fairs were also gradually shifting their focus toward appealing to an emerging consumer society. Hence, many of the national pavilions presented themselves as shop windows for products of their industries and crafts. The rather modest Finnish pavilion offered the most explicit example of this approach. Designed as a showcase for Finnish design (furniture, household utensils, and the like), one wing of the pavilion was nothing more than a display window geared towards exclusive observation from the outside. Products with a specific nationalist connotation got particular emphasis in the exhibits. A display of watches and clocks opened the Swiss pavilion, while in the interior of the Brazilian pavilion, completely dedicated to the country's national drink, coffee, high glazed columns full of coffee beans could be seen. Remarkable emphasis was put also on the theme of tourism, considered by many countries as a promising economic activity. In some cases, the choice of a regionalist

BULLETIN OFFICIEL DE L'EXPOSITION UNIVERSELLE
ET INTERNATIONALE DE BRUXELLES

AVEC PROGRAMME DU 21 AU 27 OCTOBRE

MET PROGRAMMA VAN 21 TOT 27 OCTOBER

OFFICIEEL BLAD DER ALGEMEENE
WERELDTENTOONSTELLING VAN BRUSSEL

1.50 FR. LE Nº HEBD.   19 OCTOBRE · Nº 50

The cover design of this program from the Brussels exposition shows the prevailing Art Deco style, even if the Italian pavilion that is shown is of a different style (courtesy Johan Lagae).

architecture of pavilions can in part be understood as a form of tourist propaganda, as in the Egyptian case, but more often this was done by means of appealing photomontages or dioramas, as in the Soprocol pavilion that was completely dedicated to promoting tourism in the Belgian Congo.

As the 1935 fair aimed at appealing to the masses, entertainment played a crucial role. The exhibition grounds contained a large amusement park, with a water chute, several roller coasters, an entire zoo, as well as educational presentations such as a demonstration of television. The exhibition grounds also contained a historical, albeit fictional, reconstruction of a part of seventeenth-century Brussels, complete with bars, restaurants and actors in historic costume. Called Old Brussels, this highly successful attraction continued the tradition of such habitat-displays at previous Belgian exhibitions. Several other habitat-displays were to be seen at the 1935 fair, such as a privately run Indian village and an African Souk, a reconstruction of a Moroccan market adjacent to the French colonial section. Throughout the event, historical and folkloristic parades and festivities were organized, the kind of activities in which Belgium had a long-standing tradition.

Organized and realized in a time of economic hardship, the 1935 fair bears some traces of limited financial means. In spite of being one of the key themes of the event, the presentation of the Belgian Congo gave many visitors an impression of *déjà vu*, because the colonial government had been reluctant to invest large sums in new displays. Nevertheless, in terms of attendance, the Brussels 1935 fair was a great success, the most visited exhibition in Belgium to date. The immense marketing machine developed for the event (illustrated press, radio broadcasting) no doubt forms part of the explanation for this success. Yet, the devaluation of the Belgian franc in March 1935 also had a major impact on attendance as it made traveling abroad too expensive for the majority of Belgian citizens, while it made Belgium an inexpensive destination for foreigners. Furthermore, some 300 congresses were organized in the context of the fair, bringing a large scientific and academic audience to the country.

In financial terms, the exhibit was considered a break-even operation, which in times of economic hardship could be called a success. Furthermore, economic conditions would considerably ameliorate in the years after the fair, although it remains difficult to assess to what extent this was actually due to the event itself. A continuing feeling of national mourning related to the death of King Albert I in 1934 and Queen Astrid during the fair, however, tempered the enthusiasm and national pride that was to be gained for Belgium as a result of the successful organization and good attendance.

The Brussels 1935 fair has left an important physical legacy, albeit more in terms of site than of buildings. While the fair formed the catalyzing force for developing the Heysel Plateau, the intended future use of the exhibition ground as a new urban area after the fair was never realized, due to economic limitations, the impact of World War II and other priorities in Brussels' urban policy. The site became reused and extended for the world's fair of 1958 and now forms a key exhibition and entertainment site for Belgium's capital city to date. The Grand Palais and some adjacent buildings still serve as exhibition spaces, while the stadium was renovated in 1994–95 and hosts major sports events. Currently, the site is mainly linked with Expo 58, which as the first postwar world's fair still acts as a powerful Belgian *lieu de mémoire*. Memories of the fascinating 1935 fair that highlighted the complexities of Europe (and the world) in the 1930s, on the contrary, have largely faded.

Bibliography

The archives of the former Commissariat Général de l'Exposition of the Brussels' 1935 fair are to be found in the State Archives in Brussels, and contain correspondence, drawings of various constructions, some visual documentation, etc.

Currently, no detailed inventory of these archives is published, but a handwritten document giving insight in the material can be consulted in the Reading Room. On specific sections, complementary archives are located elsewhere as, for instance, in the African Archives (Ministry of Foreign Affairs) that preserve detailed information on the organization and planning of the extensive section of the Belgian Congo. Original visual documents on the design of some of the pavilions can be found in the funds of specific architects preserved at the Archives d'Architecture Moderne in Brussels, which also hold a collection of printed sources on the fair in its library.

The event produced an immense array of published sources that form a crucial source for research. They can be found in various archives and public libraries in Belgium. Apart from the hard-to-find 3-volume *Rapport Général du Commissariat Général du Gouvernement* (1935), a wealth of both textual and visual information, is provided by the *Livre d'Or de l'Exposition Universelle et Internationale de Bruxelles 1935* (1937), as well as by the 52 issues of the *Bulletin Official de l'Exposition Universelle et Internationale de Bruxelles 1935* that appeared between August 1933 and November 1935. Numerous official guidebooks were published, most of them in French, and several participating countries produced their own catalogue (France, Great Britain, Brazil, Switzerland, for example). General accounts were provided in popular magazines, substantial ones being the theme issue on the 1935 fair by *L'Illustration* (June 1935) and the *Almanach illustré du Soir* (1936). Contemporary Belgian periodicals on art and architecture devoted much attention to the fair, especially *L'Emulation*, which had several contributions during 1935 on the design of a variety of pavilions. In addition, the exposition received substantial coverage in major Belgian and European newspapers.

Secondary sources and historical analysis remain scarce. Thomas Coomans presents a popular synthesis in *De Heizel en de wereldtentoonstellingen van 1935 en 1958* (1994). In his survey book, *World's Fairs* (1998) Erik Mattie underlines the architectural interest of the event, while this topic is also discussed in some book contributions by Françoise Deville and by Johan Lagae, who also wrote on 1930s Belgian Congo pavilions. A profound historical analysis of the overall organization of the fair and the section of the Belgian Congo in particular (paying attention to the contemporary political, economical, social and cultural context) is found in Philippe Delhalle's unpublished master's thesis "l'Exposition Universelle et internationale de Bruxelles 1935 et la participation du Congo Belge" (Université Catholique de Louvain, 1984). Two works place the 1935 Brussels exposition in the context of other Belgian and international fairs. See Paul Greenhalgh, *Ephemeral Vistas: Expositions Universelles, Great Exhibitions, and World's Fairs, 1851–1939* (1988), and A. Cocks and J. Lemmens, *Les Expositions universelles et internationals en Belgique de 1885 a 1958* (1958). Finally, a substantial visual documentation on the fair, with some general essays and a select number of brief texts on specific pavilions is available on a website produced at the Department of Architecture and Urban Planning of the Ghent University (Belgium) by Jef Vervoort and Johan Lagae under the supervision of Mil De Kooning (*http://archarch.ugent.expo35*).

San Diego 1935–1936

Matthew Bokovoy

California-Pacific International Exposition

In July 1934, San Diego decided to stage another world's fair to overcome the economic depression that had descended upon the city. San Diego thus joined a small company of American cities that had held both a Victorian and Century-of-Progress Exposition, such as Chicago, New York City, San Francisco, and Philadelphia. In 1931, local progressive leaders like George W. Marston, Carl Heilbron, Ernest Dort, and David C. Collier had tried to organize a municipal centennial fair for 1934 to commemorate the founding of San Diego civil government in 1834. The civic fair was meant to herald San Diego's Mexican heritage, but a conservative city council deemed the event too expensive, there was little local enthusiasm, and the leaders did not have enough political clout to organize the event.

It took an outsider to propose San Diego's Century-of-Progress Exposition. Scripps-Howard newspaperman Frank Drugan moved to San Diego after his home was destroyed in the Long Beach earthquake of 1933. Arriving in San Diego, he believed a world's fair might promote economic prosperity and uplift the collective morale of the city. The 1915 fair had promoted economic development and lifted San Diego out of the recession of 1907–09. The depression conditions in the city left 23,000 people unemployed in a city of roughly 150,000. With frequent labor protests and strikes, it was only the naval presence that kept San Diego somewhat stable. Drugan was a politically connected Angeleno in the Democratic party and a close personal friend of Franklin D. Roosevelt and Norman Davis, FDR's ambassador-at-large. He traveled to Chicago to visit the Century of Progress Exposition of 1933–1934 and inquire

about an exposition for San Diego. His friend, Cyrus McCormick, Jr., heir to the reaper corporation and a member of Santa Fe's Spanish Colonial Arts Society, introduced him to Paul Massman, the director of exhibits. Massman arranged for exhibitors at San Diego should there be a fair, and Drugan went to Washington, D.C. to meet with Jesse H. Jones, head of the Reconstruction Finance Corporation (RFC). Jones told him that the fair could procure a guaranteed note from the RFC to begin construction, should the event be run by competent staff.

Drugan received support from his contacts in San Diego, particularly congressman George Burnham and liberal Republican state senator Ed Fletcher, Jr. On July 24, 1934, San Diego businessmen met and named the event the California-Pacific International Exposition. The fair committee hired Zack Farmer, head of the Los Angeles 1932 Olympic Organizing Committee, to plan and organize the exposition. Oscar Cotton of the local All-Year-Club told his colleagues that the fair, "in addition to procuring profits, is intended to advertise San Diego," much as the first fair had done." With solid support from Gilbert A. Davidson and Frank Belcher, Jr., head of the Spreckels' corporations, Burnham and U.S. Senator Hiram Johnson lobbied Congress in front of the House Committee on Foreign Affairs. They told the committee the "exposition will tend to inspire national confidence and a higher appreciation of American institutions, stimulate business and industry, and assist the government in bringing a more abundant life to its people." Davidson especially assured the committee that Spanish and Mexican heritage would enliven the event "because it is desirable to make this a great California-Mexican affair" with participation of Mexico and Latin American nations.

Secretary of State Cordell Hull and Secretary of Agriculture Henry Wallace used their influence to support congressional recognition of the fair. After returning to San Diego, Burnham explained to city leaders that the world's fair would begin a "cycle of progress," and the "Federal Government should put up a building to the New Deal, explaining to people the great works that have been accomplished — by the various agencies — A, B, C, D of the Government." By March 1935, Burnham had received interest from Roosevelt himself, who was no stranger to San Diego. He had been instrumental in bringing the Eleventh Naval District to the city when he accompanied Josephus Daniels to the Panama-California Exposition in 1915 as assistant secretary of the Navy. The president released $350,000 for the California-Pacific International Exposition and $125,000 for a special federal building. With abundance as the theme of the fair and with the New Deal featured prominently, the exposition would portray a modernized version of the California Dream. An idealistic goal to be sure, the "culture of abundance" meant the productive capacities of the industrial economy would supply the goods and needs for ever more Americans, eliminating previous generations' experience of scarcity and want.

The California-Pacific International Exposition opened on May 29, 1935, with tens of thousands of visitors despite the depression doldrums. Completed in less than a year, the exposition had received $800,000 from the federal government and $1.2 million from private subscribers. The majority of exhibitors were drawn from both industrial and consumer enterprises, and many had prominent buildings and displays, such as the Ford Motor Pavilion, the Ford Bowl, the General Motors Building, the Standard Oil Tower, and the Firestone Singing Fountains. The Federal Building proved popular, as well as the Palace of Water and Transportation. All these buildings and displays belonged to the only new addition to Balboa Park, named the Palisades Group, and conceived by San Diego architect Richard Requa and his assistant Juan Larrinaga. By blending Art Deco and Mesoamerican styles, Requa believed the Palisades embodied modernism, "yet remain[ed] in historical harmony with the old buildings" created by Bertram G. Goodhue in 1915. Other exhibitions included the House of Pacific Relations, created by Frank Drugan, and meant to promote world peace, the Spanish Village, the Old Globe Theater, the Women's Palace, a nudist colony called "Zoro's Garden," the Gold Gulch, and the Federal Housing Administration's Palace of Better Housing that included two exhibits named "Modeltown" and "Modernization Magic." The popular entertainment area was known as the Zócalo, which contained entertainments like Crime Never Pays, Ripley's Believe-It-Or-Not, the End-of-the-Trail, the Hollywood Hall of Fame, Monsters Alive, a burlesque show called "Sensations," and a Midget City and Farm. The most popular entertainments, especially for young sailors, were the burlesque shows, Zoro's Garden, and the antics of Gold Gulch Gertie, who performed a Lady Godiva ride daily. During the 1936 season after some intrigue and a management shakeup, the Zócalo featured three shows by Fanchon and Marco to offer more wholesome, family oriented entertainments. Nonetheless, local authorities became chagrined when Sally Rand, the famous fan dancer who had achieved notoriety at the Century of Progress Exposition, performed numerous shows in the Lily Pond in April 1936.

Tourists and local visitors gravitated to certain exhibits, thus making them the most significant and popular. The Palace of Better Housing drew record crowds, since Modernization Magic and especially Modeltown showcased the latest federally approved housing designs and new twenty-year mortgages created by the National Housing Act of 1934. The Federal Housing Administration hoped to democratize housing and spur economic recovery, since America's housing stock had not kept up with demand during the 1920s. Among 56 miniature models of different home styles, the most popular were the "Mission Style" with red tile roofs and the "Santa Fe Style," an Americanized version of Pueblo Indian architecture. There were also other American regional styles, the avant-garde International Style, and a "developer vernacular" that resembled the drab and bare suburban home of today. Acclaimed architects, such as Richard Neutra, Reginald Johnson, Leland Fuller, George Adams, and the local modernists Kenneth Messenger and Antonio Ruocco, provided cutting edge designs as well,

The Ford Motor Pavilion also proved

Zoro's Gardens, a nudist colony, was a popular attraction along the midway at the California-Pacific Exposition (editors' collection).

This views shows the Palace of Better Housing with a lily pond in the foreground (editors' collection).

popular with audiences, especially the "Earth of Auto" display and a special historical automobile ride called "Roads of the Pacific," which re-created the roadside landscape of the world's imperial highways. "Earth to Auto" highlighted Henry Ford's nostalgic belief that agriculture would be a key supplier of materials to industry, telling audiences "a greater proportion of tomorrow's automobile will be produced on the farm," uniting both producers and consumers.

"Roads of the Pacific" recounted the imperial history of the Americas, asking visitors to imagine the "hurrying feet of conquerors; the stately tread of rulers followed by a long train of servants and retainers; the weary plodding of men and beasts loaded down with the burdens of commerce." Riding in a new Ford V-8, key to the company's new middle class image, one woman remembered how she and her friends went "traipsing around the world. And be back in about fifteen minutes." By displaying the new consumer tenor of industry, both federal and corporate exhibitors portrayed the theme of abundance, with equal parts of middle class entitlement and a faith in the restoration of industrial capitalism to health by their stewardship.

Beyond uplifting exhibits, visitors found Zoro's Garden, Sensations, and the Gold Gulch the most interesting popular entertainments. The Zoro's Garden nudists caused enough controversy locally that it likely kept the ailing San Diego *Herald,* the competitor to the *Union,* with enough front page copy to carry the paper through the depression. Queen Zorine, the first leader of the nudists, resented insinuations that the nudists were burlesque girls. While the burlesque shows were located on the Zócalo, Zoro's Garden was located in the canyon east of the Casa del Prado. Queen Zorine and George Barr, the exercise director of the colony, both believed the "Nudist program is perhaps the simplest in the world, and yet it takes intensive discipline and determination — And so when I give you the general points of our program, I mean day in and day out. One cannot be a Nudist intermittently." When the "fallen" evangelist Aimee Semple MacPherson came to the fair for speaking engagements in late July 1935, Zorine smelled a fraud and issued an invitation to the preacher, knowing full well it would be declined. Tired of the hypocrisy of local moral leaders, police censors, and poor management of the colony, Zorine resigned and left San Diego. "Queen Tanya" assumed leadership as the exhibit became transformed into a strip show, a form of male entertainment known as "cheesecake" that had developed in the 1920s. The local furor over the burlesque and strip shows of the Zócalo and Gold Gulch, surprisingly, forced the resignation of the entire Los Angeles management team. With too many residual, working class amusements, the new

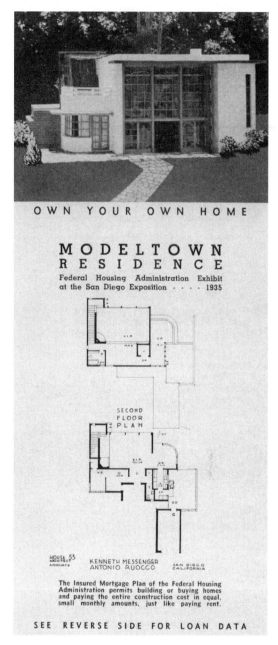

Kenneth Messenger and Antonio Ruocco's contribution to Modeltown, 1935 (courtesy Special Collections, San Diego Public Library).

team cleaned the Zócalo for middle class respectability.

The 1936 season of the California-Pacific International Exposition closed on September 9. Roughly 3.2 million people had visited during the two seasons of the event, and the first season left a cash surplus of $400,000, with the second season posting a $44,000 surplus. It had not been quite as successful as the Panama-California Exposition, but the fair brought steady employment for thousands of San Diegans due to the New Deal agency money that

OWN YOUR OWN HOME

**MODELTOWN
RESIDENCE**
Federal Housing Administration Exhibit
at the San Diego Exposition - - - - 1935

HOUSE I
ARCHITECT REGINALD D. JOHNSON LOS ANGELES

The Insured Mortgage Plan of the Federal Housing
Administration permits building or buying homes
and paying the entire construction cost in equal,
small monthly amounts, just like paying rent.

SEE REVERSE SIDE FOR LOAN DATA

Reginald Johnson's contribution to Modeltown, 1935 (courtesy Special Collections, San Diego Public Library).

financed the event. The exposition helped renovate and restore the original buildings in Balboa Park with the help of RFC and State Emergency Relief Administration money. The fair helped restore local faith in both the capitalist system and the nation. The powerful vision of America as a consumer democracy emerged through the regional promotion of the California Dream, stamped for approval by the federal government and corporate America. Through New Deal infrastructure, projects in California and branch plant industrial relocations from the east and midwest, the California Dream imagery fused with the theme of abundance at the fair to symbolize the high-wage, suburban, white collar, and consumer-oriented industrial democracy that awaited the United States after World War II. Like similar Century-of-Progress Expositions in Chicago, San Francisco, and New York, the California-Pacific International Exposition previewed the American Dream for millions of locals and tourists during a time of economic hardship and social dislocation.

Bibliography

The principal records for the California-Pacific International Exposition are housed in the California Room research archives at the San Diego Public Library. There are 33 boxes of organizational documents, including the minutes of the managers, the finance committee, and all other divisions of the management structure. There are also contracts, exhibitor correspondence and information, and other ephemera. These documents are the only extensive record of the fair, however, duplicate copies of these records can be found at the San Diego Historical Society (SDHS). Two memoirs are useful for understanding the fair. They are Oscar Cotton, *The Good Old Days* (1962) and Daisy Lee Worthington Worcester, *Grim the Battles* (1954). SDHS has many other collections, such as the George Marston Papers and Vesta Muehleisen Papers, that recount the CPIE, in addition to general ephemera collections and scrapbooks covering the event. U.S. Government publications like the *Congressional Record* contain the House of Representatives and Senate committee hearings on the CPIE.

General histories of San Diego during the 1930s include Richard Pourade, *The Rising Tide* (1967); Mike Davis, Jim Miller, and Kelly Mayhew, *Under the Perfect Sun: The San Diego Tourists*

Never See (2003); and the city guide created by the Federal Writers Project of the Works Progress Administration, *San Diego: A Californian City* (1937). For the history of the CPIE, see Richard Amero, "San Diego Invites the World to Balboa Park for a Second Time," *Journal of San Diego History* 31, 3 (Fall 1985). Robert Rydell discusses technological fantasies at the CPIE in *World of Fairs: The Century-of-Progress Expositions* (1993). Matthew Bokovoy has written a history of the two San Diego expositions, *The San Diego World's Fairs and Southwestern Memory, 1880–1940* (2005), and interested researchers should consult its bibliography. Bokovoy has also written numerous articles on the fairs, urban planning, and the development of modern Spanish heritage in the San Diego and the Southwest, "'The Peers of Their White Conquerors': The San Diego Expositions and Modern Spanish Heritage in the Southwest, 1880–1940," *New Mexico Historical Review* 78, 4 (Fall 2003); "The Federal Housing Administration and the 'Culture of Abundance' at the San Diego California-Pacific International Exposition of 1935–1936," *The Journal of the American Planning Association* 68, 4 (Autumn 2002); and "Ghosts of the San Diego Rialto," in Jim Miller, ed., *Sunshine/Noir: Writing from San Diego and Tijuana* 1, 1 (2005). The architect Richard Requa wrote an organizational and architectural history of the CPIE in *Inside Lights on the Building of San Diego's Exposition, 1935* (1937) and it should be read against the organizational records found at SDPL. There are also two popular histories of Balboa Park, one by Florence Christman, *The Romance of Balboa Park* (1985) and the other by Roger Showley, *Balboa Park: A Millennium History* (1999). For understanding the Great Depression in San Diego, and the role of the Navy and the city of Tijuana locally, see the dissertations by Abraham Shragge, "Boosters and Bluejackets: The Civic Culture of Militarism in San Diego, California, 1900–1945" (unpub. Ph.D. diss., University of California at San Diego, 1998) and Vincent Z.C. de Baca, "Moral Renovation of the Californias: Tijuana's Political and Economic Role in

Architect Richard Neutra poses next to his contribution to Modeltown, 1935 (courtesy San Diego Historical Society, UT 4052).

American-Mexican Relations, 1920–1935" (unpub. Ph.D. diss., University of California at San Diego, 1991). In addition, one should consult Paul Vanderwood, Juan *Soldado: Rapist, Murderer, Soldier, Saint* (2004), and Lawrence Taylor, "The Wild Frontier Moves South: U.S. Entrepreneurs and the Growth of Tijuana's Vice Industry, 1908–1935," *Journal of San Diego History* 48, 3 (Summer 2002), for additional information on San Diego and Tijuana. From a more literary point of view, the legacy of the CPIE and Balboa Park figures in two works, one literary biography, the other fiction. Father of American crime *noir* Jim Thompson lived near Balboa Park during the 1940s, and enjoyed walking there in the evenings. See Thompson's acclaimed novel, *Now and on Earth* (1942) about wartime San Diego. Robert Polito's biography of Thompson, *Savage Art: A Biography of Jim Thompson* (1995) evokes 1940s San Diego in ways that cannot be glimpsed in other articles and books about San Diego.

Johannesburg 1936–1937

Deborah L. Hughes

Empire Exhibition

The year 1936 marked the fiftieth anniversary of the founding of the city of Johannesburg, in southern Africa. In its short history, Johannesburg grew from a mining outpost to one of the most important communities in sub–Saharan Africa almost entirely from the wealth generated by gold. Situated in the Transvaal province, Johannesburg became the hub of a vast mining industry that came to represent South Africa's contribution to an ailing global economy. Initial considerations to mark the anniversary with a citywide Jubilee celebration were met with great enthusiasm, but reflective of the city's international and imperial relevance, these plans evolved into an event of even greater proportions. By 1935, city leaders joined forces with leading industrialists from around the British Empire to produce the first British empire exhibition in Africa.

That the Union of South Africa should propose to celebrate the imperial connection during this period may seem at first a historical curiosity. National politics throughout the 1920s and 1930s revealed the extent to which the majority white settler community, the Afrikaners, wished to distance themselves from the British empire. As the empire evolved into the Commonwealth of Nations, the leading National Party government sought to establish the Union's independence from the British government in steps that were often perceived within imperial circles to be provocative. The South African prime minister, General J.B.M. Hertzog, built his political career on promising South Africans emancipation from British over-lordship and the elevation of the Afrikaner people. During his tenure, South

Africa emerged rapidly from the economic slump that disrupted the global economy in the 1930s, and the wealth of the country's mines and associated industries gave it the power to engage in rapid industrialization. The nation could only benefit from increased promotion of its trading potential. The International Convention Relating to International Exhibitions, signed in Paris in 1928, however, limited the Union's options for engaging the international trading community. If it wished to pursue an international exhibition, it would have to be imperial.

The empire exhibition that evolved from these political considerations was held at the Witwatersrand Agricultural Society fairgrounds at Milner Park in an area of Johannesburg now occupied by the University of the Witwatersrand, and ran from September 16, 1936, to January 15, 1937. As it was an imperial exhibition, the opening day event was marked by introductory speeches from the king of England, the prime ministers of the dominions and Great Britain, as well as the governor general of South Africa. However, the event was largely national in scope and attempted to strike a delicate balance between recognizing South Africa's imperial connection and promoting its economic, military, and political autonomy within the empire. Event organizers outlined six specific objects of the exhibition. The first was to "present a striking picture of the history and development of the Union." The second, third and fourth objects focused primarily on displaying the Union's mining, manufacturing, agricultural, and commercial resources, encouraging development of the country's communication and transportation networks, as well as "cultivating friendly and active trade relations" with other African countries. It is only in the fifth stated object that organizers admitted the significance of securing "the interest and participation" of other commonwealth nations. The last stated object spoke to the real ambition of event organizers: "to gain world-wide publicity for the Union and develop tourist and other traffic to it from other countries."

While event propagandists traveled throughout South Africa and the British empire encouraging participation from leading manufacturers, trade groups, industrialists, and agriculturalists, the city of Johannesburg worked to build the exhibition. Typical of events of this type in this period, the grounds included major government pavilions, a central parade arena, as well as structures built solely for the display of the country's major industries, most notably mining. The Johannesburg Empire Exhibition is especially notable, however, for building the first ice rink in all of Africa, one of its major entertainment features.

In spite of an extensive advertising and propaganda campaign, the Johannesburg Empire Exhibition did not succeed financially. Although the event received positive reviews by the sympathetic English-language press and those who were able to make it to Johannesburg from across South Africa and the surrounding African countries, the imagined audience of regional and oversees visitors, estimated in the development stage at between 2 and 2.5 million, failed to materialize. This may be contributed first to racial politics in South Africa that put restrictions on the attendance of indigenous Africans, and second to the amount of travel required to reach Johannesburg from around the world. Whatever the reason, gate receipts failed to recoup expenses and the Union government was forced to bail out the city to pay its creditors.

It is difficult to determine the extent to which the exhibition succeeded in its less tangible aims. Some exhibitors reported general pleasure with the contacts they made while in Johannesburg, but others admitted that the cost of display would probably not be recovered in future trade and sales with these new contacts. From the imperial perspective, the exhibition did little to influence anti-imperial sentiment in South Africa, even though for a short time that sentiment seemed to lose its potency. Perhaps the most conclusive statement that can be made about the event's lasting political, cultural or economic value on South Africa is that historical recognition of the exhibition is almost entirely obscured by the Great Trek Centenary that took place in Pretoria two years later.

Bibliography

Basic information about the exhibition and its attractions for visitors can be found in the *Official Guide to the South African Empire Exhibition* (1936). Local newspapers doubtless covered the fair, but these are not readily accessible. However, the *Times* of London ran several articles on the event between 1935 and 1937. In particular, see the issues of July 16, September 16, and December 19, 1936, and January 18–19, 1937. The New York *Times* published a feature article on the exhibition on September 3, 1936.

The exhibition was also the subject of a number of contemporary magazine articles that, for the most part, dealt with specific exhibits or features of the event. See, for example, "Gold and Diamond Mining Exhibits," *Engineering and Mining Journal* 137 (October 1936): 523*ff*; "Johannesburg Exhibition: Survey of the Electrical Exhibits," *Electrician* [London] (October 16, 1936): 457–58; "Some Impressions of the Lighting at the Empire Exhibition," *Light & Lighting* [London] 30 (January 1937): 8–10; and, finally, J. Phillips, "Rock Garden at the Empire Exhibition, Johannesburg," *Journal of the Royal Horticultural Society* [London] 61 (August 1936): 333–37. A more general view is presented in "South Africa's Empire Exhibition," *Engineer* [London] October 9, 16, and November 13, 1936.

A contemporary assessment of the Empire Exhibition is Jennifer Robinson, "Johannesburg's 1936 Empire Exhibition: Interaction, Segregation and Modernity in a South African City," *Journal of Southern African Studies*, 29, 3 (September 2003): 759–789. Also, consult Deborah L Hughes, "A Nation Negotiates Empire: Promoting the Union of South Africa at the Johannesburg Empire Exhibition, 1936–37" (unpublished paper, University of Illinois).

Paris 1937

Arthur Chandler, updated by Philip Whalen

Exposition Internationale des Arts et Techniques dans la Vie Moderne

In 1937, the Queen City of Expositions held court for the last time. World War I was scarcely two decades past. The most catastrophic war in the history of the human race loomed less than two years away. Paris, France, Europe, and all nations of the earth seemed poised in the eye of a hurricane, between the winds of World War I and World War II. The Exposition internationale would be the final European enactment of the ritual of Peace and Progress before the deluge.

To their credit, the exposition officials recognized that they were celebrating in a deeply troubled world and did their best to confront the actual and impending disasters within the framework of the exposition itself. The 1937 Exposition internationale faced some of the most important dualisms that divided humanity against itself: the split between Paris and the provinces, between France and her colonies, between art and science, between socialism and capitalism, between fascism and democracy. The official philosophy of the exposition still paid homage to the twin gods Peace and Progress, as all parties at the great ceremony in Paris intoned the faith: no matter how bleak the world seems to be, the twin gods will see humanity through to a glorious future. "This great lesson in international cooperation will not be forgotten," predicted Fernand Chapsal, the French Minister of Commerce, in the official public report on the exposition.

In fewer than three years, Paris would belong to the conquering Nazis.

On December 28, 1929, the French Chamber of Deputies passed a resolution calling for an "Exposition of Decorative Arts and Modern Industry," in 1936, to be placed under the direction of the Minister of Commerce. The exposition was first conceived as a follow-up to the Exposition des Arts Decoratifs Modernes of 1925. Though the attendance at the "Art Deco" fair was only a tenth of the number that visited the 1900 Exposition Universelle, France congratulated itself on having taken a decisive step in maintaining her leadership in cultural affairs. The 1925 exposition, though not as ambitious as the five previous Parisian world's fairs, was pronounced a *succès d'estime* for France. Even if France was losing her place in the first rank of economic and political power, Paris could at least prevail in matters of taste. France planned the new exposition with an eye toward consolidating her claims to cultural authority.

Conceived during the victorious optimism of the 1920s, the Exposition internationale of 1937 (the original opening year was set back) was carried out in the anxious zeitgeist of the 1930s. The Great Depression, unemployment, and runaway currency inflation forced a change in the government's original plans for a decorative arts exposition. Given the precarious state of the national economy, the decorative arts did not seem a serious enough concern to justify the labor and expense of a major international exposition. Instead, the government announced in the *Livre d'Or Officiel* that it would integrate the exposition with "the overall plan of economic recovery and the struggle against unemployment."

Though the decorative arts would not be the major focus of the new exposition, the exposition planners believed that the arts themselves should take an active part in the "struggle against unemployment." Because of the Great Depression — and the trend among painters and sculptors towards "unpopular" abstract art — the number of buyers to support the arts had declined sharply. To alleviate the widespread and growing poverty among artists— an embarrassment to the city which prided itself as the home and center of fine art — the nation of France and the city of Paris commissioned 718 murals, and employed over 2,000 artists to decorate the pavilions.

If the decorative arts were not to be the major subject of theme of the great exposition, What would take their place? As time went on, the objectives themselves wavered and shifted in the political storms. Some legislators thought the exposition should celebrate "Workers and Peasants" in an attempt to heal the split between Paris and the provinces and to give an egalitarian cast to the exposition's theme and purpose. Others wanted to see the artisan exalted, in an attempt to ennoble colonial craftsmen and to fix the status of art as a decorative auxiliary to social concerns.

It was finally decided that the world's fair would take as its theme the division that had grown up between the arts and technology. The very title — "International Exposition of Arts and Technics in Modern Life" — shows the decisive split from the spirit of the earlier expositions universelles. The fairs of the earlier era and the event of 1937 are all "expositions"— shows of the products of human ingenuity, under the aegis of Peace and Progress— but the "universal" is gone from the name and nature of the newest fair. All previous expositions had been international; but national rivalries were supposed to be subordinated to larger, "universal" concerns: the elevation of taste through the arts and the improvement of everyday life by science through industry. The title of the 1937 exposition breaks down the real meaning inherent in the earlier term "universal" into its component parts: the nationalism inherent in the competition for prestige, the fundamental duality between the arts and technology, and the transforming power of art and science.

The title of the 1937 exposition suggests another change in the thinking of the planners, a change as fundamental as the shift from "universal." Now "Art" and "Science" no longer exist as absolute values. Art become artisanship, science becomes technology. The value of art and science derives from its social utility, the exposition planners announced at Paris

1937. Application to daily life is the highest measure of worth.

By 1935, the new exposition had a theme and a name, but as 1936 drew closer, detailed plans for the event had still not been drawn up. The opening date was moved up to 1937, and a commission set to work in earnest on the grand schemes and finer details. But the compressed time frame hurried the commission into hasty decisions and improvisational planning.

When the American correspondent for the *Architectural Record* surveyed the exposition, he could compliment the "cheerful magnificence of conception, peculiarly French," while at the same time lamenting that the overall objectives of the exposition were "foiled by a lack of coordination between the idea and the realization." Looking back to the exposition of 1937 half a century later, François Robichon concluded that "the scheme of the whole was undiscoverable, since the placement of the 200 pavilions was made without any overarching plan, with the exception of those in the Trocadéro Esplanade."

As always with Parisian expositions, the work proceeded slowly, and the exposition opening time was pushed back again and again. It was an embarrassment for the French government to watch the Italians, the Germans, the Russians, and many others complete their pavilions while bureaucratic delays and strikes drove the French commissioners to despair. At one point Edmond Labbe, chief commissioner of the exposition resigned his post with a despairing outburst: "I am a dishonored man, and I herewith tender my resignation. The French Pavilion will not be ready in time for the inauguration. The workers pay no attention to me. In spite of all my appeals to their honor and power, they still go on strike."

Workers are not always swayed by the fine words Peace and Progress. Parisian laborers in 1937 demanded a pledge from the government that if they helped build the exposition, they would be guaranteed employment thereafter. Labbe was persuaded to continue, and the work proceeded. But would the fair ever open its gates to the public? Just a few weeks before the actual opening date, one of the commissioners approached the director of works and asked him: "Since you're the builder of all this," the official asked, "can you tell me when the fair will be ready to open?"

"Well," replied the director, "I can't tell you exactly. But I do know that, according to the contract, I have to start demolition on November 2."

The major architectural event of 1937 — the official "spike" of the whole exposition — was to be a splendid new modern art museum. There was little public outcry over the proposed demolition of the Trocadéro Palace, the principal legacy from the 1878 exposition universelle. It was leveled in 1934 without ceremony. "The old Trocadéro will be mourned," remarked one French architect, "but only by those who habitually mourn the dead."

The new Chaillot Palace was to be the triumphant vindication of the present age over the past. Unfortunately, as Robichon noted, "The reconstruction of the Trocadéro palace took place in total disorder. After having first decided to demolish the old structure, they opted instead for camouflage. Jacques Carlu, Louis-Hippolyte Boileau; and Léon Azema were awarded the commission to rebuild the new Chaillot Palace along the same lines as the colonnade of the old Trocadéro. The idiom of the new building would be modern, but not too much so. As deputy commissioner Julien Durand assured the legislature during the budgetary hearings: "The old Trocadéro will be replaced by a monument whose lines, in spite of their modernism, will fit well within the monumental tradition of Mansart, Gabriel, Ledoux, Percier, Fontaine, etc." Both Carlu and Azema had been winners of the traditionally prestigious Prix de Rome in architecture, and could be counted on to design a building not too far out of the mainstream. The radical modernism of Le Corbusier was passed over in favor of a style which mixed traditionalism and the international style.

This return to the past by way of neoclassicism has been seen by some observers as a prime symbol of fascism in architecture. Indeed, Albert Speer, chief architect of the Third Reich, thought so, and his German pavilion at the 1937 exposition was carried out in a spirit quite close to that of the Chaillot Palace. The wide, impersonal sweep of the colonnade conjured up for many a feeling of totalitarianism, a subjection of the individual to the state — in short, an architecture of fascism.

As it turned out, the new Chaillot Palace was not the most exciting architectural event at the exposition. Le Corbusier, whose *Pavillon de l'Esprit Nouveau* had created such an uproar at the 1925 Art Deco fair, was excluded from all the design terms of the 1937 exposition. One of his students, Junzo Sakakura, designed the Japanese pavilion. But Le Corbusier himself was too uncompromisingly visionary for the exposition planning commissioners. Undaunted, and following the tradition of "refuse" painters from earlier expositions (Courbet in 1855, Manet in 1867, Matisse in 1889), Le Corbusier and his followers erected a huge tent outside the exposition grounds, just beyond the Porte Maillot. Inside, they set forth his models and plans for the ideal city of the future. Said the writer for the *Architectural Record:* "It was one of the most exciting, convincing, and most easily remembered exhibits of 1937 Paris."

At the earlier French national fairs held in the first decades of the nineteenth century, the artists refused to lower themselves by appearing in the same expositions as the "lower" mechanical arts. Painters and sculptors displayed their work at their own annual and biennial salons, where patrons and purchasers entered the "higher" world of aesthetic beauty, far from clanking machinery. Since the 1855 exposition, though, artists agreed to compete with each other side by side with the industrialists. But for painters and sculptors, gold medals awarded at world's fairs never had the status comparable to awards from the annual *salons*. Artists felt that the fine arts were more noble and refined products of the human spirit.

Though art and industry had coexisted at world's fairs, there were never any systematic attempts to integrate the two. Applied ornament might dress up the perceived graceless functionality of the machine; and machinery might serve as a subordinate subject for art (the first painting with a motorcar appeared in the frescoes at the 1900 exposition). But art and science remained separate in the nature and application of their basic values.

The 1937 Exposition internationale was designed in part to effect a unification between these forms of knowledge. In this case, though, the unification meant a subordinate position for art. There was fine art to be seen at the exposition, of course — in the retrospective gallery. And Picasso's *Guernica,* on display in the Spanish pavilion, showed that painters were

The architecture of the food products building reflects the modernism prevalent at the 1937 Paris exposition (photograph by Gorsky Freres).

still capable of making powerful statements about the moral dimension of the contemporary world. But the overall presence of art at the 1937 exposition was as decoration. The term "artisan" is used again and again in the official literature; and the word is used with the kind of respect that indicates the writers felt at artisanship was every bit as worthy as artistry. In the modern view, easel painting was elitist. The muralists and sculptors who adorned the walls of the industrial galleries were the artists truly in phase with the official philosophy of the fair.

The most telling sign that art had declined into servitude was the manner in which artisanship was exalted over art, and the condescending admiration bestowed upon the artisans of colonial cultures by their rulers. In 1931, Paris had staged a modest party for the colonies of France — an exposition coloniale that presented the natives, in a picturesque encampment out by the Chateau de Vincennes, for scrutiny and appreciation by the citizens of the governing nation. Now the colonials were brought back and placed in isolated splendor on the Ile des Cygnes in the Seine. This was the

familiar French 1001 Nights dreamland, the exotic Orient and darkest Africa made real by theme pavilions and dusky natives hawking wares in the *Quartier d'Outre Mer*. Here primitive artisanship thrived. Beneath the imported totem poles, between the fronds of the newly planted banana trees, palms and cacti, the colonial artisans weaved fabrics and sang their songs.

As he surveyed the exhibit of tribal masks from Gabon and the Ivory Coast, the official chronicler of the colonial exhibit, Marc Chadourne, has a vision of the message crying out from these wares: "I am black, but I am beautiful." Chadourne could not see that the "but" was a mountain over which the entire world would one day have to cross.

France had her colonies, Paris her provinces. What the Isle de Cygnes was to France, the Regional Center, located in a remote corner of the Esplanade des Invalides, was to Paris. Here the French borrowed from the Chicago World's Columbian Exposition, which devoted a portion of the fairgrounds to the states of the union. The idea was transferred to Paris, where the "Provinces" seemed to the French as the equivalent of states. But Chicago does not signify to America what Paris signifies to France. No on came away from the Columbian exposition with the notion that the other states were provinces of Chicago. At the Regional Center of the 1937 exposition, the fundamental distinctions of prestige and power between Paris and the rest of France were made manifest.

In the Regional Center, picturesquely clad artisans from the provinces displayed their native crafts in pavilions designed as hybrids that wedded French regional traditional styles — the Norman, the Gothic, the Renaissance — with the cool lines of the International Style. The visual aspect of these regional pavilions was in effect miniaturized grandeur: reductions of older styles meant for larger buildings. In a spirit of cooperation, even the Ile de France — the province that includes Paris — participated with a structure that resembled the top part of one tower in the City Hall of Paris.

In the domain of ideas, the 1937 exposition attempted to reconcile, symbolically, art and industry. From the political vantage point, the fair was a vehicle of nationalistic propaganda. The word "propaganda" had not yet acquired connotations of deception, and one saw the word everywhere, in French and foreign pavilions alike. Propaganda continued the tradition of national displays at all previous world's fairs. Each country did its best to show the world the superiority of the political and economic system that had produced the marvels on view in its national pavilions.

Each country stressed the virtues of its home government but added allurements to promote tourism. The French erected a special Pavilion du Tourisme, where the beauties of France could be admired without the distractions of industrial or artistic exhibits. The Italian building showed how lovely Italy had become even lovelier under the benign reign of Il Duce. The Soviet Union mounted the most expensive display of all: a map of mother Russia made entirely of gold studded with rubies, topazes, and other precious stones — a luxurious and luxuriant illustration of the country's industrial growth in recent years.

But the most striking feature of the Soviet pavilion was not the exhibits of gold and propaganda — it was the placement of the building face to face with the Nazi pavilion. Nothing in

any international exhibition has ever matched this dramatic architectural confrontation. In the shadow of the Eiffel Tower, the two opponents faced off with self-aggrandizing monuments to their nationalistic spirits. According to his own account, Albert Speer, Hitler's architect-in-chief and designer of the German building, accidentally stumbled into a room containing a sketch of the Soviet Pavilion. This ostensibly innocent accident enabled Germany to dominate its rival on the Esplanade. Facing the heroically posed Russian workingman and peasant woman brandishing hammer and sickle, the German eagle, its talons clutching a wreath encircling a huge swastika, disdainfully turned its head and fanned out its wings. At the ground level, a massively naked Teutonic couple stare at the Russian monument with grim determination.

When the gates to the exposition closed in November 1937, they closed on the final Ritual of Peace and Progress in the queen city of expositions. A total of 16,704 prizes had been distributed to participants. Over 600 congresses had been held on an unprecedented number of topics. Thirty-four million people had attended the fair, and the final balance sheet showed a loss of 13 million francs. But the officials pointed out that, during the year of the exposition, over four million more people attended theatrical and musical performances than in 1936, producing an estimated profit of 40 million francs; admissions to the Louvre and Versailles doubled; the Metro collected 59 million more fares; train travel increased 20 per cent; and hotels registered 112 per cent more guests. Clearly, the monetary goals of the exposition, taken in the larger context of the French economy, had been met.

In spite of these encouraging statistics, most observers counted the exposition as something less than an unqualified success. Only 34 million visitors — half the attendance of the 1900 exposition — attended this elaborate ceremony of the unification of Arts and Technics. The mood of the 1937 exposition carried none of the buoyant optimism that prevailed in 1900. Some enthusiasts talked of continuing the exposition into the next year; but the plan failed to win popular support.

Amidst the technological wonders and charming pavilions of artisanship, there lurked an unpleasant feeling of tension, suspicion, and hostility at the Exposition internationale in 1937.

No one could mistake the brute confrontation between the Russian and German buildings. And there were other tangible evidences of mistrust. Almost none of the major nations distributed information about the materials and processes used in their industrial exhibits. Knowledge was the hoarded property of the nation that discovered and applied it. Guards in every pavilion were posted to stop visitors from photographing the exhibits. Even apparently public displays were to be appreciated, not studied. One architect was making sketches of the night-time illumination patterns of the French buildings—only to have his drawings confiscated and destroyed by the exposition gendarmes.

The ritual of Peace and Progress was over. The medals were distributed, and the conquering exhibitors of 44 nations politely applauded each other during the closing ceremonies on November 2, 1937. Soon the participants departed to their fortified cities and prepared to arm human pride with the tools of technology for the forthcoming tournament of blood. In the City of Light, the lamps were extinguished. The ultimate confrontation was at hand.

The Soviet pavilion was one of the great iconic symbols at the 1937 Paris exposition. Located directly opposite the German pavilion, the Soviet building appeared to challenge its future wartime adversary (photograph by Gorsky Freres).

Bibliography

The mammoth *Rapport Général* (10 volumes) is the most comprehensive document, produced under the imprint of the French government from 1938–1940. More accessible, and admirably illustrated, is the *Livre d'Or Officiel de l'Exposition Internationale des Arts et Techniques dans la Vie Moderne* (1937). This volume is especially valuable for information about how the commissioners of each section felt about the moral, social, and aesthetic implications of their part of the exposition. The exposition's promotional *Official Guide* (1937) provides a detailed overview of the event's attractions. The *Livre d'Or Officiel de l'Exposition Internationale des Arts et Techniques dans la Vie Moderne* (1937) provides a wealth of information of the organizer's intentions and expectations. More reflective, Paul Dupay's *L'Exposition Internationale de 1937* (1938) discusses the event's overall accomplishments and notable disappointments. Good photographs may be found in the twelve volumes of the *Exposition Paris 1937* magazine published through 1936 and in the souvenir album, *Exposition Internationale des Arts et Techniques Appliqués à la Vie Moderne*

The Eiffel Tower hovers over the dramatic Photo Cine Phono theatre, an attraction at the 1937 world's fair in Paris (photograph by Gorsky Freres).

Architecture (April 1936). The U.S. and major foreign pavilions are described in detail in two articles in *Architectural Record*: "1937 International Exhibition," 82 (October 1937): 81–91, and "U.S. Pavilion Carries Skyscraper Motif to Paris," 82 (December 1937): 20–23. James D. Herbert addresses the ideological implications of the exposition's high modernist aesthetic the rough the examination of various pavilions in *Paris 1937: Worlds on Exhibition* (1998). The political implications of the Exposition's folk aesthetic are examined in Shanny Peer, "French Uses of Folklore: The Reinvention of Folklore in the 1937 I of Folklore in the 1937 International Exposition," *Folklore Forum* 22 (1989): 62–77, and Elise Marie Moentmann, "Conservative Modernism at the 1937 International Exposition in Paris" (unpub. Ph.D. diss., University of Illinois, Urbana-Champaign, 1998).

The regional dimensions of the 1937 exposition have received increased attention during the past decade. Shanny Peer, *France on Display: Peasants, Provincials, and Folklore in the 1937 Paris World's Fair* (1998) underscores the nature and extent of the exposition's regional, rural, and provincial agendas. Philip Whalen provides an in-depth examination of the Burgundian contribution in "Burgundian Regionalism and French Republican Commercial Culture at the 1937 Paris International Exposition," *Cultural Analysis* 6 (2007). The tensions between national and regional interests is examined in Serge Wolikow and Annie Bleton-Ruget, "Le Front Populaire et les Composantes Agrariennes de l'Identité Nationale Française: Autour de l'Exposition Internationale de 1937," *Antifascisme et Nations* (1998).

The most comprehensive assessment of the 1937 exposition is Bertrand Lemoine, ed., *Cinquantenaire de l'Exposition internationale des arts et des techniques dans la Vie Moderne,* published in 1937. Its 510 pages are admirably organized, lavishly illustrated (including many color photos), with essays on virtually every aspect of the fair. Also quite good is the substantial and wittily written section on the exposition in Philippe Bouin and Christian-Philippe Chanut, *Histoire Française des Foires et des Expositions Universelles* (1980).

(1937). A French counterpart to this essay is found in Marc Gaillard, *Les Expositions Universelles de 1855 à 1937* (2003): 158–183. A special issue of *Le Monde*, "Paris 1937 Exposition," was published May 29, 1937, and also contains useful general information.

For the English-speaking student, the best sources for facts and criticism of the 1937 exposition are the essays in architecture magazines. See T. F. Hamlin, "Paris, 1937: A Critique" in *American Architect* (November 1937): 25–34; Henry R. Hitchcock, Jr., "Paris 1937: Foreign Pavilions," *Architectural Forum* (September 1937): 158–74; Elizabeth B. Mock, "Paris Exposition," *Magazine of Art* (May 1937): 266–73; and an anonymous article, "Paris International Exposition of 1937: Views and Plan,"

Glasgow 1938

John M. MacKenzie

British Empire Exhibition

The idea for an Empire Exhibition in Glasgow was conceived in 1931 at the height of the depression in a conscious effort to promote employment and to advertise the industries of Scotland. After 1936 it was planned and promoted by the Scottish Development Council, backed by a guarantee fund of £750,000. The exhibition cost £10 million to construct. The objects of the exhibition were fivefold: to illustrate the progress of the British empire; to reveal the resources and potentialities of the empire to new generations; to stimulate Scottish work and production and to direct attention to Scotland's historical and scenic attractions; to foster empire trade and closer friendship among the peoples of the Commonwealth of Nations; and to emphasize to the rest of the world the peaceful aspirations of the peoples of the British empire.

The exhibition was built around a hill, 170 feet high, at Bellahouston Park, southwest of the Glasgow city center, and covered 175 acres. The architect was Thomas S. Tait, and the civil engineers were Crouch and Hogg. The exhibition was arranged on three main axes: Scottish Avenue, on which were placed the Scottish pavilions, the concert hall, and the palace of art; Dominions and Colonial avenues, which ran between the pavilions of the imperial territories, together with the palaces of engineering and industries and a range of other buildings devoted to specific industries and companies; and Kingsway, on which stood the pavilions of the British government, the city of Glasgow, and a notable exhibit of the Women of the Empire. Scottish industries like shipbuilding, steel and coal, agriculture, fisheries, and forestry were prominent. There was a Scottish model dairy, an Empire Tea Pavilion, and

a Scottish Highland village, An Clachan, which was intended to covey the rugged Scottish spirit that had helped to build the empire. Specific associations (like the Bee-keepers) and companies (like Shell-Mex, ICI and Dunlop) had their own buildings.

Whereas previous British exhibitions had adopted pastiche, eclectic, or antique styles, Glasgow was unashamedly modern. The buildings were in a distinctive thirties style —flat roofed, angular, with smooth surfaces, metal frames, and strongly accented glazing, the vertical elements being provided by pylons, flagpoles, and ribbed frontages. It was a great deal more satisfying than the stolid, almost windowless concrete of Wembley.

The exhibition was open from May 3 to October 29, 1938, and received 12,593,232 visitors (plus another 600,000 who attended events in the stadium, outside the exhibition grounds, and did not visit the exhibition itself). It suffered a loss of £118,691, which was amply covered by sums received from the guarantors.

The exhibition set out to place Scottish industrialism, notably the heavy industries of the Clyde Valley, into the context of the international, though distinctively imperial, economy. But the historic national identity presented was the contrasting one of rural Highland life, which had supposedly formed the Scottish character at home and, through emigration, abroad. The exhibition therefore presented an interesting three-tiered structure: empire, metropole, and Celtic periphery. The Palace of Arts concentrated on Scottish art, and there was a retrospective of the Glasgow school, a significant movement of the late nineteenth and early twentieth centuries.

Although the exhibition was overshadowed by the growing European crisis, attendance was remarkable for a country with a

A photograph of the tower at the British Empire Exhibition in Glasgow. This was the first exhibition in Britain that utilized the modernistic architecture of the 1920s and 1930s (editors' collection).

capital of culture for 1990 represented a wholly new strategy in the late twentieth century.

Bibliography

Collections of material relating to the Glasgow Empire Exhibition can be found in the Mitchell Library, Glasgow, the University of Glasgow, and the Glasgow Art Galleries and Museums Service. Among these, the report of Sidney Graham to the Administrative Committee (January 11, 1939) is particularly important. The exhibition produced large quantities of ephemera, and there were special supplements to Scottish newspapers like the *Glasgow Herald.*. The Imperial Institute in London was the main coordinator of the dominions and colonial exhibits, and the papers relating to these can be found in the institute's records in the Public Record Office (particularly PRO 30/76/161–70).

The most complete accounts of the exhibition can be found in Alistair Goldsmith, "The Glasgow International Exhibitions, 1888–1938" (M. Litt. thesis, University of Strathclyde, 1986), and in a more accessible survey of all of Glasgow's fairs, Perilla Kinchin and Juliet Kinchen, *Glasgow's Great Exhibitions* (1989). Colin McArthur, "The Glasgow Empire Exhibition of 1938," in Tony Bennett et al., eds., *Popular Culture and Social Relations* (1986), offers an interpretation of the exhibition in terms of the location of Scotland in the cultural and economic periphery. John M. MacKenzie, *Propaganda and Empire* (1984), places the exhibition in its propagandist and ethnic context, while Paul Greenhalgh, *Ephemeral Vistas* (1988) surveys the design, cultural, artistic, national, and gender implications of the exhibits.

population of little more than 5 million. Ironically, the industries it celebrated were to experience their last great flourishing during the war and the era of reconstruction that followed. Within two or three decades, as the empire also slipped away, Scotland was in search of a new identity. The Glasgow Garden Festival of 1988 and the emergence of the city as a European

New York 1939–1940

Paul T. Sayers

New York World's Fair

That all of the forces needed to pull it off could come together in such unanimity of effort seems absolutely remarkable. Over the years, talk of a world's fair in New York had cascaded in endless quantities from many mouths. To actually pull off the world's fair of 1939–1940, however, required a sheer collective sense of determined ambition that was in many ways unprecedented.

New York was the second largest city in the world at the time. Its seven and a half million people constituted a massive potential audience, one that trailed only London's. The intense planning, debates, building, and implementation of its agenda was done in a way and on a scale that fully justified its venue.

The fair would run for two seasons: April 30 to October 31, 1939 and May 11 to October 27, 1940. That the show could go on at all under the sheer force of the pressure of world events was notable. The world was viciously and literally ripped apart at its seams as the show that had to went on. Its builders had pulled out all the stops for many years to make it happen and would not let it die.

It was timed to open on the 150th anniversary of the inauguration of George Washington. Toward that end, James Earl Fraser created a 60-foot sculpture of Washington mounted on a 12-foot pedestal. Macy's T. Percy Straus and George MacAneny of Title Guarantee and Trust Company early on secured the support of President Franklin D. Roosevelt. With New York's Governor Herbert Lehman and the city's Mayor Fiorello H. La Guardia, a group of some 96 people — including architects, scientists, and social critics— started to thrash out the possibilities in earnest.

The men and women who brought the fair to Queens were dreaming of a far reaching enterprise that would captivate, educate, and entertain on a scale that, in its own way, was as bold as some of Roosevelt's legislative initiatives to combat the Great Depression. The years before the fair's conception had been drenched in doubt, suffering, and despair. The fair's creators knew about the heartbreak endemic to the age and, more importantly, about the promise of tomorrow, too. Their hearts were so open that they would devote the best years of their lives to bringing it off. They dared to take inspiration from its conception and make it live vibrantly for about a year. They did so that millions would feel their dream resonate, lose their bearings, and dream that they were dreaming, too.

Joseph Shadgen, a Jackson Heights civil engineer, is most often credited with coming up with the idea of having a world's fair in Flushing Meadows. It came to him in 1934, the year of the General Textile strike, the largest in the nation's history. Initially, Shadgen had landed at a $625-a-month job at the fair. Fired for incompetency, he sued the fair corporation for $2 million, and eventually settled for $45,000. The notion that this section of Queens was a viable site took a highly imaginative perspective.

The Long Island Railroad Company had long used the marshy area, known as the Corona Dumps, as a scrap yard. It was three and a half miles long and more than a mile wide. The logistical challenges to be met in a mere three years were daunting and included draining the marsh, cleaning and rerouting the Flushing River, putting down water and electrical mains, and transplanting 10,000 large trees. These trees came from five states from Maryland to Connecticut and weighed up to thirty tons each. It was estimated that the landscaping effort alone cost $1,500,000. When the fair opened, there were 200 buildings on 1,216 acres— an area 50 percent larger than Central Park — to plan and build and, for the most part, to demolish when it was over.

Robert Moses, head of New York City's Park Commission, drove the landscaping effort and a transportation concept involving both modification and creation that guaranteed accessibility. He was instrumental in seeing to it that 250 acres were made available to park 35,000 cars, that 300 boats could be moored in Flushing Bay, and that 575 buses could be parked on Roosevelt Avenue. Fairgoers entered the grounds through one of ten gates, their security monitored by a police force of some 2,000 and health safeguarded by six first aid stations in 1939 and five the next year.

Moses wanted to keep the site as a park after the fair and had shrewdly maneuvered to have the first $2 million of the fair's profits devoted to this transition. The widespread expectation that the fair would make money would prove false. In consequence, Moses' dream of a new park was deferred until after his own stewardship of the 1964 world's fair at the same location.

A contagious optimism had grown that the fair's purposes were powerful enough to secure multiple ends. Its organizers were powerful, their aims lofty, and the converging international forces imposing. That the fair lost some $19 million was far from its most vital characteristic. Besides, organizers estimated that it would bring New York City $1 billion, though there was and is no way to measure accurately that effect.

The Chicago Century of Progress Exposition of 1933–1934 was an important inspiration in many ways, particularly in its intense promotion of commercial interests and a brilliant ingenuity in using colors. Perhaps most importantly, in a time of economic devastation and precious little entrepreneurial drive, it made a profit. The New Yorkers, nothing if not hugely ambitious, covered the ante, but rose the stakes impressively.

Grover Whalen was chosen fair president. A former New York police commissioner, he was president of Schenley Distilleries at the time. The joyously extroverted and indefatigable Whalen was a wise choice. He had led the city's reception for Charles Lindbergh in 1927

and the massive National Recovery Act parade in September 1933. In September 1935, Whalen, McAneny, and Straus were joined in incorporating the fair by the heads of 23 banking and trust companies, 30 corporations, 15 Wall Street law firms, eight insurance companies and retail firms, and eight business associations.

Though usually described as a private business enterprise, the fair was non-stock, non-profit, and paid no taxes. A $1.6 million loan by 16 Manhattan banks got things rolling. Subsequent funding came largely from interest paying bonds, federal and state funds, and foreign investment. It was an expensive venture. While the Chicago exposition had been put on for slightly more than $33 million, the New York fair had already cost some $155 million on the day it opened.

The theme of the first season was "Building the World of Tomorrow with the Tools of Today." Business wanted to show that very powerful companies could build such a world. Lavish commercial displays garnered unprecedented attention. Seemingly at every turn in the planning and implementation of policy, the interests of business were promoted. Critics complained that the best sites went to business, that the more idealistic plans of its committees were weighed accordingly, and that even the guide book for the first season was replete with commercial hucksterism. Doubtless, those intellectuals advocating their viewpoints most fiercely within the fair's policymaking elite, such as social analyst and architectural critic Lewis Mumford, wished that the corporate interests would take a secondary place during the first season.

On June 29, 1936, groundbreaking ceremonies for the fair were held in Queens. By March 1937, Flushing Meadows Park had been completed ahead of schedule and construction at the site began The seemingly untiringly energetic Whalen was relentless in his efforts to bring talented individuals into the enterprise. George Gershwin wrote the music and his brother Ira the lyrics to "Dawn of a New Day," the fair's theme song. Whalen persuaded Howard Hughes to paint the fair's symbols, the trylon and perisphere, on his plane when he circled the globe on his legendary flight. He convinced Westinghouse — a company involved on many fronts— to develop a time capsule to be opened in 6939. It contents included millions of pages of text on microfilm and a pack of Camel cigarettes. The atomic bomb was only a dream then, too, and the expectation that there would be people — and smokers at that — left with the patience to make use of it all seems somewhat optimistic in retrospect.

The unions had emerged from the labor unrest of the 1930s whole and a collective force to be reckoned with. They injected desperately needed balance into what had very nearly disintegrated into feudalism. The fair, a little like the country as it regained its confidence under Roosevelt, also grew stronger. Somehow it managed to surmount the controversies and passions and worker complaints — the fair employed some 50,000 — that attended its transformation from shadowy, contentious, and often idealized conceptualization into riveting, dynamic, but still often contentious reality.

The bitter disillusionment and distrust of America's involvement in world affairs that had gripped much of the nation in the wake of World War I was very much alive during the fair's planning stages and had scarcely receded by opening day. In 1937, Germany, amid howls of complaint, had signed the contract that would have allowed it to build its own pavilion. That same year, the pugnacious Mayor La Guardia proposed a "Chamber of Horrors" for the fair that triggered vicious invective in the Nazi press. A later effort to exhibit the works of exiled Germans came closer to fruition. But the combined efforts of Whalen, Lehman, Moses, Harry Guggenheim, Treasury Secretary Henry Morgenthau, and Herbert Bayard Swope could not pull it off.

In April 1938, Whalen was informed that the German government was unable to raise the foreign exchange to proceed with construction. Wherever the whole truth lay about the German withdrawal, the fair was spared the ongoing controversy and accusations of moral cowardice that would have attended Germany's participation. After Czechoslovakia had been

The Trylon and Perisphere, perhaps the best known world's fair symbols, are shown in a night view with the statue of George Washington in silhouette (editors' collection).

annexed in late 1938 and 1939, La Guardia sponsored a committee to collect funds to furnish and operate its pavilion in the face of Nazi attempts to quash the process. The last president of the country, Edvard Benes, spoke at the still unfinished, pavilion on opening day. The protests that arose because of the participation of Italy and Japan were mitigated by a sense that Roosevelt was working both for peace and to make the country ready for war if peace could not be had.

A geometric concept of Beaux-Arts origin structured the main exhibit area into a fondpoint system of radiating streets and fanlike segments. Its layout, sculptures, and murals were carefully calibrated in terms of tone, effect, and coordination. The sculptor Lee Lawrie's strikingly colored pylons at the Century of Progress had drawn Nelson A. Rockefeller's attention. Lawrie worked with the Design Board to bring in such artists as Paul Manship and Malvina Hoffman. Among over thirty other sculptors, they produced such innovative and graceful works as the Bridge Plaza leading into the Entertainment Zone and Manship's famous "Time and the Fates of Man," the largest sundial in the world.

Axes along symmetrical lanes led to the Fair's central theme structures, the Trylon and Perisphere. They were the most famous and instantly recognizable symbols of s world's fair since Eiffel built his tower for the Paris Exposition of 1889. The New York *Times* famously called the twin symbols the "the egg and the folk."

Architects Jacques Fouilhoux and Wallace Harrison had promised a practical design where the theme of the fair would find dramatization. They worked with Henry Dreyfuss, the designer responsible for Democracity, the exhibit within the Perisphere. The architectural designs of the Trylon and the Perisphere, a point of orientation throughout the Fairgrounds, had their genesis in a hairpin and ball of putty of Harrison's.

Because a ball was judged optimal for enclosing the largest amount of space with the smallest amount of surface, a sphere was chosen. The Perisphere had a 628-foot circumference and was as high as an 18-story building. The design of the Trylon, a three-sided 610-foot tower, was chosen largely because of its contrast with the sphere. Since a freestanding sphere was an architectural novelty, there was no engineering precedent on which the work could be modeled. Notable for their sheer beauty, the two forms were greeted upon publication of the plans in March 1937 as an "icon of the future," and were reproduced on countless posters, brochures and other publications, and every imaginable kind of souvenir.

At night, lights projected cloud patterns on the globe. In its colored mist, it seemed that the sphere was revolving like a giant planet on its axis. At Halloween, it became a huge jack-o-lantern. The darkness brought out the fair's endlessly inventive lighting schemes and clever use of colors.

Within the Perisphere, Democracity, designer Henry Dreyfuss' hugely popular work,

was permeated with idealistic aims and served as a powerful magnet to draw visitors. There were no slums, strip-mined hillsides, or garishly designed bridges in Democracity. It was staged to represent society in 2039 — a century in the future. It urban area encompassed 10,000 square miles and a million and a half residents. The city's heart was located at Centerton and was surrounded by suburbs and towns, such as Millville where industrial workers happily toiled.

Centerton was the base of the metropolitan area's corporate, educational, and cultural life. The suburbs were given special prominence, not to mention names such as Pleasantville. This concerted effort not to overcrowd the city might be viewed as oddly prescient in view of the urban flight that swept the nation a quarter century later. The gleaming representation of a shining future was applied so thickly that it proved an irresistible target to future generations of sharp-tongued critics. The unkindest among them even drew analogies between its vision of harmony and the carefully manipulative choreography practiced by the Nazis at the Nuremburg rallies.

To get to Democracity, fairgoers first entered the Trylon. From there, the crowds endured a long wait and then rode two adjacent escalators, the world's longest, to the Perisphere There they left the escalators for one of two circular platforms that revolved in opposite directions for the six-minute presentation. Above was the great dome of the Perisphere lit in blue; below the beautifully crafted diorama of Democracity, viewed as though from seven thousand feet. A noted black composer of the day, William Grant Still, had composed orchestral music that accompanied the narration of radio's celebrated H.V. Kaltenborn. At the performance's climax, daylight faded, and lights came out on throughout the metropolitan area. The stars came out above. Processions of workers appeared from ten equidistant points on the interior dome. A choir sang an anthem by Al Stillman built around the fair's theme of Building the World of Tomorrow. At the conclusion of the performance, visitors left using the Helicline, a 950-foot ramp that circled the Perisphere.

There were more than 100 exhibit buildings and 1,500 exhibitors. The technological advances that commercial exhibits displayed at the fair were breathtaking. None was more successful or popular than General Motors' Futurama. Designed by Norman Bel Geddes, it featured a ride through 408 dioramas set in the year 1960. Another popular draw was Voder, AT&T's groundbreaking voice operations demonstrator. It mimicked human speech through sound vibration and modular hiss and initiated a tidal movement in communications clearly evident today. Perhaps the most notable technology unveiled in connection with the fair, however, involved television and the political process. Although television had been seen at earlier fairs, including the Century of Progress, this was the first time it was used to broadcast a presidential address. On opening day, Roosevelt spoke before a small television audience in the New York metropolitan area. NBC broadcast the speech on the same day that regular commercial broadcasting commenced. Television was widely used in other exhibits, too. Politics, culture, and the world would never be the same again.

Some 58 nations and two international bodies gave the fair a remarkable international flavor, given the fragility of the world's peace. The Soviet government's announcement that it would support a $4 million pavilion provided a heady precedent. Foreign governments put up some $31 million for buildings and $100 million worth of exhibits.

The Soviet pavilion, designed by Boris Iofan and Karo S. Alabian, was adorned with Vyacheslav Andreyev's bombastic steel figure, "The New Soviet Citizen." The star in the hand of this 79-foot figure glowed red at night, warning low-flying planes of its presence. The figure was nicknamed "Big Joe" and "the Bronx Express Straphanger," and dominated the semicircular building.

During the fair's first season, the Soviet-German August 1939 nonaggression pact had shocked the world. The next month, the Germans had invaded Poland from the west, the Soviets slightly later from the east. The announcement of the German invasion was made over the fair's loudspeakers and the fair closed for the day. In the two months that remained in the first season, the Polish pavilion became a major attraction.

World events moved swiftly and dramatically between the fair's two seasons. Changes in the fair from one season to the next were also

extensive and at least largely due to this rapidly evolving international situation. Even as they transpired, Whalen traveled to Europe between the fair's seasons, cajoling head of states to ensure that their national exhibits would remain for 1940. The huge sums of money at stake, however, were probably the second biggest factor in those changes.

In comparison with the traumas of World War II, the fair's changes between seasons were hardly earth shattering. They were vital for the fair, though, and included reducing the general admission price from 75 cents to 50 cents in the hopes of boosting attendance — though estimates of what an average individual might spend during a day at the fair during the first season were closer to $15. The cost of an adult season ticket was reduced from $15 to $10. Children were charged only a quarter daily admission during both seasons, could get in for only a dime one day a week, and could get a season's ticket for five dollars.

There were other changes. A Negro week was initiated. Harvey Gibson, the president of the fair corporation for the 1940 season, brought in rowdier entertainment, not that a bare breast or two was an unknown sight in the first season. The Amusement Zone was rechristened the Great White Way and, as in the first season, continued to close at 2 A.M., four hours after the fair's exhibit buildings. The new motto, "For Peace and Freedom," reflected the fair's relentless optimism and the nation's hopeful spirit. In November 1939, the Soviets invaded Finland. They pulled out of the fair for the 1940 season, and their pavilion was dismantled and shipped back to the Soviet Union. In its place, an American Common celebrated free speech through occasional programs and performances.

Other nations with notable exhibits included Greece, Great Britain, Japan, and Italy. The Japanese had launched a vicious war in China in 1937. It continued as the fair began and the Chinese had no official exhibit. They had exhibited a replica of the Golden Temple of Jehol at the Century of Progress. This replica of the Golden Temple represented them again in Queens. Sadly, it was located in the Amusement Zone.

Still, other smaller countries, such as Lebanon, Luxembourg, Iceland, and Iraq, sponsored beautiful pavilions. Though the fair's architecture was largely modern, buildings such as the Hall of States— the site of a celebration of cultural evolution by 33 American states and three territories— were allowed a more traditional architectural approach.

To the men and women who propelled their fair forward, it might have sometimes seemed that, like the country struggling to get on its feet again, they were riding the crest of a very large wave. They radiated relentless optimism and compelling visions of how much better the future could be in science, communication, business, and the arts. The organizers had put on a show that was adorned with strikingly original art, new products ideas, and the art of compromise amid spirited and endless debate.

There is no other world's fair in history that had its proceedings as profoundly influenced by international politics and war as the New York World's Fair of 1939–1940. The questions that these forces projected included those of who could participate and how they could continue their participation and the fair's viability when their very existence as nations was threatened. The wonder was not that the fair failed to live up to the great expectations of those that thought that it could both fulfill its boundlessly ambitious agenda and generate a profit, but that it managed to survive intact for a second season under the unparalleled stresses of having much of the world fall to pieces all around it.

Its legacy sprang from the fact that although a commercial endeavor, its ambitious program was born because of a special interaction between intellectual, creative, and commercial forces. Its birth had coincided with the emergence of the nation from the most severe economic calamity in its history. It was the beneficiary of emerging new technologies that promised breathtaking improvements for consumers whose psyches had been thoroughly pummeled by the rigors of the Great Depression. The way that the fair brought together such disparate forces to forge its way was a harbinger of how the war would be fought to its victorious conclusion, and if the consumer and technological benefits promised at the fair had to be postponed until the war was over, they were awesome in their impact when they finally arrived.

When it was over the fair corporation declared bankruptcy. Some 44 million had attended the fair — about 6 million fewer than anticipated — and their memories were so vivid that the able and imperious Robert Moses competed with them a quarter century later when New York tried to recreate the magic of 1939–1940

In the amusement zone at the 1939 New York World's Fair, one of the favorite attractions was the Parachute Jump (editors' collection).

in 1964. By most reports, including those who had attended both world's fairs, the creativity, excitement, and collective effort in the earlier world's fair left the grander imprint on their memories.

The architects and designers of the New York World's Fair in 1939–1940 had created a place where the millions whose names have often been forgotten might have rubbed shoulders with others whose names sometimes still resonate. Though celebrities like Babe Ruth and Eddie Rickenbacker served the fair actively and well, it was staged for those who had survived the worst of the hard times. Soon they were to be challenged to the limits of their emotional and physical strength. In the interim, they were offered a visionary festival of how things could be and from it they took joy, knowledge, inspiration, and awe.

Bibliography

The records of the New York World's Fair are held in the Manuscripts and Archives Division of the New York Public Library in New York City. They are extensive, consisting of 1,174 record cartons, 192 volumes, and other materials that cover every aspect of the fair. The papers include administrative, legal, financial, and departmental files, public relations materials, press releases and clippings, photographs, artifacts and memorabilia, and phonographic recordings of events at the fair. Fortunately, there is a finding aid, published in 1985, that researchers can access on-line through the New York Public Library website (*www.nypl.org*).

Other manuscript collections that contain material of interest about the New York World's Fair include the Papers of James F. Byrnes at Clemson University, the Papers of Harry Frank Guggenheim, Arthur B. Spignam, Lee Lawrie, and Harold B. Ickes, all at the Library of Congress, the Papers of George McAneny at Princeton University, and the Papers of Robert Moses, at the New York Public Library.

Frank Monaghan, *Official Guide Book of the New York World's Fair 1939* (1939), is useful, as is Kathryn Maadrey's revised edition of the guidebook for the 1940 season. The New York *Times* and other New York newspapers covered the fair on a daily basis and frequently editorialized about its costs, administration, and other issues of the day. .Many contemporary magazines and journals published articles about the fair; check the *Reader's Guide to Periodical Literature* for specific journals or titles.

Secondary works include Ed Tyng, *Making a World's Fair* (1958), on the planning and development of the event; Helen Harrison, curator, *Dawn of a New Day* (1980), the catalogue of an exhibit prepared for the fortieth anniversary of the fair that contains several good analytical essays; Richard Wurts, *The New York World's Fair 1939/1940* (1977), a large-format pictorial record, and Andrew F. Wood, *New York 1939–40 World's Fair* (2004), a smaller-format pictorial history. The fiftieth anniversary of the fair produced two nostalgic books of interest: Larry Zim, Mel Lerner, and Herbert Rolfes, *The World of Tomorrow: The 1939 New York World's Fair* (1989), and Barbar Cohen, Steven Heller, and Seymour Chwast, *Trylon and Perisphere* (1989). Finally, Grover Whalen's autobiography, *Mr. New York* (1955), presents his perspective on the fair in which he was so deeply involved.

Two popular novels give some insight into the ambience of the fair: E.L. Doctorow, *World's Fair* (1985), and David H. Gelertner, *1939: The Lost World of the Fair* (1995).

A website of note is *www.newyorkgames.org/news/archives/000262.html*.

San Francisco 1939–1940

Donald G. Larson

Golden Gate International Exposition

The nineteen thirties were years of depression across the nation, and San Francisco was particularly hard hit. Two great building projects, the Golden Gate Bridge and the San Francisco-Oakland Bay Bridge, stimulated the economy in the Bay area. In honor of these two monumental engineering feats, city leaders promoted holding a world's fair. San Francisco had previously hosted two world's fairs, the California Midwinter Exposition of 1894 and the Panama-Pacific International Exposition of 1915. Both had been successful and had shown that a world's fair would provide jobs and stimulation to the local economy as well as boost tourism in California. Both San Francisco and New York were planning fairs in 1939. New York partisans in the federal government attempted to force San Francisco to postpone its fair, but President Franklin D. Roosevelt maintained support for the west coast. Eventually New York City Mayor Fiorello La Guardia came to the San Francisco fair for dinner.

By the 1930s, open space had all but disappeared in San Francisco. Where could a world's fair be held? Engineers devised perhaps the most innovative approach for the location of any world's fair to that date, a man-made island in the middle of San Francisco Bay. The Bay Bridge went through Yerba Buena Island, and it would provide auto access by a causeway from the bridge. A 400-acre rectangular site was dredged and filled over the shoals of Yerba Buena Island with a cove between the two islands for boats and a seaplane launching area. Unlike the previous fairs in San Francisco, where automobile parking was not an issue, the parking now needed was provided at the north end of the island. Ferry slips were also built, giving water access from various cities around San Francisco Bay to what would become Treasure Island.

Treasure Island glittered in the sunlight by day and glowed gloriously by night, clearly visible from both sides of the bay. Its design was the culmination of world's fair design in America, stretching back as far as the 1876 Centennial. The exposition company built the buildings and created courts and vistas in harmonious patterns, and the exhibitors displayed their wares in these palaces. Subsequent fairs have allowed the exhibitors to construct buildings to their own design, consequently losing the cohesive design of earlier world's fairs.

Treasure Island had a Pacific Basin theme. Western and oriental motifs were used in the design of the exposition palaces and grand courts. Visitors could enter the site through two great towers reminiscent of Angkor Wat called Portals of the Pacific, but nicknamed

"Elephant Towers" by President Roosevelt when he toured the site. This was one of two entrances through the western wall of the exposition, designed to shelter fairgoers from the bay breezes. Baffle entrances between the towers led directly into the Court of Honor with the 400-foot Art Deco Tower of the Sun rising in the center and capped by a golden phoenix. A carillon, now located in San Francisco's Grace Cathedral, rang out the hours and was often used for concerts.

Moving north from the Court of Honor, one entered the Court of the Seven Seas, which stretched 1,000 feet between the exposition palaces to the Court of Pacifica. Great prows of sailing ships lined the walls, honoring the glories of exploration. Bright banners on ships' masts and crow's nest lights brightened the avenue at night. The Court of Pacifica was a circular court with the Fountain of Western Waters at its center. Sculptures representing the various cultures of the Pacific Basin adorned the fountain. At the northern edge of the court, Pacifica, an 80-foot statue created by Ralph Stackpole, stood in front of an oriental prayer curtain that chimed in the breeze. At night the revolving illumination of the prayer curtain doubled as a background for the white-lit Pacifica. The names of the great discoverers who had opened the Pacific Ocean to the western world lined the walls.

Moving south from the Court of Honor and the Tower of the Sun, one entered the Court of the Moon. Colored "Evening Star Blue" by day, it became cobalt blue and indigo at night. A long rectangular pool stretched its length with arches of water crisscrossing the pool glowing at night in golden light provided by underwater illumination.

East of the Tower of the Sun fairgoers entered the Court of Reflections. Two rectangular pools reflected the Tower of the Sun from the east and the great Arch of Triumph from the west. The Arch of Triumph separated the Court of Reflections from the Court of Flowers, a square court surrounded by arches with a tiered fountain rising to a statue, Girl and Rainbow. Continuing east through the Court of Flowers one arrived at the Lake of Nations. Two great oriental Towers of the East dominated the outer wall of the Court of Flowers and reflected in the Lake of Nations before them. At night they glowed orange, orchid,

A picturesque view of the 1939–1940 Golden Gate International Exposition on Treasure Island, taken from nearby Yerba Buena Island.

This is an aerial view of Treasure Island in San Francisco Bay, site of the 1939—1940 Golden Gate expo. (Both photographs by Roberts and Roberts, Berkeley, California. Larson Collection, Special Collections Library, California State University, Fresno.)

pink, and gold. Great Thai lanterns illuminated the walkways.

East across the Lake of Nations and perpendicular to the Tower of the Sun stood the Federal Building. Forty-eight columns represented the forty-eight United States at that time. Colorful murals decorated the walls. On either side of the Federal Building and around the Lake of Nations were various state and international exhibits.

On the north side of the Lake of Nations stood the extremely modern and critically acclaimed Pacific House, the theme building of the fair. Six large murals by Miguel Covarrubias, displaying the economy and culture of the Pacific Rim, adorned the walls. In the center of

The Larson family outside the Court of Flowers (courtesy of Donald Larson).

the great hall was an oceanic relief map of the Pacific Basin with spouting dolphins. White in 1939, its walls became red the next year when the exposition company brightened the colors for the 1940 season.

Behind the Pacific House was the amusement center called the Gayway. Numerous venues separated the fairgoers from their money. In the dinosaur exhibit children were excited to watch the moving animatronic creatures. Other attractions included a diving bell in a pool of fish, a carousel with hand carved creatures, twin ferris wheels, a roller-coaster, a Scottish village, and most notoriously, Sally Rand's Nude Ranch, which was definitely off limits for adolescents. Free outdoor variety shows were a regular occurrence.

A great amphitheatre was built behind the Court of Pacifica to show "The Cavalcade of the Golden West" (1939) and "The Cavalcade of a Nation" (1940). On a stage 400 feet wide and 200 feet deep with a water curtain spraying some 30 feet high, a cast of 300 actors and 200 animals displayed the history of the west in these pageants.

Billy Rose brought his highly popular Aquacade from New York to San Francisco in 1940. It was a profitable venture, and featured Johnny Weissmuller, Esther Williams, and Gertrude Ederle along with the Aquabelles and Aquabeaux.

Julius L. Girod, a San Francisco park superintendent, worked his magic in creating gardens and floral displays of incredible beauty on a budget of $1.8 million from the Works Progress Administration. Sparkling fountains and breathtaking views of San Francisco and the East Bay across the water gave visitors a marvelous display. It was a wonderful place to walk, but other forms of transportation were provided. There were Elephant Trains, Swan Boats on the Lake of Nations, rickshaw rides, and rolling cars. Air flight was still relatively new to most people in 1939, so it was quite exciting to watch the Pan-American China Clipper take off from Yerba Buena

Cove outside the Hall of Transportation on its way to the Orient.

The various exhibit palaces held a myriad of displays. Model trains were displayed in the Hall of Transportation. Mr. Peanut was hawking his wares in the Food Building. People got their first look at television in the Communication Building. General Motors displayed a translucent Pontiac among its exhibits, and Westinghouse introduced a robot, "Willie Vocalite." A $40 million exhibit of classical paintings was displayed in the Palace of Fine and Decorative Arts in 1939, which was subsequently replaced by a show called "Art in Action" in 1940.

The Golden Gate International Exposition opened February 18, 1939, and closed September 29, 1940, with a six-month break in the middle. Leland W. Cutler served as exposition president in 1939, and Marshall Dill assumed the post in 1940. George Creel was the U.S. commissioner for both years. The fair closed with a gross attendance of 17,410,999 and debts totaling $539,423. Plans to turn the island into an international airport were abandoned when the U.S. Navy took over the island. The building's architectural embellishments were quickly torn down. Pacifica, the personification of peace, had a chain tied around her base and was pulled over on her face, broken into pieces. World War II had begun.

Bibliography

While there are numerous sources available for a detailed study of the Golden Gate International Exposition 1939–1940, the following sources are particularly helpful. Beginning in 1937, fair organizers published a newsletter publicizing the fair and detailing its progress, *Golden Gate International Exposition Bulletin*. The *Official Guide Book* (1939), edited by Gladys Tilden Walker, has a pull-out color map of the site. A revised guide was pub-

lished for the 1940 season. The catalogue of the 1939 art exhibit is *Masterworks of Five Centuries* (1939). H.C. Bottorff, *Closing Report: San Francisco Bay Exposition, Sponsor for the Golden Gate International Exposition* (1942), is the official history of the fair. Bottorff, the executive vice-president and general manager, includes a wealth of statistics for the fair, ranging from daily attendance figures to gardening costs. Jack James and Earle Weller, *Treasure Island, the Magic City* (1941) is a heavily illustrated description of the exposition, with information on activities and special events during the two-season run of the fair and statistical appendixes. There is even a list of all the fair employees during the two years. The art and architecture of the fair is described and explained in Eugen Neuhaus, *The Art of Treasure Island* (1939), and in "San Francisco Exposition 1939," *Architectural Forum* 70 (June 1939): 463–500. Richard Reinhardt, *Treasure Island, San Francisco's Exposition Years* (1973), is a fascinating and well-illustrated reminiscence by a modern authority on fairs who visited the Golden Gate International Exposition numerous times when he was eleven years old. Reinhardt has also written a fiftieth-anniversary retrospective of the fair, "The Other Fair," *American Heritage* 40, 4 (May/June 1989): 42–53. Other modern work on the exposition includes Robert W. Rydell, "The 1939 San Francisco Golden Gate International Exposition and the Empire of the West," in Rob Kroes, ed., *The American West asb Seen by Europeans and Americans* (1989), Richard H. Dillon, "Treasure island: Our Other 1939–1940 World's Fair," *American History Illustrated* 25, 2 (May/June 1990): 52–69, and Lisa Rubens, "Re-presenting the Nation: The Golden Gate International Exposition," in Robert W. Rydell and Nancy E. Gwinn, eds., *Fair Representations: World's Fairs and the Modern World* (1994). Finally, in the Donald G. Larson World's Fair Collection 1851–1940, Special Collections Department, Henry Madden Library, California State University, Fresno, there are numerous items dealing with the Golden Gate International Exposition, including written material, reports, memorabilia, photographs, motion pictures, records and postcards.

Wellington 1939–1940

Conal McCarthy

New Zealand Centennial Exhibition

The last world's fair in New Zealand

marked the "one hundred crowded years" since the signing of New Zealand's founding document the Treaty of Waitangi in 1840. There were many advocates for this exhibition: the

A certificate of attendance from the New Zealand Centennial Exhibition (courtesy Alexander Turnbull Library, Wellington, New Zealand, Zoe Martin–Carter collection).

mayor of Wellington, Thomas Hislop, Labour Party politicians such as William Parry, and government officials such as J.W. Heenan. Heenan, from the Department of Internal Affairs, wanted to "create a national spirit." The exhibition was the centerpiece of an array of events organized by the National Centennial Committee, including books, monuments, re-enactments, festivals, art exhibitions and a film. The certificate of attendance depicted "Zealandia" as Britain's handmaiden of the South Seas, draped in a Union Jack and surrounded by native flora and fauna such as the kiwi. This image of New Zealand as a vital offspring of the mother country that had reached maturity, a modest expression of national identity, did not shake New Zealand's unquestioning loyalty to Britain.

With considerable financial support from the government, the exhibition was organized by a private company, led by an experienced manager in Scotsman Charles Hainsworth, who had come to New Zealand to manage the Dunedin exhibition of 1925–1926. The exhibition upstaged the rest of the official pageantry in early 1940 by opening in November 1939 in front of a large crowd of 40,000 people. Though it attracted local and national support, the timing was unfortunate, with the outbreak of the war limiting participants and attractions. There were few overseas visitors, some events were cancelled, and the company eventually lost money. The site on the Miramar peninsula in the Wellington suburb of Rongotai was accessible to the city but not ideal — it was an exposed and windswept place, with building curtailed by height restrictions due to the nearby aerodrome.

The contemporary Art Deco architecture was one of the most memorable features of the fair. The architect was Edmund Anscombe, who had worked on the Dunedin exhibition fourteen years earlier. Here the buildings were laid out on a similar axial plan with a broad avenue leading to a central hall with a striking tower which "symbolized the progress and ambition of the young nation." This tower became the exhibition's main symbol, and was reproduced on everything from souvenir books to crockery and teaspoons. The tower was lit at night so that visitors were entranced by the clean modern lines and curving forms reflected in the pools, with the Maori motifs adding a distinctive local flavor. Plaster sculptures and decorative art played their part in creating this vision of a bright, promising future. On the base of the tower was a stucco bas-relief frieze by Alison Duff which showed the march of progress like a Parthenaic procession. In contrast to the utilitarian exhibition halls, the interiors of the main courts boasted false ceilings, linoleum floors and artificial lighting. Intricately constructed displays announced by stylish Art Deco lettering were integrated into a flowing design that led visitors from booth to booth like a department store. William Toomath argues that the exhibition's extensive complex was one of the most complete manifestation of the streamlined art deco style in the world, probably inspired by the sweeping futuristic pavilions at the New York World's Fair of 1939. Another building of note was the Australian pavilion, designed in a stern modernist style by architect Arthur Stephenson.

The tower block of the New Zealand Centennial Exhibition, was the tallest building and the centerpiece of the fair (Alexander Turnbull Library, Wellington, New Zealand, Eileen Deste collection ½-036219-F).

With respect to its contents, this fair was oriented more toward the future than earlier ones in Dunedin and Christchurch, emphasizing the material and technological progress of the modern age. Another theme was the beneficent role of the government in the lives of its citizens. The extensive government court included an extraordinary range of exhibits: armed forces, transport, education, internal affairs, external affairs (including Pacific Island dependencies Samoa, Niue, and the Cook Islands), health, housing, industry and commerce, labor, land development, post and telegraph, broadcasting, public works, state advances, public trust, tourism, and publicity. In the women's section there were arts and crafts, classes on cooking, and other activities that reflected the conventional domestic roles of women, something that was about to change dramatically with the wartime manpower shortage. Despite the generally serious tone of these exhibits, there was time for recreation and even fun. The social security department used a mechanised robot called "Dr. Well-and-Strong" who led a tour along the "Highway to Health and Happiness." Among the most popular exhibits were the miniature model of New Zealand and the underground replica of the famous Waitomo caves. As usual the entertainment was popular with the public. Some 150,000 people flocked to the cinema, the concerts at the band shells were well attended, and at "Playland," the big hit was the Cyclone roller coaster. Overall the trend was towards a different style of leisure attraction, a total experience for the whole family in an immersive world of its own that pointed the way towards the theme parks and shopping malls of the post-war period.

Despite the fact that the exhibition emphasised the cultural dimension of nationalism, it did not include fine art aside from historical murals in the government court, as recent centennials of Australian states had. The Centennial Exhibition of International and New Zealand art was staged at the National Art Gallery and the Academy of Fine Arts in Wellington, far from the fairgrounds. This large show was made up mostly of British art loaned by artist-dealer Mary Murray Fuller. Meanwhile, A.H. McLintock arranged a more adventurous historical survey of the country's best art, the National Centennial Exhibition of New Zealand Art, which toured the country in 1940–1941.

If the exhibition's official imagery was guilty of celebrating the nation's progress by contrasting a Maori past to a *Pakeha* (European) present, influential Maori politician Apirana Ngata set out to challenge this view through the Native Department display. The Maori court featured an unnamed *whare runanga* (council house). Though designed and built in some haste, its mixture of modern and traditional elements, particularly the interior design and decoration, nevertheless expressed the dynamism of Maori culture. It could be argued that the recent revival of customary arts and crafts, part of a wider "Maori renaissance," represented an indigenous attempt to create a place for themselves in modern New Zealand. As Ngata wrote in the guide to the Maori court, "It may be claimed that no object or exhibit with its blend of a beautiful ancient form with modern adaptations could more suitably symbolise the present stage of development of the Maori people."

Bibliography

The primary documents relating to the New Zealand Centennial Exhibition are extensive. The records of the New Zealand Centennial Exhibition Company are held in the Wellington City Archives. The minutes of the National Centennial Committee and other exhibition-related material are kept in the files of the Department of Internal Affairs, Archives New Zealand, Wellington. Relevant correspondence and other papers may be found in the J.W. Heenan Collection, Alexander Turnbull Library, Wellington. Clippings from daily newspapers as well as the official exhibition newspaper, *New Zealand Centennial News,* can also be found in the Turnbull Library. Edmund Anscombe's color film of the exhibition can be found at the National Film Archives, Wellington. Short clips of this film, plus a rich selection of other visual resources, may seen online in the Centennial Exhibition section of the website *NZHistory.net http://www.nzhistory.net. nz/*. Photographs and other images of the exhibition may be found by searching on the Alexander Turnbull Library's database *Timeframes http:// timeframes.natlib.government.nz/*

Secondary sources on the exhibition are also extensive. The views of politicians at the time on the exhibition can be gleaned from speeches recorded in *New Zealand Parliamentary Debates* (1937–1940). The most comprehensive coverage is provided in N. Palethorpe, *Official History of the New Zealand Centennial Exhibition, Wellington, 1939–40* (1940). The major published report is *Official Guide to the Government Court: New Zealand Centennial Exhibition 1939–40* (1939). The best photographic coverage of the exhibition and its contents can be found in *Pictorial Souvenir of the New Zealand Centennial Exhibition 1939–40* (1939). Fascinating insights into the Maori section of the exhibition can be found in a booklet issued by the Native Department, Apirana Ngata, *New Zealand Centennial Exhibition: The Maori Court Souvenir* (1940).

Among modern studies, a good starting place is William Renwick, ed., *Creating a National Spirit: Celebrating New Zealand's Centennial* (2004), which covers the exhibition in the context of all the other centennial events. Renwick's book includes useful chapters on the background to the exhibition (Gavin McLean) architecture (William Toomath), the Maori court (Bernie Kernot), and the art exhibitions (Roger Blackley). For a study of Anscombe's architecture, see G. Bowron's "A Brilliant Spectacle: the Centennial Exhibition Buildings," in John Wilson, ed., *Zeal and Crusade: the Modern Movement in New Zealand* (1996). A recent study of the Maori displays in the context of a longer history of Maori exhibitions can be found in Conal McCarthy, *Exhibiting Maori: A History of Colonial Cultures of Display* (2007). The most recent general histories of New Zealand are

James Belich, Paradise *Reforged: A History of the New Zealanders from the 1880s to the Year 2000* (2001), and Tom Brooking, *The History of New Zealand* (2004). For useful biographies of the people involved in the exhibition, consult the *Dictionary of New Zealand Biography http://www.dnzb.govt.nz/.*

Lisbon 1940

John E. Findling

Exposição do Mundo Português

The idea for a Lisbon world's fair came from Antonio Ferro, the national secretariat of propaganda or Portugal, and the fair was organized by Captain Henrique Galvão, a close friend of dictator Antonio de Oliveira Salazar but later an opponent of the regime. Its purpose was to glorify the fascist regime of Salazar, although the official rationale was to "set forth in pageant, dance, and patriotic community gatherings, the story of eight centuries of Portuguese history." The fair celebrated the anniversaries of the founding of Portugal in 1140 and independence from Spain after sixty years of rule in 1640.

Located in the Belém district near the Hieronymite Monastery in Lisbon where Vasco da Gama and the poet Luiz Vaz de Camões were buried, the fair celebrated three eras of history. The first cycle, which took place in the spring of 1940, had medieval history as its theme. The events included town meetings on opening day, June 2, a speech by Salazar, an exhibit of primitive art in the Museum of Ancient Art, and a Navy Day festival with a reception aboard a replica of a fifteenth-century caravel, a naval procession on the River Tagus complete with a scheduled landing of a Pan-Am Clipper, a review of international fleets, and an exhibit of the exploits of the first navigators on the Rock of Sagres.

The second cycle's theme, which took place during the summer months, was imperial history. It featured an exhibit of arts and crafts, a garden containing colonial designs from Africa, China, and India, a pageant of twenty-one imperial provinces, a festival for Camoes, and an Olympic week in a stadium newly built for the fair.

The final phase commemorated the Brigantine Epoch, from 1640 on, and took place in the fall. It featured gala performances in the reconstructed opera house and tours of the restored seventeenth-century quarter of Lisbon.

The fair's opening on June 2 coincided with the British evaluation of Dunkirk, which almost completely crowded it out of the newspapers. Because of World War II, the fair had much less foreign participation than had been planned. In particular, the review of international fleets suffered because of the war and tensions among those countries still neutral. At the opening, Salazar and the colonial patriarch attended services at the Lisbon Cathedral while the town council and the National Assembly had ceremonial meetings. On June 30, the British, anxious to keep Portugal neutral, commissioned the duke of Kent, brother to King George VI, to award Salazar the Grand Cross of the Most Distinguished Order of St. Michael and St. George, an award usually reserved for a Briton. The fair, overshadowed by the war, attracted nowhere near the attention given to the competing New York World's Fair. When it closed on December 3, there were rumors that the director of colonial fairs and exhibitions and national broadcasting had profited from the fair. Salazar dismissed the charges as communist-inspired and declared his satisfaction with a fair O. H. de Oliveira Marques described as "a typical Fascist display in its manner of interpreting the past and abusing it to herald the present."

Bibliography

The records from the exposition are kept in the archives of the Calouste Gulbenkian Foundation Library in Lisbon (*www.gulbenkian.pt*). In addition, the Museu de Arte Popular in the Lisbon district of Belém has on display many of the folk art exhibits from the 1940 fair. There is very little information on the Lisbon world's fair in English, either in books or newspapers. There is some mention of the fair in the New York *Times* and the *Times* of London, but the former was more occupied with the New York World's Fair and the latter with World War II and England's precarious situation. Nor does it rate more than a passing note in most histories of Portugal and is often omitted from histories of world's fairs.

The best source of information on the fair, once the propagandistic element is discounted, is the *Portuguese Bulletin of Political, Economic and Cultural Information*, no. 30/31, which is completely devoted to the Exhibition of the Portuguese World. Two books in Portuguese contain much information about the fair. The first is Gustaro do Matos Sequeira, *Mundo Português — Images de uma Exposição Historica 1940* (1956). As the title suggests, this book is an illustrated retrospective of the fair that provides a sense of the design of the exposition. The other work is by Augusto de Castro, the general commissioner of the fair. Entitled *A Exposição do Mundo Português* (1940), it is a general history of Lisbon and the Portuguese empire and discusses the preexhibition planning.

Finally, three general histories provide the necessary political and social context for the exposition: O. H. de Oliveira Marques, *History of Portugal,* vol. II (1972) is a broad treatment, while Antonio de Fegueiredo, *Portugal: Fifty Years of Dictatorship* (1976) concentrates on the mid-twentieth century era of Salazar rule. A more recent history, James M. Anderson, *The History of Portugal* (2000), is a short general survey.

Port-au-Prince 1949–1950

Kimberly D. Perle

Exposition Internationale du Bicentenaire de Port-au-Prince

The international exposition in Haiti in 1949 was planned to celebrate the bicentennial of the founding of Port-au-Prince, but the main idea behind what came to be known as the "little world's fair" was to attract tourists and stimulate the economy.

Plans for the exposition arose in 1948 while Haiti, with the help of some international financial aid, was undergoing a period of modernization. President Dumarsais Estime wanted to show off the "new Haiti" and its culture and hoped that a world's fair would entice tourists and pleasure seekers. Estime committed approximately $1 million, close to three-fourths of Haiti's entire annual budget, to the bicentennial.

In the latter part of 1948, the Haitian government reclaimed 60 acres of waterfront land on La Gonave Bay, relocated some 20,000 people who lived in this impoverished area, and began converting the land into a scenic wonderland surrounded by lush gardens, beautiful parks, and an abundance of tall coconut and palm trees. The site curved 2 miles along the bay and was divided by a boulevard named in honor of President Harry S Truman.

August Ferdinand Schmiedigen, an architect from New York, whose experience included the Paris 1937 and New York 1939 — 1940 world's fairs, oversaw the construction of the exposition. Modernistic white and gray buildings were erected along the boulevard, their exteriors boasting colorful murals of Haitian life. All of the buildings were permanent structures designed to be used as government offices after the exposition. Although Schmiedigen had time constraints to worry about and unskilled native labor to direct, he ensured that every detail was just right. The Haitian section of the fair, however, was designed by architect Albert Mangones and was said to have had a "pleasing disregard for straight lines."

Throughout the site's strategically placed gardens and parks were an array of statues and sculptures. In the central garden a "super-electric-musical-luminous" fountain was installed. Westinghouse experts said it was one of the most impressive fountains they had ever seen, surpassing even the New York World's Fair fountain for special effects. According to most visitors, the transformation of the swampy slum was breathtaking, and this gave the Haitian citizens feelings of pride and enthusiasm for the upcoming events.

The exposition opened in two sections. On December 8, 1949, the national section, including the agricultural, fine arts, and folklore pavilions, and the amusement area opened along with the government-sponsored National Casino of Haiti. At the opening ceremony, a telegram from President Harry S Truman to President Estime was read, followed by a parade of U. S. soldiers and marines. During the parade a squadron of nine U. S. Air Force B-29s flew over the line of march.

Ceremonies dedicating the international section were held on February 12, 1950. On the following day, the U.S. pavilion opened along with other official and foreign pavilions. President Estime and his wife, after presiding over the opening ceremonies, took a guided tour of the U.S. exhibit. Other pavilions displayed the exhibits of Cuba, France, Venezuela, Guatemala, Italy, Mexico, Argentina, and other participating nations, as well as the Pan American Union and the United Nations. The Vatican contributed a small, permanent chapel to grace the exposition grounds.

Visitors could walk through the scenic exposition grounds and enjoy native exhibits, consisting of works of art, handcrafted articles of mahogany, needlework, pottery, silver, historical documents, furniture, and agricultural products. The principal attraction for most visitors was the Haitian folklore troupe, which presented a program of folk dancing several times a month that portrayed the customs and yearnings of the Haitian people. Programs involved voodoo rituals and beliefs, accompanied by drum beating and songs that told stories of primitive religions. These shows were held in an open-air theater, also known as the "voodoo amphitheater."

Other points of interest included a cockfight stadium, a botanical garden, an aquarium of tropical fish, a model banana and sisal plantation, and a burlesque show imported form the United States. The midway, named Les Palmistes because it was built in the heart of a palm tree forest, was also a crowd pleaser. The park was operated by Ross Manning Shows, an amusement company from the United States, and featured carousels, carnival pitchmen, and a variety of thrilling rides and sideshows.

The theme of the exposition, Peace and Progress, was only partially appropriate. Although Haiti's program of modernization was closely linked to the idea of progress, the country's political conflict with neighboring Dominican Republic was a constant threat to peace. The small attendance figure was attributed to Haiti's political problems. It is estimated that approximately 250,000 people attended the bicentennial celebration before it closed on June 8, 1950.

Haiti's exposition failed to attract as large a number of tourists from the United States as hoped; most of those attending were Haitians. But despite the political unrest and low attendance figures, the exposition was not a complete loss. Haiti, often looked upon as a Third World country, seemed to have a future in the modern world. The exposition created more jobs, new businesses, better roads, beautiful parks, and much-needed government office buildings. Most importantly the bicentennial exposition lifted the spirit and morale of the Haitian people.

Bibliography

Primary sources regarding Haiti's bicentennial exposition are few. For an in-depth study of U.S. participation in this fair, refer to U.S. Senate, Foreign Relations Committee, 81st Cong., 2d sess., *Port-au-Prince Bicentennial Exposition* (1950). For those who are able to read French, Augustin Mathurin, *Bicentenaire de la fondation de Port-au-Prince, 1749–1949* (1975), is an interesting book on the historical aspects of the fair, written in memory of President Dumarsais Estime. Selected articles in the *New York Times* provide good background information. See especially the issues dated October 4, 16, 23, 25, 1949. Additional information can be found in George S. Schuyler, "Haiti Looks Ahead," *Americas*, 1 (December 1949): 6–8; and "Unparalleled Fair," *Time*, 54 (October 17, 1949): 40.

London 1951

Harriet Atkinson

The Festival of Britain

The 1951 Festival of Britain was first proposed by the Royal Society of Arts in London as a way of marking the centenary of London's 1851 Great Exhibition. Prime Minister Clement Attlee's Labour government agreed to hold and pay for the Festival and set up a department to oversee it. Early in its development, however, its organizers decided that the event would differ from its predecessor of 1851 in one crucial respect: it would exclusively be a celebration of British achievement or, in the phrase used at the time, an "autobiography of the nation." While the factors encouraging this decision were connected to the immediate economic pressures that Britain was experiencing in the aftermath of the World War II, the consequences for the established form of the international exhibition were significant. The Festival marked the emergence of a new type of exhibition that turned the world's fair model on its head, by putting a nation state on show to the world.

Inverting the practice of gathering all exhibits from across the world in one place, the Festival assembled exhibits from just one country — Britain — into a single narrative of achievements for the world to observe (significantly without reference to the British colonies or Commonwealth). As a consequence, the structure of the exhibition also changed. While the Great Exhibition had been an exhibition of all nations on a single site at London's Crystal Palace, the Festival of Britain became in its organizers' words "a constellation of events" across Britain.

The government organised eight official Festival exhibitions with the professed aim of displaying Britain "at home to the world." The Festival exhibitions each differed in style and content, with that at London's South Bank forming the spectacular centrepiece, opening on May 4, 1951. Set by the south side of the River Thames, with the Houses of Parliament as backdrop, it was structured around 27 pavilions dedicated to every aspect of British life from "Power and Production" to "Homes and Gardens." Among many structures, two were singled out for particular praise: Ralph Tubbs's monumental aluminium-roofed Dome of Discovery (at 365 feet in diameter, it was the largest dome in the world) and Powell & Moya's feat of engineering the towering, aluminium-clad Skylon (standing 320 feet high). Elsewhere in London, a Pleasure Gardens at Battersea gave visitors light relief from the more didactic content of the South Bank exhibition; a major exhibition at South Kensington explored the possibilities of science; and an exhibition of 'Live Architecture' set out through pavilions and new housing, schools, and churches to show the possibilities for designing areas under reconstruction. Major Festival exhibitions were also held in Glasgow and Belfast, and two travelling exhibitions toured Britain, one by land and one by sea on a decommissioned World War II aircraft carrier.

The idea uniting all Festival exhibitions was that each told an aspect of a British "story." This so-called story was told both through the placement of buildings on the sites and through the words, images, and objects of the exhibitions. The Festival marked the apotheosis of British exhibition design's experimentation with narrative structuring, and displays were heavily dependent on words, as well as images and objects, to communicate their message; a legacy from wartime government poster and exhibition design and from public information films.

The events were conceived to appeal to an international audience, and marketing was aimed particularly at Europe and North America. Four London buses were shipped to mainland Europe early in 1951 to drive across the continent on an advance marketing tour; numerous articles and advertisements were placed in U.S. newspapers and magazines. Most notable, in the context of post war privations in Britain, was the Festival organisers' decision to spend $100,000 on the first ever four-page full color advertisement in *Life* magazine; inviting Americans to come to Britain in 1951.

While the Festival itself marked a dramatic departure from the structure of previous international expositions, its designers drew their inspiration from earlier fairs including the 1930 Stockholm Exhibition, the 1938 Glasgow Empire Exhibition and the 1939 New York World's Fair. Indeed, several Festival designers had made significant contributions to these earlier exhibitions. Eminent Festival exhibition designer Misha Black, for example, had worked on pavilions at both the 1938 Glasgow Exhibition and the 1939 New York World's Fair. Self-consciously departing from the axial site plans they associated with the Beaux-Arts school, seen previously at the 1893 Chicago World's Fair and successive Paris expositions, the Festival's designers chose a plan based more on informal, meandering circulation around the site. The landscaping of the site signalled British architects' renewed conviction in the validity of the eighteenth-century English Picturesque as a viable aesthetic for post-war British public planning. An eighteenth-century English visual category hugely influential throughout Europe, the Picturesque was concerned with contriving landscapes to appear like painted compositions in order to provide

visual variety. Originally developed and shaped by the landowners of English private country estates, it was identified around the time of the Festival as applicable within the new context of British urban public planning. The focus on the possibilities for visual play and informality at the Festival's South Bank Exhibition in London, rather than on grand spatial axes, was necessitated by its relatively small area of 29 acres by comparison with previous international exhibition sites, such as the 1939 New York World's Fair site, for example, with its 1,216 acres.

By the time the Festival closed on September 30, 1951, more than one in three Britons were estimated to have attended, with a total of almost 13 million people visiting events around the country and over eight million visiting the London exhibitions. The Festival's organizers noted later that they had failed in their initial idea of making this a true celebration of the whole country: the central London events were by far the most popular, capturing the imagination of press and public by virtue of their sheer visual impact and scale, and it is these that have since become synonymous with the Festival. The Festival's design was heavily referenced in the subsequent 1958 Brussels World Expo. At home it also spawned a derivative aesthetic — "Festival style" — which referenced the atomic structures favored in textiles and products produced for the events; this was at once emulated and vilified. Architects and town planners regarded the Festival's exhibitions as a pattern book for national reconstruction, particularly of the New Towns of the early 1950s. The Festival of Britain was based in a long tradition of international exhibitions but it subverted that tradition to meet the needs of the British post-war context.

Bibliography

Following the close of the Festival exhibitions, their contents were widely dispersed and sold at auction. Unfortunately, no single museum collection holds a large number of Festival items. Important alternative primary sources are the multiple guides and catalogues that were produced to accompany each of the government sponsored exhibitions. Most of the local events were also accompanied by leaflets and guides;

these are held by many major British libraries. Festival of Britain archive records can be found at the National Archives at Kew, London; the Public Records Office of Northern Ireland in Belfast; the Royal Society of Arts, London; the National Art Library and Archive at the Victoria and Albert Museum, London; the Design Archives at Brighton University; the Museum of London Archives; and the Royal Institute of British Architects, London. A large number of contemporary publications devoted special editions to the Festival, including *Architects Journal, Architectural Review* and *Picture Post.*

Many films were commissioned for the Festival, to be shown both in cinemas and at various exhibition sites. These include *Family Portrait: A Film on the Theme of the Festival of Britain* (written and directed by Humphrey Jennings and Wessex Films, 1950); *Festival in London* (Crown Film Unit, 1951); *The Magic Box* (Festival Film Production, 1951); *David* (directed by Paul Dickson, World Wide Pictures, 1951). The majority can be viewed at the British Film Institute, London. *Brief City* (written and directed by Hugh Casson and Patrick O'Donovan, 1951), a short valedictory

film, made as the South Bank Exhibition closed, aimed to sum up the Festival's achievements. The British Broadcasting Corporation archives also hold a very large number of Festival broadcasts (which number around 2,700). Key secondary sources include Michael Frayn, "Festival," in Michael Sissons and Philip French, eds., *Age of Austerity* (1963); Mary Banham & Bevis Hillier, eds., *A Tonic to the Nation: The Festival of Britain 1951* (1976); Barry Curtis, "One Continuous Interwoven Story (The Festival of Britain),' *Block,* 11, (1985–86), reproduced in *Block Reader in Visual Culture* (1996); Inyang Isola Ime Ebong, "The Origins, Organisation and Significance of the Festival of Britain, 1951" (unpub. Ph.D. thesis, University of Edinburgh, 1986); Becky E. Conekin, *Autobiography of a Nation* (2003); Elaine Harwood and Alan Powers, eds., "Twentieth Century Architecture 5, Festival of Britain" in *The Journal of the Twentieth Century Society* (2001); Harriet Atkinson, "Imaginative Reconstruction: Designing Place at the Festival of Britain, 1951" (unpub. Ph.D. thesis, Royal College of Art and Victoria & Albert Museum, London, 2006).

Brussels 1958

Robert W. Rydell

Brussels Universal and International Exposition

Between April 17 and October 19, 1958, nearly 42 million visitors toured the Brussels Universal and International Exposition, the first major world's fair held in the postwar years and the first since the 1939–40 New York World's Fair. Like earlier Belgian fairs, the 1958 exposition was intended to promote Belgian economic growth and the development of Belgium-controlled Africa. But the 1958 fair rapidly acquired broader significance as tensions of the cold war increased and doubts deepened about the validity of the longstanding Western habit of equating progress with science and technology. By the time the fair opened, the exposition, with its towering Atom-

ium as centerpiece, had become a place for testing and shaping the possibilities of human existence under the shadow of nuclear destruction.

First proposed in 1947 and financed by the Belgian government, including a grant from the colonial lottery, and various corporations, the fair immediately fell victim to the rumblings of the cold war. Promoters of the event, including powerful Belgian metal and mining industries, initially set 1955 for the exposition's opening, but the Korean War disrupted international financial markets and political relations, forcing postponement until 1958. The cold war was equally in evidence once the fair opened as the United States and the Soviet Union built pavilions dedicated to propagandizing their rival political systems. The era's nuclear umbrella also provided cover for other exhibitors bent on defining the socioeconomic contours of the postwar world: scientists and engineers used the fair to promote the uses of nuclear power in energy development; the Belgian government relied on the fair to reaffirm domestic support for its crumbling imperial policies in the Congo; and multinational corporations, following the pattern of corporation-sponsored exhibits at the 1933–1934 Chicago Century of Progress Exposition, saw the fair as a public relations paradise for promoting the purported benefits to follow from global economic consolidation.

Direction of the fair was set by Baron George Moens de Fernig, the exposition's commissioner-general, and Charles Everaerts de Velp of the government's Ministry of Economic Affairs. In addition to securing royal lands to add to Heysel Park for purposes of expanding the 1935 exposition grounds, exposition directors set up an organization that oversaw exhibit development, architectural planning, and the supervision of as many as 15,000 Belgian and foreign construction workers.

The exposition grounds were vast, covering nearly 500 acres of undulating parkland that proved to one of the most beautiful settings for a world expo. The layout of exposition assumed an odd form. From a bird's-eye perspective, the design of the fair resembled nothing so much as a child's rendering of a large barnyard animal. Forming the head and shoulders were the Foreign Buildings; the main body was devoted to the Belgian and Belgian colonial exhibits; and the hindquarters was given over to scientific and cultural displays. Standing at the heart of the fair as well as at the intersection of four major arterial avenues was the Atomium.

The expo's architect-in-chief, Marcel van Goethen, determined that the main exhibit halls would be designed along modernist lines and that no effort would be made to establish a rigid formula similar to the one imposed at earlier fairs. The result was striking, if not especially significant architecturally. Exhibition halls represented an eclectic range of modernist styles that emphasized the playful possibilities of structures that seemed to defy gravity. "The fair of roofs," was how one critic described the archi-

At the 1958 Brussels exposition, the Atomium signaled the coming of the atomic age. It was the signature structure at this fair and remains an important tourist attraction (photograph by John E. Findling).

tectural landscape, while another noted the "glass-box-curtain-wall" effect of the buildings. Notable designes included Le Corbusier's Philips Pavilion (complete with the "Electronic Poem," composed by Edgard Varèse), often likened to a "collapsed aluminum tent" or to a "serious airline accident"; Egon Eiermann's West German Pavilion, a "necklace" of small two- and three-story exhibition halls; Edward Stone's U.S. Pavilion, "a merry-go-round of latticed plastic"; Alexander Boretski's Soviet Pavilion, which bore an uncanny resemblance to a refrigerator; Guillaume Gillet's steel-roofed French Pavilion; and J. van Dooselaere's beaklike Belgian Civil Engineering Building.

While it is easy to trivialize the architecture of the fair, it would be a mistake to overlook the ideological scaffolding that gave it form. Few critics missed the importance of the Soviet Pavilion — the first Soviet structure at any world's fair to break away from the heavy-handed socialist realist style that had guided the design of Soviet exhibition structures at fairs held in Paris (1937)

The U.S. pavilion, shown here amidst an array of state and territorial flags, earned criticism for its poor showing in the cold war propaganda contest with the U.S.S.R. pavilion (courtesy Peter M. Warner).

and New York (1939). For the first time, heroic statues of workers and party founders were located inside the building and not joined to the structure's exterior. While Russians were relying on a new architectural design to improve the image of the Soviet Union, Americans were engaged in similar public relations. Located diagonally across from the "closed-in" Soviet pavilion, the American pavilion, according to Western critics, placed a premium on "light, strength, and freedom." Not surprisingly, representatives of other nations watched nervously to determine if the transformation of the fair into an architectural rutting ground between the superpowers carried implications for international relations and noted the irony of locating the smaller pavilions of Middle Eastern countries between those of the United States and Soviet Union.

In addition to making a spectacle of cold war politics, the fair also permitted politicians in countries like Germany, Japan, and Italy, losers in the Second World War, to refurbish their national images and soothe memories of bat-

tle wounds among the victors. The small and unimposing German pavilion, often referred to as a jewel, contrasted sharply to Albert Speer's monument to Nazism at the 1937 Paris exposition. Instead of representing an exhibition of German power, German exhibits stressed "a Germany striving for a life which is cheerful, friendly and free, unhampered by anxious reference to danger in the world at large." Japan followed suit and seemed bent on exhibiting a new openness through the timber and glass construction of its pavilion, while the modesty and economy of scale of the Italian pavilion seemed light-years away from anything proposed by Mussolini in his plans for the E-42 fascist world expo.

Architecture was not alone in reflecting broader political configurations. Exhibits within the pavilions often became sources of controversy that reflected the anxieties about the Cold War. The U.S. government divided bitterly over the fair. President Dwight Eisenhower felt so strongly about the need for the

U.S. to make a strong showing that he included a special request for funds in his budget message to Congress, only to encounter strong opposition in the House of Representatives because of a portion of the exhibit dedicated to America's "Unfinished Business," especially with respect to civil rights for African Americans. Southerners termed this part of this exhibit a "gross insult to the South" and forced cuts to the budget for the exhibit. When these cuts forced the reduction of U.S. scientific exhibits in the International Hall of Science and the Soviet Union took over the space occupied by the Americans, American anxieties about competing with the Russians deepened. When it eventually took form, the American pavilion housed exhibits that equated the promise of consumerism with the meaning of freedom and democracy. Of all the exhibits in the American pavilion, the most popular was Circarama, a large exhibition hall with a 360-degree screen that enveloped visitors with a Walt Disney motion picture tour of the United States.

The Soviet Union treated the propaganda opportunity provided by the fair as seriously as did the Americans. Devoted to the "unseen blooming in Soviet science and culture," exhibits in the Soviet pavilion told the story of forty years of Russian technological and scientific progress since the revolution and were explicitly intended to counter efforts by the West to smear the Soviet Union. At the core of the exhibit were models of Sputnik, surrounded by displays intended to convince fairgoers that the Soviet Union would shortly surpass the U.S. in the production of material goods. Equally important to the Soviet display was its emphasis on the peaceful uses of atomic energy, which the exhibit catalog contrasted to the American use of nuclear power "for the undoing of mankind."

While the Brussels World's Fair shed light on — and, at times, basked in the light of — cold war political struggles between the superpowers, it also unshuttered another development of the postwar years: decolonization. The end of the British and French empires was already in sight in 1958. Indeed, the absence of expansive British and French colonial exhibits at the Brussels fair that had characterized those nations' participation at earlier world's fairs made the Belgian colonial exhibits seem all the more impressive — and anachronistic. Intended to demonstrate the "civilizing mission" of Bel-

gian colonial rule in the Congo (Zaire) and Rwanda-Urundi (now the separate nations of Rwanda and Burundi), the colonial show covered 19 acres of tropical gardens and consisted of seven pavilions dedicated to colonial government, energy and transportation, Catholic missions, agriculture, natural history, mining, and commerce. As a display of imperial aims, the exhibit was a success, but as a display of colonial realities, it masked more than it revealed, as Belgians and the rest of the world would discover two years later when the Congo erupted in a bloody struggle for independence.

Other exhibitors proved similarly adept as re-presenting realities. In the face of a spiraling arms race and profound skepticism about the contributions of science to human progress, exposition planners, with the cooperation of scientific organizations in fifteen nations, set aside one of the permanent palaces from the 1935 exposition for a Hall of International Science dedicated to demonstrating how scientific research would contributed to a resurgence of humanism.

Underscoring the importance of science to this fair was the exposition's towering, permanent monument to the atom. The idea for the Atominium was first proposed by André Waterkeyn, an engineer with the Belgian metals consortium Fabrimetal. Waterkeyn never lost sight of promoting the metal industry in the course of designing his representation of a crystal molecule of iron — a design construction that immediately captured the fancy of exposition managers. Waterkeyn's plan for a 334-foot-high structure with nine 59-foot-diameter spheres large enough for scientific exhibits and restaurants and connected by escalator tubes symbolizing binding molecular forces was compelling. His Atomium concept was perfectly attuned to the exposition's twin goals of building public support for the rapid development of nuclear energy facilities and of promoting the idea that human beings were in control of their own destiny. At once instructive and awesome, the Atomium crystallized concerns about the atomic threat while suggesting that the future of atomic energy could be left to the control of scientists and engineers who had the good of humanity uppermost in their minds. At the same time, the Atomium reinforced claims by the burgeoning nuclear power industry that nuclear power was safe — despite the fact that the plans to power the exposition with a nuclear generator had to be abandoned because of health concerns.

The role of the fair in promoting nuclear energy development cannot be underestimated. In the Electrical Energy pavilion, a consortium of Belgian industries displayed models of reactors scheduled to begin operation in 1960. Meanwhile, planners of various national pavilions vied with one another to demonstrate the rapid progress of nuclear energy development. Photographs and models of nuclear reactors under development were prominently displayed in the U.S. pavilion. Not to be outdone, the French government unfolded plans to use nuclear power to meet at least one-fourth of France's energy needs by 1967. The British pavilion included a hall devoted to British nuclear industries, and the Soviet Union proudly displayed its nuclear models as well.

To find relief from the anxieties of the atomic age, fairgoers could turn to midway areas located in various parts of the exposition. In the area of the fair given over to Gay Belgium, a reconstruction of a typical Belgian village circa 1900, visitors could retreat into nostalgia for the past while enjoying a variety of cabaret and nightclub entertainments. Or fairgoers could escape to the future in various midway attractions like the Interplanetary Rocket that supposedly had the capacity to transport visitors to Mars. Flying cards, a centrifugal force machine, plus a variety of other technological amusements located in the Jardin des Attractions translated fear of atomic age technology into pleasurable experiences associated with leisure and mass consumption.

Promoters of the Brussels Universal Exposition tried to provide a "balance sheet of the modern world," constantly emphasizing the possibilities for human beings under the threat of nuclear annihilation to direct menacing scientific and technological advances toward human-centered goals. The dominant note of the fair was optimistic and upbeat, but the fair probably stimulated cold war competition as much as it muted conflict. And for all of the rhetoric about the fair's ushering in a new humanism, the exposition probably reinforced pervasive feelings of loneliness and despair as visitors tried to reconcile the exposition's promise of a better future with evidence that the future would be ever more determined by large-scale industrial and political organizations.

Was the exposition a success? As with all other world expos, the answer is more complex that determining whether the ink on the bottom line of exposition ledger books was black. The best estimates available suggest that expenditures for the fair substantially outstripped income, but the indirect economic benefits of the fair were significant. Construction jobs and employment on the fairgrounds provided significant relief from unemployment. In the course of building the fair, Brussels acquired 30 miles of new roads and 5 miles of tunnels. Tourists numbering in the millions spent money for hotels, food, and transportation in Brussels. And once the fair was completed, many of the prefabricated buildings were disassembled and shipped around Belgium and Europe for permanent structures. The city of Liège bought the Transportation Hall for use as a covered market, an Antwerp firm bought the Finnish pavilion, and a Dutch firm purchased the Vatican's exhibit hall. Other exhibition buildings were returned to their countries of origin where they added to urban landscapes around the world. Most visibly, Brussels acquired several hundred additional acres of parkland and a permanent addition to its skyline, the Atomium, as a lasting reminder of an exposition that did as much to shape as it did to reflect the political culture of the atomic age.

Bibliography

The best port of entry into the Brussels Universal Exposition is Rika Devos and Mil Kooning eds., *L'Architecture moderne à l'expo 58* (2006).

In the primary literature, a good starting point is the *Guide officiel: Exposition universelle bruxelles 1958* (1958). See also the eight-volume *Le Memorial official de L'Exposition universelle et internationale de bruxelles* (1958–1962), which provides detailed information about the fair's organization and exhibits and includes a volume that bears the ambitious title *Synthèse*.

Most of the nations that exhibited at the exposition also produced their own catalogs. See, for instance, *This Is America* (1958) and *USSR: World's Exposition in Brussels* (1958). For an insightful treatment of the American pavilion, see Robert Haddow, *Pavilions of Plenty* (1997). For information about the exposition's financial success, see H. de Meyer and P. H. Virenque, *Brussel '58 in Cijfers* (1959).

Seattle 1962

John M. Findlay

Century 21 Exposition

The first U.S. world's fair after World War II, the Seattle world's fair of 1962 played a pivotal role in the development of American international expositions. It marked a turn away from sprawling fairs held in such major metropoles as New York and Chicago toward more focused events staged by smaller cities in the southern and western states. During this period, world's fairs served host cities primarily as tools of urban renewal and magnets for outside investment. Seattle (1962), San Antonio (1968), and Spokane (1974) had mostly positive experiences with this model of the international exposition. However, the problems experienced by Knoxville (1982) and New Orleans (1984) helped bring an end to the era. Thereafter, international expositions disappeared from the American scene.

Seattle had hosted its first world's fair, the Alaska-Yukon-Pacific Exposition, in 1909. During the mid–1950s, downtown interests proposed another international exposition for 1959 to mark the fiftieth anniversary of the AYP. As in many other American cities during the twentieth century, a world's fair in Seattle was seen in large part as a means to help overcome economic and cultural underdevelopment. Downtown leaders' plans were in some ways a response to the prominence of the Boeing Airplane Company in the city's life. A major defense contractor as well as the nation's leading manufacturer of commercial jets, Boeing was the main reason for Seattle's substantial industrial and demographic growth after 1940. Yet many thought it played too large a role in the town. Proponents of a world's fair saw the event as a way to diversify the economy and make it less dependent on aerospace. They expected an international exposition to adver-

tise the city, attract investors and new industry, and stimulate the tourist trade. And by making Seattle less of a cultural backwater, the fair would help companies' efforts to recruit employees from other parts of the country. Both during and after the proposed exposition, promoters hoped, the fairgrounds would serve as a complex of new cultural institutions — theaters, museums, sports arenas, and so on — capable of elevating Seattle into the nation's cohort of major-league cities.

Boeing compounded a spatial problem as well. With its plants located away from the city center, the airplane manufacturer was a powerful force for suburbanization. And as in so many other metropolitan areas during the postwar period, Seattle's downtown was threatened by the growth of sprawling subdivisions, the construction of outlying shopping malls, the embrace of automobiles and new highways, and the beginnings of inner-city decay. Those who wanted to bring a second world's fair to Seattle were intending to counteract the effects of suburban development on downtown, particularly on retail trade and property values. By locating a world's fair somewhere in the vicinity of the central business district, downtown leaders hoped to direct greater attention and resources to a part of the city that seemed to be getting passed by.

Downtown Seattle itself did not contain enough available acreage to host a world's fair. Given the orientation of local promoters of an international exposition, however, it is no surprise that the fairgrounds were located as close to the central business district as possible. Planners chose a 74-acre site in the Warren neighborhood, about a mile north of downtown, as the location of Century 21. The parcel included land and structures that, because they were owned by municipal and state governments, proved relatively easy to convert into a fairgrounds. The Warren neighborhood had some signs of blight, which lent credence to planners' claims that development for a fair represented a kind of urban renewal. And fair promoters envisioned the exposition's new and renovated buildings as a lasting legacy that would serve downtown populations. To ensure a stronger connection between the central business district and the fairgrounds, developers of the fair arranged for the construction of an elevated monorail line between the downtown and the site of Century 21. After it was done ferrying fairgoers between downtown hotels and restaurants and the exposition in 1962, the monorail was expected to become the nucleus of a city-wide transit system centered on downtown.

For local proponents, then, a mid-century world's fair would serve many urban needs—provided it could attract enough outside recognition. Yet when planners first imagined the event in 1955 and 1956, there was little reason to think that the exposition would attain much significance at the national or international level. Although it was going to host the first U.S. world's fair in two decades, Seattle was so isolated from most American centers of population that it would have been unreasonable to expect the project to attract many visitors or much media coverage. Why would foreign nations, large corporations, or the federal government find worthwhile an investment in an exposition staged in the remote Pacific Northwest? For the initial two years of planning, it is hard to see why Seattle had much chance of getting the world's attention or attracting substantial resources. The theme that local planners proposed for the fair—a "Festival of the West"—underlined just how limited were the horizons of local proponents. Unless it came to be regarded as a more significant event, Seattle's fair would not be able to accomplish the goals that downtown leaders had set for their city.

In October 1957 the Soviet Union's successful launch of *Sputnik I*, the world's first artificial satellite, changed everything by creating the perception that the United States lagged behind its cold war rival in space and science. American statesmen, politicians, and scientists suddenly became desperate both to assert the nation's strength in scientific advance-

ment and the mastery of outer space, and to devise means to close the supposed gap between Soviet and U.S. achievement. In response to *Sputnik*, politicians and scientists attempted to reshape the contents of the U.S. Pavilion at the Brussels world's fair of 1958, but the timing and setting of that exposition did not permit much chance to make their case. Subsequently, they seized upon the international exposition being planned in Seattle as a vehicle for affirming U.S. abilities and leadership in the realms of science and space.

What had been imagined locally as a Festival of the West suddenly became America's Space Age world's fair. Noting the futuristic nature of the focus on science and space, local organizers adopted The Century 21 Exposition as the fair's official name. An event that local planners had once envisioned as a counterbalance to the effects of Boeing on Seattle now became, among other things, a monument to the aerospace industry. Locals had to change their plans, but the resulting benefits to Seattle—in the form of a much more important, better funded, well-attended, and widely recognized exposition—were substantial. As a new site for the claims and counterclaims of the cold war, the fairgrounds gained a prominence they otherwise would never have had. The ideas of science and space lent thematic cohesion to the exposition, and attracted greater participation by the U.S. government, foreign nations, and large companies. A more important fair required more time for preparation, too, so the event was ultimately scheduled to run from April 21 through October 21, 1962. During those six months the fair attracted 9.6 million visitors.

Once the Seattle world's fair began to loom larger in importance, it attracted international attention. In 1959–1960, the Bureau of International Expositions sanctioned Century 21 as a "second-category" fair. Whereas a first-category event, such as Brussels in 1958, required hundreds of acres so that each participating nation could build its own exhibit building, a second-category exposition grouped exhibits together in structures provided by the host city and state. This ranking suited Seattle's event and relatively small fairgrounds quite well. Sixteen foreign governments, plus contributors to the African Nations, European Economic Community, and United Nations exhibits, participated in the Century 21 Exposition. Communist countries in eastern Europe and the Soviet Union declined invitations to send official exhibits. In authorizing federal funding for the event, Congress prohibited participation by any "Communist de facto government holding any people of the Pacific Rim in subjugation." This barred attendance by North Korea, North Vietnam, and the People's Republic of China. The exposition could have been named America's Cold War World's Fair.

As a pawn in U.S. geopolitical maneuvering, the Seattle exposition gained a level of support it otherwise would have found difficult to attain. With scientists and others testifying about the important role the fair had to play in winning the cold war and the space race, Congress (prodded by the very adept delegation from Washington state) agreed to invest an unprecedented amount of federal money in the event. It appropriated slightly less than $10 million for the U.S. Science Exhibit, a structure designed by architect Minoru Yamasaki. This five-part complex, arranged around a group of arches, housed a series of displays and experiences that attested to the positive impact of scientific research and space exploration on the world. Science and space were prominent themes in the other key structures. The state of Washington built a large sports and entertainment arena, named the Coliseum and designed by modernist architect Paul Thiry (who also served as principal architect for the grounds). The Coliseum housed an exhibit known as the World of Tomorrow. Designed to predict the nature of life in the year 2000, this group of displays mainly demonstrated how scientific research was generating practical benefits for men, women, and children in the form of more comfortable and automated homes, better planned and climate-controlled cities, and more efficient schools, workplaces, and transportation systems. Toward the end of fair planning, almost as an afterthought, a group of private investors erected the building that became Seattle's chief landmark, the Space Needle (designed by architects John Graham and Co. and Victor Steinbrueck). This signature structure contained a restaurant and platforms for viewing the city and its surroundings. More than 600 feet high, the Space Needle attested to the theme of space exploration, although it offered no substantive exhibit or information to fairgoers.

Because the themes of space and science emerged in the context of geopolitical competition between superpowers, the events and exhibits of Century 21 included some sharp edges that bespoke cold war tensions. For example, George Meany, president of the AFL-CIO, critiqued the Soviet empire in a Labor Day speech that juxtaposed Seattle's Space Needle, "a towering monument to the aspirations of humanity for a better life," to the recently constructed Berlin Wall, which represented "the basic cruelty of the Communist conspiracy and its utter disregard for human life and human values." Similar rhetorical jousting occurred during the visits of Russian and American space travelers. The Soviet cosmonaut Gherman Titov, the second man to orbit the earth, traveled to Century 21 in early May and was asked whether he saw a divine presence in outer space. Titov replied, "I don't believe in God. I believe in man — his strength, his possibilities, his reason." Local newspapers naturally described Titov as "indoctrinated." U.S. astronaut John Glenn, who visited a few days later, responded differently: "The God I pray to is not small enough that I expected to see him in outer space." Americans pointedly contrasted Glenn's successful flight, a public spectacle in an open society, to the secretive space program of the "closed, totalitarian" Soviet Union. Other displays that touted the productivity of American capitalism implicitly — sometimes explicitly — critiqued communist economies.

As difficult as it was to separate the Seattle world's fair from cold war rivalry, by the time the exposition opened in 1962 some of the fears that *Sputnik* had provoked among Americans had subsided. Moreover, the scientists and industrial designers who played such a large role in creating exhibits ultimately muted international tensions and played up the idea of science as a source of harmony, a universal means of expressing creativity, a tool for mastering nature, and a method of producing worldwide abundance. In these ways, the Seattle world's fair of 1962 reiterated the sense of progress, the optimism, even the utopianism so common at international expositions. When the science exhibits were unveiled, especially at the federal pavilion, their hopefulness made it clear that those in charge had prioritized peaceful messages over displays that reminded audi-

This nighttime view of the 1962 Seattle world's fair shows the Space Needle, the Washington State Coliseum, the U.S. Science Exhibit and the Monorail line, which connects the fairgrounds to downtown Seattle (University of Washington Libraries, Special Collections UW856).

entific achievement, in space exploration, but in God!" It appears that most visitors did not share Graham's sense that faith and science were somehow at odds. Without truly compromising their religious beliefs, they made the U.S. Science Exhibit the most popular part of the fair. It attracted more than 6.7 million guests; the Space Needle and the World of Tomorrow exhibit ranked next, with fewer than 3 million guests apiece.

Century 21's focus on science and space placed a higher premium on *ideas* than had been common at American world's fairs. The director of Chicago's 1933–34 Century of Progress exposition, Lenox Lohr, had written in 1952 that world's fairs ought to emphasize "high entertainment value" and target the "low income family group" as the primary audience. By 1962, however, the American population was both more affluent and better educated. The planners and designers of Century 21, inspired in part by the federal government's commitment to the theme of science and in part by the host city's own orientation to the aerospace industry, took ideas quite seriously. They presented "middlebrow" fare to mainly middle-class audiences.

As a result, more commercial features seemed to lack luster. Show Street, which featured adult entertainment, and the Gayway, which featured rides and other amusements, met with relatively little enthusiasm. One observer identified Century 21 as "a thinking man's world's fair." The gendered bias of this appraisal had some basis in fact. Throughout planning, designers assumed that ideas surrounding science and space would appeal to men but not women, and wondered what the fair could offer "for the ladies." Their answer was fashion shows and push-button kitchens in the "Home of the Future." Women visitors, of course, defied such expectations and flocked to the scientific

ences of Cold-War competition. Science as presented at Century 21 seemed rather like a universal religion capable of bringing different peoples together and helping solve the problems that divided them.

Of course, some Christian displays and spokespersons at Century 21 expressed uneasiness at the prominence of science. The evangelist Billy Graham, for instance, worried that the Seattle fair exemplified how modern civilization was putting too much faith in science. "Our scientific advancement is progressing out of all proportion to our moral and spiritual progress," Graham claimed. "As the sands of our age are falling in the hour glass, our hope and confidence should not rest alone in our mighty sci-

The U.S. Sciencce Exhibit, which cost $10 million, consisted of five exhibit halls clustered around a series of arches and pools of water and was motivated by cold war competition with Soviet Union in the realms of space and science (University of Washington Libraries, Special Collections UW13106).

exhibits along with men. Yet the sexism of planners and designers was captured forever in the Century 21 motto, "Man in Space."

Putting on the 1962 world's fair required organizers to deviate from earlier American models of the international exposition. The Century 21 Exposition did employ industrial designers who had worked on the New York World's Fair of 1939–40, including the firms of Walter Dorwin Teague, Raymond Loewy, and Donald Deskey. But it also paid close attention to the changing ways of American consumers in the era after World War II. Planners recognized that the postwar United States had a larger middle class with considerably more disposable income and schooling than before, and they drew on emerging innovations in commerce and leisure in order to cater to such audiences. The shopping mall served as one

influential model for the Seattle exposition; James B. Douglas, president of the company that operated the pacesetting Northgate shopping center in Seattle, and John Graham, Northgate's architect, had substantial roles in laying out the fairgrounds.

Even more important was the influence of Disneyland, the theme park in Anaheim, California, that opened in 1955. Eventually, such places as Disneyland and Disney World would undermine the appeal of world's fairs in the United States by performing on a permanent basis many of the roles previously played by international expositions of one or two years' duration. But in 1962 Disneyland seemed less a threat to world's fairs than a model to be emulated. The designers and organizers of Century 21 relied heavily on the example of the Anaheim theme park. To build Seattle's Skyride and Monorail, they hired the same firms that had built those rides at Disneyland. To manage concessions, amusements, ticket sales, admissions, personnel, wardrobe, security, rides, and maintenance for Century 21, they hired theme-park veterans from the Disney company. Such decisions helped to make the Seattle world's fair a success in the eyes of visitors and observers. They also helped to change the tenor of the exposition. Originally intended to address some of the problems of downtown Seattle, an exposition influenced by the shopping mall and Disneyland, and geared to the themes of science and space which in a way honored the Boeing Company, attracted audiences that could in many respects be characterized as "suburban" in outlook and habits. It is doubtful that most paying customers devoted much attention to the concerns of Seattle's central business district.

Even if fairgoers did not appreciate the needs that had prompted downtown interests to propose an international exposition in the first place, Century 21 did offer advantages to Seattle. Those who owned property and ran businesses in the central business district became better organized and lobbied governments more effectively as they prepared for the fair. They spearheaded campaigns to clean up downtown, meet the need for better transportation and parking in the city center, and devise a new master plan for the post-fair period. They also ensured that Century 21 provided cultural dividends for the city. The fair provided an occasion to invite musical, literary, and theatrical performers to the city, most of which attracted substantial audiences. It also represented an opportunity to raise standards in such other areas as fine dining. Locals remember 1962 as the year when Seattle started getting notably more cosmopolitan.

The most concrete legacy to the city was the fairgrounds, which was transformed after 1962 into the district known as the Seattle Center. From the start of planning, local organizers had insisted that an international exposition should produce a cultural infrastructure for a city lacking in adequate facilities for the performing and visual arts and professional sports. Using funds earmarked for the fair by local, state, and national governments, as well as by corporate exhibitors, Seattle added new buildings and converted older ones into a single complex capable of supporting opera, the symphony orchestra, theater, ballet, and museums. Although it would take a few years for Seattle to nurture impressive companies of musical and theatrical performers, the city now had venues that were appropriate for a substantial metropolis. In time Seattle would become renowned for its opera and theater. The U.S. Science Exhibit became the Pacific Science Center, a successful museum devoted to making science accessible and enjoyable to families. And in 1967 Seattle literally attained "major-league" status when it acquired a franchise in the National Basketball Association. The aptly named SuperSonics played in the Seattle Center Coliseum, which had been built with state funds for Century 21 as the home for the World of Tomorrow exhibit. Within another ten years the city had acquired major-league football and baseball teams as well. The 1962 world's fair marked a significant turning point in the cultural history of Seattle.

To the extent that the growing urban sophistication was focused on the Seattle Center after 1962, the benefits to the central business district were limited. Downtown interests had wanted to locate the fairgrounds as close to their properties and businesses as possible, but the site of the exposition and the Seattle Center remained one mile away from the major stores, hotels, and offices concentrated downtown. Those who attended musical, sporting, and theatrical events at the former site of Century 21 did not need to travel through downtown to do so. Indeed, although the Monorail continued to run between the two districts, going back and forth between them was not that easy. So while the cultural blossoming occurring at the Seattle Center benefited the metropolitan area overall, it did not particularly help downtown. And downtown was not especially supportive of the Seattle Center. That the two neighborhoods sometimes actually competed against one another became apparent during the 1980s and 1990s. Fair planners had anticipated that Century 21 would create convention facilities at the Seattle Center capable of attracting large gatherings to the city, but their expectations were disappointed. When Seattle and the state of Washington decided to build a new convention center during the early 1980s, they located it downtown, closer to major hotels and department stores, and rejected the idea of putting it near the Seattle Center. During the 1990s the Seattle Symphony Orchestra and ACT Theatre actually relocated away from the vicinity of the Seattle Center to new buildings downtown. The old fairgrounds remained a vital part of the city, as is attested by new homes for the city's ballet and opera company, the controversial Experience Music Project museum designed by Frank Gehry, the presence of two of Seattle's three major theater companies, the renovated Coliseum (now known as Key Arena) which hosts NBA basketball and large concerts, and the year-round activity throughout the grounds. Yet many in the city felt that the mixed-use, mixed-design Seattle Center was long overdue for a large-scale overhaul. It had not undergone systematic renovation since 1962. Similarly, the Monorail connecting the Center to downtown remained an unreliable relic of the world's fair, and never became incorporated into a modern transit system.

Although the fairgrounds eventually became dated, they did not go out of fashion nearly as quickly as the some of the fair's messages. Century 21 was to some extent successful in predicting the future when it spoke about space travel, computers, microwave ovens, and other technological wonders. But its overall vision proved to be rather limited. This became apparent at the end of the fair. President John F. Kennedy had agreed to attend closing ceremonies on October 21, 1962, but he canceled on short notice, claiming that he had a cold. In fact, he needed to return to the White House to manage the Cuban Missile Crisis. The day after the world's fair ended, he announced the blockade of Cuba. Scientists and designers had spent years trying to downplay for the exposition the anxieties surrounding *Sputnik*; now the specter of nuclear war and fallout shelters belied the fair's messages about global harmony and the universal benefits of science and space exploration. As the rest of the decade unfolded, the naiveté of Century 21 became steadily more apparent. In its attitudes toward women, its obliviousness toward matters of race relations, and its confidence about the desirability of science producing greater mastery over the environment, the Seattle world's fair guessed wrong about some of the key changes in store for the United States. In retrospect the 1962 event seems to

have been more a culmination of "1950s" thinking than an accurate forecast of the 1960s. As with so many other international expositions, Century 21's optimistic ideas about tomorrow became obsolete quickly.

If the fair's ideas did not have a long shelf life, the world's fair itself as a tool of urban renewal fared better. First San Antonio and then Spokane consulted Seattle when planning their own expositions for 1968 and 1974 respectively. They particularly liked the fact that the Seattle world's fair had made money for organizers (who claimed a net profit of $100,000), provided positive advertising while stimulating trade and tourism for the host city, and attracted substantial outside capital to assist in redeveloping the city's infrastructure. During the latter part of the twentieth century, the Seattle's world's fair of 1962 — with its smaller host city, its limited theme, its site of fewer than 100 acres, and its devotion to urban renewal — became the model for American world's fairs, as long as they lasted. By contrast, the huge New York World's Fair of 1964, which attracted 27 million visitors to fairgrounds of 646 acres while losing millions of dollars, was the last of its kind in the United States.

Bibliography

For scholarly treatment of the Seattle world's fair of 1962, and the material on which this essay is based, John M. Findlay, *Magic Lands: Western Cityscapes and American Culture After 1940* (1992), see especially chapter 5 ("The Seattle World's Fair of 1962: Downtown and Suburbs in the Space Age," pp. 214–264). Additional details regarding Century 21 as urban renewal can be found at John M. Findlay, "The Off-Center Seattle Center: Downtown Seattle and the 1962 World's Fair," *Pacific Northwest Quarterly* 80 (January 1989): 2–11. For more popular accounts, turn to Murray Morgan's history commissioned by the fair organizers, *Century 21: The Story of the Seattle World's Fair, 1962* (1963) and to Don Duncan's book commissioned by the operators of the Seattle Center, *Meet Me at the Center: The Story of the Seattle Center from the Beginnings to the 1962 World's Fair to the 21st Century* (1992).

Rich collections of primary sources concerning the Seattle world's fair of 1962 may be found in several locations. Records documenting participation by the state of Washington are located in the Papers of the Seattle World's Fair of 1962, Record Group 138, at the Puget Sound Regional Branch of the Washington State Archives, Bellevue, Washington. Records documenting participation by the U.S. government are located in Records of International Conferences, Commissions, and Expositions, Record Group 43, at the Pacific Alaska Region of the National Archives and Records Administration, Seattle. The largest and most diverse collection of records may be found in the Special Collections division of the University of Washington Libraries, Seat-

tle. See in particular the Ewen C. Dingwall Papers; Dingwall was the general manager of Century 21, and materials concerning most aspects of planning and operations crossed his desk. The exposition produced an *Official Guide Book, Seattle World's Fair, 1962, Century 21 Exposition* (1962). And it provided the backdrop for a 1963 movie — part musical, part adventure — starring Elvis Presley: *It Happened at the World's Fair*, directed by Norman Taurog.

New York 1964–1965

Andrew V. Uroskie

New York World's Fair

While New York lawyer Robert Kopple initiated the planning of a second New York World's Fair in 1958, he was soon succeeded by New York's veteran builder and deal-maker, Robert Moses, the head of the Triborough Bridge and Transit Authority. Moses made it clear that he cared little for the fair *per se*, but considered it rather a means through which to generate permanent civic improvements on the site of Flushing Meadows Park. The financial difficulties of the 1939 fair had left him unable to fulfill his grand vision there, and Moses considered the 1964 event as an opportunity to crown his fifty year career of urban development. By keeping fair construction to a minimum and overall costs low, he hoped to generate enough of a profit to build a permanent zoo and botanical garden, as well as improved roadways to his newly erected 55,000-seat sports stadium at Flushing Meadows. The second world's fair in New York was scheduled for 1964 and 1965, in order to mark the tercentenary of the English acquisition of the area from the Dutch in 1664, as well as the twenty-fifth anniversary of the 1939–1940 New York World's Fair.

In contrast to the triumphant cultural success of the 1939 New York World's Fair, its sequel 25 years later was widely perceived as a

colossal failure. At least part of the reason rested in the irascible leadership of Robert Moses, the president of the fair board. One of his first battles was with the Bureau of International Expositions (BIE). The BIE was reluctant to sanction the New York fair, because it had already given its blessing to Seattle's Century 21 exposition of 1962. It set certain guidelines for New York as a condition to granting its approval for the fair, but Moses, who likened the BIE to "three little men in a cheap hotel room in Paris," refused to accept the guidelines. The BIE refused its sanction, and as a consequence, foreign participation was greatly limited at New York, although some foreign nations were unofficially represented by private commercial interests. Many of the foreign nations that did participate were newly independent African and Asian states, happy to have an independent presence at a world's fair for the very first time. They came to a world's fair whose theme was "Peace through Understanding," and whose signature structure was the Unisphere, a huge steel globe, 120 feet in diameter, situated not far inside the main entrance to the fairgrounds.

Nevertheless, the New York World's Fair remains instructive for its dramatization of the massive social, cultural, and political transformations then taking place. Planned and designed in the spirit of the 1950s, the fair had become a cultural and social curiosity by the time it ended in the fall of 1965. In the early 1960s, history was apparently moving faster than the organizers' imaginations. One area of concern to the organizers was the contemporary civil rights movement, near its peak of activity when the fair opened in April 1964. By this time, public demonstrations by civil rights activist were commonplace at most public functions, and the announcement that President Lyndon Johnson was officially dedicating the U.S. pavilion was sure to generate a large crowd of protestors. Indeed, many hundreds of demonstrators gathered at strategic places on or just outside the fairgrounds, waving signs, shouting slogans, and heckling the president. More than three hundred were arrested, and many white fairgoers were clearly annoyed at all the commotion. Financially, it was a blow to the fair as well, since the extensive publicity

deterred people from coming to the fair, and that, combined with bad weather in the early weeks of the fair's run, created a deficit from which the fair never really recovered. The 1964 season registered a $20 million loss, and another $1 million was added to the loss column at the close of the 1965 season.

Even before the fair opened in the spring of 1964, critics were complaining that, far from inhabiting the requisite future temporality, it had failed even to keep up with the present. Despite the fair's self-conception as a showcase for future technologies, the cultural aspirations of the technologies on display were fundamentally oriented towards the past. As such, the fair became a kind of living relic — a museum in reverse. Rather than familiarizing viewers with things produced long ago or far away, it defamiliarized that which had seemed natural only a few years back. Yet it is precisely this tempo-

The New York World's Fair of 1964–1965 promoted "Peace Through Understanding" and constructed the Unisphere as a visual symbol of the fair's theme (editors' collection).

ral dissonance that makes the 1964–1965 World's Fair such an evocative bridge between the past, present, and future.

Consider the "Jungle Road Builder." General Motors' acclaimed "Futurama" exhibit at the 1939 World's Fair was able to inspire millions because, at the close of the Great Depression, cars and superhighways were still the stuff of future dreams. Yet for the baby-boomer generation of the 1960s, burgeoning suburbs and long commutes had begun to force a reconsideration of the automotive romance. *Life* magazine — hardly a bastion for radical social thought — compared the fair's layout to the suburban sprawl of gas stations and fast food places on highways connecting cities. "Why go to their fair," it sarcastically queried, "when you can see it at home?" For their unambiguously titled "Futurama II" in 1964, General Motors presented its "Jungle Road Builder," a three-football-field-long, five-story tall, atomic-powered machine that would delve deep into the untrammeled forests of the world and eviscerate everything in its path with lasers, saws, and chemical toxins, leaving behind a barren asphalt superhighway in its wake. Alongside underwater cities, desert farming, and lunar colonies, the Jungle Road Builder upheld an ethos of expansion and development at any price, a "Manifest Destiny" that defined progress in terms of the conquest and industrialization of the natural world. Yet for the youth of the 1960s, who increasingly shared a commitment to environmentalism and social justice, these technologies must have seemed the proverbial "road to nowhere" — a future world better left in the past.

The esteemed modernist architect Gordon Bunshaft initially proposed housing all the exhibits within a giant, donut-shaped pavilion similar to Baron Georges Haussman's idea for the 1867 Paris Exposition Universelle a century before. Yet Moses's frugality, combined with his disdain for modernist aesthetics, quickly caused Bunshaft and other architects and designers to resign in protest. Eschewing both the thematic coherence and the modernist aspirations of the 1939 World's Fair, Moses envisioned the 1964 event in baldly populist and commercial terms, deliberately favoring no aesthetic period or style in his attempt to offer "something for everyone." Moses's laissez-faire approach to planning, together with the "cor-

porate and religious stranglehold he had encouraged," kept most critics contemptuous of the art and architecture on display. One standout was the IBM Pavilion, designed by Eero Saarinen & Associates together with Charles and Ray Eames. There, "a large white ellipsoid ... seemed to rest like an egg in a nest, on a grove of stylized trees."

The egg-shaped theater was less about architecture than information-processing: the repetition of the company logo in relief over the surface of the ovoid mimicked the character-covered ball of their new Selectric typewriter on display inside. Moreover, the theme of the pavilion was the interaction of man and computer: rendering the computer more familiar, but also conceptualizing human experience as fundamentally computational. The "people wall" rose up into the "information center" like recordable media into a drive while the audience, thus enclosed within the nine screen theater, was bombarded with *Think!* (1964), an Eames-authored multimedia spectacle emanating from fourteen linked projectors.

While multiscreen cinema was certainly not new (having been introduced in the 1900 Exposition Universelle in Paris), the 1964 New York World's Fair had an unprecedented number of exhibits utilizing various widescreen and multiscreen technologies. In addition to *Think!*, viewers could see *Man in the 5th Dimension* at Billy Graham's Christian Evangelical Pavilion, *The Searching Eye* by Saul Bass at the Kodak Pavilion, *American Journey* at the U.S. Pavilion, *The Triumph of Man* at the Travelers Insurance Pavilion, *To the Moon and Beyond* in the Transportation and Travel pavilion, and Francis Thompson and Alexander Hammid's *To Be Alive!* in the Johnson Wax Pavilion. This last work, a seventeen-minute film presented on three linked screens, "played to capacity audiences every day of the fair" generating more than five million viewers and prompting "requests to see the film from throughout the world" according to the company.

Yet if the cinema of view displayed some relative novelty, the same could not be said for the fair's display of the plastic arts. One might imagine that Pop art, then emerging in New York to international acclaim, would be a natural representative of the fair's aesthetic. But Moses's idea of fine art could comprehend neither abstraction, nor minimalism, nor representation's ironic reinvention within Pop. In place of the limited degree of aesthetic modernism one could find in 1939, art critics generally agreed that the 1964 event had simply turned its back on art and embraced kitsch — or worse. Passing over dozens of highly respected sculptors, Moses gave pride of place on the mall entrance to an unsolicited proposal by an unknown sculptor wanting to "protect the fair from artistic desecration." *The Rocket Thrower*, by Donald De Lue, recalled nothing so much as the fascist aesthetics of the 1930s. John Canady, chief art critic for the New York *Times*, described the piece as a "lamentable monster, ... an absurdity that might be a satire of the kind of sculpture already discredited at the time of the 1939 fair."

While individual pavilions stepped up to do what they could — the New York State Pavil-ion exhibited a range of contemporary American painting and sculpture, while the Spanish Pavilion exhibited paintings by Goya, Velázquez and El Greco — the artistic treasure of the fair was something no one could have expected. Negotiating directly with Pope John XXIII, Moses was able to secure a loan of Michelangelo's *Pietà* from St. Peter's Basilica in the Vatican, where it had remained unmoved for more than 450 years. As might be expected, it was displayed in truly tasteless fashion: in front of blue velvet drapes, behind bulletproof glass, and lit by a spotlight in a darkened room, as viewers rode past on a conveyer belt.

While Moses adopted a laissez-faire attitude toward corporate exhibit planning, he involved himself much more closely with the amusement aspect of the fair. Never an enthusiast for the traditional midway attractions or

Architectural critics thought that the roof of the IBM pavilion resembled a large egg (editors' collection).

Sinclair Oil brought back new and improved animatronic dinosaurs at the New York world's fair. As the photograph shows, the dinosaur did not seem to scare visitors (editors' collection).

the titillating shows often seen at earlier fairs, Moses allowed only a limited number of family oriented amusements at the fair. There were a few rides, a puppet show, and a porpoise show. The Belgians constructed their usual typical village, complete with a fifteenth-century church, a town hall, and a canal, and it cost fairgoers an extra $1.25 to enter. For twenty-five cents, visitors could ride to the top of a ferris wheel, eighty feet tall, disguised as a giant Firestone tire. While the Century of Progress had featured (and profited from) Sally Rand, and other fairs had nude tableaux or other forms of adult entertainment, the New York World's fair in 1965 closed down a show in the Bourbon Street New Orleans attraction because of alleged exotic dancing, although the performers were described as wearing "oversized bikinis" and cocktail dresses.

Moses's hostile relation with the press was generally blamed for keeping attendance low, but a final surge of visitors in the closing weeks of the second season helped the fair to break attendance records for international exhibitions at the time with a total of 51 million people. Though it never achieved the profits that would have allowed Flushing Meadows Park to be completed in grand style, Moses did find other funds to complete the botanical garden, zoo, and roads he had promised.

Bibliography

Primary documentation of the fair's development is detailed in the ten issues of the New York World's Fair 1964–65 Corporation progress reports, 1961–1965. These and many other documents from the fair's administration are housed in the Rare Books and Manuscripts Division of the New York Public Library. The papers of fair president Robert Moses are also at the New York Public Library, and researchers should consult Series 12 of these papers, which contains correspondence, clippings, and other printed matter related to Moses's involvement with the fair. The Queens Museum, originally the New York State Pavilion for the 1939–1940 fair, and reused in 1964–1965, contains many items of interest from both fairs. The museum organized an exhibit for the fair's twenty-fifth anniversary in 1989, and by far the best single reference on the fair is the catalogue created for that exhibition, *Remembering the Past: The New York World's Fair, 1939–1964* (1989). The catalogue contains an extensive bibliography for both fairs, as well as individual essays on aspects of art, architecture, and cultural politics.

The *Official Guide, New York World's fair, 1964–1965* (1964, 1965), contains basic information about the fair and its attractions and was published in several different editions at various times during the two seasons of the fair. Time-Life

Books, *Official Souvenir Book, New York World's Fair, 1964/1965* (1964) is a heavily illustrated book about the fair that also includes articles by celebrities. The fair was extensively covered by the New York *Times,* the other New York newspapers, and the popular magazines of the day, and references to these articles may be found in the standard indexes.

Apart from the Queen's Museum catalogue, there has not been much modern work done on this fair. Robert Caro, *The Power Broker: Robert Moses and the Fall of New York* (1974), is a long, critical look at the career of the individual who dominated this fair. Walt Disney Productions, which had a role in creating some of the attractions at the fair, celebrated the fair in *20th Anniversary, New York World's fair 1964–1965: A Disney Retrospective* (1984).

The documentary film *Re-Live the Magic: The '64 World's Fair* (1981) features rare footage of some exhibits, while the website at *http://www.nywf64.com/* contains a rich variety of visual data and individual perspectives on various exhibits.

Montreal 1967

Krista L. Bennett

The Universal and International Exposition of 1967 (Expo 67)

Proposed as the flagship of Canada's yearlong centenary celebrations, Expo 67 marked Canada's "coming of age." The theme, *Man and his World,* blended human technological ingenuity with demonstrations of Utopian optimism. As cold war animosities, Vietnam protests, and uncertainty and "Summer of Love" possibilities framed North America's present, Canada constructed a futuristic vision of modernity and transformation, one that *Life* magazine pronounced "a stunning leap into tomorrow."

From its inception, Expo 67 was an enactment of stunning leaps. First proposed by Canadian Senator Mark Drouin while attending Canada's nation day festivities at the 1958

World's Fair in Brussels, Canada's bid to the Bureau International des Expositions (BIE) was officially endorsed by Prime Minister John Diefenbaker in February 1960. However Canada did not win; Moscow did. Two years later financial concerns forced Moscow's withdrawal and Canada tried again. On November 13, 1962, the BIE awarded the 1967 world's fair to Montreal. It was only the third category one exhibition ever granted, and the first awarded in North America.

On March 22, 1963, the newly established Canadian Commission of the 1967 World Fair, the governments of Quebec and the city of Montreal agreed upon a program to transform islands in the St Lawrence River across from Montreal's downtown for the exposition site. Island construction started in August 1963 and the handover of the site to the Expo Commission occurred June 30, 1964. Recriminations of

This overview shows a variety of pavilions at Expo 67, including Habitat, a new concept in urban housing designed by Moshe Safdie, and seen in the background (courtesy Peter M. Warner).

land produced brought the site to 988.7 acres of parkland, building sites, lakes, canals, and parking lots — the largest Expo site in history.

Expo organizers endeavored to create coherent concrete and conceptual routes through the exhibition. In addition to supporting services, facilities and landscaping, the Expo Commission was responsible for the construction of 847 pavilions and buildings (121 acres of floor space), 27 bridges (Concordia Bridge, Bridge des Isles and the Canal Bridges won engineering and architectural awards), 51 miles (82 km) of road and pathways, and an integral full-size rapid rail transit system. Known as the Expo-Express, the train traversed the three focal points of the site from its main gate at Place d'Accueil at Cité-du-Havre to the pavilions of Île Notre-Dame and to its northernmost extremity, the 135 acre *La Ronde* amusement park — approximately 21 miles (34 km) of track. The eight Expo-Express computer-controlled trains of six cars carried an estimated 44 million passengers at a capital and operating cost $18.3 million. Additionally, three small monorails previously used at the Swiss International Exhibition at Lausanne in 1964 carried an estimated 16 million passengers along approximately 6.5 miles (10.5 km) of track. The minirail lines were named for the color of their cars: The Blue mnirail connected Île Sainte-Hélène and Île Notre-Dame and passed beneath scenic waterfalls, through the U.S. pavilion, over and under its own tracks and beneath the Expo-Express. The cost per passenger was 50 cents. The two smaller Yellow minirails served Île Sainte-Hélène and Île Notre-Dame separately at a cost of 40 cents per passenger. Capital and operating costs for the three minirails was approximately $10.5 million. This built-in transit system was augmented by trackless trailer trains, Vaporetto canal boats, Hovercraft, helicopters and pedicabs operated by concessionaires.

profligate handling and the protracted start-up moved several members of the Expo Commission, including the chief planner, the com-mis-sioner, the deputy commissioner and one director to resign for fear the project could not be completed in time.

The new commissioner general, diplomat Pierre Dupuy, and the deputy commissioner general, construction engineer Robert Shaw, drove a monumental transformation. A total of 17.6 million cubic yards (28 million metric tons) of material from the river bed, as ell as excavations for the Montreal *Metro* and the St. Lawrence Seaway project were used to create the site. The Mackay Pier area was extended to become Cité-du-Havre, while Île Sainte-Hélène was expanded to encompass two islets, Îles Ronde and Verte, and a second island, Île Notre-Dame, was created. The 297 acres of new

Together with the efforts of Dupuy and Shaw, the director of operations, Philippe de Gaspé Beaubien, and the director of public relations and communications, Yves Jasmin, ensured plentiful media coverage and public awareness of Expo 67. In addition to their public relations efforts, advertising and publicity through print and television advertisements provided by friends of Expo was estimated at $250 million resulting in over 8 billion exposures — far outstripping that of most previous world exhibitions. Furthermore, there were some 200 major and nearly 1,500 minor displays in Canadian and American department stores viewed by an estimated 30 million shoppers. And Expo 67 was covered by news media. More than 7,000 groups visited Expo before it opened, approximately 4,000 were present for the opening day ceremonies on April 27, 1967, and over 500,000 press visits were made over the duration of the exhibition.

French author Antione Saint-Exupéry's *Terre des Hommes*, translated as "Man and his World," inspired the theme of Expo 67. Unlike previous world exhibitions where the theme was expressed by an iconic structure or symbol, the theme at Expo 67 was conceived as the physical and emotional nuclei of the exhibition and along with world fair classification rubrics, international decorum, and site function, the theme was the basis of the fair's organization both physically and conceptually. The theme conveyed not only contemporary humanism's integration of creative expression and understanding in the fields of science, technology, art and philosophy, but it also promoted awareness of belonging to the "community of man" — a concept that Canadian communications theorist Marshall McLuhan contemporarily called the "Global Village." Fittingly, consultation with many international scholars and officials contributed to the development of the theme.

Man and his World was presented in four major themes with seventeen sub-themes arranged at the site's three focal points. The first, Man and the Community was centered at Cité-du-Havre. Here the Man in the Community, Labyrinth, Habitat 67 and Man and his Health presented ways in which people lived together. Labyrinth was one of the most popular and ambitious exhibits at Expo. The story of progress — from the cave to space presented

as a contemporary adaptation of Theseus' disorienting yet triumphant challenge in the mythic labyrinth — was the National Film Board's attempt to transform cinema into *gesamtkunst* through the integration of film, multi-screen projection, shadows, architecture, music, and sound. The 5-story, square, windowless, reinforced concrete Labyrinth building, designed by Blaud, Lemoyne, Edwards, Shine contained three chambers: The first was designed with balconies overlooking a 38 foot (11.6 metre) vertical screen with a similarly sized floor area where visitors needed to lean over the balcony to view both screens and complete the narrative (i.e., girl feeding goldfish). The second employed maze-like mirrored corridors with light and sounds that responded to visitors' movements. The third used five screens in crucifix form; "vertical editing" connected images across the horizontal and vertical screens.

Conceived as Israeli-Canadian architect Moshe Safdie's undergraduate thesis, Habitat 67 was a revolutionary high-density housing system based on prefabricated modules intended to combine the best of suburban and urban living and was considered "the soul, the genius" of the fair. Built by stacking 354 pre-cast concrete cubes, each weighing 70 to 90 tons, Habitat 67 was composed of 158 apartment units, each with a private entrance and garden, connected by a series of aerial walkways and bridges accessed by elevators. During Expo 67, several units were open to the public, and many were used by exhibitors and dignitaries. Habitat 67 was not built to the scale originally intended (Safdie's original plan called for 12,000 units and included a school, a hotel, and a shopping area) resulting in a high cost per unit and a total cost of $21 million. Habitat 67 won several design and construction awards.

Located between Labyrinth and Habitat 67, the Arthur Erickson-designed Man in the Community pavilion focused on the historical emergence of the "city-community." The pavilion was a tapered geometric cone of alternately stacked cedar hexagons. The tip of the cone was open and allowed sunlight and rain to fall onto a large pond at the center of the pavilion.

Man and his Health included the Meditheater, a six-screen, in-the-round theatre demonstrating medical procedure; pre-natal blood transfusions, kidney dialysis, nuclear medicine, artificial limbs, the iron lung and brain surgery to ameliorate the symptoms of Parkinson's disease. It also featured transparent models of the human body, polygraph technology, medical training and the effects of heroin, marijuana and LSD on animals as illustrated by spider webs.

The Man the Explorer complex on Île Sainte-Hélène included exhibits related to Life; the Planet Earth and Space; the Oceans; and the Polar Region. Filmmakers Ferguson and Kerr, who produced the film *Polar Life*, along with Kroitor and Low from Labyrinth went on to form the IMAX Corporation.

Île Notre-Dame was the site of Man the Producer. This pavilion explored uses of natural resources and technologies through the subthemes of Resources for Man, Progress, and Man in Control? and presented a confident narrative of abundance and development. Man the Provider, also on Île Notre-Dame, featured the role of agriculture and farming, particularly food production, in establishing adequate living standards for all earth's peoples.

The fourth theme, Man the Creator, featured expressions of self in the fields of fine arts and crafts, photography, contemporary sculpture, and industrial design and was shown throughout the exhibition site. In Cité-du-Havre, the Expo 67 Museum of Fine Arts housed 188 works (insured at a value of $39 million) spanning the ancients to the moderns loaned from thirty nations; in the Photography and Industrial Design Pavilion, 500 photographs affirmed "The Camera as Witness" and projects conceived and executed by students of 18 major schools were exhibited. On Île Sainte-Hélène, the International Rose Garden and Parc Hélène de Champlain provided the outdoor setting for the 55 works in the International Exhibition of Contemporary Sculpture. Nearby, the Du Pont of Canada Auditorium lecture series and film elucidated the role of industry in contemporary society, including industrial design. While the fine arts were regarded as universal and international collections were showcased, crafts were seen to be more regional and ethnic and were shown in most national pavilions and the Women's pavilion.

Nations, industries, and private participants were asked to interpret these themes relative to their exhibitions so that the theme would guide and organize potentially disparate contributions into a unified coherent whole. Organizers also suggested the materials used in pavilion construction be evident and invited architects to "explore the decorative possibilities of film-like materials stretched over bold frames or the frank assembly of mass-produced components fastened together in patternful ways" to create a "interesting, complex and fragile quality" according to the *Master Plan: Design Intent* by the Canadian Corporation (p. 9), to reflect the temporality of Expo 67.

Canada set the example. The south tip of Île Notre-Dame was the site of the Canada Pavilion and Place des Nations, where national and special day ceremonies were held. The central feature of the eleven-acre (30,285 sq. meters) $21 million Canada pavilion was a 100 foot (30.5 meters) inverted pyramid called Katimavik (an Inuit word for gathering place). The steel grid structure with blue-green translucent skin had iconic sculptures of "things universal to all men" affixed to the sloping walls. Cast shadows and accompanying electronic music created otherworldly atmosphere. The promenade around the top of Katimivik offered extraordinary views of the entire expo site. Beside it was a six-story, stylized "People Tree," its 1,500 fall-colored leaves displaying photographs of Canadians. The surrounding complex of pyramidal roofed structures, held exhibit areas devoted to the Land of Canada, the People of Canada, and the Challenges to Canadians, and Canada and the World, a 500 seat Arts Centre, a 1,200 seat outdoor amphitheatre, a Children's Creative Centre, a post office and the Tundra Restaurant, critically acclaimed for its arctic specialties and décor of tapestries, carvings, pottery, and murals by Native artists. The Canada pavilion was designed by Ashworth, Robbie Vaughn and Williams, Schoeler, Barkham, and Heaton/Z. M Stankiewicz.

Near the Canada pavilion were Canada's provincial pavilions. Notable among them was the on-site replica of the schooner *Atlantica* at the Atlantic Provinces pavilion, the floating, vegetation crowned mountain that was the Western provinces pavilion, and the Ontario Pavilion's angled structure of pyramid shapes made of opaque vinyl glass fiber membrane stretched over cigar-shaped steel booms. Michael Snow's *Walking Women* and Josef Drenters' *Pioneer Family* were displayed here and the multi-image film "A Place to Stand"—which was awarded an Oscar for best live action short film — was screened. The 50 foot (15 meter) glass-faced Quebec Pavilion presented exhibits of Quebec's unique and dynamic French history and culture under the headings *Challenge*, *Struggle*, and *Drive*. Built as a permanent structure, the Quebec pavilion now functions as an arts center.

Some 60 foreign nations were represented at Expo 67. Dominating the Expo skyline and public imagination, the most popular and globally recognized pavilion was architect philosopher Buckminster Fuller's geodesic dome built for the United States. Fuller and Sadao Inc. and Geometrics Inc., built the 250-foot diameter, 200-foot high (76×61 meter) hexagonal grid frame of steel pipes covered by a transparent skin of 1,900 moulded acrylic panels for $9 million. Inside, exhibition areas were created through a series of platforms supported by concrete columns and connected by stairs and escalators, including the longest escalator ever constructed at 125 feet (40 m). Titled Creative America, the pavilion showcased American technology through four sub-themes. The first section, The American Spirit contained cultural artifacts, such as a Native American headdress, a New England patchwork quilt, and presidential election ephemera. The second and most popular section, Destination Moon, illustrated the Apollo space program exhibiting several actual capsules, including *Freedom Seven Mercury* used by Alan Shepard in 1961 and *Gemini VII*. Life-size models of satellites and rockets hung on enormous multicolored parachutes from the roof of the pavilion, and a model lunar landscape showed space expedition equipment. The third, American Painting Now, held twenty-three colossal commissioned works by prominent American modernists and lauded American individualism and dominance in the contemporary art world. The largest and most prominently placed, Barnet Newman's *Voice of Fire* was to spark fierce controversy and ongoing dialogue upon its acquisition by the National Gallery of Canada in 1989. The last section celebrated American cinema and showed giant photographs of famous actors including Mary Pickford, Marilyn Monroe, Marlon Brando, and Orson Wells. The U.S. pavilion was heavily damaged by fire in 1976, but since 1995 has functioned as Biosphère, a center for observation of the St. Lawrence River and the Great Lakes.

Across the LeMoyne Channel from the American dome on Île Notre-Dame, evoking the standoff of the Paris 1937 exposition, was the USSR pavilion. A large structure with a curved roof supported by glass and aluminium walls was dominated by an exterior sculpture of the hammer and sickle, and a giant bust of Lenin within. At $15 million, it was the most expensive pavilion at Expo. The theme, In the name of Man for the Good of Man, framed Soviet commemoration of its accomplishments in the 50 years since the Revolution of 1917. The first to put a human in space, the Soviets represented their space program with a replica of the *Vostok* satellite and several other satellite prototypes. They also featured their atomic and hydroelectric power programs, advances in agriculture and mining, and traditional and contemporary culture.

For the pavilion of the Federal Republic of Germany, architects Rolf Gutbrod and Frei Otto, with structural engineer Fritz Leonhardt, constructed a series a of masts, the highest being 125 feet (38 m) over which a PVC-coated polyester fabric was stretched to create the translucent tent-like structure. The innovative design won the Prix August Perret from the International Union of Architects. Inside German scientific and technological contributions from Gutenburg's press to Otto Han's Nobel Prize-winning work with uranium fission and Albert Einstein's educational toy designs were featured alongside Berlin style restaurants and music performances by German artists.

The pavilion of Czechoslovakia was a simple rectangular structure with walls of glass and ceramic tile. Its section devoted to children, and its Kino-automat, a small, interactive theater where viewers could vote on how a branching-narrative would unfold, contributed to its great popularity.

The French pavilion, a large concrete and steel structure wrapped in a vortex of aluminum fins was built almost completely over water. One of the few permanent structures built for Expo 67, it became the Casino de Montreal in 1993.

In addition to national pavilions there were private participants. The United Nations pavilion, designed by Eliot Noyes and Associates, was a circular form of concrete, steel, and glass on a 140-foot by 110-foot plaza (43×31.5 m) of flagpoles with the flags of the United

Nations and its 122 member nations. Inside the pavilion was a 330-seat movie theater and exhibits featuring the UN Charter and the work of United Nations agencies around the world.

The Telephone Association of Canada distinguished itself from the outset. The order to the pile driver that broke ground for the pavilion came live via satellite form the Paris office of the BIE; the pavilion itself featured Disney technologies. A Circle Vision 360° movie theater placed viewers in the center of the action, while videophones and hands-free speakerphones were also great crowd pleasers.

The Indians of Canada Pavilion was the first revisionist approach to the display of native culture at a world exhibition. Smiling hostesses sporting fashionable hairdos and uniforms stood beside the statement, "You have stolen our native land, our culture, our soul..." at the pavilion entrance and greeted visitors. Native leaders, headed by Chipewyan painter Alex Janvier, were involved in the planning and execution of the pavilion and ensured that the stories of awful losses suffered by native peoples as a result of European settlement and governmental strategies of managing Native populations were not overshadowed by propagandistic rhetoric. They also worked to see that limited, historicized notions of Native culture neither dominated nor denied contemporary native struggle and achievement. The pavilion was designed collaboratively by Architect Joseph Whitefield Francis and First Nations artists. A 65-foot (20 meter) totem pole carved by the Hunt Brothers of British Columbia marked the entrance to a giant wood and metal teeepee-like structure. Inside, a massive mural titled *Mother Earth and Her Children* by Ojibway painter Norval Morriseau and traditional craft objects were displayed not as ethnographic samples, but as artworks. Photographic works depicting the difficulties of life on Native reserves, idealized crafts people creating traditional objects, and native lawyers, doctors and business people complicated stereotypical notions of "Indianness." A great grizzly with symbols of Native religion carved on its body was lit with a shaft of light in the form of a cross to present the physical and metaphoric superimposition of Christianity. The provocative position the Indians of Canada pavilion presented challenged visitors to reconsider the role of Native people in Canadian society.

The Hospitality pavilion was Expo 67's manifestation of previous fairs' women's pavilions and featured a comfortable lounge, meeting rooms, and a small theater. Exhibits and demonstrations of handicrafts and fashion, pageants, and baby-sitting services were featured. The amusement park *La Ronde* added pure entertainment to the didactic overtures of Expo. Rides ranged from the spectacular $3 million Gyrotron — a large pyramid within which riders were taken on a simulated space voyage before plummeting into a fiery volcano — to the more traditional ferris wheel and go-carts. The Youth pavilion was strategically placed beside *La Ronde* and Expo's security offices on the far side of Parc Héléne de Champlain away from the other pavilions.

Expo 67 employed many innovations in its concept and actualization. The omnipresence of film and new film technologies presented at Expo gained it the nick-name "celluloid city." Sound was also everywhere, with formal performances of classical and operatic favorites to interactive sound pieces and sonic experimentations presented against a ubiquitous soundtrack of piped music. A modular system of site furniture, designed by Luis F. Villa/ Frank Macioge Assoc. (including benches, trash receptacles, drinking fountains, mailboxes, outdoor lighting, phone booths, and public address components), constructed with triangular bases that allowed highly flexible combinations of single and multiple elements. While it created a thread of visual unity throughout the site, it also gave visitors consistent points of reference for amenities. A system of universal signage was similarly employed to simplify and unify directions across language barriers. Tickets to Expo were also new. A single day admission was a regular ticket, but the "Expo 67 Passport to Man and his World" admission ticket, issued to visitors who purchased seven-day or season passes was in the form of a booklet resembling a passport with the holder's personal information, photo and privileges and responsibilities itemized within. Beneath the heading "visas," passport text encouraged visitors to "have these souvenir pages stamped at the pavilions you visit." Popular among visitors and pavilions alike, the passport has played a part at every subsequent world exhibition.

While most of the festivities surrounding the more than 100,000 performances, 62 national and 32 special days ran smoothly, there were some unexpected incidents. French President Charles De Gaulle's proclamation "Vive le Québec Libre!" in Montreal the day before celebrating France's national day at Expo fuelled passions around the issue of Quebec sovereignty. Demonstrators opposing U.S. policy in Vietnam created occasional trouble, prompting the banning of protests on the site. Higher than anticipated visitor volume caused sundry adjustments from limiting minirail travel per admission to increasing garbage collection schedules. Outside the fair a month-long Montreal transit strike impeded attendance and significantly reduced access to Expo. With *Metro* stops nonfunctional, the only access point to Expo was Place d'Accueil. Estimated admission losses were 5 million.

By the end of 1968, the liquidation of Expo 67 was, on the whole, completed. In addition to leaving Montreal with a new municipal infrastructure, new islands, and an international presence, national pavilions expected to be demolished were instead donated to Montreal to be incorporated in Mayor Jean Drapeau's permanent exhibition called Man and his World. Expo 67's reputation and momentum carried Montreal to win the 1976 Olympic Summer Games and acquire a major league baseball franchise. The team was named the Montreal Expos to capitalize on fan support and brand recognition. The *La Ronde* amusement park continues to operate in the summers.

As much as the exclusivity of the title Man and his World grates the sense and sensibility of contemporary audiences, it was the language of an era. This is certainly not to say that women had not begun to contest male social and economic privilege or were not actively contributing to the fields featured at Expo, but the separate treatment of women through the limited purview of the Women's pavilion and the general lack of representation elsewhere reflected the prevalent relationship of women to the established notions of power and dominance. Where most of Expo's emphasis was forward thinking, the title marked the end of an era when the systemic marginalization of women was largely uncontested

Expo 67 was a resounding success. The more than $500 million spent by the city of Montreal, the province of Quebec and the fed-

eral government of Canada to bring Expo 67 to the world did indeed bring the world to Expo 67. In the six months between the official opening of Expo 67 on April 28 and its close on October 28, a nation of 20 million had brought over 50 million to Expo 67. The Expo Commission's summary documents counted 60,845 participants, more than 60 foreign governments, three U.S. states, 15 cities, 18,051 private participants and over 42,000 sponsors, lenders, and concessionaires. Widely praised by the architecture and design press (*Architectural Record*, *Architectural Review*, *Japan Architect* and *Progressive Architecture* all devoted issues to Expo 67) and covered extensively in the popular press, Expo 67 had carried its message of international community and understanding far beyond the constructed islands of the St. Lawrence.

Bibliography

The exposition's records are held at the Public Archives Record Centre in Montreal, under the name of the Canadian Corporation for the 1967 World Exhibition. The corporation final report on Expo 67 is *General Report on the 1967 World Exhibition*, 5 vols. (1969). This report contains financial reports, attendance tables, departmental reports, and much more in its 2,000 pages, and it is clearly the basic primary research source for the expo. The corporation also published annual reports for the years from 1963 through 1968. The *Official Guide, Expo 67* (1967) gives the basic information about the exposition and its attraction that visitors needed.

Other contemporary published sources include Jean-Louis de Lorimer, ed., *Expo 67 Memorial Album of the First Category Universal and International Exhibition, Montreal* (1968), a huge pictorial album that contains illustrations and much information on the various pavilions at the expo, as well as essays on the origins and development of the event. Another commemorative book, Robert Fulford, *This Was Expo* (1968) provides instant nostalgia. Anthony Clegg, *The Minirail at Expo 67 and Man and His World* (1968) deals with the fairgrounds' transportation system.

A number of articles discussed the innovative architecture of Expo 67. Most helpful are "The Architect's Expo," *Progressive Architecture* 48, 6 (June 1967): 126–67; "Brilliantly Ordered Visual World: Expo 67," *Architectural Record* 142 (July 1967): 115–26; and the *Architectural Review* and *Japan Architect,* both of which devoted their entire August 1967 issues to the expo.

The expo's art exhibit catalogue is *Man and His World: International Fine Arts Exhibition* (1967), while Philip J. Polock, *The Camera As Witness* (1967) is the illustrated catalogue of the photography exhibit that portrayed the theme of Expo 67. For sculpture, see Guy Robert, intro., *International Exhibition of Contemporary Sculpture* (1967).

At the turn of the century, a number of retrospective projects placed 1960's Canada as a moment of transition from one era to another and focussed their attention on Expo 67. Particularly helpful are the Canadian Museum of Civilization's

Cool 60's Design and the accompanying text *Made in Canada: Craft and Design in the Sixties* (2005); The Canadian Centre for Architecture's exhibitions *Not Just a Souvenir* and *The Sixties: Montreal Thinks Big,* The Confederation Centre Art Gallery's *From Our Land: The Expo 67 Canadian Craft Collection*; and McGill University's online digital collection *Habitat.* The CBC Home Video publication *Expo 67: Back to the Future,* Yves Jasmin's personal memoir, *La Petit Histoire d'Expo 67* (1997) and Sandra Alfoldy, *Crafting Identity* (2005), especially chapter 3, "Negotiating a Separate Identity: The Indians of Canada Pavilion at Expo 67," are all useful.

San Antonio 1968

Shirley M. Eoff

Hemisfair '68: A Confluence of Civilizations of the Americas

On April 4, 1968, Martin Luther King, Jr.'s assassination highlighted racial tension and discord in the United States. While much of the nation mourned, the city of San Antonio, Texas, prepared to celebrate its 250th anniversary with a world's fair designed to capitalize on the city's ethnically mixed heritage and dedicated to strengthening unity and understanding among the nations of the Western Hemisphere. The genesis of this first officially designated international exposition in the southwestern United States began a decade earlier with San Antonio businessman Jerome Harris' suggestion that a world's fair would draw attention to the city's unique ethnic heritage and culture and serve as a catalyst for community pride, consensus-building, and economic revitalization.

Harris's idea for a celebration of hemispheric relations quickly captured the attention of the local and state political elites. Texas Governor John Connally led the lobbying effort for official sanction and for state and local funding. As commissioner-general of the fair,

he personally traveled to four continents to solicit exhibitors. U.S. Senator John Tower, Congressman Henry B. Gonzalez, and Lieutenant Governor Ben Barnes assisted Connally in his efforts, and President Lyndon Johnson, a Texan himself, lent his considerable political clout to the cause. Mayor Walter McAllister and the 167 board members of the non-profit San Antonio Fair, Inc., who represented a cross-section of the city's population, orchestrated local efforts. Prominent businessmen, headed by construction magnate H.B. Zachry, pledged $10 million to begin construction and San Antonio voters approved bond measures totaling $35.5 million to support the project. The state of Texas contributed $10 million for construction of the Institute of Texan Cultures while the U.S. Congress appropriated $7.5 million for the U. S. Pavilion.

Despite broad support, the decision to locate the fair in the heart of an urban renewal district in downtown San Antonio created considerable tension between "progressives" who saw an opportunity to resurrect a blighted area and "preservationists" who desired to protect the area's historic integrity. Original recommendations to preserve 129 historic structures were rejected in favor of a much scaled-down agreement to preserve and restore only twenty-two structures, which would be used as restaurants, boutiques, fair offices, and industrial pavilions for the duration of the fair. The local flavor and Spanish ambience of these remnants of old San Antonio proved to be one of the most distinctive and charming features of the 92.6 acre HemisFair site.

The compact size of the site created minor logistical problems in housing some fifty-five exhibitors representing twenty-five nations, the states of Texas and Arkansas, and twenty-one U.S. corporations. In keeping with the theme of celebrating the confluence of peoples and cultures from four continents in the Americas and to promote San Antonio as a center of commercial and cultural exchange between the U.S. and Latin America, fair organizers arranged corporate sponsorships to ensure the largest contingent of Latin American participants at any world's fair to date. To highlight pan-American unity and cooperation and to compensate for space limitations, five Central American states shared a single pavilion as did eleven representatives of the Organization of American States.

To alleviate potential congestion, fair promoters created a multifaceted transportation system. Particularly notable was the quarter-mile extension of the city's famed River Walk into the convention center complex, achieved by diverting the river's natural course. This not only allowed leisurely access via river taxis but also introduced visitors to one of the city's unique charms. Elevated walkways, a mini-monorail, and a sky rail facilitated internal traffic flow within the compact site.

Despite some remarkable housing and transport features, critics charged that the fair's architecture and physical conception lacked originality and creative flair. A rather conservative $13.5 million convention center, composed of three distinct buildings filled with state-of-the-art equipment and technology, anchored the site. Organizers billed the fair's theme structure, the 622-foot Tower of the Americas, with its revolving restaurant and two magnificent observation decks, as the tallest observation structure in the Western Hemisphere, but it struck many as reminiscent of Seattle's Space Needle. Since this was a special category fair, exhibits were set up in standard

fair-provided space rather than the elaborate pavilions associated with larger fairs. Focal points included the Institute of Texan Cultures, the U.S. Pavilion, an international exhibition space designated as "Las Plazas del Mundo," and a commercial exhibition area featuring major corporate sponsors. Returning to the international exhibition scene for the first time in many yeas was a women's pavilion, which purported "to capture the essence of womanhood." The exhibit chronicled women's role in the development of the Americas and highlighted specific achievements in government, the arts, and the sciences.

Six years of preparation came to fruition when HemisFair '68 opened its gates to the public on April 6, 1968, at an estimated cost of $156 million. During its six-month run ending on October 8, almost 6.4 million visitors experienced a wide array of cultural events, entertainment venues, and technology exhibits. Performances by Mexico's Ballet Folklórico, exhibits of priceless Spanish art never before shown outside Spain, a display of Latin American village life built from Santa Fe designer Alexander Girard's folk art collection, and ceremonial dancing by Indian tribes exemplified the cultural diversity of the Americas and entertained visitors of all ages.

Despite much acclaim, attendance fell short of expectations and costs exceeded all estimates, leaving the city of San Antonio with a deficit of $7.5 million. Heavy rains delayed construction and increased costs by as much as $3 million, and legal fees and damages resulting from a tragic monorail accident added unanticipated financial obligations. Periods of national mourning for Martin Luther King and Robert F. Kennedy, unseasonably wet weather, and damaging publicity from the monorail accident limited attendance to 85 percent of the projected number.

While it was not considered a financial success, HemisFair '68 nonetheless stands as a watershed event in San Antonio's history and development. The event propelled the city into the international spotlight, allowing it to display its unique ambience and embrace its multicultural and multiethnic heritage. Besides employing some 8,000 people directly, the fair stimulated considerable growth in the hotel and retail sectors and generated an estimated $500 million economic impact to the region's

Hemisfair '68's location on the San Antonio River made it possible for the fair to have many beautiful fountains (photograph by John E. Findling).

economy. The fair left a legacy of physical improvements and permanent structures in the form of the restored historic buildings, the convention center complex, the Institute of Texan Cultures, and a federal courthouse complex that added significantly to the city's infrastructure needs. These, plus the hotel and retail expansion, laid the foundation for a booming tourist and convention industry, commercial success, and the city's emergence as a center for inter-American business and political exchange that could rival Dallas and Houston.

Bibliography

Official records for HemisFair '68 became available to researchers in 1998. The Archives of the San Antonio Fair, Incorporated, housed at the University of Texas at San Antonio Library, doc-

ument planning, lobbying, financing, and construction aspects of the fair. The bulk of the records consist of correspondence, committee reports, financial records, minutes, and press releases from 1964–1968.

Timothy James Palmer's unpublished 1990 University of Texas at Austin M.A. thesis, "HemisFair '68: The Confluence of Politics in San Antonio," provides a useful overview of the political debates, boosterism, financial struggles, and urban renewal efforts associated with the fair. *HemisFair '68 and the Transformation of San Antonio* (2003), a collection of oral histories edited by Sterlin Holmesly, discusses the pivotal role the fair played in altering the city's image and generating tourism and business expansion. Useful material also exists in David R. Johnson's edited collection, *The Politics of San Antonio* (1983).

Fair publicity guides provide details of the layout, exhibits, and site development. The best are *HemisFair 1968: Official Souvenir Guidebook* (1968) and "HemisFair '68," an 88-page supplement to the San Antonio *Express News*, April 2, 1968. Also useful is the U.S. Department of Commerce's report, *Federal Participation: HemisFair '68* (February 1971), which focuses on the building of the U.S. Pavilion but provides valuable insight into federal-state participation and efforts to use the fair to promote international trade and improve hemispheric economic relations. Contemporary overviews include Jim Davis, "San Antonio's Big Show," *Humble Way* 7 (1968): 1–8, and Keith Elliott, "HemisFair," *Texas Parade* 18 (April 1968): 12–19.

Excellent coverage appeared in the *San Antonio Express News* and the *New York Times* between March and October 1968. The fair's problems are succinctly highlighted in Juan Vasquez's "Troubled HemisFair Becomes Amusement Center" New York *Times,* October 20, 1968, while the immediate impact is best expressed in

Kemper Diehl, "Fair Ends—Was It Worth It?" New York *Times*, May 5, 1968.

Two articles dealing with the important urban renewal aspects of the fair are James L. McKay, "HemisFair '68 and Paseo del Rio," *American Institute of Architects Journal* 69 (April 1968): 48–58, and Roger Montgomery, "HemisFair '68: Prologue to Renewal," *Architectural Forum* 129 (October 1968): 84–89. Interesting retrospectives and assessments appear in the April 7, 1988, edition of the San Antonio *Express News* and in Carlos Freymann, "The Fair That Changed San Antonio," *San Antonio Business Journal* (April 7, 2003). On the occasion of the twenty-fifth anniversary of Hemisfair, John Lund Kriken, "Hemisfair 68: Its Impact on San Antonio," *World's Fair* 13, 4 (October-November-December 1993): 20, summarizes the positive legacy that the fair brought to San Antonio's downtown.

Osaka 1970

David Anderson

Japan World Exposition

The Japan World Exposition, Osaka, 1970 (Expo 70) was a Category One–Universal Exposition held on an 815-acre site in the Senri Hills in Osaka Prefecture, Japan. The exposition ran for 183 days, from March 15 to September 13, 1970. Expo 70 was the first international exposition to be held in Asia, and attracted a total attendance of over 64 million—the largest attendance of any world fair since their inception in 1851.

Expo 70 attracted international representations from a total of 76 countries, one territory (Hong Kong), three U.S. states, three Canadian provinces, two U.S. cities, one German city, four organizations and two corporations. Domestic participation included 32 organizations represented in 32 pavilions: one each for the Japanese government, the Preparatory Committee of the Local Governments' Pavilion for the Japan World Exposition, two public enterprises, and 28 private companies.

The themes of two of the previous post-

World War II expositions, Brussels in 1958 and Montreal in 1967, centered on drawing attention to human society. Expo 70's theme, "Progress and Harmony for Mankind" was deliberately Oriental in character in that its focus was about the quintessential commonalities of humanity, irrespective of the difference between East and West. The official emblem was patterned after the cherry blossom with five petals symbolizing the five continents of the Earth and the central circle symbolizing Japan. The emblem was also the architectural pattern for the Japanese Government pavilion.

Japan's interest in staging a world exposition arose from a number of national and local government authorities as part of the planning for the 2600th anniversary of Japan, Osaka Prefecture and the commemoration of the centennial of Japan's modernization and opening up to the world. On April 23, 1964, Gisen Sato, governor of Osaka Prefecture, Kaoru Chuma, mayor of Osaka, and Daizo Odawara, president of the Chamber of Commerce and Industry, submitted a request on behalf of the residents of Osaka to host a world exposition to Prime Minister Hayato Ikeda and his cabinet. On June 9, 1964, the cabinet agreed to study the matter further, and on September 1, 1964, a World Exposition Investigation Room was established by the government. Japan's capacity to hold great international events was bolstered through the highly successful staging of the Tokyo Olympics later that same year. In April 1965, the government examined and subsequently approved an application from the recently formed Osaka International Exhibition Preparatory Council to host a First Category World Exposition in Senri Hills, in 1970. Shortly after, the Ministry of International Trade and Industry requested the Ministry of Foreign Affairs to send an application for Japan to host the exposition to the Bureau of International Expositions (BIE). The BIE officially accepted Japan's proposal on May 12, 1965.

The staging of the exposition was highly significant for Japan. It represented and demonstrated many important things for the country. First, the exposition was staged at a time when there was a developing national self-realization of hope given that Japan had emerged just twenty-five years earlier from the devastation of World War II. The exposition provided a sense of the Japanese people's capacity to take a positive role on the world stage, with a sense of pride in their country and connection with the world. This sense of emergence had certainly been bolstered by the successful staging of the 1964 Olympic Games. Second, the year 1970 marked the beginning of unprecedented economic growth and development and a period of historic prosperity. Expo 70 was both a marker of the beginning of considerable prosperity, and also likely a contributor to it.

The site for the exposition was planned by the world-renowned Japanese architect Kenzo Tange, who fused the architectural traditions of his native Japan with the contemporary philosophy and traditions of the western world. The Expo '70 site was spatially arranged in a manner that portrayed the theme of the exposition. The central area of the site was the Symbol Area, 500 feet wide and three-quarters of a mile long running north and south and dividing the site into two sections. It was designed to be a place to meet the people of the world and also represent and depict the theme of the exhibit. Air conditioned, moving side-walks extended out in four directions from this Symbol area to other parts of the expo site. The Symbol area was metaphoric, a tree trunk, the moving walkway branches, and the foreign and domestic pavilions flowers in full bloom. The centerpiece of the exposition was the Tower of the Sun by famous Japanese sculptor Taro Okamoto (1911–1996) — a 230 foot tall sculpture, which remains today in the Banpaku Koen (Expo 70 Commemorative Park). The Sun Tower was built near the Festival Plaza (within the Symbol Area) at which concerts, national days, staged performances, and the opening and closing day ceremonies were held. The Festival Plaza was covered by the world's largest translucent roof, one hundred feet tall, 350 by 1,000 feet in area, supported by six pillars, and weighing 6,000 tons. The other key icon of the Exposition was the extensive Japanese Gardens covering an area of 64 acres containing four thematic representations: *Garden of Ancient Times* (Heian Period — 8th to 11th centuries); *Garden of the Middle Ages* (Kamakura Period — 12th to 13th centuries); and *Garden of Modern Times* (Edo Period — 17th to 19th Centuries); and *Garden of Present Day*.

The architecture of Expo 70 was spectacular by scale and striking in terms of visual appeal; for instance, the Australian Pavilion featured a great suspended circular roof measuring 158 feet in diameter and weighing 240 tons that was suspended in the air by twenty parallel wire strands hung from the tip of the "Sky Hook." The Sumitomo Pavilion was made up of nine "floating spheres" (flying saucers) each of which was a polyhedron dome made of triangular steel pieces connected by steel-frame bridges. The Toshiba IHI Pavilion was composed of a giant space-like framework produced by welding 1,476 tetrahedron metal units. A red dome called the Global Vision Theater, 131 feet in diameter was suspended from the tetra-unit framework.

The most popular pavilions on site were those of the United States and the Soviet Union. The popularity of these pavilions were the product of these two nations' political domination of the world in 1970, the large physical size and impressive architecture of their pavilions, and their exhibition themes, which portrayed their nations' technical superiority and achievements in space technologies. The U.S. Pavilion, 86,000 square feet of floor space, was at the time the largest air-supported roof ever built. On display was the "Moon Stone" brought back to Earth from the Apollo 11 lunar mission only eight months before the opening of the exposition. The pavilion also featured as its centerpiece a large exhibition about the Apollo project that included the actual Apollo 8 spaceship which, in December 1968 had made the first manned voyage around the moon. In addition, visitors could see a full-scale model of the Apollo 11 Lunar Lander. Like the U.S. pavilion, the Soviet pavilion was a dominant architectural spectacle. It was the largest foreign pavilion, was 360 feet in height and contained 270,000 square feet of floor space. Exhibits also focused on space and space technology. The Soviet pavilion also celebrated the centennial of V.I. Lenin's birth.

The pavilion also featured a piano that once belonged to Tchaikovsky and a huge screen that displayed 10 films simultaneously.

The exposition featured numerous visions of the future. For example, the telecommunications pavilions featured "dream telephones"—wireless handheld telephones where visitors could call any part of the country. The Furukawa Pavilion presented a world of cashless shopping, using customer voice prints. The expo had a "lost and found" department that utilized "TV-telephones" with which one could browse among lost articles or communicate audio-visually when a lost child was located. The site was interlinked with a futuristic monorail system, mirroring the monorail systems of fairs in the 1960s.

Looking much like a giant pincushion, the U.S. pavilion featured an innovative air-supported fiberglass dome (courtesy of Martin Manning and the Public Diplomacy Archives, U.S. Department of State).

The Japanese Government pavilion, consisted of five cylindrical exhibit halls arranged in the shape of the petals of a cherry blossom. Each of the halls was 190 feet in diameter and 89 feet high, and elevated 21 feet above ground level by three pillars to allow free passage of visitors underneath. The exhibits of the pavilion were divided into three sections—the Past (Hall 1), the Present (Halls 2 and 3) and the Future (Halls 4 and 5) covering two thousand years of history and evolution of Japanese culture, present day society, and Japan in the 21st century. The exhibits also showed how the Japanese were building an advanced culture and economy by absorbing Western as well as Eastern cultures, and combining these with their own culture. The Matsushita Pavilion featured the "Expo '70 Time Capsule" to be opened in the year 6970. Perhaps more comprehensive then the Westinghouse Time Capsule of the 1939 New York World's Fair, the Expo 70 capsule is window into the past, reflecting the 20th Century's greatest achievements, such as the Apollo space missions and heart transplant surgery, in addition to more controversial representations of the century such as a special collection of mementos of the Hiroshima atomic bomb and a list of endangered species. Other interesting items among the 2,008 objects contained within the capsule include a silk condom, false teeth, a glass eye, insects encased in resin, pamphlets on how to brew sake, handcuffs, an origami instruction book, a string of fake pearls, and a "micromini" television set.

In the history of world's fairs, art exhibitions have often played a significant role. In this tradition, Expo 70 had its Museum of Fine Arts. The title of the exhibition was "Discover the Harmony," and it portrayed ancient, classic and modern representation of the arts. Since this was the first exposition hosted in Asia, emphasis was placed on bringing together art from both the East and the West. Works by European artists Salvador Dali, Pablo Picasso, Paul Gauguin, Pierre Auguste Renoir, Paul Rubens, Vincent Van Gogh and Paul Cézanne, and Japanese artists Sesshu and *Kano* were considered highlights of the museum.

Festive events held in the outdoor spaces and halls proved perfect representations of "the harmony of mankind." Many of the 2,880 performances were staged at the Festival Plaza, while others were held at the Expo Hall, the Water Stage, the Festival Hall, or the outdoor theater. The Festival Plaza, serving as a point of interaction for people from around the world, was host to some 270,000 performers and more than 10 million guests.

Expoland consisted of a 42.5 acre section of the exposition that contained a wide variety of amusement park rides and experiences, including a giant ferris wheel, a fun house, a minirail, and a water park. Daidarasaurus, the most popular ride at Expoland, was a three-quarter mile long roller-coaster that traveled at a top speed of 40 mph. Expoland also contained Expo Tower—a 417-foot high observation tower with nine cabins used as observation rooms from which a panoramic view of the entire exposition site could be gained. The tower remained as a symbol and memorial to Expo '70 until its deteriorated state forced its demolition in 2002.

Expo 70's total attendance was more than 64 million over the six months of operation. According to the *Japan World Exposition Official Report* (1972), the average daily attendance on the site on peak days was 641,000 with a high of 835,000. The record attendance day was later called "Black Saturday" because of serious concerns of overcrowding on the expo site and the gridlock of human traffic. Newspapers of the day depicted hundred of visitors stranded overnight at Expo 70 because of the inability of the public transport systems to cope with so many visitors leaving the site at closing time. The sheer volume of people attending Expo 70 also presented problems at opening time each day. Crowds would rush through the entry gates in order to get to the popular pavilions and avoid long lines. The rush became affectionately know as the "Buffalo Run."

The event cost 87,800 million yen for construction and operation (the equivalent of approximately $1.25 billion in 2006 dollars). However, this figure does not include the considerable expenditure on city transportation and other infrastructure projects leading up to the staging of the exposition. The Japan World Exposition is considered to have brought a credit balance of about $100 million to Japan's international balance of payments mainly by boosting the trade surplus during its run.

Shortly after the conclusion of Expo 70, the 815-acre exposition site was converted into public recreational parklands— Banpaku Koen (Expo 70 Memorial Park). The extensive parklands are a combination of walking trails, forested areas, and open air fields in which concerts and community events are frequently staged. The Banpaku Koen has 11 different types of sports facilities, including tennis courts, an athletics field, and a sports plaza. The parklands are also currently home to the National Museum of Ethnology, which showcases materials on ethnology from around the world; the Japan Folk Crafts Museum, and the International Institute for Children's Literature. The gardens and a few of the original buildings and architectural features remain, including the central icon of the exposition, the impressive Sun Tower which still stands near the entrance of Banpaku Koen.

The Expoland Amusement Park continues to operate as a fully functional amusement park attraction. The former International Art Museum pavilion was used as the building for the National Museum of Art (moved to downtown Osaka in November 2004) until March 2004. Additionally, there remains the Matsushita Electric Industrial Company time capsule. Expo '70 was a remarkable event by virtue of its shear scale, architecture, attendance, and significance for the nation of Japan.

Bibliography

Non-Japanese speaking researchers will profit most from the excellent records collected by the United States Information Agency (USIA), the organization that had responsibility for the U.S. presence at foreign expositions. The USIA has been subsumed by the State Department, and its USIA Historical Collection now forms part of the State Department's Public Diplomacy Historical Collection. In this collection, researchers will find congressional records, correspondence, newspaper clippings, and various reports. In addition, the Library of Congress has guides and other publications related to the exposition.

The three-volume *Japan World Exposition, Osaka, 1970: Official Report* (1972) and the guide book, *Expo '70 Official Guide* (1970) are available in English and provide details about the staging and operation of the exposition and its attractions. What visitors thought of Expo '70 is the subject of David Anderson and H. Shimizu, "Memories of Expo '70: Visitor's Experiences and the Formation of Vivid Long-Term Memories," *Curator: The Museum Journal* 50, 4 (2007): forthcoming.

The exposition was covered quite extensively in U.S. newspapers and periodicals, and has attracted some scholarly interest. Edward H. Teague has collected works on the exposition published before the early 18980s in *Expo '70: the World Exposition, Osaka, Japan: A Bibliography of Monographs and Articles* (1984). Among popular accounts of the expo, see David Butwin, "Meet Me at the Fair (If You've Got the Yen)," *Saturday Review* (September 13, 1969): 44–45, 96–97, and Bill Hosokawa, "Expo '70: SuperShow in Japan," *Reader's Digest* (January 1970): 149–53. Among other contemporary articles, the most useful and interesting are E. J. Kahn, "Letter from Osaka," *New Yorker* (June 6, 1970): 88, 91–94, 96–102, which analyzes the fair's role on Japan's economic development. Eleanor C. Munro, "The Orient Express," *ARTnews* 69, 4 (Summer 1970): 48–51, 72–75, found Expo '70 "automated, electronic, and jingling with lights and music." The art at the exposition is critiqued in "The Osaka Fair Expo '70," *Craft Horizons* 30, 3 (May-June 1970): by James Platt, who noted that very few participating nations honored their national artistic heritage. Finally, "The U.S. Pavilion at Expo '70," *Art in America* 58, 2 (March-April 1970): 60–79, brings together six essays detailing U.S. contributions to various contemporary art forms, including the "new technological art."

On the architecture of the fair, the best source is the entire May-June 1970 issue of *Japan Architect*, with excellent illustration and commentary by architects who designed various pavilions. Also, Peter Blake, "Expo '70," *Architectural Forum* 132, 3 (April 1970): 30–41, presents a critical view of the fair's architecture, while Ervin Galantay, "Designing the Environment," *Nation* (August 31, 1970): 134–38, argues that the fair is a worthy attempt on the part of the designers to show that an urban environment could be hospitable. Dedicated architectural students will want to consult *Structure, Space, Mankind: Expo '70* (1970), published in connection with the Second Architectural Convention of Japan. This work consists of one volume of text, including an essay by Kenzo Tange, the chief architect, and one volume of illustrations. Tange has been the subject of several biographies and studies of his work. His autobiography, *Kenzo Tange* (1998) is probably the place to start, but see also Robin Boyd, *Kenzo Tange* (1980) and Anthony G. White, *Kenzo Tange: A Selected Bibliography* (1990).

Most histories of post-war Japan pay attention to the impact of Expo '70 on Japan's economic development. A good source for this context is T. Nakamura, *The Postwar Japanese Economy: Its Development and Structure, 1937–1994* (1995), but there are many others.

Spokane 1974

Arlin C. Migliazzo

Expo '74: The International
Exposition on the Environment

The Spokane World's Fair began as an effort by downtown business leaders to revitalize the city's urban core. They formed Spokane Unlimited in 1958 and commissioned a New York City consulting firm (Electric Bond and Share Company) to develop a comprehensive proposal for that purpose. Completed in June 1961, the Ebasco plan focused on massive downtown renovation anchored by restoration of the polluted Spokane River as it sliced through the city. Civic leaders hired urban planner King Cole to spearhead the renewal effort and formed the Association for a Better Community to maximize grassroots support. By the late 1960s after a number of failed attempts to secure funding for the colossal project from Spokane taxpayers, activists decided to pursue the possibility of staging an environmentally themed celebration of Spokane's centennial to generate dollars for urban redevelopment. Economics Research Associates (ERA) of California was retained in 1970 to conduct a feasibility study. The firm expressed doubts about the centennial celebration, but encouraged Spokane to consider the possibility of hosting a world's fair focused on the environment. In July 1970 an ERA contact in Paris checked with Réné Chalon, the director of the prestigious Bureau of International Expositions (BIE) and discovered there were no competing fairs in 1974. In short order the centennial celebration plan gave way to the grander vision of a Spokane world exposition on the environment and the centennial committee transformed itself into the Expo '74 Corporation with local banker Rod Lindsay as chair. King Cole assumed the presidency of the fair's corporation and Mel Alter became gen-

eral manager. The leadership team mounted a campaign to raise needed capital in order to press forward with planning the fair. Pledges ranging from $100 to $100,000 by local benefactors and businesses allowed the corporation to surpass its $1 million goal by June 1971 and secure initial financing. Almost simultaneously, support for the exposition began building in Washington, D.C., as Spokane's congressional representative (Thomas Foley), Washington's U.S. senators (Warren Magnuson and Henry "Scoop" Jackson), and officials in the Departments of State and Commerce were brought on board. Over the ensuing months, Spokane's bid to host a world's fair received official sanction from the BIE, the U. S. government, and the state of Washington. Back in Spokane delicate negotiations with railroads and other prime riverfront titleholders secured 100 acres on both banks of the Spokane River, as well as Havermale and Crystal Islands, for the exposition. Business leaders voted to tax themselves to get the project underway, and as federal and state dollars began to pour into the city, voters approved needed bond issues. Construction began in 1972. In late summer 1973 the Expo '74 Corporation board reassigned Alter to administer the fair's environmental symposia and hired Petr Spurney as the new general manager. Cole retained his title and continued to be the public figure most identified with the international exposition.

Expo '74 was the first U.S. world's fair to be sanctioned by the BIE since the United States joined in 1968. The fair's classification as a single theme or Category II Exposition by the BIE meant that the host city bore the responsibility for site development and construction. This allowed local architects and engineers to design functional pavilions that took advantage of the fair's unique riverine setting and theme. Plan-

Ducks swimming in the foreground of the Spokane River illustrate the theme of Expo '74 World's Fair, "Celebrating Tomorrow's Fresh, New Environment" (photograph by Walter Hodges, Expo '74 press release).

ners color coded the site in zones of yellow, magenta, orange, red, and purple. The hue of each sector was softer on the fringes but grew progressively brighter as fairgoers were drawn into the focal center of each area. Fifty pavilions provided homes for 103 exhibitors, including 10 nations, 43 commercial participants, more than 80 Native American groups, an amusement park, and a number of states, Canadian provinces, and private organizations. Countless entertainers, artists, musicians, and craftspeople from around the world contributed to the "global village" appeal of the fair. The environmental theme, the Folklife Festival, and the African American pavilion were firsts for a world exposition. The environmental theme was ubiquitous, if unevenly apparent throughout the fairgrounds as exhibitors addressed ecological concerns from their own

particular, sometimes problematic perspectives. A series of symposia on the environment, though not fully attended, when coupled with the overall ecological ethos of the fair, provided a pivotal international focus on the environment unparalleled at the time. The United Nations recognized the role Expo '74 played in promoting ecological awareness by designating the fair the center for World Environment Day activities on June 5.

Long before the gates closed for the final time at 6:00 P.M. on November 3, Spokane's world's fair had already been heralded a success. A total of nearly 5.2 million visitors passed through one of the five colorful gates since opening day on May 4, exceeding the projected break-even point. Unfortunately, a higher than anticipated ratio of season pass admissions to individual ticket purchases and double-digit

Showing the more commercial side of world's fairs, this model promotes the virtues of modern bathroom fixtures (photograph by Walter Hodges, Expo '74 press release).

celebration and showcased the first bicentennial exhibit. Beyond these contributions to national and international concerns, Expo '74 trans-formed Spokane, the smallest city yet to host a world's fair. The Spokane Opera House and Convention Center emerged from Expo's Washington State Pavilion and Art Center. The site opened to a new function in 1976 as Riverfront Park, a 100-acre "living space" in the center of a city reborn. The Spokane River sparkled again, and the city anticipated a future bright with new possibilities.

Bibliography

Significant collections pertaining to the Spokane World's Fair are located at three different facilities in Spokane County. The Eastern Washington State Historical Society Library and Archive at the Northwest Museum of Arts and Culture is the primary repository for the records of the Expo '74 World's Fair Corporation (1965–1975) and of its president (1968–1974), King F. Cole. The EWSHS collection includes incoming and outgoing correspondence, planning documents, financial forecasts and assessments, blueprints, audiovisual records, promotional materials, interviews, and other relevant documents. Library holdings also include manuscript records germane to Expo '74 from the Northwest Mining Association, the Spokane Council of Churches, and the public interest group Save Our Station Fund. The Pacific Northwest Room at downtown branch of the Spokane Public Library houses materials generated by the exhibitors and official published reports on the fair. Also included are environmental impact studies on the fair and an exhaustive collection of newspaper clippings and rare pamphlets on nearly every aspect of Expo '74. The Kennedy Library at Eastern Washington University contains records pertaining to Spokane Unlimited, the Folklife Festival, King Cole, and various other fair-related materials, chief among them interviews with

inflation resulted in a revenue shortfall of $723,961, which was, however, easily covered by calling in a percentage of each of the not-yet-collected pledges made in the early 1970s. The fair generated 4,000 jobs and an immediate economic benefit to Spokane of between $125 million and $139 million. The estimated long term $699 million return to the Spokane area in revitalized downtown commerce and increased tourism over the ensuing decade was nearly nine times the cost of the exposition ($78 million).

The impact of Expo '74 went far beyond the familiar measurement of dollars and cents. The environmental theme ("Celebrating Tomorrow's Fresh, New Environment") and related symposia educated fairgoers and international experts alike. Spokane's world's fair officially opened the two-year American Bicentennial major figures as well as fair employees and fair-goers.

Based on painstaking research in archival materials and related secondary literature as well as dozens of interviews with major figures, fair employees, and fairgoers, J. William T. Youngs, *The Fair and the Falls: Spokane's Expo '74 — Transforming an American Environment* (1996) is a noted historian's definitive study of all aspects of the fair and the community which staged it. Besides Youngs' monumental study, the best secondary sources of comprehensive statistical and background information on Expo '74 are Claude Bekins' official *Report of the United States Commissioner ...* (1974); Dawn Bowers, *Expo '74: World's Fair Spokane* (1974) which was underwritten by the Expo '74 Corporation, and the *Expo '74 Official Souvenir Program* (1974). William Stimson, A *View of the Falls: An Illustrated History of Spokane* (1985, 1999) does an admirable job of placing Expo and its regional impact in the context of Spokane's twentieth-century development. Willis B. Merriam's brief but informative pamphlet, *Spokane: Background to Expo '74* (1974), emphasizes the linkages between Expo and the urban renewal efforts of the late 1950s. The April 1974 issue of *Passages*, the magazine of Northwest Orient Airlines, contains numerous articles on the exposition, which provide various perspectives on the genesis and goals of Expo, as well as intriguing details on the pavilions. Dorothy Kienast examines the fair from an aesthetic vantage point in "Spokane and Expo '74: A Designer's Viewpoint," *Creative Communicator* 5, 6 (1974). These laudatory articles are somewhat balanced by a critical assessment of the environmental theme of the fair by Rosa Gustaitis in her feature article, "Expo '74: The Environment as Commercial," *Washington Post* (May 12, 1974). Numerous articles highlighting one aspect or another of Expo '74 appeared in newspapers such as the *New York Times*, the *Wall Street Journal*, the *Chicago Sun-Times*, the *New York Daily News*, the *Chicago Tribune*, the *Miami News*, the *Las Vegas Review-Journal*, the *Milwaukee Journal*, the *Seattle Times*, the *Tampa Tribune-Times*, and the *Cleveland Press* and in magazines and journals such as *Sunset*, *The New Yorker*, *Moody Monthly*, *U.S. News and World Report*, *The Christian Century*, and *Parade*. There are scores of newspaper articles on Expo '74 reaching back into the decade before the fair in the two Spokane newspapers, the *Spokesman-Review* and the *Spokane Daily Chronicle*.

Okinawa 1975–1976

Martin Manning

International Ocean Exposition (Expo '75)

The International Ocean Exposition grew out of the Japanese government's desire to rectify, upon Okinawa's reversion to Japan in 1972, disparities with the other prefectures and to improve the social climate, utilizing the natural and cultural resources of Okinawa. The exposition was held from July 20, 1975, to January 18, 1976, on a 247-acre site on Motobu Peninsula, near the northern end of Okinawa, the main island of the Ryukyu chain. Ocean Expo '75 was originally scheduled to open on March 2, 1975, and run through August 31, but the international petroleum crisis preoccupied participating countries, exacerbated an already critical exposition logistics problem, and greatly reduced stocks of petroleum-based construction materials. The Japanese government successfully appealed to the Bureau of International, Expositions (BIE) for a postponement.

In November 1971, the Japanese government formally applied to the BIE for permission to hold a "Special Category" exposition on an oceanographic theme. The master plan was approved by the Japan Association for the Ocean Expo in October 1972. Major construction began in mid–September 1973 for expo interface projects, such as roads, reservoirs and airport facilities, but several radical groups on

Okinawa resisted the exposition. The teachers' union discouraged students from attending the show and environmentalists objected to despoiling the landscape with new roads and other works as well as with the development of the Motobu site. Objections abated in spring 1975 when the show began to materialize. The very low silhouette maintained by American military personnel with respect to Expo '75, their quiet assistance, and other help rendered to the Japanese for the expo, all helped defuse the issue of U.S. military presence on Okinawa. The very visible and dynamic U.S. Pavilion distracted the attention of antagonists and the positive and peaceful impression made by the United States neutralized any enmity which might have been directed at the U.S. military presence.

The exposition's theme was "The Sea We Would Like to See." There were four basic subthemes: "Fish" expressed the ecology of sea creatures and their role in marine industry; "Ethnic and History" emphasized the cultures of the world's ocean-going people along with their traditions and future; "Ships" focused on adventure and exploration; and "Science and Technology" showed various facilities and apparatus for ocean research and development and called attention to the need for international cooperation when protecting and utilizing ocean resources.

Expo '75 was the largest Special Category exposition to that date, with participation by 35 countries; three international organizations (European Community, United Nations, Seacentre); seven Japanese and Okinawa facilities, including Aqua Farm, Aquapolis, Marine Life Park, Oceanic Cultures Pavilion, Shore Park, Expo Beach, and the Okinawa Prefecture Pavilion; and eight corporate pavilions (Fuyo Group, Hitachi A/V Marine Library, Kaiyo Midori Kan, Mitsubishi, Mitsui Children's Science Pavilion, Sumitomo, World Oceans Group, and Visual Exhibition by Matsushita). Perhaps the most spectacular attraction was the Aquapolis, touted as the future city on the sea. It was the world's largest floating structure: 100 meters long, 100 meters wide, and 32 meters high; it weighed 16,500 tons and could accommodate 2,400 people. Built by the Japanese government at a cost of more than $41 million, it was easily one of the most impressive and dominating structures at the exposition.

Since Expo '75 was a Special Category exposition, pavilions were leased to official national exhibitors and then reverted back to the Japanese organizers at the end of the expo. Some participants, such as Denmark and Sweden, had no pavilions of their own. There were pavilions for Australia, Brazil, Bulgaria, Cameroon, Canada, Central America [Costa Rica, El Salvador, Guatemala, Honduras, Nicaragua], Colombia, Cuba, Egypt, German Democratic Republic, Holy See (Vatican City), Hungary, Indonesia, Iran, Italy, Kenya, Republic of Korea, Malta, Monaco, Morocco, Netherlands Antilles, Philippines, Spain, Thailand, United Arab Emirates, United Kingdom, United States of America, U.S.S.R., Uruguay, and Western Samoa. As was customary at most of the cold war expositions, the United States and the Soviet Union had the two largest pavilion sites.

Official American participation in Ocean Expo '75 was based on the theme, "Ocean Earth," and had five main objectives: 1) to demonstrate American interest in the economic welfare of Okinawa; 2) to illustrate the American spirit of cooperation with the Japanese central government through support of its initiative in developing Ocean Expo; 3) to enhance the psychological acceptance of the American military presence on the island; 4) to further the growing awareness of the oceans' potential; and 5) to promote the rational use of marine resources in order to avoid conflicts and confrontations. The U.S. pavilion occupied an area of 55,000 square feet and received a total of 1,750,000 visitors during the six-month of the expo.

Two international oceanic symposia were held at the expo site. The first was "Pacem in Maribus VI" (The Sixth Conference on Peace on the Oceans), held October 1–3, under the co-sponsorship of the International Ocean Institute, Malta, and the Japan Association for the International Ocean Exposition. For background on the issues discussed at the conference, see: Elisabeth M. Borgese and David Krieger, eds. *The Tides of Change: Peace, Pollution, and Potential of the Oceans* (1975) which contains selected papers of convocations and research projects sponsored by Pacem in Maribus in preparation for the United Nations Conference on the Law of the Sea. The second major symposium was called "Man and the

Ocean," held November 17–22, 1975, which underlined the urgent need for a reasonable and well-balanced policy of ocean development and preservation. The symposium gave theoretical depth to the unifying theme of the exposition and generated material for the establishment of a new concept of the sea itself.

Expo'75 benefited from its topical theme and the conscientiousness of all participants in their interpretation of that theme. Most important, the exposition boosted tourism and brought needed improvements, such as highways, waterworks and hotels, to Okinawa. Direct expenditures for the exposition came to about 90 billion yen, including 46 billion yen in operating expenses. In addition, another 250 million yen was spent on related public works. Final attendance was estimated at 3,485,750 visitors, about one million fewer than anticipated but the exposition closed without a deficit.

All pavilions of official national participants were dismantled and the Motobu site was rebuilt into a park-like setting. A major part of the 247-acre site was preserved as the Ocean Exposition Memorial Park. Along with using the government pavilion as a museum, new facilities were constructed as a center for cultural interchange of youth around the world. The northern part of Okinawa and the exposition site were developed into a resort area. The park is located in Motobu Township. After the exposition ended, the site became a park operated by the national government. Within the park, there is the Okinawa Pavilion, a large red roofed building modeled after typical traditional Okinawan houses. The pavilion exhibits the history and spirit of Okinawa.

The Oceanic Cultures Hall displays the history and lifestyles of the people of the South Pacific who have been influenced greatly by the ocean. There is also a Ryukyuan village with full-scale representations of buildings reflecting the lifestyle of old Okinawa. On the southern side of the park, there was the Aquapolis, which was sold to an American scrap company in 2000 and taken apart. The Tropical Dream Center, where tropical and sub-tropical flora and orchids bloom in profusion, was built in the Ocean Exposition Memorial Park.

Night view of the main promenade of the 1975 Okinawa exposition with the U.S. pavilion in the background.

Bibliography

Most of the official records of the exposition were published by its host, Okinawa International Ocean Exposition Foundation, rather than by the Japanese government. The best place for the official records of the International Ocean Exposition is the Okinawa Prefectural Archive, whose website is <*http://www.archives.pref.oki nawa.jp*> (Japanese only). The archive has some 129 items, including the official guidebook, budget report, operations report, catalogue, photographs, and other ephemera. The Ocean Exposition Commemorative Park Management Foundation, which manages the Ocean Exposition Commemorative Park where the exposition was held, transferred all relevant documents on the exposition to the Okinawa Prefectural Archive.

The Okinawa Prefectural Library has other publications relating to Expo '75, including official records, books, and posters. Japanese readers may consult the library's homepage at <*http:// www.library.pref.okinawa.jp/*>. The Ryukyu University Library also holds expo-related materials, including the guidebook and various reports on Expo '75 planning, exhibits, and the observance of the twentieth anniversary of the expo. .

Information on this exposition may also be found in various publications of the Japan Association of the International Ocean Exposition. See especially *Okinawa: Expo'75 — A Review of the International Ocean Exposition* (n.d.) and *Okinawa International Ocean Exposition* (1976). *Expo '75 Pictorial Report* (n.d.) is a convenient guide with bilingual captions. For the architecture of the fair, see the October-November 1975 issue of *Japan Architect*, which is devoted to the event.

A history of the Okinawa Exposition in English remains to be written. Although most of the publications on the fair are in Japanese, English editions do exist. See *Expo'75 — International Ocean Exposition, Okinawa, Japan, 1975, July 20, 1975-January 18, 1976: The Sea We Would Like to See* (1975), which contains a master plan of Expo '75. It is also available as *Expo '75 Bulletin no. 18: Supplement*.

Original English-language materials on Expo '75 are hard to locate. There was extensive press coverage, but with the exception of travel and science writers, most foreign correspondents focused on the political aspects of Okinawa and its reversion back to the Japanese government in 1972. The Public Diplomacy Historical Collection [formerly the USIA Historical Collection] of the U.S. Department of State has files on Expo '75, including BIE minutes of the commissioner-general meetings, newspaper clippings, photos, official correspondence, and various reports. The official records of U.S. participation are at the National Archives and Records Administration, College Park, Maryland.

Most countries that participated in Tsukuba prepared their own final reports For U.S. participation, see: United States Information Agency. *Ocean Expo '75: Final Report to the President from the Director of the United States Information Agency on the First International Ocean Exposition, Motobu Peninsula, Okinawa, Japan, July 20, 1975-January 18, 1976.* (1976).

More popular accounts of the expo may be found in *Sunset* magazine. See especially "You Must Plan Well Ahead for Expo '75 on Okinawa," *Sunset* 153 (November 1974) and "Surprise World's Fair... Okinawa's Expo '75," *Sunset* (September 1975): 46–51.

Knoxville 1982

Carl E. Kramer

Knoxville International Energy Exposition

The 1982 Knoxville World's Fair, formally known as the Knoxville International Energy Exposition (KIEE), symbolized the triumph of urban boosterism and pork-barrel politics in the context of a national energy crisis. Organized around the theme, "Energy Turns the World," KIEE was conceived in 1974 by W. Stewart Evans, executive director of the Downtown Knoxville Association, after attending a presentation on the 1974 Spokane World's Fair. The following year, convinced that a world's fair could jump start development in Knoxville's central business district, he persuaded Mayor Kyle Testerman, a Republican, to appoint a bipartisan committee to conduct a feasibility study of the idea. The committee consisted of seventeen local financial and political power brokers chaired by Jake Butcher, chairman of United American Bank, Knoxville's largest financial institution, and a former Democratic candidate for governor of Tennessee. The study committee's favorable report recommended that the city apply for a world's fair in 1980. Meanwhile, Democrat Randy Tyree upset Testerman in his re-election bid. But Tyree quickly endorsed the concept.

In 1976 fair advocates organized the not-for-profit Knoxville International Energy Exposition, elected Jake Butcher as chairman of the board of directors, and hired public relations executive S. H. (Bo) Roberts as president. Mirroring the support of mayors of both parties, the exposition won strong backing from U. S. Senators Howard Baker, a Republican, and James Sasser, a Democrat. The Knoxville *News-Sentinel*, the city's largest newspaper, quickly became an unabashed advocate, not only on the editorial page but in the news pages as well. Confident in their vision, KIEE applied to the U. S. Department of Commerce for a fair in 1980. The DOC rejected the application for 1980, stating that four years did not allow sufficient preparation time. Undaunted, KIEE resubmitted the application for 1982, and it was approved.

The expo gained critical political and international support in 1977 with endorsements by President Jimmy Carter, the Tennessee General Assembly, and the Bureau of International Expositions. In October 1978, after intense lobbying by Butcher and Sasser and the intervention of federal Budget Director Bert Lance, President Carter approved a $12.4 million, four-agency federal assistance package, and two months later he formally endorsed the expo and directed the secretary of state to issue invitations to appropriate foreign nations to participate in the event.

With a 1980 population of barely 175,000, Knoxville hardly seemed the logical site for an international exposition. But fair organizers had a highly appealing rationale. At a time when energy consciousness was at its height because of recent price hikes by oil producing countries, they argued that Knoxville's proximity to Oak Ridge's National Atomic Laboratory, the American Museum of Science and Energy, the Tennessee Valley Authority's huge power generating facilities, the University of Tennessee's energy research center, and the state's rich coal fields made the city a natural site for an exposition focused on energy. From an entertainment perspective, Knoxville offered the advantage of immediate access to the Great Smoky Mountain National Park and the popular resorts at Gatlinburg and Pigeon Forge.

In addition to the appeal of the energy theme and popular entertainment venues, fair organizers argued that the event's proposed 72-acre site provided an opportunity to redevelop and revitalize the Lower Second Creek valley, a blighted, trash-clogged neighborhood located between downtown Knoxville and the University of Tennessee (UT) campus. Along with the anticipated publicity generated by media coverage and millions of visitors, boosters also envisioned new hotels and office buildings, increased retail sales and tax revenues, raises for city employees, thousands of new jobs, and extensive transportation improvements, including elimination of "Malfunction Junction," a traffic bottleneck at the interchange of I-40 and I-75.

Not everyone accepted the organizers' vision. Among the dissenters were city Councilwoman Bernice O'Conner and UT political scientist Joseph Dodd, who spearheaded an ongoing campaign for a referendum on the matter. But KIEE organizers, backed by powerful political leaders and the *News-Sentinel,* skillfully fended off their efforts and moved ahead with their program. In 1979 they secured a $30 million loan package from a group of national and local banks. The lenders included Chemical Bank of New York City, Butcher's United American Bank, and several others that he and his brother, C. H. Butcher, controlled. The same year, President Carter approved a congressional appropriation of $20.8 million to build the U. S. Pavilion, and Italy became the first foreign nation to sign a participation contract.

The exposition movement continued to gather momentum during 1980. Construction began in May with the groundbreaking for a Hilton Hotel and a city-financed parking garage developed by the Pegasus Company, a local firm whose owners included Lionel Wilde, Jake Butcher's brother-in-law. Soon thereafter the U. S. government awarded an additional $9.9 million for site development and associated urban redevelopment. The national political environment changed markedly in November when Republican Ronald Reagan was elected president of the United States and his party captured control of the Senate. When the GOP took command in January, Howard Baker became Senate majority leader and began taking a more active role in promoting his state's interest in the fair. Over the months that followed, he encouraged executives of major corporations to become exhibitors and lobbied Secretary of State Alexander Haig to promote international participation. Twenty-four nations, thirty corporations, and seven states ultimately committed to sponsor exhibits.

Although their political connections enabled the fair's organizers to overcome a succession of obstacles, controversies continued to erupt as opening day neared. Construction cost overruns, the evictions of residents of apartments and rental properties near the fair grounds, and ballooning charges for motels and campgrounds generated unfavorable press coverage. A major target of public ire was a requirement that reservations be routed through a central housing office operated by the Knoxville Visitors Bureau. Its operations proved both inept and inefficient, provoking anger from operators of local hotels and other visitor accommodations and their customers.

Despite these and other distractions, President Reagan opened the Knoxville International Energy Exposition as scheduled on May 1, 1982. The controversies surrounding KIEE's development, compounded by visitor anger over slow ticket lines and inefficient gate operations during the early days, heightened anxieties for the fair's ultimate success. Based purely on paid visitation, however, it was a resounding success. On October 9 the fair attracted 102,842 visitors, surpassing the previous one-day attendance record set at the Seattle World's Fair in 1962. On October 30 KIEE recorded its eleven millionth visitor, and it closed the following day, having attracted more visitors than any other international theme fair in North American history. Only universal-class events such as those in New York City in 1964 and Montreal in 1967 recorded more visitors.

KIEE's centerpiece was Sunsphere, a gold-tinted glass globe sitting atop a 192-foot steel tower, symbolizing the sun, Earth's ultimate source of energy. True to the fair's theme, many exhibits emphasized sources and production of energy. The cantilevered glass and steel U. S. pavilion, the fair's largest and most expensive venue, hosted a series of robot- and laser-operated exhibits depicting the history of energy use and development in America. The Japan pavilion, the largest foreign entry, featured a domed theater with a multi-media presentation that showcased the nation's energy challenges and also included presentations of Japanese folk art. Giant solar collectors were a central feature of Saudi Arabia's pavilion, which highlighted the nation's role as a major energy producer and banker for third-world

nations. West Germany's pavilion featured models of nuclear reactors, and West Virginia's highlighted the history of coal mining, including a replica of a coal camp and a display on the history of the United Mine Workers Union.

But some of the most popular exhibits were only remotely related to energy. The Peoples' Republic of China pavilion presented a broad array of Chinese art works and bricks from the Great Wall. Hungary showcased the popular Rubik's Cube puzzle, and the inventor, Dr. Ermo Rubik, made a special appearance on August 17, Hungary's National Day. The popular Egyptian pavilion featured a 3,000-year-old collection of chariots and statuary, while curators at Peru's pavilion exhibited a 700-year-old mummy.

In addition to its exhibits, KIEE attracted popular entertainers such as comedians Bob Hope and Bill Cosby; musicians Debbie Boone, Johnny Cash, Lynn Anderson, Roberta Peters, Chet Atkins, and Victor Borge; and larger ensembles including the Knoxville Symphony Orchestra, Japan's Grand Kabuyki Theatre, and numerous international theatrical, musical, and dance organizations. Daily entertainment included fireworks displays, magicians, clowns, mimes, parades, and a host of small regional and international groups. For fans of professional sports, KIEE offered exhibition games between the New England Patriots and Pittsburgh Steelers football teams and the Boston Celtics and Philadelphia 76ers basketball teams.

Despite KIEE's popularity with the public, its aftermath proved as problematic as its development. Just days after it closed, the Federal Deposit Insurance Corporation initiated an audit of the United American Bank and others owned by Jake Butcher. He was arrested for bank fraud in late 1982. Soon thereafter his empire collapsed, forcing him into bankruptcy. In 1985 he pled guilty and ultimately spent several years in a federal prison. About the same time as Butcher's arrest, the Tennessee attorney general sued KIEE and its central reservation agencies for consumer fraud, alleging that they had overcharged many customers, failed to make proper refunds, and provided inadequate accommodations. It took more than four years to close out the case following a settlement in March 1983.

KIEE also failed to deliver in a timely

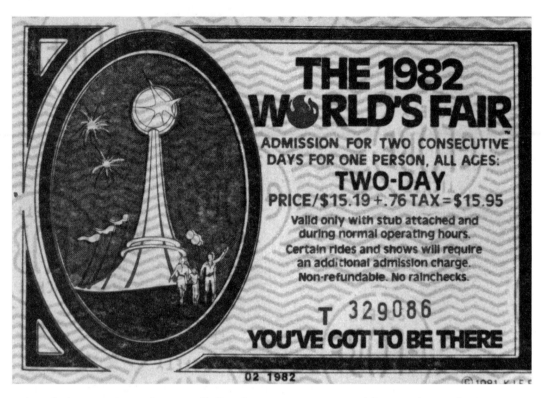

This admissions ticket to the Knoxville fair shows a representation of the Sunsphere and indicates that the price of a two day pass was $15.95 (editors' colection).

fashion on most of its promises of post-fair public improvements, particularly the revitalization in downtown Knoxville. A $224 million expansion of the local interstate highway system significantly improved traffic flow. Likewise, within five years after the fair closed, local arts groups developed an old candy factory and several nearby Victorian homes into a small artists' colony with shops, studios, and galleries. But the U. S. pavilion, which originally cost $21.1 million, could not be sold. The government transferred it to the city for one dollar, but the city could find no use for it and finally demolished it in 1992. The Sunsphere remained open until 1984, when its restaurant closed because of inadequate patronage. It remained shut until 1987, when it reopened as the home of the local arts council. Other facilities suffered similar financial difficulties. Over the next two decades several development groups proposed a succession of multimillion dollar redevelopment schemes. Each failed, however, to muster the capital necessary to bring its proposal to fruition.

The city of Knoxville finally launched its own initiative in 2001, when it appropriated $14 million to develop the World's Fair Park. The new Knoxville Convention & Exposition Center, located next to the still underutilized Sunsphere, opened in July 2002, and the World's Fair Park followed a year later. While much remained to be accomplished, nearly a quarter of a century after it closed, the Knoxville area had begun to realize the benefits promised by the boosters of the 1982 world's fair.

Bibliography

Official records of the Knoxville International Energy Exposition are housed in the McClung Collection of the East Tennessee Historical Center in Knoxville. Materials include financial and personnel records as well as videotapes, slides, and papers. The University of Tennessee's 1982 Knoxville International Energy Exposition Collection, held at the Hoskins Library, contains correspondence, technical reports, and documents from many organizations involved in bringing the fair to the city, including the Greater Knoxville Chamber of Commerce, KIEE, and the Downtown Knoxville Association. Other essential documents include the *Official Guide Book, The 1982 World's Fair* (1982) and the U. S. Department of Commerce, *Final Report of the United States Commissioner General for the Knoxville International Energy Exposition ... to the President of the United States* (1982).

The most useful secondary account is Joseph Dodd, *World Class Politics: Knoxville's 1982*

World's Fair, Redevelopment and the Political Process (1988). While Dodd's evaluation is highly critical, particularly of the exclusion of the public from the planning process, the high-stakes wheeling and dealing by Jake Butcher and his associates, and the failure to deliver on downtown revitalization, he concludes that KIEE ultimately broke even financially. Also useful is Robert Doak, "Knoxville 1982: Knoxville International Energy Exposition," in John E. Findling, editor, and Kimberly D. Pelle, assistant editor, *Historical Dictionary of World's Fairs and Expositions, 1851–1988* (1990): 352–55.

New Orleans 1984

Miki Pfeffer

Louisiana World Exposition

In 1984, New Orleans gave a magnificent party, but too few visitors came. Promoters of the Louisiana World Exposition expected 12 million people, but only 7,335,279 attended, and some of those were season pass holders who returned 25, 50, even 100 times. Although the fair was well conceived and executed, it was overbuilt, under funded, and poorly marketed with strategic missteps that caused negative reviews in the press. Apologists and critics claimed that the New Orleans event was too distant from urban centers, too soon after Knoxville's World's Fair of 1982, and too much a victim of shifting national priorities and local funding demands. It has the distinction of being the only world's fair to declare bankruptcy while still open, and it killed hopes of another American fair for the rest of the century. Yet, legions of devotees were infatuated with its theme-park atmosphere, world-class entertainment and nightlife, food and beverage choices, variety of exhibits and folklife demonstrations, daily fireworks, and the spectacle of its 4,000-foot access to the Mississippi River. The Louisiana World Exposition captured the city's festivity and pageantry and lifted community spirits, and it also inspired considerable urban renewal.

The fair's official guide credits Edward Stagg, executive director of the Council for a Better Louisiana in 1974, with the idea that a world's fair would revive the city's sagging economy and psychic doldrums. Governor Edwin Edwards supported the scheme and in 1977 created the Louisiana Exposition Authority, a consortium of businessmen. By 1981, planners met with Reagan administration Secretary of Commerce Malcolm Baldrige who announced that the government was not going to approve the fair because promoters had failed to secure sufficient financial backing. Republican Governor David Treen convinced Baldrige to allow more time for fund raising, and a compromise was struck: President Ronald Reagan would approve the fair, but the government would spend only $10 million — one-twentieth of what it had spent in Knoxville — and would wait to invite foreign countries until another $12 million was raised and until planners presented a proposal to finance a U. S. pavilion. The Bureau of International Expositions (BIE) gave approval in 1981 as long as a matching $30 million secured the development. These early financial hurdles were a harbinger of the fair's troubles throughout its six-month run from May 12 to November 11, 1984, but the private, non-profit Louisiana

World Exposition, Inc. forged ahead, hiring Petr Spurney as president and chief executive officer. Spurney's credentials included having been general manager of the 1974 Spokane World Exposition and other celebrations, but he had never directed a large event from start to finish. Promoters also assembled leases on more than 80 acres along a stretch of neglected riverfront wharves, railroad yards, and historic but dilapidated warehouses near the central business district and the French Quarter. It was an exceptional location within walking distance of three-quarters of the city's hotels.

Nevertheless, troubles came early as start-up funds were quickly depleted, as extravagant plans escalated beyond contractors' ability to keep up, and as expectations inflated past the chance to materialize. In addition, without federal participation, New Orleans Mayor Ernest N. Morial and city government demanded funds for site development and infrastructure from already-slim coffers, and they expected that a planned New Orleans Convention Center be left behind as the centerpiece for future expanded tourism. This permanent building was the fair's Great Hall and housed a renovated authentic New Orleans cottage, Woman's Pavilion, African-American Pavilion, television station, large art exhibit, three-story beating heart identifying Ochsner Hospital's medical station, and a few state, religious, and federal displays.

Inexplicably, when advance sales were disappointing, planners added more features. They assumed New Orleans was an "easy sell" to corporate investors, but few came forward, and without the nudge of the president, foreign governments were slow to commit. Planners also miscalculated the need for early marketing. Tour agents around the country complained that promotion was too little, too late, and aimed at adults instead of families, although the fair had many amusements for children. Perhaps the greatest strategic error was promoters' invitation to journalists to preview the fair the day before it opened, when construction, painting, and debris were still evident. Although the fair was ready for opening day, reporters already had logged negative reports of incompleteness that exacerbated the fairs mounting financial problems. Promoters claimed that President Reagan's absence from the fair sent a message of benign neglect and robbed it of free international press.

The official theme was a rather abstruse "The World of Rivers: Fresh Water as a Source of Life," and it was carried out in each of six "neighborhoods" with inventive fountains, water-related pavilions and exhibits, water gardens and lagoons, and a popular kiddie wash (resembling a car wash) in which even adults frolicked during the steamy summer months. A variety of ships docked at or departed from the riverfront, reinforcing the fair's theme, but some exhibits stretched to comply, as when the Union Pacific Railway's movie touted "Rivers of Steel," and America's Electric Energy Exhibit claimed its "overall message" was "Rivers of Electricity." Surprisingly, no exhibit focused on transforming contaminated water to fresh, healthy water, although the Mississippi River gathers the nation's pollutants as it flows southward toward New Orleans.

According to CEO Spurney, the mission of World's Fairs had changed in the 1980s from showcases of technology to the technology of entertainment. Fantasy and nostalgia, razzmatazz and piety became unofficial themes of the New Orleans fair, reflecting the city's own Janus-like quality. Through two colossal entrance gates created by Mardi Gras float designers and strewn with alligators, sea gods, and bare-breasted mermaids, visitors came for the impressive opening day ceremonies on the riverfront, and they encountered the hurly burly of the fair's signature symbol, the Wonderwall, a meandering architectural montage that both honored and mocked centuries of architecture. The eleven-feet-wide, half-mile-long wall was a diversionary tactic to camouflage huge power lines overhead and was a "frozen parade" with playful nooks for street performers, sculptures, fountains, and food vendors. Painted in a pastel palate resembling that of traditional New Orleans homes, it included Gothic windows, Greek temples, Roman aqueducts, gates, arcades, and stairs, art deco ornamentation, and domes, turrets, and flags "reminiscent of the great royal festivals of the Renaissance." Conceived by California architects Charles Moore and William Turnbull in collaboration with Perez Associates, the major architects of the fair, it was to be a "mythic wall-as-city," a "tribute to the persistence of memorable architecture," and a "representative of the commerce and pleasure that nourish a city." It cost approximately $3.9 million, and its frequent surprises charmed visitors.

Sea figures surround one of the two entrance gates at the 1984 New Orleans World's Fair (courtesy Historic New Orleans Collection, Williams Research Center, Claire de la Vergne, photographer).

of Billy Rose's hit show at the 1939 New York World's Fair. In the Fulton Street Mall neighborhood, amid folk music from an Italian Village and a raucous oom-pah-pah German Beer Garden, was the serenity of the Vatican Pavilion, as quiet as a church. This "crown jewel of the fair" with its rare art treasures drew large crowds, although the Archdiocese of New Orleans charged an additional $5 to the $15-a-day fair entrance fee. During the final week, the Archdiocese invited all in at no charge, and low-income families flocked to the exhibit. Also, for twelve hours a day on nine stages, a smorgasbord of entertainment greeted fairgoers in every neighborhood (over 1,000 acts over the course of its 184-day run), and even a silly pelican mascot, Seymour D. Fair, amused visitors. In a city acclaimed for its food and drink, fairgoers made some new discoveries: sushi, Belgian waffles, fresh-fruit daiquiris.

For the best views of the grounds, visitors chose the elevated monorail or a tram system that ran high along the riverfront. Crossing the Mississippi River on the 350-foot-high Mississippi Aerial River Transit (MART) offered breathtaking views of the landscape, especially each night when brilliant fireworks lit the sky. Another favorite vantage point was the Giant Wheel rising to the height of a 15-story building, and at night it was "aglow with over 4,000 lightbulbs." Just as at the 1884 Cotton Centennial where newly invented electric lights captivated fairgoers, the 1984 Louisiana World Exposition presented a spectacle of computerized alternating light shows each night, especially tracing through the Wonderwall and Centennial Plaza.

This fair, this "city within a city," had the flair of street festivals and a focal point in each neighborhood. For example, from a particular spot in Centennial Plaza, sections of the Wonderwall formed an "optical illusion" of the façade of the Main Building at the World's Industrial and Cotton Centennial Exposition held in New Orleans a century earlier. It was reflected in a Centennial Lagoon near a 1904 antique carousel. A major attraction in the Bayou Plaza neighborhood was the nostalgic Aquacade with musical extravaganzas of synchronized swimming and diving reminiscent

Visitors also developed favorites among the few corporate and foreign exhibits. The Liggett & Myers Tobacco Company's twelve-story-high amphitheater on the river, designed by Frank O. Gehry, was home to nightly big-name entertainment and other celebrations.

A section of the Wonderwall in the Centennial Plaza at the 1984 New Orleans World's Fair. It nostalgically recalls the Main Building of the Cotton Centennial 100 years earlier (courtesy Historic New Orleans Collection, Williams Research Center, photographer Claire de la Vergne).

When the canvas backdrop behind the stage was raised, it spectacularly framed movement on the Mississippi River. Gehry claimed to have taken inspiration for the structure from the river's industrial cranes and barges. Chrysler's pentagon-shaped building (like the symbol of the company) depicting automotive technology also attracted attention. The International Riverfront neighborhood was built on old river wharves, and this series of spaces for foreign exhibitors became an international showplace and busy bazaar, especially in China's freestanding pavilion. Canada's gigantic-screened IMAX film of its many rivers was a crowd-pleaser. Only these countries and Australia, Egypt, France, Italy, Japan, Liberia, Peru, and Korea sent separate exhibits; others showed collectively: countries of the Caribbean Basin and those of the European Economic Community. The Army Corps of Engineers' dredgeboat *Kennedy,* near the U. S. Pavilion and NASA's Space Orbiter *Enterprise*, was a popular demonstration of the Corps's ability to transfer Mississippi River silt to needed spots. Also fasc-

inating to visitors was a working "offshore" oil derrick, complete with shifts of roustabouts and a 50,000-gallon aquarium at its base. Despite the fair's successes, critics claimed that it had too few corporate exhibits to make it profitable and too few foreign exhibits to qualify as a legitimate world's fair.

Although the Louisiana World Exposition declared bankruptcy before the end of its six months, it limped to the end with a closing ceremony sponsored by private donations. However, the harsh reality of financial reports does not reveal lasting benefits for the city. After costs of nearly $350 million, including fees for transporting the *Enterprise,* building the U. S. Pavilion, and renovating the city's sidewalks and lighting in the French Quarter, the exposition lost approximately $120 million. Bankruptcy court sold off whatever assets were available, including sections of the Wonderwall, and for at least three years, lawsuits plagued the private corporation, its board members, and particularly Spurney. Nevertheless, the city gained a Riverwalk shopping mall where the international pavilions had stood, and the Mississippi River again became part of life in the city. The Ernest N. Morial Convention Center was ready for a large convention the month after the fair's closing and has been expanded into a mammoth trade venue with more than a million square feet of exhibit space covering eleven blocks. (In 2005, the Convention Center became notorious as a site of human misery in the floods of hurricane Katrina.) In the surrounding area, a Riverfront Historic District with firm zoning controls held developers accountable to preserve architecturally significant buildings, and it accelerated the revival of the entire district into hotels and condominiums, galleries and museums, food and beverage venues, and rejuvenated office spaces. Reclamation of the riverfront continued on the lower side of Canal Street and now includes a world-class aquarium and IMAX theater — evocative of exhibits at the Louisiana World Exposition — and a riverfront park that is the scene of many New Orleans festivals and family gatherings.

Bibliography

The New Orleans *Times-Picayune* provides the most complete coverage of the Louisiana World Exposition. The newspaper was criticized for a lack of support, but it offers a balanced view, even of the fair's problems. To locate specific articles, use *Bell & Howell Newspaper Index to the Times-Picayune/The States-Item*. The *1984 World's Fair, New Orleans: The Official Guidebook* (1984) offers as precise an overview as is possible when created well in advance of the event. *World's Fair New Orleans* (Picayune Publishing, Inc., 1984) is a small picture book that attractively captures the color and whimsy of the event, and *The World's Fair, New Orleans* by Joshua Mann Paliet (1987) unwittingly leaves a poignant record of the dearth of visitors. The book's foreword by Kent Bloomer and Charles Moore provides a chronicle of the creation of the Wonderwall, and weekly *Gambit* publisher, Gary Esalen, offers a cogent assessment of the fair's "Residual Effects." In an appendix, Pailet also lists every performer and entertainment act during the six months.

The Historic New Orleans Collection houses the papers of the U. S. Commissioner General John G. Weinmann, including correspondence, monthly status reports, financial documents, photographs, and memorabilia. Congressional approval is outlined in *Authorization for the 1984 Louisiana World Exposition, Ninety-seventh Congress, second session, on H.R. 6409* (1982). For an architectural overview by the fair's major architects, Perez Associates, see *Master Plan: Louisiana World Exposition, May 12-Nov. 11, 1984* at East Jefferson Parish Library. Louisiana Collections at the city's universities and New Orleans Public Library also include a variety of useful reports and plans. After a decade, Peter Edward Hagan assesses the outcomes of the fair in *The History and Impact of the 1984 Louisiana World Exposition* (1994), and in the videocassette "A World's Fair to Remember," public television station WYES looks back two decades and includes interviews with principals and frequent visitors of the event.

Tsukuba 1985

Tatsushi Narita

The International Exposition, Tsukuba, Japan, 1985 (Tsukuba Expo '85)

The city of Tsukuba, lying on the southern slopes of Mount Tsukuba and located about 33 miles northeast of Tokyo is a national project city. In creating a satellite capital city in accordance with the national population dispersion policy, the Japanese government narrowed down the selection to the area of Tsukuba as early as 1960s. Complicated interests hindered the smooth transition of the core

The editors wish to thank Martin J. Manning for providing additional information on Tsukuba '85 included in this essay.

central government functions to the new community. To put it rather bluntly, only educational and research institutions were forced to relocate from Tokyo. Promotion of science was the best decision left to Tsukuba. In 1978, the Science and Technology Agency, a branch of the world-famous Ministry of International Trade and Industry (MITI) announced its concept for a science exposition. However, the Bureau of International Exposition (BIE) did not endorse the concept of focusing narrowly on scientific technology that the agency proposed. For this reason, a task force, composed of Jiro Ushio (chair), Jun Shimokawabe, Takemochi Ishii and Yoichiro Murakami, was created to work out an acceptable theme. The exposition theme the task force hammered out successfully was "Dwellings and Surroundings: Science and Technology for Man at Home." The BIE approved it in 1980 and registered the exposition as a Special Exposition in 1981.

The International Exposition, Tsukuba, more popularly known as "Tsukuba Expo '85" was prepared, organized and operated by the Japan Association for the International Exposition, Tsukuba, 1985. It ran from March 17 to September 16, for a total of 184 days.

The site covered an area of about 100 hectares (246 acres). Heavily promoted by big Japanese corporations and the national government, Expo '85 attracted 20,334,727 visitors, a figure larger than that of any other Special Expositions of the time. The importance that the national government attached to the exposition was seen in the fact that Crown Prince Akihito (now the emperor) opened the fair, and Emperor Hirohito paid an official visit on June 16, 1985.

The architecture of the fair was a colorful collection of massive geometric-shaped pavilions. (Kisho Kurokawa, Japan's leading architect, designed several of them, including the Toshiba Pavilion, the Mitsui Pavilion, the Japan IBM Pavilion and the Kuruma-kan Pavilion.) The expo's master site plan called for eight self-contained blocks. The fair's tallest structure was Technocosmos, an 85-meter ferris wheel; the most popular amusement area was Children's Plaza, created to help children understand, through amusement and recreation, the principles of science and technology. Japanese government exhibits consisted of the Theme Pavilion, the History Pavilion, Children's Plaza, Expo Plaza and Tsukuba Expo Center (designed as the one and only permanent facility). Among the exhibits shown the most popular was hydroponically grown tomatoes, famous for its maximum yield of 13,312 tomatoes. There were 28 Japanese corporate participants. The Fujitsu Pavilion showed a computerized, graphic rendition of the micro-world of DNA molecules and featured a huge intelligent robot called Fanucman. The robots, in the Fuyo Robot Theater, not only vacuumed the floor and played soccer but also staged a musical play. Emphasizing a biotechnological vision, the Midori-kan Pavilion was dedicated to a bright future of human longevity. Sony presented a huge LED display device called Jumbotron. Japan Air Lines and Sumitomo together combined to give a superbly silent and smooth ride on a magnetically levitated High Speed Surface Transit (HSST) train that flew a half-inch above the track. International participants included 47 countries and 37 international organizations. They were all housed in four groups of identical modules. The United States featured what computers might become in an age to come. Dedicated to "Artificial Intelligence: Amplifying the Mind," the U.S. Pavilion intended to exemplify the great potential of AI. The exhibit made heavy use of robots under the rubric "Robots That Think," and presented an array of computer-related systems that could solve the Rubik's Cube puzzle or perform complex mathematical tasks. The federal government's efforts to involve the private sector in the U.S. exhibit paid off as four major corporations contributed $6 million, some 40 percent of the congressional appropriation for American participation. The Canadian Pavilion featured a television station that broadcast views and information on Canada to Japanese visitors. The Soviet and British pavilions touted their scientific and technological achievements, while China emphasized its culture and folk arts. Many other countries present took advantage of the opportunity to showcase their export products and tourism. In hammering out the fundamental vision of this expo, the task force led by Ushio seems to have succeeded in placing emphasis on ways to improve human society in the near future. But at Tsukuba, the foremost priority was given to the presentation of

At the U.S. pavilion in Tsukuba, the Mind Machine captured the imagination of visitors as it portrayed computers of the future (courtesy of Martin J. Manning and the Public Diplomacy Archives, U.S. Department of State).

positive images of science and technology. The result was an overriding concentration on "high-tech," particularly the foreshadowing of the new technology of robotics and biotechnology. Tsukuba Expo was surreptitiously known as Dentsu Expo. Of 28 private pavilions, 18 were produced by Dentsu, the giant advertising agency while four were produced by Hakuho-do, Dentsu's formidable rival.

Only five pavilions, including the Mitsubishi Future Pavilion, the Fuyo Robot Theater and the Suntory Pavilion, were built by the participants themselves. Masterminded by public relations experts, most of the pavilions followed similar patterns in the presentation of themes and exhibits, causing alert-minded visitors to surrender to monotony. At the TDK Pavilion, however, Masanori Hata, a multi-talented Japanese designer, devised a unique presentation called "Elephinsect Bird," which he said combined the sensitivity of an elephant's keen nose, the vision of an insect's compound eyes, and the flying capabilities of a bird. The popularity of Hata's presentation suggested that high-spirited expositions of the late twentieth century would succeed only with active involvement from a wide range of people rather than from an overt reliance upon large corporations spending huge amounts of money.

Bibliography

Records of Tsukuba Expo '85 are housed at the Ibaraki Prefectural Library and the Tsukuba Banpaku Kinen Zaktan (Tsukuba Expo Memorial Foundation), located at the Tsukuba Expo Center, which became a permanent memorial site after the fair ended. Both archives have federal government and prefectural records on the exposition, artifacts, visual materials, and other material related to the fair. The essential book about the Tsukuba Exposition is *Tsukuba Expo '85: Official Report* (1986), published by the Japan Association for the International Exposition with the cooperation of Dentsu Inc. For the architecture of the fair, see *Expo '85: Architecture* (1985) and *Quest Tsukuba Exposition: A Source Book* (1985), a beautiful publication, complete with thorough architectural descriptions. Good guidebook materials include *Tsukuba Expo '85: Pictorial Report*, a convenient book captioned by Japanese and English. See also Alfred Heller's chapter on the Tsukuba Expo in his *World's Fairs*

and the End of Progress: An Insider's View (1999). Those conversant with Japanese may consult Toshiya Yoshimi's thought-provoking discussion of the fair in his *Banpaku genso: Sengo seijino jubaku (Illusions of Expositions: The Spellbinding by Post-War Era Politics)* (2005).

Records for the U.S. participation at this fair are at the Public Diplomacy Historical Collection of the U.S. Department of State and at the National Archives and Records Administration in College Park, Maryland. There was some coverage in English-language newspapers and magazines. Among the most useful are John Allwood, "Tsukuba," *World's Fair* 4, 1 (Winter 1984); David Tracey, "Tsukuba Expo 85: High-Tech Dazzle as an Instrument of Government Policy," *World's Fair* 5, 1 (Winter 1985), and Milton Meskowitz, "A Powerful Message from Japan," and Alfred Heller, "Caution! You Are Approaching a Black Hole: Expo '85 and the Promises of Technology," both in *World's Fair* 5, 3 (Summer 1985). See also E. J. Kahn, "Our Far-Flung Correspondents: The Boom-Boom Fair," *New Yorker* (August 5, 1985). Other articles can be found through the standard indexes, but Lewis Simons, "A High-Tech Expo Opens in Japan's City for Science," *Smithsonian* 16, 1 (April 1985): 158–62, 164–65, is especially recommended.

Among contemporary views of Tsukuba Expo, the following articles are useful: Marc Mancini, "Shadows of '39," *Film Comment*, 21, 2 (September-October 1985), in which Mancini claimed that the scientific extravaganza of Expo '85 traced its roots directly to the New York World's Fair of 1939; and "Japan's Celebration of the Future," *Futurist* 19 (December 1985): 29–32, which noted that the expo communicated a special message to the Third World that "the Western model is not the *only* model of development."

Vancouver 1986

John E. Findling

Expo 86: The 1986 World Exposition

Following on the success of two previous Pacific Northwest expositions, Seattle's Century

21 expo in 1962 and Spokane's environmentally themed Expo '74, Vancouver civic leaders began thinking in 1978 of an exposition of their own to celebrate the city's centennial in 1985. In March 1978, the National Harbours Board

announced a development plan for Vancouver that included a new convention center on the harbor. In December, notified the Bureau of International Expositions (BIE) of its plan to host an exposition, changing the date to 1986 when it realized that Tsukuba (Japan) had 1985 locked up. A formal application for BIE sanction was submitted in June 1979 that called for an expo split between a small 5-acre site on the harbor (for the convention center), and a 170-acre site in a decaying industrial area along the north bank of False Creek. Transpo 86, as planners called it at this time, would serve to bring about the development of the False Creek area, prompt a needed upgrade of the public transit system, and encourage the replacement of aging Empire Stadium.

By early 1981, the BIE had sanctioned the event, and an expo board of directors had been formed, with Jim Pattison, a well-known local businessman, as president, and Patrick Reid, a career diplomat and former head of the BIE, as commissioner-general. In May 1982, the official name was changed from Transpo 86, to the more conventional Expo 86 to get rid of the trade show connotation of "Transpo." An expo logo, consisting of three circles representing land, water, and air, and also integral parts of the number 86, was adopted, and planning for the expo began in earnest.

The expo board of directors settled on the theme of "World in Motion, World in Touch," for Espo 86. The exposition would emphasize all forms of the movement of people and goods from both technological and economic viewpoints. Four theme pavilions were constructed. The first, called "Now and the Future," exhibited present and future forms of transport and communication, and was opened several moths prior to the exposition as a "preview center." A second pavilion, "Imagination in Motion," showed artistic renditions of futuristic and fantastical transportation and communication, while a third pavilions, "Moving Traditions," looked backward, displaying historic and traditional modes of transportation and communication. A final theme pavilion, "Retrospective," was housed in the historic 1888 roundhouse of the Canadian Pacific Railroad, where visitors could see an exhibit on significant technological breakthroughs in transportation and communications. In addition to the four theme pavilions, Expo 86 had four theme plazas scattered along the site, where outdoor exhibits on aviation, automobiles, boats, and trains could be seen. Finally, expo organizers planned a series of symposia on the broad theme of "goals and opportunities in transportation and communication." These were held between January 1984 and May 1986. In addition, other conferences and conventions related to the theme occurred during the expo itself.

Prince Charles and Princess Diana opened Expo 86 in a private ceremony on May 2, 1986, and 104,000 visitors attending the public opening the next day were treated to the most expensive (C$1.6 billion) specialized (Category II) expo to date, with 55 participating nations, seven Canadian provinces, two territories, three U.S. states, and "a bevy" of Canadian and international corporations. The large and permanent Canadian pavilion was located on Burrard Inlet on the harbor and was connected with the rest of the site by a four-minute monorail ride. The Victoria *Times* noted that visitors would enjoy the colorful carnival-like atmosphere more than the transportation and communication theme, and it was probably right. Expo 86 was a bright, colorful affair, with plenty of street entertainment and special cultural events scheduled throughout its run. The architecture was originally to be classically derived, but when that proved too expensive, planners adopted the flexible modular structures becoming common at expositions by this time. The most distinctive structure was probably Expo Centre, the first theme pavilion, which was a geodesic-domed building that, perhaps, was too reminiscent of the U.S. pavilion at Expo 67 in Montreal.

To its credit, Expo 86 worked hard to showcase Canadian Indians, or First Nations people. The Northwest Territory pavilion featured more than 200 musicians and artisans and a regular schedule of concerts and craft demonstrations. In May, visitors could see a traditional Indian summer camp, where natives made clothing from animal skins and demonstrated handgames and drumming. In August, fairgoers met Looti Pjamini from Gries Fiord and watched him build an Inuit sled and carve spears for fishing. The pavilion restaurant served traditional northern food, including musk ox, caribou, and Arctic char. At the Folklife Festival Complex, a First Nations restau-

This geodesic dome, known as Expo Centre, represents a style of architecture first seen in the U.S. pavilion at Montreal 1967 (courtesy Peter M. Warner).

rant also served traditional Indian food. And feature 25 Salish elders who chatted with diners about past and present Indian traditions. A nearby gallery displayed arts and crafts from 23 different British Columbian tribal groups.

As the mid–October closing date neared, Greg Joyce wrote in the Victoria *Times* that expo observers were debating about whether the fair would be just a "pleasant memory," or whether it would result in an "economic nightmare." Some thought the theme had been presented superficially, while others praised what they regarded as a genuine effort at educating visitors. Although some had anticipated horrendous traffic problems and a significant increase in crime, neither happened. A run of fifty rainless days helped bring attendance up to about 22 million for the expo, and most local agreed that the fair had been good for the local economy and international visibility of Vancouver. Ted Allan, president of the BIE noted that, "Expo has reversed the feeling by some in

Europe that Canada stopped at Toronto" (quoted in Victoria *Times*, October 12, 1986). One reason for the exposition's good attendance was a skillful marketing campaign directed to the Pacific Coast of the United States, where managers of tourist attractions as far away as the San Diego Zoo complained about lower-than-expected numbers of visitors. Even a deficit announced as C\$ 336 million did not dampen the mood much and was eliminated within two years by receipts from a government-run lottery.

After the close of Expo 86, a part of the site became known as BC Place, a tourist destination made attractive by retaining some of the buildings, plazas, and walkways. Expo Centre became BC Place, a museum and tourist information center, and the BC Pavilion and restored railroad roundhouse remained on the site. A 25-year long-range plan called for turning much of the expo site into a mixed residential and commercial neighborhood. As of 2007, the main attraction at BC Place is the inflatable domed BC Place Stadium, with a capacity of 60,000. It is home to the BC Lions of the Canadian Football League and hosts many concerts and other sporting events annually. The Canada pavilion on the harbor became a permanent convention center, as planned. Not everyone was so sanguine, however, about the economic impact of Expo 86. Dennis Capozzo, an economist at the University of British Columbia, argued that the long-term impact of the expo on Vancouver would be minimal He noted that the expo had no lasting effect on the local real estate market and that the experience of Expo 67 suggested that tourist revenue in Vancouver would soon return to pre-expo levels He did concede that with the new Canada Place convention center and more hotel rooms, Vancouver could experience a permanent increase in conventions and conferences.

Bibliography

The official records of Expo 86 are housed in the British Columbia Provincial Archives in Victoria. They include correspondence, minutes of board and committee meetings, reports, planning documents, financial records, and a great deal of printed material and ephemera about the fair. The official report for the expo is *General Report of the 1986 World Exposition, May 2-October 13, 1986* (1986). Much basic information can be found in the guidebook, *Expo 86: Official Souvenir Guide*

(1986). A pictorial souvenir book is *The Expo Celebration: The Official Retrospective Book* (1986). Two other semi-official publications may be of interest: *Expo Design 86* (1986) and *Expo: Something's Happening Here* (1986), a promotional videotape. The Victoria *Times* and other local newspapers and magazines covered the fair on a daily basis, although four feature articles merit special mention: Robert Fulford, "Only Fair," *Saturday Night* (October 1986): 9–12, appraises the fair from a political perspective; E. J. Kahn, Jr., "Letter from Vancouver," *New Yorker*, "July 14, 1986, 73–81," is a critique of the expo by the same individual who wrote letters from Knoxville and Tsukuba for *New Yorker*. The architecture of Expo 86 is analyzed in K.D. Stein, "Vancouver Better than Fair," *Architectural Record* 174 (July 1986): 120–31. See also Robert Lindsay, "A World in Motion, a Wait in Line," New York *Times*, June 15, 1986. On the Pacific National Exhibition that preceded Expo 86, see David Henry Breen and Kenneth Coates, *Vancouver's Fair: An Administrative and Political History of the Pacific National Exhibition* (1982). For a more critical look at Expo 86, see Robert Anderson and Eleanor Wachtel, *The Expo Story* (1986), published while the fair was going on, is a full-length study of all the political and economic factors that went into the organizing and staging of the event. A condensed version of their arguments can be found in their essay in the earlier version of this book, "Vancouver 1986," in John E. Findling, ed., *Historical Dictionary of World's Fairs and Expositions, 1851–1988* (1990). Finally, researchers should consult the quarterly journal *World's Fair*, which ran numerous articles on Vancouver in the early and mid–1980s.

Brisbane 1988

Martin Manning

World Expo 88

World Expo 88 was held from April 30 through October 30, 1988, in Brisbane, the capital of Queensland, the gateway to the outback, the Great Barrier Reef, and the splendid beaches along the Gold and Sunshine coasts. The exposition was the largest single event of

Australia's bicentennial celebration, with its opening day ceremonies held in the presence of Queen Elizabeth II. Expo 88 was officially sanctioned by the government of Australia and declared an Official Bicentennial Event by the Australian Bicentennial Authority. It was registered in December 1983 by the Bureau of International Expositions (BIE), which classified it as an "international specialized exposition" that focused on a particular theme, "Leisure in the Age of Technology."

The exposition organizers were the Brisbane Exposition and the South Bank Redevelopment Authority, which was established and constituted by the Queensland state government under a legislative act, Expo 88 Act 1984. The 98-acre exposition site, on the south bank of the Brisbane River, was directly across from Brisbane's central business district. Through its exhibits and entertainment, World Expo 88 examined how leisure is pursued in other countries and provided a unique insight into the way it has influenced man's cultural development all over the world. Central to the World Expo 88's theme was the way technology is changing man's pursuit of leisure and shaping his future. Because of the tremendous scope of this subject, three secondary themes were identified: Leisure — The Universal Pastime; Technology — Creating and Created for Leisure; and Leisure and Technology — The Future Together.

For Expo 88, the national government and the state of Queensland transformed a run-down, industrial area in the port city of 1.2 million into a holiday fantasyland. Brisbane's exposition aimed to have a distinctive Australian character and to provide a memorable experience unlike other events of the Bicentennial year. The tropical character of the exposition was everywhere apparent, from its riverside setting, lush vegetation and giant tent-shaped "sun sails," to its tropical fish blimps and abundance of outdoor entertainment and eateries. The sun sails, affording protection from the Queensland sun, were the inspiration of James Maccormick of the Expo architects, Bligh Maccormick 88, and formed one of the world's largest and most complex series of tension membranes.

George Fetting, one of the designers, was so successful that he was engaged later to design the Australian exhibit for the Osaka International Garden Expo (1990), but Brisbane's exposition offered more than gardens. Following the example of Expo 86 in Vancouver, Expo 88 was sitescaped to add a sense of celebration. The decorations included neon lighting, banners, flags, and a large collection of sculpture, both international and Australian. The most popular sculptures were locally produced and

included a series of about 100 "human factor" figures by Brisbane artist John Underwood and his Artbusters team. These light-hearted works, molded in white fiberglass, portrayed people in everyday activities mingling with the exposition crowd.

The exposition attracted 52 government participants and 34 corporations, with the strongest representation from Asia and the Pacific, which marked the participation of many of its new nations. Vanuatu, Tonga, and the Solomon Islands were part of the Pacific Lagoon, which included the Cook Islands, Fiji, Papua, New Guinea, and Western Samoa. All were lashed together by traditional thatch-and-wood structures.

There were exhibitions by the United Nations and the European Community, by the six Australian states and two territories, and by three American states (Alaska, California, Hawaii), one Canadian province (British Columbia), one Japanese prefecture (Saitama, Queensland's sister state), and a Japanese city (Kobe, Brisbane's sister city).

As host state, Queensland had the largest pavilion and for many visitors it was the "showstopper." There was a staged presentation of aboriginal legends inside the Australian pavilion and a tower-like structure modeled after Ayers Rock, a widely known landmark in the central Australian desert. To achieve maximum impact, the exposition's monorail was routed through the building but the centerpiece of the pavilion was a "people mover" that took visitors on a Disneyland-like ride around the exhibits. The novel transport system, with eight electronic open carriages each carrying 49 people, was purchased from the Mitsubishi corporation of Japan after it had been used, with great success, in the company's pavilion at Expo 85 in Tsukuba. The Queensland Pavilion at World Expo 88 presented a dynamic and progressive state and one that could offer the holiday of a lifetime. It aimed to give Queenslanders a new vision of their state, encompassing people as well as commodities, while directing an "unashamedly hard-sell message" to interstate and overseas visitors.

New Zealand made its first appearance at an international fair since 1970; it had one of the biggest exhibits. To underscore the close cultural ties between New Zealand and Australia, the pavilion included representations of an animal familiar to both countries, sheep gathered in a woolshed. Canada had a multi-million-dollar L-shaped pavilion built under the titular direction of Canadian wheelchair marathoner Rick Hansen, who at 30 was the fair's youngest delegation head. Hansen had logged thousands of miles on Australian roads during a two-year fund-raising world tour that ended in May 1987. Canada's pavilion displayed exhibits that showed Canadians working and playing during the country's four distinct seasons. Part of that effort included an underwater sound-and-light show displaying advances in deep-sea technology. There was also a Fitness Arcade that challenged visitors to undergo such tests as pedaling an exercise bicycle and striving to generate enough electricity to operate a radio. On the Thunderbird Stage, more than 200 Canadian entertainers delighted visitors with a variety of shows. Japan produced an electronic display which depicted tea ceremonies and other pastimes that were popular in Tokyo in 1788, while the Germans had a beer garden, the Swiss-built a 44-yard ski slope, the Soviets opened a borscht parlor accompanied by gypsy music played on balalaikas, and the Chinese offered bricks from the Great Wall.

The United States, with its theme "Sport and Its Science," had one of the most popular pavilions at Expo '88. Since the expo was held the same year as the 1988 Seoul Olympics, the U.S. planning staff was able to schedule many athletes either before or after the Games to perform on the popular outdoor sports court or to make appearances inside the American pavilion. The U.S. presence was headed by Commissioner General Art Linkletter. As visitors approached the American exhibit, they saw American athletes performing on the outdoor court, which featured such sports as gymnastics, basketball, double dutch jump roping, and wrestling. Among the more than 60 teams participating were the USA Deaf Basketball Team, the Hawaii Powerlifting Association, the U.S. Table Tennis Association, the Wheelchair Tennis Association, and the Greater Massachusetts Girls Soccer Club. The U.S. Information Agency (USIA) also sent a number of sports experts and specialists to offer programs and seminars. They included Bart Connors, former Olympic gold medalist and gymnastics coach; and Andy Fleming,

national sports coordinator for the Paralyzed Veterans of America.

Inside, visitors were impressed with a diverse group of artifacts from the various sports halls of fame in the United States, including Babe Ruth's baseball glove and Lou Gehrig's bat. In addition, the exhibition focused on the role of technology and medicine in improving athletic performance and making competition safer. Inside the pavilion in the "Match the Athletes" section, visitors could throw a baseball and have the speed measured by a radar gun so that they could compare their performances with those of professional and college athletes. Joining the United States in the pavilion were the states of Alaska, California and Hawaii, which presented exhibits on their major sporting centers.

Corporate pavilions included Ansett Airlines of Australia; Australia Post; Cadbury Schweppes Pty. Ltd.; Communities of Australia; Pavilion Ford Motor Company of Australia Ltd.; Fujitsu Australia Ltd.; IBM Australia Ltd.; Japan External Trade Organization; and the Office of Economic Development for the City of Brisbane Pavilion of Promise Ltd.; while primary Australian industries were represented by Queensland Newspapers Pty. Ltd.; Queensland Teachers Credit Union; Royal Australasian College of Surgeons; Suncorp Building Society; Service Clubs of Australia; Univations; and the Universal Telecasters Pty. Ltd.

Expo 88 was also the catalyst for several important conferences built around the sports theme. A conference on the History of Sport and Leisure, organized by the Department of Human Movement Studies, University of Queensland, in association with the Australian Society for Sport History, was held during the exposition at the university from June 26 to July 1, 1988, with sessions on the expo site and at the University of Queensland. The U.S. pavilion and the Alcohol and Drug Foundation of Queensland co-sponsored an international conference on "Drugs, Society, and Leisure," also from June 26 to July 1, which addressed numerous issues related to alcohol and to drug abuse with particular emphasis on drug in sports.

As the largest single event of Australia's Bicentennial, Expo 88 must be considered a success. It had a fun theme that appealed to the average visitor, and final attendance was 18,560,447.

The tendency toward modular, prefabricated national pavilions at world's fairs is seen with the U.S. pavilion at the Australian exposition (courtesy of Martin J. Manning and the Public Diplomacy Archives, U.S. Department of State).

Bibliography

The Brisbane exposition was well-covered in the Australian media; along with newspapers, there were visual records from television broadcasts and film. The official records for Expo 88 appear in several repositories: Foundation Expo 88 [*http://www.foundationexpo88.org*]; National Archives of Australia [*http://www.naa.gov.au/ the_collection/recordsearch.html*]; Queensland State Archives [*http://www.archives.qld.gov.au/search/ default.asp*]; and Libraries Australia [*http://lib rariesaustralia.nla.gov.au/apps/ks*].

For secondary sources, see Silvia Correia, "World Expositions:Planning for World Expo 88" (unpub. thesis (B. Plan.), University of New South Wales, 2002); Harry Gordon, "Expo Exposed," *Time* (April 13, 1987): 33–36; John Howse, "Australia's Bash," *Maclean's* (May 2, 1988): 36–41; Judith McKay, *Showing Off: Queensland at World Expositions, 1862 to 1988* (2004); "Now the Frosting on Australia's Bicentennial Cake: Expo 88," *Sunset: The Magazine of Western Living* (April 1988): 114–119; and *World Expo 88, Brisbane-Australia, April 30-October 30, 1988* (1988), a lavishly illustrated official guidebook. *World's Fair*

coverage was continuous throughout the run of the fair but the most complete overview article was William Kahrl. "The Surprising Success of World Expo 88," *World's Fair*, 8, 3 (Summer 1988): 13–20.

Each country produced its own final report. For the United States, see United States Information Agency, *Final Report, United States Pavilion, World Expo 88, Brisbane, Australia* (1988?). Also see United States Information Agency, Office of Research. East Asia and Pacific Branch. *Visitor Reaction to the U.S. Pavilion at Expo88, Brisbane, Australia*; prepared by James S. Marshall (1988). The official records of U.S. participation are in the National Archives and Records Administration, College Park, Maryland. Since the Seoul Olympics were being held the same year as Expo 88, Andrew Jay, the program officer, was able to get many prominent athletes going or coming from the Games. The Brisbane records have correspondence with the various athletes or their agents, the halls of fame, and various other athletic organizations and groups that were asked to participate or to contribute funds. For Italy, see: Expo '88 (Brisbane, Qld.), Italian Section, *Expo '88 Brisbane : Sezione italiana = Italian Section*

(1988), with notes in both English and Italian. For Spain: *El Pacífico Español de Magallanes a Malaspina* (1988).

During the exposition, special exhibits, outside the national shows, were displayed, often accompanied by a published catalogue: See Margie

K.C. West, ed., *The Inspired Dream: Life as Art in Aboriginal Australia* (1988), an exhibit held at the Queensland Art Gallery. Another exhibition catalogue was *Sculpture: the World Expo 88 Collection* (1988) that accompanied a presentation of modern twentieth-century sculpture.

Genoa 1992

Martin Manning

Colombo '92

The Genoa, Italy, exposition, called Colombo '92, was held from May 15 to August 15, 1992, in the birthplace of Christopher Columbus. The specialized international exposition was one of two held in 1992 for the quincentenary of Columbus' first voyage to the New World. Genoa originally hoped to be the site of a universal exposition, but it was late in presenting its proposal to the Bureau of International Expositions (BIE). Instead, it was allowed to hold a smaller exhibition. It is not usual practice for two fairs to take place in the same year, but the BIE chose 1992 to honor Columbus with a universal exposition in Seville, the port from which Columbus sailed on his famous voyage; and with a smaller exposition in Genoa, his birthplace. The Genoa theme reflected this: "Christopher Columbus: The Ship and the Sea." The BIE classified it as an "international specialized exposition," meaning that it focused on this particular theme.

Prior to the exposition, the old docks in the harbor seemed abandoned and inaccessible behind rusting fences, with empty warehouses and broken windows. This changed as plans were developed for the exposition in the ancient port sector of the city, which was opened up, redesigned and renovated, an urban renewal project that cost the Italian government $470 million (585 billion *lire*). The renowned Genoese architect, Renzo Piano, was commissioned to provide the comprehensive

design for the fair and its horseshoe-shaped site. According to Piano, the fair was "the first of a new exhibition type which is inside a city," referring to the fair's location on Genoa's Old Port, below the historic center of the city that rivaled Venice as the leading port of Italy's Renaissance and acquired the dubious reputation of declining to sponsor the explorations of Columbus, who was born there in 1451. Piano used the exposition to restore and expand Genoa's impressive architectural heritage with permanent improvements, including a new underground rail system, a vehicle underpass, pedestrian areas, and plazas built to link the harbor area to the rest of the city.

Alberto Bemporad, the commissioner general for Expo 92, was a citizen of Genoa. Under his leadership, Ente Colombo, an organization consisting of representatives of five constituencies: the region, the province, the city government, the Chamber of Commerce, and the port authority, organized and managed the many facets of the exposition.

Over an area of approximately twelve acres (five hectares), the Old Port of Genoa included a pier (the current Ponte Soinola) on which the Italian Pavilion, featuring a large aquarium; was built, as well as a floating platform, also a part of the Italian Pavilion, located next to the pier. There was a long dock extending from the pier ("sea way") that connected the shore to an island of floating platforms, designed to be used as a terminal for boats arriving and departing the exhibition; another pier (Ponte Embriaco), parallel to the Italian pavilion pier, with an array of metallic nests that resembled the old ship cranes or "booms"; and a metallic tower in the center, with two elevators taking fairgoers up to see a panoramic view of Genoa. Sails and flags covered these structures and a representation of these formed the symbol of the exhibition. There was also an outdoor theatre and four seventeenth-century buildings (the old Customs area), two designed for services and two designed to host foreign exhibitors; a sixteenth-century gateway, designed by Galeazzo Alessi (called Porte Siberia because it was through this structure that provisions were brought to ships); and a four-story building, built in the eighteenth century, that had been a cotton warehouse until just a few years before the fair.

As a specialized exposition, the Genoa organizers provided pavilions for the exhibitors. The entire event was held in the renovated cotton warehouse and in the four seventeenth-century merchant homes (*palazzina*) so most of the exhibiting nations were able to put up relatively inexpensive booths and still make coherent statements on the exposition theme. About 80 percent of the warehouse housed foreign exhibitors over four floors; while the terminal portion, facing the sea, was turned into a 1,500-seat conference center, one of the largest in Europe. An elevated parking lot, behind the service area; and two other parking areas were located in the area behind the "booms" and the Italian Pavilion. At the request of the sponsors, the U.S. exhibit was housed in one of the *palazzina*, San Desiderio, a short distance from the central section of the exposition site. Because directional signs were few and small, in keeping with the aesthetic demands of the expo's designer, relatively few visitors found the U.S. exhibit. However, the San Desiderio *palazzina* was described as a "small jewel" by Commissioner General Alberto Bemporad in his remarks at the pavilion's opening.

The U.S. Pavilion had displays on the sea and the environment. The 5,000-square foot exhibit produced by the United States Information Agency (USIA), "Beyond the Horizon," made use of multi-media effects in three galleries to depict the importance of waterways to the history, growth, and culture of the United States. One of the galleries focused on the Chesapeake Bay ("The People of the Chesapeake: A Mirror of America") and on the port

of Baltimore, a sister city to Genoa, as illustrative of America's maritime culture. The exhibit carried an environmental message: the importance of preserving and protecting the waters of the world. However, the Baltimore connection had a definite relevance. The Genoa exposition provided its organizers with an opportunity to open up the old port of the city. Much of what was developed and planned, including a new aquarium, was modeled on what had been done in Baltimore, a point highlighted by the governor of Maryland and former mayor of Baltimore, William Schaefer, during his visit to Genoa in June 1992. Unlike the other displays in Genoa, the U.S. exhibit was "pulsed": visitors were required to remain in each of the three galleries for a five to eight minute period and were walked and talked through the presentation by young American guides, all fluent in Italian.

The Genoa and Seville expositions marked the first time that U.S. participation in world fairs was a joint endeavor of the private and public sectors. The U. S. government (through the USIA) provided a little over $2 million while private sector donations amounted to almost $800,000. Amway was the principal corporate sponsor; its chairman, Jay Van Andel, was the U.S. commissioner general for the exposition. Corporate patrons included Ameritech, Delta Air Lines, Ford Motor Company, Hatteras Yachts, Llykes Brothers Steam-ship Company, Coca-Cola, Coors Brewing Company, National Geographic, and Rand McNally.

Including the United States, there were 53 participating countries and organizations. Most Latin American countries were part of the Italian-Latin American Institute Collective Pavilion, while major European and Asian nations had their own space. International organizations present were the Community of Independent States, the European Community, the International Committee of the Red Cross, the National Federation of [Italian] Unions, the Organization of American States (OAS), the Scientific Italian Community, the Military Sovereign Order of Malta, and the United Nations.

The Italian pavilion included an aquarium, still unfinished when the exposition opened, but which, when fully functional, was expected to be the largest in Europe. It was designed to become a permanent visitor attraction and research center but much of the

The logo of the U.S. pavilion clearly depicts the theme of the expo (courtesy of Martin Manning and the Public Diplomacy Archives, U.S. Department of State).

multimedia show. There was a talking robot dressed as a samurai who described his visit to Italy in 1613. The German pavilion in the old cotton warehouse extended outdoors to include a forty-foot submarine designed for research. The British exhibit was appropriately dedicated to Great Britain's maritime past; it told visitors about Greenwich Mean Time and Lloyd's Register of Shipping. There was also David Bushnell's wooden one-man submarine, built in 1774, with propellers driven by the man inside pedaling as if he were on a bicycle. Switzerland sold Swiss army knives, watches and chocolates, while the Bahamas peddled little jars of its "original" sand for $6.00. Egypt sent former King Farouk's royal yacht. Israel's exhibit, on the upper floor of the warehouse, included the remains of a typical fishing boat from the time of Jesus and an ancient stone fragment with the word "*janua*," the Latin name for Genoa, once a Roman trading settlement at St. Jean d'Acre.

Genoa must be considered a success despite unfavorable comparisons to the larger event in Seville. Though not large by international exposition standards, Genoa represented an immense effort on the part of local, regional, and national governments. It encountered management and administrative problems and attendance there was lower than anticipated; with just under one million visitors. However, the fair did offer a pleasing combination of entertainment and education. Visitors included the president and the prime minister of Italy; the presidents of Portugal and of Honduras, Marilyn Quayle, wife of the U.S. vice president; the Duke of Kent; Princess Elena of Spain; and Prince Rainier of Monaco. A purpose of international expositions is to demonstrate a linkage between peoples and nations as a means of encouraging cooperation in the resolution of mutual problems and concerns. In a video presentation within the U.S. exhibit, the point was made that the Chesapeake Bay is distant from the Mediterranean but not separated from it. As Columbus knew, the waters of the earth are in a single cup.

aquarium space was eventually required for the Italian national exhibit, the biggest at the exposition. There was a hollowed-out freighter floating at dockside with a grand selection of artifacts representing various aspects of the theme: silver ship models used for ducal table decorations, carved bowsprit figures, maps and charts; jewels, and navigation instruments. In their exhibits, Russia and Tunisia highlighted arts and crafts instead of a focused maritime theme but most other countries followed the exposition's theme closely, such as Japan which brought a small cargo ship, the *Yotei Maru*, that had recently plied the coastal waters of that nation on a leisurely journey from Japan to Genoa. Part of that ship was converted into Japan's Colombo '92 exhibit, which included graphic displays on the expo's theme, and a

Bibliography

The Genoa exposition was well-covered in the Italian media; along with newspapers, there were visual records from television broadcasts and film. In theory at least, all documents of national interest in Italy should be collected by the National Library system, SBN (Servizio Bibliotecario Nazionale), but there is no guarantee all documents are there. Apart from the "Sistema Bibliotecario Nazionale" (*www.sbn.it*), there are some other organizations where expsoition documents could be found. These include the Fondazione Regionale Cristoforo Colombo (*www.fondazionecolombo.it*); the Fiera di Genoa (*www.fiera.ge.it*) ; the Biblioteca de Amicis (*www.portoantico.it*). This library contains information on the exposition architect, Renzo Piano and his work at the fair. Finally, consult the website of the Genoa City Admninistration (*www.comune.ge.it*).

The official records of U.S. participation are in the National Archives and Records Administration, College Park, Maryland. There are files on U.S. participation at Genoa in the Public Diplomacy Historical Collection, formerly the USIA Historical Collection. Participating countries produced their own final reports. For the United States, see *Beyond the Horizon: Final Report* (1993?).

Contemporary documentary publications in Italian are abundant. See *Cristoforo Colombo, La Nave e Il Mare: Esposizione Internazionale Specializzata Genova '92: Padiglione Italia* (1992); *Cristoforo Colombo: La Nave e Il Mare: Genova, 15 Maggio–15 Agosto 1992: Relazione Finale, Genova, Maggio 1993* (1993?); *España y Genova: El Mediterraneo y America: Cristóbal Colón: La Nave y el Mar* (1992); Lucia Bronzan, *Genova, Ragusa, Mare = Genova, Dubrovnik, More: Esposizione Internazionale Specializzata Cristoforo Colombo: La Nave e il Mare, Genova, 15 Maggio–15 Agosto 1992, Padiglione della Croazia* (1993) and Alberto Bemporad, *Colombo '92, la Città, il Porto, l'Esposizione: Il Progetto di Renzo Piano per il Recupero alla Città del Porto Antico di Genova: Modello per una Nuova Generazione di Esposizioni: l'Architettura, gli Allestimenti* (1992).

On the architecture of the fair, see William Weaver, "Genoa Holds an Expo, Too," New York Times, June 7, 1992. There was coverage of Genoa in the specialized journal World's Fair See especially William Kahrl, "La Superba: Genoa's Colombo 92 in Progress," World's Fair, 11, 3 (July-September 1991): 1–3; and "Two Reactions to Colombo 92, World's Fair, 12, 3 (July-September 1992.

International study conferences were held at the same time as the exhibition developed the themes of the Genoa exposition. A special scientific committee, consisting of scholars and upper management executives of companies related to the field of the ship and the sea, worked to define the contents of the exhibition and the specific themes of the conferences. Also during the exposition, temporary exhibits, outside the national shows, were displayed within the *palazzos* or within the site. For example, in the Palazzo Ducale (Ducal Palace), there was "Christopher Columbus and the Age of the Great Discoveries" which closed on October 1992, two months after the official closing of the exposition. Other exhibits focused on sea-related topics, such as ancient shipbuilding techniques, underwater archaeological discoveries, evolution of navigation systems, balanced use of sea for its resources, evolution of coastal communities, water sports and environmental protection of seas. In the United States, the Smithsonian Institution created a special exhibit, "Trinkets to Treasure: Souvenirs from the 1893 and 1992 World's Fairs," which opened at the National Museum of American History in November 1993 and continued for several years. This little exhibition included the stuffed animal, Gatto Cristoforo, or Christopher the Cat, the official mascot of the Genoa exposition that adorned many toys and games from the fair.

Seville 1992

Veronique Marteau

Expo '92

The first full scale universal exposition since Osaka twenty-two years earlier, Expo '92, whose theme was "The Age of Discoveries" was held in Seville from April 20 to October 12, 1992. It broke all previous records for participation with 111 countries, 23 international organizations and 30 multinational companies, five of which had their own pavilions.

King Juan Carlos first brought up the idea of a world exposition in May 1976, a few months after the death of Francisco Franco, Spain's right-wing dictator for thirty-six years. Juan Carlos, on a visit to the Dominican Republic, gave a speech at the Cathedral of Santo Domingo in which he suggested hosting a new Ibero-American International Exposition in Spain to celebrate the quincentenary of Christopher Columbus' first voyage to the New World.

But in 1981, the American delegation to the Bureau of International Expositions (BIE) formally solicited the authorization to organize a world's fair in Chicago in 1992. Spain responded in March 1982 by presenting to the BIE a proposal for a world's fair in Seville in 1992. Eventually a compromise was reached: the Spanish government and the Chicago organizers offered to hold the 1992 world's fair simultaneously in Seville and in Chicago. In December 1983, for the first time in its history, the BIE authorized the organization of a universal exposition in two cities. However, funding problems led Chicago to bow out in 1987, and Seville remained the sole site of the 1992 world's fair.

In Seville, a 530-acre site on the island of La Cartuja was selected. A reclaimed flood plain, this large, unused piece of land, located between two branches of the Guadalquivir River, was within walking distance of the historical city center. It was endowed with high symbolical value since it harbored the Carthusian monastery of Santa María de las Cuevas which Columbus had often visited and where his body had been briefly buried in the sixteenth century.

An extensive campaign of public works, whose cost was estimated at about $10 billion, was carried out in Seville and in the surrounding autonomous district of Andalusia in preparation for the world's fair. The Guadalquivir was returned to its original course: the "Chapina plug," an earthen causeway-dam, built in the fifties as a flood-control measure, was removed. A 950-yard long canal and an artificial lake were added. Riverside railway tracks were dismantled and replaced by a landscaped promenade. Six bridges were constructed, four of them connecting the island of La Cartuja to the city of Seville. The Alamillo

Bridge designed by Santiago Calatrava, resembling a harp with its 140-meter high oblique pylon with suspended cables stretching down, was the most spectacular.

Great emphasis was put on the improvement of transportation: a new airport and a new railway station were built. Airports in Jerez and Malaga were modernized and enlarged. A high-speed train line, the first one in Spain, linking Madrid to Seville in less than three hours and dropping the visitors right at the gate of Expo '92, was constructed. Two ring roads around Seville and a new network of highways connecting southern Spain to major intercontinental routes were built.

The historical monuments in the center of Seville were renovated and the cobblestones of the old streets replaced. An impressive opera house, the Teatro de la Maestranza, was erected along the Guadalquivir, close to the eighteenth-century bullring. The old riverside train station was turned into an exhibit hall. Nineteen hotels in and around the city and "Expo City," a 2000-unit residential complex intended to house the foreign participants, were built.

The island of La Cartuja was equipped with a state-of-the-art telecommunication infrastructure. The monastery of Santa María de las Cuevas was painstakingly restored, along with the cone-shaped kilns of the porcelain factory that operated in the cloister from the nineteenth century until 1982. These cones were adopted as one of the symbols of the expo. Parking space for 40,000 cars and 1,100 tour buses was provided.

The site, laid out like a city with a grid of streets and avenues, was organized into three main areas of interest: the thematic pavilions which were distributed along the Route of Discoveries, the 1.6-mile axis running from the southern gate of Triana, to the northern gate of Italica; the ensemble made of the Spanish pavilion, located on the western shore of the artificial Lake of Spain, and the 17 pavilions of the autonomous communities of Spain standing in a semicircle around the lake; and the national and corporate pavilions situated along five avenues (Avenue 1, Avenue of Europe, Palm Avenue, and Avenues 4 and 5) bisecting the Route of Discoveries and the Acacia Way.

Even though walking was the best way to see the expo in detail, free buses circling the site behind the pavilions were available to the

Lake of Spain and pavilions of Extremadura, the Balearic Islands, Madrid and Castilla y León at the Seville Expo '92 fair (photograph by Jean-Luc Bilhou-Nabera).

visitors. For a fee they could use the cable car system offering spectacular panoramic views, the monorail, small motorized tourist trains, or the boats plying the Guadalquivir.

Considerable effort was devoted to keeping visitors cool and comfortable in a region where temperatures can exceed 110°F in summer. Vegetation and water, two key elements in the traditional Andalusian patios, and plazas were used extensively. Some 25,000 trees and 300,000 shrubs were planted. A large garden, the "Jardines del Guadalquivir," where visitors could relax, was created in the area behind the Pavilion of the Future and the river. Fountains, waterfalls, water walls, and pools were scattered all around the fairgrounds. Shade was provided in the main streets by a system of pergolas covered with leafy plants, irrigated by drip systems. On Palm Avenue the giant bio-climatic sphere formed by a metal mesh full of tiny water nozzles produced a refreshing mist. The twelve funnel-shaped 100-foot-tall towers on the Avenue of Europe, each representing a member country of the EEC, drew the hot air in and expelled cool mist. Throughout the site, thousands of water micronisers sprayed droplets of water.

The theme of Expo '92, "the Age of Discoveries," was explored in the thematic pavilions of the 15th Century, Navigation, Discovery, Nature, and Future. The organizers' ambition was to trace the pattern of progress in the fields of science, technology, and culture that humankind followed over five centuries from the voyages of Christopher Columbus to the present day. The Pavilion of the 15th Century, located within the Monastery of Santa María de las Cuevas, presented an exhibit of art and culture from around 1492 when the population on the planet was still fragmented into isolated groups. The Pavilion of Navigation, resembling the inverted keel of a ship, related the history of navigation from the Vikings to the twentieth century, putting a special emphasis on the great navigators. On the pavilion's river side, visitors could climb over replicas of Christopher's Columbus' *Niña*, *Pinta* and *Santa María* ships. Unfortunately, an accidental fire destroyed the exhibits of the Pavilion of Discovery in February 1992,* a few weeks before the opening of the expo. In an effort to camouflage the damage, large black silhouettes of giant chimney sweeps and mul-

The destruction of the Pavilion of Discovery by fire was unfortunately not the only one. A few days before the opening of Expo '92, the Pavilion of the Pacific Islands— home to Figi, Kiribati, Solomon Islands, Tonga, Tuvalu, Vanuatu and Western Samoa— was also burned to the ground. Pavilions such as Australia, New Zealand and Papua New Guinea offered space for the countries to put on live performances.

ticolored ladders were plastered on the outer walls. The hemispheric Omnimax theater, spared by the fire, showed a film entitled "Eureka! The passion to know" that summed up five centuries of discoveries. The Pavilion of Nature, the first ever at a universal exposition, included a greenhouse and the Garden of the Americas planted with hundreds of American species, which, entering mostly through the port of Seville, had changed the diet and the vegetation of the Old World. The Plaza of the Future was divided into four pavilions: Energy, Telecommunications, Environment, and the Universe. The Pavilion of Energy presented energy-saving machines and showed the vast disparities in the amounts of energy used in different countries. The Pavilion of Telecommunications looked at the technology behind communications and how it affected everyday life. A huge wall of some 115 video-screens recounted all the inventions in the field. The highlight of the Pavilion of the Environment was a 3-D Showscan movie entitled "Concerto for the Earth." The first part of the film, projected in 2-D, showed the beauty of the earth. Then, rendered all the more shocking by being shown in 3-D, the various aspects of man-made pollution such as deforestation and toxic waste shattered the idyllic vision of the beginning of the movie, making pollution impossible to ignore. The Pavilion of the Universe, the most popular, embarked the visitor on a "Cosmic Adventure," soaring through galaxies in its digital planetarium. On leaving the pavilion, one could send a message to the stars via interactive video screens.

Some countries linked the contents of their pavilions to the theme of the expo. Italy, the birthplace of Christopher Columbus, took the expo theme to heart, dedicating its exhibits to science through the ages. Portugal documented its major role in the European discovery of the New World. Japan featured an exhibit on Japan in the age of Columbus. France chose the theme of discovery through knowledge, from medieval manuscripts to computer images. Latin American countries displayed pre–Columbian artifacts. But in some pavilions, the relation to the "Age of Discoveries" was far from obvious. A good example was the pavilion of Hungary, considered one of the most inspired pieces of architecture of the expo. Designed by Imre Makowecz, its

church-like wooden structure with seven slate-roofed spires exhibited a single item: a barren oak tree whose roots were visible through a transparent floor. Another example was the pavilion of Switzerland, designed by Wirth Architekten Ag in cooperation with Vincent Mangeat. A 30-meter-high tower made of recyclable paper polygons beside a broad wooden staircase, it was decorated with six three-and-a-half meter long fiberglass Alpine horns. Visitors entered the pavilion through a gift shop selling cowbells, Swiss watches, penknives, and cuckoo clocks. But the conventionality of the contents ended with a painting by Ben Vautier proclaiming "Swiss doesn't exist," After videos showing cow wrestling, bicycle football, and other amusing pastimes, the message changed to "*Je pense donc je Suisse*," a take-off on Descartes' famous statement, "I think, therefore I am." This self-mocking stand set off a controversy in Switzerland, but the visitors obviously relished the humor and playfulness of the pavilion.

Another instance of a pavilion whose contents did not really tally with the theme of Expo '92 was the curvaceous wooden Chilean pavilion by José Cruz Ovalle and German del Sol. Its star attraction was an iceberg brought from Antarctica that diffused a cold air stream, which visitors appreciated. Another intriguing structure was the pavilion of Kuwait, by Santiago Calatrava, whose row of tusk-like segmented roof-pieces, reminiscent of palm trees, moved at different angles, creating a changing sculpture against the sky. Close by, a nomadic tent was pitched on the small esplanade in front of the truncated pyramid of rusty metal of the Mauritanian pavilion. The Saudi Arabian pavilion, designed by SITE in conjunction with Fitch RS, was also evocative of the desert, with its crumbling mud-brick wall and its roof canopy made of hand-woven Bedouin rugs. Inside, exhibits ranged from pre–Islamic art to detailed models of Mecca and Medina. The Moroccan pavilion, by Michel Pinseau, was a modern version of a Moorish palace with arches surrounding a glass cube adorned with multi-level fountains tiled with mosaic. As for the pavilion of Finland, it was admired for its sculptural architecture. Called "Hell's Gorge" by its designers, a group of five architectural students collectively known as Monarch, it was composed of two contrasting vertical structures: a tall, thin box-like edifice of steel and glass and a lower rounded pine-sheathed building, separated by a narrow passage. This shaft-like void created a space of luminosity and shadow intended to bring a Finnish kind of light to Seville. The pavilion of Czechoslovakia also took a poetic approach. Its architecture by Martin Nemec and Jan Stempel was simple and straightforward. The box-like shape was covered with layers of black wire gauze hung on the basic structure with oak beams. In the large hall inside, visitors were invited to experience a presentation of day and night, a symbol of the everlasting cycle, thanks to scenographic effects mixing Bohemian glass sculptures with light, color and sound effects.

The twelve European pavilions were gathered around the Avenue of Europe with the pavilion of Spain at one end and the pavilions of Great Britain and Germany at the other end. The funnel- shaped tower of the pavilion of the European Economic Community, whose form echoed the kilns of the Monastery of Santa María de las Cuevas, was imprinted with the flags of the European countries merging into colorful stripes. It stood in the middle of the avenue, surrounded by twelve white cooling towers of similar shape, each symbolizing a European country. The British pavilion, by Nicholas Grimshaw, was a large semitransparent box with rooftop sails, and water pouring down the façade, behind which a huge Union flag hung. Rivulets of water also flowed on the surface of the three white sails walls of the Danish pavilion by KHRAS Architects, a sleek structure made of modular units. Visitors flocked to the German pavilion, by Harald Mühlberger and Georg Lippsmeir, shaded by a giant oval inflated roof that looked like an enormous painter's palette, to contemplate a graffiti-splattered chunk of the Berlin wall. Other attractions were the flying machines of Leonardo da Vinci in the Italian pavilion, an immense white fortress by Gae Aulenti and Pierluigi Spadolini, with a globe-shaped theater and planets suspended in the middle of its gigantic atrium. By contrast, the French pavilion by Viguier, Jodry and Seigneur, was almost immaterial. A transparent platform made of 500 glass squares, open on three sides, led to a narrow blade-like building whose mirrored facade reflected the busy life of the expo. It was topped by an artificial "sky," a thin blue canopy held by four very slender pencil-shaped steel pillars, vir-

tually fading into the Andalusian sky. The main attraction was the "well of images," located under the glass platform, a seventeen-meter-deep rectangular pit whose mirrored walls acted like a big kaleidoscope, multiplying the images of the three IMAX movies alternatively projected on the floor. Directly across the pavilions of its neighbors France and Portugal, the pavilion of Spain by Julio Cano Lasso, the largest of the expo, was imposing. A huge white cube housed an exhibition entitled "Spanish Art Treasures," bringing together paintings by masters such as Goya, El Greco, Picasso and Miró. Visitors crossed courtyards and patios of white marble to enter a dome topped by a gleaming metallic cupola. Inside there was an exhibition of works of contemporary artists such as Arroyo, Barceló, Chillida, Saura and Tapies, and a theater which featured one of the star attractions of the expo, a Moviemax film entitled "Winds of Spain." Thanks to the seats moving in synchrony with the action, spectators embarked on a vertiginous tour of Spain, using every possible means of transportation from horse carriages to hot air balloons. Also popular was the multi-media exhibit, "Routes of Spain," that celebrated the diversity of the country and of the Spanish language.

Caribbean, Central American, and South American countries had had the choice between constructing a pavilion of their own or occupying a space in the Plaza of America, a multi-level office-like edifice by Jesus Castañon, Eduardo Gomez, and Ernesto Sanchez Zapata, provided by Spain. Chile, Cuba, Mexico and Venezuela elected to build their own pavilions, located in different parts of the fairgrounds. Mexico was awarded the most privileged spot, close to the Spanish Pavilion. The work of Pedro Ramírez Vásquez and Jaime Ciovannini, it was a plant-covered flattened pyramid connected to a long white bridge-like concrete structure ending with two 50 foot-high X's. Mexico thus proclaimed it was the sole country in the world with an X in its name. Sixteen other countries, eager to hold down the cost of their participation, opted for the Plaza of America, conveniently located near the Lake of Spain. For the first time at a world's fair, Puerto Rico had its own pavilion, whose dominant feature was a sleek copper and green glass cylinder by Segundo Cardona Colom, Luis Sierra and Alberto Ferrer.

Cooling towers on the Avenue of Europe, looking toward the French pavilion (photograph by Jean-Luc Bilhou-Nabera).

As for the U.S. pavilion, the original project by Barton Myers had to be abandoned when Congress cut funding for participation in the expo. Instead, a huge water wall was installed as a facade. Two geodesic domes, used in European trade shows, were assembled on each side of a central courtyard. They were masked by two 153-by-30 foot panels by Peter Max that faced each other. One of them depicted the first five hundred years in American history with Columbus' three caravels, and portraits of Sitting Bull, and a cowboy on his horse; and the other reflected the next five hundred years with images of spaceships and whirling planets. Three shade sails carrying the American colors, the sole remnants of the original design, towered above the courtyard. An exhibit entitled "Where liberty dwells, there is my country," whose centerpiece was Connecticut's copy of the Bill of Rights, was housed in one of the domes. A movie called "World Song," celebrating life around the world from birth to old age was shown in the other dome. Sports events and demonstrations and small concerts held in the courtyard drew large crowds. The dramatic

rivalry that had existed between the American and Soviet pavilions at the world's fairs of Brussels, Montreal, and Osaka was obviously gone in Seville. Several months before the opening of the expo, the letters USSR were torn down from the front of the Russian pavilion. The building, by Yuris Poga and A.Sparans, whose sloping façade was animated with rows of rotating multi-colored panels, housed sparse exhibits organized around three themes: "Man discovers the earth," "Man discovers the cosmos," and "Man discovers himself," Of particular note were a scale model of the Siberian town of Tobolsk, a miniature wooden church, and a fifteenth-century icon of the Holy Trinity by Andrei Rubliov. The theme of spirituality was further highlighted on Russia's day of honor when a Russian Orthodox pope christened the pavilion.

Across Acacia Way, the Canadian pavilion, by Bing Thom, was extremely popular. It was a simple and massive zinc-clad box whose façade bore geometrical indentations creating changing shades and patterns in the Seville sun. Visitors entered through an open-air courtyard layered with waterfalls. They walked by a turquoise reflecting pool surrounding an island stage featuring live entertainment. In this cooling atmosphere, they were entertained by a witty little film shown on video monitors entitled, "The Taxpayers of Canada present another Government Movie," as they waited to be ushered into the 500-seat theater where a film using the new technique of IMAX HD (high definition) was projected on a 60-foot screen. Entitled "Momentum" it offered spectacular panoramas of Canada from the high Arctic to Niagara Falls. Also very popular, Tadao Ando's Japanese pavilion, billed as one of the largest timber buildings in the world, was inspired by the aesthetic of *kinari*, or unadorned beauty. Its rectangular structure, with gently tapering concave walls and a roof supported by an intricate arrangement of columns, was reminiscent of the architecture of medieval Buddhist temples. To enter the pavilion, visitors ascended an escalator alongside a wide and steep wooden staircase forming an impressive arched bridge symbolizing the passage from West to East, as well as the link between Japan's past and future. Inside, a compendium of Japanese culture and history was presented. There were traditional Shinto and Buddhist effigies, samurai suits of armor, displays of origami, a full-size replica of the two upper floors of the Castle Azuchi, holographic images and art generated by computer graphics and lasers. In the back of the pavilion, a revolving theater showed a movie featuring cartoons, film, and computer graphics. It offered an insight into the past, present and future of Japan in the company of Sasuke, a legendary ninja, Don Quixote, and Sancho Panza.

The pavilion of New Zealand, by Logan Brewer and Peter Hill, also resorted to historical reference in the design of its façade, which, thanks to *faux* rocks and mechanical seagulls, recreated the landscape seen by Captain Cook when he first visited the islands.

As for the Australian Pavilion by Philip Page and David Rendon, a large edifice surrounded by canvas panels covered with aboriginal and contemporary designs, its centerpiece was the reproduction of a rain forest including fifty palm trees transported from Tasmania. The pagoda-shaped pavilion of South Korea by Hak-Sun Oh, welcomed visitors with the motto "joined hands." Its exhibits focused on the relationship between East and West and the eco-

nomic miracle achieved in the country over the past thirty years, and then offered a glimpse of the next world's fair, the Taejon International Exposition '93. The five member states of the Association of Southeast Asian Nations (ASEAN), Malaysia, Singapore, the Philippines, Thailand, and Indonesia shared a plot. Lined up side by side, their small pavilions formed a picturesque and festive street scene. They attracted numerous visitors thanks to their traditional dance performances and their shops offering jewelry, scarves, carvings and other handicrafts.

If the theme of the Age of Discoveries was not always strictly observed by the participants, the sub-theme of Expo '92, "A world wide fiesta," certainly was. Many pavilions had their own entertainment venues. Some had a cultural program unfolding throughout the six months of expo, whereas others offered the same shows every day. Argentina, for instance, featured spirited demonstrations of tango in its theater; New Zealand had Maori performers entertain the waiting crowds on a stage built inside its façade, and Brazil presented scantily clad carnival dancers and drummers who pranced around the alleys of the Plaza of America.

Some participating countries staged events that took over the entire site of Expo '92. Portugal recreated the embassy of King Manuel I to Pope Leo X in 1514, complete with elephants and horses laden with gifts of exotic goods from the new territories discovered by Portuguese navigators. Puerto-Ricans celebrated the shortest night of the year, La Noche de San Juan, by transforming the expo into a gigantic party with bands playing salsa and merengue all over the site. Ireland used the backdrop of the expo to present the story of Gulliver's travels with a huge 72-foot-high, 4.5-ton figure that floated down the Guadalquivir.

Expo organizers clearly encouraged street entertainment, which was plentiful, and provided an elaborate daily parade called La Cabalgata. Conceived by Joan Font, the leader of the Catalan theater group Els Comediants, it was an allegory of the twelve months of the year, each represented by a float, animated by about 200 actors and acrobats and several musical bands. Curro, a large white bird with a rainbow-colored crest, was the Expo mascot and marched at the end of the parade, which closed with a huge iron bull with percussion elements. La Cabalgata was based on Mediterranean traditions such as Christmas, carnivals, popular pilgrimages, and summer fiestas. True to Els Comediants' well-known spirit of transgression, it took a mischievous pleasure in stressing the pagan aspects of Catholic tradition. The presence of a drunken bishop in the parade roused the ire of the archbishop of Seville but continued nonetheless until the end of the fair.

Expo '92 was different from other previous expositions in that the show went on until the early hours of the morning.* An elaborate special effects spectacular on the Lake of Spain and its surroundings announced the start of Expo-Night. Created by Yves Pépin, it was a combination of computer-controlled fireworks, sound, lighting and smoke effects, water jets, laser graphics, and images and holograms projected on six water screens.

The organizers' avowed goal was to make of Expo '92 the "greatest stage on earth, with representations of every artistic genre from all over the world." Several venues were constructed for that purpose. Cine Expo was an open-air movie theater: equipped with a spectacular giant 288-square-meter screen with stereo sound, it had a capacity of 1,200 spectators and showed a different film every day. The Sony Plaza which could hold audiences of up to 10,000, offered live pop-rock concerts, broadcast on the Jumbotron, a gigantic television screen as high as an eight-story building, towering above the plaza. The Auditorio, an immense open-air theater built in white Andalusian marble and seating 5,400 people, featured shows as varied as dance, recitals, flamenco, zarzuela operetta, and rock. The Teatro Central Hispano played host to representatives of the avant-garde theater and dance. The Palenque, a huge, 9000-square-meter covered plaza whose eye-catching textile canopy looked like a forest of huge tilted umbrellas, served various functions in the course of each expo day. In the morning it held the ceremonies of the National and Honor Days of all the countries, companies and autonomous regions represented at Expo '92.

In the afternoons, there were folk singing and dancing groups, fashion shows, and children's entertainment. At night, after the multimedia show on the lake, the Palenque became a dance hall with live music.

The cultural program of Expo '92 extended beyond the confines of the site. The world's leading opera companies and symphony orchestras were invited to the newly built Teatro de La Maestranza. The Teatro Lope de Vega, built along the María Luisa Park for the Ibero-American Exposition of 1929, hosted a festival of classical theater in which some of the most renowned Spanish and international companies took part. Last but not least, the Itálica Roman Amphitheater on the outskirts of Seville hosted a particularly brilliant edition of its yearly International Dance Festival.

During the first four months of Expo '92, there was an average of only 161,369 visits per day that caused concern to the organizers. Hoping to welcome large crowds of out-of-town and foreign visitors, the organizers had suspended the sale of season passes[†] mainly bought by Sevillanos, a week after the opening. Even though this measure aroused a lot of anger among the townspeople, it was not rescinded. In August, attendance picked up with an average of 261,513 visits per day. In September, the average daily attendance was 363,511, and for the last twelve days of the fair in October, it was 405,021. On Saturday October 3rd, some 629,845 visitors literally jammed the site. The total count was 41,814,571 visits, which Expo organizers considered equivalent to 15,540,628 visitors. According to the organizers, Expo '92 broke even, presenting a small surplus of 25,605 million pesetas.

In 1992, Spain celebrated its integration in the European single market. Along with the Summer Olympics in Barcelona and Madrid's designation as the European Capital of Culture, Expo '92 was a successful showcase for the accomplishments of post–Franco Spain.

However, the recession that hit in 1993 undermined the post-expo project of Cartuja

---

*The site opened at 9 A.M. and closed at 4 A.M. The price for a full day ticket was 4,000 pesetas (about $40 U.S.). Children between 5 and 14 paid 1,500 pesetas. Expo-Night tickets were valid from 8 P.M. to 4 A.M. and cost 1000 pesetas for adults and children alike. Pavilions were opened from 10 A.M. to 9:30 P.M.

†The season passes were 30,000 pesetas (about $300 U.S.) for adults, and 15,000 pesetas for children between 5 and 14. Expo-Night passes were 10,000 pesetas.

93, which was to use the highly qualified infrastructure and space produced by Expo '92 to create three new areas: an technopolis of scientific research and development on the site occupied by the international pavilions; a theme park around the Lake of Spain, the Spanish pavilion, the pavilions of the autonomous communities of Spain, the thematic pavilions, and the cultural venues such as the Auditorio; a service zone in the World Trade Center and the Press Center. For a few years the fairgrounds seemed to revert to wilderness. But the situation improved gradually. Fifteen years after the expo, the building surface of Cartuja 93 Scientific and Technological Park is completely taken up. Companies or institutions now occupy the international pavilions that were not torn down at the end of Expo '92. The Pavilion of Italy, for instance, is a center for small and medium companies. At the end of 2004, Cartuja 93 had a leading position among all the Spanish scientific and technological parks in terms of number of companies (291) and economic activity (1,393 million euros).

Two Curros, the mascots of the Expo '92 in Seville, serve as a backdrop in this photograph of a tired baby after an extended visit to the fair (photograph by Jean-Luc Bilhou-Nabera).

A theme park called "The Park of Discoveries" opened in the summer of 1993. There visitors rediscovered some of the thematic pavilions and enjoyed roller coaster rides and video games. It closed in 1995. Two years later, La Isla Mágica, an amusement park divided into six areas was inaugurated and remains quite popular with local teenagers and summer tourists.

Bibliography

The archives of Expo '92, which include documents, photos, and videos produced before and during Expo '92, are housed in the buildings of the Sociedad Estatal de Gestion de Activos (AGESA), a public company created in 1993 to administer the heritage of Expo '92. As of 2007, they are still being catalogued. The address is: Edificio N-1. Américo Vespucio 43. Isla de la Cartuja. Sevilla 41092.

The daily *ABC* had a section entitled "Diario de la Expo," which chronicled the every day life of Expo '92 and sometimes included small articles in English. On the occasion of the national and honor days of the countries, companies and autonomous regions represented at Expo '92, *ABC* gave a thorough account of their participation and of the contents of their pavilions. Another daily, *Diaro 16 Andalucia*, also had a detailed section devoted to Expo '92 called "Crónica de la Expo 92."

The official guide to the fair is *Guía Oficial Expo '92*. In more than 330 pages, it provided information on the thematic pavilions, the participating countries, the participating companies and the cultural venues. Since it was put together for the opening of Expo '92, it relied heavily on photos of scale models of the pavilions and even on drawings and was rather vague about the contents of the national pavilions. There was an independent guidebook: a paperback entitled *The Best of Expo* (1992) . The Spanish edition is *Lo Mejor de la Expo*. There were no illustrations, but each pavilion was given a rather accurate if sketchy description of its architecture and contents and rated from one to five stars

The exposition committee also published a booklet entitled *Programa de Espectaculos* (1992), listing the cultural events offered on site and in the city of Seville as well as at the Itálica Roman amphitheatre as part of the "greatest stage on earth" program.

As far as the iconography of Expo '92 is concerned, *Expo '92 Sevilla Arquitectura y Diseño* (1992) documents with precision every pavilion and structure at the fair. The book *No Digas Que Fue un Sueno* (1992) also offers photographs of the pavilions. The picture book *Abierta al Mundo, todas las fotos del primer dia de la Exposición Universal Expo '92* (1992) captures the beauty, the colors, and the fun atmosphere of the opening day in particular and of Expo '92 in general. *Dernières Lumières du Siècle, The Limelights of a Waning Century* (1992) provides great pictures of the expo

and interesting commentary in French and English. For the tenth anniversary of Expo '92, *ABC* published a small book of black and white photographs culled from its archives, *La Expo desde el recuerdo* (2002).

The architecture of Expo '92 was widely commented upon in contemporary architecture journals. For instance, see *Architectural Review* 190, 1144 (June 1992); the entire issue is devoted to Seville and the exposition.

The official report on Expo '92, *Memoria General de la Exposición Universal Sevilla 1992* (1993), criticized the balance sheet as being overly optimistic Another book containing statistics is *Expo '92 — Seville in Numbers: How were countries doing?* (1992) presents data on the number of visits and cost of participation for each participating country.

Anthropologists showed a keen interest in Expo '92. John Knight gives an overview of the fair in "Discovering the world in Seville: the 1992 Universal Exposition," *Anthropology Today*, 8, 5 (October 1992): 20–26. In *Hybrids of Modernity*, (1996), Penelope Harvey explores the connections between anthropology, the nation state, and the world's fair as exemplified by Expo '92. In *The Best of All Possible Islands: Seville's Universal Exposition, the New Spain, and the New Europe* (2004), Richard Maddox uses the world's fair in Seville as a vantage point from which to examine Spain's developing democracy and its integration into Europe. Another useful article is Marina Perez de Mendiola, "The Uniuversal Exposition Seville 1992: Presence and Absence, Remembrance and Forgetting," in M. Perez de Mendiola, ed., *Bridging the Atlantic: Toward a Reassessment of Iberian and Latin Amrican Cultural Ties* (1996).

Last but not least, Expo '92 proved a source of inspiration to novelist Ariel Dorfman, who said he conceived the idea behind *The Nanny and the Iceberg* (1999) on learning that the Chilean pavilion exhibited an iceberg from Antarctica.

Taejon 1993

John R. McGregor

Taejon International Exposition

The 1993 Taejon International Exposition, commonly known as Expo '93, was a specialized international exposition sanctioned by the Bureau of International Exhibitions (BIE) at its 108th General Assembly on December 12, 1990. The exposition celebrated the centenary of Korea's inaugural participation at the 1893 World's Columbian Exhibition in Chicago. It was the first exposition hosted by Korea, and the first to be held by a developing nation. The exposition attracted a record participation of 108 international governments, 33 United Nations-level organizations, several multi-lateral organizations (European.Community, the International Olympic Committee, and others), and a bevy of Korea's largest corporate conglomerates.

A city of 1.1 million, Taejon is a central transport, research, and development hub of the Republic of Korea, located 100 miles south of the capital, Seoul, host of the 1988 Summer Olympic Games. The expo site was located on a 246-acre parcel of land on the northern bank of the Kapchon River, nestled in the gentle shade of U-Sung-Yi-San Mountain, and consisted of five major elements:

The Korean Corporate Zone, a "universal expositions"—style architectural and technology wonderland;

The Central Zone, with the 93-meter symbol tower 'Han'Bit'Ap'—the "Tower of Great Light" in the center;

The International Zone, home to the 108 international participants, included local governments and other Korean and international conglomerates such as IBM Korea, Fujitsu, and Lotte, among others.

The amusement zone, "Kum'dori Land"— some of Korea's most up-to-date roller-coasters and other high-tech rides, including a majestic large-scale ferris wheel.

Expo Town — a brand new village of high density apartment living for all Expo staff— three kilometers from the Expo site.

The Korean Corporate Zone — with its themed pyramid, sphere, and crystal-shaped pavilions highlighting the latest in exhibitions technology — took visitors on a terrestrial and inter-stellar voyage of wonder. The most memorable of these pavilions were the Daewoo Pavilion, with its several-stories high, 3-D IMAX movie on the history of civilization; the Samsung "Starquest" Pavilion, with its mammoth representation in bronze and steel of a 2093 Moon Base and the transport needed to get there; and the stunning Sanyoung "Earthscape" Pavilion, where visitors were taken on a tour of the majestic microcosm of nature's world on a extra high-resolution IMAX screen seven stories high.

At the expo's Central Zone, the extended cone shape of the flagship Korea Pavilion took fairgoers on a voyage through Korea's past, present, and future, ending with a humanoid robot quintet playing traditional Korean court instruments, in much the same way that Korean musicians entertained the audiences at the Korean pavilion at the World's Columbian Exposition a century earlier. The 303-foot high expo symbol tower, "Han'bit'ap" (the Tower of Great Light), based on the design of an ancient Korean observatory, gave one a memorable overview of the exposition from two viewing platforms. The tower's powerful light beam also searched the Taejon skies every evening and was an adjunct to the fireworks show before closing time each weekend evening. The Tower Plaza space was also the site of the national and corporate day flag-raising and other ceremonies.

The other side of the Tower Plaza featured the distinctive United Nations pavilion, possibly the largest and most impressive representation by the UN at a world exposition, a beautiful three-story glass rendition of a dove in flight. The pavilion is today the Expo '93 Museum, where uniform-clad "dou-mi's" (special helpers, as the official Expo '93 hosts and hostesses were called) still maintain their presence and charming smile as they guide visitors through a collection not only of all the official gifts from participating Korean, international and corporate pavilions at the expo, but also some of the more popular commercial exhibits, such as a solar car.

The International Zone was a lively fair of world culture and was for many governments, the first opportunity to become known to the Korean public. Bound together in a festival-like cluster of three-story pre-fabricated units, participating nations tackled the challenge of development that is sustainable and friendly to the environment and sustainable. Their exhibit fit in with the expo theme of "The Challenge of a New Road to Development," Emergent technologies at the expo focused on generating power from environmentally friendly renewable energy sources and advances in recycling technology, including a "maglev" (magnetic levitation) train which floated on its several meters of track; and electric and solar-powered vehicles.

The exposition's extensive cultural pro-

This aerial view of the Taejon fair shows many of the principal pavilions (Taejon Expo '93 press photograph).

The Tower of Great Light was the centerpiece of Expo '93 (Taejon Expo '93 press photo).

gram included performing and visual arts from all over the world, as well as a celebration of traditional and modern Korean culture. Some of the expo-themed highlights included computer graphics opera, electronic music, work by renowned Korean digital/video artist Nam June Paik at the Recycling Pavilion, and an international collection of plastic environmental art located throughout the site under the name, "Future Lies Ahead.'

More than 14 million visitors came to the expo over its 93 day run, a healthy tally of some 147,000 visitors per day and more than 40 percent higher than estimated. Nearly half of the visitors were Korean students, and 4.8 percent were international visitors, as opposed to a projected total of 500,000. Daily visitor totals ranged from a hight of 222,000 on October 31 to a low of 55,000 on September 29.

Soon after the expo's closing on November 7, the city of Taejon (now anglicized and known as Daejon) was welcoming visitors again, this time to the new Korea Expo Park. Here people can re-live the expo experience, view the Corporate Zone, attend some of the pavilions much as they were in 1993, and enjoy coffee and cake on the first level of the Tower of Great Light. "Kum'Dori," the friendly beanbag shaped yellow "cosmic elf" mascot of the Expo, still welcomes people at the West Gate of the expo site, albeit as a Legoland rendition in a guarded glass box. And one can still see the blue and red, yin and yang renditions of the official expo logo in the two high-spanning arches of the Expo Bridge. "Ku Nal Un," or "That Great Day" in English, the official theme song that looks towards a time of harmonious global unity, can still be heard as faint background music through the parkland.

Bibliography

Much basic information about the Taejon International Exposition can be found in the documents prepared by the exposition organizing committee, including the *Taejon Expo '93 Update* (the monthly newsletter), the *Taejon Expo News* (the weekly newsletter published during the

Many world's fairs' host cities build their own pavilions. Shown here is Taejon's pavilion for its 1993 exposition (from *A Stamp Collection in Commemoration of Taejon Expo 93,* 1993).

expo), and a summary book, *A Comprehensive Review of Taejon Expo '93* (1993), as well as the guidebook.

The expo received little attention in the U.S. press, but a few articles may be helpful. *World's Fair* covered the exposition in several articles. Jack James, "What Korea Wants from Expo 93," *World's Fair* 12, 3 (July-August-September 1992): 6–9, argues that Korea wants to achieve the status of an advanced industrial nation as a result of the expo. Kim Chong Tae, "Korean Expo Lands 112 Nations," *World's* Fair 13, 2 (April-May-June 1993): 4, reviews preparations for the far, and Alfred Heller, "Expo 93 Marries a Theme Park

Before a Large Audience," *World's Fair* 13, 4 (October-November-December 1993): 8–12, reviews the fair and notes how it resembles a contemporary theme park, while BIE president Ted Allan, "Expo 93 Threatens to Break the Mold," in the same issue, evaluates the expo from the perspective of the BIE. See expo-related articles in the *Rocky Mountain News* (August 1, 1993), the Washington *Post* (October 25, 1993), and the New York *Times* (September 5, 1993). See also Ellen Hoffman, "Korean Expo and Science Town: A Peek into the Future?" *Omni* 10, 2 (November 1993): 31.

Lisbon 1998

Laura Huntoon

Expo '98 — The Lisbon World Exposition

The Lisbon Expo 98 ran from May 22 to September 30 in the Portuguese capital city.

The official theme was Oceans: A Heritage for the Future, celebrating the oceans of the world and Portugal's historic role in the European Age of Discovery, while its mascot was a drop of ocean water named Gil in honor of the fifteenth century Portuguese navigator Gil

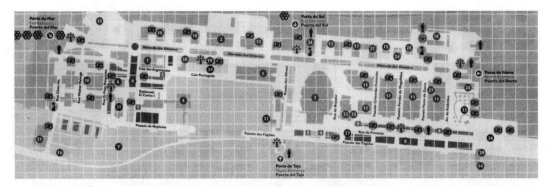

Site plan of Expo '98: (*from press kit, Expo '98, Lisbon, Portugal*).

Eanes. This whimsical mascot with a boy's name was criticized for not being a universal symbol. In response a female counterpart, Docas, was added during the fair. Both an iconic bridge and tower were named in honor of the Portuguese explorer Vasco da Gama to commemorate his arrival in India in 1498. Total visits reached just under 11 million.

Expo 98 represented a reuse of land, a shift from industrial usage to residential, commercial, and recreational land uses. The site of Expo 98 was a 123-acre parcel along the Tagus River in a former brownfield east of central Lisbon, part of a larger redevelopment area. A master plan covering the 812-acre "Intervention Zone," incorporating land from the municipalities of Lisbon and Loures, was approved in 1994. While each municipality welcomed the plan for its infusion of investment, both lost control of land use to the Expo 98 management organization, Parque Expo, and felt that their interests had been ignored.

Two groups, the Exposition Commissariat, representing the Portuguese state; and a subordinate corporate entity, Parque Expo 98, the agency responsible for carrying out the world's fair, were approved as part of this plan. Powers authorized by the national government included compulsory land acquisition, special tax exemption until 1999, and exemption from an environmental impact assessment, although an impact study was conducted for the site. These powers allowed Expo 98 planners to dispense with much local review although local and special district planners were consulted in Lisbon.

The timing and scale of Expo 98 provided a rationale for many related investment projects and public activities that national and met-

ropolitan governments and business had been seeking. Urban redevelopment, environmental rehabilitation, protection of the national heritage, defining national identity, and building event capacity in metropolitan Lisbon were all seen as important expo goals. As the *Official Expo 98 Guide* enthused:

> Antiquated industrial facilities, a tank farm, old military warehouses, an obsolete abattoir and even a huge rubbish tip were to give way to a new concept of the use of urban land that would, in the future, give back to the city a large strip of land, about 5 kilometers in length, located along the Tagus, the river that bathes Portugal's capital [p. 24].

Most expo-related communication and transportation infrastructure addressed regional integration. Lisbon(s metropolitan government co-operated with the Portuguese national government to focus European spending on Lisbon. The European Union (EU) and the Portuguese national government provided funding for off-site infrastructure, including a bridge across the Tagus River and the second ring road around metropolitan Lisbon. A new metro line connecting the site to the city center ended at a new bus, train, and metro station, Oriente Station, designed by architect Santiago Cavaltrava, with parking, commercial space, and new bus routes from this station.

The central entrance to the expo site, called the Sun Entrance, was directly across from Oriente Station. This entrance was subsequently refitted as a retail center, the Vasco da Gama, after the expo. During the run of the fair, the Sun Entrance led to a central axis landscaped with an *allée* of poplar trees and a reflecting pool adjacent to the Utopia Pavilion. The site as a whole was organized on a modified orthogonal grid oriented around a basin, Olivais Dock, on the Tagus River. Two main axes bisected the site. The principal east-west axis led from Oriente Station to the river bank, just north of the dock. The principal north-south axis, parallel to both the river and the railroad tracks, was the route for evening parades and connected two secondary entrances as well as leading to the national pavilion areas. The southern International Pavilion was a temporary structure, while the northern International Pavilion, designed by architects Antonio Barreiros Ferreira and Alberto Franca Doria, became an exhibit hall for the Lisbon International Fair. Careful attention was paid to landscaping and sidewalks. Landscaping reflected both local flora and former Portuguese territories, while sidewalks were embellished with mosaics reminiscent of Portuguese tiles.

Five principal pavilions destined for post-expo use were located adjacent to the Olivais Dock and the banks of the Tagus, providing a dramatic setting for the expo and for public facilities after the exposition. One of the largest and busiest exhibits, the Oceans Pavilion, was built on a platform extending from the southern dock of the basin, while the Luís de Camões Theatre and the Vasco da Gama Tower both overlooked the water.

A major emphasis was placed on daily programs. A variety of street entertainment was programmed to help visitors pass time spent in line. One group of performers was dubbed the Olharapos, or monsters of the depths. These sixty imaginary monsters, inspired by illustrations of sea creatures from discovery-age maps, roamed the site. Another open-air performance was the evening parade called *Peregrinação*, or Pilgrimage, consisting of mechanical contraptions parading to the banks of the Tagus to encounter the Rhinoceros, a simulation of a rhino in a metal cage. Acqua Matrix, a multi-media show with the theme of the "Birth of a New Man for the New Century" was staged around midnight each night at the Olivais Docks.

Re-use and redevelopment were an integral part of the expo program. The expo grounds were designed as two related sites: *Parque das Nações*, (Park of Nations), a mixed-use area incorporating government offices, and commercial and recreational space, including a marina, and *Expo Urbe* (Expo City), a residential development directed toward middle- and upper-income residents.

A relatively large share of the central core of the expo site was designated for public uses. The initial bid proposal included a detailed site plan with an inventory of post-expo uses for the major pavilions, including the Portuguese Pavilion, converted for the Council of Ministers; the Oceans Pavilion a salt-water aquarium now an independent tourist attraction; and the Utopia Pavilion, renamed the Atlantic Pavilion, now an arena and event space. The area adjacent to the arena with a large reflecting pool and rows of poplar trees remains as a small park.

Redevelopment of the site continues. In 2004 the successor agency to Parque Expo, Parque das Nações, sold the Pavilion of the Future to Estorial Sol, a Portuguese gambling and tourism company, which reopened it as Casino de Lisboa. Many observers noted an increase in Lisbon's international profile after the expo, indicated, perhaps, by Lisbon's playing host to the European Football Cup in 2004.

Although Expo 98 had relatively low attendance compared with the 1992 exposition in Seville, it produced significant post-expo site development. These developments transformed the built environment and created a relatively open social environment on part of the expo site. Although pre-bid site planning did not attract a record number of tourists to the expo, it influenced the site's subsequent development as a tourist attraction. Estimated yearly visits to the cluster of museums, restaurants, gardens, and public facilities on the former expo site now are greater than attendance at Expo 98 itself. Like most other modern expos, Expo 98 was not a financial success, finishing with a loss of $ 1.32 billion through the end of 1998. Continuing operations however, have contributed to reducing this shortfall. Expo 98 did expedite a major urban redevelopment, bring European Union subsidies for infrastructure, and assist in tourist marketing. Expo 1998, however, produced this new section of the city with limited public participation.

International expos' potential contributions to urban redevelopment could represent an increase to the value-added to a region after the exposition closes. Lisbon 1998 represented this potential for city-building embodied in the expo process. The exposition resulted in improved

The Luso American Wave is an outdoor sculpture 60 feet long and 8.5 feet high that the United States gave to Portugal as part of its participation in Expo 98 (press photo, U.S. section, Expo 98, Lisbon, Portugal).

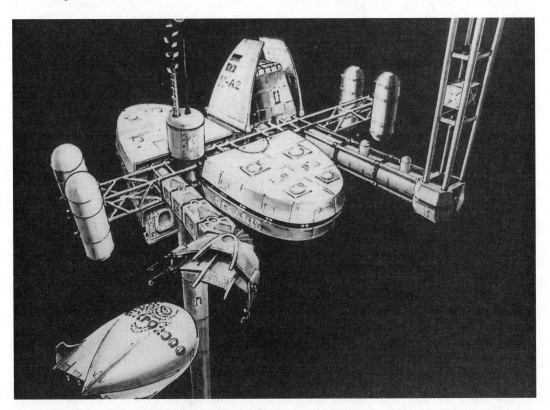

The German pavilion at Expo 98 was modeled after the German underwater research station OCEA-NIS. Visitors experienced the sense of being 300 feet below sea level as they learned about the scientific work done at the station (press photo, German section, Expo 98, Lisbon, Portugal).

regional infrastructure, increased tourist marketing, and enhanced connectivity to global markets. Improved infrastructure and media attention are common expo outcomes, while the large-scale urban redevelopment started by Expo 98 is much harder to achieve.

Bibliography

Although there is no organized archival collection of Expo 98 papers, the Parque des Nações, the successor organization to Parque Expo '98 S.A., has primary documents related to the expo, including the annual reports, *Relatorio de Contas,* published by Parque Expo from 1994 through the expo. The national government of Portugal, through its *Tribunal de Contas,* published *Auditoria ao Projecto Expo '98: Actos do Tribunal: O Relatorio de Auditorio* (2000), a five-volume audit of the exposition through the end of 1998. It is available on-line at *www.tcontas.pt/pt/actos/rel_auditoria/2000/audit2000.shtm.* For the redevelopment of the expo site, J. Cabral, B. Ruto, and J. Reis, *Lisbon — Portugal: The Expo '98 Urban Project* (2000) is a survey of the planning process and institutions of Expo '98 that includes a detailed description of the metropolitan context of the expo, European Union support for expo-related infrastructure, and design of the site.

For basic information on the expo, see the guidebook, *Expo 98 Official Guide* (1998), published in various languages, including English. The expo organization published a monthly newsletter for more than two years before the expo opened that followed site development, participant news, and other plans for the event. Another Expo '98

publication, *The Oceans, a Heritage for the Future: Press Information* (1998) has useful information on the expo's theme, its theme pavilions, and its entertainment program. On the architecture of the expo, Steven Spier, "Redefining Expo," *Architectural Review,* 204 (July 1998): 26–27, provides basic information. A subsequent look at the post-expo site is provided by Timothy, Brittain-Catlin, "View from Lisbon," *Architectural Review* 214 (July 2003): brings the story of the expo area's redevelopment forward to five years after the expo. A scholarly approach to the same issue is Mark I. Wilson and Laura Huntoon, "World's Fairs and Urban Development: Lisbon and EXPO98," *International Review of Comparative Public Policy* 12 (2001): 371–93. Another article in English is Jean-Paul Carriere and Christophe Demaziere, "Urban Planning and Flagship Development Projects: Lessons from EXPO 98, Lisbon," *Planning Practices & Research* 17, 1 (2002): 69–79, which posits Expo 98 as a model for urban regeneration.

Hanover 2000

Larry Maloney

Expo 2000— The World Exposition

Germany emerged from the rubble of World War II as Europe's economic powerhouse. With efficiency as its middle name, Germany seemed capable of anything, so no one blinked when the superpower pushed its selection as host of a universal exposition. What surprised many, however, was the outcome of the country's successful bid —failure. Germany's Expo 2000 showed that even the most organized and efficient countries can make critical mistakes. In fact, Expo 2000 may well prove to be the ultimate case study in the strategic mishandling of an international event.

Germany's exposition odyssey began in 1988 when Hanover proposed hosting a world exposition in 1998 — the fiftieth anniversary of the founding of the federal republic. The

prospect of an international event in Hanover seemed odd and perfect all at once. Hanover, a city of 500,000, could not be called an international tourist destination by any stretch of the imagination. However, the city had established a reputation as having the largest permanent fairground in the world, used for its annual trade shows; existing infrastructure could be used, thus lowering the cost of hosting the event. Hanover's dream gained acceptance in the capital, and plans began in earnest to bid for the exposition.

The Bureau of International Expositions (BIE), however, interfered with the plan. In 1989, BIE changed the rules governing international expositions so that they occurred every five years, and the next available opportunity was not until 2000. Hanover was not deterred; plans shifted quickly from celebrating the federal republic's anniversary to welcoming the new millennium. In spite of the new plan, Hanover faced an uphill battle given that Toronto and Venice were also preparing to bid for the 2000 exposition. Prior to the vote at the BIE meeting in 1990, Venice unexpectedly withdrew its candidacy, leaving long shot Hanover a 50 percent chance of winning. Toronto, the city expected to win, lost by one vote.

With ten years to plan, Hanover began preparations in earnest for Expo 2000. Based on the apparent success of the 1992 exposition in Seville, organizers set a budget of $1.6 billion for the event, a record for a universal exhibition. Organizers intended Expo 2000 to be the first exhibition in history to operate solely on private sector funds. They expected to pay for the mammoth event through an anticipated 40 million visitors during the six month event. Early market research indicated that the majority (60 percent) of visitors would be Germans with nearly all the remainder (35 percent) coming from elsewhere in Europe. Organizers expected those tourist numbers to generate $870 million in gate receipts with $460 million secured from corporate sponsors and $145 million from licensing fees, and they believed these figures to be realistic, given that the exposition would take place on a site with pre-existing infrastructure, the first time this would occur in the history of international exhibitions. Even with the prospect of a healthy revenue stream and the use of a pre-existing site, Expo 2000 planned to lose an estimated $190 million. While the loss would be covered with a contingency fund, the German government and the state of Lower Saxony agreed to pay for any remaining deficit with taxpayer funds.

This exposition was structured on a theme common to all on the planet: "Humankind — Nature — Technology, a New World Arising." Early on, Commissioner General Birgit Breuel and her staff of 500 had a vision for bringing the expo's theme to life — that mankind must find a way to live in harmony with nature. The Agenda 21 pro-clamation for sustainable development provided the conceptual framework for their expo concept. Agenda 21 had been the most visible outcome of the 1992 Earth Summit in Rio de Janeiro. Germany and 177 other countries signed Agenda 21, and the city of Hanover adopted the Agenda 21 principles in 1994. Expo 2000 accepted Agenda 21 in 1995 as the binding theme for all participating nations.

Expo 2000 planned to invite the entire world to participate in showing how mankind could thrive while protecting the environment. The organizers extended invitations to 185 countries and 173 accepted, making Expo 2000 the largest gathering of nations in the history of universal exhibitions. Germany achieved this task through unprecedented outreach to many of the world's least developed nations, which represented two-thirds of the participating nations. Many of these countries accepted invitations to participate even though they had no previous exhibition experience. The Federal Ministry for Economic Cooperation and Development contributed DM 100 million to assist 65 of the poorest countries with their exhibition planning. The umbrella of planning for the poorest nations paid off as a number of African nations pooled resources and combined their exhibitions into one hall under a unifying theme of "The Gift of Africa," a decision that increased visibility for all the African countries.

In addition to the record-setting country participation, Expo 2000 reached out to international organizations such as the International Olympic Committee, the International Red Cross and the World Bank, all of which agreed to exhibit at the expo.

For all its success in bringing the world to Hanover for this event, the United States's decision not to participate startled the organizers and the country. The United States had participated in every universal exhibition from the inaugural event in London in 1851 through Lisbon in 1998, so its participation seemed assured. However, after embarrassment with the quality of the pavilion and exhibitions displayed in Seville in 1992, the federal government passed a law in 1994 prohibiting the use of public funds for U.S. pavilions.

The U.S. government planned to raise $40 million in corporate donations to fund the country's presence at the fair and Expo 2000 granted the United States one of the most prominent sites on the fairgrounds. In what should have been the first sign of trouble for the exposition, many companies approached by the U.S. embassy in Germany did not even know of Hanover's existence. In the end, sufficient corporate funding could not be raised, and the United States scrapped its plans to participate officially in one of the largest international endeavors ever.

In spite of the snub from America, organizers continued to look for ways to enhance their expo experience in ways that had not been undertaken previously. The organizers sought to break free of the traditional confines of physical exhibition space so that the overarching theme of sustainable development could be experienced around the globe. The organizers developed the theme, Projects Around the World — the first attempt by any exposition to expand the reach of an exhibition globally, and staged a competition to find innovative ideas that either could be replicated in other regions of the world or that represented a unique approach to addressing a local problem.

Ricardo Diez Hochleitner, president of the Club of Rome, which in recent years has focused on the issue of sustainable development, chaired a committee to evaluate more than 3,000 entries. An International Advisory Board selected 487 of these entrants from more than 100 countries as Expo 2000 International Projects Around the World, and they were given the right to identify their programs as Expo 2000 events. The projects represented innovative approaches to important issues, such as:

• Barefoot College of India submitted an initiative that teaches poor illiterate farmers through puppet shows.

• SEKEM was an Egyptian initiative focused on biodynamic farming that today encompasses 800 farmers and 8,000 hectares of farmland.

• Village of Dolls was an effort from Pakistan that provides a livelihood to women in the Punjab region.

• More importantly, 120 of the most promising programs received assistance from the Federal Ministry for Economic Cooperation and Development (BMZ), and more than half of the programs were integrated into exhibitions at the expo.

• In addition to showcasing promising programs from the around the globe, expo organizers planned a series of Global Dialogue events: several three-day forums designed to highlight critical issues related to mankind's place in the world. Global Dialogue topics included:

• Sustainability and Natural Resources.

• Responsible Governance in a Global Society.

• Science and Technology — Thinking the Future.

• Fighting Poverty: Social Innovations and New Coalitions.

• The Role of the Village in the 21st Century.

• Health.

• Building Learning Societies.

• Culture on the Move.

• The Future of Work and Sustainable Business.

• Shaping a Future of Global Partnership

The Global Dialogue sessions were made possible through unprecedented cooperation from 60 international organizations that helped to organize and promote the conferences, which involved more than 4,500 conference participants. Given the importance of the topics, plans included broadcasting sessions throughout Europe.

In the end, organizers filled the 320 acre site — roughly the size of Monaco — with exhibits from more countries than ever before. In addition to a record 51 individual pavilions, the exposition included a thematic area of five interconnected buildings tied to the Agenda 21 strategy. And in keeping with Agenda 21, only one-third of the site involved any new development.

As is the custom with universal expositions, the participating nations constructed pavilions to dazzle the anticipated throngs of visitors, some of which accentuated the theme of sustainable development. Japanese architect Shigeru Ban designed the Japan pavilion completely from cardboard and paper. The Netherlands constructed a five-level structure of "landscapes," including a forest irrigated by rainwater captured on the pavilion's roof. The United Arab Emirates recreated a desert fort complete with sand and camels. Even the Duales System Pavilion found a unique way to engage visitors by creating a tornado every hour through a giant ventilation system.

In addition to the pavilions, organizers planned a series of events and activities to titillate the expo tourist. More than 200 ensembles and orchestras performed during the six-month event. Deutsche Telecom set up the largest mobile screen in the world (14 meters by 32 meters) for a film festival, as well as to

A view of the Duales System pavilion, one of the corporate participants in the Hanover 2000 exposition. Inside this glass and steel building, visitors could watch a simulation of a tornado (Expo 2000 press photo).

broadcast the Sydney Olympic Games. The Karstadt Fun Sports Hall provided youth with an outlet through skateboarding and beach volleyball. Organizers expected a nightly water and light show to draw in tourists during evening hours, and even planned the complete production of Goethe's Faust. In all, more than 15,000 cultural events were scheduled during Expo 2000. It seemed that the organizers had thought of everything possible to draw tourists to the site.

And then, the fair opened. The pomp and circumstance of opening day showed no precursor of the calamity awaiting organizers that began to unfold the next day and for months to come when the site remained alarmingly empty of the anticipated visitors. The Expo 2000 planning team expected approximately 260,000 visitors daily to the 320-acre site. The first week closed with approximately 70,000 visitors per day. The impact on expo finances could be felt immediately. One week after the

opening, 523 employees on the expo site received pink slips, mostly those working in concessions, as there were so few customers.

The visitor numbers did not improve after the first week, and the sport of finger pointing began almost instantly, particularly from those holding the responsibility to cover the shortfall — the federal government and the state of Lower Saxony. Calls for a drop in admission prices fell on deaf ears, with the organizers stating that the pricing structure was not the problem and that a reduction in prices now would not be fair to those who had bought their tickets in advance.

The public disagreed. Some 40 percent of Germans polled felt the exposition prices were too high. Reluctantly, expo organizers responded with a drop in evening ticket prices to "celebrate" the birthday of Hanover's selection as the expo host. Other price reductions were offered five weeks into the event, when organizers stopped charging extra for parking and for buying a ticket on site. Children under the age of 12 were admitted free when accompanied by an adult. Senior citizens could buy a day pass for $5 instead of $35, and new rates were provided for family passes. Yet, attendance numbers did not respond accordingly.

Desperate to attract visitors, the management team approved an additional infusion of $25 million for advertising to showcase the fun awaiting at expo—3,000 television, print and radio advertisements began running at the end of July, the beginning of the summer vacation period for many Europeans. The team also approved an additional $10 million for advertisements in six neighboring countries.

The new pricing strategy presented a dreadful paradox to the organizers, however. Reductions in ticket prices might bring in the long hoped-for tourists, but the exposition budget could not be met with lower ticket prices. With new advertising, attendance numbers improved marginally, and the deficit ballooned. By July, the commissioner general began to reset expectations on total attendance to the exposition, from 40 million to fewer than 14 million, and in August, the federal government and the state of Lower Saxony poured $430 million into the expo to avoid financial collapse. Upon hearing this news, Bernhard Zentgraf, chairman of the Lower Saxony Federation of Taxpayers, stated that the "expo was the greatest miscalculation in German history."

Conditions at the fair improved only slightly over the remaining months. Poor publicity from the early days of the fair regarding the cost to pass through the gates and then for extras inside such as food continued to dampen attendance numbers. By the end of October, however, attendance finally spiked. Organizers hyped the new numbers. Two days prior to the close of the exposition, they issued a press release that showed 95 percent of expo visitors recommended a visit. But, it was too late. Expo 2000 closed with 18.1 million visits instead of the projected 40 million, making it the second most poorly attended universal exposition of the post-war era.

Of course, the attendance numbers wreaked havoc on the exposition's budget. Organizers had projected $1.6 billion in revenue; they generated a third of what was expected, leaving the federal government and the state of Lower Saxony with a deficit of $1.2 billion.

What went wrong? Organizers made several mistakes before the gates even opened, and decisions made once disaster struck were too late to influence an abysmal outcome. First, the organizers built a universal exposition on a difficult theme. "Humankind—Nature—Technology" proved to be a hard sell to a public deciding how best to spend money on a summer vacation. The motto gave the exposition the appearance of an educational crash course on environmental problems. As a German marketing firm described the dilemma, "the organizers have failed to convey to the public a clear image of what Expo 2000 is going to be: an entertainment park, a blown-up museum or a nature reserve."

Second, organizers compounded this problem when they did not hire a head for the Department of Tourism and Ticketing until two years before the gates opened. With a key position left unfilled, expo management pursued development of the fair and its themes without professional guidance as to how those decisions would affect the exposition's ability to attract tourists.

Third, the management team decided to defer advertising until the year 2000 as the ticketing system planned for Expo 2000 would not be operational until spring 2000. The small amount of advertising approved prior to the media blitz, all print media, posters and brochures, made the exposition seem more educational than entertainment oriented. Once the organizers poured money into emergency advertising, it had little effect. Analysis of attendance prior to and after the new media campaign indicated an increase of 375,000 more visitors per week, still dramatically below the attendance numbers needed to pull the fair out of the red.

Finally, organizers continued to rely on attendance projections based on those achieved by Seville in 1992 (41 million) even though Hanover lacked the traditional tourist draw of Seville. This was confirmed by a post-fair analysis of the tickets sold; 83 percent of visitors to Expo 2000 were German, so there were few international visitors to spread the word about how mankind could live in harmony with nature. More importantly for the city of Hanover, fewer international visitors meant a dampened economic boom for the city through overnight stays.

In spite of its mammoth failure to live up to its expectations, Expo 2000 produced tangible benefits for the city of Hanover and the surrounding region. Improvements valued between $5 and $8 billion modernized the city, including the largest open span exhibition hall in Europe, new subway lines, upgrades to train stations and freeways, as well as a new terminal at the airport. In the short term, the University of Frankfurt estimated that the exposition helped to generate $1.35 billion in tax revenue for the federal and local economies. Even with the layoffs that occurred, more than 100,000 jobs were created due to the fair. Additionally, Expo 2000's Projects Around the World produced concrete benefits for many of those initiatives with $12 billion in capital investment and the creation of 25,000 new jobs.

Expo 2000 also resulted in the creation of a new vehicle to assist future exposition cities: AVE, the Association of Cities and Regions Hosting an International Exposition. The BIE and several exposition cities created AVE to promote regional development through the exposition process and to disseminate management knowledge to future host cities. One can only hope that knowledge transfer includes lessons on visitor projections and effective budgeting.

Post-mortems on the fair, particularly ones originating from Germany, proved critical of press accounts that stated the Expo was a "megaflop" when viewed in terms of attendance and ballooning deficit projections. True, Expo 2000 provided a glimpse into the future mankind can achieve if we learn to use the planet's resources wisely. Organizers orchestrated the largest gathering of nations at a universal exhibition in history, and they highlighted innovative approaches to conserving resources. But, even the most innovative approaches mean little if the public does not witness and learn from the experience. Additionally, financing is a resource, and Hanover's mismanagement raised a note of caution for future cities interested in universal expositions. Hanover left a debt of $15 per person for every man, woman and child in the country — a debt many felt could have been put to use in better ways in the newly reunited country. Just as cities steered clear of bidding for the 1984 Olympics after the financial debacle of the 1976 Games in Montreal, a debt that took Canada 28 years to pay off, Hanover may have contributed sufficient doubt as to the economic viability of universal expositions to discourage capable cities from seeking bids in the future. That is a legacy no city should leave to the next generation.

Bibliography

Official Expo publications provide basic information about the event. The guide book, *The EXPO-Guide: The Official Guide to EXPO 2000* (2000) contains short descriptions of the pavilions and other basic information of use to visitors. A much more elaborate publication, published under the name of Birgit Breul, the commissioner general of Expo 2000, is *The EXPO-Book: The official Catalogue of EXPO 2000* (2000), with more detailed information about the themes, participants, and cultural program of the exposition.

Expo 2000 failed to generate sufficient press in the United States due in part to the country's absence from the fair. However, British media outlets provided more coverage, particularly the BBC, The *Guardian*, and The *Observer*. English coverage of Expo 2000 also can be found through *Deutschland* magazine and the English edition of the daily, *German News*. The most useful English document regarding Expo 2000, however, is the *Report by the Federal Minister of Economics and Technology on the World Exposition Expo 2000 in Hanover, Nr. 489* (2001). Other articles that may be of use is K. Loeffler, "EXPO-2000 Hannover: The World Exposition June 1-October 31, 2000 in Germany: The Austrian and German Pavilions," *Österreichische Zeitschrift für Volkshunde* 103, 4 (2000): 517–21, Aaron Betsky, "Dutch Pavilion, Expo 2000 Hannover, Germany...." *Architecture* 87, 10 (1998): 56–58, and "Japan Pavilion," *Interiors* 160, 1 (January 2001): 58–59.

The exposition web site contains remnants of information in English and can be found at *http://www.expo2000.de/expo2000/index_e.htm*. Finally, the German daily *Die Welt* provided extensive coverage of Expo 2000 in German.

Aichi 2005

Alfred Heller

The Japan World Exposition

Nagoya City had failed to secure the Olympic Games early in the 1980s, but a strong desire remained in the region to hold an important international event. A national development plan, adopted by the central government of Japan in 1987, had designated Nagoya and surrounding towns as an important "industrial and technological nucleus zone." Manufacturers in the area, including Toyota Motor Corporation, were working with the city and the prefecture to secure major research institutions for the area.

In Tokyo, the trade ministry that had put on the great Expo 70 in Osaka was talking about holding another such event in Japan. Thus it followed that in October 1988 regional and local forces, public and private, combined to push for a world exposition in Aichi as a further way to promote and develop the region. Two months after that, the Japanese delegate to the General Assembly of the Bureau of International Expositions (BIE) told the assembly that his country was prepared to host the first international exposition of the twenty-first century, in the eastern outskirts of Nagoya, in Aichi Prefecture.

The BIE's selection process continued until June 1997, when the assembly chose Japan (Aichi) over Canada (Calgary) to hold Expo 2005. Japan had reportedly waged a vigorous, expensive campaign to secure the prize.

Within a month after the decision, a working group formed by the Japanese government, chaired by Shoichiro Toyoda, honorary chair of Toyota, set to work to create the expo's governing body, the Japan Association for the 2005 World Exposition (referred to below as the organizers, or the association). Subsequently, Toyoda became chair of the associa-tion itself. Taizo Watanabe was the government's choice for Commissioner General of the expo. The governmental official in charge of the expo was Shoichi Nakagawa, who was Minister of Economy, Trade and Industry.

The scope and character of the expo and its site planning underwent drastic changes as the preparations went forward. Probably the most important catalyst for change was that "nesting by goshawks was identified within the proposed site area (Kaisho Forest) on May 12, 1999," according to an official report of the association.

Clearly, the endangered hawks and their habitat had to be protected to satisfy environmental demands, and equally important, the expo had to go forward. After much discussion, and prodding from the BIE, the organizers decided to scale back the expo, leave the forest and natural features largely intact, and shift development to already-used or less sensitive ground in several widely separated areas. Furthermore, the environmental theme would take center stage as never before. In 2001, all of this was codified in a master plan incorporating a "concept story" prepared by the Japanese philosopher Taichi Sakaiya.

The theme finally selected for Expo 2005 was "Nature's Wisdom," with several subthemes. It did, in fact, turn out to be a green expo, the greenest ever. It protected open spaces and natural areas containing endangered plants and animals. It had nature trails. Its exhibits taught lessons in ecology. The expo's fabric was a product of its 3R motto: Reduce, Reuse, Recycle. After the expo much of the land would become a park. The steel-framed pavilions would be dismantled and reused. The pathways were paved with industrial detritus. Restaurant eating utensils were made of recyclable plastic. Clusters of trash cans invited visitors to separate out their waste, to the point where attendants had to explain to them where to put this and where to put that. The expo was conservative and innovative in its use of energy.

The means of getting around were intended to adumbrate urban transport of the future: Intelligent Multimode Transit System (IMTS) vehicles, a magnetic levitation train (not new for expos), fuel-cell-powered buses, bicycle taxis. But in truth, the vaunted energy-efficient onsite transportation was notable for its infrequency. Some visitors never did spot an IMTS bus. The queues for gondolas between major points were long and winding. Conventional transport wasn't much better. People stood in the heat of summer for a half hour to board an occasional tram that crawled around the 2.6 kilometer Global Loop. The Global Loop was the name of a pedestrian boulevard that traversed the grounds. The organizers created the elevated loop to help visitors move through the site's uneven, forested terrain to the various development clusters, without leveling every hill and dale for the short-lived event. It was a grand skyway, and became the dominating image of the expo.

The loop was convenient for those who stayed on it, but it was mostly uncovered, and visitors who wanted to avoid the sticky heat of the open, 21-meter-wide deck got off, to seek out shadier if longer routes from one Global Common to the next — or ice cream at one of the food courts, or a bench overlooking the koi-pond.

The loop wound its way to and through six separated areas called Global Commons. Each Common contained temporary warehousing erected by the organizers, for exhibits from countries in specific geo-political regions: Asia (17 countries); the Americas (17); Europe (two Commons with 34 countries divided between them); Africa (30); and Oceania and Southeast Asia (22). Altogether, 120 countries were represented.

Japan had two pavilions at the expo. In addition, there were several local government exhibits. The United Nations and a handful of other international entities also had exhibits. Two corporate zones dominated the northern approach to the fair.

The organizers carried on a variety of special projects. Global House featured the 12,000-year-old head and tusks of a woolly mammoth,

discovered recently in Siberia. On the Expo Plaza the Bio Lung was a wall of plants that, proponents claimed, lowered the temperature in the area several degrees. The NGO Global Village had ever-changing exhibits from environment-oriented nongovernmental groups around the world, and representatives of those groups more than willing to talk with visitors. A children's interactive fun zone near the NGO area got kids wet and muddy.

Because half the expo grounds were given over to more or less unspoiled terrain, the organizers carried on a many-faceted nature education program in a "forest experience zone" and a "trail zone." Activities ranged from self-guided tours to crafting with natural materials to tree climbing. As at other expos, there was a heavy schedule of concerts and world-level entertainments.

One of the two Japan pavilions was in the main 158-hectare (390-acre) Nagakute area and the other was over the hill in Seto (15 hectares). Each pavilion demonstrated a commitment to "rekindling the relationship between mankind and nature," in quite different ways. A visit to the Nagakute pavilion, which was surrounded by a sun- and heat-deflecting woven bamboo cocoon, started in an atrium with flashing images depicting natural crises facing us, such as acid rain and global warming. Then a moving belt took visitors past scenes of how the Japanese incorporate nature in their lifestyles. Visitors moved through the inside of a sphere — presumably it was earth — and looked out at clouds and birds wheeling around. Then they could walk through a simulated forest, to experience daily life there. It was a technically busy exhibit.

By contrast, the Japan pavilion at the Seto area used performers and artists to send its messages. In an arena, actors recited the epic poem "One Seed," incorporating traditional Japanese words and songs of nature. Produced by Akiko Kitamura, it was a powerful show, replete with prancing, shouting, grappling and declaiming. As visitors spiraled up towards the exit they saw some fine installation art by Toshihiro Sakuma and Takemi Nishimoto. The architect and executive creative director of the Japan Pavilions was Yutaka Hikosaka.

To an unusual degree, the official theme infused the exhibits of participating nations. The organizers encouraged this phenomenon.

At Expo 2005 in Aichi, an elevated walkway called the Global Loop enabled visitors to move from one group of pavilions to the next (photograph by Alfred Heller).

Working with the BIE, they established the Nature's Wisdom Award. The award was presented to national pavilions for excellent design and for the effectiveness of their message, especially in relation to the theme. The last time official awards were given at an expo was in Brussels in 1958. In Aichi, the host country pavilions were not eligible for the awards, nor were the exhibits of local governments. An international jury of nine members, including Wu Jianmin, president of the BIE and Vicente González Loscertales, secretary-general of the BIE, produced two sets of awards during the course of the expo.

Winners of gold prizes for large pavilions (4 or more 18 square meter modules) were Korea and Germany; for medium-size pavilions (1.5 to 3 modules), Turkey and Mexico; for small pavilions (a single module or less), the Philippines and the Netherlands; and for group exhibits, Venezuela and the Andean Amazonian pavilion.

Korea's motif, "Light of Life," was expressed through symbolism evoked from five basic colors: blue, red, yellow, black and white. Blue was intended to convey a clear and cheerful life, with animated fish swimming on a screen of water. The red section emphasized the sun, the beginning of life, and the fire and heat of the Korean people and Korean industry. Yellow symbolized the earth. Clay pots and semiconductors inhabited this section. In the black section, visitors saw their own images on a screen, morphed into trees by charcoal artistry, suggesting a perennial interaction between people and nature. In the white section, lighting and white paper combined to create a world of brightness.

Germany offered visitors a ride in a six-person capsule, traveling under the sea, through the air, through a thunderstorm, into a hydraulic power-generating turbine, along the beautiful Rhine River, above a park of wind generators, to a presentation about technolo-

Crowds of visitors wait to enter the innovative pavilion of the Netherlands at the 2005 Aichi exposition. Inside visitors watched a video projected on the surface of a pool of water (photograph by Alfred Heller).

gies that emerge from the natural world. Turkey showed how traditional forms in Turkish art were inspired by natural forms such as spider webs and snowflakes. Mexico stressed its natural diversity in a tour of four ecosystems: sea, desert, forest and jungle. In a rich and compelling exhibit, art and crafts, ancient to modern, added an impression of the diversity within Mexican culture. The Philippines showed the many uses of the coconut, expressing "the Filipino sense of wholeness, interconnectedness." Coconut parts were made into flooring and walls on which were projected images of the country. Upstairs, visitors could avail themselves of a massage with virgin coconut oil. The Netherlands presented a mural of Delft tiles in a space surrounding a small pond. Visitors saw a film, projected from inside the pond, about the country, titled "Land of Water." Venezuela was one of four countries represented in the Andean Amazonian Pavil-

ion. Each one showed its natural attractions, elements of its culture, and efforts to combat environmental damage.

In Aichi, the national pavilions in general, and the prize winners in particular, reached a level of quality that had rarely been seen among national pavilions at expos in the final decades of the twentieth century, when few such pavilions bothered to contribute new perspectives to an expo's theme. Then some nations presented little more than elaborate gift shops, and apparently did not bother to give serious thought to their presentations. The theme-oriented attitude of the Aichi organizers, actively encouraged by the BIE, resulted in a continuum of cohesive, focused, attractive national pavilions.

Nevertheless, the biggest attractions at Expo 2005 were in the corporate zone. First among these was the Toyota Group pavilion, the best placed, most dominating pavilion at the world's fair, with a show produced by Yves Pèpin, renowned for extravaganzas such as the fireworks at the Eiffel Tower on the occasion of the French Bicentennial in 1989.

Inside the pavilion was an indoor arena surrounded by banked seats. A master of ceremonies came in and started to play the trumpet. Big mistake. It screeched and sputtered. Then a robot, called a partner robot, walked in — really walked, arms and legs articulating smoothly. Then he — it — started playing the trumpet, flawlessly. The robot was joined by six others that marched in, carrying brass instruments, and they all played "When the Saints Come Marching In," a swinging version with varying rhythm and dynamics. Goodbye New Orleans, hello Nagoya, home of Toyota.

Then in came the so-called i-units, mean-looking little bugs about the size of people that ran back and forth as children do, sometimes with people sitting in them, sometimes not. It didn't seem to matter; humans became the machines and the machines became human. These i-units zipped around at great speeds, dodged each other artfully, and made an observer's eyes swim. A partner robot called i-foot that could climb stairs with a person in its arms appeared in another part of the show.

The Toyota partner robots and the Toyota i-unit robots made the show exhilarating. Its message was akin to the dominating messages of automotive exhibits at previous expos — the Highways and Horizons show by General Motors at the Futurama in New York in 1939, and the more modest but still powerful Spirit Lodge, also by GM, at Vancouver in 1986. The two earlier shows were essentially advertisements for more highways. The pitch in 2005 was for "the best forms of mobility for each of us," within the constraints of environmental reality. The show suggested that a major automobile manufacturer had a corporate strategy that was going beyond the traditional mindset of the industry. Nevertheless, at Expo 2005 cars were calling the tune, as ever. Commented Douglas M. West, the U.S. pavilion's deputy commissioner-general for the private sector, on loan from Toyota North America for the duration: "Personal transportation and mobility have dominated modern world's fairs as they have dominated our lives. It's natural for auto companies to play big roles."

A number of other corporations put on lively shows in their pavilions. For example, the Hitachi Group pavilion caused visitors to interact with endangered species through virtual reality: a bird would seem to sit on a spectator's hand, then fly away when he or she moved. At the Mitsui-Toshiba pavilion, photos of audience members were transferred to a film which showed them returning by spaceship from the distant future to save the earth.

The U.S. pavilion was mainly about Benjamin Franklin, who had come back to earth, thanks in part to his own imagination and wizardry, but also to that of BRC Imagination Arts, which produced the American show as they have so many other successful features, including Vancouver 86's Spirit Lodge. Franklin was cited as a prime example of how Nature's Wisdom, in this case a lightning bolt that hit a kite he was flying, could be used by creative, entrepreneurial people, to pioneer new industries such as those based on electricity — certainly an oblique approach to the expo's environmental theme, but good enough apparently to win the United States a bronze award for its large pavilion.

Appearing as a 3-D apparition, Franklin touched on an array of American achievements, with charm and humor and a few magic tricks. The United States had not participated in Expo 2000 in Hanover, Germany, the first time the country had not exhibited at a major expo. Now here it was back again, cutting a swath as if nothing had happened. But pavilions costing more than $30 million, as this one did, don't just appear. Douglas West, who was intimately and centrally involved in the pavilion's development, including fund-raising, emphasized that none of the funds used to plan, build and operate the pavilion came from the federal government. Toyota, he admitted, made a "substantial" contribution, as did many others — corporations, foundations, and some states.

Shoichiro Toyoda, as the Expo 2005 chairman and its sparkplug, helped enlist a variety of political and financial support for the U.S. pavilion, feeling that the success of the expo depended on American involvement. Former Senator Howard Baker of Tennessee, then U.S. ambassador to Japan, got behind the project (Senator Baker had also helped bring Expo 82 to Knoxville). Toyoda leveraged his company's power and influence to bring in North American corporate sponsors and partners.

They contributed tax-deductible funds to the charitable entity that produced the pavilion: Aichi USA 2005.

Douglas West said the United States had one of the most "disadvantaged" locations at the expo, at the back end of Global Commons 2. It was relatively hard to reach. Because the six commons were widely dispersed, other countries suffered similar fates. As things turned out, however, crowds sought out the U.S. pavilion, and respectable queues occupied the entryway.

The expo's balance sheet, covering the period of 1997 through June 2006, showed total expenditures of ¥256 billion ($2.17 billion), total income of ¥268.9 billion ($2.28 billion), and a net surplus of ¥12.9 billion ($109 million). The enterprise benefited from national and regional subsidies of various kinds, including lottery receipts, and corporate donations.

Expo 2005 was a friendly reminder, if any were needed, of Japan's continuing eminence in eastern Asia and the world at large. The Japanese liked their fair, and attendance was strong.

Most pavilions had waiting lines. A system of advance reservations cut down the waiting time for popular venues, but getting into the liveliest shows could entail a wait of two to three hours. On closing day, September 25, a final total of 22,049,544 visitors was posted for the five-month run, far exceeding the predicted 15 million.

Bibliography

Expo records, including the archives of the Japan Association for the 2005 World Exposition, are to be maintained by Global Industrial Progress and Research Institute, Tokyo, successor organization to the association.

Individual publications of value, produced by the Japan Association, include: *The 2005 World Exposition, Aichi, Japan, Official Report* (2006); *The 2005 World Exposition, Aichi, Japan, Official Guidebook* (2005); and *Nature's Wisdom Award* (2006). *Toyota Group Exhibition Guide*, 3 vols. (2005) presents the vision and intended message of a major exhibitor.

Zaragoza 2008

Bureau of International Expositions

Expo Zaragoza 2008

From June 14 to September 14, 2008, the first international exposition organized according to the recognized model of the Bureau of International Expositions (BIE) was to be held in Zaragoza, Spain. The theme of Expo Zaragoza 2008 will be "Water and Sustainable Development." Zaragoza is the administrative and financial capital of the Aragon region and the fifth largest Spanish city, with a population of 650,000. With its enviable and accessible geographical position in the northern part of Spain, it is the functional capital of the Ebro Valley, the dynamic centre of the region with the most socio-economic potential of Spain. The exposition site is located in the Ranillas

Meander, to the west of the city, along the banks of the River Ebro. It is the meeting point between two densely populated Zaragoza districts: ACTUR and Delicias-Almozara.

The exposition is supported by sound principles and motives at international, national, regional, and local levels. Spain's development and stability, its consolidation as a world-class tourist destination, and its experience in organizing large-scale international events, such as the Summer Olympic Games in Barcelona (1992) or the international exposition in Seville (1992). Expo Zaragoza 2008 takes place between the expositions of Aichi 2005, "Nature's Wisdom," and Shanghai 2010, "Better City, Better Life." The official mascot of the exposition is Fluvi, whose name was chosen by popular election. and whose design was chosen in a competition with 120 entries.

Sub-themes: The general theme, "Water and Sustainable Development," is developed and organized into three sub-themes to be displayed in three theme pavilions: Water, a Scarce Resource (Bridge Pavilion); Water for Life (Water Tower); and Water Landscapes (River Aquarium). And a fourth sub-theme running throughout, which is particularly relevant at international expositions, deals with issues affecting the entire planet: Water, the Element Linking Peoples.

Participants: One hundred participants are expected, including countries, international and national organizations, NGO's, and corporations.

The Water Tribune is designed as a forum for reflection and debate on the theme of the exposition, which will promote scientific knowledge and contrast it with experiences, demands, and expectations of society. The Tribune will be a joint experience that through awareness, conversation, and emotion, aims to produce social, personal, and cultural transformations in the perception of water and its sustainability, use and management, through:

• Themed weeks, consisting of seminars and meetings.

• Forums for citizen participation.

• Parallel events that will utilize the existing structures and dynamics of international bodies and associations

• An Information and Communication Platform that will recognize pioneering projects in technology and sustainable water management

• The Zaragoza Charter

Water Park: As of 2007, the exposition site will be complete with the building of the new Water Park, set in the Ranillas Meander. With an area of 1,200,000 square meters, it will become a first-class green space for the city and its surroundings. Alday Jover Architects are responsible for the project. This area will have different spaces: water enclosures, metropolitan facilities area, a leisure area, a whitewater channel, river beaches and swimming pools, a spa center, a 9-hole golf course, and hotels.

Volunteers: By early 2007, a total of 22,807 people had agreed to participate in the volunteer program of Expo Zaragoza 2008, a number that continues to grow and to enrich

the human capital of this world expo. What stands out most about this large group is its diversity. Volunteers come from all regions in Spain and from all continents. Their ages range between 14 (they will be 16 by the time the expo takes place) and 94. They will be the voices, the eyes and the added value of Expo Zaragoza 2008; they will create awareness and promote the Expo and they will help and inform visitors. Volunteers will be placed in specific locations according to their experiences and preferences. All volunteers will undertake a basic information and training program, either in person or via an online program.

General layout of the participants' pavilions: The pavilions for official participants will be located in eight large buildings, connected by a landscaped area and served by a logistics area below street level, which will house the Internal Services Department. The national pavilions are located in the International Participants Area (61,667 square meters), which is divided into eight eco-geographical areas within the site, designed to organize and separate the participating countries:

• Islands and Coasts
• Oasis
• Ice and Snow
• Temperate Forests
• Tropical Rainforests
• Mountains and High Plains
• Grasslands, Steppes and Savannahs
• Rivers and Flat Plains

The joint pavilions corresponding to the eco-geographic areas of Grasslands, Steppes and Savannahs, Tropical Rainforests, and Islands and Coasts, are being built by the organizers to house the pavilions of countries of Sub-Saharan Africa, Latin America and the Caribbean Community (CARICOM), respectively.

Main elements: The principal architect, Zaha Hadid, and the engineer, Ove Arup, are responsible for the design of the Bridge Pavilion, one of the landmarks of the exposition. Built on a base shaped like of a drop of water and 73 meters high, the Water Tower will be one of the major symbols of the exposition. The aquarium project has been designed by the MC Engineering Company and architect Enrique de Teresa. The River Aquarium will be part of the facilities that Zaragoza will receive following the exposition, adding to the tourist attraction of the city. The aquarium contract has been awarded to the company Coutant Acuariums, headed by Philippe de Lacaze.

Themed Squares: Located between the Bridge Pavilion and the Spain Pavilion, these exhibitions aim to enrich and intensify the message of the vital link with water from various perspectives. The design contract for the riverfront development project and the themed squares was awarded to Batlle i Roig architects. Six independent themed squares are planned, each with a useful exhibition space of approximately 1,000 square meters and with detailed monographic treatment based around water and sustainable development.

Cultural Program and Shows: The expo plans to stage an extensive array of shows and events for all kinds of visitors, with water as a source of inspiration. Different programming blocks have been organized depending on the programmer: Expo Zaragoza 2008, participating countries, or other organizations. More than 3,400 activities are to be staged over 93 days, many of them during the Expo Night (from 9 P.M. until 3 A.M.). As a way of generating publicity, Expo Zaragoza 2008 is to sponsor the new tour of *Cirque du Soleil* in seven

European cities: Berlin, Brussels, London, Frankfurt, Düsseldorf, Paris, and Madrid before the expo, and during the expo, members of the famous company will take part in the daily parade at the expo site.

Art: EXPOAGUA Zaragoza 2008 is holding a competition to find artworks for a major exhibition along the banks of the river Ebro. A total of 25 art installations by artists from all over the world are to be chosen and installed. One of the essential conditions stipulated in both the management plan for the expo site and surrounding area and the expo accompaniment plan is the recovery and improvement of the banks of the Ebro, the Water Park, and the river bank areas in the city. The artistic program aims to emphasize the most significant and meaningful public spaces along the city's main road, accentuating on the one hand the unifying nature of the project and on the other hand the diverse landscape created by different interactions between the river and the city.

Budget: The total investment by the Spanish government, the Aragon government and the town council of Zaragoza is around 1,650 million euros, including not only the expo site but also improvements in city facilities. In early 2007, private investment had reached 60 million euros and was expected to grow as the opening day got closer.

Post-Expo: The exposition's commitment does not end with the closing ceremony on September 14, 2008. Organizers want to go beyond the expo itself, expressing the hope that Zaragoza, its inhabitants, and its visitors will continue to be a first-class tourist destination with sustainable environmental development. The expo site will become a cultural and scientific park that will coexist with adjacent sporting facilities and parkland and accommodate both cultural and popular leisure activities. Modular spaces will be included for use as offices and services in the former international pavilions. The aim is to prioritize the corresponding advanced tertiary

This photograph of a model of the Bridge Pavilion, designed by Zaha Hadid, echos the exposition's water related theme (courtesy of Bureau of International Expositions).

uses and top-level productive spaces, a funda-mental objective that is supported by the high-quality of the urban and architectural sur-roundings. In addition to these modular spaces, the buildings that will house the themed exhibits during the exposition (Bridge Pavil-ion, River Aquarium and Water Tower), as well as the Spain Pavilion, will be turned into cul-tural amenities by the city. The conference cen-ter will continue to be used as a state-of-the-art convention center. The Aragon Pavilion will be converted into an office building for the regional government of Aragon. The commer-cial and catering areas, as well as the hotels, will increase the attractiveness of the city for tourists. In short, beyond 2008, Zaragoza will have a metropolitan park complex, providing an attractive combination of educational and leisure elements, with the use of the adjacent business area.

The Zaragoza Charter: The Zaragoza Charter will consist in a set of principles that will contribute to the development of a univer-sal ethics about the sustainable use of water. Its values will assume that the old approaches to water management are to be overcome. The result of the intense activity the Water Tribune is performing from June 2006 until September 2008 will be conceptually expressed in this dec-laration of principles, a charter that the sign-ing countries will be committed to act upon. It will essentially guarantee that all regions pro-vide access to water in adequate quantity and at a fair price. An institution will be established to watch over the legacy of Expo Zaragoza 2008.

Bibliography

It has not yet been determined where the records of the Zaragoza exposition will be perma-nently housed. However, the archives of the BIE in Paris have a substantial amount of informa-tion regarding the origins and planning of the exposition, and researchers should make inquiries there as to specific published and unpublished documents

Shanghai 2010

Susan Fernsebner

World Exposition 2010

In Shanghai's World Exposition of 2010, officials of the People's Republic of China (PRC) have embraced the opportunity to intro-duce the world to a twenty-first century metrop-olis, and, moreover, to present the process of a metropole's construction itself. Exposition organizers presented the theme "A Better City, a Better Life" in their winning bid before the Bureau of International Expositions (BIE), promoting this theme amidst a claim as the very first officially recognized world exposition to be held in a developing country. The World Expo of 2010, like the Summer Olympic Games to be hosted by Beijing in 2008, has been cele-brated in the People's Republic of China as rep-resentative of China's true arrival on a global stage.

In many ways, the thematic focus of the event is intended to unite both the local and the global. As planned, the exposition is to offer a site at which all can study issues related to urban development, including architecture, environmental concerns, and "eco-friendly" methods of urban planning, as well as the rela-tionship "between cities and their rural hinter-land." Celebrating new methods for development on multiple levels, then, the exposition is intended as take a closer look at urban space within the city as well as a city's relationship to the broader terrain that surrounds it, region-ally and globally. Exposition planners have advertised their intent to explore the ways in

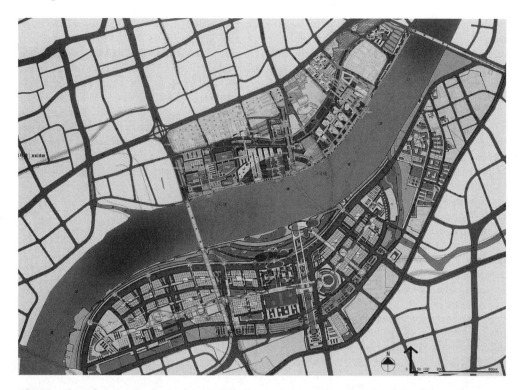

This site plan of Expo 2010 shows that it will be located along both sides of the Huangpu River, south of the central business district of Shanghai (courtesy Bureau of Shanghai World Expo Coordination).

which cities are reinvented, spatially and socially, from within. This concern is not limited to the Pudong district's shining towers, but also to less celebrated areas of the city. Indeed, the event has been advertised as a site for addressing urban poverty in the course of rebuilding a city, and, as such, an event that will answer the United Nations Millennium Declaration advocating the reduction and elimination of urban slums.

These thematic concerns naturally coincide with the planned location and design for the space occupied by the world exposition. Planners chose a declining district of the city that sits along both banks of the Huangpu River, an area that has been home to aging factories, warehouses, and residences. This location is one that invokes both history and a vision of the future as it bridges older quarters of town including the Shanghai Bund, the famous historical home to the old foreign concessions (and current tourist centers), and the new post-modern palisades of Pudong that now dwarf the older banking houses from across the

river banks. In choosing this site, expo designers intend to explore urban development in light of social, architectural, economic, and environmental concerns as well as to promote a new vision of China itself. The choice of location is directly tied to the theme of reinventing old and historical urban centers as a new metropolis, a concern that is presented through Shanghai organizers' vision of "remodeling communities in a city." The site of the exposition is intended as a laboratory for experimentation and collective examination of the ways in which an urban space might be remade. The process of its construction, moreover, is already presented as a case in point. Run-down factories in the area will be renovated and recycled for use as exposition offices, display and retail space (and the construction of a museum), while urban residents of the area have been promised opportunities for relocation to new and improved neighborhoods in other parts of the city.

The logistics of the process are substantial. The expo grounds alone will cover more than 795 acres. The architecture of the exposition will, in many ways, directly embody themes related to its own construction. Major pavilions planned for the event include five theme pavilions, all devoted to urban concerns, with the titles "Eternal City," "Dynamic City," "Innovative City," "Evergreen City," and "Livable City." Global attention to urban concerns will also be encouraged at the site of a "City of Harmony" Experimental Center. This center is planned to offer both indoor and outdoor exhibits, with a specific invitation for other cities from around the world to present their own displays on the broad theme of designing urban centers and communities. This "City of Harmony" Center will be included within a ten-hectare (24 acres) space at the exposition devoted to interactive display that is intended to allow visitors to learn more about the process of urban design through direct experimentation. Among film and computer animated displays, the fairground will also highlight related documentaries on the subject of urban space. Indeed, exposition organizers have specifically advertised the exposition as its own object of study. As plans have it, visitors will have the opportunity to survey the mechanics of creating this particular urban environment in both its architecture and green space, the provisions of its energy and material supplies, as well as the logistics of transport and refuse management. The exposition is also intended to offer a world expo museum as a permanent attraction on the grounds, its directors working in partnership with other museums around the world to present traveling exhibits of art and historical pieces borrowed from other countries. The global array of objects in all of these sites at the exposition will be matched with a parade of special days and holiday celebrations at the exposition (including days devoted to the environment, issues of labor, the anti-tobacco movement, and the United Nations, among others, as well as traditional holidays such as China's Mid-Autumn Festival).

The PRC government has made substantial investments in the project. The total budget has been set at approximately $3.6 billion dollars, with funding provided by the central government and Shanghai municipal government, as well as bonds and bank loans. $2.75 billion is intended for construction projects, with

another $1.35 billion anticipated for operation expenditures. In keeping with such scale of outlay, in both funding and the expanse of the site itself, organizers also anticipate a substantial audience for the event. Roughly 70 million visitors are expected to attend, with a general estimate of 400,000 to 600,000 visitors touring the grounds on any given day. The exposition is already celebrated as a welcome boost to the tourist industry for Shanghai and the People's Republic of China more broadly. A similar boost appears to have been anticipated by corporate entities as well. For example, the Coca-Cola Corporation publicly endorsed the People's Republic of China in its bid for the exposition before the BIE (other rivals included Moscow as well as cities in South Korea, Mexico, and Poland).

Indeed, the prominent endorsement provided by Coca-Cola fits with a legacy to which the World Exposition of 2010 in Shanghai, like the city itself, already advertises a clear claim. Organizers have directly noted that the year of the exposition will mark the thirty-second year since the beginning of China's reform policies in 1978. Marking both the end of the Cultural Revolution and the beginning of market reform, these policies presented new definitions of "socialist modernization" that celebrated a new culture of management and development, new policies for production, and mandated reaffirmation of a system of laws and standards that would serve the goal of modernization itself. The year 1978 thus was a watershed in China's political and economic history, and, as it happens, was the same year that Coca-Cola announced it would open a bottling plant in Shanghai. The World Exposition of 2010 thus appears to herald the success of these reforms with a celebration of modern development and a culture of "business dynamism." Most significantly, for audiences at home and abroad, the world exposition of 2010 in Shanghai is intended to confirm a second development—namely China's prominence upon a global stage and claim to all the modernist metaphors that accompany a twenty-first century.

Bibliography

In keeping with the world expo organizers' embrace of the cutting edge, minute details of preparation for the event has been presented in online publications, reports, bulletins, and promotional news accounts available at the exposition's extensive website. (*www.expo2010china.com*). Key newspaper sources for exploration of both the upcoming event and its context can be found in Shanghai's newspapers, particularly the *Jiefang ribao* and *Wenhui bao*, as well as national news sources such as the Xinhua news service and the *Renmin ribao (People's Daily)*. Abroad, both the BBC news service as well as the Los Angeles *Times* and New York *Times* have also offered coverage to issues of development, management of local dislocation, architecture, and general organization for the event.

Appendix A: The Bureau of International Expositions

Vicente González Loscertales

Exhibitions are not a recent invention. They date back to the times when large-scale markets were regularly held in cities which, because they were located at major route intersections, attracted visitors and brought prosperity. Crowds of people, some of whom had travelled great distances, would visit these markets, stay at the site, and exchange a wide variety of articles. These events thus provided a forum for expressing and evaluating ideas and for demonstrating and comparing skills.

Through these gatherings, a highly beneficial atmosphere of mutual understanding and fellowship developed between people of different nations and often conflicting cultures. Buyers and sellers would flock to the cities of Lyon, Frankfurt, and Leipzig in particular from all over medieval Europe.

The commercial transactions of long ago thus paved the way for the international exhibitions of today, which play an educational role and are instrumental in promoting understanding throughout the world.

The first international exhibition in the modern sense of the term took place in 1851 in London, capital of England, the world's leading industrial power, which with its vast empire had profited handsomely from free trade and the prosperity of the Victorian era. The exhibition was an overwhelming success.

Every nation was invited to contribute to the exhibition, which constituted an inventory of all branches of human endeavour. Paris took over and organised brilliant exhibitions in 1867, 1878, 1889 and 1900. Soon other large centres were also eager to welcome craftsmen and manufacturers from all over the world, and among the most successful international exhibitions were those held in Vienna, Amsterdam, Brussels, Barcelona, St. Louis, Turin, and Philadelphia.

These events inevitably gave rise to numerous conflicts of interest and were often characterized by very poor organization. This state of confusion caused the participating governments serious problems and, as a result they felt the need to establish regulations to prevent the proliferation of exhibitions and provide participants with certain guarantees. As interest and experience in exhibitions grew it became apparent that the various parties had to be brought together and their differences aired in an attempt to solve common problems.

An international agreement seemed necessary. Paris had been calling for one since 1907. In 1912 the German government took the initiative and called interested governments together in order to work out the basis for an agreement.

The governments were quick to respond and they expressed the desire to establish regulations to improve relations between organizers and participants and between inviting governments and official or private exhibitors.

It was the Berlin Diplomatic Conference

411

that established the basis for an international convention governing international exhibitions. However, the diplomatic decision that resulted could not be ratified because of World War I.

The governments took up the matter again in 1920, but it was not until November 22, 1928, at another conference in Paris, that delegates of thirty-one countries signed the first convention governing, in a constructive manner, the organisation of international exhibitions.

The International Convention of 1928 brought order to the world exhibitions' situation by regulating their frequency and outlining the rights and obligations of the exhibitors and organisers. At the same time the International Exhibitions Bureau (BIE) was created in order to ensure compliance with the provisions of the Convention.

Subsequently two protocols -one concluded in 1948 and the other in 1966 — amended the Convention on the key issue of exhibition frequency.

In view of the precedents that had been set during the International Exhibitions Bureau's forty years of existence and also in view of new economic data (faster rate of progress, decreased travel time, and the appearance of new countries on the world scene), a thorough revision of the 1928 Convention was necessary.

This revision was undertaken in 1965 and resulted in the signing of the Protocol of November 30, 1972, which has since governed the organization of international exhibitions. Since the beginning of its regulatory activity in 1931, over 40 expos that have attracted more than 500 million visitors have been organized under the auspices of the International Exhibitions Bureau.

From the earliest date, the BIE has accepted the need to differentiate between two categories of exhibitions; major events having a theme of a general nature and smaller, more economical events, where the theme is more precise and specialized.

But the nomenclature and precise definition of these have changed over the years, as the BIE has seen the need for the exhibition medium to adapt to changing international circumstances. Under the 1972 amendment to the protocol, the title of universal or international exhibitions now describes registered exhibitions.

These exhibitions last up to six months, have no limitation of the size of the site and are the major events of the future. They have a frequency of every five years.

In the intervening years between two registered exhibitions, member states can organise on recognized exhibition which is restricted to 25 hectares for the site, has a duration not exceeding three months and has a specialized theme.

The BIE also continues to recognize the Horticultural Exhibitions such as the Netherlands Floriade in 2002, which are recommended by the International Association of Horticultural Producers.

It is important to note that it is not only the international nature of the participants that makes an expo an international event. Expos are also international events because the rules and regulations of an expo are internationally agreed upon by all the member states of the BIE.

Controlling not only the frequency and quality of exhibitions but, in particular, also the conditions of participation for international participants is a continuous process carried out by the BIE from the inception of a project to its close. During an exhibition, the BIE maintains its control function through the College of Commissioners General at the exhibition and an elected Steering Committee, which maintains not only a close liaison with the exhibition organizers but, if needed with the BIE.

The International Exhibitions Bureau also represents the commitment of its member states to pursue the cultural, economic and political mission connected to events that are unique for their breadth, their drive to innovate and their force of attraction.

The BIE is the guardian of the memory and values of expos, and ensures the innovation and evolution of Expos. It promotes the network of cities that have hosted expos (AVE) which favors the exchanges between organizers, contributes to the preservation of their legacy and inspires the future.

Through its unique experience in the organization and follow-up of expos, the BIE supports the organizers and the participants during the preparation, ensures the respect of the theme, advises the organizer on the reuse of the site and of how to transmit the expo message.

Appendix B:
Fair Statistics

This appendix lists the opening and closing dates for the fairs included in this volume, the size of the site, the paid attendance and total attendance, and the profit or loss incurred by the fair organizers. Although we have included what we believe to be the most accurate figures available, readers should be aware that substantial discrepancies abound in the literature. The date of the formal ceremony opening of a fair may differ from the date the public was first admitted; generally, we have used the latter. Attendance figures may vary considerably as well. It is not always clear whether they include free or discounted admissions, employees passing through the gates, tickets sold but not used, or artificial inflation carried out by promoters. Where information was available, we have tried to distinguish between total attendance and paid attendance; unfortunately, this distinction is not often made in fair records. Profit and loss figures present even greater problems because of different accounting procedures over the years, whether the sale of fair assets are included in the final figures, and whether or not underwriters' guarantees are factored in. Therefore, these figures should be used with prudence.

Site/Year	Open Date	Close Date	Size (acres)	Attendance Paid (+000)	Attendance (+000)	Profit/(Loss)
London 1851	May 1, 1851	October 15, 1851	19	6,039		£186,437
Dublin 1853	May 12, 1853	October 29, 1853	2.5	956	1,156	£19,000
New York 1853–1854	July 14, 1853	November 1, 1854	4		1,150	($300,000)
Paris 1855	May 15, 1855	November 15, 1855	29	5,162		(FF 8.3 million)
London 1862	May 1, 1862	November 15, 1862	23.5		6.211	broke even
Dublin 1865	May 9, 1865	November 10, 1865	17	956		£10,074
Paris 1867	April 1, 1867	October 1, 1867	215	9,063		FF 2.9 million
London 1871–1874	May 1, 1871	September 30, 1871	100		1,142	£17,671
	May 1, 1872	October 19, 1872	100		647	(£ 5,780)
	April 14, 1873	October 31, 1873	100		498	(£12,126)
	April 6, 1874	October 31, 1874	100		467	(£17821)
Vienna 1873	May 1, 1873	November 1, 1873	280	5,058	7,250	(15 million gldn)
Philadelphia 1876	May 10, 1876	November 10, 1876	285	8,004	9,789	($4.5 million)
Paris 1878	May 1, 1878	November 10, 1878	185	13,000	16,032	(FF31 million)
Sydney 1879–1880	September 17, 1879	April 20, 1880	24	850	1,117	(£103,615)
Melbourne 1880–1881	October 1, 1880	April 30, 1881	21		1,459	(£277,292)
Atlanta 1881	October 5, 1881	December 31, 1881	19	196	290	loss
Amsterdam 1883	May 1, 1883	Ocotber 31, 1881	62		1,439	
Boston 1883–1884	September 3, 1883	January 12, 1884	3		300	($25,000)
Calcutta 1883–1884	December 4, 1883	March 10, 1884	22		1,000	profit?
Louisville 1883–1887	August 1, 1883	November 10, 1883	45	770	971	
New Orleans 1884–1885	December 16, 1884	June 1, 1885	249		1,159	($470,000+)
Antwerp 1885	May 2, 1885	November 2, 1885	54.3		3,500	broke even
Edinburgh 1886	May 6, 1886	October 30, 1886	25		2,770	£5,555
London 1886	May 4, 1886	November 10, 1886	24		5,551	£34,642
Adelaide 1887–1888	June 21, 1887	January 7, 1888	18		767	
Barcelona 1888	May 20, 1888	December 9, 1888	115		2,240	$1,737
Glasgow 1888	May 8, 1888	November 10, 1888	70		5,748	£41,000
Melbourne 1888–1889	August 1, 1888	January 31, 1889	35		2,200	(£238,000)
Paris 1889	May 6, 1889	November 6, 1889	228	27,722	32,350	$600,000
Dunedin 1889–1890	November 26, 1889	April 19, 1890	12.5		625	£579
Kingston 1891	January 27, 1891	May 2, 1891	23		303	(£4,500)
Madrid 1892	October 30, 1892	January 31,1893				
Chicago 1893	May 1, 1893	October 30, 1893	686	21,477	27,529	$1.4 million
Antwerp 1894	May 5, 1894	November 5, 1894	86.5		3,000	profit
San Francisco 1894	January 27, 1894	June 30, 1894	160		1,356	$66,851
Hobart 1894–1895	November 15, 1894	May 15, 1894	11		290	loss

Site/Year	Open Date	Close Date	Size(acres)	Attendance Paid (+000)	Attendance (+000)	Profit/(Loss)
Atlanta 1895	September 18, 1895	December 31, 1895	189	780		($25,000)
Brussels 1897	May 10, 1897	November 8, 1897	148		6,000	loss
Guatemala City 1897	March 15, 1897	June 30, 1897	800			$39
Nashville 1897	May 1 1897	October 31, 1897	200	1,167		
Stockholm 1897	May 1 1897	October 3, 1897	514			
Omaha 1898	June 1 1898	October 31, 1898	200	1,778	2,614	
Paris 1900	April 5, 1900	November 12, 1900	553	39,027	50,861	FF7.1 million
Buffalo 1901	May 1 1901	November 13, 1900	350	5,307	8,120	($3 million)
Glasgow 1901	May 2, 1901	November 9, 1901	75		11,560	£35,216
Charleston 1901–1902	December 1, 1901	June 1, 1902	160			
Torino (Turin) 1902	May 1902	November 12, 1902				
Hanoi 1902–1903	November 16, 1902	February 16, 1903	41			
St. Louis 1904	April 30, 1904	December 1, 1904	1,271.80	12,804	19,695	$1.02 million
Liège 1905	April 27, 1905	November 6, 1905	52		7,000	BF75,117
Portland 1905	June 1 1905	October 15, 1905	400	1,588	2,554	$84,840
Milan 1906	April 28, 1906	October 31, 1906	250		5,500	
Christchurch 1906–1907	November 1, 1906	April 15, 1907	14		1,968	(£81,430)
Dublin 1907	May 4, 1907	November 9, 1907	52		2,750	(£103,345)
Jamestown 1907	April 26, 1907	November 30, 1907	400	1,481	2,851	($2.5 million)
London 1908	May 14, 1908	October 31, 1908	140		8,400	profit
Seattle 1909	June 1 1909	October 16, 1909	250	2,766	3,741	$63,676
Brussels 1910	April 23, 1910	November 1, 1910	220		13,000	(BF10,000)
Nanking 1910	June 6, 1910	December 1960	90 – 100			
London 1911	May 12, 1911	October 28, 1911	200+		11,000	loss
Ghent 1913	April 26, 1913	December 1, 1913	309	13,128	18,876	
San Francisco 1915	February 20, 1915	December 4, 1915	635			$2.4 million
San Diego 1915–1916	January 1, 1915	December 31, 1916	400		2,050 (1915)	
Rio de Janeiro 1922–1923	September 7, 1922	July 31, 1923	62	3,626		
Wembley 1924–1925	April 23, 1924	November 1, 1924	216	15,081	17,403	(£1.6 million)
	May 9, 1925	October 31, 1925	216	7,590	9,699	
Paris 1925	April 30, 1925	October 15 1925	72		14,000	
Dunedin 1925–1926	November 17, 1925	May 1, 1926	65		3,200	(£16,217)
Philadelphia 1926	May 31, 1926	November 30, 1926	1,000	5,853	6,408	($5.6 million)
Long Beach 1928	July 27, 1928	September 3, 1928	63		1,100	broke even
Barcelona 1929–1930	May 19, 1929	January 15, 1930	291.5			
Seville 1929–1930	May 9, 1929	June 21, 1930	494		1,500	
Antwerp 1930	April 26, 1930	November 5, 1930	170.5	468		(BF7 million)

Site/Year	Open Date	Close Date	Size (acres)	Attendance Paid (+000)	Attendance (+000)	Profit/(Loss)
Liège 1930	May 3, 1930	November 3, 1930	165			BF15 million
Paris 1931	May 6, 1931	November 16, 1931	148	32,000	33,489	FF29,000
Chicago 1933–1934	May 27, 1933	November 12, 1933	427	22,566	27,303 (1933)	$160,000
	May 29, 1934	October 31, 1934	427	16,486	21,066 (1934)	
Brussels 1935	April 27, 1935	November 6, 1935	250	20,000	26,000	BF45 million
San Diego 1935–1936	May 26, 1935	November 11, 1935	185		4,785	$44,000
	February 12, 1936	September 9, 1936	185		2,004	
Johannesburg 1936–1937	September 15, 1936	January 15, 1937	100		1,500	(£70,000)
Paris 1937	May 24, 1937	November 2, 1937	259	31,412	34,000	(FF495 million)
Glasgow 1938	May 3, 1938	October 29, 1938	175		12,593	(£118,691)
New York 1939–1940	April 30, 1939	October 31,1939	1,216.50		25,817 (1939)	($18.7 million)
	May 11, 1940	October 27, 1940	1,216.50		19,116 (1940)	
San Francisco 1939–1940	February 18, 1939	October 29, 1939	400		17,042	($559,423)
	May 25, 1940	September 29, 1940	400			loss
Wellington 1939–1940	November 8, 1939	May 4, 1940	55		2,641	
Lisbon 1940	June 2, 1940	December 2, 1940	29			
London 1951	May 4, 1951	September 30, 1951	65		8,000	
Port-au-Prince 1949–1950	December 8, 1949	June 8, 1950	500	250+		
Brussels 1958	April 17, 1958	October 19, 1958	74		41,454	(BF3 billion)
Seattle 1962	April 21, 1962	October 21, 1962	646		9,640	
New York 1964–1965	April 22, 1964	October 18, 1964	646		27,148	($21 million)
	April 21, 1965	October 17, 1965	646		24,459	
Montreal 1967	April 28, 1967	October 29, 1967	988.7	50,306	54,992	(C$274 million)
San Antonio 1968	April 6, 1968	October 6, 1968	92.6		6,384	($5.5 million)
Osaka 1970	March 15, 1970	September 13, 1970	815		64,219	$146 million
Spokane 1974	May 4, 1974	November 3, 1974	100		5,600	$47 million+
Okinawa 1975–1976	July 17 1975	January 18, 1976	247.1		3,480	
Knoxville 1982	May 1, 1982	October 31, 1982	72		11,150	loss
New Orleans 1984	May 12, 1984	November 11, 1984	81.4		7,300	($121 million)
Tsukuba 1985	March 17, 1985	September 16, 1985	250		20,335	
Vancouver 1986	May 2, 1986	October 13, 1986	175		22,000	(C$336 million+)
Brisbane 1988	April 30, 1988	October 30, 1988	98		15,760	
Genoa 1992	May 15, 1992	August 15, 1992	12		1,000	
Seville 1992	April 20, 1992	October 12, 1992	531		41,815	25,605 million pesetas
Taejon 1993	August 7, 1993	November 7, 1993	247		14,005	
Lisbon 1998	May 22, 1998	September 30, 1998	123		11,000	($1.32 billion)

Site/Year	Open Date	Close Date	Size (acres)	Attendance Paid (+000)	Attendance (+000)	Profit/ (Loss)
Hanover 2000	June 1, 2000	October 31, 2000	320		18,100	($1.2 billion)
Aichi 2005	March 25, 2005	September 23, 2005	427.5		22,049	$109 million
Zaragoza 2008*	June 14, 2008	September 14, 2008	57		est. 6,000	
Shanghai 2010*	May 1, 2010	October 31, 2010	1359		est. 70,000	($120 million)

*projected statistics

Appendix C: Fair Officials

This appendix lists the principal individuals responsible for the management and operation of each of the fairs included in this volume. Wherever possible, titles carried by those individuals are also indicated. In some cases, a lack of sufficient reliable information precluded the listing of more than one individual or the officials' titles for a particular fair.

London 1851. Prince Albert, Chairman, Royal Commission; Henry Cole.

Dublin 1853. William Dargan; Richard Turner.

New York 1853–1854. Theodore Sedgwick, President of the Association (1852–1854). Phineas T. Barnum, President of the Association (1854).

Paris 1855. Prince Napoleon, Chairman of Exposition Committee; Frederic Le Play, committee member; Michael Chevalier, committee member; Emile Pereire, committee member.

London 1862. Earl Granville, Royal Commissioner; Wentworth Dilke, Commissioner; Colonel Lawrence Shadwell, General Manager; William Fairbairn, Commissioner; Marquis of Chandos, Commissioner; Thomas Baring.

Dublin 1865. Duke of Leinster; Lord Talbot de Malahide; Benjamin Lee Guinness.

Dunedin 1865. John Hyde Harris, President of the Executive of the New Zealand Exhibition; James Hector, Commissioner and Juror; Alfred Eccles, Secretary; Thomas Forrester, Superintendent.

Paris 1867. Frédéric Le Play, Commissioner General.

London 1871–1874. Prince of Wales, President of Royal Commission; Marquis of Ripon, Chair of General Purposes Committee; Earl Granville, Chair of Finance Committee.

Vienna 1873. Baron Wilhelm von Schwarz-Senborn, General Director; Archduke Charles Ludwig, Fair Protector; Archduke Rainer, President.

Philadelphia 1876. John Welsh, President of the Board of Finance; Joseph R. Hawley, President of Centennial commission.

Paris 1878. Jean Baptiste Krantz, Commissioner General; Charles Dietz-Monnin, Director of the French Section; Georges Berger, Director of Foreign Section; Marquis of Chennevières, Director of Fine Arts.

Sydney 1879–1880. Lord Augustus Loftus, President of the Exposition Committee.

Melbourne 1880–1881. William Clark, Committee President; J. J. Casey, Executive Vice-President; James Munro, Executive Vice-President; Sir Graham Berry, Prime Minister.

Atlanta 1881. Hannibal Ingalls Kimball, Chairman, Executive Committee of the International Cotton; Exposition Association and Director General; Joseph E. Brown, President of the International Cotton Exposition Association.

Amsterdam 1883. Edouard Agostini, Technical Advisor; Oliver Claude Sainte-Foxe, French Commissioner.

Boston 1883–1884. Nathaniel J. Bradlee, President; Charles Benjamin Norton, Secretary, Foreign Exhibition Association; Frederick W. Lincoln, Treasurer.

Calcutta 1883–1884. Augustus Rivers Thompson, President of the Executive Committee; S. T. Trevor, Vice-President of the Executive Committee; Jules Joubert, General Manager.

Louisville 1883–1887. J. H. Lindenberger, Committee Chairman; Bidermann du Pont, Exposition President; J. M Wright, General Manager.

New Orleans 1884–1885. Edmund Richardson, President; Albert Baldwin, Vice-President; William B. Smith, Vice-President; Edward A. Burke, Director General; F. C. Morehead, Commissioner General.

Antwerp 1885. Victor Lynen, President of the Executive Committee; Auguste Beernaert, Director of Central Committee.

Edinburgh 1886. Queen Victoria, Royal Patroness; Edward, Prince of Wales, Royal Patron; Marquis of Lothian, Honorary President; Sir James Gowans, Chairman of the Executive Council; Henry Anthony Hedley, Manager of the Exhibition; James Marchbank, Secretary; Thomas Gaff, Treasurer.

London 1886. Prince of Wales, President of Royal Commission; Sir Philip Cunliffe-Owens, Secretary to Royal Commission; Edward Cunliffe-Owens, Assistant Secretary; J. R. Royle, Assistant Secretary for India.

Adelaide 1887–1888. Sir Edwin T. Smith, Vice-President; Sir Samuel Davenport, Executive Commissioner; Jonathan Fairfax Conigrave, Secretary.

Barcelona 1888. Francesc de P. Ruis I Taulet, President of Central Committee; Manel Girona I Agrafel, Royal Delegate.

Glasgow 1888. Sir Archibald Campbell, President; Sir James King, Chairman of the Executive Council; Henry Anthony Hedley, Manager of the Exposition; W. M. Cunningham, Secretary; Alfred Brown, Treasurer.

Melbourne 1888–1889. George Higinbotham, President of the Exhibition Committee; Sir James MacBain, successor to Higinbotham; Sir Graham Beny, Agent General.

Paris 1889. Pierre Tirad, Commissioner General; Charles Adolphe, Minister of Public Works; Georges Berger, General Manager of the Exposition.

Dunedin 1889–1890. John Roberts, President; R.E.N. Twopeny, Executive Commissioner; Jules Joubert, General Manager.

Kingston 1891. Governor H. Al Blake, President; S. Lee Bapty, General Manager; A. C. Sinclair, Promoter.

Chicago 1893. Thomas W. Palmer, President of World's Columbian Commission; Harlow Higinbotham, President of World's Columbian Exposition Corporation; Daniel H. Burnham, Chief of Construction.

Antwerp 1894. Count of Ursel, Commissioner General; Count of Pret Roose of Calesburg, President of the Executive Committee.

San Francisco 1894. Michael H. de Young, President and Director General.

Hobart 1894–1895. Jules Joubert, General Manager; William Moore, President and ex officio chairman of all committees; Russell Young, Solicitor.

Atlanta 1895. Charles A. Collier, President and Director-General; W. A. Hemphill, First Vice-President; Samuel H. Inman, financial Director.

Brussels 1897. Adrien d'Outremont, Commissioner-General; Emile Demot, Executive Committee member; Maurice Lemonnier, Executive Committee member; Nigor Thys, Executive Committee member; Senator Georges Dupret, Executive Committee member.

Guatemala City 1897. Juan F. Ponciano.

Nashville 1897. John W. Thomas, President; V. L. Kirkman, First Vice-President; W. A. Henderson, Second Vice-President; John Overton, Third Vice-President.

Stockholm 1897. H.R.H. The Crown Prince, Chairman of the Central Committee; H.R.H. Prince Eugene, Chairman of the Art Exhibit Department; Governor Baron Gustaf Tamm, Chairman of the Administration Committee; Oscar Bjorck, Commissioner of the Art Exhibit; Arthur Thiel, Commissioner for the Industrial Arts.

Omaha 1898. Gurdon W. Wattles, President; Alvin Saunders, Vice-President; Herman Kountze, Treasurer; John A. Wakefield, Secretary; Edward Rosewater, Publicity.

Paris 1900. Alfred Picard, Commissioner General; Henri Chardon, Secretary-General; M. J. Bouvard, Director of Architecture and of Parks and Gardens; Ferdinand W. Peck, Commissioner General of the United States.

Buffalo 1901. John G. Milburn, President; William I. Buchanan, Director General; C. Y. Turner, Director of Color; Karl Bitter, Director of Sculpture.

Glasgow 1901. Lord Blythswood, President; Henry Anthony Hedley, General Manager of the Exhibition; James Hunter Dickson, Treasurer.

Charleston 1901–1902. F. G. Wagener, President.

Torino 1902. Raimondo D'Aronco, Chief Architect.

Hanoi 1902–1904. Paul Bourgeois, Secretary of French Commission on Foreign Expositions; Guillame Capus, Director General.

St. Louis 1904. David R. Francis, President; William H. Thompson, Treasurer; Walter B. Stevens, Secretary.

Liège 1905. Richard Lamarche, Commissioner General; Count of Flanders, President of Honor of the Superior Patronage Commission; Prince Albert, President of Exposition Commission.

Portland 1905. Henry Corbett, President (1902–1903); Harvey Scott, President (1903–1904); Henry Goode, President (1904–1906); Theodore Hardee, Assistant to the President; John Wakefield, Director of Concessions and Admissions; Ion Lewis, Director of Architecture; Oskar Huber, Director of Works; Henry Reed, Secretary and Director of Exploitation.

Milan 1906. Senator C. Mangili, President of Executive Committee; Conte Crivelli Serbelloni, Vice President of Executive Committee.

Christchurch 1906–1907. Sir Joseph G. Ward, President; W. Hall Jones, Commissioner.

Dublin 1907. Marquis of Ormonds, President; William M. Murphy. Chairman of Finance and General Purposes Committee; James Shanks, Chief Executive Officer.

Jamestown 1907. Fitzhugh Lee, President of Exposition Company; Henry St. George, successor of Lee.

London 1908. Imre Kiralfy, Director of Exposition Company; John Belcher, Managing Architect; Marius Tondoire, Managing Architect.

Seattle 1909. John E. Chilberg, Head of the Executive Committee; Ira A. Nadeau, Director General; John Langley Howard, Chief Architect.

Brussels 1910. Emile Demot, Presiding Officer of the Executive Committee; Eugène Keyon, Director General; Count Adrien van der Burch, Director General; Robert d'Ursel, Commissioner General.

Nanking 1910. Tuan Fang, Governor-General; Chang Jen-chun, Successor of Fang; H. E. Chin Chi, Director General; Yang Shih-chi, Adjudicator General.

London 1911. Forbes Dennis, Honorary Secretary; Frank Lascelles, Master of the Pageant; H. W. Matthews, General Business Manager.

Ghent 1913. Gerard Cooreman, President of the Executive Committee.

San Francisco 1915. Charles C. Moore, President; William H. Crocker, Vice-President; Reuben B. Hale, Vice-President; I. W. Hellman, Jr., Vice-President; M. H. de Young, Vice-President; Leon Sloss, Vice-President; James Rolph, Jr., Vice-President.

San Diego 1915–1916. G. Aubrey Davidson, President; D. C. Collier, Director General; Frank P. Allen, Jr., Director of Works.

Rio de Janeiro 1922–1923. Carlos Sampaio, Commissioner General.

Wembley 1924–1925. Prince of Wales, President; Lord Stevenson, Chairman of the Board; Sir Travers Clark, Chief Administrator; Sir John W. Simpson, Architect; Maxwell Ayrton, Architect; Sir E. O. Williams, Consulting Engineer.

Paris 1925. Fernand Davy, General Commissioner; Charles Plumet, Chief Architect.

Dunedin 1925–1926. J. Sutherland Ross, President and Chairman; Charles Speight, Deputy Chairman; Charles P. Hainsworth, General Manager.

Philadelphia 1926. Erastus Long Austin, Business Manager, Controller, and Director in Chief; W. Freeland Kendrick, President of the Sesqui-Centennial Exhibition Association; Mrs. J. Willard Martin, Chair of the Women's Committee.

Long Beach 1928. J. David Larson, General Manager; Paul C. Graham, General Chairman.

Barcelona 1929–1930. Sr. Marques de Foronda, Director; Sr. Don Eduardo Aunos, Minister of Work.

Seville 1929–1930. Sr. Don José Cruz Conde, Royal Commissioner of the Exposition; Sr. Don Nicolas Diaz Molero, Honorary President; Sr. Don Eduardo Aunos, Minister of Work.

Antwerp/Liège 1930. Emile Dignefer, President; Baron Delvaux de Feuffe, Special Commissioner.

Stockholm 1930. Gregor Paulsson, Commissary-General; Gunnar Asplund, Chief Architect.

Paris 1931. Marshal Hubert Lyautey, General Commissioner; Governor General Marcel Oliver, General Delegate.

Chicago 1933–1934. Rufus G. Dawes, President of the Fair Corporation; Charles C. Peterson, Vice-President; Daniel H. Burnham,

Secretary; George Woodruff, Treasurer; Lenox R. Lohr, General Manager.

Brussels 1935. Adrien van der Burch, Commissioner General; Réné Fonck, Director General; Joseph van Neck, Chief Architect.

San Diego 1935–1936. Frank G. Belcher, President; Zack Farmer, Managing Director; Philip Gildred, Managing Director; Wayne M. Dailard, Managing Director.

Johannesburg 1936–1937. Councilor Maldwyn Edmund, President; Major Colin C. Frye, Chairman of Executive Committee.

Paris 1937. Edmond Labbe, Commissioner General; Paul Leon, Commissioner General adjoint; Pierre Mortier, Director of Propaganda; Jacques Greber, Chief Architect.

Glasgow 1938. Earl of Elgin, President Cecil M. Weir, Convenor of the Administrative Committee; S. J. Graham, General Manager; Thomas S. Tait, Architect.

New York 1939–1940. Grover Whalen, President; George A. McAneny, Chairman; Harvey D. Gibson, successor to McAneny.

San Francisco 1939–1940. Leland W. Cutler, Exposition President (1939); Marshall Dill, Exposition President (1940); George Creel, U.S. Commissioner (both years).

Wellington 1939–1940. The Hon. D. G. Sullivan, President; T.C.A. Hislop, Chairman of Directors.

Lisbon 1940. Captain Henrique Galvão, Organizer.

Port-au-Prince 1949–1950. Dumarsais Estime, President; Jean Fouchard, Commissioner General; John Shaw Young, U.S. Commissioner; Warren Kelchner, Deputy Commissioner; August F. Schmeidigen, Chief Architect.

Brussels 1958. Georges Moens Fernig, Commissioner General; Charles Everaerts de Velp, Secretary General, Andre Waterkeyn, Chief Engineer, Designer of the Atomium.

Seattle 1962. Edward Carlson, Chairman of Century 21 Corporation; Ewen Dingwall, Director; James N. Faber, Assistant Director.

1964–1965, New York. Robert Moses, President; Major General William E. Potter, Executive Vice-President; Brigadier General William Whipple, Jr., Chief Engineer; Thomas J. Deegan, Jr., Chairman of Executive Committee; Charles F. Preusse, Counsel to the Fair.

Montreal 1967. H. E. Pierre Dupuy, Ambassador and Commissioner General; Robert F. Shaw, Deputy Commissioner General; Jean Drapeau, Mayor of City of Montreal.

San Antonio 1968. John Connally, Commissioner General; Marshall Stevens, President; John H. White, Vice-President; Boone Powell, Chief Architect.

Osaka 1970. H.R.H. Crown Prince Akihito, Honorary President; Eisaku Sato, President; Toru Haguiwara, Commissioner General.

Spokane 1974. King F. Cole, President; Petr L. Spurney, General Manager; Roderick A. Lindsay, Chairman, Expo '74 Corporation.

Okinawa 1975–1976. Jiro Takase, Commissioner General of Japanese Government; Nobumoto Ohama, President, Japan Association; Takashi Ohki, Supervisor.

Knoxville 1982. Jake F. Butcher, Chairman of the Board; S. H. Roberts, Jr., President; Roger F. Hibbs, Treasurer.

New Orleans 1984. Floyd W. Lewis, Chairman; Petr L. Spurney, President and Chief Executive Officer; Lester E. Kabacoff, Vice-President.

Tsukuba 1985. Katsuichi Ikawa, Commissioner General; Toshiwo Doko, Chairman.

Vancouver 1986. Jimmy Pattison, Chairman; Patrick Reid, Commissioner General.

Brisbane 1988. Sir Llewellyn Edwards, Chairman; Sir Edward Williams, Commissioner General; Bob Minnikin, General Manager.

Genoa 1992. Alberto Bemporad, Commissioner-General.

Seville 1992. Manuel Olivencia Ruiz, General Commissioner (1984–1991); Emilio Cassinello Auban, General Commissioner (1991–1992); Emilio Cassinello Auban, President, Sociedad Estatal Expo '92 (1985–1991). Jacinto Pellon Diaz, President, Sociedad Estatal Expo '92 (1991–1992).

Taejon 1993. Oh Myung, Chairman, Organizing Committee.

Lisbon 1998. Jose Torres Campos, Commissioner-General.

Hanover 2000. Birgit Breul, Commissioner-General.

Aichi 2005. Shoichiro Toyoda, President, Expo 2005; Tanzo Watanabe, Commis-sioner-General.

Zaragoza 2008. Zaha Hadid, Chief Architect.

Shanghai 2010. Hua Junduo, Commissioner General.

Appendix D:
Fairs Not Included

This appendix lists, by year and city, fairs and exhibitions held after 1851 that fell short of meeting the qualifications to be included in the main body of this book. Many of them were very specialized in nature, while others lacked a suitable international scope. Yet each was important to its host city, and the list, taken as a whole, demonstrates the pervasiveness of such fairs, especially in the nineteenth century. The name of the fair is given in the language of the host country unless that language is not a common Western tongue.

Year	City (Country)	Name
1852	Cork	Irish Industrial Exhibition
1853	Brussels	Exposition d'art industriel
1853	Fredericton, New Brunswick	Native Industry Exhibition
1854	Christiania	Exhibition of Norwegian Arts and Manufactures
1854	Madrid	Exposición de Artes Industriales
1854	Melbourne	International Exhibition
1854	Munich	Allgemeine deutsche Industrie-Ausstellung
1855	Madras	Exhibition of Arts, Manufactures and Raw Materials of the Presidency
1856	Bern	Exposition des arts et des manufactures Suisses
1857	Lausanne	Exposition industrielle
1857	Manchester	Art Treasures Exhibition
1858	New York	American Industry Exhibition
1858	Turin	Esposizione Nazionale de Prodotti d'Industrie
1859	Athens	National Exhibition
1859	Hanover	Industrie-Ausstellung
1860	St. Petersburg	Exhibition of Russian Products
1860	Stockton, England	Stockton Polytechnic Exhibition
1861	Haarlem	Dutch Industries Exhibition
1861	Melbourne	Victorian Exhibition
1861–1862	Edinburgh	Exhibition of Industrial and Decorative Art
1962	Rome	Esposizione nazionale
1863	Constantinople	Exhibition of Turkish Produce and Foreign Machinery
1864	Amsterdam	Exhibition of Dutch Produce, Art, and Industry

1864	Calcutta	Agricultural Exhibition
1864	London	North London Industrial Exhibition
1864	Lucknow, India	Agricultural Exhibition
1864	Valletta, Malta	Exhibition of Local Arts and Industry
1864	Merseburg, Thuringen, Germany	Industrie-Ausstellung
1864	Turin	Esposizione del cotoni Italiani
1865	Birmingham	Metals and Trades Exhibition
1865	Bordeaux	Exposition industrielle et artistique
1865	Boulogne	Exposition internationale de peche
1865	Cologne	Landwirtschaft und gartenbau Ausstellung
1865	Freetown, Sierra Leone	Industrial Exhibition
1865	Oporto, Portugal	Exposição das Artes, Fabricantes, e Agricola
1865	Stettin, Prussia	Industrie-Ausstellung
1866	Copenhagen	Danish Industrial Exhibition
1866	Melbourne	Intercolonial Exhibition
1866	Rio de Janeiro	Exposição das Materias Primas
1866	Saigon	Cochin China Exhibition
1866	Stockholm	Scandinavian Industries Exhibition
1866	Vienna	Landwirtschaft Ausstellung
1866–1867	Melbourne	Intercolonial Exhibition of Australia
1867	The Hague	Fishery Exhibition
1868	Bucharest	National Exhibition
1868	Le Havre, France	Exposition maritime internationale
1868	Santiago	Exposición de Productos de Chile
1869	Amsterdam	International Exhibition of Domestic Economy
1869	Beauvais, France	Exposition d'agriculture et d'industrie
1869	Chartres, France	Exposition d'art et d'industrie
1869	Hamburg	Industrie- und Gewerbeausstellung
1869	Naples	Esposizione marittimo
1869	Wolverhampton, England	South Staffordshire Industrial and Fine Arts Exhibition
1870	Gujarat	Indian Cotton Exhibition
1870	Liège	Exposition internationale d'art industriel
1870	London	Workmen's International Exhibition
1870	St. Petersburg	Russian Industrial Exhibition
1870	Sydney	Intercolonial Exhibition
1870	Turin	Esposizione de prodotti d'Italiane
1870–1871	Cordova	Exposición Nacional Argentina
1871	Georgetown	Exhibition of Natural Products
1871	Lima	Exposición Nacional del Peru
1871	Naples	Esposizione internationale maritimo
1871	Saigon	Exposition agricola et industrielle
1871	Turin	Esposizione industriel del prodotti naturale
1972	Athens	National Industrial Exhibition
1872	Bogotá	Exposición de las Productos de America Sud
1872	Copenhagen	Scandinavian Art and Industry Exhibition
1872	Dublin	Arts, Industries, and Manufactures Exhibition
1872	Kyoto	Japanese Exhibition
1872	Louisville	Industrial Exhibition
1872	Melbourne	Exhibition of Natural Products and Works of Art
1873	Nashville	Industrial Exposition
1873	Chicago	Interstate Exposition

1873	Madrid	Exposición de Productos Naturales
1874	Brussels	Exposition d'art industriel
1874	Cincinnati	Industrial Exhibition
1874	Marseille	Exposition d'inventions modernes
1874	Rome	Esposizione de prodotti d'industrie Italiano
1875	Geneva	Exposition international
1875	Kyoto	Exhibition of Japanese Manufactures
1875	Melbourne	Intercolonial Exhibition
1875	Nizhni Novgorod	Nizhni Novgorod Fair
1875	Santiago	Exposición Internacional de Chile
1875–1876	Algiers	Exposition universelle
1875–1876	Montevideo	Exposición Nacional
1876	Helsinki	Finland Universal Exhibition
1876	Munich	Deutsch-österreichische Kunst- und Industrie Ausstellung
1876	New Orleans	Southern States Agricultural and Industrial Exposition
1876	Thurso, Scotland	Exhibition of Arts and Industry
1877	Capetown	South African International Exhibition
1877	Hamburg	Internationale Milchwertschafts-ausstellung
1878	Ballarat, Victoria, Australia	International Exhibition
1879	Copenhagen	Kunstindustrielle Udstilling
1879	Milan	Esposizione internazionale
1880	Berlin	Internationale Fischerei-Ausstellung
1880	Brussels	Exposition nationale
1880	Dusseldorf	Gewerben- und Kunst- Ausstellung
1881	Adelaide	International Exhibition
1881	London	International Medical and Sanitary Exhibition
1881	Milan	Esposizione industriale Italiana
1881	Paris	Exposition internationale d'électricité
1882	Biella, Italy	Esposizione generale
1882	Bordeaux	Exposition de produits industriels et agricole
1882	Christchurch	New Zealand International Exhibition
1882	Edinburgh	International Fisheries Exhibition
1882	Lille	Exposition internationale d'art industrielle
1882	Munich	Internationale Elektricitats-Ausstellung
1883	Caracas	Exposicion Nacional de Venezuela
1883	London	International Fisheries Exhibition
1883	Madrid	Exposición de Mineria y Metalurgia
1883	Prague	Industrial and Electrical Exhibition
1883	Vienna	Internationale Electrische Ausstellung
1883	Zurich	Schweizerische Landes-Ausstellung
1883–1884	Marseille	Exposition internationale maritime
1883–1884	Nice	Exposition internationale
1884	Brussels	Exposition d'art industriel
1884	Charleston, South Carolina	Industrial Exposition
1884	Edinburgh	International Forestry Exhibition
1884	London	International Health Exhibition
1884	Melbourne	Intercolonial Exhibition
1884	Philadelphia	International Electrical Exhibition
1884	Turin	Esposizione Generale Italiana

1885	Budapest	Hungarian National Exhibition
1885	Konigsberg, Prussia	Internationale Ausstellung für Polytechnik und Industrie
1885	Montenegro	Universal Exhibition
1885	Montevideo	Exposición Nacional de Uruguay
1885	Nuremberg	Internationale Ausstellung
1885	Wellington	New Zealand Industrial Exhibition
1886	Edinburgh	International Exhibition of Industry, Science, and Art
1886	Liverpool	International Shipping Exhibition
1887	Atlanta	Piedmont Exposition
1887	Le Havre, France	Exposition internationale maritime
1887	Liverpool	Royal Jubilee Exhibition
1887	London	American Exhibition
1887	Manchester	Royal Jubilee Exhibition
1887	Parma, Italy	Esposizione industriale e scientifica
1887	St. Louis	St. Louis Exposition
1888	Berlin	Landes Ausstellung
1888	Bologna	Esposizione internationale
1888	Brussels	Grand concours internationale des sciences et de l'industrie
1888	Copenhagen	Nordiske Industri-Landbrugs og Kunstudstilling
1888	Minneapolis	Industrial Exposition
1888	Jacksonville	Sub-Tropical Exposition
1888	Richmond	Virginia Agricultural, Mechanical, and Tobacco Exposition
1889	Ocala	Florida Inter-National and Semi-Tropical Exposition
1890	Boston	International Maritime Exhibition
1890	Bremen	Nord-West Deutsche Gewerbe- und Industrie-Ausstellung
1891	St. Etienne, France	Exposition d'art et d'industrie
1891–1892	Detroit	International Fair and Exposition
1891–1892	Launceston	Tasmania International Exhibition
1891–1892	Palermo	Esposizione nazionale
1892	Buffalo	International Exposition
1892	Kimberley	South Africa and International Exhibition
1892	London	International Horticulture Exhibition
1894	Luxembourg	Exposition du travail
1894	Lyons	Exposition internationale
1894	Manchester	British and Colonial Industrial Exhibition
1894	Milan	Eposizione internationale
1894	Odessa	National Exhibition
1895	Amsterdam	International Exposition
1895	Dublin	Arts and Crafts Exhibition
1895	Kyoto	National Japanese Exhibition
1895	Rio de Janeiro	Exposição National
1896	Berlin	Berliner Gewerbe-Ausstellung
1896	Budapest	Hungarian Millenary Exposition
1896	Geneva	Exposition nationale Suisse
1896	Kiel	Internationale See-Ausstellung
1896	Nishni Novgorod	Pan-Russian Exhibition

1896	Rouen	Exposition nationale et coloniale
1897	Arcachon, France	Exposition international
1897	Brisbane	Queensland International Exhibition
1897	London	Imperial Victorian Exhibition
1897	Madrid	Exposición de las Industrias de España
1898	Dijon	Exposition universelle et internationale
1898	London	Universal Exhibition
1898	Turin	Esposizione generale italiana
1899	Coolgarlie	Western Australian Internation Mining and Industrial Exhibition
1899	Ghent	Provincial Exhibition of East Flanders
1899	Philadelphia	National Export Exhibition
1899	Venice	Esposizione internationale
1900	London	Women's International Exhibition
1901	Calcutta	Indian Industrial and Agricultural Exhibition
1901	Ponta Delgada	Exposição Internacional
1901	Riga	Jubilaums-Ausstellung
1902–1903	Cork, Ireland	International Exhibition
1902	Lille	Exposition de Lille
1902	Wolverhampton	International Exhibition
1903	Madras	Madras Industrial and Arts Exhibition
1903	Nottingham	Home and International Exhibition
1903	Osaka	National Industrial Exposition
1903–1903	St. Petersburg	Exposition internationale scientifique, pedagogique et industrielle de St. Petersburg
1904	Bradford, England	International Exhibition
1905	London	Indian and Colonial Exhibition
1905	London	Naval, Shipping, and Fisheries Exhibition
1906	Bucharest	Bucharest Jubilee Exhibition
1906	London	Imperial Austrian Exposition
1906	Marseille	Exposition coloniale
1907	Amsterdam	International Exhibition
1907	Bordeaux	Exposition internationale maritime
1907	Ghent	Exposition internationale de la boulangerie et les industries connexes
1908	London	Imperial Hungarian Exhibition
1908	Zaragoza	Exposición Hispano-Française
1909	Copenhagen	Exposition française d'art decoratif
1909	London	Imperial International Exhibition
1909	Quito	National Ecuadoran Exposition
1910	Buenos Aires	Exposición Internacional de Agricultura
1910	Frankfurt	Exposition internationale des sports et de jeux
1910	London	Japan-British Exhibition
1910	Vienna	International Shooting and Field Sports Exposition
1911	Charleroi	Exposition Nationale de produits et industrie de Belgie
1911	Dresden	Internationale Hygiene Ausstellung
1911	Glasgow	Scottish National Exhibition
1911	London	Coronation Exhibition
1911	Rome	Esposizione internazionale d'arte
1911	Roubaix, France	Exposition internationale de nord de France
1911	Turin	Esposizione internationale d'industria e de laboro

1912	London	Latin-British Exhibition
1913	Auckland	Auckland Exhibition
1913	Liverpool	Liverpool Exhibition
1914	London	Anglo-American Exhibition
1915	Panama	Exposición Nacional de Panama
1918	New York	Bronx International Exposition
1921	Riga	Jubiläums-Ausstellung
1922	Marseille	Exposition nationale coloniale
1922	Singapore	Malaya-Borneo Exhibition
1923	Gothenburg	Gothenburg Tercentennial Jubilee Exposition
1925	La Paz	Exposición Industrial
1925	Tel Aviv	Palestine and Near East Exposition
1930	Dresden	Internationale Hygiene Ausstellung
1931	Berlin	Internationale Baugewerbe Ausstellung
1931	Rio de Janeiro	Exposição Internacional
1932	Bucharest	International Children's Exposition
1933	Tokyo	Women's and Children's International Exhibition
1934	Oporto	Exposição Internacional
1936	Cleveland	Great Lakes Exposition
1936	Dallas	Texas Centennial Central Exposition
1937	Dallas	Greater Texas and Pan-American Exposition
1937	Dusseldorf	Reichausstellung Scheffendes Volk
1939	Liège	Exposition internationale et technique de l'eau
1946	London	"Britain Can Make It" Exhibition
1950	Rotterdam	International Maritime Exposition
1951	Lille	International Textile Exposition
1954	São Paulo	Fería Internacional Comercial do São Paulo
1955–1956	Ciudad Trujillo, Dominican Republic	Fería Internacional para el Paz y la Fraternidad
1967	Fairbanks	Alaska 67 Centennial Exposition
1988	Glasgow	Glasgow Garden Festival
1990	Osaka	International Horticultural Exposition
1999	Kunming, China	International Horticultural Exposition
2000	London	Millennium Exhibition
2004	Barcelona	Universal Forum of World Cultures

Appendix E: Fairs That Never Were

From time to time, major world's fairs have been planned but never held. Reasons for these nonoccurrences range from the onset of a world war to the realization that the financial demands of the fair were beyond the ability of the host city and other sponsors to meet. More recently, cities have planned fairs as part of the submission process to the BIE. If they lose out in the selection process, the fair is never held. This appendix provides brief histories of a number of these fairs that once seemed so promising to their planners yet died as dreams.

New York 1913

In early 1910, the New York Advancement Company suggested that a world's fair be held to celebrate the three-hundredth anniversary of the settlement of Manhattan. In June, Mayor William Gaynor appointed a committee headed by John Clafin to look into the feasibility of a 1913 fair for the city. The committee met later that month, with most members opposed to the idea, asserting that there were too many taking place, that New York could not afford a fair that would match the recent St. Louis exposition, and that a fair would bring no permanent benefits to the city. After further study by a subcommittee, Clafin recommended to the mayor that a fair not be held. Proponents then began talking about a permanent world's fair, similar to Earl's Court in London, but the advisory committee also declined to endorse this idea. Still others suggested that New York host a spectacular reception to "parliaments of the world," an event that would be hosted by a giant committee composed of New Yorkers, New Jerseyites, and 100 others appointed by the president. This idea failed to generate any enthusiasm, and the New York *Times* editorialized in December 1910 that New Yorkers would be perfectly content to get along without the bother and expense of hosting a fair.

Baltimore 1914

Talk of a major world's fair to celebrate the centennial of the "Star-Spangled Banner" and the successful defense of Baltimore in the War of 1812 was relatively short-lived, and civic leaders instead put on a week-long celebration centered on Fort McHenry, then in a state of considerable neglect. It was hoped that the celebration, to include events such as religious services, parades, and an appearance by the president (the secretary of state came instead), would generate enough interest to restore the area and make it into a national landmark.

New Orleans 1915

New Orleans had hoped to host a world's fair to celebrate the completion of the Panama Canal. The city mounted a large publicity campaign to win public support for its fair, basing its case on the fact that it was the U.S. port nearest to the canal. San Francisco, however, won the battle, and the New Orleans fair was never held.

Tokyo 1917

A world's fair planned for Tokyo in 1912 had been postponed until 1917, when a larger exposition, formally titled the Grand Exhibition of Japan, was to be held. It was cancelled because of World War I.

Portland 1930

A Portland (Oregon) exposition was chartered in 1925 but failed to raise sufficient capital to begin preparations for the fair, which was to have been called the Pacific American International Exposition. The Great Depression halted further planning after 1930, and the company was dissolved in 1945. The only tangible result of this effort was the striking of a commemorative medal, using bronze from the U.S.S. *Oregon,* then berthed in Portland and used as a museum.

Havana 1932

A French syndicate proposed to the Cuban national tourist commission that a fair be held in Havana between December 1931 and April 1932. Mayor Tirso Mesa of Havana liked the idea and appointed a committee of ten prominent businessmen to carry on the planning. The site was to be a parcel of reclaimed land at the foot of the Pardo that would extend along the Seine River. Eight nations were to participate, and the plans called for a Parisian restaurant and an amusement park. A lack of preparation time, the worldwide economic crisis, and political instability in Cuba conspired to keep this fair from happening.

New York 1932

In 1927, a world's fair organizing committee revealed plans for a major world's fair to commemorate the two-hundredth anniversary of George Washington's birth. The site chosen was the 2,000-acre Marine Park, at the south end of the Flatlands in Brooklyn, on Jamaica Bay. The committee's plans included digging a 30-foot channel in front of the site to accommodate visits of large warships. In addition, 5 million square feet of exhibition space, a stadium seating 200,000, and a bid for the 1932 Olympic Games were all contem-

plated. Planners anticipated participation by over forty nations, as well as Puerto Rico, Alaska, Hawaii, and the Philippine Islands. Post-fair projections included a permanent marine park on the site, as well as an ongoing international exposition and possibly an airport. After a round of initial enthusiasm and preliminary planning, the organizing committee ran into difficulties, first from civic leaders in Chicago, upset about the possibility of their Century of Progress fair, set for 1933, being upstaged, and then from the Merchants Association of New York City. This important organization announced its opposition to the 1932 fair in December 1929, two months after the stock market crash, asserting that technological advances of the 1920s—movies, radios, and automobiles—had made world's fairs all but obsolete and that, given the lack of time for proper planning and the competition from Chicago, a New York fair in 1932 was certain to fail. This viewpoint was echoed by the George Washington Bicentennial Commission of New York State. In a report published during the summer of 1930, the commission sought suggestions for appropriate bicentennial celebrations but clearly stated that no national or international expositions would be held. In February 1931, Sol Bloom, the treasurer of the original organizing committee, announced that no world's fair would take place but that the bicentennial would be celebrated across the nation throughout the year 1932. In the end, the Washington bicentennial was celebrated with a series of smaller events, such as pageants, parades, and colonial balls, around the country, and with the issuance of a set of twelve commemorative stamps and a new twenty-five cent piece, all portraying Washington's likeness.

Vancouver 1936

In 1930, plans were announced for the first great Canadian world's fair, to be held in Vancouver in 1936. Prime Minister Mackenzie King, various provincial premiers, and officials of the Canadian National Railroad and the Canadian Pacific Railroad expressed their initial support for the endeavor. The principal object of this fair was to focus the benefits of Far East trade to North America, and especially to the Pacific coast ports of Vancouver, Seattle,

San Francisco, and Los Angeles. The estimated cost of the fair was $15 million, but planners were certain that this would be an excellent investment.

Cologne 1940

A world exposition based on the broad theme of communication was registered with the BIE in 1938. The organizers wanted to emphasize advances in transportation with special sections on road traffic, trains, river navigation and port facilities, and (with less emphasis) aviation. In addition, conferences on communication issues were to be held. Organizers selected an exposition site along the Rhine River, across from the great cathedral of Cologne, but the onset of World War II halted plans.

Los Angeles 1940

A permanent "World Mart and Exhibition" was to have been built in Los Angeles harbor, but the onset of World War II forced the abandonment of plans. The fair, called the Pacific Mercado, was to have included all the nations of the Western Hemisphere in an effort to promote a spirit of friendship and cooperation based on mutual trade. A similar venture, the "First Great Exposition Featuring the Pacific Basin and the Americas," was planned for 1942. It was to have been open year round and have foreign consulates, an international office complex, and administrative space in permanent buildings. The war undermined these plans as well, and no buildings were ever constructed.

Tokyo 1940

Japan had been interested in hosting an international exposition since the beginning of the century. Plans for fairs in 1912 and 1917 had not materialized, and after World War I, it was hoped to host a fair in conjunction with the Tokyo Peace Memorial Exposition in 1922, but preparations could not be made in time. The exposition date was then pushed forward to 1940, with the fair, called the Grand International Exposition of Japan, to be held in conjunction with the Games of the Twelfth Olympiad. The fair was to be sited in both Tokyo and Yoko-

hama, and it was planned around the celebration of the 2,600th anniversary of the accession of the Emperor Jinmu. A site was laid out on landfill in Tokyo Bay, with a subsidiary site at Yokohama Harbor for maritime products exhibits, an aquarium, and a music hall. The exposition was scheduled to run from March to August, centered on the theme of the "fusion" of eastern and western cultures, and 40 million visitors were expected. Once again war intervened and caused plans to be postponed indefinitely. Tickets sold for the 1940 exposition were honored at the Osaka 1970 fair.

Rome 1942

Originally to be known as E42, this fair was planned for Tre Fontano, a site 3 miles south of Rome. Formally titled the Esposizione Universale di Roma, it was to have commemorated the twentieth anniversary of the fascist march on Rome, and Benito Mussolini planned to make it a great showplace of fascist political philosophy. The principal architect of fascist Italy, Marcello Piacentini, designed the fair buildings, highlighted by a concrete arch over 300 feet high. Work began in 1938 on a site in the San Paolo district of Rome near Tre Fontano, and some of the major buildings were constructed, including a church, the Palazzo della Civiltà (also known as the Square Colosseum), and the Palace of Congress. The exposition appears to have been planned as a general exhibition with no specific theme, apart from the glorification of Italy, with exhibits in the arts, sciences, agriculture, mining, and other traditional categories. The war halted further development, and the site was vandalized in the immediate postwar years. In 1951, the buildings were restored, and the rest of the buildings in Piacentini's original plan were constructed. The giant sports arena was used in the 1960 Olympics, and many of the other buildings became museums.

St. Louis 1953

An exposition to commemorate the sesquicentennial of the Louisiana Purchase aroused no particular opposition when it was first announced in 1948. When a site in Forest Park was chosen, however, most city officials objected on the grounds that such a fair would aggravate the housing shortage, and a citizens' group, led by Mrs. William A. Schubert, protested the use of any parkland for a world's fair.

Paris 1955

In May, 1950, the government announced that Paris would host an international exposition in 1955 to mark the centennial of the first Exposition Universelle. Six months later, however, the date of the proposed fair was pushed back to 1961 because of the higher priorities of the government in reconstruction, modernization, and rearmament that would preclude any financial commitment to a world's fair.

Houston 1956

A state-chartered philanthropic organization known as Houston's World's Fair, Inc. revealed plans in 1953 to hold a fair in Houston three years later. The corporation bought 935 acres of land adjoining the San Jacinto battlefield, 25 miles east of Houston, and announced that the fair would promote peace and the restoration of free trade among all nations. In addition, the fair would display the achievements of the atomic age and bring to the city important economic benefits.

San Francisco 1956

In 1954, George Christopher, a member of the San Francisco Board of Supervisors and candidate for mayor of the city, proposed a world's fair that would celebrate the centennial of the official establishment of the city and county and observe the fiftieth anniversary of the great earthquake and fire. Civic, business, and financial leaders, however, felt that such a fair would be a financial disaster, citing a lack of preparation time and unfavorable world political conditions. In addition, critics noted problems that had plagued the San Francisco fair of 1939–1940 and suggested that world's fairs were obsolete.

Boston 1976

Boston competed with Philadelphia for the distinction of hosting America's bicentennial exposition. Boston's fair was to be based on the theme of the interdependence of man, with a specific focus on problems brought about by urbanization and population growth. The site was to be on Boston Harbor, in a shallow area that could be reclaimed with landfill and adjacent to a 30-acre island that offered good opportunities for post-fair benefits. Plans for the expo never progressed beyond very preliminary stages, since Philadelphia received the sanction of the federal government in 1971.

Philadelphia 1976

Planning for Philadelphia's participation in the national bicentennial began with the appointment of a citizens' committee in 1962. A major part of early planning was an international exposition, an "occasion where the dual goals of celebrating the past and recognizing the future can be brought together." Philadelphians felt their city was the most logical place for such a fair, given its historical legacy and its central location. To that end the Philadelphia Bicentennial Corporation was formed. Initial plans called for the fair to be sited in the city on the west bank of the Schuylkill River, centered on Penn Central's Thirtieth Street station, where up to 390 acres were available. There were to be no national pavilions but rather a "total environment that is responsive to the theme." Planning for the fair was to be coordinated with many other civic improvements underway for the bicentennial—renovating of historic sites, constructing a tourist center, scheduling numerous international conferences. International performance was to be emphasized, and there would be performance pavilions rather than country pavilions.

For more than six years, the bicentennial corporation wrestled with its plans, moving the proposed fair to a second site at Port Richmond and debating over many other details. The exposition received a presidential recommendation in 1971 and was registered with the BIE the same year. But further complications arose in early 1972 when newly elected mayor Frank Rizzo rejected the Port Richmond site in favor of one of 240 acres in Fairmount Park, with additional land in Society Hill and along the river. In May 1972, all fair plans were buried by the American Revolution Bicentennial committee, which refused to sanction the event on the grounds of cost, too little preparation time, and the fact that poor people would not be able to afford the cost of admission. The committee recommended that 1976 bicentennial observances resemble those of 1932—a national celebration made up of a large number of small events.

Los Angeles 1981

Planning for an international exposition in 1981 that would celebrate the bicentennial of the founding of Los Angeles began in the early 1970's, and the proposed fair, which adopted a theme of "Simultaneous Dialog between All Peoples," received the sanction of the Bureau of International Expositions in November 1976. Planners wanted to build the fair at the Ontario Motor Speedway, a very accessible site 38 miles east of downtown Los Angeles that already had utility service and parking lots. By 1977, however, planners were encountering major financial difficulties. A $38 million bond issue proposal seemed dead in the state legislature, and efforts to raise private funds lagged badly. City and county money was not forthcoming either, although governments of both had endorsed the concept of a fair, which would commemorate the two-hundredth anniversary of the city's founding. Opponents pointed to major environmental and public transportation problems in and around the site and accused promoters of using the idea of the fair to bail out the financially troubled speedway. In May 1978, the Los Angeles fair received a death blow when Commerce Secretary Juanita Kreps announced that she did not support the fair and that the Carter administration would not send out official invitations to foreign nations to participate.

Paris 1989

The idea of celebrating the bicentennial of the French Revolution and the centennial of the 1889 exposition with another world's fair was first suggested in September 1981 and gained parliamentary approval in July 1983. Original plans called for the fair to have four themes: the sources of liberty, the solidarity of mankind, biology, and living in the year 2000. Planners located two sites—one in the west end and one in the east end of the city—for the fair and envisioned building some of it on a giant floating island in the Seine River. Shortly after winning parliamentary approval, however, the proposed fair was abruptly cancelled by French president François Mitterand, who blamed popular Paris mayor Jacques Chirac's opposition to the fair as too costly and disruptive.

Chicago 1992

The idea for a world's fair to celebrate the quincentennial of Columbus's first voyage of America and the centennial of the World's Columbian Exposition was first publicly suggested by Chicago architect Harry Weese in 1977. In 1980, a group of prominent Chicago business leaders began discussing the idea seriously and in 1981 organized themselves as the Chicago World's Fair—1992 Corporation, with Thomas G. Ayers, the recently retired head of Commonwealth Edison Company, as chairman. Working in considerable secrecy and with haste, the Fair Corporation put together a specific proposal for a universal category fair for 1992 that would be sited south of the Chicago Loop, near the location of the Century of Progress exposition, that would draw over 54 million people, and would earn an $8 million profit. Over the next two years, however, the planners hurt themselves with a condescending attitude toward anyone who dared criticize or question their plans and by their inability to refute veiled hints that their plans concealed a substantial degree of potential profiteering on property development in and around the fair site. Although Mayor Jane Byrne was very much in favor of the fair, Mayor Harold Washington, who entered office in 1983, was far more skeptical, as was the city council in his administration. By this time, a public action group, the 1992 Committee, had also been formed to demand public accountability on the part of the fair planners; this group eventually became an important lobby in opposition to the fair. Questions were raised about the financing for the fair, the choice of a site, the number and quality of jobs that would be created, and, perhaps most important, whether public funds could be better spent on a variety of neighborhood improvement projects. Although the fair corporation hired John Kramer, a young and dynamic publicist, as general manager and scaled down its plans somewhat, important questions still remained unanswered. Some answers were revealed by an independent advisory committee appointed by state House Speaker Michael Madigan, which reported in June 1985 that there was every likelihood that the fair would lose hundreds of millions of dollars and that the fair was far too risky a proposition for the city to take on. When Governor James Thompson and most city officials endorsed the Madigan report, the fair corporation abandoned its plans.

Vienna/Budapest 1995/1996

The idea for a 1995 exposition in Vienna, Austria, grew out of meetings and conferences in the late 1980s. The purpose of this fair was to heighten regional economic development and reduce political tensions between east and west Europe. Organizers chose a site near the Vienna International Center and the Austrria Canter Vienna, both existing venues that could be adapted for exposition use. A secondary theme was the "demarginalization" of Austria and the opportunity for Vienna to regain its former glory as a great capital of Europe. In 1987, as a gesture of *perestroika*, Austria invited Budapest to join forces and hold an expo situated in both cities, which would be connected by a high-speed rail line and by cruise ships plying the Danube.

In 1991, however, Vienna abandoned its plans for an expo, but the Budapest organizers, after receiving BIE permission to delay the expo by a year, dcided to proceed with an expo on their own. Plagued by financial problems, however, the Budapest fair was canceled in July 1994, shortly after the anti-expo Socialist-Liberal government under Prime Minister Gyula Horn had come to power in Hungary.

Tokyo 1996

Tokyo civic leaders planned an exposition, to be called World Cities Expo, for 1996 to accompany the construction of a new community, Tokyo Teleport Town, which was to be located on a nearly 1,000-acre island created by reclaimed land from Tokyo Bay, 6 miles south of the city center. The development of Tokyo Teleport Town began in 1987, but a recession in Japan during the early 1990s slowed

progress by lowering real estate prices.and diminishing the investment value of land in the new town. But by mid–1994, construction was well underway on the ¥200 billion exposition. The expo, not registered with the BIE, was to be held at the Tokyo International Exhibition Center and the Teleport Tower, permanent structures that would continue to be used for exhibitions and conferences. Another area that was largely completed was Orkos Park, or Cities of Antiquities Garden, where artifacts from ancient civilizations would be displayed.

By the summer of 1994, the World Cities Expo had persuaded 20 cities to participate, with the prospect of another 15 coming in before the December deadline. Planners anticipated 20 million visitors during the March 24-October 13 run of the expo. However, in the spring of 1995, Tokyo Governor Yukio Aoshima abruptly canceled the expo, leaving the city government with large compensation payments to participating cities and corporations that had spent a great deal of money preparing for the expo. The future of Tokyo Teleport Town was also uncertain, although most observers felt that its development would continue.

Toronto 1998

Toronto, after losing out to Hanover for the 2000 expo, applied to the BIE to host a smaller "recognized" exposition on the theme of "Communities: The Spirit of Tomorrow." The fair would have emphasized the appreciation of the value and importance of one's own and other communities and encouraged trade and cultural exchange between communities. The expo would have been located on the Canadian National Exhibition grounds, with considerable post-expo renovation planned. The BIE, however, selected Lisbon to host the 1998 exposition.

Toronto 2000

Toronto began planning for a millennium exposition in the late 1980s. The theme was to be "Peace with Our Planet: Visions of a New Millennium," inspired by the United Nations Commission on the Environment study, "Our Common Future," dealing with sustainable development. The fair would have been situated on the existing Canadian National Exhibition grounds in downtown Toronto. In the BIE vote for the 2000 expo, however, Toronto lost out to Hanover by one vote.

Venice 2000

Like Toronto and Hanover, Venice applied to the BIE to host a millennium exposition in 2000, but its application was unsuccessful. The theme of the exposition was to deal with "the construction of a world equilibrium," an equilibrium between available resources and their exploitation. Organizers planned to place the expo on three separate sites in Venice, but these had not been determined by the time the application was submitted to the BIE. The exposition would have been divided into three parts: 1) The Network of Ideas: a workshop on the theme of the expo; 2) The Network of Production: an exhibition of technological achievements; and 3) The Nations Area, where participating nations would place their exhibits. The first part would consist of a series of conferences between March 1 and June 30, while the second and third parts, open for the same period of time, would be more traditional exhibitions. The expo was slated to end June 30, just before Venice's high tourist season, but organizers were convinced that a four-month run would be sufficient to guarantee the expo's success.

Manila 2002

Planning for a 2002 exposition in Manila began in 1993 under the leadership of Commissioner-General Mina T. Gabor, who had headed the Philippines pavilion at Expo '92 in Seville, and the World Expo 2002, as it came to be called, received BIE sanction in the mid–1990s. Expo 2002 would have been the first sanctioned international fair to be hosted by a developing country. Its theme was to have been "Ecotourism: Growing with Nature," and the fair would probably have been built at Quezon Memorial Park in Quezon City, a Manila suburb.

Organizers canceled the expo in January 1999 because they could not obtain the necessary financial support from the private sector. Financial problems for the Philippine expo became apparent soon after Expo '98 in Lisbon; the organizers were deep in debt and there were allegations of corruption. There were also rumors of political discord pitting Gabor and her main ally, former President Fidel V. Ramos against the current president, Joseph Estrada. These dampened enthusiasm in the local business community that led to the abandonment of the project.

Queensland, Australia 2002

The loser to Manila in the BIE deliberation for a 2002 expo, Queensland reconsidered its bid after the Manila effort collapsed in January 1999. The Queensland expo, based on the broad theme of information technology and its role in society, was to be situated near the tourist area known as the Gold Coast. The organizers, who had planned for a 35-month building schedule and who had to find an alternative site since the original one was no longer available, requested that the BIE allow them to delay the expo until 2003. The BIE, however, refused the request, and the organizers, realizing that to do all that needed to be done by 2002 was not feasible, dropped their plans.

Calgary 2005

A loser to Aichi in the competition for the 2005 exposition, Calgary's expo would have celebrated the centennial of organization of both Alberta and Saskatchewan as Canadian provinces. A site of between 150 and 200 acres, located on the Bow and Elbow Rivers near the city center was selected, in part because it included Fort Calgary Historic Park and Stampede Park, existing facilities. The theme, never fully developed, dealt vaguely with issues facing the world in the twenty-first century.

General Bibliography

Each entry in the Encyclopedia has its own specific bibliography

In searching out primary and secondary material for research on world's fairs, the place to begin is Robert W. Rydell, *Books of the Fairs* (1990). This long essay, published as part of a Smithsonian Institution project, "The Books of the Fairs," to gather together and microfilm its holdings of some 2,000 books, pamphlets, and journals on world's fairs and expositions between 1834 and 1915, constitutes a comprehensive and analytical discussion of exposition bibliography. Rydell's work, divided into three major sections, first traces the general evolution of fairs. The second section concerns itself with the historiography of fairs and expositions and contains commentary on a wide variety of published works. The final section deals with the literature of fairs as found in the Smithsonian and other archival and manuscript collections. The Smithsonian project, published in four stages by Research Publications, Ltd., in 1989 and 1990, includes Rydell's bibliography as an introduction. This work was supplemented by Bridget J. Burke, "World's Fairs and International Expositions: Selected References 1987–1993," in Robert W. Rydell and Nancy E. Gwinn, *Fair Representations: World's Fairs and the Modern World* (1994): 218–47, a well-annotated and extensive list of books and articles on fairs published between 1987 and 1993, and, in turn, Burke's article was updated by the Smithsonian Institution in Martha Higgins, comp., "Revisiting the World's fairs and International Expositions: A Selected Bibliography, 1992–2004," an on-line publication available at *www.sil.si.edu/silpublications/worlds-fairs/* This work includes articles, monographs, and a great many dissertations, many of which are annotated.

Other bibliographies and checklists are far less comprehensive. The Library of Congress's Division of Bibliography published *A Selected List of References on Fairs and Expositions, 1928–1939* (1938); it is very complete for those years and also includes mention of some general works, but it is of limited usefulness because of its short time span and early date of publication. "International Expositions, 1851–1900," in volume 4 of *American Asso-*

ciation of Architectural Bibliographers (1967), contains short summaries of major nineteenth-century fairs, with substantial bibliographies, including some archival sources following each. As might be expected, the emphasis is on architecture. Alva W. Stewart and Susan J. Stewart, *World's Fairs since 1960: A Bibliographic Overview* (1983), covers seven fairs between 1962 and 1982, listing, without annotation, bibliographic citations for each. Another bibliography dealing with recent fairs is John Hill and Beverly Carron Payne, comps., *World's Fairs and Expos: The Modern Era* (1982), a publication of the Canberra College of Advanced Education. This work lists sources for fairs between 1962 and 1982, also without annotation and with a strong emphasis on planning, construction, traffic, architecture, and post-fair use. Marvin R. Nathan, *San Francisco's International Expositions: A Bibliography, including Listing for the Mechanics' Institute Exhibitions* (1995), is useful for those studying the fairs and exhibitions of the San Francisco area.

More recent bibliographical works and *World's Fairs: A Guide to Selected English-Language Resources* (2005), an Indiana University project done under the guidance of Robert Goehlert. It lists works, including theses and dissertations that for the most part were published between 1995 and 2004 on a wide variety of U.S. and foreign fairs and includes films and other video material and websites. Most of the entries are annotated. A much more ambitious project is Alexander Geppert, Jean Coffey, and Tammy Lau, "International Expositions: A Bibliography" (2002). It is an exhaustive listing of almost 1,500 books, websites, and articles on fairs and expositions from the late eighteenth century until 1940. Though not annotated, its thoroughness and clear citations make it an especially valuable work. It is available at the website of the library at California State University, Fresno. See also Ken Harman, "A List of World Exhibitions, Parts I-IV," in *Exhibition Study Group Journal* 37 (1995): 23–28; 38 (1995): 20–27, 29; 39 (1995): 62–68; 40 (1996): 12–14.

Archival Holdings

U.S. GOVERNMENT

Material related to world's fairs and expositions may be found in at least four different federal repositories. The most extensive body of information is to be found in the Smithsonian Institution archives, since the Smithsonian and the U.S. National Museum, whose records are in these archives, were responsible for preparing U.S. government exhibits for most fairs between 1876 and 1939. The records of the Smithsonian, described more fully in *Guide to Smithsonian Archives* (1983) and in Rydell's *Books of the Fairs* (1990), are primarily found in Record Groups 70 and 192 and consist of documents illustrative of the financial and technical aspects of exhibiting at world's fairs. In addition, there are several collections of photographs; particularly valuable are those relating to Chicago 1893, Atlanta 1895, Nashville 1897, and Buffalo 1901.

The U.S. National Archives contains some fair records, principally within Record Group 46 (Records of the United States Senate) and Record Group 223 (Records of the United States House of Representatives). Here researchers may find official reports from U.S. commissioners to various fairs, mandated by Congress at the time money was appropriated for U.S. participation in the fair. Accompanying these reports may be correspondence, State Department reports, and other documents concerning the political and diplomatic aspects of U.S. participation.

A number of manuscript collections in the Library of Congress contain material relating to various world's fairs. Of particular significance are the papers of Frank Lamson Scribner, a botanist and exhibit specialist, who was instrumental in preparing the U.S. exhibits for the Department of Agriculture between 1900 and 1934 and who was a technical adviser at a number of U.S. fairs. Other important collections include the papers of Frances B. Johnston, a photographer at the Chicago 1893 and St. Louis 1904 fairs, and the papers of William John McGee, who was the director of the history and anthropology exhibit at the St. Louis fair.

From 1958 until it was folded into the State Department in the 1990s, the U.S. Information Agency (USIA) was responsible for U.S. participation in foreign expositions, while the Department of Commerce handled domestic expositions. The USIA archives are now part of the State Department's Public Diplomacy archives and include material on those fairs in which the agency had a role; this includes final reports, guides, clippings, and survey questionnaires, as well as internal correspondence. The material in the collection is quite extensive for international fairs between 1958 and 1992, but the government's decision to curtail participation in later fairs has obviously limited the availability of records from later fairs. There is also a general clippings file with material from all fairs, domestic and foreign from 1958 forward.

STATE, LOCAL, AND UNIVERSITY ARCHIVES

The locations of the records of many individual fairs are noted in the annotated bibliographies for those fairs, as supplied by their authors. This section deals with archival holdings that contain information on a number of different fairs, although if a particular collection has especially useful resources for one fair, it may also be included in the bibliography for that fair.

The best collection of world's fair material outside Washington, D.C., is the Donald G. Larson Collection of Expositions and Fairs, 1851–1940, housed in the Special Collections Department, Henry Madden Library, California State University, Fresno. This collection consists of printed material concerning both foreign and domestic world's fairs during the time period indicated, including guidebooks, catalogues, maps, and pamphlets, as well as academic work on fairs, including theses and dissertations. In addition, the Larson Collection contains fair-related items of material culture—photographs and glass negatives, awards, souvenir medals, badges, and postcards, for example. Altogether, these are more than 6,300 items in the collection. Much of the collection is searchable online, and many of the photographs have been scanned and can be viewed online at the library's website,

The Hagley Museum and Library, near Wilmington, Delaware, which emphasizes science and technology in its holdings, contains a substantial amount of fair-related material in its various sections. The library is rich in material on pre-1851 mechanics' institutes in the United States and also boasts much on the early Paris expositions—technical reports, official reports, and proceedings of scientific congresses and conferences held in conjunction with fairs. There are more than 50 books and pamphlets on the Paris 1878 exposition alone. The Hagley Photographic Archives contains a number of items from the Chicago 1893, Paris 1900, and New York 1939–1940 fairs, while the Manuscripts Department, which contains the papers of the large DuPont family, has material of interest to researchers on the New York 1853 and New York 1939–1940 fairs, among others.

Near the Hagley Museum is the Winterthur Museum and Library, whose holdings include a large number of commercial exhibit catalogues and advertisements, especially from the Philadelphia 1876 and Chicago 1893 expositions. The archives at Winterthur is another good source for material on the Chicago 1893 fair; the catalogue lists more than 900 items, including a large number of photographs.

The Robert A. Feer Collection of World Fairs

of North America is located at the Boston Public Library. Donated by a private collector, this collection includes books, articles, prints, and memorabilia from fairs between 1853 and 1968. Earl R. Taylor, comp., *A Checklist of the Robert A. Feer Collection of World Fairs of North America* (1976) is a useful finding aid.

Other repositories containing world's fair materials include the University of Maryland Architecture Library, whose collection is strongest in late nineteenth-century fairs, the University of Maryland, Baltimore County Special Collections library, which has a small selection of material, also dealing with late nineteenth-century fairs, the Henry Ford Museum and Greenfield Village, near Dearborn, Michigan, which houses a collection of brochures, souvenir booklets, and ephemera from a variety of fairs, and the Yale University library, which purchased most of the extensive Alfred Heller Collection in 2006, which consists of rare books, paintings and prints, and other scarce material from many different fairs. Many of these libraries and museums have websites where researchers can go to obtain more detailed information about relevant materials.

BUREAU OF INTERNATIONAL EXPOSITIONS

The headquarters of the Bureau of International Expositions is located at 34 Avenue d'Iena in Paris. In addition to administrative offices and a small conference center, the BIE maintains a useful library of research materials on expositions. Much of the material relates to fairs that have been held or proposed since the creation of the BIE in 1928. Of particular interest are the bidding documents from would-be host cities competing for the BIE's sanction. In addition, the library also has a collection of books, pamphlets, and other printed material about earlier fairs.

OFFICIAL PUBLICATIONS

The Bureau of International Expositions (BIE) in Paris publishes a periodic newsletter but also has published monographs and handbooks on its regulations and activities. Of particular importance is Marcel Galopin, *Les Expositions internationales au XXe siècle et la Bureau Internationale des Expositions* (1997) for its history of the evolution of the BIE, but see also Roger Meizoz, *La Reglementation des expositions sur le plan international* (1965) and Charles Piat, *Les Expositions internationales relevant de Bureau International des Expositions* (1983). An older work with information and documents about the BIE is Maurice Isaac, *Les Expositions internationales* (1936)

WORLD'S FAIR ORGANIZATIONS

In the United States, the principal, and perhaps the only, organization devoted to world's fairs generally is the World's Fair Preservation Society. Founded in 2003, this group is dedicated to "pre-serving the history of world's fairs and promoting current or future fairs. Its website, with more information, is *www.crystalpalace51.org* . A number of indivudal fairs have their own support organizations that publish newsletters and carry on other activities designed to keep their fair's history in the public eye. For the Omaha 1898 exposition, the organization is the Trans-Mississippi Historical Association, 2708 S. 13th St., Omaha, NB 68108, and its newsletter is the *Trans-Miss News.* For the 1901 Buffalo fair, the organization is the Pan-American 1901 Exposition Club, 183 Lamarck Drive, Snyder, NY 14226, and its newsletter is the *Pan American Herald.* The organization also has a website, *www.panamexpo.org.* For the 1904 St. Louis fair, the organization is the 1904 World's Fair Society, 2605 Causeway, St. Louis, MO 63125, and its newsletter is *World's Fair Bulletin.* The organization also has a website, *www.1904.1904worldsfairsociety.org* Finally, the World's Fair Collectors Society, founded in 1968, which had published the informative newsletter, *Fair News,* went defunct in 2006.

In Great Britain, the principal organization is the Exhibition Study Group, founed in 1978 and "dedicated to the conservation and study of all matters relating to exhibitions. It publishes the *Exhibition Study Group Journal* four times a year and holds an annual two-day conference at various sites in the United Kingdom. Its website, which contains links to an index of its journal and to books its members have published, is *www.studygroup.org.uk*

General Works

For many years, the most comprehensive book on world's fairs and expositions was John Allwood, *The Great Exhibitions* (1977). Still a standard work, this book touches on some seventy fairs up to and including Osaka 1970, with interesting and insightful commentary and an abundance of excellent illustration. There is also an appendix on the Bureau of International Expositions (BIE) and a checklist of international exhibitions with an array of statistical information. Unfortunately, Allwood's book is now out of print and hard to find. Of interest also is John Allwood, "How the Great Fairs Came to Be: A Short Illustrated History," *World's Fair* 3, 2 (Spring 1983): 7–11.

Another important general work is Kenneth Luckhurst, *The Story of Exhibitions* (1951). This survey is particularly useful on the art and industrial exhibitions and the French national exhibitions prior to 1851. The book contains a chapter on national, local, and specialized exhibitions and another on exhibition buildings and display techniques. Tony Bennett, *The Birth of the Museum:*

History, Theory, Politics (1995) and "The Exhibitionary Complex," *New Formations* 4 (Spring 1988): 73–102, deals with some of the more theoretical questions concerning fairs, as does Maurice Roche, *Mega-events and Modernity: Olympics and Expos in the Growth of Global Culture* (2000), unfortunately bogged down by postmodernist jargon, and Reesa Greenberg, Bruce Ferguson, and Sandy Nairne, eds., *Thinking about Exhibitions* (1996). Other theoretical aspects are discussed in Robert Lumley, ed., *The Museum Time-Machine: Putting Cultures on Display* (1988), and Sharon MacDonald, ed., *The Politics of Display: Museums, Science, Culture* (1997). Both of these books also highlight the close relationship between expositions and museums. Also worth consulting is Keith Walden, *Becoming Modern in Toronto: The Industrial Exhibition and the Shaping of a Late Victorian Culture* (1997), which focuses principally on the annual Canadian National Exhibition but provides insights that are applicable to many early world's fairs. Philippe Hamon, *Expositions: Literature and Architecture in Nineteenth-Century France* (1992) attempts to draw some parallels between expository literature and the architecture of expositions in the cultural development of France during the height of its exposition era. Even the most recent world's fairs have found their way into cultural research. Penelope Harvey, *Hybrids of Modernity: Anthropology, the Nation-State, and the Universal Exhibition* (1996), takes the 1992 Seville exposition as a basis for discussion about what she calls "auto-anthropology," and Carl Malamud, *A World's Fair for the Global Village* (1997), suggests that world's fairs had a role in the development of the World Wide Web.

A number of general works deal only with nineteenth-century fairs. The most recent of these are Robert Brain, *Going to the Fair: Readings in the Culture of Nineteenth-Century Exhibitions* (1993) and Meg Armstrong, "'A Jumble of Foreignness': The Sublime Musayums [*sic*] of Nineteenth-Century fairs and Exhibitions," *Cultural Critique* 23 (Winter 1992): 199–250. Werner Plum, *World Exhibitions in the Nineteenth Century: Pageants of Social and Cultural Change* (1977), a Marxist analysis of early expositions, which Plum describes as "pageants of the world of rising bourgeois society, as it prepared itself for the universal expansion of its technology, its economic sinews, and its political power." Less analytical is Christian Beutler, *Weltausstellung im 19. Jahrhundert* (1973), a heavily illustrated catalogue of building and decorative art exhibits for the ten major fairs between 1851 and 1893.

Earlier works on nineteenth-century fairs include C.B. Norton, *World's Fairs from London 1851 to Chicago 1893* (1892), a survey of major fairs since the Crystal Palace with some good engravings of various fair buildings. The book also previews the upcoming World's Columbian Exposition of 1893.

An article, "International Exhibitions from 1851 to 1874: A Retrospect," in *Practical Magazine* 4 (1875): 448–54, contains a good discussion of the topic, with particular emphasis on British fairs but some mention of smaller, more obscure fairs held in the 1850s and 1860s. An early effort to work world's fairs into the mainstream of historical scholarship is Merle Curti, "America at the World Fairs, 1851–1893," *American Historical Review* 55 (1950): 833–56. Curti's article emphasizes how the exhibits sent to these early fairs reflected the "emergence of a new and powerful America" that won praise from Europeans earlier than had been presumed. Italian readers may wish to consult Linda Amone and Carlo Olmo, *Le esposizioni universali, 1851–1900: Il progresso in scena* (1990). Finally, the *Encyclopedia Britannica*, in its earlier editions, contained excellent articles on world's fairs and expositions, under the heading "Exhibitions." See the Ninth Edition (1889), vol. 8, pp. 803–5, and the Eleventh Edition (1911), vol. 10, pp. 67–71.

Several volumes in French, German, and Spanish contain useful information for the generalist researcher. Brigitte Schroeder-Godehus and Anne Rasmussen, *Les Fastes du progrès* (1992) is an encyclopedia treatment of fairs between 1851 and 1992 that contains a wealth of statistical and bibliographical information on 29 major world's fairs, as well as chapters on such matters as the classification of expositions, and the rules that have governed them over the years. *Le Livre des expositions universelles, 1851–1989* (1983), a publication of the Paris Museum of Decorative Arts, is a coffee table book on 29 expositions held between 1851 and 1970, with many illustrations and short articles on specific aspects of each fair. The book also contains a more substantial chapter on general world's fair topics such as architecture, the sciences, and organization, and concludes with a chapter on the prospects for a 1989 Paris exposition. Rene Poirier, *Des Faires, des peuples, des expositions* (1958), written for the Brussels 1958 exposition, is a survey of fairs from 1851 to 1939, with additional chapters on the origins of fairs, national and colonial fairs, the organizations of fairs, and the "social and spiritual" life of fairs. Florence Pinot de Villechenon, *Les Expositions universelles* (1992), Ruprecht Vondran, *Stahl ist Zukunft: Von der Weltausstellung London 1851 bis zur EXPO 2000 in Hannover* (1999), and Luis Calvo Teixeira, *Exposiciones universales: el mundo en Sevilla* (1992) are three other comprehensive histories of fairs that were written in conjunction with recent expositions. Another general work is Winfried Kretschmer, *Geschichte der Weltausstellung* (1999).

An important recent work, especially for those interested in the impact of exhibitions (and other large-scale events) on their urban setting is John R. Gold and Margaret M. Gold, *Cities of Culture: Staging International Festivals and the Urban Agenda, 1851–2000* (2005), which deals not only with world's fairs, but also with the Olympic Games and the European Cities of Culture. Another general work that merits consideration is Alfred Heller, *World's Fairs and the End of Progress: An Insider's View* (1999), a memoir by the founder and editor of the influential journal *World's Fair* (1981–1995) and a long-time authority on the subject. Robert W. Rydell and Nancy E. Gwinn, eds., *Fair Representations: World's Fairs and the Modern World* (1994), is an anthology with essays that range from bibliographies to fair legacies. Other, older general works include W. Waters, *History of Fairs and Expositions: Their Classifications, Functions, and Values* (1939), and George Jackson, *History of Centennials, Expositions, and World Fairs* (1939). Both books, published in conjunction with the New York World's Fair of 1939–1940, contain a hodgepodge of information on fairs of various kinds. Waters's book combines some superficial history with practical information on promotion and organization of fairs and discusses state fairs, trade fairs, and agricultural fairs, in addition to world's fairs. Jackson also discusses some of the practical aspects of fair management; his book, moreover, contains Rufus Dawes's report on the Century of Progress Exposition in Chicago (1933–1934) and short chapters on both the New York and San Francisco fairs of 1939–1940.

Among other publications, *The Great World's Fairs and Expositions* (1986) is an illustrated catalogue of the Mitchell Wolfson, Jr., Collection of Decorative and Propaganda Arts, exhibited in 1986 at Miami-Dade College, Miami, Florida. Colin Simkin, *Fairs* (1944), is a special publication of the Travelers Insurance Company, containing a short essay, "Fairs Past and Present," by Simkin, along with many pictures and ephemeral information. Maurice Isaac, *Les expositions internationales* (1936), is an exhaustive three-volume analysis of the organization and regulation of fairs by the BIE and of what the author calls the "judicial milieu" of fairs. Finally, Robert K. Landers, "World's Fairs: How They Are Faring," *Editorial Research Reports* (April 18, 1986): 291–308, includes a brief survey of past fairs, with emphasis on those of the 1980s, and their financial problems. More modern general works include John R. Davis, "From the Great Exhibition to EXPO 2000: The History of Display," *Bulletin of the German Historical Institute London* 22, 2 (November 2000): 7–19; and Alexander Geppert, "Weltheater: Die Geschichte des europaischen Ausstellungs-wesens im 19. und 20. Jahrhundert Ein Forschunghsbericht," *Neue Politische Literatur* 47, 1 (2002): 10–61.

With the advent of video recording, a number of fairs have become generally available in a visual format. Two videos treat multiple fairs: "Come to the Fair!" From *A Walk through the Twentieth Century with Bill Moyers* (1985), which deals with U.S. fairs from Buffalo 1901 through Knoxville 1982, and "World's Fairs," from the *Modern Mar-vels* series (2001), which includes both foreign and domestic fairs. Films and videos of many individual fairs have been made and are widely available on DVD on in other formats. Many of these are listed in the bibliographical essays following each fair.

Collective and Thematic Works

A number of books dealing with fairs in one location have been published and provide a convenient source for comparative history. Fairs in the United States and France have attracted the most attention. For those wishing to explore fair held in the United States, a good starting place is Robert W. Rydell, John E. Findling, and Kimberly D. Pelle, *Fair America: World's Fairs in the United States* (2000), which includes a narrative history of major American fairs and analyzes how the rationale for world's fairs has changed through the years. John E. Findling, *Chicago's Great World's Fairs* (1994), surveys both the World's Columbian Exposition and the Century of Progress Exposition and discusses the links between them, while Robert W. Rydell, "Visions of Empire: International Expositions in Portland and Seattle, 1905–1909," *Pacific Historical Review* 52, 1 (February 1993): 37–65, compares two U.S. fairs in the Pacific Northwest that projected a burgeoning American imperialism. Other books on U.S. fairs will be found below in sections dealing with topics such as nationalism, anthropology, photography, and philately. For France, Adolphe Demy, *Essai historique sur les expositions universelles de Paris* (1907), is a general work on world's fairs through its publication date, but it contains separate chapters on each of the five great Paris fairs between 1855 and 1900. A more recent work is Pascal Ory, *Les Expositions universelles de Paris* (1982), which surveys each of the six major Paris fairs (1855–1900, 1937) and includes a final chapter on the legacies of these fairs. Also of interest is Wolfram Kaiser, "Vive la France! Vive la Republique? The Cultural Construction of French Identity at the World Exhibitions in Paris, 1855–1900," *National Identities* 1, 3 (1999): 227–44. Sylvain Ageorges, *Sur la trace des expositions universelles* (2006), contains chapters on each of the great Paris expositions, along with information and photographs on buildings and other stuructures that remain from those expositions. Ageorges is a professional photographer, and the book is well illustrated with both historical images and those he has taken himself of surviving structures.

A number of useful publications deal with other countries or cultures and their experience with either hosting or exhibiting at fairs. Mauricio Tenorio-Trillo, *Mexico at the World's Fairs* (1996), surveys that country's participation in many fairs. For the various Belgian fairs, consult A. Cockx and J. Lemmens, *Les Expositions universelles et internationals en Belgique de 1885 á 1958* (1958). Written for the 1958 Brussels fair, this short volume surveys the Belgian fairs that preceded it, with separate chapters for each of the twentieth-century events. A work dealing solely on the Antwerp fairs is *De panoramische droom/The Panoramic Dream: Antwerpen en de wereldtentoonstellung/Antwerp and the World Exhibitions, 1885–1894–1930* (1993). Glasgow's five exhibitions (not all world's fairs) are described in Perilla Kinchin and Juliet Kinchin, *Glasgow's Great Exhibitions: 1888, 1901, 1911, 1938, 1988* (1988), an attractive book with many illustrations and site plans. Austria is handled in Ulrike Felber, Eike Krasny, and Andreas Rapp, *Smart Exports: Österreich auf den Weltausstellungen 1851–2000* (2000), and Finland in a book by the Finnish Ministry of Trade and Industry, *The World Exhibitions and Their Effects on Finland* (2002), the result of a study to determine how much benefit Finnish companies derive from participation in an exposition and how these events affect Finland's international image. The German area of Schleswig-Holstein is discussed in Erich Maletzke, *Spurensuche-Schleswig-Holstein auf den Weltausstellungen 1851 bis 2000* (2000). Tunisia's involvement with world's fairs is covred in CEPEX (Centre de promotion des expositions), *La Tunisie aux Expositions Universelles* (2000). Zeynep Celik, *Displaying the Orient: Architecture of Islam at Nineteenth-Century World's Fairs* 1992) explains the pavilions and other structures representing Islam that looked so strange to most fairgoers, while Barbara Kirschenblatt-Gimblett, "A Place in the World: Jews and the Holy Land at World's Fairs," in Jeffrey Sandler and Beth S. Wenger, eds., *Encounters with the "Holy Land": Place, Past and Future in American Jewish Culture* (1997), discusses the ways in which Jewish culture was portrayed at fairs.

Two significant works discuss the world's fairs of the 1930s but from different points of view. Robert W. Rydell, *World of Fairs: The Century-of-Progress Expositions* (1993) discusses the fairs of the 1930s with regard to the ways in which fair planners used science and technology to project fairgoers into a future world of prosperity. In "Utopia Realized: The World's Fairs of the 1930s," an article in Joseph J. Corn, ed., *Imagining Tomorrow: History, Technology, and the American Future* (1986), Folke T. Kihlstedt notes how fairs of the 1930s, especially the New York World's Fair of 1939–1940, stressed the future in terms of optimism and material progress within the context of corporate capitalism and individual opportunity. For visitors, the future was actualized by forward-looking architecture and industrial design. Also useful is Pierre-Gerlier and Brigitte Schroeder-Gudehus, "L'Internationalisme et les expositions dans les annes trente," in Regine Robin, ed., *Masses et cultures de masse dans les annes trente* (1991).

Several books concern themselves with architectural and design aspects of world's fairs. One of the more comprehensive is Wolfgang Friebe, *Architektur der Weltausstellungen, 1851 bis 1970* (1983), also available in an English edition, *Buildings of the World's Exhibitions, 1851–1970* (1985). This is a heavily illustrated book highlighting architectural innovations at many world's fairs and including site plans for number of those fairs. A more recent general work that focuses on architecture is Erik Mattie, *World's Fairs* (1998), which includes some statistical and general information about major fairs, in additional to good architectural photographs and site plans. Wolfgang Clasen, in *Expositions, Exhibits, Industrial and Trade Fairs* (1968), cites noteworthy pavilions and well-designed exhibits that have appeared at various world's fairs and lesser events. In an article on fair architecture, "Seven Eras of World's Fairs," *Progressive Architecture* 55 (August 1974): 64–73, L. G. Zimmerman establishes a seven-part taxonomy for fairs: the Crystal Palace, 1851–1876; the Centennial era, 1876–1889; the Neoclassic era, 1889–1893; the Art Nouveau era, 1893–1925; the Modern era, 1925–1940; the Atomic/Pop era, 1940–1967; and the Expo era, 1967–1976. John R. Mullen, *World's Fairs and Their Impact upon Urban Planning* (1972), is primarily a bibliography, but in a short introductory essay, Mullen emphasizes the role fairs can play in bringing about urban benefits. A recent general work in German on fair architecture is Terje Niels Dahle, *Architektur der Weltausstellungen* (2000). Finland's often innovative pavilions are discussed in P.B. Mackeith and Kerstein Smeds, *Finland Pavilions* (1993), while Spain's receive attention in David Canogar, *Pabellones españoles en las Exposiciones Universales* (2000). Foreign exposition architecture in general is surveyed in Lisa Schrenk, "From Historic Village to Modern Pavilion: The Evolution of Foreign Architectural Representation in International Expositions in the 1930s," *National Identities* 1, 3 (1999): 187–312. For aspects of landscaping at fairs, see Felix Driver and David Gilbert, eds., *Imperial Cities: Landscape, Display and Identity* (1999).

Fine arts have been a staple at nearly every world's fair, and many books have been written about the art at one particular fair. Elizabeth Gilmore Hoff, *The Art of All Nations* (1981), is a collection of documents about art in the mid-nineteenth century, with chapters on London 1851, Paris 1855, London 1862, Paris 1867, and Vienna 1873. For the decorative arts, see Yvonne Brunhammer, "National, International, and Universal Exposition and the French Decorative Arts," in *L'Art de Vivre: Decorative Arts and Design in France, 1789–1989* (1989). Several books dealing with photography at an exposition are listed in the bibliography following the essay on that exposition, but Anna Maxwell, *Colonial Photography and Exhibitions: Representations of the "Native" and the Making of European Identities* (1999), deals more generally with photography, especially with regard to the way in which natives were portrayed.

A recent book that covers several different themes with respect to world's fairs is Paul Greenhalgh, *Ephemeral Vistas: The Expositions Universelles, Great Exhibitions, and World's Fairs, 1851–1939* (1988, 2000). Although there is an underlying constant of nationalism, seen in chapters devoted to imperial display and "human showcases," Greenhalgh's book also considers such diverse topics as funding, women, and fine arts. On the theme of nationalism, Peter Hoffenberg, *An Empire on Display: English, Indian, and Australian Exhibitions from the Crystal Palace to the Great War* (2001), emphasizes the contribution of exhibition to the development of the British empire in the late nineteenth century. Another take on nationalism is seen in Stephen Wildman, "Great, Greater, Greatest? Anglo-French Rivalry at the Great Exhibitions of 1851, 1855, and 1862," *RSA Journal* 137, 5398 (1989): 660–64.

The participation of women at world's fairs was the subject of Virginia Grant Darney's 1982 Ph.D. dissertation at Emory University. In "Women and World's Fairs: American International Expositions, 1876–1904," Darney notes how the fairs of that era reflect women's progress from "gender segregation" to "gender integration and individualism." Jeanne Madeline Weimann, *The Fair Women* (1981) deals principally with the Women's Building at the 1893 World's Columbian Exposition in Chicago but also mentions briefly women's participation at other fairs.

Robert W. Rydell discusses the manner in which American fairs between 1876 and 1916 were used to confirm the prevailing anthropological notion of Anglo-Saxon racial superiority in his monograph, *All the World's a Fair* (1984). His book treats twelve different fairs, giving particular attention to the zoolike displays of nonwhites that visually stressed the social and cultural differences among the races. Another work that is highly anthropological in nature is Burton Benedict, ed., *The Anthropology of World's Fairs* (1985). While much of this work deals with the Panama-Pacific International Exposition in San Francisco, Benedict's lengthy introductory essay does mention numerous other fairs in a discussion of the "rituals" and "rules" governing world's fairs and their exhibits. Howard P. Segal, in *Technological Utopianism in American Culture* (2005), argues that world's fairs, especially in the 1930s, presented an idealized view of the promise of technology to their visitors that was significant in shaping how they thought of themselves and their future.

Edo McCullough treats the entertainment aspects of fairs informally in *World's Fair Midways* (1966), a book that discusses not only the entertainment areas but also the nature of the entertainment. A more recent article that also touches on entertainment is Paul Greenhalgh, "Education, Entertainment, and Politics: Lessons from the Great International Exhibitions, in Peter Vergo, ed., *The New Museology* (1989). The use of fairs by filmmakers to showcase innovative cinematic techniques is surveyed in Marc Mancini, "Pictures at an Exposition," *Film Comment* 19 (January-February 1983): 43–49. In a well-illustrated book, *Glass from World's Fairs, 1851–1904* (1986), Jane Shadel Spillman surveys the glass exhibits from eleven major fairs. K.G. Beauchamp, *Exhibiting Electricity* (1997), a publication of the Institution of Electrical Engineers in Great Britain, and David Nye, "Electrifying Expositions, 1880–1939," in Rydell and Gwinn, *Fair Representations* (1994): 140–56, discuss that spectacular feature of late nineteenth and early twentieth-century fairs. Those interested in fair ephemera may wish to contact Victor E. Annaloro, in Flushing, N.Y., who has compiled a CD called "The Great American Expositions," and containing more than 500 images of exposition tickets of various types, medals, posters, and many other types of ephemera for a wide variety of U.S. fairs.

Finally, William J. Bomar, *Postal Markings of United States Expositions* (1986), presents an exhaustive survey of special cancellations used either to promote upcoming fairs or to cancel postcards and letters at exposition postal stations. The book also contains information on specially printed envelopes, postcards, and seals used in conjunction with fairs. Postcards were also a staple of early world's fairs, and Robert W. Rydell analyzes them in "Souvenirs of Imperialism: World's Fair Postcards," in Christraud M. Geary and Virginia-Lee Webb, eds., *Delivering Views: Distant Cultures in Early Postcards* (1998). A related book is Frederic Megson and Mary Megson, *American Exposition Postcards, 1870–1920* (1992), a catalogue of the souvenir picture postcards that accompanied each world's fair after the World's Columbian Exposition of 1893. British exposition postcards are catalogued in F.A. Fletcher and A.D. Brooks, *British Exhibitions and Their Postcards: Part I: 1900–1914; Part II: 1915–1979* (1978–79).

Internet Resources

Websites come and go. The following list of general websites, websites for U.S. fairs, and websites for foreign fairs reflects the widespread interest in fairs that has developed in recent years. All of the sites on this list were accessible and operating in May 2007. Researchers should be aware that information found on websites (as opposed to books and articles in peer-reviewed journals) may not be accurate or up-to-date, since anyone can place anything on the worldwide web. Nevertheless, many of these website contain excellent information and wonderful images of many different fairs, and those interested in a particular fair should not hesitate to pay visits to relevant sites.

Websites — General Information

Bureau International des Expositions (Bureau of International Expositions), http://www.bie-paris.org/. The Library of the Bureau of International Expositions provides information on many international exhibitions. The Bureau International des Expositions was created in 1928 to set standards and outline obligations of exhibitors at world expositions. This site provides information on past, present and future expositions.

Revisiting the World's Fairs and Expositions, a Selected Bibliography, 1992–2004 by the Smithsonian Institution Libraries, http://www.sil.si.edu/silpublications/worlds-fairs/. Excellent selection of images and a bibliography of sources including articles, dissertations, monographs, and additional websites. See the general bibliography for more information.

Expomuseum, http://www.expomuseum.com/. Site contains a collection of information, photos, timelines, and memorabilia for world's fairs and expositions. A new feature has been added in the form of a web blog to provide news about former and upcoming fairs.

University of Maryland, Essays for Online Exhibition on World's Fairs, http://www.lib.umd.edu/ARCH/honr219f/home.html. Collection of honors seminar essays, some with images, which focus on fairs and expositions from 1851 to 1967. The university also offers an overview of fairs held from 1851 to 1970 at http://www.lib.umd.edu/ARCH/exhibition/.

National Gallery of Art, Image Collections of International Expositions, http://www.nga.gov/resources/expositions.shtm, the NGA maintains a large collection of photographs, albums, and postcard booklets from various international expositions held from 1851 to 1958.

University of Delaware Library, American World's Fairs and Expositions, http://www.lib.udel.edu/ud/spec/exhibits/fairs/index.htm. The University of Delaware Library possesses a variety of primary source materials relating to world's fairs and expositions held in the United States between 1876 and 1939.

Scouting at the World's Fair, http://www.stefford.com/jjmsr/. This site, created and maintained by James J. Miller, Sr., focuses on the participation of Boy Scout Service Corps at world's fairs and expositions.

The World's Fair and Exposition Information and Reference Guide, http://www.earthstation9.com/index.html?worlds_2.htm. This long-existing internet source contains 430 listed exhibitions, expositions and world's fairs, with 1,024 Links. Information is also available for a charge on CD-ROM.

World's Fair and Exposition Collectibles, http://www.the-forum.com/COLLECT/worldfai.htm. This site maintains a collection of memorabilia from several important fairs and expositions that are available for purchase online.

Library of Congress, American Memory Collection. http://memory.loc.gov/ammem/index.html. The American Memory Collection contains maps, manuscripts, motion pictures, sheet music, photos, prints, sound recordings, and other texts. These are searchable by keyword, topic, collection or time period. For example, a search for the 1939 Bew York World's Fair returns 688 items of relevance.

Donald G. Larson Collection on Interna-

tional Expositions and Fairs, 1851–1940, http: //www.csufresno.edu/library/subjectresources/specialcollections/worldfairs/index.html. Though this site from California State University-Fresno does not contain many online images or memorabilia, it is an excellent reference tool, and even includes fairs scheduled but never held.

Cornell University Library, Making of America, http://cdl.library.cornell.edu/moa/. This extensive online collection provides over two thousand book and journal items related to world fairs prior to 1926.

Internet Archive, http ://www.archive.org/ index.php. IA provides free access to moving images, audio, text, and archived webpages with numerous search options. It contains many amateur and professional films made at world's fairs and expositions during the twentieth century.

International Exhibitions, Expositions Universelles and World's Fairs, 1851–1951: A Bibliography, http://www.tu-cottbus.de/BTU/Fak2/Theo Arch/Wolke/eng/Bibliography/ExpoBibliography. htm. This site is an excellent source for students or others researching international fairs and expositions. It contains research aids, internet sources, and other extensive resource listings for events held from 1851–1951, and some resources for events held after 1951.

Fairs and Expositions in American History, http://www.geometry.net/detail/basic_f/fairs_&_ex positions_american_history.html. A detailed listing of websites focusing on fairs in America including some very unusual sources.

Websites — U.S. Fairs

PHILADELPHIA 1876

Centennial Exhibition of 1876, Pennsylvania Historical and Museum Commission, http:// www.phmc.state.pa.us/ppet/centennial/page1.asp?s ecid=31. Provides the history of the 1876 exhibition with a few photos.

Centennial Exhibition of 1876, Library of Philadelphia, http://libwww.library.phila.gov/Cen Col/. Unique online collection of silver albumen photographs and history of the exhibition

1876 Centennial Exhibition in Philadelphia, Architecture, http://www.bc.edu/bc_org/avp/cas/ fnart/fa267/1876fair.html. Boston College's collection of images scanned from *The Illustrated History of the Centennial Exhibition*, by James D. McCabe, published in Philadelphia, 1876, and Frank Leslie's *Illustrated Historical Register of the Centennial Exposition* 1876. New York, 1877.

The Railroads and the Centennial Exhibition of 1876, http://cprr.org/Museum/Centennial_Exhibition_1876/. Central Pacific Railroad Photographic History Museum's history and memorabilia.

Centennial Exposition, Philadelphia, 1876,

http://www.digitalhistory.uh.edu/learning_history/worlds_fair/centennial_resources.cfm. University of Houston's collection of digitized articles from *Scribner's Monthly, Manufacturer and Builder, Appleton's Journal*, and others.

NEW ORLEANS 1884–1885

The World's Cotton Centennial Exposition, http://penelope.uchicago.edu/Thayer/E/Gazetteer/ Places/America/United_States/Louisiana/New_Orl eans/_Texts/KENHNO/29*.html. This webpage reproduces a chapter of *History of New Orleans* by John Kendall (1922), describing the history and development of the Cotton Exposition in New Orleans.

1884 World's Industrial and Cotton Centennial Exposition. http://www.earthstation9.com/ index.html?1884_new.htm. Earth Station 9's site is devoted to the 1884 fair, containing 158 facts and trivia nuggets plus 10 links to external resources, but no images.

New Orleans: Gateway to the Americas-Cotton Exposition, 1884, http://nutrias.org/ex hibits/gateway/1884.htm. This site focuses on the contributions of Central and South America and offers information about the Panama Canal.

CHICAGO 1893

1893 World's Columbian Exposition, Chicago Public Library, http://www.chipublib. org/digital/lake/CFDWCE.html. Collection of photos, links, and primary source material.

The World's Columbian Exposition, Chicago Historical Society, http://www.chicago-history.org/history/expo.html. Site provides a bibliography, photos, artifacts, and text about the Columbian Exposition. Site also includes a small section about the Pullman railroad car.

Interactive Guide to the World's Columbian Exposition, http://users.vnet.net/schulman/Col umbian/columbian.html#TOP. Site includes admission statistics, pricing, transportation, architecture, construction materials and costs, Chicago history, and exposition legislation among many other important topics.

ATLANTA 1895

Cotton States and International Exposition, Atlanta, 1895. http://www.georgiaencyclopedia. org/nge/Article.jsp?id=h-2913. New *Georgia Encyclopedia* features information on Cotton Expositions held in Atlanta in the nineteenth century.

Speech Before the Atlanta Cotton States and International Exposition, http://teachingameri-canhistory.org/library/index.asp?document=69. Text of Booker T. Washington's speech given September 18, 1895, and recognized as one of the most important and influential speeches in American history. The audio of the speech is available online at http://americanradioworks.publicradio.org/features/sayitplain/btwashington.html.

Cotton States and International Exposition, Atlanta, 1895, http://www.digitalhistory.uh.edu/learning_history/worlds_fair/cotton_states_resources.cfm. University of Houston's digital history site provides a collection of links for the 1895 exposition.

Africa and the American Negro : addresses and proceedings of the Congress on Africa held in connection with the Cotton States and International Exposition December 13–15, 1895, http://docsouth.unc.edu/church/bowen/menu.html. Covers the colonial partition of Africa and promotes the generally held view of the Congress's speakers that colonization provided an opportunity to promote Christianity and its civilizing influence in Africa.

NASHVILLE 1897

Tennessee Centennial and International Exposition, http://tennessee.gov/tsla/history/manuscripts/findingaids/1785.pdf. Tennessee State Library collection for the 1897 exposition contains some history and a description of archive holdings available.

Tennessee at 100, http://pr.tennessee.edu/alumnus/winter96/centenn.html. An account of the contributions made by the University of Tennessee to the fair.

Tennessee Centennial Exposition Nashville, http://memory.loc.gov/service/pnp/ppmsca/03300/03354v.jpg. Lithograph by The Henderson Litho. Co., 1897

OMAHA 1898

Trans-Mississippi International Exposition of 1898, http://www.omaha.lib.ne.us/transmiss/. Omaha Public Library's collection of sources on the 1898 fair, including a section about the Indian Congress

Trans-Mississippi Exposition: Omaha, Nebraska, 1898 http://www.historicomaha.com/transmis.htm Site contains four galleries of images from the 1898 fair. All images have been scanned in grayscale.

The Year 1898, http://www.npr.org/templates/story/story.php?storyId=1010542 National Public Radio's archived audio file that explores events of the year 1898 including the Trans-Mississippi Exposition.

BUFFALO 1901

William I. Buchanan Collection, Buffalo and Erie County Historical Society, http://www.bechs.org/exhibits/exhibits.htm. The collection features Buchanan's correspondence as director general, along with other documents related to the exposition.

Theodore Roosevelt Inaugural National Historic Site, National Park Service http://www.nps.gov/archive/thri/PanAmExhibit.htm. A permanent and virtual collection to commemorate the 100th anniversary of the Pan-American Exposition.

Films of McKinley and the Pan-American Exposition, 1901, Library of Congress. http://memory.loc.gov/ammem/papr/mckhome.html. These films include footage of President William McKinley at his second inauguration; of the Pan-American Exposition in Buffalo, New York; of President McKinley at the Pan-American Exposition; and of President McKinley's funeral.

Illuminations: Revisiting the Buffalo Pan-American Exposition of 1901, University of Buffalo, http://ublib.buffalo.edu/libraries/exhibits/panam/. This site presents a wide range of both primary texts and original essays on the history of the Pan-American Exposition.

"Do the Pan," http://www.panam1901.bfn.org/. Virtual tours, documents, and stories from the 1901 exposition.

McKinley Assassination, http://www.npr.org/templates/story/story.php?storyId=1128584. National Public Radio's archived audio file that revisits McKinley's assassination at the 1901 exposition in Buffalo.

Buffalo, New York, http://www.npr.org/templates/story/story.php?storyId=1125189. National Public Radio's archived audio file includes a discussion with author Mark Goldman, (*City on the Lake: The Challenge of Change in Buffalo, New York*) about the 1901 Exposition.

CHARLESTON 1901–1902

Panoramic view of Charleston exposition, http://memory.loc.gov/mbrs/awal/2132.mpg.

Thomas A. Edison's 1902 film of the Charleston Exposition. Other films in the Library of Congress collection include President Roosevelt reviewing the troops http://memory.loc.gov/mbrs/trmp/4135.mpg **and the Midway** http://memory.loc.gov/mbrs/awal/0176.mpg. *Photographs of the Charleston Exposition* http://www.boondocksnet.com/gallery/wfe1902/. Excellent collection of images from the exposition.

ST. LOUIS 1904

University of California-Riverside, Keystone-Mast Collection, Expositions and World Fairs, http://138.23.124.165/collections/permanent/projects/stereo/immigration/worldfair.html#. Small collection of prints from the 1904 world's fair at St. Louis.

The Louisiana Purchase Exposition, http://washingtonmo.com/1904/index.htm. Collection of articles and photos of the 1904 St. Louis Fair.

Agricultural Events at the 1904 St. Louis World's Fair, http://www.lyndonirwin.com/1904fair.htm. Missouri State University site that includes photos and text describing agriculture at the fair.

1904 World's Fair, Missouri Historical Society, http://www.mohistory.org/content/fair/wf/html/index_flash.html. Excellent site with numerous resources including programs for educators.

Also contains an interactive virtual tour of the fairgrounds.

"Living Exhibits" at 1904 World's Fair Revisited, http://www.npr.org/templates/story/story.php?storyId=1909651. National Public Radio's audio file and photo gallery that revisits tribal displays at the 1904 fair.

From the Belgian Congo to the Bronx Zoo, http://www.npr.org/templates/story/story.php?storyId=5787947. National Public Radio's audio file and photos that tell the story of Ota Benga, who was among a group of pygmies brought to the United States to be displayed at the St. Louis world's fair in 1904.

PORTLAND 1905

A Fair to Remember: The 1905 Lewis and Clark Exposition, http://www.ohs.org/exhibits/fair.cfm. Oregon Historical Society's online exhibit companion for the 1905 fair that includes photographs and ordering information for additional resources.

Lewis and Clark 1905 Exposition, Portland, Oregon, http://www.iinet.com/~englishriver/LewisClarkColumbiaRiver/Regions/Places/lewis_clark_1905_exposition.html. Collection of text and high quality color images including maps and postcards.

1905 Lewis and Clark Exposition, http://www.history.pdx.edu/guildslake/topics/mainfair.htm Portland State University's site dedicated to the 1905 fair includes general history, the world's fair movement, and fun items like the "World's Largest Log Cabin."

JAMESTOWN 1907

Jamestown Exposition of 1907, http://www.rkpuma.com/ov/nickel22expo.htm. Collection of scanned color images of buildings used for the 1907 exposition.

The Jamestown Exposition 1907, http://www.npl.lib.va.us/sgm/oldlobby/archives/james.html. Norfolk Public Library's online exhibit of text and images about the 1907 exposition. Additional images available at http://www.npl.lib.va.us/absoluteig/gallery.asp?categoryid=92

Jamestown Exposition, http://www.vahistorical.org/onthisday/2501.htm. Brief history of the exposition from the Virginia Historical Society.

Jamestown Exposition Illustrated, http://www.countyhistory.com/gwf/jamestown/index.html. Scanned fair guide available online in addition to postcards.

Enduring Legacy of the Jamestown Exposition, http://www.hrnm.navy.mil/1907exposition/. Hampton Roads Naval Museum's site dedicated to the 1907 exposition. Site includes film clips, images, and an interactive tour of the fairgrounds.

SEATTLE 1909

Alaska-Yukon-Pacific Exposition (Seattle), http://content.lib.washington.edu/aypweb/index.html. 660 photographs from the Alaska-Yukon-Pacific Exposition document the fair held on the campus of the University of Washington during the summer of 1909. Images include depictions of the buildings, grounds, entertainment, and exotic attractions at the fair.

Alaska-Yukon-Pacific Exposition, 1909, http://www.historylink.org/essays/output.cfm?file_id=7082. This site provides a slide show of Seattle's first world's fair, which opened on June 1, 1909. An essay about this fair can be found at http://www.historylink.org/essays/output.cfm?file_id=5371.

Open: A World of Wonders, http://seattletimes.nwsource.com/centennial/february/exposition.html. This story ran in the Seattle *Times* on February 18, 1996, and tells the history of the fair in addition to photos and classroom resources.

Hard Drive to the Klondike: Promoting Seattle during the Gold Rush, http://www.nps.gov/archive/klse/hrs/hrs3e.htm. This site from the National Park Service provides a unit of historical study and resources for the 1909 Alaska-Yukon-Pacific Exposition with a few images.

SAN FRANCISCO 1915

Panama Pacific International Exposition, http://www.sanfranciscomemories.com/ppie/panamapacific.html. Great collection of images, souvenirs, maps, and links.

Panama-Pacific International Exposition, http://www.sfmuseum.org/hist9/ppietxt1.html. San Francisco Museum's collection offers a PowerPoint presentation of hand-colored prints and a virtual tour.

Panama-Pacific International Exposition, http://userwww.sfsu.edu/~scottrau/index.htm. San Francisco State University's archive of exposition history and artifacts.

The 1915 Panama-Pacific International Exposition http://www.nps.gov/archive/prsf/history/ppie/ppie.htm. National Park Service, Presidio's history site for the exposition that contains a pdf file of the brochure created by the NPS.

Mabel and Fatty at the World's Fair, http://memory.loc.gov/mbrs/lcmp003/33488s1.mpg. The comedy stars of the silent era visit the Panama-Pacific Exposition.

PHILADELPHIA 1926

Sesqui-Centennial Exposition, 1926, http://www.lib.udel.edu/ud/spec/exhibits/fairs/sesqui.htm. University of Delaware's site provides brief history with images of the 1926 Expo.

1926 Sesqui-Centennial International Exposition http://www.libertybellmuseum.com/WorldsFair/1926sesqui.htm. Liberty Bell Museum's site devoted to the 1926 Expo includes numerous images of Liberty Bell memorabilia from the fair.

**The Past is Present: Historical Representation at the Sesquicentennial International Expo-

sition, http://repository.upenn.edu/dissertations/ AAI9953514/. University of Pennsylvania student dissertation available for download, which explores the tensions between politicians, middle-class white women, corporations, civic and fraternal organizations, immigrants, and African Americans at the Sesquicentennial Expo.

CHICAGO 1933–1934

University of Chicago Library's Century of Progress 1933–34 World's Fair Collection, http://century.lib.uchicago.edu/. Three hundred and fifty pamphlets from the collection have been digitized and made available for on-line viewing. Also available is a searchable database of the *Checklist of Official Publications of the Century of Progress International Exposition and Its Exhibitors*

Century of Progress 1933–34, http://www.chicagohs.org/history/century.html. Chicago Historical Society's site devoted to the 1933 fair. Site offers a bibliography, photos, artifacts, and a quiz about Chicago firsts.

Images from a Century of Progress, http://www.sjsu.edu/faculty/wooda/chicago/. Site offers photos, postcards, panoramic views, and online resources for the 1933 fair.

Century of Progress Exposition, http://www.encyclopedia.chicagohistory.org/pages/225.html. *Encyclopedia of Chicago*'s site offers text and a few photos with links to more in-depth information on specific topics, including race relations and civil rights during the Great Depression.

SAN DIEGO 1935–1936

California Pacific Exposition, San Diego 1935–1936, http://www.sandiegohistory.org/calpac/35expo11.htm. San Diego Historical Society's site for the 1935 Expo includes stereocards, postcards, detailed maps, audio files, and several video clips including Zoro's Gardens Nudist Colony

Crosby Exhibit of 1935 California Pacific International Exposition, http://epicovers.com/crosby/collections/cpie/. Walter Garfield Crosby's covers for the 1935 Expo (stamps).

Ford Building History, http://www.sandiegoairandspace.org/organization/buildinghistory.html. San Diego Air and Space Museum's site dedicated to the history of the Ford exhibit at the 1935 fair.

NEW YORK 1939–1940

Welcome to Tomorrow, 1939 New York World's Fair, http://xroads.virginia.edu/~1930s/DISPLAY/39wf/frame.htm. Excellent site with artifacts, photos, resources, and text about the 1939 fair.

New York's 1939–1940 World's Fair, http://www.sjsu.edu/faculty/wooda/nywf.html. Andrew F. Wood's site, created from research for his book, *New York's 1939–1940 World's Fair*, has images of postcards, comics, advertisements, and history.

1939 New York World's Fair, http://www.pmphoto.to/WorldsFairTour/home.htm. This site organizes its information by the seven zones of the fair. Excellent organization makes a virtual tour very informative and user-friendly.

The 1939 New York World's Fair- Early Television http://www.earlytelevision.org/worlds_fair.html This site is devoted to the introduction of television at the 1939 fair. Linked text allows user to view the original programming schedule, learn about the marketing campaign, or read an audience survey letter from NBC.

SAN FRANCISCO 1939–1940

The Treasure Island World's Fair (The San Francisco Golden Gate Exhibition 1939–1940), http://www.sfmuseum.net/views/ggieviews.ppt. This PowerPoint presentation offers 24 images of the fair. It is included as part of San Francisco Museum's online resources for world's fairs. Numerous sources for the 1939 fair are available at http://www.sfmuseum.org/hist1/index0.1.html.

Hard Times, High Visions, http://bancroft.berkeley.edu/Exhibits/Looking/hardtimes.html. Images and text about the 1939 Golden Gate Intrenational Exposition.

SEATTLE 1962

Seattle Center at 40, http://seattlepi.nwsource.com/specials/worldsfair/. Site features art, architecture, pop culture, history, and commentary about the 1962 World's Fair in Seattle.

Century 21: The 1962 World's Fair, http://seattletimes.nwsource.com/photogallery/gen/worldsfair/. Seattle *Times* site offers a photo gallery of the fair.

Seattle Space Needle, http://www.spaceneedle.com/. Site offers history and fun facts about the 1962 World's Fair and the Space Needle.

Century 21— The 1962 Seattle World's Fair, http://www.historylink.org/essays/output.cfm?file_id=2290, http://www.historylink.org/essays/output.cfm?file_id=2291. Online encyclopedia of Washington State offers a great essay and artifacts for the 1962 fair.

NEW YORK 1964–1965

1964 New York World's Fair, http://www.nywf64.com/. Site provides artifacts, memorabilia, postcards, and souvenirs of the 1964 fair.

1964–1965 New York World's Fair, http://www.worldsfairphotos.com/nywf64/index.htm. Buy CDs of prints, view postcards, souvenirs, and advertising, or take a tour of the fair.

New York City Transit system, http://world.nycsubway.org/us/worldsfair/. Great collection of photos of the monorail system at the 1964 fair.

SAN ANTONIO 1968

HemisFair '68, http://www.lib.utexas.edu/taro/utsa/00050/utsa-00050p1.html. University of

Texas, San Antonio's guide to San Antonio Fair, Inc., Records, 1963–1995, which also contains a concise history and timeline of preparation for this fair. HemisFair Park http://hotx.com/hot/hillcountry/sa/tours/hemisfair/. History and renovation of the HemisFair Park in San Antonio.

SEATTLE 1974

Expo 74 Spokane World's Fair, http://www.historylink.org/essays/output.cfm?file_id=5133. Washington State History Online Encyclopedia offers text and a few photos for the 1974 expo.

A Virtual Visit to Expo '74, The Spokane World's Fair, http://expo74.brandx.net/. This site includes a first-hand account of visiting the fair, information about rides at the fair, music tributes, country pavilions, and performers at the fair.

KNOXVILLE 1982

Energy Turns the World- Knoxville 1982, http://users.vnet.net/schulman/1982/fair.html. Site includes section about the developers of this exposition, a history of Knoxville, fair statistics, adaptive re-use of the fair site, and memories of the fair. Site is part of a web-ring devoted to world's fairs.

Knoxville International Energy Exposition, http://tennesseeencyclopedia.net/imagegallery.php?EntryID=K026. *Tennessee Encyclopedia of History and Culture*'s brief history of the 1982 expo.

Key figures in Knoxville's Energy Expo: Then and Now, http://web.knoxnews.com/advertising/worldsfair/news_keyfigures.html. Part of the Knoxville *News-Sentinel*'s site to celebrate the twentieth anniversary of the Energy Expo. The main page can be found at http://web.knoxnews.com/advertising/worldsfair/index.html.

No Knocks for Knoxville, http://www.time.com/time/magazine/article/0,9171,953482,00.html. *Time* magazine's 1982 article about the Knoxville International Energy Exposition

NEW ORLEANS 1984

The Wonder of the 1984 World's Fair, http://www.ogdenmuseum.org/exhibitions/exhibition-worldsfair.html. Ogden Museum, University of New Orleans exhibit dedicated to the 1984 fair, featuring photographs by Joshua Mann Pailet.

Foul Times for a Fair, http://www.time.com/time/magazine/article/0,9171,954394,00.html *Time* magazine's article about the 1984 Louisiana World Exposition and its financial losses.

Websites — Foreign Fairs — General

Minor American and International Expositions, 1867–1939 http://siarchives.si.edu/findingaids/faru0070.htm#FARU70s23. Index to Series

23 collection from the exposition records of the Smithsonian Institution. More information about using collections is available at http://siarchives.si.edu/research/main_collectionaid.html

Making of America, http://cdl.library.cornell.edu/moa/. Cornell University Library's collection of digitized primary sources offers numerous items for American and European fairs and expositions. Browse the collection by publication or search for a particular fair at http://cdl.library.cornell.edu/moa/moa_search.html

Design, Politics and Commerce: International Exhibitions 1851–1951, http://special.lib.gla.ac.uk/teach/century/index.html. University of Glasgow's Special Collections Department provides resources and online images from several exhibitions including London (1851, 1862), Vienna (1873), Paris (1855, 1878, 1889), Glasgow (1888, 1901), as well as information about Art Nouveau and Art Deco.

Mettlach Beer Steins, http://www.steincollectors.org/library/articles/Mettlach/mettlach.htm. Article contains images and discusses the display of steins at world's fairs that made Mettlach factories famous.

Expo 2000, http://www.expo2000.de/expo2000/geschichte/detail.php?wa_id=2&lang=1. This website contains information of various kinds about many major international expositions.

Websites — Foreign Fairs — Specific

LONDON 1851

Industrial Arts and the Exhibition Ideal, http://www.vam.ac.uk/vastatic/microsites/1159_grand_design/essay-industrial_new.html. Article by Peter Trippi discusses the Victoria and Albert Museum and the start of the exhibition movement.

DUBLIN 1853

Fairs of the Past, http://columbus.iit.edu/bookfair/ch1.html. Chapter from *The Book of the Fair* that briefly describes the 1853 exhibition in Dublin and many other early fairs.

PARIS 1855

Books On the Exposition Universelle, World's Fair of 1855, http://cec.chebucto.org/Books/WFB/WFB-1855.html. Bibliography listing sources for study of the 1855 exposition.

Fanfare for the New Empire, http://charon.sfsu.edu/publications/PARISEXPOSITIONS/1855EXPO.html. Essay reproduced from *World's Fair*, 6, 2 (1986) by Arthur Chandler, but link to images may not work.

LONDON 1862

Great London Exhibition 1862 Stereo Cards, http://www.the-forum.com/collect/ster1862.htm. Small collection of stereo cards from 1862 fair.

DUBLIN 1865

Fairs of the Past, http://columbus.iit.edu/bookfair/ch1.html. Chapter from *The Book of the Fair* that briefly describes the 1865 exhibition in Dublin and many other early fairs.

Dublin International Exhibition, 1865, http://www.scienceandsociety.co.uk/results.asp?image=10243044&wwwflag=2&imagepos=1. Site includes an engraving by the Leighton Brothers, showing the interior of the Exhibition Hall.

DUNEDIN 1865

Exhibition Art Gallery, http://www.historic.org.nz/Register/ListingDetail.asp?RID=2149&rm=Full&sm=advanced. New Zealand's Historic Places Trust register that provides history of the art gallery created for the 1865 fair.

PARIS 1867

1867: Empire, http://ml.hss.cmu.edu/courses/mjwest/Chapter_2_1867.htm. Student essay from Carnegie Mellon University's Modern Languages Department about the 1867 fair in Paris.

Empire of Autumn, http://charon.sfsu.edu/publications/PARISEXPOSITIONS/1867EXPO.html. Essay reproduced from *World's Fair,* 6, 3 (1986), by Arthur Chandler.

Post-war Paris http://www.retropolis.net/exposition/postwarparis.html. Reprint from *World's Fair* 8, 3 (1988), by Arthur Chandler, with images and text about the 1925 fair but also discusses the 1867 and 1900 fairs.

Expositions Universelles, Paris 1867, http://www.sil.si.edu/silpublications/Worlds-Fairs/WF_selected.cfm?categories=Expositions%20Universelles%2C%20Paris%201867. Smithsonian Institution's bibliography of sources for the 1867 exposition.

Paris Exposition Universelle 1867 and 1878, http://www.photoart.plus.com/expos/p556778.htm. Small collection of images from 1867 and 1878 fairs.

LONDON 1871–1874

Elias Howe sewing machine, 1871, http://www.scienceandsociety.co.uk/results.asp?image=10321354. Plate taken from the official catalogue of the London International Exhibition of 1871.

Gilbert and Sullivan Archive, http://diamond.boisestate.edu/gas/other_sullivan/shore_sea/index.html. Sullivan's *On Shore and Sea*, was composed for, and performed at, the opening of the London International Exhibition, May 1, 1871. This site has MIDI and karaoke files of the music for download and other sources.

PARIS 1878

Heroism in Defeat, http://charon.sfsu.edu/publications/PARISEXPOSITIONS/1878EXPO.html. Reprint from *World's Fair* 6, 4 (1986) by Arthur Chandler, describing the Paris Exposition Universelle of 1878.

Paris Exposition Universelle 1867 and 1878, http://www.photoart.plus.com/expos/p556778.htm. Small collection of images from 1867 and 1878 fairs.

1878: Hearts and Minds, http://ml.hss.cmu.edu/courses/mjwest/Chapter_3_1878.htm. Student essay from Carnegie Mellon University's Modern Languages Department about the 1878 fair in Paris.

SYDNEY 1879–1880

Sydney International Exhibition, http://www.lib.umd.edu/ARCH/exhibition/1879/. Pamphlet from the 1879 exhibition as digital image.

Sydney Lights up the International Exhibition Building, 1879, http://www.cityofsydney.nsw.gov.au/history/linksinthechain/Zoom/lg_89060.html. City of Sydney website discusses use of electric lights.

Curators of the Colonial Idea: the museum and exhibition as agents of bourgeois ideology in nineteenth century New South Wales, http://www.teachingheritage.nsw.edu.au/lviews/wphr3_rigg.html. Valda Rigg's article discusses colonial ideology in the nineteenth century and the impact of world exhibitions.

In Sight of Sydney's Garden Palace, http://www.music.unimelb.edu.au/about/csam/13_royle.pdf. Book review discusses history of the 1879 exhibition

MELBOURNE 1880–1881

Curators of the Colonial Idea: the museum and exhibition as agents of bourgeois ideology in nineteenth century New South Wales, http://www.teachingheritage.nsw.edu.au/lviews/wphr3_rigg.html. Valda Rigg's article discusses colonial ideology in nineteenth century and the impact of world exhibitions.

AMSTERDAM 1883

World Expositions in Amsterdam—1883, http://parallel.park.org/Netherlands/pavilions/world_expositions/index 2.htm. History and images of the 1883 exposition.

International Exhibition at Amsterdam, http://moa.cit.cornell.edu/cgi-bin/moa/sgml/moa-idx?notisid=ABS1821-0015-157. *Manufacturer and Builder*, 15, 3, (1883) includes an article about the exhibition.

CALCUTTA 1883–1884

Indian Museum, Calcutta, http://userpages.umbc.edu/~achatt1/Calcutta/indmus.html. Association of museum with international exhibition of 1883.

Calcutta Exhibition, http://www.stampsofindia.com/readroom/510.htm. Stamp collecting website that discusses the 1883 exhibition.

The Calcutta International Exhibition, http://moa.cit.cornell.edu/cgi-bin/moa/sgml/moa-idx?notisid=ABS1821–0015–169 and http://moa.cit.cornell.edu/cgi-bin/moa/sgml/moa-idx?notisid=ABS1821–0015–473. *Manufacturer and Builder* articles about the 1883 exhibition.

ANTWERP 1885

International Exhibition at Antwerp, http://moa.cit.cornell.edu/cgi-bin/moa/sgml/moa-idx?notisid=ABS1821–0016–539. *Manufacturer and Builder*, 16, 9 (September 1884) article about the Antwerp exhibition.

Ambitious project by De Porceleyne Fles, http://www.rijksmuseum.nl/collectie/aanwinsten%202004/delfts-tegeltableau?lang=en. History of a tile plate in relief exhibited at the Antwerp fair.

EDINBURGH 1886

Old Edinburgh Exhibit, http://www.edinphoto.org.uk/PP_V/pp_wane_international_exhibition_1886.htm. Collection of postcards, book prints, cabinet prints and *carte de visites*.

Exhibition: Edinburgh 1886, http://www.arthist.arts.gla.ac.uk/int_ex/exhibitions/1886edinburgh/edinburgh_1886.html. Virtual collection of artifacts and photographs.

International Exhibition of Industry, Science and Art, http://members.fortunecity.com/gillonj/edinburghinternationalexhibition/. Site offering only a brief history of the exhibition.

LONDON 1886

A Critical History of Architecture, http://architronic.saed.kent.edu/v6n1/v6n1.05b.html. Discussion of architecture at the 1886 Colonial and Indian Exhibition

The Restoration of the Jaipur Gate, http://www.hove.virtualmuseum.info/jaipurgate.asp.

The Jaipur Gate was made for the Colonial and Indian Exhibition of 1886. Website describes the gate and the restoration efforts.

The Journal of the Manchester Geographical Society, http://books.google.com/books/pdf/The_Journal_of_the_Manchester_Geographic.pd?. Article is about tobacco brokers and others interested in the trade, held in the Conference Hall of the Colonial and Indian Exhibition.

ADELAIDE 1887

Curators of the Colonial Idea: the museum and exhibition as agents of bourgeois ideology in nineteenth-century New South Wales, http://www.teachingheritage.nsw.edu.au/lviews/wphr3_rigg.html. Valda Rigg's article discusses colonial ideology in nineteenth century and the impact of world exhibitions.

Adelaide Jubilee International Exhibition 1887–1888, http://www.pictureaustralia.org/apps/pictureaustralia?action=PASearch&mode=search&complete1=true&attribute1=subject&term1=Ade-laide+Jubilee+International+Exhibition%2C+%28 1887%29. High quality images from the 1887 exhibition from the State Library of South Australia.

Adelaide Jubilee International Exhibition, http://www.musicaustralia.org/apps/MA?function=searchResults&term1=Adelaide%20Jubilee%20International%20Exhibition,%20(1887)%20Songs%20and%20music.%20&scope=scope&parameter1=phrase&location1=Anywhere. View the scores of two songs written for the Adelaide Jubilee.

BARCELONA 1888

Modernisme and the 1888 Universal Exposition of Barcelona, http://www.artnouveaunet.eu/data/PROCEEDINGS_DOWNLOAD/BRUSSEL/Lluis_Bosch_Pascual.doc. Article describing how the Barcelona exposition made the Modernisme Movement known to the general public.

MELBOURNE 1888–1889

Medals of Melbourne International Exhibition, 1888, http://www.museum.vic.gov.au/coins/1880/international_exhibition_medals.html. The gold, silver and bronze medals awarded as prizes and for services by the Melbourne 1888 International Exhibition.

Centennial Extravaganza, http://www.museum.vic.gov.au/windows/worldfair/index.asp.

PARIS 1889

1889 Paris Exposition Universelle, http://www.nga.gov/resources/expo1889.shtm. National Gallery of Art's online images from the 1889 exposition.

DUNEDIN 1889–1890

New Zealand and South Seas Exhibition, http://www.lib.umd.edu/ARCH/exhibition/1889–90/gallery1.html. Image of the exhibition building.

Welcome to the Exhibition: "What a Show" http://www.cityofdunedin.com/city/?page=feat_osm_showingoff. City of Dunedin's site devoted to the history of world expositions including those held in Dunedin. Includes images.

KINGSTON 1891

The Great Exhibition of 1891, http://www.jamaica-gleaner.com/pages/history/story0018.html. Images and detailed history about the 1891 exhibition in Jamaica.

Jamaican Elegance with a Jewish Twist, http://www.jewishjournal.com/home/preview.php?id=13348. Article tells the story of George Stiebel, son of a German Jew and a Jamaican housekeeper, born in the 1820s, whose monetary donation helped stage the Great Exhibition of 1891 and introduced tourism to Jamaica.

MADRID 1892

Columbian Historical Exposition (Madrid, 1892–1893), http://siarchives.si.edu/findingaids/

faru0070.htm#FARU70s9. Index to Series 9 collection from the Exposition Records of the Smithsonian Institution. More information about using collections is available at http://siarchives.si.edu/research/main_collectionaid.html.

The Columbian Historical Exposition in Madrid. *American Anthropologist*, Vol. 6, No. 3 (Jul., 1893), pp. 271–278

Exhibit of Games in the Columbian Exposition, *The Journal of American Folklore*, Vol. 6, No. 22 (Jul.– Sep., 1893), pp. 205–227. Both articles available at http://www.jstor.org/.

The Recall of Columbus, http://a257.g.akamaitech.net/7/257/2422/28june20040851/www.gpo access.gov/serialset/cdocuments/sd107–11/pdf/314–315.pdf. Artist Augustus Heaton's work was exhibited at the Columbian Exposition to commemorate the 400th anniversary of the discovery of America.

ANTWERP 1894

Antwerp International Exhibition, http://www.slv.vic.gov.au/miscpics/0/0/6/doc/mp006678.shtml. Image of a wood engraving gives overview of the exposition grounds.

HOBART 1894–1895

Tasmanian International Exhibition Building, http://images.statelibrary.tas.gov.au/Search/Search.asp?Letter=T&Title=Tasmanian+International+Exhibition+Building%2C+Domain%2C+Hobart+1894–95. Image from State Library of Tasmania, excellent quality.

Tasmanian International Exhibition (1894–1895 : Hobart, Tas.)— Songs and music, http://greenstone.statelibrary.tas.gov.au/cgi-bin/library.exe?e=d-000–00—-0music—00–0–0–0prompt-10—-4———0-1l—1-en-Zz-1—-10-home —-00001–001–0-0utfZz-8–0&a=d&c=music&cl=CL3.4.24. State Library of Tasmania, Collection of songs and music from the exposition.

BRUSSELS 1897

Exposition Internationale de Bruxelles, http://www.lib.umd.edu/ARCH/exhibition/1897/gallery1.html. This postcard features a bird's-eye rendering of the Exposition Internationale de Bruxelles of 1897.

A Dark Reminder of Belgium's Colonial Past, http://www.iht.com/articles/1997/11/05/colo.t_0.php. *International Herald Tribune* article about Belgium's celebration of colonialism.

Philippe Wolfers' Japonism in Belgium, http://www.ascasonline.org/ARTICOLOF51.html. Article discusses how Wolfers introduced his delicate and original new designs at the exposition in Brussels. Includes images.

GUATEMALA CITY 1897

Central American Exposition, http://www.nationalanthems.info/gt.htm. Music and lyrics of the National Anthem, written and performed as one of the main events of the 1897 exposition

STOCKHOLM 1897

The 1897 Stockholm Exposition, http://www.martinkarlsson.net/pdf/oldstockholmtext.pdf. Article that provides history of the exposition and describes it as the "culmination of innovation."

Spectacular Articulations of Modernity: The Stockholm Exhibition of 1897. *Geografiska Annaler. Series B, Human Geography*, Vol. 73, No. 1, Meaning and Modernity: Cultural Geographies of the Invisible and the Concrete (1991), pp. 45–84. This article available from http://www.jstor.org/.

Unspeakable Spaces: Racism's past and present on exhibit in Stockholm, or the unaddressable addressed. By Allan Pred, *City & Society* 2001, Vol. 13, No. 1, pp. 119–159, http://www.anthrosource.net/doi/abs/10.1525/city.2001.13.1.119?journalCode=city. Article available for purchase and download from anthrosource.

PARIS 1900

1900 Paris Exposition Universelle, http://www.nga.gov/resources/expo1900.shtm. National Gallery of Art's online images from the 1900 exposition.

Post-war Paris, http://www.retropolis.net/exposition/postwarparis.html. Reprint from *World's Fair*, 8, 3 (1988), by Arthur Chandler, with images and text about the 1925 fair, but also discusses the 1867 and 1900 fairs.

GLASGOW 1901

Glasgow International Exhibition, http://www.nga.gov/images/decor/dpaglas2_fs.shtm. National Gallery of Art's online images from the 1901 exposition.

Glasgow International Exhibition, http://special.lib.gla.ac.uk/exhibns/month/oct1999.html. University of Glasgow's library online exhibit of history and images from the 1901 fair.

TURIN/TORINO 1902

Esposizione Internazionale de Disegno, Turin 1902, http://www.sil.si.edu/silpublications-/Worlds-Fairs/WF_selected.cfm?categories=Esposizione%20Internazionale%20de%20Disegno%2C%20Turin%201902. Bibliography from the Smithsonian Institution with sources in English and Italian.

International Exhibition of Modern Decorative Art, Turin, http://wolfsonian.fiu.edu/collections/c2/art2.html. Postcard, *Esposizione Internazionale d'Arte Decorativa Moderna, Torino*

The Work of Antonio Sant'Elia: Retreat Into the Future, http://books.google.com/books?id=ENizos1KJEgC&pg=PA11&lpg=PA11&dq=torino+1902+exposition&source=web&ots=04an3JPKw6&sig=y0mxHa8uSGnayFt-eEWAZ_MWOK0#PPA12,

M1. This book features information about and works from Antonio Sant'Elia, an Italian architect. Chapter 1 discusses the Torino Expo.

HANOI 1902–1903

L'exposition de Hanoi 1902, http://belleindochine.free.fr/expoHanoi1902.htm. Site offers history and images, though text is in French.

Hanoi Exposition Inauguration Ceremony, http://dlxs.library.cornell.edu/cgi/t/text/pageview-eridx?c=sea;idno=sea057;view=image;seq=121. Large image from Cornell University showing the arrival of Monsieur Doumer.

LIÈGE 1905

Expositions of Belgium, http://pageperso.aol.fr/__121b_DOOIUlLhI4SOhBSmqjSHSjLnm3yUs8j0r2oJjPsTcGQ=. Images from each of the international expositions held in Belgium. Text in French.

MILAN 1906

International Exposition in Milan 1906, http://finemedals.com/ovide_yencesse1.htm. Large images of the bronze plaque for the French section of the international exposition.

Report of the Commissioner of Education, http://books.google.com/books/pdf/Report_of_the _Commissioner_of_Education.pdf? Report from the United States Office of Education, 1907. See Chapter IV for a report on educational progress in Italy and a section devoted to the educational exhibits at the exposition.

CHRISTCHURCH 1906–1907

New Zealand International Exhibition of Arts and Industries, http://library.christchurch.org.nz/Heritage/Publications/1906InternationalExhibition/OfficialRecord/SectionIV.pdf. Official record of the New Zealand International Exhibition of Arts and Industries held at Christchurch.

Simplicity and Splendour: The Canterbury Arts & Crafts Movement from 1882, http://www.achome.co.uk/internationalac/index.php?page= new_zealand. History of New Zealand 's arts and crafts movement, on display at Christchurch.

Penny Claret stamp, 1906, http://tpo.tepapa.govt.nz/print/PrintTopicExhibitDetail.asp?Type= Exhibit&ID=0x000a4fdd&Language=English. Article and images describing the series of stamps to commemorate the Christchurch Exhibition.

The Mona Vale Fernery, http://www.ccc.govt.nz/parks/Trees/protected_22.asp. This brief history describes fernery that was originally part of the New Zealand International Exhibition.

DUBLIN 1907

Irish International Exhibition, http://www.victoriansilk.com/grant/bookmarks/gb175.html. Image of silk bookmark to commemorate the 1907 expo. There is also an image of a silk postcard at http://www.victoriansilk.com/grant/postcards/gc236.html.

Dublin—1907, http://www.studygroup.org.uk/Exhibitions/Pages/1907%20Dublin.htm. History of the 1907 exposition, no images.

LONDON 1908

1908 London Olympics, http://www.historytalk.org/News%20and%20Events/1908%20Olympics.pdf. Discusses the Olympic Games as well as international expositions.

Postcards of the White City, http://www.studygroup.org.uk/White%20City/Part%2020.htm. Discussion of Valentine's postcards of the Franco-British Exhibition 1908, no images.

NANKING 1910

China's World's Fair of 1910: Lessons from a Forgotten Event. Michael R. Godley *Modern Asian Studies*, Vol. 12, No. 3 (1978), pp. 503–522. Article available from http://www.jstor.org/

Souvenir of Nanking, http://dsr.nii.ac.jp/toyobunko/III-2-C-b-75/index.html.en. Souvenir booklet from Nanking, 1910.

Zhang Jian and Nanyang Industrial Exposition in 1910, http://www.sal.tohoku.ac.jp/~kiri-hara/public_html/cgibin/shibusawa/Ma_Min_and _Ai_Xianfeng__paper.pdf. Article discusses the exposition in terms of the economical, cultural and civil diplomatic interaction among China, Japan and America.

LONDON 1911

Olympiads and Empire Games, http://www.teara.govt.nz/1966/A/AthleticstrackAndField/OlympiadsAndEmpireGames/en. Article describes the forerunner of the Empire Games, the 1911 Festival of Empire meet.

Lewis Evans and the White City Exhibitions, http://www.mhs.ox.ac.uk/sphaera/index.htm?issue11/articl4. Scientist Lewis Evans's collections and contributions to Londn exhibitions.

White City Exhibitions, http://www.20thcenturylondon.org.uk/server.php?show=conInformationRecord.262. Imre Kiralfy, builder of the Great White City and Stadium.

IRVING (Coronation Year Souvenir), http://www.civilization.ca/tresors/cigares/images/cigar545.jpg. Montreal cigar maker J. Hirsch & Sons produced a series of three tins in 1911 commemorating the coronation of King George V.

GHENT 1913

Exposition Universelle 1913, http://www.finemedals.com/godefroid_devreese12.htm. Image of bronze plaque for the Exposition Universelle 1913 in Ghent.

RIO DE JANEIRO 1922–1923

1922 International Exposition, http://finemedals.com/godefroid_devreese7.htm. Image of the bronze medal created for the International Exposition in Rio de Janeiro in 1922.

Architecture and History — Exposition 1922–1923, http://www.museuhistoriconacional. com.br/ingles/mh-h-300.htm. Brief history and images from the Rio de Janeiro expo.

A Tropical Cuauhtemoc, http://www.analesiie.unam.mx/pdf/65_93–137.pdf. This article discusses examines Mexico's presence at the 1922 International Exposition in Rio de Janeiro

WEMBLEY 1924–1925

The British Empire Exhibition Wembley 1924–1925, http://www.gosschinaclub.demon.co. uk/exhibitions.htm. Brief history and images from the 1924 exhibition.

The Fiji Pavilion at the British Empire Exhibition at Wembley, http://www.justpacific.com/ fiji/fijianart/empireexhib1924.html. Maps, photos and text describing the Fiji Pavilion.

British Empire Exhibition, Wembley 1924, http://www.sil.si.edu/silpublications/Worlds-Fairs/WF_selected.cfm?categories=British%20Em pire%20Exhibition%2C%20Wembly%201924. Smithsonian Institution's bibliography of sources for the 1924 exhibition at Wembley.

British Empire Exhibition 1924, http://www. 20thcenturylondon.org.uk/server.php?show=Con MediaFile.1462. Good quality images of program and map that were produced for the British Empire Exhibition.

PARIS 1925

Post-War Paris, http://www.retropolis.net/ exposition/postwarparis.html. Reprint from *World's Fair* 8, 3, (1988), by Arthur Chandler, with images and text about the 1925 fair and discussion of the 1867 and 1900 fairs.

From Czech Cubism to the Paris Expo of 1925, http://www.modernista.cz/english/ma_czech_ modernism.html. Article describes how the Paris Expo was the climax of the Czech decorative style.

Paris 1925, http://www.vam.ac.uk/vastatic/ microsites/1157_art_deco/virtual/gallery1/paris192 5.htm. Virtual Tour and history of the 1925 Paris exposition.

DUNEDIN 1925–1926

Anscombe, Edmund 1874 — 1948, http:// www.dnzb.govt.nz/dnzb/default.asp?Find_ Quick.asp?PersonEssay=4A17. Architect for the 1925 — 26 New Zealand and South Seas International Exhibition

New Zealand Archives, www.archives.govt. nz/docs/pdfs/ArchivesDirectory.pdf. Manuscripts and other archived items for the 1925 — 26 New Zealand and South Seas International Exhibition.

BARCELONA 1929–1930

Barcelona Pavilion, http://www-vrl.umich. edu/project/barcelona/. University of Michigan's virtual reality laboratory that provides the history and virtual imaging of the pavilion building.

Barcelona Pavilion, http://www.bluffton. edu/~sullivanm/spain/barcelona/mies/pavilion.ht ml. Photographs of the pavilion.

Panoramic view of the Barcelona Exposition, http://www.archives.gov/exhibits/panoramic_ photography/images/barcelona_exposition_1929.h tml. National Archives and Records Administration, *Records of the Bureau of Foreign and Domestic Commerce.*

The Barcelona Chair, http://www.moma. org/collection/browse_results.php?object_id=4369 . Museum of Modern Art's history and image of a Barcelona chair made for the German Pavilion by Ludwig Mies van der Rohe.

SEVILLE 1929–1930

Seville Exposition, http://www.time.com/ time/magazine/printout/0,8816,723639,00.html. 1929 *Time* article about the 1929 exposition.

ANTWERP/LIÈGE 1930

KBC Tower, Antwerp, http://www.ecocam. com/MB12/MB12087m.jpg. Image of the first skyscraper on the European continent built in Art Deco style, for the universal exposition.

1930 Exposition International, http://www. simmonsgallery.co.uk/2001site/medals/exhibition_medals2005/imagepages/1930.htm. Medals from the 1930 exposition.

STOCKHOLM 1930

Scandinavian Moderne, 1900–1960, http:// www.artsmia.org/modernism/e_SM.html. Article includes discussion of the Stockholm exhibition as an international showplace for Swedish design.

Erik Gunnar Asplund, http://www.moma. org/collection/browse_results.php?criteria=O%3A DE%3AI%3A%A1&page_number=181&template_id=1 &sort_order=1. This image of Gunnar Asplund's design for an advertising tower was signature element for the 1930 Stockholm exhibition.

PARIS 1931

Empire of the Republic: The *Exposition Coloniale Internationale de* Paris 1931. Article from *World's Fair* 8, 4 (1988), by Arthur Chandler.

Exposition Coloniale Internationale, Paris 1931, http://www.sil.si.edu/silpublications/worlds-fairs/WF_selected.cfm?categories=Exposition+Col oniale+Internationale%2C+Paris+1931. Bibliography from the Smithsonian Institution with resources for the 1931 exposition.

The 1931 Paris Exposition Coloniale Internationale, http://www.chez.com/gamelan/expo1931. htm. Collection of images for the 1931 exposition.

BRUSSELS 1935

1935 Bruxelles Exposition Poster, http:// www.modernism.com/prod_one.cfm?id=1513&sro

w1=0. Belgian art deco poster by Leo Marfurt (1894–1977) promotes the 1935 Bruxellles exposition universelle.

Czechs at World Expositions — Part IV, http://www.expo2005.cz/en/magazine/magazine_200404/article_05.shtml. Preparation for Czech participation at the Exposition Internationalle et Universelle de Bruxelles.

JOHANNESBURG 1936–1937

Empire Exhibition, Johannesburg, South Africa, 1936, http://www.sil.si.edu/silpublications-/Worlds-Fairs/WF_Selected_PF.cfm?categories=Empire+Exhibition,+Johannesburg,+South+Afric a,+1936. Bibliography from the Smithsonian Institution with resources for the 1936–1937 Exposition.

Historical Notes on Northern Rhodesia, http://www.greatnorthroad.org/livingstone/history.shtml. Excerpts on Northern Rhodesia from *The British South Africa Company Historical Catalogue and Souvenir of Rhodesia,* Empire Exhibition, Johannesburg, 1936 —1937.

PARIS 1937

Exposition Paris 1937, http://www.travel-brochuregraphics.com/France_Pages/France_2/Par is1937–4.htm. Official magazine published by the general committee.

GLASGOW 1938

Exhibition Glasgow 1938, http://www.arthist. arts.gla.ac.uk/int_ex/exhibitions/1938glasgow/glas gow_1938.html. Virtual collection of artifacts and photos.

Symbol of Unity, http://www.time.com/ time/printout/0,8816,759687,00.html. 1938 *Time* article about the Glasgow exhibition.

WELLINGTON 1939–1940

New Zealand Centennial Exhibition, 1939, http://www.teara.govt.nz/NewZealanders/NewZeal andPeoples/TheNewZealanders/8/ENZ-Resources/ Standard/4/en. Certificate of attendance, New Zealand Centennial Exhibition, 1939.

New Zealand Centennial Exhibition 1939–1940, http://library.christchurch.org.nz/Heritage/Photos/disc16/IMG0041.asp. Archived image of the 1939 exhibition.

The Centennial Exhibition — New Zealand, http://www.nzhistory.net.nz/culture/centennial-/centennial-exhibition. Site includes essays, film clips, radio broadcasts and photographs.

LISBON 1940

History of Science in Portugal (1930–1940), http://www.brown.edu/Departments/Portuguese_ Brazilian_Studies/ejph/html/issue4/pdf/fnunes.pd. Article includes discussion of science exhibits and celebrations at the 1940 Exhibition.

PORT-AU-PRINCE 1949–1950

Bicentennial at Port-au-Prince, 1949, http:// www.trumanlibrary.org/photographs/view.php?id =20465. Image of plaque of President Truman dedicated at the 1949–50 exposition.

LONDON 1951

Festival of Britain, http://www.museum oflondon.org.uk/archive/exhibits/festival/intro.ht m. Museum of London's history and images of construction for exposition.

1951: King George opens Festival of Britain, http://news.bbc.co.uk/onthisday/hi/dates/stories/may/3/newsid_2481000/2481099.stm. BBC's history of the 1951 exposition.

1951 Festival of Britain, http://www.national-archives.gov.uk/films/1945to1951/filmpage_fil.ht m. UK National Archives history and film collection of the 1951 exposition.

BRUSSELS 1958

Brussels Universal and International Exposition, http://usinfo.state.gov/journals/itps/0406/ ijpe/brussels.htm. U.S. Department of State history and images of the 1958 exposition.

MONTREAL 1967

Expo 67: Montreal Welcomes the World, http://archives.cbc.ca/300c.asp?IDCat=69&IDDos =100&IDLan=1&IDMenu=69. CBC Radio Canada's archives for the 1967 exposition.

Expo 67, http://www.canadiandesignre-source.ca/officialgallery/?cat=48. Canadian Design Resource site for the 1967 exposition.

OKINAWA 1975

Description of the Japanese Computer-controlled Vehicle System, http://faculty.washington.edu/jbs/itrans/cvs1.htm. Description and images of the Rapid Transit System, first demonstrated at the International Ocean Exposition in Okinawa.

TSUKUBA 1985

Tsukuba Expo '85 Japan; the tools with which to dream, http://www.atarimagazines.com/ creative/v11n8/64_Tsukuba_Expo85_Japan_th.ph. Article from *Creative Computing,* 11, 8 (August1985), about the important of world expositions generally, with specific attention to the 1985 exposition.

3D for the 21st Century — The Tsukuba Expo & Beyond, http://www.3dmagic.com/pdf/21-ST-CEN.PDF. Article about science at the 1985 exposition, with focus on 3D imaging.

Samantha Smith, http://www.time.com/ time/magazine/article/0,9171,952319,00.html. Article about an 11 year old who traveled to address a children's symposium on the 21st century, sponsored by organizers of the technology and science fair Tsukuba Expo '85. In her opening message

Smith said, "the year 2001 can be the year when all of us can look around and see only friends—no opposite nations, no enemies and no bombs." Samantha was famous as a Disney host and for her correspondence with Soviet leader Yuri Andropov. She died in a plane crash at age 13 in 1985. See also http://www.samanthasmith.info/kobe,_japan.htm

Vancouver 1986

Westward Ho to Expo 86, http://www.time.com/time/magazine/article/0,9171,961308,00.html. *Time* article about the 1986 exposition.

Expo 86, http://www.canadianencyclopedia.ca/index.cfm?PgNm=TCE&ArticleId=A0002692. The Canadian's Encyclopedia's article and images of the 1986 exposition.

Brisbane 1988

Expo 88, http://www.ozbird.com/oz/OzCulture/expo88/default.htm. Collection of articles and images from the 1988 exposition.

Genoa 1992

Christopher Columbus: International Exposition 1992, http://web.utk.edu/~archinfo/a489_f02/PDF/Cole%20-%20piano_genoa.pdf. Architecture article about the 1992 exposition.

Seville 1992

The Dark Side of Spain's Fiesta, http://www.time.com/time/magazine/article/0,9171,975997,00.html. *Time* article describing how Expo's construction introduced a new level of envy and conflict.

All's Fair in Seville, http://www.time.com/time/magazine/article/0,9171,975368,00.html. *Time* article describes the Expo 92 as a "comparatively backward-looking affair, a pageant of past progress."

Taejon 1993

Taejon 1993, http://www.bie-paris.org/~bieparis/main/pages/files/expos/1993-bis.pdf. BIE's file of resources for the 1993 exposition.

Lisbon 1998

The Age Of Aquariums, http://www.time.com/time/magazine/article/0,9171,988428,00.html.

Time article about the largest aquarium in Europe, built as the centerpiece of Expo '98.

The Oceans a Heritage for the Future, http://www.solo-photography.com/oriente.htm. Collection of images from the 1998 exposition.

Hanover 2000

Expo 2000, http://expomuseum.com/2000/. Expo Museum's collection of resources for the 2000 Exposition.

Expo 2000:Discordant Themes, http://www.time.com/time/magazine/article/0,9171,998058,00.html

The Battle of Venice, http://www.time.com/time/magazine/article/0,9171,970233,00.html.

He Builds with a Really Tough Material: Paper http://www.time.com/time/magazine/article/0,9171,997495,00.html. *Time* articles about the 2000 exposition.

Aichi 2005

Expo 2005; Japan Loves Nagoya, http://www.time.com/time/magazine/article/0,9171,1042504,00.html.

Global Visions, http://www.time.com/time/magazine/article/0,9171,1118361,00.html. *Time* articles about the 2005 exposition.

Expo 2005, http://www.expo2005.or.jp/en/. The official website of the 2005 exposition.

Zaragoza 2008

Expo Zaragoza 2008 Consortium, http://www.expozaragoza2008.es/index.jsp?seccion=57&seccionRaiz=47&seccionDesplegar=48&idioma=en_GB. Official website of the Zaragoza 2008 Consortium.

Eastward Bound and Trading Up, http://www.time.com/time/europe/secret/trieste.html. *Time* article about the 2008 exposition.

Shanghai 2010

Expo 2010, http://www.expo2010china.com/expo/expoenglish/index.html. Official website for the 2010 Expo.

Civic Envy, http://www.time.com/time/magazine/article/0,9171,1597553,00.html. *Time* article about the 2010 exposition.

About the Editors
and Contributors

Carl Abbott teaches urban studies and planning at Portland State University. He has authored a number of books on such topics as the rise of the Sunbelt, the urbanization of the American West, and the growth of Washington, D.C. His most recent book is *Frontiers Past and Future: Science Fiction and the American West* (2006). In the works is "How Cities Won the West: Four Centuries of Urban Change in Western North America" (in which he will talk about as many world's fairs as he can fit in, from San Diego to Vancouver).

David Anderson is an associate professor in the Department of Curriculum Studies, University of British Columbia, Canada. His consultative and research activities focus on helping museum-based institutions optimize the experiences they provide their visitors and also center on further refining the theoretical frameworks through which educational researchers conceptualize and investigate visitors' behavior.

Lara Anderson is lecturer and convenor of Spanish studies in the French, Italian, and Spanish Department of the University of Melbourne in Parkville, Victoria, Australia. She received her Ph.D. from the University of Auckland, and is researching the themes of decadence and consumerism in late-nineteenth and early-twentieth century Spanish novels, and has published *Allegories of Decadence in Fin-de-Siècle Spain* (2006).

Harriet Atkinson received a Ph.D. from the joint history of design department of the Royal College of Art and Victoria & Albert Museum, London. She has contributed essays to the *Design History Journal, Studies in the Twentieth Century Environmental History* and *Cambridge Architecture Journal: Scroope 18*. Her research is funded by the U.K. Arts & Humanities Research Council.

Reid Badger is professor emeritus of American studies at the University of Alabama and adjunct professor of humanities at New York University. He is the author of *The Great American Fair:*

The World's Columbian Exposition and American Culture (1979), *A Life in Ragtime: A Biography of James Reese Europe* (1995), and coeditor of *Alabama and the Borderlands: From Prehistory to Statehood* (1985). He is also the author of "World's Fairs and Other Recipes for Progress," the introduction to *Favorite Dishes: A Columbian Autograph Souvenir Cookery Book* (1893, rpt., 2001).

Volker Barth completed his Ph.D., a joint doctoral degree (co–tutelle) in history from the Ludwig-Maximilians-Universität, Munich, and the École des Hautes Études en Sciences Sociales (EHESS), Paris, in 2004. From 2001 to 2007, he worked in an interdisciplinary research group dealing with the project "The cultural staging of the other in the 19th century," financed by the Deutsche Forschungsgemeinschaft (DFG). He is a postdoctoral research fellow at the EHESS and the scientific advisor for the Bureau International des Expositions (BIE).

James M. Beeby is assistant professor of history at Indiana University Southeast. His research interests encompass the American south, populism, African American history, and the gilded age and progressive era. He has published articles on Jim Crow, disfranchisement, and the Populist Party. He is revising his book on the Populist Party in North Carolina.

Burton Benedict is professor emeritus of anthropology at the University of California, Berkeley, and lives in Berkeley.

Krista L. Bennett is a doctoral candidate in art history at Queen's University, Canada. Following a BFA, BEd, MEd and a detour through ten years of public school teaching, curriculum development and administration, her research investigates representations of Canadian identity through presentation and reception of craft at world's exhibitions at the turn of the 19th and 20th centuries.

Susan Bennett worked as librarian, archivist,

and latterly as curator for the Royal Society for the encouragement of Arts, Manufactures and Commerce for nearly twenty-five years. In 2001 Susan helped organize, in conjunction with the Prince Albert Society and the Victorian Society, an international conference on "The Legacy of the Great Exhibition." Susan is now writing up the life and times of "A thankless child," Georgiana Keate (née Henderson), the subject of her M.A. history of art, and is a founder member and honorary secretary for the William Shipley Group for RSA History (www.williamshipleygroup.btik.com).

Astrid Böger is associate professor of American studies at Radboud University in Nijmegen, the Netherlands. She has published two monographs on documentary literature, photography, and film, as well as numerous scholarly articles on a range of subjects in contemporary American culture. She has also been a cocurator of an exhibit on Chicago New Bauhaus artist Nathan Lerner. Böger is completing a book on the early American world's fairs as important sites of nation-formation.

Matthew Bokovoy is an independent historian and editor. He has worked for the University of Oklahoma Press and was editor of the *Journal of San Diego History*. Bokovoy is the author of the *San Diego World's Fairs and Southwestern Memory, 1880–1940* (2005). Bokovoy is writing a book titled "Twilight of Ideals: America in Conservative Times" that examines the rightward drift of the country in the last 25 years.

Bruno Bontempi, Jr. is a professor in the Programa de Estudos Pós-Graduados em Educação: História, Política, Sociedade at Pontifícia Universidade de São Paulo. He is a historian who researches educational theory, intellectuals, and the historical patterns of secondary school and professional education in Brazil.

J.D. Bowers is an assistant professor of history at Northern Illinois University where he teaches U.S., religious, and public history and is the director of secondary history education.

Kristen L. Brackett received her M.A. degree in history from the University of Cincinnati and is an adjunct professor of history for the State University of New York system.

Kaye Briegel is a lecturer in the Oral History Resource Center at California State University, Long Beach. She has researched and written widely in Long Beach history. Among her publications is *Bixby Land Company: A Centennial History* (1996).

Robert W. Brown is professor of history and chair of the History Department at the University of North Carolina at Pembroke. He teaches modern European history, and his research interests include the social history of art and architecture in nineteenth-century France; the history of Paris; modern European cultural history; and the history of Nazi Germany. He visited his first world's fair in 1964, when he went several times to the New York fair.

Cristina Carbone completed her Ph.D. on the American National Exhibition in Moscow of 1959 at the University of California at Santa Barbara. Formerly the curator of the Architecture, Design and Engineering Collections at the Library of Congress, she now teaches art and architectural history at Western Kentucky University and the University of Louisville. She is researching the surviving architecture from North American world's fairs.

Arthur Chandler is a professor of humanities at San Francisco State University. He drives a red 6-speed 2005 Corvette, goes ballroom dancing twice a week, and teaches courses on the cultural histories of San Francisco, Paris, and Vienna.

Laurie Dalton is working on her Ph.D. in Canadian studies at Carleton University. Her dissertation focuses on Canadian pavilions at world expositions and her research areas are in visual culture, heritage, museums, and tourism. She is a contract lecturer in the department of art history at Carleton and also works in the Education and Public Programs department at the National Gallery of Canada.

John R. Davis is reader in modern European history and director of graduate studies at Kingston University in the United Kingdom. His research has focused on commercial liberalization, Anglo-German relations, and British and German history. He has published widely, including books on *Britain and German Zollverein 1848–1866* (1997) and *The Great Exhibition of 1851* (1999).

Catherine Dibello received her doctorate from Indiana University in 1983. Since then, she has divided her time between Shippensburg University of Pennsylvania, where she is professor of English, and Tunghai University in Taichung, Taiwan. Her recent publications include *Everyday English in Taiwan* and *Composing Our World*.

David Dunstan is senior lecturer and formerly director of the National Centre for Australian Studies at Monash University Australia. He is a graduate in history in Monash and Melbourne Universities and has long-standing interests in Melbourne's history and material culture and the Exhibition Building. His book *Victorian Icon: Melbourne's Royal Exhibition Building* (1996) was commissioned by the Exhibition Trustees prior to relinquishing their charge, the Royal Exhibition Building, to Museum Victoria.

Shirley M. Eoff is professor of history at Angelo State University in San Angelo, Texas, where she has taught British and United States history for a quarter century. She has authored *Viscountess Rhondda: Equalitarian Feminist* (1991) and is researching media relations to the entry of the Northern Ireland Women's Coalition into the Irish peace process. She has also published articles on the 1949 San Angelo polio epidemic and the local World War II era bombardier school.

Susan Fernsebner is a historian of China and

assistant professor of History at the University of Mary Washington. Completing a book manuscript on China's participation in world's fairs, her research on material culture and nationalism can also be found in recent publications in the journals *Late Imperial China* and *Postcolonial Studies*.

John M. Findlay is professor of history at the University of Washington, Seattle. He teaches and writes about the American West and Pacific Northwest. His publications include *Magic Lands: Western Cityscapes and American Culture After 1940* (1992) and *People of Chance: Gambling in American Society from Jamestown to Las Vegas* (1986).

John E. Findling is professor emeritus of history at Indiana University Southeast. As a pensioner, he helps manage a small business in Louisville, Kentucky, that sells stamps and old postcards to collectors and waits ever less patiently for the Chicago Cubs to win a World Series, or even a National league pennant.

Charlene G. Garfinkle, an independent scholar from Santa Barbara, California, wrote her dissertation on the design and decoration of the Woman's Building at the World's Columbian Exposition and recently published an article on the Dutch National Exhibition of Women's Labor in 1898. She earned her Ph.D. in history from the University of California, Santa Barbara, in 1996, and is secretary-treasurer of the Association of Historians of American Art.

Alexander C. T. Gepppert is assistant professor at Freie Iniversität Berlin where he teaches modern European history. His publications on international expositions include a number of articles, including a comprehensive bibliography compiled with Jean Coffey and Tammy Lau of the Special Collections Library at California State University, Fresno. As a fellow at Harvard University, he is working on a large-scale study of outer space and extraterrestrial life in the European imagination of the twentieth century.

David Glassberg, a Philadelphia native, teaches history at the University of Massachusetts, Amherst, and is the author of *Sense of History: The Place of the Past in American Life* (2001). In addition to writing about the colonial revival at the Philadelphia world's fair of 1926, he once lived in a house purchased from a man named George Washington.

Lewis L. Gould is professor emeritus at the University of Texas at Austin and lives in Austin. He is co-author of *The Modern American Presidency* (2004) and occasionally writes commentary on the institution of the presidency.

Paul Greenhalgh is director of the Corcoran Gallery of Art in Washington, D.C., and has been president of the Nova Scotia College of Art and Design. He is the author of *Ephemeral Vistas* (2000) and has contributed articles to a spectrum of scholarly journals.

Alfred Heller has attended seventeen world's fairs, beginning with the Golden Gate International Exposition in 1939. He wrote *World's Fairs and the End of Progress* (1999). From 1981 to 1995 he edited and published *World's Fair* magazine.

Deborah L. Hughes is a Ph.D. candidate at the University of Illinois at Urbana-Champaign working toward the completion of her dissertation titled, "Whose Commonwealth? Citizenship and the Political Economy of Imperial Exhibitions, 1924–1938." Her scholarship explores the ways that empire exhibitions in the United Kingdom, South Africa, Jamaica, and Australia were constitutive of interwar imperial politics and served as dramatic ideological sites of conflict over the changing nature of imperial identity within the emerging Commonwealth.

Laura Huntoon is an associate professor of planning in geography and regional development at the University of Arizona. She holds degrees from Harvard and the University of Pennsylvania. She has been a visiting professor at the University of Seville. Huntoon teaches and conducts research in the areas of international city planning, informal and formal nonprofit organizations and migration and population changes. She has worked as a planner in Seville, Spain, and served as an advisor to the Spanish Ministry of Labor's Forum for the Integration of Immigrants. Her research on the urban spatial impact of large-scale one-time events received a national Planning Award from the American Planning Association.

Miglena Ivanova is an assistant professor in English and world literature at Coastal Carolina University. She holds a Ph.D. in comparative literature from the University of Illinois at Urbana-Champaign and specializes in the dramatic traditions of Ireland, Britain, Scandinavia, Russia, and Japan.

Lars F. Johansson is a graduate of Georgetown University's School of Foreign Service, Washington, D.C., and Lund University, Sweden. He immigrated to the United States in 1996 and resides in Fresno, California, where he is department chair of the social sciences department at McLane High School.

Iane Kimber qualified as an archivist in 1973. She has spent most of her career as a local government archivist in London and is borough archivist of the London borough of Hammersmith and Fulham.

Carl E. Kramer is visiting assistant professor at Indiana University Southeast and vice president of Kramer Associates, Inc., a public history consulting firm in Jeffersonville, Indiana. An urban historian, Mr. Kramer is the author of *Capital on the Kentucky: A 200-Year History of Frankfort and Franklin County* and *This Place We Call Home: A History of Clark County, Indiana.* He attended the 1964 New York world's fair and the 1982 Knoxville world's fair.

Johan Lagae is assistant professor of architectural history at the Department of Architecture and Urban Planning of the Ghent University, where he graduated as an engineer-architect in 1991. He holds a Ph.D. on 20th century colonial architecture in the Belgian Congo (2002) and has widely published on this topic, as well as on Belgian modernism and on 1930s (colonial) exhibitions in books and journals. He also authored a *catalogue d'oeuvre* of architect Claude Laurens and was one of the curators of *Memory of Congo: The Colonial Era*, a major exhibition on Congo's colonial past (Royal Museum of Central Africa, Tervuren, 2005). His recent work deals with issues of built heritage as well as urban history in former colonial territories in Africa.

Marc Lagana was born in Versailles, France, and graduated in 1974 with a Ph.D. in history from the University of Wisconsin, Madison. From 1975 to 2006 he was professor of history at Université du Québec à Montréal. An historian of contemporary France, Lagana is particularly interested in the social and political history of colonial imperialism, socialism and communism. He lives in Paris.

Donald G. Larson was born in San Francisco and grew up in the Kerman area in the San Joaquin Valley near the city of Fresno on a family farm. He attended local schools with his twin brother, Phil, and graduated from the College of the Sequoias in Visalia, 1952, and the University of California, Berkeley, with a degree in history in 1954. He received his master's degree from Fresno State College in 1960. He taught history for forty-five years, the last thirty-five years as a professor at Fresno City College, the oldest community college in California. Don was married for forty-six years to his late wife, Carol, and has a daughter and son-in-law, Lynn and Dan Roth, and two granddaughters, Jennifer and Jessica. Don's family is the major focus in his life. He remains active in local sociopolitical affairs and does political analysis for local television stations. His love for world's fairs began when he attended the Golden Gate International Exposition in San Francisco in 1940 and has continued to be a major hobby since that time. The Donald G. Larson World's Fair Collection 1851–1940 is housed under his name at the Special Collections Department of the Henry Madden Library, California State University, Fresno.

Tammy Lau is the head of the Special Collections Library at California State University, Fresno, which houses the Donald G. Larson Collection on International Expositions and Fairs, 1851–1940, one of the largest collections encompassing all world's fairs within this time frame.

Ursula Lindqvist is on the Nordic studies faculty at the University of Colorado at Boulder, where she is also a faculty affiliate in women and gender studies and in the Center for the Study of Ethnicity and Race in the Americas. She earned her Ph.D. in comparative literature from the University of Oregon in 2005. Her research interests range from modernist poetry and poetics to critical studies of race, gender and ethnicity in popular culture. Her book-in-progress is titled "Nordic by Design: Nationalism and the Colonial Imagination in Sweden, Denmark, and the Caribbean."

Vicente González Loscertales is secretary-general of the Bureau International des Expositions (BIE), headquartered in Paris. A native of Madrid, he received a Ph.D. in history from the University of Madrid and served in the Spanish diplomatic corps before moving to the BIE.

John M. MacKenzie is the author of *Propaganda and Empire* (1984) and *The Empire of Nature* (1988), and co-author of *The Railway Station: A Social History* (1986). His most recent book is *The Scots in South Africa* (2007), of which he is a co-author. He is editor of the Studies in Imperialism series for Manchester University Press and has a large collection of fair-related ephemera.

Ronald J. Mahoney lives in genteel retirement in New Mexico after long service as curator of the Donald G. Larson Collection of International Expositions and Fairs, 1851–1940, in the Henry Madden Library at California State University, Fresno.

Larry Maloney developed a passion for travel after working for the Peru and Egypt pavilions at the 1982 World's Fair in Knoxville. He has a master's degree in international service from the American University in Washington, D.C., where he now resides. He also has written several essays for the editors' publications, the *Historical Dictionary of the Modern Olympic Movement* and *Encyclopedia of the Modern Olympic Movement*.

Martin Manning is a research librarian in the Bureau of International Information Programs, U.S. Department of State, and curator of its public diplomacy archives, which includes the international exposition files of all BIE-approved fairs held abroad since World War II in which the U.S. government participated. Manning was born in Boston, Massachusetts, not far from the site of the 1883 American Exhibition of the Products, Arts and Manufactures of Foreign Nations, and has degrees from Boston College and Catholic University.

Veronique Marteau caught the expo bug as deputy commissioner general of the French section of Expo'92 in Seville. She later attended the world's fairs of Lisbon, Hanover, and Aichi. A graduate of the Ecole Normale Supérieure, she holds an "agrégation" in English and was a Fulbright scholar at Columbia University. She served as cultural attaché for the French government in Boston and New York, taught American history at the University of Caen, and is working on a dissertation on U.S. public diplomacy, with an emphasis on American participation at world's fairs, at the Institut d'Etudes Politiques de Paris.

Conal McCarthy was appointed director of the museum and heritage studies program at Victoria University of Wellington in early 2005. He has worked as a teacher, art educator, curator, and lecturer. His research interests include New Zealand art and architecture, museum history and theory, visitor research and heritage issues. His first book, a study of colonial architecture in North Otago, was published in 2002, and his second book, *Exhibiting Maori*, appeared in 2007. He has presented papers at several international conferences and has written numerous articles.

Gary McDonogh is professor and director of the program in Growth and Structure of Cities at Bryn Mawr College. His work has focused on the culture and imagery of urban conflict in Barcelona, *Good Families of Barcelona* (1986), the American South, *Black and Catholic in Savannah* (1993), *The Florida Negro: A Federal Writers' Project Legacy* (1993), and Hong Kong, *Global Hong Kong* (2005). He is working on issues of suburbanization outside the U.S. as well as global Chinatowns.

John McGregor is a veteran of three world expositions—Brisbane World Expo '88, where he worked for the Japanese Government Pavilion; the Universal Exposition of Seville, 1992, where he worked as a multilingual guide for the VIP Visitors Department of the Seville Expo Authority; and Taejon Expo '93, Republic of Korea, where he worked as a press writer for the Expo Press Center. He founded Foundation Expo '88 in 2004 after attending a World Expositions conference in Seville. He has a bachelor of arts in Asian studies from Griffith University, Brisbane. He speaks Mandarin, Korean, Japanese, Spanish, and Australian Sign Language.

Arlin C. Migliazzo is professor of history at Whitworth University. His publications include studies on the Pacific Northwest, colonial South Carolina, church-related higher education, and comparative democratic development. The University of South Carolina Press published his latest book, *Community, Identity and Social Adaptation: A Social History of Purrysburg Township, South Carolina, 1732–1865* (2007). He has been a Fulbright/Hays Scholar and a Washington Centennial Scholar. He first visited Spokane as the Expo '74 site was under construction and returned as a fairgoer in the summer of 1974.

Tatsushi Narita is professor of British and American studies in the Graduate School of Humanities at Nagoya City University, Nagoya City, Japan. He is a member at large of the executive council of the international American Studies association. He is founding president of the Nagoya Comparative Culture Forum. His main interest is in the development of Transpacific American studies. He is preparing a book on the young T.S. Eliot and is editing a book in the area of Transpacific American studies.

Marvin Nathan is emeritus professor of humanities, San Francisco State University. He taught at San Francisco State in interdisciplinary humanities for 35 years. His teaching fields included ancient and medieval culture and history, religious studies, nineteenth-century American culture, and the visual arts. He is the author of books and articles on world's fairs, the history of photography, medieval England, and California literature, architecture and politics. For many years he taught a graduate seminar in American international expositions from 1853 to 1940. Since his retirement in 2000 he has written fiction and has coauthored a book on how photographers framed the narrative of the 1906 San Francisco earthquake and fire.

Kirsten Orr is an architect who is a lecturer in the School of Architecture at the University of Technology, Sydney. She has completed a Ph.D. at the University of New South Wales. Her dissertation is titled "A Force for Federation: International Exhibitions and the Formation of Australian Ethos (1851–1901)."

Kimberly D. Pelle, sliding gracefully into middle age, manages the Adult Student Center at Indiana University Southeast and is excited about the birth of her first grandchild. She hopes to attend her first world's fair in Spain.

Miki Pfeffer is a New Orleans native with an abiding interest in the city's world's fairs. Her thesis, "Exhibiting Women: Sectional Confrontation and Reconciliation in the Woman's Department at the World's Exposition, New Orleans, 1884–85," is at the University of New Orleans. Miki continues to do independent research, focusing especially on the 1884 Cotton Centennial's Woman's and Colored departments. She lives in Thibodaux, Louisiana.

Thomas Prasch has been writing about world's fairs and international exhibitions ever since John E. Findling offered him an essay in the earlier version of this book. Assistant professor and chair of the Department of History at Washburn University, Topeka, he received his Ph.D. in British history from Indiana University, writing a dissertation on Victorian photography of working-class subjects. He has published on a range of subjects in Victorian history, international exhibitions, and film and history, and he continues to plug away at a research project on the development of London's South Kensington museum/exhibition complex.

Barrie M. Ratcliffe has been a university professor in Britain, Canada, France and the United States. A specialist in later modern European history and especially nineteenth-century France, his latest book is *Vivre la ville: Les classes populaires à Paris (1ère moitié du XIXe siècle)* (2007).

Andrea C. Roeber graduated from Humboldt-Universität zu Berlin with an M.A. in art history in 2002 and worked in a museum specializing in porcelain. Her Ph.D. project deals with the significance on international exhibitions for the development of applied arts, fitting neatly in with her main research fields: nineteenth-century decorative arts, design, and exhibition history.

Nadine Rottau studied art history and history in Münster, Vienna and Hamburg, where she finished with an M.A. in 2002 and started her Ph.D. project, "Concepts of a truth to material in 19th century applied arts and architecture in Germany and Britain." Since 2005 she has been a member of the graduate study group Kunst & Technik at the Technical University Hamburg-Harburg. Her general fields of research are art history of the 19th century with a focus on applied arts, the iconography of materials, and art and fashion.

James M. Russell is professor of history at the University of Tennessee at Chattanooga. He has published several articles of Atlanta history, a monograph, *Atlanta 1847–1890: City Building in the Old South and the New* (1988), and has written several online publications.

Robert W. Rydell is professor of history at Montana State University. He has written several books and many articles about world's fairs, including *Fair America* with John E. Findling and Kimberly D. Pelle. He is working on another book about world's fairs and several museum exhibitions about the past, present, and future of world expos.

Paul T. Sayers was born in Beaufort, South Carolina, on July 24, 1956, the son of transplanted northerners. He grew up as the only boy among six sisters in a storytelling Irish-American family. Receiving degrees in history and international studies, he embarked on a career as a diplomat, but in libraries. He is with the Cataloging and Policy Support Office of the Library of Congress, and he continues to write on twentieth-century American historical themes and short fiction.

Noah W. Sobe is an assistant professor of cultural and educational policy studies at Loyola University Chicago. He is a historian of education and comparative education researcher whose work on world's fairs centers on their significance to the international circulation of models of school organization, curricula, and theories of teaching and learning.

Matthew G. Stanard is associate professor in the Evans School of Humanities and Social Sciences at Berry College. He received his Ph.D. in modern European history at Indiana University-Bloomington in 2006. Stanard has been a Belgian American Educational Foundation Fellow, a Future Faculty Teaching fellow at Indiana University-Purdue University Indianapolis, and a Chancellor's Fellow at Indiana University-Bloomington. He is working on turning his dissertation, "Selling the Tenth Province: Belgian Colonial Propaganda 1908–1960," into a book.

Ivan D. Steen is associate professor of history at the University at Albany, State University of New York, where he is the director of the graduate program in public history and the co-director of the Center for Applied Historical Research. He is the author of *Urbanizing America: The Development of Cities in the United States from the First European Settlements to 1920* (2006) and numerous articles and essays. He has been interested in world's fairs ever since attending the 1939 New York fair on his father's shoulders.

Anthony Swift is senior lecturer in history at the University of Essex in Colchester, England. He is the author of *Popular Theater and Society in Tsarist Russia* (2002), various articles on Russian history and world's fairs, and is working on a general history of world's fairs.

Andrew V. Uroskie is assistant professor of modern and contemporary art in the graduate program in Art History and Criticism at Stony Brook University in New York. He received his Ph.D. from the University of California–Berkeley's Department of Rhetoric, where he was awarded the Chancellor's Dissertation Fellowship for his work on the historiography of the moving image in late modernist art. His first book, *Between the Black Box and the White Cube: The Emergence of the Moving Image in Contemporary Art*, explores the moving image as medium and metaphor within the postwar neo-avant-gardes of the 1950s and '60s, and is being published by the University of Chicago Press.

Jennifer Wagelie received her Ph.D. in art history from the Graduate Center, City University of New York. Her area of specialization is art of the Pacific Islands and she wrote her dissertation on the history of displaying and collecting Maori art in the United States. She works in the department of academic programs at the National Gallery of Art in Washington, D.C.

David R. Watters is curator-in-charge of the Section of Anthropology at Carnegie Museum of Natural History, Pittsburgh, Pennsylvania. His research focuses on circum-Caribbean archaeology. His interest in the 1892 Madrid exposition developed from his investigations in the history of archaeology and anthropology, particularly the career of Swedish archaeologist Carl V. Hartman, Carnegie Museum's first anthropology curator (1903–1908).

Philip Whalen is an assistant professor of history at Coastal Carolina University in Conway, South Carolina. He teaches courses in French history and is co-director of the honors program.

Index

Numbers in **bold** refer to the main entry for the fair.
Numbers in ***bold italics*** refer to pages with illustrations.